Glossary of Terms and Principles

-This **glossary of terms and principles** will hopefully provide a quick aid to those unfamiliar with some of the phrases, topics or principles that are frequently discussed in this book. Since we feel it is more beneficial, this glossary has been arranged topically rather than alphabetically.-

Papacy – the office of a pope, the successor of St. Peter, which was founded by Jesus Christ (Mt. 16:18-20; John 21:15-17) upon St. Peter as head of the Christian Church. The bishops of Rome are the successors of St. Peter. They hold the same primacy in the Christian Church that St. Peter held in the apostolic Church.

Magisterium – the teaching authority of the Catholic Church, exercised by a pope when proclaiming a dogma with the authority of the Papacy. Not every pronouncement of a true pope is a teaching of the Magisterium. A pope speaks magisterially when he meets certain conditions (as defined by Vatican I). Those who are faithful to the Magisterium are those who are faithful to what all the popes throughout history have dogmatically taught or set forth as what the Catholic Church has always held.

Ex Cathedra – Latin for *"from the Chair."* This refers to when a pope speaks infallibly from the Chair of St. Peter when he has fulfilled the conditions for an infallible pronouncement. It is heresy and mortal sin to deny an *ex cathedra* pronouncement of a pope, which is irreformable (unchangeable), since it constitutes the dogma that Christ revealed to the Church.

> Pope Pius IX, Vatican Council I, 1870, Session 4, Chap. 4:
> "…the Roman Pontiff, <u>when he speaks ex cathedra</u> [from the Chair of Peter], that is, when carrying out the duty of the pastor and teacher of all Christians in accord with his supreme apostolic authority he explains a doctrine of faith or morals to be held by the universal Church, through the divine assistance promised him in blessed Peter, <u>operates with that infallibility</u> with which the divine Redeemer wished that His Church be instructed in defining doctrine on faith and morals; and so such definitions of the Roman Pontiff from himself, but not from the consensus of the Church, are unalterable."[1]

Divine Revelation/Dogma – Jesus Christ's truth is the teaching of Divine Revelation. The Catholic Church teaches that the two sources of Divine Revelation are Sacred Scripture and Sacred Tradition; their true content is set forth by the Magisterium of the Catholic Church. Divine Revelation ended with the death of the last apostle. Dogma is unchangeable. When a pope defines a dogma, he doesn't make a dogma true from that point forward, but rather solemnly declares without erring that *which has always been true since the death of the last apostle*. Dogmas are to be believed as the Church has "once declared them," without any recession from that meaning to a "deeper understanding."

> Pope Pius IX, *First Vatican Council*, Sess. 3, Chap. 2 on Revelation, 1870, *ex cathedra*:
> "Hence, also, that understanding of its sacred dogmas must be perpetually retained, which Holy Mother Church <u>has once declared</u>; and there must never be a <u>recession</u> from that meaning under the specious name of a deeper understanding."[2]

> Pope Pius IX, *First Vatican Council*, Session 3, Chap. 4, Canon 3:
> "If anyone says that it is possible that at some time, **given the advancement of knowledge**, a sense may be assigned to the dogmas propounded by the church which is

Glossary of Terms and Principles

different from that which the Church has understood and understands: **let him be anathema.**"3

Heretic – a baptized person who rejects a dogma of the Catholic Church. Heretics are automatically excommunicated from the Church (*ipso facto*) without any declaration for rejecting an authoritative teaching of the Faith.

> Pope Leo XIII, *Satis Cognitum* (# 9), June 29, 1896:
> "No one who merely disbelieves in all (these heresies) can for that reason regard himself as a Catholic or call himself one. For there may be or arise some other heresies, which are not set out in this work of ours, and, **if any one holds to a single one of these he is not a Catholic.**"4

> Pope St. Pius X, *Editae Saepe* (# 43), May 26, 1910: "It is a certain, well-established fact that **no other crime so seriously offends God and provokes His greatest wrath as the vice of heresy.**"5

Schismatic – a baptized person who refuses communion with a true pope or with true Catholics. Schismatics are almost always also heretics. Schismatics also incur automatic excommunication.

Apostate – a baptized person who doesn't merely deny one or more truths of the Catholic Faith, but gives up the Christian Faith altogether. Apostates also incur automatic excommunication.

Antipope – a false claimant to be the pope (i.e. a false claimant to be the Bishop of Rome). There have been over 40 antipopes in Church history, including some who reigned in Rome. This book proves that the Vatican II revolution was brought in by men who are and were antipopes falsely posing as true popes.

Sedevacante; sedevacantist position – *Sede* is Latin for "chair" and *Vacante* is Latin for "empty." A *sedevacante* period is a period when there is no pope: the Chair of St. Peter is empty. This usually occurs after the death of a pope or after a pope's resignation; this has occurred over 200 times in Church history, and has lasted for years at times. The doctors of the Church also teach that the Chair of Peter would become vacant if a pope were to become a manifest heretic. The sedevacantist position describes the position of traditional Catholics who hold that the Chair of St. Peter is presently vacant because the man in Rome can be proven to be a public heretic, and therefore not a true pope.

Vatican II – a council which took place from 1962-1965. Vatican II purported to be a general council of the Catholic Church, but actually was a revolutionary "robber council" which taught doctrines condemned by the Catholic Church. Vatican II brought in a new religion, and was responsible for the incredibly rotten fruits and revolutionary changes that ensued in its aftermath.

Vatican II Sect – this phrase describes the counterfeit Church that has arisen since Vatican II, which was prophesied in Catholic prophecy and Sacred Scripture. This counterfeit sect is rife with heresy, apostasy and the most outrageous scandals, as this book proves in tremendous detail. This book proves that the Vatican II sect is <u>not</u> the Catholic Church, but the Devil's counterfeit to lead people astray during the Great Apostasy.

Glossary of Terms and Principles

Novus Ordo Missae - Latin for *New Order of the Mass*; it refers to the New Mass promulgated by Paul VI on April 3, 1969.

Novus Ordo Church – as it is referred to in this book, is basically synonymous with the term "Vatican II sect," which describes the counterfeit Church of Vatican II, the New Mass and those who adhere to it.

Traditional Catholic – a person who is simply a Catholic who adheres to the Catholic Faith of all times, who adheres to all the dogmas proclaimed by popes, and the traditional rites of the Church. A traditional Catholic doesn't accept the false Vatican II religion or the New Mass (the Novus Ordo) because they are novelties opposed to Catholic teaching.

False Traditionalist – a person who adheres to the traditional Catholic Faith *in certain ways* (such as in the resistance to ecumenism or parts of Vatican II), but also holds some allegiance to the false Vatican II sect. The allegiance of "false traditionalists" to the Vatican II sect is usually because they accept the post-Vatican II "popes" as true popes when the post-Vatican II "popes" can be proven to be antipopes (as shown in this book).

Ecumenism – this refers to the teaching of Vatican II and the "popes" after Vatican II to respect, unite with, pray with, and esteem false religions. "Ecumenism," as practiced and taught by the Vatican II sect, is directly condemned by Catholic teaching, the popes and the whole tradition of the Church. It puts the true religion on a par with false religions, and the true God on a par with false gods. The Ecumenism of the Vatican II sect is exposed in tremendous detail in this book. Some say that, strictly speaking, Ecumenism refers to the heretical practice to unite with Protestant and schismatic sects, while interreligious dialogue refers to the same practice with non-Christian religions. But the two terms are basically synonymous today.

CATHOLIC CONCEPTS CONCERNING NON-CATHOLIC RELIGIONS

Non-Catholic religions are false/There is no Salvation Outside the Catholic Church – The Catholic Church teaches as a dogma that there is only one true religion and one true God. The Church teaches that all non-Catholic religions are false and belong to the Devil. It is a dogma of the Catholic Faith that Outside the Catholic Church There is No Salvation (*extra ecclesiam nulla salus*). This has been defined seven times by popes speaking *ex cathedra*.

> Pope St. Gregory the Great, quoted in *Summo Iugiter Studio*, 590-604:
> "The holy universal Church teaches that it is not possible to worship God truly except in her <u>and asserts that all who are outside of her will not be saved</u>."[6]

> Pope Eugene IV, *Council of Florence*, "Cantate Domino," 1441, *ex cathedra*:
> "The Holy Roman Church firmly believes, professes and preaches that all those who are outside the Catholic Church, not only pagans but also Jews or heretics and schismatics, cannot share in eternal life and will go into the everlasting fire which was prepared for the devil and his angels, unless they are joined to the Church before the end of their lives; that the unity of this ecclesiastical body is of such importance that only for those who abide in it do the Church's sacraments contribute to salvation and do fasts, almsgiving and other works of piety and practices of the Christian militia produce eternal rewards; and that nobody can be saved, no matter how much he has given away in alms and even if he has shed blood in the name of Christ, unless he has persevered in the bosom and unity of the Catholic Church."[7]

Glossary of Terms and Principles

Paganism/the worship of other gods- The term paganism refers to the false, polytheistic religions, such as Buddhism, Hinduism, etc. The Catholic Church teaches that the gods worshipped by members of pagan religions (who worship various gods) are demons.

> Psalms 95:5- "For all the gods of the Gentiles are devils…"

> 1 Cor. 10:20- "But the things which the heathens sacrifice, they sacrifice to devils, and not to God. And I would not that you should be made partakers with devils."

> Pope Pius XI, *Ad Salutem* (#27), April 20, 1930: "…all the compulsion and folly, all the outrages and lust, introduced into man's life by the demons through the worship of false gods."[8]

Islam – a false religion revealed by the false prophet Muhammad. Its followers are called Muslims, who follow the book called *The Koran*. Muslims reject the Trinity and the Divinity of Christ. According to Catholic teaching, Islam is an abomination and a diabolical sect (i.e. a sect of the Devil). Muslims are unbelievers (infidels) who need to be converted for salvation.

> Pope Eugene IV, *Council of Basel*, 1434:
> "… there is hope that very many from **the abominable sect of Mahomet** will be converted to the Catholic faith."[9]

> Pope Callixtus III: "I vow to… exalt the true Faith, and to extirpate **the diabolical sect of the reprobate and faithless Mahomet** [Islam] in the East."[10]

The Vatican II sect heaps praise on Islam and considers it a good religion.

Judaism – the religion which rejects Jesus Christ as the Messiah and attempts to practice the Old Law given through the mediation of Moses. Judaism holds that the Messiah is still to come for the first time. The Catholic Church teaches that the Old Law was revoked with the coming of Christ, that it is a mortal sin to continue to observe it (Council of Florence), and that the adherents of the Jewish religion will not be saved unless they convert to Jesus Christ and the Catholic Faith.

> Pope Eugene IV, *Council of Florence*, 1441, ex cathedra:
> "The Holy Roman Church firmly believes, professes and teaches that the matter pertaining to the law of the Old Testament, the Mosaic law, which are divided into ceremonies, sacred rites, sacrifices, and sacraments… after our Lord's coming… ceased, and the sacraments of the New Testament began... All, therefore, who after that time (the promulgation of the Gospel) observe circumcision and the Sabbath and the other requirements of the law, the holy Roman Church declares alien to the Christian faith and not in the least fit to participate in eternal salvation."[11]

> Pope Benedict XIV, *A Quo Primum*, June 14, 1751: "Surely it is not in vain that the Church has established the universal prayer which is offered up for the faithless Jews from the rising of the sun to its setting, that they may be rescued from their darkness into the light of truth."[12]

Orthodoxy/Eastern Orthodox – the followers of the schism from the Catholic Church that occurred in the year 1054. The "Orthodox" reject the dogma of the Papacy, Papal Infallibility and the last 13 dogmatic councils of the Church. They also allow divorce and remarriage. They are

Glossary of Terms and Principles

considered heretics and schismatics in Catholic teaching. They need to be converted for unity and salvation.

> Pope Benedict XIV, *Allatae Sunt* (#19), July 26, 1755:
> "First, the missionary who is attempting with God's help to <u>bring back Greek and eastern schismatics to unity should devote all his effort to the single-objective of delivering them from doctrines at variance with the Catholic faith.</u>"[13]

However, the Vatican II sect says "the Orthodox" don't need to be converted for salvation. It teaches that they are part of the true Church and on the road to salvation (as proven in this book).

Protestants – the followers of the sects which split from the Catholic Church after Martin Luther's revolt in 1517. Protestants are those who reject Catholic dogma in one or more areas. One who rejects or protests against any Catholic dogma is a heretic and *ipso facto* excommunicated. Protestants usually reject Catholic dogma in the areas of the priesthood, the Mass, the sacraments, the Papacy, the necessity of faith and works, the intercession of the saints, etc.

> Pope Pius XI, *Rerum omnium perturbationem* (#4), Jan. 26, 1923: "… <u>the heresies begotten by the [Protestant] Reformation</u>. It is in these <u>heresies</u> that we discover the beginnings of that apostasy of mankind from the Church…"[14]

> Pope Leo XII, *Ubi Primum* (# 14), May 5, 1824:
> "It is impossible for the most true God, who is Truth itself, the best, the wisest Provider, and the Rewarder of good men, to approve all sects who profess false teachings which are often inconsistent with one another and contradictory, and to confer eternal rewards on their members… by divine faith we hold one Lord, one faith, one baptism… This is why we profess that there is no salvation outside the Church."[15]

The Vatican II sect, however, holds that Protestantism is not heresy, that Protestants are not heretics, that their sects are means of salvation and part of the true Church.

OTHER IMPORTANT CATHOLIC CONCEPTS USED THROUGHOUT THE BOOK

Catholics cannot partake in non-Catholic worship – Prior to Vatican II, all Catholic moral theology manuals reiterated the traditional teaching of the Church that it is a mortal sin against the divine law to partake in non-Catholic worship. After Vatican II, this mortally sinful activity is officially encouraged (e.g., see *The Vatican II sect vs. the Catholic Church on partaking in non-Catholic worship* section of this book).

> Pope Pius XI, *Mortalium Animos* (# 10): "So, Venerable Brethren, it is clear why this Apostolic See <u>has never allowed</u> its subjects to take part in the assemblies of non-Catholics…"[16]

Heresy can be manifested by deed – While some people manifest their heresy by written statements or oral declarations, most heresy and apostasy is manifested by deed, not word. People manifest their heresy and apostasy by going to non-Catholic temples to worship, such as the synagogue or the mosque, or by joining the Protestants and schismatics in their worship at their churches.

> St. Thomas Aquinas, *Summa Theologica*, Pt. I-II, Q. 103., A. 4: "All ceremonies are professions of faith, in which the interior worship of God consists. <u>Now man can make profession of his inward faith, by deeds as well as by words</u>: and in either profession, if he makes a false declaration, he sins mortally."[17]

That's why St. Thomas Aquinas taught that if anyone were to worship at the tomb of Mohammed, he would be an apostate. Such an **action** alone would show that he does not have the Catholic Faith, and that he accepts the false Islamic religion.

> St. Thomas Aquinas, *Summa Theologica*, Pt. II, Q. 12, A. 1, Obj. 2: "… if anyone were to… worship at the tomb of Mahomet, he would be deemed an apostate."[18]

> Pope Pius IX, *Ineffabilis Deus*, Dec. 8, 1854, defining the Immaculate Conception: "… by their own act they subject themselves to the penalties established by law, if, what they think in their heart [contrary to this decree], **they should dare to signify by word or writing or any other external means**."[19]

We see here that heresy against the dogma of the Immaculate Conception can be signified by word, writing and "other external means." In fact, in his book *Principles of Catholic Theology*, Benedict XVI admitted that the actions and gestures of ecumenism, which the post-Vatican II sect has made toward the Eastern schismatics, signify precisely that (according to the Vatican II sect) the schismatics don't need to accept the Papal Primacy:

> Benedict XVI, *Principles of Catholic Theology* (1982), p. 198: "**Nor is it possible, on the other hand, for him to regard as the only possible form and, consequently, as binding on all Christians the form this primacy [the Papal Primacy] has taken in the nineteenth and twentieth centuries.** <u>The symbolic gestures of Pope Paul VI and, in particular, his kneeling before the representative of the Ecumenical Patriarch [the schismatic Patriarch Athenagoras] were an attempt to express precisely this</u>…."[20]

This will be discussed more in the book, but this is an astounding admission by the current leader of the Vatican II sect that the actions of ecumenism signify heresy against the Papal Primacy. This is a clear example of heresy manifested by deed.

The Catholic Church rejects all who have opposing Views – Those who reject the Catholic Church's dogmatic teaching are condemned, anathematized and rejected by the Church.

> Pope Pelagius II, epistle (1) *Quod ad dilectionem*, 585:
> "If anyone, however, either suggests or believes or presumes to teach contrary to this faith, let him know that he is condemned and also anathematized according to the opinion of the same Fathers."[21]

> Pope Eugene IV, Council of Florence, "Cantate Domino," 1441: "Therefore it [the Church] condemns, <u>rejects</u>, anathematizes and declares to be outside the Body of Christ, which is the Church, <u>whoever holds opposing or contrary views</u>."[22]

To reject one dogma of the Catholic Church is to reject all Faith, since Christ is the guarantor of its dogmas

> Pope Leo XIII, *Satis Cognitum* (# 9), June 29, 1896:

"… can it be lawful for anyone to reject any one of those truths without by that very fact falling into heresy? – without separating himself from the Church? – <u>without repudiating in one sweeping act the whole of Christian teaching</u>? For such is the nature of faith that nothing can be more absurd than to accept some things and reject others… But he who dissents even in one point from divinely revealed truth absolutely rejects all faith, since he thereby refuses to honor God as the supreme truth and the *formal motive of faith*."[23]

Pope Leo XIII, *Satis Cognitum* (# 9), June 29, 1896: "The Church, founded on these principles and mindful of her office, has done nothing with greater zeal and endeavor than she has displayed in guarding the integrity of the faith. <u>Hence she regarded as rebels and expelled from the ranks of her children all who held beliefs on any point of doctrine different from her own</u>. The Arians, the Montanists, the Novatians, the Quartodecimans, the Eutychians, did not certainly reject all Catholic doctrine: they abandoned only a certain portion of it. Still who does not know that they were declared heretics and banished from the bosom of the Church? In like manner were condemned all authors of heretical tenets who followed them in subsequent ages. There can be nothing more dangerous than those heretics who admit nearly the whole cycle of doctrine, and **yet by one word, as with a drop of poison**, infect the real and simple faith taught by our Lord and handed down by apostolic tradition."[24]

Catholics do not hold communion with heretics
– All who reject the Faith of the Catholic Church are outside of and alien to her communion; true Catholics must hold no communion with them.

Pope Leo XIII, *Satis Cognitum* (# 9), June 29, 1896:
"The practice of the Church has always been the same, as is shown by the unanimous teaching of the Fathers, who were wont to hold as outside Catholic communion, AND ALIEN TO THE CHURCH, WHOEVER WOULD RECEDE IN THE LEAST DEGREE FROM ANY POINT OF DOCTRINE PROPOSED BY HER AUTHORITATIVE MAGISTERIUM."[25]

Pope St. Leo the Great, *Sermon 129*: "Wherefore, since outside the Catholic Church there is nothing perfect, nothing undefiled… **we are in no way likened with those who are divided from the unity of the Body of Christ;** *we are joined in no communion*."[26]

Clerics, including bishops and popes, must be resisted if they stray from the Faith; they lose their offices automatically if they become public heretics

Canon 188.4, *1917 Code of Canon Law*:
"There are certain causes which effect the tacit (silent) resignation of an office, **which resignation is accepted in advance by operation of the law, and hence is effective without any declaration**. These causes are… (4) <u>if he has publicly fallen away from the faith</u>."[27]

Pope Leo XIII, *Satis Cognitum* (#15), June 29, 1896:
"No one, therefore, unless in communion with Peter can share in his authority, since **it is <u>absurd to imagine</u>** that he who is outside can command in the Church."[28]

What is a public defection from the Faith?

Canon 2197.1, *1917 Code of Canon Law*:

Glossary of Terms and Principles

"A Crime is *public*: (1) if it is already commonly known or the circumstances are such as to lead to the conclusion that it can and will easily become so…"[29]

St. Robert Bellarmine, *De Romano Pontifice*, Book II, chap. 30: "Finally, the Holy Fathers teach unanimously not only that heretics are outside of the Church, but also that they are "ipso facto" deprived of all ecclesiastical jurisdiction and dignity."

Dom Prosper Guéranger, *The Liturgical Year*, Vol. 4, p. 379, on how a layman of the 5th century resisted and condemned Nestorius, his bishop, when he demonstrated manifest heresy: "It was then that Satan produced **Nestorius… enthroned in the Chair of Constantinople**… In the very year of his exaltation, on Christmas Day 428, Nestorius, taking advantage of the immense concourse which had assembled in honor of the Virgin Mother and her Child, **pronounced from the Episcopal pulpit the blasphemous words**: 'Mary did not bring forth God; her Son was only a man, the instrument of the Divinity.' The multitude shuddered with horror. <u>Eusebius, a simple layman, rose to give expression to the general indignation, and protested against this impiety</u>. Soon a more explicit protest was drawn up and disseminated in the name of the members of this grief-stricken Church, **launching an anathema against anyone who should dare to say**: 'The Only-begotten Son of the Father and the Son of Mary are different persons.' **This generous attitude was the safeguard of Byzantium, and won the praise of popes and councils**. When the shepherd becomes a wolf, the first duty of the flock is to defend itself."[30]

Pope St. Celestine, quoted by St. Robert Bellarmine:
"**The authority of Our Apostolic See** has determined that the bishop, cleric, or simple Christian who had been deposed or excommunicated by Nestorius or his followers, **after the latter began to preach heresy** *shall not be considered deposed or excommunicated.* <u>For he who had defected from the faith with such preachings, cannot depose or remove anyone whatsoever</u>."[31]

St. Robert Bellarmine, Cardinal and Doctor of the Church, *De Romano Pontifice*, II, 30:
"**A pope who is a manifest heretic automatically (*per se*) ceases to be pope and head**, just as he ceases automatically to be a Christian and a member of the Church. Wherefore, he can be judged and punished by the Church. *This is the teaching of all the ancient Fathers* who teach that manifest heretics immediately lose all jurisdiction."

St. Robert Bellarmine, *De Romano Pontifice*, II, 30:
"**This principle is most certain. The non-Christian cannot in any way be Pope, as Cajetan himself admits (ib. c. 26). The reason for this is that he cannot be head of what he is not a member;** now he who is not a Christian is not a member of the Church, **and a manifest heretic is not a Christian, as is clearly taught by St. Cyprian (lib. 4, epist. 2), St. Athanasius (Scr. 2 cont. Arian.), St. Augustine (lib. De great. Christ. Cap. 20), St. Jerome (contra Lucifer.) and others;** <u>therefore the manifest heretic cannot be Pope</u>."

St. Francis De Sales (17th century), Doctor of the Church, *The Catholic Controversy*, pp. 305-306 : "<u>Now when he [the Pope] is explicitly a heretic, he falls ipso facto from his dignity and out of the Church</u>…"[32]

St. Antoninus (1459): "**In the case in which the pope would become a heretic, he would find himself, by that fact alone and without any other sentence, separated from the Church.** A head separated from a body cannot, as long as it remains separated, be head of the same body from which it was cut off. A pope who would be separated from the Church by heresy, therefore, would by that very fact itself cease to be head of the Church. He could not be a heretic and remain pope, because, since he is outside of the Church, he cannot possess the keys of the Church." (*Summa Theologica*, cited in *Actes de Vatican I. V.* Frond pub.)

St. Robert Bellarmine, *De Romano Pontifice*, Book II, Chap. 30, concerning judging those who are heretics: "… for men are not bound, or able to read hearts; but **when they see that someone is a heretic by his external works, they judge him to be a heretic pure and simple, and condemn him as a heretic.**"[33]

Indefectibility – refers to the promise of Christ that He would always be with His Church (Mt. 28) and that the gates of Hell cannot prevail against the Church (Mt. 16). Indefectibility means that the Catholic Church will, until the end of time, remain essentially what she is. The indefectibility of the Church requires that *at least a remnant* of the Church will exist until the end of the world, that the official teachings of the Church will not err, and that a true pope will never authoritatively teach error to the entire Church. It does not exclude antipopes posing as popes *or a counterfeit sect that reduces the adherents of the true Catholic Church to a remnant in the last days*, which is precisely *what is predicted* to occur in the last days and what happened during the Arian crisis.

St. Athanasius: "Even if Catholics faithful to tradition are reduced to a handful, they are the ones who are the true Church of Jesus Christ."[34]

Endnotes for *Glossary of Terms and Principles* section

[1] Denzinger, *The Sources of Catholic Dogma*, B. Herder Book. Co., Thirtieth Edition, 1957, no. 1839.
[2] Denzinger 1800.
[3] Denzinger 1818.
[4] *The Papal Encyclicals*, by Claudia Carlen, Raleigh: The Pierian Press, 1990, Vol. 2 (1878-1903), Vol. 2 (1878-1903), p. 393.
[5] *The Papal Encyclicals*, Vol. 3 (1903-1939), p. 125.
[6] *The Papal Encyclicals*, Vol. 1 (1740-1878), p. 230.
[7] Denzinger 714.
[8] *The Papal Encyclicals*, Vol. 3 (1903-1939), p. 381.
[9] *Decrees of the Ecumenical Councils*, Sheed & Ward and Georgetown University Press, 1990, Vol. 1, p. 479.
[10] Von Pastor, *History of the Popes*, II, 346; quoted by Warren H. Carroll, *A History of Christendom*, Vol. 3 (*The Glory of Christendom*), Front Royal, VA: Christendom Press, p. 571.
[11] Denzinger 712.
[12] *The Papal Encyclicals*, Vol. 1 (1740-1878), pp. 41-42.
[13] *The Papal Encyclicals*, Vol. 1 (1740-1878), p. 57.
[14] *The Papal Encyclicals*, Vol. 3 (1903-1939), p. 242.
[15] *The Papal Encyclicals*, Vol. 1 (1740-1878), p. 201.
[16] *The Papal Encyclicals*, Vol. 3 (1903-1939), p. 317.
[17] St. Thomas Aquinas, *Summa Theologica*, Pt. I-II, Q. 103., A. 4
[18] St. Thomas Aquinas, *Summa Theologica*, Pt. II, Q. 12, A. 1, Obj. 2:
[19] Denzinger 1641.
[20] Benedict XVI, *Principles of Catholic Theology*, San Francisco: Ignatius Press, 1982, p. 198.
[21] Denzinger 246.
[22] Denzinger 705.
[23] *The Papal Encyclicals*, Vol. 2 (1878-1903), p. 394.
[24] *The Papal Encyclicals*, Vol. 2 (1878-1903), p. 393.
[25] *The Papal Encyclicals*, Vol. 2 (1878-1903), p. 393.

[26] Quoted in *Sacerdotium*, # 2, Instauratio Catholica, Madison Heights, WI, p. 64.
[27] *The 1917 Pio-Benedictine Code of Canon Law*, translated by Dr. Edward Von Peters, Ignatius Press, 2001, p. 83.
[28] *The Papal Encyclicals*, Vol. 2 (1878-1903), p. 401.
[29] *The 1917 Pio-Benedictine Code of Canon Law*, translated by Dr. Edward Von Peters, p. 695.
[30] Dom Prosper Guéranger, *The Liturgical Year*, Loreto Publications, 2000, Vol. 4, p. 379.
[31] Quoted by St. Robert Bellarmine, *De Romano Pontifice*, II, 30.
[32] St. Francis De Sales, *The Catholic Controversy*, Rockford, IL: Tan Books, 1989, pp. 305-306.
[33] St. Robert Bellarmine, *De Romano Pontifice*, II, 30.
[34] *Coll. Selecta SS. Eccl. Patrum. Caillu and Guillou*, Vol. 32, pp. 411-412.

Detailed Table of Contents

PART I – OUTLINING THE PRESENT SITUATION OF THE CATHOLIC CHURCH AND THE POST-VATICAN II APOSTASY IN TREMENDOUS FACTUAL DETAIL

note: While this Table of Contents is extremely detailed (in order to make it as easy as possible to find particular sections a reader may be looking for), it does not cover even all of the subjects that are addressed in this 600-plus page book; and it does not do justice to the depth and specificity into which each section of this book goes. We hope that reading the Table of Contents does not substitute for reading in full the sections of this book.

1. The Great Apostasy and a counterfeit Church predicted in the New Testament and in Catholic Prophecy – *Page 1*

▶ Jesus Christ predicts that there will hardly be any faith on Earth when He returns (Lk. 18:8). – *Page 1*
▶ The New Testament teaches that the Great Apostasy will happen "in the Temple of God" (2 Thess. 2) and "in the holy place," (Mt. 24:15) which clearly indicates a takeover of Catholic buildings in a religious deception. – *Page 1*
▶ The Great Apostasy will be worse than the Arian Crisis (4th cent.), in which 97% of the bishops became Arian and the true Catholic Church was reduced to a remnant who were considered the outsiders at the time. – *Page 2*
▶ Our Lady of La Salette appeared in 1846 and prophesied that Rome will lose the Faith and become the Seat of the Antichrist – a prophecy which has been fulfilled before our eyes. – *Page 3*

2. Pope Leo XIII's Original Prayer to St. Michael - a prophecy about the Future Apostasy in Rome – *Page 6*

3. The Message of Fatima: a heavenly sign marking the beginning of the end times and a prediction of apostasy from the Church – *Page 10*

• An explanation of the Miracle of Fatima and its significance to this topic… – *Pages 10-13*
• The Masonic Daily Paper, *O Seculo*, stunningly confirms without even knowing it that Our Lady was the woman clothed with the sun of Apocalypse 12:1. – *Page 13*
▶ Fatima, the sign of Apoc. 12:1, and the great red dragon (Communism), the sign of Apoc. 12:3, both come on the seen in 1917…– *Page 14*
• Sister Lucia of Fatima told Fr. Fuentes in 1957 that we are in the last times. – *Page 15*
• Testimonies that Heaven asked that the third secret of Fatima be revealed by 1960 at the latest. – *Page 16*
• Why would the third secret of Fatima be clearer in 1960? Because it has to do with Vatican II. – *Page 17*

4. A complete list of the Antipopes in History – *Page 19*

▶ Jesus Christ founded His Church upon St. Peter (Mt. 16) and made him the first pope.
▶ It's a fact that there have been many antipopes in Church history: a full list of the 41 antipopes in Church history.

Detailed Table of Contents

5. The Great Western Schism (1378-1417) and what it teaches us about the post-Vatican II apostasy – *Page 21*

• During the Great Western Schism, there were three claimants to the Papacy at one time (two antipopes), with the true pope holding the least support of the three. [SEE TABLE] – *Page 21*
• At one point during the Great Western Schism the entire College of Cardinals rejected the true pope and recognized an antipope. – *Page 22*
• During the Great Western Schism there was massive confusion, with multiple antipopes and antipopes reigning from Rome. [SEE DETAILED DISCUSSION]
• A pre-Vatican II theologian, commenting on the Great Western Schism, said that God could have left the Church without a pope for the whole period of the Great Western Schism. – *Pages 28-29*

6. The Catholic Church teaches that a heretic would cease to be the pope, and that a heretic couldn't be validly elected pope – *Page 31*

• Quotes from St. Robert Bellarmine, St. Francis De Sales and St. Antoninus that a pope who would become a heretic would cease to be the pope... – *Pages 31-32*
• The Church's teaching that a heretic cannot be a pope is rooted in the dogma that heretics are not members of the Catholic Church. – *Page 32*
• Pope Paul IV issued a Papal Bull solemnly declaring that the election of a heretic as pope is null and void. – *Page 33*
• In line with the truth that a heretic cannot be the pope, the Church teaches that heretics cannot be prayed for in the canon of the Mass. – *Page 35*

7. The Church's enemies, Communists and Freemasons, made an organized effort to infiltrate the Catholic Church – *Page 37*

• Statements from Communists and Freemasons about their plan to infiltrate the Catholic Church and attempt to get their own men to the highest levels...

8. The Vatican II Revolution (1962-1965) – *Page 40*

THE MOST SPECIFIC HERESY IN VATICAN II – *Page 41*

• Vatican II uses the same verb as the Council of Florence to teach just the opposite. – *Page 42*

THE OTHER PRINCIPAL HERESIES OF VATICAN II IN THE FOLLOWING DOCUMENTS: – *Page 43*

Unitatis Redintegratio – Vatican II's Decree on Ecumenism – *Page 43*
 • Vatican II longs for the universal Church. – *Page 43*
 • Vatican II says the Church is not fully Catholic. – *Page 44*
 • Vatican II teaches that heretics and schismatics are in communion with the Church. – *Pages 45-46*
 • Vatican II says no one born into Protestantism can be accused of the sin of separation (i.e. heresy). – *Page 46*
 • Vatican II says the life of grace exists outside the Church. – *Page 46*
 • Vatican II says non-Catholic sects are a means of salvation. – *Pages 46-47*
 • Vatican II says heretics must be looked upon with respect ... and more. – *Page 48*

Orientalium ecclesiarum – Decree on Eastern Catholic Churches – *Page 49*

Detailed Table of Contents

    • Vatican II teaches that non-Catholic schismatics may lawfully receive Holy Communion, which is totally condemned by Catholic teaching and a host of popes. – *Page 50*
    • Vatican II says Catholic churches should be shared with non-Catholics. – *Page 52*

Lumen Gentium – "dogmatic" Constitution on the Church – *Page 52*

    • Vatican II says that bishops have supreme power over the Church together with the pope. – *Page 52*
    • Vatican II teaches that Muslims and Catholics together worship the true God. – *Page 53*
    • Vatican II teaches one can be an atheist through no fault of his own. – *Page 54*
    • Vatican II teaches that the Church is united with those who don't accept the Faith or the Papacy. – *Page 55*

Dignitatis Humanae – Declaration on Religious Liberty – *Page 56*

    ▶ An explanation of Catholic teaching against religious liberty… – *Pages 56-57*
    • An explanation of how Vatican II teaches just the opposite… – *Pages 57-58*
    • Benedict XVI admits that Vatican II's teaching on Religious Liberty contradicts the teaching of the Syllabus of Errors of Pope Pius IX! – *Page 58*
    ▶ Detailed refutations of the attempted defenses of Vatican II's teaching on this issue: refuting the "coercion" subterfuge, the "within due limits" subterfuge, "the issue is not dogmatic" objection, etc. – *Pages 59-62*
    • Vatican II's teaching on religious liberty rejects the entire history of Christendom and destroys Catholic society. – *Page 62*
    • Changes to the Spanish Catholic law as a result of the teaching of Vatican II… – *Pages 63-64*
    • Vatican II teaches the condemned heresies of liberty of speech and of the press. – *Page 64*

Ad Gentes – Decree on Missionary Activity – *Page 65*

    • Vatican II teaches that the Catholic Church is insufficient as a means of salvation. – *Page 65*
    • Vatican II teaches that we should work with heretics in missionary projects. – *Page 65*

Nostra Aetate – Decree on Non-Christian Religions – *Page 66*

    • Vatican II praises Muslims, and teaches that the "god" of the Muslims created heaven and earth. – *Page 66*
    • Vatican II uses the same language as the Council of Florence on the fasts, almsgiving, etc. of non-Catholics, but with an opposite meaning. – *Page 66*
    • Vatican II teaches that in Buddhism a way is taught by which man can reach the highest illumination. – *Page 68*
    • Paul VI confirms Vatican II's heretical teaching. – *Page 68*
    • Vatican II praises the false religion of Hinduism, and uses language which directly contradicts the teaching of Leo XIII against Hinduism. – *Pages 68-69*

Gaudium et Spes – Constitution on the Church in the Modern World – *Page 70*

    • Vatican II teaches that in the Incarnation Christ united Himself in some way with every man. – *Page 70*
    • John Paul II used this heresy to repeatedly teach universal salvation. – *Page 70*
    • Vatican II teaches that birth control can be virtuous. – *Page 71*
    • Vatican II teaches that man is superior to everything, and that everything should be directed to him as its center and crown. – *Page 72*

Sacrosanctum Concilium – Constitution on the Sacred Liturgy – *Page 72*

    • Vatican II put into motion the liturgical revolution we are dealing with now. – *Pages 72-73*
    • Vatican II officially called for changes to the liturgical books, including revising the rite to every sacrament. – *Page 74*

Detailed Table of Contents

- The disastrous fruits of Vatican II's policy are clear. *Pages 75-76*
- Vatican II called for the customs of pagan peoples in the liturgy, something explicitly condemned as Modernism by Pope St. Pius X. – *Page 75*
- Vatican II called for the simplification of the rites, something condemned by Pope Pius VI. – *Page 76*
- Vatican II called for "bodily self-expression," radical adaptations, and pagan musical traditions to be incorporated into the liturgy. – *Page 76*

9. The Liturgical Revolution – A New Mass – *Page 82*

▶ The traditional Roman Rite of Mass was codified by Pope St. Pius V, who declared that it cannot be changed. – *Page 82*

- The New Mass is a new 1969 creation promulgated by Paul VI. – *Page 82*
- Since the New Mass has been instituted, in the Vatican II churches the world has seen every kind of aberration, sacrilege and liturgical outrage imaginable, including Rock concerts, etc., etc., etc. [MANY PHOTOS] – *Pages 82-92*

▶ *The Ottaviani Intervention*, authored by cardinals, says the New Mass represents a striking departure from the theology of the Council of Trent. – *Page 92*

- The New Mass was created by Paul VI with the help of six Protestant ministers. [PHOTO] – *Page 93*
- Paul VI admitted to his good friend, Jean Guitton, that he wanted to change the Mass to make it more Protestant. – *Page 93*
- Only 17% of the traditional orations were not deleted or modified in the New Mass. Traditional orations describing traditional concepts of Hell, sin, temptations, God's wrath, dangers to the soul, etc., etc., were specifically eliminated. – *Pages 93-94*
- The horrifying results of this policy are clear for all to see. [PHOTOS] – *Pages 94-95*
- Almost every traditional sign and rubric demanding respect for the Body and Blood of Christ has been removed from the New Mass. [PHOTOS] – *Pages 95-96*
- The requirements for sacred vessels and that the altar be of fitting dignity have been abolished with disastrous results. [PHOTOS] – *Pages 96-97*
- When the Protestants split from the Church in 16th century England, they implemented basically the same changes to the Mass that are seen in the New Mass. [PHOTOS] – *Pages 97-99*
- The definition of the Mass in the 1549 Anglican Prayer Book is the same as in the New Mass. – *Page 99*

Detailed Table of Contents

• The specific prayers which have been deleted from the Mass bear a striking resemblance to those deleted by the Protestants, and those retained are most of those which the Protestants retained. [PHOTOS] – *Pages 99-103*
• The Novus Ordo offertory is taken from a Jewish table prayer. – *Page 101*
• The official Good Friday prayer in the New Mass is for the Jews *to grow* in faithfulness to God's covenant, while the traditional Church prays that they accept Christ since the Old Covenant has ceased. [SEE TABLE] – *Page 101*
• The Protestants implemented Communion in the hand and Communion under both kinds, and so does the New Mass. [PHOTOS] – *Pages 101-102*
• It is beyond dispute: the New Mass destroys the Roman Rite. – *Page 103*
• Novus Ordo (New Order of Mass) churches bear a striking resemblance to Freemasonic lodges. [PHOTOS] – *Pages 103-104*
• The primary architect of Paul VI's New Mass was Cardinal Annibale Bugnini, a Freemason. [PHOTO] – *Page 104*

PROOF THAT THE NEW MASS IS NOT VALID – THE ESSENTIAL WORDS OF CONSECRATION HAVE BEEN CHANGED – *Page 105*

▶ An explanation of what is needed for a valid sacrament based on Catholic teaching…
▶ The Catholic Church's teaching on the form of consecration, from Pope Eugene IV and Pope St. Pius V…
▶ Pope St. Pius V teaches that changing the meaning of the form renders the Mass invalid.
• The changes to the form of consecration in the New Mass: the removal of "mysterium fidei" and the change of "many" to "all" change its meaning.
▶ *The Catechism of the Council of Trent* teaches that "all" cannot be used in the form of consecration in place of "many."

ANOTHER ANGLE TO THIS ISSUE ABSOLUTELY PROVES THAT THE NEW MASS IS INVALID – *Page 107*

▶ Pope Leo XIII teaches that sacraments must signify the grace which they effect and effect the grace which they signify.
▶ The grace which must be signified in the Eucharistic form is the union of the faithful with Christ (Pope Eugene IV).
▶ The words "for you and for many unto the remission of sins" signify this grace; the words "for you and for all" do not.
▶ All approved consecration formulas in rites of the Church signify the union of the faithful with Christ in the consecration, while the New Mass formula does not.

10. The New Rite of Ordination – *Page 112*

• Promulgated in 1968, the New Rite of Ordination is missing a word declared to be essential by Pope Pius XII.
• The biggest problem with the New Rite is not the form, but the surrounding ceremonies and prayers which have been deleted.
▶ Pope Leo XIII declared the Anglican Rite of Ordination invalid because of its removal of all references to the true sacrificing priesthood.
• The New Rite suffers from the exact same defects as the Anglican Rite; in fact, the pattern of deletion is almost identical.
• Some of the important prayers and ceremonies that have been abolished…
▶ The New Rite is invalid, and the consequences for "priests" ordained in it and confessions made to "priests" ordained in it…

Detailed Table of Contents

11. The New Rite of Consecration of Bishops – *Page 120*

▶ A comparison of the traditional form of consecration of bishops with Paul VI's radically different form for the New Rite of Consecration of Bishops…
• The traditional rite unequivocally signifies the power of the episcopacy, while the new rite does not.
• Some of the important prayers and ceremonies that have been abolished…
▶ The New Rite cannot be considered valid: an explanation of the consequences for "bishops" consecrated in it and "ordinations" of "priests" by such "bishops"…

12. New Sacraments: the Changes to the Other Sacraments – *Page 122*

▶ A look at the changes made by Paul VI to the rites of baptism, confirmation, confession, extreme unction, and marriage…
• A summary of the validity or lack thereof of Paul VI's new sacramental rites…

13. The Scandals and Heresies of John XXIII – *Page 126*

-The Man who called Vatican II and claimed to be pope from 1958-1963 –

• "Suspected of Modernism" as a professor…
• Said Catholics and schismatic "Orthodox" are in the same Church.
• Disagreed with Outside the Church There is No Salvation.
• Friend of Freemasons, internationalists, and schismatics…
• Demonstrated low moral character…
• Chose to receive his "cardinal's" hat from notorious anticlerical, Vincent Auriol. [PHOTO]
• Friendly with Soviet killer of Catholics, M. Bogomolov. [PHOTO]
• Friendly with radical Ed Herriot. [PHOTO]
• Said one could be a Christian by deed without Faith.
• Told a member of a non-Catholic monastery that he is in the Church.
• Suppressed the prayer against Islam, and said he would have always remained a Muslim if he had been raised in the religion.
• Removed Catholic saints from the Calendar.
• Brokered the Vatican-Moscow agreement that Vatican II wouldn't condemn Communism so that schismatics could attend its proceedings. [PHOTO]
• Praised dissidents and made many other statements offensive to Catholic teaching.
• His encyclical *Pacem in Terris* taught the condemned heresy of religious liberty, and was praised by Masonic leaders as a Masonic document.
• Blessed Jews attending the synagogue, indicated that he is one of them, and said the Church has crucified them.
• Removed the prayer for the "perfidious Jews" from the Good Friday Liturgy.
• Praised by Jews, Freemasons and non-Catholics after his death…
• John XXIII was a manifest heretic and could not have been a valid pope, according to Catholic teaching.

Detailed Table of Contents

• The stunning parallels between Antipope John XXIII of the Great Western Schism (Baldassare Cosa) and Antipope John XXIII of Vatican II (Angelo Roncalli)…

14. The Heresies of Paul VI (1963-1978), the man who gave the world the New Mass and the Teachings of Vatican II – *Page 140*

• Paul VI claimed to be pope from 1963-1978. He was the man who promulgated Vatican II and the New Mass, and changed the rites of all seven sacraments.

PAUL VI ON NON-CHRISTIAN RELIGIONS – *Page 141*

• Promoted ecumenism as respect for false religions. – *Page 141*
• Praised false religions and religions "invented by man" as noble. – *Page 142*
• Said the Church esteems false, non-Christian religions. – *Page 142*
• Praised the Hindu Gandhi. – *Page 142*
• Taught that non-Christian religions are no longer an obstacle to evangelization – which is a new gospel. – *Page 143*
• Said that idolatrous and pagan religions of Asia are "rightly held in deep veneration." – *Page 143*
• Praised the wisdom of the images in the pagan and idolatrous Shinto temple. – *Page 143*

PAUL VI ON BUDDHISM – *Page 143*

▶ A brief explanation of the false, pagan Buddhist religion in light of Catholic teaching…
• Paul VI said that Buddhism is "one of the riches of Asia." – *Page 144*
• Paul VI admired Buddhism in its various forms and called it "noble." – *Page 144*
• Paul VI looked with respect on Buddhist way of life and wanted to collaborate with the Buddhist patriarch to "bring about the salvation of man." – *Page 144*

PAUL VI ON ISLAM – *Page 144*

▶ A brief explanation of the false religion of Islam in light of Catholic teaching…
• Paul VI spoke of the riches of the Islamic Faith, and said this "Faith" binds us to the one God. – *Page 145*
• Paul VI taught that Muslims and Catholics together adore the true God. – *Page 145*
• Paul VI had "high respect" for the faith they profess. – *Page 145*

Detailed Table of Contents

• Paul VI had laudatory words for Anglican and Mohammedan "martyrs"! – *Page 145*

PAUL VI ON RELIGIOUS LIBERTY – *Page 146*

• Paul VI promoted the heresy of religious liberty. – *Page 146*
• Paul VI said the Church endured persecutions in history not to maintain Christian Faith without compromise, but to ensure the right to religious liberty for every man. – *Page 146*

PAUL VI ON THE "ORTHODOX" – *Page 146*

• Paul VI gave a Masonic handshake to the schismatic Patriarch of Constantinople on Jan. 5, 1964. [PHOTO] – *Page 146*
• Paul VI attempted to lift the excommunications against the schismatics. – *Page s 146-147*
• Paul VI praised the schismatic patriarch for his "great ministry." – *Page 147*
• Paul VI praised the "piety" and "excellence" of other schismatic patriarchs. – *Page 147*
• Paul VI praised schismatic sects and councils as "venerable" and "holy." – *Page 148*
• Paul VI held that schismatics could be saved and considered them part of the faithful. – *Page 148*
• Paul VI rejected proselytism (conversion) of the schismatics in a joint declaration with a schismatic "pope." – *Page 148*
• Paul VI indicated that a schismatic is the legitimate holder of the See of St. Mark. – *Page 148*

PAUL VI ON OTHER PROTESTANT SECTS – *Page 149*

• Paul VI said that opposition to Protestantism has been transformed into mutual respect. – *Page 149*
• Paul VI encouraged Protestants to continue to profess their faiths loyally. – *Page 149*
• Paul VI said the World Council of Churches manifests the communion of faith and love that Christ gave to His Church! – *Page 149*
• Paul VI called Lutherans "brothers" and hoped for an Anglican Church united but not absorbed (i.e. not converted). – *Page 150*
• Paul VI praised Anglican "martyrs" and spoke of the "martyrdom" of Protestant heretic Martin Luther King, Jr. – *Page 150*

PAUL VI ON BIRTH CONTROL – *Page 150*

• Paul VI repeatedly encouraged "natural" birth control. – *Page 150*
• In *Humanae Vitae*, Paul VI taught that couples are free to have zero children by "natural" birth control methods if they choose to. – *Page 150*

PAUL VI ON THE UNITED NATIONS – *Page 151*

▶ A brief explanation of why the United Nations is evil…– *Page 151*
• Paul VI said "we have Faith in the U.N." – *Page 151*
• Paul VI said the principles of the U.N. should be put into effect. – *Page 151*
• Paul VI said the U.N. is the path that must be taken for modern civilization. – *Page 151*
• Paul VI deliberately attempted to replace the Church with the U.N. as the universal organization that represents hope for the world. – *Page 151*

PAUL VI PROMOTING THE NEW WORLD ORDER – *Page 151*

• Paul VI repeatedly promoted a new world order and a new international order. – *Page 151*

Detailed Table of Contents

PAUL VI ON THE WORSHIP OF MAN – *Page 152*

• Paul VI encouraged meditation on man, a cult of man, the primacy of man, faith in man and the general worship of man. – *Pages 152-153*
• Paul VI on Christmas as a feast of man…– *Page 153*

OTHER CHANGES MADE BY PAUL VI – *Page 154*

• Paul VI gave away the triple-crowned Papal Tiara, which represents a true pope's authority. [PHOTO] – *Page 154*
• Paul VI frequently wore the breastplate of the ephod, a vestment used by Freemasons and Jewish High-Priests. [PHOTOS] – *Page 155*
• Paul VI removed the Index of Forbidden Books and abolished the Oath Against Modernism. – *Page 156*
• Paul VI removed saints from the calendar and many other changes. – *Page 156*

PAUL VI ON "MAGIC" – *Page 158*

• Paul VI repeatedly spoke of magic. – *Pages 158-159*

PAUL VI BASICALLY ADMITTED THAT HIS CHURCH IS THE WHORE OF BABYLON – *Page 159*

• Paul VI made statements which reveal that his Church is the false bride, the Whore of Babylon, predicted in chapters 17 and 18 of the Apocalypse. – *Page 159*

ANOTHER PICTURE OF ANTIPOPE PAUL VI WEARING THE RATIONAL OF A JEWISH HIGH PRIEST [PHOTO] – *Page 160*

ANTIPOPE PAUL VI'S SIGNATURE CONTAINING THREE 6'S – *Page 161*

• Paul VI had a very odd way of writing his name which, when turned upside-down, comes out to three clear 6's. [PHOTOS]
• This kind of thing reveals the type of man Paul VI was.

15. The Scandals and Heresies of John Paul I (1978-1978) – *Page 164*

• John Paul I claimed to be pope for 33 days in 1978.
• John Paul I was a committed defender of the heresies of Vatican II, and held many other novel and heretical things.

Detailed Table of Contents

16. The Heresies of John Paul II, the most traveled man in history and perhaps the most heretical (1978-2005) – *Page 169*

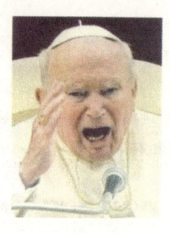

• Karol Wojtyla (John Paul II) claimed to be pope from 1978-2005.

JOHN PAUL II REPEATEDLY TAUGHT UNIVERSAL SALVATION, THAT ALL MEN WILL BE SAVED – *Page 170*

• John Paul II taught that Christ is united with each man forever, that no one is in mortal or original sin, and that all men are saved in various ways. [PHOTO] – *Pages 170-171*

JOHN PAUL II TAUGHT THAT THE HOLY GHOST IS RESPONSIBLE FOR NON-CHRISTIAN RELIGIONS – *Page 172*

• John Paul II taught that the belief of the followers of non-Christian religions is attributable to the Spirit of Truth, the Holy Ghost. – *Page 172*
• John Paul II with African Animists (witch doctors)… [PHOTO] – *Page 173*
• John Paul II said the Church's respect for non-Christian religions is respect for action of the Holy Spirit, and that other religions are a sign of the working of the Holy Spirit. – *Page 173*

JOHN PAUL II TAUGHT AND PRACTICED COMPLETE RELIGIOUS INDIFFERENTISM – *Page 173*

• John Paul II's writings are filled with religious indifferentism. – *Pages 173-174*

JOHN PAUL II AT THE BUDDHIST TEMPLE – *Page 174*

• John Paul II committed an act of apostasy in a Buddhist Temple in 1984. [PHOTO] – *Page 175*
• John Paul II spoke of his enthusiasm to meet "His Holiness," the Supreme Buddhist Patriarch, and of the coming of the "Lord Buddha." – *Page 175*

JOHN PAUL II RECEIVED THE MARK OF THE ADORERS OF SHIVA – *Page 176*

• In 1986, John Paul II received the *Tilac* or *Tika*, the sign of recognition of the adorers of Shiva. [PHOTO] – *Page 176*

Detailed Table of Contents

JOHN PAUL II VENERATED THE HINDU GANDHI – *Page 176*

• In 1986, John Paul II venerated a monument to the Hindu and idolater Gandhi. [PHOTOS] – *Page 177*
• He even took off his shoes in veneration for the pagan whom he called a "hero of humanity." – *Pages 176-177*

JOHN PAUL II'S APOSTASY IN ASSISI – *Page 178*

• In 1986, John Paul II held an apostate interreligious prayer service with over 150 religious leaders from various false religions (Jews, heretics, schismatics, Muslims, various pagans, etc.). [PHOTO] – *Page 178*
• At the gathering, a statue of Buddha was placed on the tabernacle. – *Page 178*
• Since the gods of the heathens are devils (Psalm 95:5; 1 Cor. 10:20), at John Paul II's gathering the pagans were praying to devils. – *Page 179*
• The Animist leaders prayed to the Great Thumb, and the Hindus prayed "peace be upon all gods [devils]." – *Page 179*
• In his 1928 encyclical *Mortalium Animos*, Pope Pius XI authoritatively condemned such interreligious prayer gatherings as apostasy. [FULL QUOTE] – *Page 179*

JOHN PAUL II'S OTHER ECUMENICAL MEETINGS – *Page 180*

• John Paul II held and participated in many other false ecumenical gatherings, totally condemned by the Catholic Church, after the Assisi event. – *Page 180*
• John Paul II being "blessed" by an Indian Shaman in a pagan ritual in 1987. [PHOTO] – *Page 180*

JOHN PAUL II PRAYED WITH AFRICAN ANIMISTS – *Page 181*

• John Paul II prayed with African Animists in 1985. [PHOTO] – *Page 181*
• John Paul II said the meeting was "striking"; it is said he even paid homage to the "sacred snakes." – *Page 181*
• In 1993, John Paul II was treated to a trance-inducing voodoo dance. – *Page 181*
• John Paul II has taken part in many events which include native pagan rituals from demonic cultures. – *Pages 181-182*
• John Paul II's 2002 "Mass" in Mexico City included pagan rituals from the demonic culture – John Paul II himself was involved in a pagan purification ritual. [PHOTOS] – *Page 182*

THE "PAN-CHRISTIAN" ENCOUNTER: JOHN PAUL II'S APOSTATE PRAYER MEETING IN 1999 – *Page 183*

• John Paul II expressed more *complete apostasy* at his interreligious prayer service in the Vatican in 1999. [PHOTO] – *Page 183*
• The meeting, called "The Pan-Christian Encounter," is exactly what Pius XI condemned in denouncing "these Pan-Christians." – *Page 183*
• Many outrageous acts occurred at the Pan-Christian Encounter, including a pagan American Indian pivoting in St. Peter's and blessing the four corners of the Earth. [PHOTO] – *Page 183*

JOHN PAUL II'S ASSISI II PRAYER-MEETING WITH FALSE RELIGIONS – *Page 184*

• In 2002, John Paul II held a repeat of his abominable 1986 event, but this one may have been even worse. [PHOTO] – *Page 184*

Detailed Table of Contents

• John Paul II arranged that the leader of each false religion was allowed to give a sermon on world peace. – *Pages 184-185*
• A Voodoo High Priest preached to the people in front of John Paul II; the Hindu told the crowd that every man is God. – *Page 184*
• John Paul II then arranged for the various false religious leaders to pray to their false gods; he gave them each a room in which to worship the Devil, a room from which all crucifixes and Catholic items were removed. [CHART OF ROOM ARRANGEMENT] – *Page 185*

JOHN PAUL II'S APOSTASY WITH THE MUSLIMS – *Page 186*

• In 1999, John Paul II bowed to and kissed the Koran, the Muslims' holy book which blasphemes the Holy Trinity. [PHOTO] – *Page 186*
• John Paul II encouraged the Muslims to live their faith abroad. – *Page 186*
• John Paul II thanked those who develop Islamic culture. – *Page 186*
• John Paul II asked St. John the Baptist to protect Islam. – *Page 187*
• John Paul II called Muhammad "the Prophet." [PHOTO] – *Page 187*

JOHN PAUL II'S APOSTASY IN THE MOSQUE – *Page 187*

• In 2001, John Paul II committed an act of apostasy in the Omayyad Mosque in Damascus, Syria. [PHOTOS] – *Page 188*
• John Paul II took off his shoes in honor of the temple of infidelity, a particular mosque that is named after a line of Muslim rulers which warred against Christianity. – *Page 188*

JOHN PAUL II TEACHES THAT MUSLIMS AND CATHOLICS HAVE THE SAME GOD – *Page 189*

• John Paul II repeatedly taught the heresy that Muslims and Catholics worship the same God, and that the false god of the Muslims will judge humanity on the last day. – *Pages 189-190*

JOHN PAUL II'S APOSTASY WITH THE JEWS – *Page 190*

• In 1986, John Paul II committed an act of apostasy in the Jewish Synagogue in Rome. [PHOTOS] – *Page 190*
• John Paul II bowed his head with the Jews as they prayed for the coming of their "messiah." – *Pages 190-191*
▶ The Catholic Church teaches that the Old Law has ceased and cannot be observed without the loss of salvation. – *Pages 191-192*
• John Paul II taught that the Old Covenant is still valid. – *Pages 192-193*
• John Paul II's unbelievable message in commemoration of the Jewish Synagogue in Rome contains many statements of heresy and apostasy. – *Pages 193-194*
• John Paul II's best-friend, Jerzy Kluger, was a Jew whom he never tried to convert [PHOTO]; Kluger credits John Paul II with making him feel more Jewish. – *Page 195*
• John Paul II's good friend, the Jewish Maestro Gilbert Levine [PHOTO], said that John Paul II never gave him the slightest indication that he wanted to convert him. – *Pages 195-196*
• John Paul II asked Levine to conduct a concert in commemoration of the Holocaust, which Levine called a "Jewish service in the Vatican," at which all the crucifixes were covered. [PHOTO] – *Page 196*
• John Paul II bestowed the Papal Knighthood on the Jew, Gilbert Levine. – *Pages 196-197*
• On CNN's *Larry King Live*, Gilbert Levine revealed the full depths of John Paul II's shocking apostasy. – *Page 197*

Detailed Table of Contents

• Levine revealed that John Paul II gave each of his sons congratulatory letters for their Bar Mitzvahs, gave them a menorah to help them practice Judaism, and encouraged them to practice Judaism to the full. – *Page 197*

JOHN PAUL II PRAYING AT THE WAILING WALL – *Page 198*

• On March 26, 2000 John Paul II prayed at the holiest site in Judaism, the Western Wall. [PHOTO] – *Page 198*
• The Western Wall is the stone remnant of the Jewish Temple; it represents the practice of the Old Law and the Jewish religion, which has been revoked. – *Pages 198-199*
• This act of apostasy by John Paul II was witnessed by almost the entire nation of Israel. – *Pages 198-199*

JOHN PAUL II'S INCREDIBLE HERESIES REGARDING BAPTIZED NON-CATHOLICS (I.E. HERETICS AND SCHISMATICS) – *Page 199*

JOHN PAUL II REPEATEDLY TAUGHT THAT HERETICS AND SCHISMATICS DON'T NEED TO BE CONVERTED – *Pages 200-201*

CATHOLICS WHO WERE TORTURED AND MARTYRED BECAUSE THEY REFUSED TO BECOME EASTERN "ORTHODOX" SCHISMATICS – *Page 201*

• In his 1945 encyclical *Orientales Omnes Ecclesias,* Pope Pius XII gives examples of Catholics in history who were tortured and killed because they would not abandon fidelity to the Papacy and become Eastern "Orthodox" schismatics. – *Page 201*
• The Vatican II sect's teaching on the "Orthodox" schismatics is an utter mockery of these saints and martyrs, besides being totally heretical. – *Page 201*

THE VATICAN'S BALAMAND STATEMENT WITH THE "ORTHODOX," APPROVED BY JOHN PAUL II, REJECTS CONVERTING SCHISMATICS AS "OUTDATED ECCLESIOLOGY" – *Pages 202-203*

MORE OF JOHN PAUL II'S INCREDIBLE HERESIES WITH THE EASTERN "ORTHODOX" SCHISMATICS– *Page 203*

• John Paul II blesses the schismatic Church of the schismatic bishop of Alexandria, "Pope" Shenouda III… [PHOTO] – *Pages 203-204*
• John Paul II signs a joint declaration with schismatic Patriarch of Romania, Teoctist, in which they reject converting each other. [PHOTO] – *Page 205*
• John Paul II gives $100,000.00 to the schismatic Teoctist and sits on an equal level chair with him. [PHOTO] – *Page 205*
• John Paul II repeatedly declares that he is in communion with non-Catholic sects. – *Page 207*
• John Paul II gives a relic to Karekin II, the head of the schismatic "Church" in Armenia, and declares that his sect is "the Bride of Christ." [PHOTO] – *Pages 207-208*
• In 1982, John Paul II goes to the Anglican church [PHOTO] and takes part in the worship of the Anglican sect – formal heresy by deed…– *Page 209*
• John Paul II mocks the English martyrs by his joint prayer with the Anglican "Archbishop" of Canterbury in 1982. [PHOTO] – *Page 209*
• John Paul II kisses the ring of, and bestows the pectoral cross on, the head of the Anglican sect, a layman [PHOTO]. This action constituted a formal denial in deed of Pope Leo XIII's infallible declaration that Anglican ordinations are invalid. – *Pages 210-211*
• In 1983, John Paul II goes to the Lutheran church in honor of the 500th anniversary of Martin Luther's birth [PHOTO] – heresy by deed. – *Page 212*

Detailed Table of Contents

• John Paul II praises the greatest enemies the Church has ever known, including Luther, Calvin, Zwingli and Hus. – *Page 212*
• John Paul II approved of the heretical Joint Declaration with the Lutherans on Justification. – *Page 213*
• John Paul II repeatedly taught that non-Catholics may receive Holy Communion, including in his Catechism, new Code of Canon Law and his encyclical *Ut Unum Sint*. – *Page 214*
• John Paul II repeatedly taught that non-Catholic sects are means of salvation. – *Page 215*
• John Paul II repeatedly taught that non-Catholic sects have saints and martyrs, which is formal heresy against the Council of Florence and Pope Pius XI. – *Pages 215-217*

OTHER ACTIONS OF JOHN PAUL II

• John Paul II approved of the practice of altar girls [PHOTO], which was condemned by three different popes. – *Page 217*
• John Paul II received the Freemasonic B'nai B'rith [PHOTO], and was awarded by Freemasons. – *Page 218*
• John Paul II apologized to the satanic communist regime in China. – *Page 218*
• John Paul II promoted the fable of evolution and called it "more than a mere hypothesis." – *Page 218*
• John Paul II said that Heaven, Hell and Purgatory are not actual places. – *Page 219*
• John Paul II changed the traditional Rosary by adding five new mysteries. [PHOTO] – *Page 220*
• John Paul II taught that man is Christ. – *Pages 220-22*
• John Paul II carried the Broken Cross, an occult symbol. – *Page 223*
• Concluding points about John Paul II – *Page 223*

17. The Vatican II Sect's Protestant Revolution: the 1999 Joint Declaration with the Lutherans on the Doctrine of Justification – *Page 227*

• In 1999, the Vatican signed an agreement on Justification with the Lutheran sect which declares that the canons of the Council of Trent no longer apply.
• This agreement states that the most notorious Lutheran heresies, which were solemnly condemned by Trent, including Justification by faith alone, are not condemned by Trent anymore. [SPECIFIC DETAILS AND EXAMPLES]
• This agreement is without question formal heresy, and arguably the single most notorious act of the Vatican II sect.
• This outrageous agreement, which rejects the Council of Trent, has been publicly and repeatedly approved and endorsed by John Paul II and Benedict XVI.

18. The Vatican II Sect vs. the Catholic Church on partaking in non-Catholic worship – *Page 234*

• As Pope Pius XI taught in *Mortalium Animos*, the Catholic Church has always forbidden the faithful from taking part in non-Catholic worship.
• This prohibition comes from the divine law, has been repeated throughout all of Catholic history, and has been confirmed by the popes.
• Vatican II and the antipopes of the Vatican II sect teach just the opposite.

THE INCREDIBLE DIRECTORY FOR THE APPLICATION OF THE PRINCIPLES AND NORMS OF ECUMENISM – *Page 236*

• This incredibly heretical directory, which was specifically approved by John Paul II, sets forth an entire progam of participation in non-Catholic worship.
• Since this is a matter of the divine law and is connected with the Faith, it cannot be changed.
• The Vatican II sect's official teaching on participation in non-Catholic worship is one of its biggest heresies; it absolutely proves that it cannot be the Catholic Church.

Detailed Table of Contents

• Its teaching that it's good to participate in non-Catholic worship proves that its leaders (the post-Vatican II "popes") are manifestly heretical non-Catholic antipopes.

19. The Vatican II Sect vs. the Catholic Church on non-Catholics receiving Holy Communion – *Page 239*

• Documentation that the Vatican II antipopes have officially taught in Vatican II, the new catechism, the new code of canon law, encyclicals and speeches that non-Catholics may lawfully receive Holy Communion…
• Documentation that the popes of the Catholic Church have officially taught just the opposite…
• This alone proves that the Vatican II sect is not the Catholic Church, and that its "popes" cannot be true popes because we are dealing with two different religions.

20. The Heresies of Benedict XVI (2005-) – *Page 243*

• Joseph Ratzinger (Benedict XVI) was one of the most revolutionary theologians at Vatican II. – *Pages 243-244*
• Ratzinger showed up at Vatican II in a suit and tie [PHOTO]. He was influential in guiding the revolutionary course of the council with his compatriots, such as Karl Rahner. – *Page 244*
▶ The heresies of Benedict XVI documented in this section come from a study of 24 books written by him, as well as his speeches.
• Benedict XVI was the author of the infamous document on the Third Secret of Fatima released in the year 2000. This document of Benedict XVI promoted the obviously false Third Secret released in 2000, which almost no traditionalist holds to be authentic or complete. In the document, Benedict XVI referred to only one Fatima scholar, Fr. Dhanis, a man who attacked the message of Fatima. – *Page 245*

BENEDICT XVI'S HERESIES ON THE JEWS – *Page 245*

▶ It is a truth of Christian revelation and Catholic dogma that Jews must be converted to Jesus Christ and the Catholic Faith for salvation, and that the Old Law (the Jewish religion) cannot be observed without the loss of salvation. – *Page 245*
• In 2001, Benedict XVI wrote the preface for the book, *The Jewish People and their Sacred Scriptures in the Christian Bible,* which teaches that the Jews' wait for the Messiah is not in vain and that their position that Jesus is not the Messiah and Son of God is valid! – *Page 246*

BENEDICT XVI TEACHES THAT JESUS DOESN'T HAVE TO BE SEEN AS THE MESSIAH – *Page 246*

Detailed Table of Contents

• In his books *God and the World* and *Milestones*, Benedict XVI says that the Jewish reading of the Old Testament, which doesn't see Jesus as the Messiah, is acceptable and might even be true. He thus denies that Jesus is truly the Messiah and Son of God. – *Pages 246-248*

BENEDICT XVI'S PUBLIC ACT OF APOSTASY AT THE GERMAN SYNAGOGUE – *Page 248*

• On August 19, 2005, at a synagogue in Cologne, Germany, Benedict XVI took active part in a Jewish worship service. This is a public act of apostasy. [PHOTOS] – *Pages 248-250*
• Benedict XVI recited the Kaddish prayer with the Jews, and was applauded by the entire synagogue for his acceptance of their religion. – *Pages 248-250*
• Benedict XVI encourages the Chief Rabbi of Rome in his "mission." [PHOTO] – *Page 251*

BENEDICT XVI TEACHES THAT PROTESTANTS AND SCHISMATICS DON'T NEED TO BE CONVERTED TO THE CATHOLIC CHURCH – *Page 252*

• Benedict XVI meeting with schismatic Syrian Patriarch in 1984… [PHOTO] – *Page 252*
• In his book *Principles of Catholic Theology*, Benedict XVI explicitly addresses the issue of whether Protestants and schismatics must be converted to an acceptance of the Papacy and Papal Infallibility (dogmas of the Faith) and he says no: it's not the way for unity. – *Page 253*
• Benedict XVI not only denies the dogma that non-Catholics need to believe in the Papacy, but questions whether popes have supreme jurisdiction in the Church at all! – *Page 254*
• Benedict XVI also denies that the Papacy was even held in the first millennium, and tells us that this is why we cannot bind the schismatics to believe in it! – *Page 255*
• Benedict XVI meeting with schismatic Patriarch Mesrob II, head of Turkish-Armenian schismatic sect… [PHOTO] – *Page 255*

BENEDICT XVI AND "CARDINAL" KASPER BOLDLY REJECT THE ECUMENISM OF THE RETURN, THAT NON-CATHOLICS NEED TO CONVERT – *Page 256*

• "Cardinal" Walter Kasper, appointed by John Paul II and Benedict XVI as head of the Council for promoting Christian Unity, boldly rejects the "ecumenism of the return": that Protestants and schismatics must be converted and return to the Church. – *Page 256*
• Benedict XVI repeats almost word for word the incredible heresy of Kasper in an address to Protestants – see table comparison. This constitutes absolute proof that Benedict XVI is a manifest heretic. – *Page 256*
• Benedict XVI joins Paul VI and John Paul II in praising the overturning of the excommunications against the "Orthodox" – and therefore in denying Vatican I. – *Page 257*

BENEDICT XVI PRAYS ECUMENICAL VESPERS WITH SCHISMATICS AND PROTESTANTS AND SAYS HE HAS COME "TO LOVE" THE ORTHODOX CHURCH! – *Page 258*

• On Sept. 12, 2006, Benedict XVI took active part in the worship of non-Catholics again by praying ecumenical Vespers with Protestants and schismatics. [PHOTO] – *Page 258*
• During the meeting, Benedict XVI actually said that he has come "to love" the Orthodox Church, a schismatic and heretical non-Catholic sect. This is an outrageous heresy. – *Page 258*
• During his speech, Benedict XVI also declared that he, the schismatics and the Protestants are all in communion with each other and in the Faith of the Apostles. – *Pages 258-259*

BENEDICT XVI'S WORST HERESY? HE PRAYS WITH THE LEADER OF THE WORLD'S "ORTHODOX" SCHISMATICS AND SIGNS A JOINT DECLARATION WITH HIM TELLING HIM HE'S IN THE CHURCH OF CHRIST – *Page 259*

Detailed Table of Contents

• On Nov. 30, 2006, in Turkey, Benedict XVI signed a joint declaration with the leader of the world's "Orthodox" schismatics, Bartholomew I of Constantinople, declaring that he [the schismatic] is in the Church of Christ. [PHOTOS] – *Pages 259-260*
• Benedict XVI encouraged another schismatic patriarch to resume his ministry. – *Page 260*

BENEDICT XVI'S INCREDIBLE HERESY ON THE SCHISMATIC "ARCHBISHOP" OF ATHENS – *Page 261*

• Benedict XVI says that the schismatic leader has authority over "All Greece" and has his "demanding service" from the Lord. – *Page 261*

MORE HERESIES OF THE PROTESTANTS FROM BENEDICT XVI – *Page 261*

• Benedict XVI with Protestant Evangelical "Bishop" Wolfgang Huber in 2005… [PHOTO] – *Page 261*
• Benedict XVI explicitly rejects converting Protestants again in *Principles of Catholic Theology*, by stating that he doesn't want their religions dissolved, but strengthened in their Protestant confessions. – *Page 261*

BENEDICT XVI'S PUBLIC ACT OF HERESY IN THE LUTHERAN CHURCH: HE POWERS AHEAD WITH MAJOR ECUMENICAL HERESY – *Page 262*

• On May 25, 2006, Benedict XVI took active part in a worship service at a Lutheran church in Warsaw; this is a public act of heresy. [PHOTO] His speech contains numerous heresies, including approval of the heretical *Joint Declaration with the Lutherans on Justification*. – *Pages 262-263*

MORE HERESIES WITH THE PROTESTANTS FROM BENEDICT XVI– *Pages 263-267*

• Benedict XVI encourages the invalid head of the Anglican Church in his "ministry" and says the Anglican Sect is grounded in Apostolic Tradition. – *Page 264*
• Benedict XVI also denied that Protestants need to convert at Vatican II. – *Page 264*
• Benedict XVI praises the "greatness" of Martin Luther's spiritual fervor, and is credited with saving the *Joint Declaration with the Lutherans on Justification,* to which he hopes Methodists also subscribe. – *Page 264*
• Benedict XVI praises the non-Catholic ecumenical monastery of Taize, and says more should be formed. – *Page 265*
• Benedict XVI gave Communion to the Protestant founder of Taize [PHOTO], Bro. Roger Schutz, and said that he went straight to Heaven when he died. – *Pages 255-256*
• Benedict XVI teaches that the Protestant "Eucharist" is a saving Eucharist. – *Page 266*
• Benedict XVI teaches that Protestantism (Evangelical "Christianity") saves. – *Page 266*
• Benedict XVI teaches that Protestantism is not even heresy – ASTOUNDING DENIAL OF DOGMA. – *Page 267*
• Benedict XVI indicates again that unity with the Protestants respects, not converts, the multiplicity of voices. – *Page 267*

BENEDICT XVI'S HERESIES AGAINST THE SACRAMENTS – *Page 268*

• Benedict XVI approves attendance at "Masses" which have no words of consecration. – *Page 268*
• Benedict XVI denies that words are even necessary for a valid consecration! – *Page 269*
• Benedict XVI says infant baptism has no reason to exist, and that those who insist on its necessity are "unenlightened." – *Page 269*

BENEDICT XVI'S HERESIES AGAINST SACRED SCRIPTURE – *Page 270*

• Benedict XVI says that Sacred Scripture's creation account is based on pagan creation accounts. – *Page 270*
• Benedict XVI calls into doubt the stone tablets of the Exodus account. – *Page 271*
• Benedict XVI says that sentences in the Bible are not true. – *Page 271*

Detailed Table of Contents

- Benedict XVI promotes evolution. – *Page 271*

BENEDICT XVI'S HERESIES AND APOSTASY WITH ISLAM – *Page 272*

▶ Islam rejects the Divinity of Jesus Christ and the Trinity. The Catholic Church officially teaches that Islam is a false religion, an abomination, a "diabolical sect" from which people need to be converted and saved. – *Page 272*
- Benedict XVI has "deep respect" for the false religion of Islam. – *Page 272*
- Benedict XVI says there is a noble Islam. – *Page 272*
- Benedict XVI says that Islam represents greatness. – *Page 273*
- Benedict XVI says that Muslims are believers and that we should esteem their traditions. – *Page 273*
- Benedict XVI wishes Muslims blessings during Ramadan, thus respecting their false religious observances. – *Page 273*
- Benedict XVI esteems Islamic civilizations. – *Page 274*
- Benedict XVI says Islam and Christianity have the same God. – *Page 274*
- Benedict XVI kisses the Koran in words: he says he respects the Koran as the holy book of a great religion. – *Page 274*

BENEDICT XVI GOES INTO A MOSQUE AND PRAYS TOWARD MECCA LIKE THE MUSLIMS – *Page 275*

- On Oct. 30, 2006, Benedict XVI went into the Blue Mosque in Turkey and prayed toward Mecca like the Muslims. He was initiated into Islam. [PHOTOS] – *Pages 275-276*

BENEDICT XVI'S HERESIES WITH PAGANISM – *Page 277*

▶ The Catholic Church teaches that the gods of the pagans are devils (Psalm 95:5; 1 Cor. 10:20).
- Benedict XVI fully favors false ecumenism with pagan religions, such as the devil-worshipping ceremonies at Assisi. – *Pages 277-278*
- Benedict XVI criticizes as hotheads those who destroyed pagan temples. – *Page 278*
- Benedict XVI tells us that pagan and idolatrous religions are high and pure. – *Page 278*
- Benedict XVI has a "profound respect" for false faiths. – *Page 279*
- Benedict XVI says that the presence of false religions is a source of enrichment. – *Page 279*
- Benedict XVI says that theology must learn from the experience of false religions. – *Page 279*

BENEDICT XVI DENYING OUTSIDE THE CHURCH THERE IS NO SALVATION – *Page 280*

▶ The Catholic Church has repeatedly defined as a dogma that no one at all is saved outside the Catholic Church or without the Catholic Faith.
- Benedict XVI explicitly addresses outside the Church there is no salvation and rejects it; he says there is undoubtedly salvation outside the Church on a large scale. – *Page 280*
- Benedict XVI says there are pagan saints – directly contradicting Pope Eugene IV. – *Page 280*
- Benedict XVI says there are many ways to Heaven besides the Christian Faith. – *Page 281*
- Benedict XVI teaches that all religions can lead to God. – *Page 282*

BENEDICT XVI INSULTING CATHOLIC DOGMA – *Page 282*

- Benedict XVI says the Council of Trent's Decree on the Eucharist offends his ecumenical ears and needs to be purged. – *Page 282*
- Benedict XVI says that Trent's Doctrine on the Priesthood was weak and disastrous in effect. – *Page 282*
- Benedict XVI totally blasphemes Church Tradition. – *Page 282*
- Benedict XVI teaches that the term "original sin" is false, even though the Council of Trent used it four times. – *Page 283*

Detailed Table of Contents

• Benedict XVI criticizes the Apostles' Creed. – *Page 283*

BENEDICT XVI ADMITTING THAT VATICAN II HAS CHANGED OR REJECTED CATHOLIC DOGMA – *Page 283*

• Benedict XVI bluntly admits that Vatican II contradicts the infallible teaching of Pope Pius IX on religious liberty and false religions; he admits it is a "countersyllabus" of Pius IX. – *Page 283*
• Benedict XVI acknowledges that the Vatican II sect has abandoned the Catholic Church's traditional prohibition of cremation. – *Page 284*

BENEDICT XVI'S HERESIES AGAINST THE CHURCH – *Page 284*

• Benedict XVI says that Church teaching doesn't exclude those who hold opposing views. – *Page 284*
• Benedict XVI teaches that the Church exists outside the Church. – *Page 284*

BENEDICT XVI TOTALLY REJECTS THE UNITY OR ONENESS OF THE CATHOLIC CHURCH – *Page 285*

▶The unity or oneness of the Catholic Church is one of its four marks and a defined dogma. – *Page 285*
• Benedict XVI repeatedly rejects the unity of the Church; he asserts that the Church was united in the first millennium, but then officially divided by the Protestant revolt and the schismatic revolt. This is blatantly heretical. – *Page 285*
• Benedict XVI teaches that the unity of the Church won't be achieved until the end of the world. – *Page 285*

OTHER HERESIES OF BENEDICT XVI – *Page 286*

• Benedict XVI indicates that Judas might not be in Hell. – *Page 286*
• Benedict XVI respects Hans Kung's path of denial of Jesus Christ. [PHOTO] – *Page 287*
• Benedict XVI says that it's important for every person to belong to the religion of his choice. – *Page 288*
• Benedict XVI utters more heresy on religious liberty, directly contradicting the dogmatic teaching of Pope Pius IX. – *Pages 288-289*
• Benedict XVI repeatedly denies the Resurrection of the Body. – *Page 289*
• Benedict XVI giving the *El Diablo* satanic sign. [PHOTO] – *Page 290*

CONCLUSION ON BENEDICT XVI – *Page 290*

• Benedict XVI is without any doubt a manifest heretic; he cannot be a valid pope, according to Catholic teaching. He is a non-Catholic antipope. – *Pages 290-291*
• Benedict XVI is a deceiver: he mixes his manifest heresies with ambiguous statements and sometimes conservative actions. – *Pages 291-292*
• Pope Pius VI teaches that heretics always use such tactics; don't be deceived by them. Catholics must hold heretics to their heresies regardless of the ambiguity and deception they attempt to employ in teaching the heresies. – *Pages 291-292*
• Benedict XVI's famous statement against Muhammad (Sept. 12, 2006) was meant solely to deceive people. This was proven by his subsequent complete retraction of it, in which he declared that it doesn't "in any way" express his personal thought. This is one of his most revealing heresies; it proves that he is a complete liar and has no credibility. – *Pages 292-294*
• So don't be fooled if Benedict XVI grants a universal indult for the Latin Mass, at a time when almost all the priests are invalid anyway, or does some other conservative gesture to bring traditionalists back under the Vatican II sect. – *Page 294*
• Benedict XVI's teaching that Jews are free to reject Christ and that Christ may not be the Messiah proves that he represents antichrist in the Vatican, in fulfillment of the prophecy of Our Lady of La Salette. – *Page 294*

Detailed Table of Contents

21. Answers to the Most Common Objections Against Sedevacantism (19 Objections answered) – *Page 298*

■ **Obj. 1)** The gates of Hell cannot prevail against the Church, as Christ said (Mt. 16). He said He would be with His Church all days until the end of the world (Mt. 28). What you are saying is contrary to the promises of Christ. – *Page 298*

▶ ANSWER: Indefectibility does not mean that the Church cannot be reduced to a remnant, as happened during the Arian crisis, and as is predicted to occur at the end. It does not mean that antipopes cannot reign from Rome, as has happened, or that there cannot be a period without a pope. Heretics are defined by the popes to be the gates of Hell. It is those who assert that heretics can be popes who assert that the gates of Hell have prevailed against the Church. There is not a single dogma that can be quoted which is contrary to the situation of a counterfeit Church, headed by antipopes, opposing the true Church, which is reduced to a remnant.

■ **Obj. 2)** What's your authority for making these judgments? Your use of dogmatic statements is private interpretation. – *Page 299*

▶ ANSWER: The authority is Catholic dogma (explained). To assert that using dogma is private interpretation is condemned by Pope St. Pius X. The Council of Trent teaches that dogmas are infallible rules of Faith meant for *all* the faithful, to distinguish truth from error and Catholics from heretics.

■ **Obj. 3)** You cannot know if someone is a heretic without a trial or declaratory sentence. – *Page 300*

▶ ANSWER: This is answered and refuted from the teaching of Pope Pius VI, the case of Martin Luther, and the teaching of St. Robert Bellarmine, etc.

■ **Obj. 4)** Can't the Vatican II popes be just "material heretics"? – *Page 302*

▶ ANSWER: No, there are three reasons why it's absurd to assert that the Vatican II "popes" are "material heretics." They are absolutely formal heretics. This answer includes a detailed explanation of the meaning of "material heretic."

■ **Obj. 5)** The Church cannot exist without a pope – or at least 40 years without a pope. – *Page 308*

▶ ANSWER: The Church has existed hundreds of times without a pope, and for years. The answer includes a quote from a well known theologian writing after Vatican I who says the Church could exist decades without a pope.

■ **Obj. 6)** Vatican I's definitions on the perpetuity of the Papal Office contradict the claims of sedevacantists. – *Page 310*

▶ ANSWER: Vatican I's definitions don't in any way contradict the position of those who reject the Vatican II antipopes; answers to the specific passages are given. In fact, it is only those who reject Benedict XVI who can faithfully profess the dogmas of Vatican I, since Benedict XVI utterly rejects them. It is precisely because we believe in Vatican I and its definitions on the Papal Office that we must reject the Vatican II antipopes, who hold them to be meaningless.

■ **Obj. 7)** No one can judge the Holy See; thus the Vatican II popes are popes. – *Page 315*

▶ ANSWER: The Holy See has told us that no heretic can occupy the Holy See. To deny *that* is to judge the Holy See. The original meaning of the phrase refers to subjecting a true bishop of Rome to a trial, which has nothing to do with recognizing that a manifest heretic cannot be the pope. Pope Paul IV destroys this objection by quoting *this very teaching in the very Bull* which declared that one must not accept a heretic as the pope!

Detailed Table of Contents

■ **Obj. 8)** St. Robert Bellarmine said that no one can depose the pope, but that one may resist his bad actions. – *Page 317*

▶ANSWER: This quotation has been completely taken out of context and misapplied. In the very next chapter, St. Robert Bellarmine says that a manifest heretic cannot be the pope. In the passage given in the objection, he is talking about a bad pope, not a manifest heretic. Further, sedevacantists don't depose a pope. They recognize that a manifest heretic has deposed himself. The dishonest promoters of this argument almost never quote St. Robert's teaching in the next chapter on manifest heretics who claim to be pope.

■ **Obj. 9)** Pope Liberius gave in to the Arian heretics and excommunicated St. Athanasius; yet he remained the pope. – *Page 319*

▶ANSWER: It is not true that Pope Liberius gave into Arianism or excommunicated St. Athanasius. According to Pope Pius IX and Pope St. Anastasius, Liberius was falsely accused by the Arians and remained faithful to Catholic teaching.

■ **Obj. 10)** Pope Pius XII declared in *Vacantis Apostolicae Sedis* that a cardinal, no matter what excommunication he is under, can be elected pope. – *Page 320*

▶ANSWER: It's a dogmatic fact that a heretic cannot be the head of the Church, since it's a dogma that a heretic is not a member. A "cardinal under excommunication" presupposes that the excommunication is not for heresy, since *a heretic is no longer a cardinal*. There are numerous things for which a cardinal could be excommunicated and still remain a Catholic cardinal – the distinction between major and minor excommunications. This is made clear by the fact that Pius XII is talking about "ecclesiastical penalties." Heretics are barred from the papacy not merely by an ecclesiastical law, but by the divine law. Pius XII is talking about Catholics under ecclesiastical impediments, not heretics. Even if we grant, for the sake of argument, that Pius XII was legislating that heretics could be elected (which he wasn't), he says that a cardinal's excommunication is only suspended for the purpose of the election, and that it comes into force immediately afterward. This would mean, even if we granted for the sake of the argument that the objection was correct, that the heretic elected would lose his office immediately after the election.

■ **Obj. 11)** What does it matter whether Benedict XVI is the pope? The issue does not concern me. – *Page 322*

▶ANSWER: If this issue doesn't matter, then the New Mass doesn't matter, the non-Catholicism of the Vatican II sect doesn't matter, etc. Further, if you accept Benedict XVI, John Paul II, etc. as true popes you cannot even present the Catholic Faith as binding to a Protestant. This is explained in *The Devastating Dilemma*.

THE DEVASTATING DILEMMA PROVES THAT ONE CANNOT EVEN CONSISTENTLY TRY TO CONVERT A PROTESTANT IF ONE ACCEPTS THE VATICAN II "POPES" – *Page 322*

■ **Obj. 12)** How could all the cardinals accept an antipope, as in the case of John XXIII? – *Page 325*

▶ANSWER: Pope Paul IV explicitly declares that one cannot accept as valid the election of a heretic as pope, *even if it takes place with the consent of "all" the cardinals* – proving that such is a possibility. At the beginning of the Great Western Schism, all of the cardinals rejected Pope Urban VI and accepted Antipope Clement VII.

■ **Obj. 13)** John XXII was a heretic who was even denounced by a cardinal; yet he remained pope. – *Page 326*

▶ANSWER: John XXII was not a heretic, and his reign is no proof that heretics can be popes. This answer utterly refutes the perversion of this case that has been advanced by certain non-sedevacantists.

■ **Obj. 14)** Pope Honorius I was condemned as a heretic by a council; yet he was a true pope. – *Page 328*

Detailed Table of Contents

▶ ANSWER: In condemning Pope Honorius, no council said that he remained the pope after his lapse. Further, the case of Honorius is very different from that of the Vatican II antipopes. The very doctors of the Church who comment on Honorius saw nothing in his case to dissuade them from their position that heretics cannot be popes.

■ **Obj. 15)** The Church and the hierarchy will always be visible. If the Vatican II Church is not the true Catholic Church, then the Church and the hierarchy are no longer visible. – *Page 331*

▶ ANSWER: People misunderstand in what the visibility of the Church consists. It does not exclude the possibility of the true Church being reduced to a small remnant at the end, which is precisely what is predicted by Catholic prophecy and Sacred Scripture – and what was seen in the Arian heresy. The hierarchy remains with the few clergy who remain faithful to the fullness of the Catholic Faith. The Vatican II sect cannot be the visible Church of Christ; in fact, one of its heresies is that it denies the visibility of the Church!

■ **Obj. 16)** The Vatican II popes haven't taught manifest heresy because their statements are ambiguous or require commentary. – *Page 334*

▶ ANSWER: The Vatican II antipopes have taught many manifest heresies which are completely bold and unambiguous and require no commentary (examples). They also have many other heretical statements which are mixed with ambiguity. Pope Pius VI points out that heretics often do this. He further points out that some heresies need study and analysis to condemn, a point which directly refutes the objection.

■ **Obj. 17)** Both the 1917 and 1983 codes of Canon Law teach that a declaration is needed for one to lose his office due to heresy. – *Page 343*

▶ ANSWER: This is simply not true. Only John Paul II's 1983 Code says this; the 1917 Code says just the opposite: public heresy deposes a cleric from office without any declaration. The one who publicly promoted this objection is completely wrong.

■ **Obj. 18)** The Council of Constance condemned the idea that a heretic ceases to be pope, since he is not a member of the Church…– *Page 343*

▶ ANSWER: No, the Council of Constance condemned the idea that *a merely wicked man* (not a heretic) ceases to be pope, since he is not a member of the Church. This is very different from the truth that a heretic ceases to be pope. See explanation...

■ **Obj. 19)** The Joint Declaration with the Lutherans on Justification isn't manifest heresy because the Vatican II "popes" didn't sign it. – *Page 344*

▶ ANSWER: The Joint Declaration with the Lutherans is absolutely manifest heresy on the part of the Vatican II antipopes. They have publicly approved of it. The fact that they didn't sign it is irrelevant. James Smith could draw up a document denying the Immaculate Conception, and if John Doe publicly promotes it (even if he didn't sign it) he is a manifest heretic.

Detailed Table of Contents

START OF PART II – BY THEIR FRUITS YOU SHALL KNOW THEM: THE ROTTEN FRUITS AND INEXHAUSTIBLE SCANDAL OF THE VATICAN II SECT – *Page 348*

The Rotten Fruits and Inexhaustible Scandal of the Vatican II sect prove that it's not the Catholic Church and that we are in the Great Apostasy

A teen in leotards, in an inappropriate position, performs for an applauding John Paul II – just one of a myriad of examples of the scandal, immorality and bad fruits universally exemplified by the Vatican II sect

▶ The Catholic Church is exceptionally holy and is characterized by its inexhaustible holiness; this is one of its marks.
• The Vatican II sect is not holy, but exceptionally unholy; it is characterized by inexhaustible scandal.

22. The Massive Sexual Scandal among the Vatican II/Novus Ordo "priests" – *Page 350*

• The sexual scandal that erupted in the mainstream media beginning approximately in 2002, as a result of shuffling pedophile priests from parish to parish in Boston, has made *what people deem* to be the Catholic Church and the priesthood the mockery of the world.
• They don't realize that they are referring to the Vatican II sect, and that this scandal is *the underlying evil reality of this counterfeit sect coming out for what it is.*
• The scandal is so massive and disgusting that entire dioceses of the Vatican II sect have gone into bankruptcy. [PHOTO OF "CARDINAL" LAW]

Detailed Table of Contents

• This reaches all over the country and even all over the world; facts on the scandal in Portland, Louisville, Phoenix, L.A., Tucson, etc., etc., etc.
• The dioceses of the Vatican II sect, as even their websites reflect, are now more known for sex-abuse hotlines than promoting the true Catholic Faith.
• The "priests" of the Vatican II sect are something to protect one's children from, not to find for true spiritual instruction.

23. The Seminaries of the Vatican II Sect are unspeakable cesspools of homosexuality and heresy – *Page 355*

• Pope Pius XI on what seminaries should be like…– *Page 355*
• The 2002 book *Goodbye Good Men* documents in tremendous detail the utterly horrifying state of post-Vatican II "Catholic" seminaries. – *Pages 355-357*
• Homosexuality, sodomy, perversion and immorality are so rampant at these "seminaries" that, in certain cases, some of the professors and seminarians even cruise the gay bars. – *Page 356*
• Conservative-minded seminarians are often forced to hide their beliefs, accept liberalism and sometimes homosexuality to be admitted or remain in the seminary. – *Pages 355-359*
• These are the seminaries that have produced the "priests" that have produced the massive sexual scandal.
• The Vatican does nothing about this abominable situation, while it promptly removes as head of a more traditional seminary a man who was opposed to the New Mass. – *Pages 355-356*

AN INCREDIBLE ACCOUNT OF THE STATE OF THE SEMINARIES FROM ONE WHO SPENT TIME AT A PROMINENT NOVUS ORDO SEMINARY– *Page 357*

• A conservative-minded seminarian, who spent time at one of the nation's prominent Novus Ordo seminaries, writes about the uncatholic, blatantly heretical, immoral and scandalous atmosphere.
• The seminarian opposed the heresy and immorality and wound up being dismissed.
• The seminarian thought that the Novus Ordo "bishop" would back him, but the "bishop" backed the heretical seminary.

24. The idolatry of the Vatican II Sect, and the formation of "priests" for its idolatry in the seminaries, is connected with its rampant homosexuality – *Page 360*

• Vatican II "priests" celebrating a new liturgy… [PHOTO]
• Scripture teaches that homosexuality is a result of idolatry.
• An examination of the demonic cultures in history shows the connection between idolatry (whether of the flesh or of the work of one's hands or of oneself) and homosexuality.
• Evidence from the satanic Aztec culture and the heathen Asian culture…

25. The Vatican II Sect promotes idolatry by its general worship of man, by its particular worship of man in the New Mass, and by its acceptance of idolatrous religions – *Page 364*

• A blasphemous post-Vatican II New Mass… [PHOTO] – *Page 364*
• *Lex Orandi, lex credendi* – The Novus Ordo Law of Prayer corresponds to the Novus Ordo Law of Belief: that Man is God. – *Page 364*
• The turning around of the altar, and a replacement by a table which faces man instead of God, replaces the cult of God with the cult of man. [PHOTO and discussion] – *Page 365*

Detailed Table of Contents

• The post-Vatican II propaganda on the New Mass invariably sees the meaning of Mass in the assembly – in man rather than in God. – *Pages 365-366*
• Vatican II's constitution on the liturgy explicitly teaches that the full participation of the people *is to be considered before all else* in the liturgy; this means that attention to man is the most important thing in the Mass. – *Page 366*
• Another empty and man-centered New Mass… [PHOTO] – *Page 366*
• That's why we hear about every kind of abomination at the New Mass, including Clown Masses, Kiddie Masses, Polka Masses, etc., etc., etc., *which are all directed toward making the worship conform to the assembly.* – *Pages 366-367*
• Body-Surfing at the New Mass… [PHOTO] – *Page 367*
• The cult of man in the New Mass was strikingly captured in an exposé of a 1978 Clown Mass in the Boston Globe [PHOTO], which spoke of man as the Body of Christ. – *Page 368*
• The American "bishops" officially laid down that when distributing "Communion" a priest must not say "Receive the Body of Christ" or "This is the Body of Christ" because the congregation itself is the Body of Christ. – *Page 369*
• This worship of the assembly as the Body of Christ instead of the Eucharist is reflected in the seminaries. – *Page 369*
▶ Pope Pius XII on the distinction between Church and Lord…– *Page 369*
• A mind-boggling story of idolatry at a Novus Ordo seminary…– *Page 370*
• Two women making a blasphemous offering at another idolatrous New Mass… [PHOTO] – *Page 370*
• Pope Pius X on the distinguishing mark of Antichrist as man replacing God…– *Page 371*

26. The Deplorable State of "Catholic" Parochial and High Schools – *Page 372*

• Since Vatican II, the once-Catholic school system has been laid waste.
• Perverse sex education, condemned by Pope Pius XI, is promoted all over the Vatican II sect's "Catholic" school system.
• Some of the details on the perversion being taught to children in the "Catholic" schools from the book *Growing in Love*.
• Details on how basic Catholic morality, modesty and spirituality are trampled under foot at the "Catholic" schools.
• There is a union between pagan culture and the "Catholic" school system; it produces young men and women who are often worse than pagans.
• These schools, which are "Catholic" in name only, feature the indifferentism of the Vatican II sect, as exemplified by a "Jewish Day" at a "Catholic" primary school. [PHOTO]
• The stunning statistics on the figures of decline in the post-Vatican II school-system, including that almost all Catholic schools have closed since 1965.

27. The Deplorable State of "Catholic" Colleges and Universities – *Page 377*

• Every "Catholic" college or university in communion with Benedict XVI is rampant with heresy and indifferentism and/or the promotion of the gay agenda and/or attacks on Sacred Scripture and/or attacks on the historicity of Our Lord or all of the above.
• Many examples given from many of the most prominent "Catholic" colleges and universities… [PHOTO]
• Official websites of "Catholic" colleges and universities literally encourage people to partake of false religions at their temples and places of worship.
• "Catholic" colleges and universities say that "No" to the Gospel and conversion is part of the divine plan.
• All of this is more expression of the universal apostasy of the Vatican II sect, the Counter Church with which these "Catholic" institutions remain in communion.

Detailed Table of Contents

28. The Annulment Fiasco - The Vatican II Sect's *De Facto* Acceptance of Divorce and Remarriage – *Page 382*

▶ Catholic dogma teaches that a consummated sacramental marriage is indissoluble.
▶ An annulment is a declaration by a valid Church authority that a marriage never existed due to a hidden or known impediment.
▶ Annulments were traditionally given very rarely, are difficult to prove, and the evidence that there was no marriage must be clear; when doubt exists the validity of the marriage is presumed.
▶ Some examples of why the Church would grant an annulment (a declaration that the marriage never existed)…
• When the Vatican II apostasy settled in, the Catholic dogma on the indissolubility of marriage was laid waste with the explosion of phony annulments.
• Only 338 annulments were given in 1968, but 59,000 a year from 1984-1994!
• See the incredible statistics on how annulments are granted in the Vatican II sect to almost anyone who wants one.
• A review of some of the ridiculous cases which were given annulments by the Vatican II sect…
• The Vatican II sect allows divorce and remarriage – this is a fact.
• The Vatican II sect does nothing to stop the phony annulment fiasco or to excommunicate prominent members who are living in invalid "second marriages."
• The Vatican II sect's capitulation on the marriage issue – granting an annulment to basically anyone who wants one – is a proof of its worship of man, never being able to disappoint man.

WHILE THE VATICAN II SECT DENIES THE INDISSOLUBILITY OF MARRIAGE, THE CATHOLIC CHURCH AND THE TRUE POPES HAVE DEFENDED IT AT ALL COSTS – *Page 384*

• Details of how Pope Gregory V, Pope Innocent III, Pope Celestine III, and Pope Clement VII (just to name a few) defended the indissolubility of marriage…
• These popes opposed and *excommunicated* powerful kings and nobles because they had entered into unlawful re-marriages.
• In contradistinction to the phony Vatican II sect, which does nothing to stop the annulment crisis and excommunicates almost no one except those leaning toward traditional Catholicism, the true popes did overturn phony annulments, *excommunicate* and suspend those involved with them.
• Pope Clement VII, faithful to Catholic Tradition and dogma, excommunicated King Henry VIII and allowed an entire country to go into schism rather than violate the sanctity of the marriage bond.
• If the Vatican II sect had been around in the 16th century, the Anglican Schism would have been avoided because a phony annulment would have been granted and the Church's teaching on marriage would have been denied.
• All of this proves again that the Vatican II sect is not the Catholic Church.

29. The Figures on the Post-Vatican II Decline – *Page 387*

• The stunning figures on the bad fruits of the Vatican II sect: the decline in ordinations, religious orders, sisters, Catholic schools, Catholic marriage, traditional belief, etc…

Detailed Table of Contents

30. One can be pro-abortion and part of the Vatican II sect at the same time – *Page 389*

• John Kerry receiving "Communion" in a Vatican II church… [PHOTO]
• The Vatican II sect denies every issue of the Faith, and only claims to stand against abortion and a few other things; but the fact is that it doesn't stand against abortion.
• The Vatican II sect doesn't excommunicate pro-abortion politicians, no matter how prominent they are.
• If the post-Vatican II sect ever had a chance to excommunicate a pro-abortionist, it was in the 2004 presidential campaign, when Sen. John Kerry (who claims to be a Catholic) put his radical pro-abortion views and his claim to be Catholic at the same time *right in the world's face.*
• Not only was Kerry not excommunicated, but almost every single Novus Ordo bishop who addressed the issue denied that Kerry should *even be refused Communion.*
• After much discussion, the official policy of the "bishops" of the U.S. was that Kerry and his like need not be refused Communion, and that it should be left up to individual "bishops."
• "Cardinal" Joseph Ratzinger, as head of the Congregation for the Doctrine of the Faith, said the "bishops'" decision to do nothing to stop it was in line with the Vatican's position.
• Read statement after statement from Novus Ordo "bishop" after "bishop" (even many considered conservative) who said that pro-abortion politicians should not be refused Communion.
▶ The Catholic Church condemns such a heretical position, which gives Communion to public heretics.
▶ Quotes from Popes Pius IX, Gregory XVI, and Pius VIII; read the quote from Pope Benedict XIV on how those opposed to just one dogma must be refused Communion.
• The Vatican II sect holds that opposition to abortion is simply an opinion, not a binding teaching which must be adhered to under pain of anathema and refusal of sacramental communion.
▶ Catholic dogma and history teach that if a man is in favor of a dogma, but doesn't condemn heresy opposed to it, he is a heretic.
▶ History shows us that bishops during the Arian crisis who signed the *Council of Nicaea's* profession of Faith, but refused to condemn the Arians, such as Eusebius of Nicomedia, were considered heretics.
• The bishops of the Vatican II sect and their antipopes have officially said that pro-abortion politicians need not be condemned or even refused the sacraments. Therefore these bishops are heretics, just like the bishops who wouldn't condemn Arians.

Detailed Table of Contents

• The fact is that one can be part of the Vatican II sect and be pro-abortion.

31. The Vatican II sect literally turns away converts at the door – *Page 396*

• In 1975, Father Linus Dragu Popian, who had been raised in the Romanian Orthodox religion, risked his life to escape Communist Romania and presented himself to the Vatican for conversion. The Vatican cardinals were horrified. They told Fr. Popian that he must not flee Communism or become Catholic because this would damage relations with the schismatic Church.
• In 2005, we were contacted by an Eastern Orthodox bishop who was considering conversion. He was told by the Archdiocese of Boston, "**There is no need to Convert, there is salvation for non-Catholics.**"
• This incredibly heretical policy is perfectly in line with the teaching of John Paul II, Benedict XVI, and the Vatican II sect's handbook on ecumenism.
• This is absolute proof that the Vatican II sect is not the Catholic Church.

32. The Religious Orders in the Vatican II Sect: Totally Apostate – *Page 397*

"Trappist" priest being installed as teacher of Zen Buddhism by a "Jesuit"

• Some of the statistics on the decline of religious orders since Vatican II…– *Page 397*
• Examples of homosexuality, religious indifferentism, Pantheism and Yoga that are common in the Vatican II sect's religious orders…– *Pages 397-400*
• Novus Ordo "Trappists" and "Jesuits" are officially installed in Novus Ordo monasteries as teachers of Zen Buddhism. – *Pages 400-401*
• Cloistered nuns on Mt. Carmel pray for Jews to remain Jews. – *Page 402*
• The Apostasy of the Novus Ordo "Benedictine Nuns" – need one say more? The director of over 200 communities demonstrates the complete apostasy typical of the Vatican II sect. – *Page 403*

Detailed Table of Contents

• St. John's Abbey: a typical example of outrageous apostasy in the Vatican II sect's religious orders. Novus Ordo "monks" attend Buddhist services and meditate with Buddhists at one of the Vatican II sect's largest monasteries. – *Pages 403-404*
• An interesting article by a "Benedictine Nun," Sr. Mary Funk, further confirms the utter apostasy of the Vatican II sect's religious orders. – *Page 404*
• These examples are very interesting because they confirm that Vatican II's heresies and new religion have been *correctly* understood and implemented by these people to promote false religions and lose the Faith. – *Pages 404-406*
• Examples such as this, *which confirm the universal apostasy of the Vatican II sect by examining the beliefs of its members and groups at the local level,* could be multiplied for many pages.
• The Apostasy of Mother Teresa of Calcutta and her religious order, the Missionaries of Charity – *Page 407*
> Mother Teresa's 1989 *Time Magazine* Interview – She loved all religions! – *Page 407*
> Mother Teresa venerating the Hindu Gandhi… [PHOTO] – *Page 407*
> Mother Teresa worshipping Buddha… [PHOTO] – *Page 408*

33. Shocking News items provide a summary of the Apostasy of the Vatican II Sect's dioceses, faithful, clergy, etc. – *Page 412*

• The internet has documented the almost bottomless pit of scandal, heresy and immorality produced by the apostate Vatican II sect and its members, clergy, religious orders, etc. Here are just some of the headlines; more of the same come out almost daily:
• Novus Ordo "Cardinal" Cheong of Seoul sends greetings for Buddha's Birth and says: "We need Buddha's teaching more and more." – *Page 412*
• Buddhist Ritual in Novus Ordo Cathedral…– *Page 412*
• So-called "Catholic priest" denies that Jesus even founded a Church on *Larry King Live* – *Pages 412-413*
• New Novus Ordo "Archbishop" of San Francisco finds Gay Cowboy movie "Very Powerful." – *Page 413*
• Circus and Clown "Mass" in Florida with a bishop… [PHOTO] – *Pages 413-414*
• Vatican newspaper agrees that Intelligent Design should not be taught in schools. – *Page 414*
• With the "Bishop's" permission, Novus Ordo "priest" announces he's gay during the Novus Ordo "Mass," and declares that he will be leaving to pursue a gay relationship. – *Page 414*
• Archdiocese of Los Angeles officially invites all to ecumenical Taize prayer services. – *Page 414*
• Muslims are going to Heaven, says EWTN priest. – *Page 414*
• Rabbi made a "Papal" Knight by the Vatican II sect. – *Page 414*
• Novus Ordo "Priests" seek to adopt Hindu rituals. – *Page 415*
• Novus Ordo Diocesan Agency helps Gays Adopt children. – *Page 415*
• The official website of the Novus Ordo "Bishops" officially pays homage to pro-abortion and pro-homosexual Rabbi Balfour. – *Page 415*
• Lutheran funeral service for non-Catholic Rehnquist to be held in Novus Ordo Cathedral. – *Page 415*
• Canadian Novus Ordo Diocese to sell all of its churches to pay Sex Abuse Claims. – *Page 415*
• Diocese settles Lawsuit over accused molestation by "traditional" Society of St. John priests. – *Page 415*
• 45% of "Catholic" Hospitals in U.S. Dispense Abortion Drugs. – *Page 415*
• Novus Ordo "Bishop" of San Diego Apologizes for Not having Catholic Funeral for Gay Nightclub Owner! – *Page 415*
• St. Petersburg's "Bishop" Lynch Favors Starving Terri Schiavo. – *Page 415*
• Ecumenical Vespers held at Novus Ordo church. – *Page 415*
• Novus Ordo "Mass" with firecrackers, drums, gongs and a costumed dragon dance…– *Page 415*
• England's "Bishops" Adopt Gay Equality Agenda. – *Page 415*
• Another Pro-Gay/ "Sodomy Mass" in the Novus Ordo…– *Page 415*
• EWTN Priest says that it's okay to attend Protestant services. – *Page 415*
• "Catholic" University of Notre Dame has Gay Lifestyle Celebration. – *Page 416*
• Hundreds of Baptisms declared invalid at Novus Ordo church in Australia. – *Page 416*
• Novus Ordo "Archbishop" of Dublin favors Homosexual Spousal Rights. – *Page 416*
• Buddhists, including the Dalai Lama, defile Mexico City Cathedral with "cardinal's" permission. [PHOTOS] – *Pages 416-417*
• Novus Ordo hospitals Commit Live-Birth Abortions, condoned by bishops. – *Page 417*
• "Catholic" Loyola University Chicago invites totally pro-abortion Howard Dean to speak. – *Page 417*

Detailed Table of Contents

- Occult-like practices rampant in the Novus Ordo…– *Page 417*
- St. Joan of Arc church promotes Gay/Lesbian/Bisexual/Transgender Agenda. – *Page 418*
- Only 18 Novus Ordo "priests" to be ordained in all of England and Wales. – *Page 418*
- "Bishop" Bernard Harrington of Winona Diocese says *yes* and appoints gay predator "priest." – *Page 418*
- "Cardinal" Law's prestigious new role in Rome, given by John Paul II. – *Page 418*
- Novus Ordo Molester-"priests" Were Moved From Country to Country. – *Page 418*
- "Cardinal" Maida of Detroit OK's Tridentine Mass only to keep people away from independent Traditional Masses. – *Page 418*
- Scranton Seminary closes…– *Page 418*
- "Cardinal" Mahony, the apostate phony, says Rainbow Sash Protesters OK to receive Communion. – *Page 418*
- There are pictures of a Novus Ordo "bishop" throwing his election party at a Masonic temple. – *Page 419*
- Boston "Archdiocese" will close 65 Parishes and 60 churches. – *Page 419*
- Novus Ordo Priest Denies "Holy Communion" to Pro-life Politician because he was kneeling! – *Page 419*
- John Paul II's Envoy Favors Recognition of Sodomite Unions. – *Page 419*
- Britain's vocation crisis deepens. – *Page 419*
- Toronto "Catholic" University Alumni Magazine Boasts of Homosexual "Marriage." – *Page 419*
- Ontario "Catholic" Teachers' Union Website Promotes Transvestites and Drag Queens! – *Page 419*
- Inter-religious service at Arcadia Parish…– *Page 420*
- "Cardinal" Martini says "Catholic Church" should abandon the Papal Monarchy and become a democracy. – *Page 420*
- What a Surprise: Pro-Abort Politician Durbin Receives "Communion" in the Novus Ordo…– *Page 420*
- More Paganism in the Novus Ordo: Kansas City members celebrate the "Year of the Monkey." – *Page 420*
- The Vatican II sect is the "Church" of Sodom – so pro-homosexual that a list of "gay-friendly" parishes has been compiled. – *Page 420*
- Novus Ordo "Priests" dying of AIDS all over the place…– *Page 420*
- Novus Ordo "Franciscan" Friars in Boston angrily oppose the distribution of flyers against homosexual "marriage." – *Page 421*
- The Novus Ordo "Archbishop" of Johannesburg, South Africa, supports the offering of the blood of sacrificed animals during the Novus Ordo "Mass." – *Page 421*
- A Witch gets Novus Ordo Burial…– *Page 421*
- L.A. Cathedral features a liturgy with 50-foot dragons representing the god of rainfall! – *Page 421*
- "Bishop" of San Jose Denies Historical Accuracy of the Gospels. – *Page 421*
- Crowd erupts into wild frenzy as six Novus Ordo "Priests" sing love songs. – *Page 422*
- Novus Ordo "Church" in Australia openly promotes Occultism and Witchcraft. – *Page 422*
- Michigan Basilica Featured Buddhist Prayer Chants – traditionalist-minded protesters were opposed by members of the Basilica and the "priest." – *Page 422*
- Diocese of the Vatican II sect in Cleveland is Worried about "The Passion of the Christ." – *Page 422*
- Toronto Novus Ordo "Catholic" Priest Files Supreme Court Affidavit Supporting Gay Marriage. – *Page 423*
- Novus Ordo "Priest" has Puppet "Masses." [PHOTO] – *Page 423*
- Break-Dancers perform for Antipope John Paul II and Get His Blessing. [PHOTO] – *Page 423*
- "Fr." Stan Fortuna is the Rapping "Priest," promoted by EWTN and Franciscan University… [PHOTO GIVING THE DEVIL SIGN] – *Page 424*
- German Diocese Offers Zen Meditation…– *Page 424*
- St. Louise Novus Ordo church conducts Interfaith Service at a Synagogue With Jews. – *Page 425*
- The Official Website of the Novus Ordo Bishops Endorses Teilhardian Pagan Spirituality. – *Page 425*

CONCLUSION ON THESE SECTIONS CONCERNING THE SCANDAL OF THE VATICAN II COUNTER-CHURCH – *Page 425*

- The headlines and sections we've covered are just the tip of the iceberg; examples could be multiplied for pages; they come out almost daily.
- Since holiness is one of the four marks of the Church, the almost universal scandal and unholiness of the Vatican II sect proves that it is not the Catholic Church.
- Its inexhaustible supply of rotten fruits is a result of its apostasy and heresy.

Detailed Table of Contents

34. The Apostasy of the "bishops" and prominent members of the Vatican II sect - is this your hierarchy? – *Page 428*

THIS SECTION CONTAINS INTERESTING ITEMS AND IMPORTANT COMMENTARY ON SOME OF THE MOST SIGNIFICANT AND REVEALING HERESIES FROM THE PROMINENT MEMBERS OF THE VATICAN II SECT

▶ St. Robert Bellarmine, Dom Prosper Guéranger, Pope St. Celestine on how even laymen must resist heretical bishops and how heretical bishops lose their offices without any declaration after defecting from the Faith…– *Pages 428-429*

▼ The "Bishop" of Buffalo gets vested by the Dalai Lama in a massive ecumenical service with Jews, Muslims and heretics which expresses his complete apostasy from the Catholic Faith. – *Page 429* [PHOTO: page 428]

▼ The Head of Russian Bishops tells us that the Vatican II sect has no intention of converting Russian "Orthodox" Schismatics. – *Page 430*

▼ U.S. Novus Ordo Bishops Officially Join "Christian Churches Together in the U.S.A" – a Protestant Communion. – *Page 430*

> With this agreement, the Novus Ordo Church in the U.S.A. has officially repudiated any claim to be the one true Church of Jesus Christ, and has admitted that it is just one of many heretical denominations.

▼ John Paul II's appointment as New Bishop in Jerusalem says that the Catholic Church has no intention of converting Jews to Christianity! – *Page 431*

▼ John Paul II's "Cardinal Archbishop" of Washington, D.C. confirms John Paul II's rejection of proselytism (converting others)! – *Page 432*

▼ The "Archbishop" of Strasbourg admits that the Vatican II sect has abandoned Catholic teaching on the Jews! – *Page 433*

> He says that Vatican II revised traditional teaching on the Old Covenant being revoked, and that John Paul II repeatedly taught that the Old Covenant is permanent.

▼ The Novus Ordo Bishops Bluntly Repudiate the Dogmatic Second Council of Lyons and the Council of Florence! – *Page 433*

> In a Joint Statement with schismatics which is carried on the official website of the American Novus Ordo "bishops," they bluntly state that the dogmatic definition of the Second Council of Lyons, which condemns those who deny that the Holy Ghost proceeds from the Father and the Son, is "no longer applicable"!

▼ Vatican Commission under John Paul II again rejects trying to convert Jews…– *Page 435*

▼ Hindus worship the Devil at the Shrine of Our Lady of Fatima…– *Page 436*

▼ The Vatican II sect commemorates Mennonite "martyrdom." – *Page 437*

▼ Non-Catholic "Saints" and "Martyrs" Commemorated by the Vatican II sect, repeating John Paul II's heresy…– *Page 438*

▼ The Vatican II sect praises and celebrates John Wesley, the founder of the Methodist sect. – *Page 438*

▼ *No Words of Consecration, No Problem.* With the approval of John Paul II and Benedict XVI, approves a "Mass" as valid which has no words of Consecration! – *Page 439*

▼ The Novus Ordo Bishop of Kansas City denies the Perpetual Virginity of Our Lady. – *Page 441*

▼ At the 2003 Fatima Conference, the Novus Ordo Clergy called the dogmatic definition of the Council of Florence "horrible"! – *Page 442*

▼ Even "conservative" Novus Ordo "bishops," such as "Bishop" Fabian Bruskewitz and "Cardinal" George, are complete apostates. – *Page 443*

▼ Every year the Vatican sends a message commemorating Buddhist feast of Vesakh. – *Page 444*

▼ Every year the Vatican Congratulates Muslims for the end of Ramadan. – *Page 444*

▼ Every year the Vatican Sends a Message to Hindus on the Feast of Diwali! – *Page 445*

▼ The Vatican II sect teaches that Jews and Muslims are the spiritual seed of Abraham, which is a denial of Jesus Christ. – *Page 446*

• There are many other examples that could be given, but these suffice to prove, once again, that *the hierarchy of the Vatican II sect is not the Catholic hierarchy – and that we are in the Great Apostasy.*

Detailed Table of Contents

35. EWTN: The Global "Catholic" Network and the Charismatic Movement – *Page 449*

• Mother Angelica, foundress of EWTN, promoted false ecumenism and the evil Charismatic movement.
▶ A discussion of why the Charismatic movement is diabolical…
▶ A discussion of Mother Angelica's "mystical" experiences…
• EWTN promotes the heresies of Vatican II and the evil false ecumenism of the counterfeit sect.

START OF PART III – THE TRADITIONALIST RESISTANCE – *Page 456*

THE TRADITIONALIST RESISTANCE – SOME ISSUES PERTAINING TO THOSE WHO HAVE FIGURED OUT, TO ONE DEGREE OR ANOTHER, THAT THE POST-VATICAN II CHURCH MUST BE RESISTED OR REJECTED

▶ These sections deal with refuting some of the false positions that have been adopted by those who have recognized a problem with the post-Vatican II "Church," but still maintain that the antipopes at the head of this new Vatican II religion are true popes or that the New Mass is valid, etc.

36. The False Apparitions at Bayside, New York – *Page 458*

▶ This article exposes the lengths to which the Devil has been allowed to go to deceive people about the Vatican II apostasy, the Vatican II antipopes and the New Mass.
▶ Our Lord foretold (Mt. 24) that there will be false miracles and false revelations in the last days to deceive, if it were possible, even the elect. – *Page 460*
▶ The alleged appearance of the Mother of God at Bayside was one of those false revelations and miracles. This is proven by the false and heretical messages contained within the Bayside revelation.
• PHOTOS of the false signs at Bayside…– *Pages 458-460*
▶ False apparitions accompanied by deceiving miracles like those at Bayside have recently occurred in many places. They are meant to misdirect people during the time of the Great Apostasy.
• Bayside teaches that there are other faiths in Heaven. [HERESY] – *Page 461*
• Bayside's false prophecy on the market crash…– *Page 461*
• Bayside's false prophecy on Ball of Redemption…– *Page 461*
• Bayside's heresy on God's powers, and that John Paul II was good… [PHOTO OF JOHN PAUL II'S APOSTASY IN ASSISI] – *Pages 462-463*
• Bayside teaches clear falsehood on the television. – *Page 463*
• Bayside's false prophecy on the one following John Paul II…– *Page 464*
• The Real Purpose of the False Bayside Messages: Stay at your parish at the invalid New Mass and with the antipope. [PHOTO OF FALSE NEW MASS] – *Page 464*
• Veronica Lueken was a voice-box for the Devil. [PHOTO] – *Page 466*

37. What does Medjugorje say? The Message of Medjugorje proves that it is also a false apparition – *Page 468*

Detailed Table of Contents

38. Was Vatican II infallible? If you believe that Paul VI was a true pope, *yes.* – *Page 469*

THIS SECTION DISPROVES THE POSITION OF THOSE WHO HOLD THAT PAUL VI WAS A TRUE POPE, BUT REJECT THE HERESIES OF VATICAN II BY SAYING THAT THEY ARE NOT BOUND TO ACCEPT THEM BECAUSE VATICAN II WAS NOT INFALLIBLE EVEN IF HE WAS A TRUE POPE

▶ This section proves that the true position is that the man who imposed the heretical Second Vatican Council *could not have been* a true pope because he solemnly attempted to bind heretical Vatican II on the faithful.
• If Paul VI was a true pope (which he wasn't), he fulfilled all three conditions to speak infallibly by his confirmation of Vatican II. – *Pages 469-472*
• Each document of Vatican II begins and ends with solemn words of Paul VI – including the invocation of his "apostolic authority" – which would definitely be infallible if he had been a true pope. – *Page 470*
• When closing Vatican II, Paul VI also solemnly declared in virtue of his "apostolic authority" that Vatican II is to be religiously observed by all the faithful. – *Page 471*

■ **Obj. 1)** John XXIII said that Vatican II would only be a "pastoral council," which proves it wasn't dogmatic. – *Page 472*

▶ ANSWER: John XXIII never said that (see explanation), and it is Paul VI's solemn confirmation that matters anyway.

■ **Obj. 2)** Paul VI said in 1966 that Vatican II had avoided proclaiming dogmas affected by infallibility. – *Page 473*

▶ ANSWER: Paul VI's 1966 statement is irrelevant because Vatican II had already been solemnly closed in 1965. Paul VI made this statement after the fact to add confusion. Further, in this 1966 statement, Paul VI says that Vatican II constitutes the teaching of the Magisterium. He further declares that whoever honors Vatican II honors the Magisterium. Thus, even those who go by this statement would be bound to accept Vatican II as the teaching of the Magisterium (which is infallible and binding) – see explanation.

■ **Obj. 3)** Vatican II was not infallible because there was a note attached to *Lumen Gentium* that said it was not infallible. – *Page 475*

▶ ANSWER: This note is not part of all the documents, but only *Lumen Gentium*. This note declares Vatican II enacts the Supreme Magisterium of the Church and that Vatican II must be accepted according to the way things are said at the council. Well, Vatican II says that its (heretical) teaching on religious liberty comes from divine revelation and is to be held sacred by Christians (see examples). Thus, even if one goes by this note, one must accept Vatican II's heretical teaching on religious liberty as sacred and part of revelation, by virtue of the "Supreme Magisterium of the Church." See explanation.
▶ All of this proves that there is no way to escape the reality Antipope Paul VI could not have been a true pope and at the same time promulgate Vatican II.

ST. PETER VS. ANTI-PETER– *Page 477*

▶ In *Quanta Cura*, Pope Pius IX dogmatically condemns, proscribes (outlaws) and reprobates the idea of the civil right to religious liberty in virtue of his apostolic authority. – *Page 477*
• In *Dignitatis Humanae* at Vatican II, Paul VI solemnly approves, decrees and establishes the idea of the civil right to religious liberty in virtue of his "apostolic authority." – *Page 477*
▶ The two cannot possibly possess the same apostolic authority (the authority of the Papacy). To assert that they did (i.e. that Paul VI was a true pope) is to blaspheme the Church, reject Papal Infallibility and assert that the gates of Hell have prevailed against it. – *Page 478*

Detailed Table of Contents

39. Paul VI ends a very popular and significant false traditionalist myth by declaring that Vatican II and the New Mass are binding – *Page 480*

• As we just covered, many "traditionalists" assert that the proper position is to resist the New Mass and Vatican II, while accepting the post-Vatican II "popes" as true popes.
• In an address on the position of Archbishop Lefebvre (which is basically never quoted by false traditionalists), Paul VI himself blows this position away by declaring that the New Mass and Vatican II are binding. He further implies that those who reject them are outside the Church.
▶ The only proper position, therefore, is one which rejects Vatican II, the New Mass and Antipope Paul VI.

40. The File on the Positions of the Society of St. Pius X (SSPX) – *Page 482*

A FURTHER ANALYSIS OF THE POSITION OF THOSE TRADITIONALIST GROUPS WHO RESIST VATICAN II AND THE NEW MASS, BUT STILL ACCEPT THE POST-VATICAN II "POPES"

• In their best-selling books, the SSPX teaches that souls can be saved in false religions, which is heresy. – *Page 483*
• The SSPX recognizes as Catholic manifestly heretical bishops. – *Pages 483-484*
• The SSPX calls the Vatican II sect a New Church which it refuses active communion with; at the same time, however, it professes communion with the head of the New Church, which is illogical. – *Pages 483-484*
• The SSPX operates a world-wide obstinate apostolate outside of communion with the hierarchy it recognizes as Catholic. – *Pages 483-484*
• The SSPX holds that the post-Vatican II "popes," whom it regards as valid, have erred in canonizations. This position is false and contrary to Catholic teaching. – *Page 485*
▶ THE CATHOLIC CHURCH TEACHES THAT CANONIZATIONS ARE INFALLIBLE; HERETICS SAY THE CHURCH HAS ERRED IN CANONIZATIONS. – *Page 485*
• Some very interesting statements by Archbishop Lefebvre expressing his view that the Vatican II "popes" might not be valid popes…– *Pages 485-487*
• Bishop Fellay says that Hindus can be saved. – *Page 487*
• Bishop Richard Williamson of the SSPX says John Paul II was a "good man" and says the SSPX's religion is not the same as that of the Vatican II "popes" it recognizes!– *Page 487*
• Bishop Tissier De Mallerais of SSPX rejects the concept of Church communion and admits that Benedict XVI has taught heresies. – *Page 488*
• The Society of St. Pius X's book, *Most Asked Questions about the Society of St. Pius X*, says the Vatican II "popes" CANNOT teach infallibly. – *Page 489*
• Benedict XVI personally tells SSPX that it must accept Vatican II. – *Page 490*
• Important points refuting the claim of SSPX supporters – and those who hold similar positions – that they are justified in simply living a Catholic life, attending the SSPX (or some other independent chapel) while not worrying about these issues, such as sedevacantism…– *Page 490*
▶ Quick comments on the SSPX's possible full reconciliation with the Vatican II sect…– *Page 491*

41. Sister Faustina's Divine Mercy Devotion is something to avoid – *Page 493*

• Some of the problematic messages delivered to Sr. Faustina which serve to prove that her messages were not from God…
• Sr. Faustina's Divine Mercy Devotion (prayed on the beads of the Rosary) has been used as a substitute for the Rosary.

Detailed Table of Contents

• Sr. Faustina's Divine Mercy Devotion has never been approved by the Catholic Church, but only by the Vatican II sect; in the 1950's it was suppressed and her diary was placed on the Index of Forbidden Books.

42. Natural Family Planning is Sinful Birth Control – *Page 497*

• What is Natural Family Planning?
• Why is NFP wrong?
• The Teaching of the Catholic Papal Magisterium…
• God's Word…
• People Know that NFP is a Sin…
• Planned Parenthood and NFP of the same cloth…
• NFP has eternal and infinite consequences.
• Objections…
• Conclusion…

43. The Whole Truth about the Consecration and Conversion of Russia and the Impostor Sister Lucy – *Page 506*

THIS SECTION EXAMINES IN DETAIL THE MEANING OF OUR LADY'S WORDS AT FATIMA ON JULY 13, 1917 ABOUT THE CONSECRATION OF RUSSIA, AND EXPLAINS HOW A TRUE UNDESTANDING OF THEM DOESN'T IN ANY WAY CONTRADICT THE REALITY THAT THE POST-VATICAN II "POPES" ARE ANTIPOPES;
IT FURTHER GIVES THE EVIDENCE THAT THERE WAS AN IMPOSTOR SR. LUCY AFTER VATICAN II, INSTALLED TO GO ALONG WITH THE POST-VATICAN II AGENDA AND THE FALSE THIRD SECRET OF FATIMA

-MANY INTERESTING PHOTOS AND MAPS-

• FACT #1: POPE PIUS XII CONSECRATED RUSSIA TO THE IMMACULATE HEART OF MARY - POPE PIUS XII CONSECRATED NOT THE WORLD, <u>BUT SPECIFICALLY RUSSIA</u>, ON JULY 7, 1952
• FACT #2: **WHAT OUR LADY MEANS BY THE CONVERSION OF RUSSIA – THE STRIKING EVIDENCE**
• THIS POSITION IS FURTHER SUBSTANTIATED BY CONSIDERING PORTUGAL – "THE SHOWCASE OF OUR LADY"
• THIS POSITION IS FURTHER SUBSTANTIATED BY SR. LUCY'S SUMMARY OF THE TUY VISION
• "THE GOOD WILL BE MARTYRED" AND "VARIOUS NATIONS WILL BE ANNIHILATED" ARE PROPHECIES THAT HAVE ALREADY BEEN FULFILLED
• WHAT RUSSIA WAS CONVERTED FROM – SNAPSHOTS OF THE SATANIC REGIME IN COMMUNIST RUSSIA
• HE WILL DO THE CONSECRATION, BUT IT WILL BE "LATE"
• OUR LADY'S WORDS REVEAL TO US THAT HER TRIUMPH IS NOT A UNIVERSAL TRIUMPH OR REIGN OF PEACE, BUT ONLY A "CERTAIN" PERIOD OF PEACE
• THE CONVERSION OF RUSSIA =…
• THE EVIDENCE
• SOME LEFTOVER OBJECTIONS – AND SR. LUCY DIDN'T EVEN KNOW IF PIUS XII'S 1942 CONSECRATION OF THE WORLD WAS ACCEPTED IN HEAVEN
• **PART II: THE EVIDENCE EXPOSING THE IMPOSTOR SR. LUCY –** *Page 542*
• THE FALSE MESSAGE OF "FR." NICHOLAS GRUNER

Detailed Table of Contents

START OF PART IV – CONCLUDING SECTIONS

44. Is the Vatican II sect the Whore of Babylon prophesied in chapters 17 and 18 of the Apocalypse? – *Page 559*

"And the woman was clothed round about with purple and scarlet" (Apoc. 17:4)

THE ASTOUNDING EVIDENCE THAT THE VATICAN II SECT IS THE WHORE OF BABYLON

- 1. The whore sits upon many waters – an explanation of this based on Catholic teaching…– *Page 560*
- 2. The whore sits upon the city of seven mountains – Rome. – *Page 561*
- 3. The whore is a woman, to contrast her with the true Church (the whore's antithesis), who is also a woman. – *Page 562*
- 4. The whore is a mother, to contrast her with the true Church (the whore's antithesis), who is also a mother. – *Page 563*
- 5. The whore is clothed round about in purple and scarlet (the colors of bishops and cardinals); that is, she wears the colors of the true Church but inwardly is an apostate fraud; STRIKING PHOTOS OF PURPLE AND SCARLET…– *Page 563*
- 6. The whore has a golden cup in her hand, representing the Chalice at Mass, which is defiled by the whore's spiritual fornication in the area of the Mass; STRIKING PHOTO…– *Page 565*
- 7. The whore is characterized by fornication and whoredom, which means spiritual infidelity in Sacred Scripture. [PHOTOS OF VATICAN II SECT'S SPIRITUAL FORNICATION] – *Page 566*
- 8. The whore has separated from her Spouse, Jesus Christ. – *Page 569*
- 9. The light of the lamp shall shine no longer in the whore, which means the sanctuary lamp and the real presence of Christ in the Eucharist. [PHOTO] – *Page 570*
- 10. The voice of the pipe is heard no longer in the whore, which means the removal of traditional Catholic liturgical music from the whore, and a replacement with worldly music. [PHOTO] – *Page 571*
- 11. All the world is drunk with the wine of her whoredom, which means the spiritual fornication having to do with the wine portion of the consecration – the very part that has been changed – which makes the New Masses invalid. – *Page 571*
- 12. The whore is drunk with the blood of the saints and martyrs because false ecumenism mocks and renders meaningless all the sufferings of the saints and martyrs not to embrace false religions, which the whore does with enthusiasm. [PHOTO] – *Page 572*

Detailed Table of Contents

CONCLUSION ON THE WHORE OF BABYLON – *Page 574*

▶ The Vatican II sect is clearly the Whore of Babylon. God tells people in Apoc. 18 to come out of her; the Apocalypse contrasts the whore with another woman (the true Catholic Church reduced to a remnant) which has fled to the wilderness (Apoc. 12). – *Page 575*

45. The Antichrist Code: The Shocking truth that John Paul II was preaching that Man is God – the Doctrine of Antichrist – right in the Vatican – *Page 577*

• John Paul II in Israel sitting in a chair with an upside-down cross over his head… [PHOTO AND EXPLANATION] – *Page 577*
• John Paul II, as a bishop, wearing an upside-down cross vestment… [PHOTO] – *Page 578*

Contents:
1. Our Lady Prophesied that Rome would lose the Faith and become the Seat of Antichrist – *Page 579*
2. Antichrist Defined – *Page 579*

Antipope John Paul II Preached:
3. Each Man Must Take Possession of the Incarnation – *Page 582*
4. The Gospel is the Good News of Man – *Page 583*
5. Man is the Christ, the Son of the Living God – *Page 584*
6. The Truth About Man is that he is Christ – *Page 585*
7. And the Word became Flesh in Every Man – *Page 586*
8. The Incarnation is the Truth About Man – *Page 586*
9. The Mystery of the Word Made Flesh is the Mystery of Man – *Page 587*
10. Mary is Blessed because she had faith in Man – *Page 587*
11. Every man is the Christ Child Born on Christmas – *Page 587*
12. The Epiphany is the Manifestation of Man – *Page 588*
13. Man is the Way – *Page 589*
14. Man is the Truth – *Page 591*
15. Man is the Life – *Page 591*
16. Each Man is the Eucharist – *Page 592*
17. Each Man is the Crucified Christ – *Page 593*
18. Man is Indeed God – *Page 594*
19. Man is the Man from Above – *Page 595*
20. Man's true reality is that he is God – *Page 596*
21. Man is the Messiah – *Page 597*
22. The New Evangelization – *Page 597*
23. Man must discover that he is God – *Page 598*
24. The Rosary of Man – *Page 599*
25. The Unsearchable Riches of Christ are Everyone's Property – *Page 599*
26. Man is the Risen Christ – *Page 599*
27. Antichrist Revealed – *Page 600*

PAUL VI AND BENEDICT XVI ALSO REPRESENTED ANTICHRIST IN THE VATICAN, IN FULFILLMENT OF LA SALETTE – *Page 601*

Detailed Table of Contents

46. What Catholics can and should do in the present apostasy – *Page 606*

▶ The difficult question of where to go to Mass or Confession; Catholics cannot attend the invalid New Mass for any reason… – *Page 606*
▶ The Profession of Faith for converts from the Council of Trent, which should also be used by those leaving the New Mass and the Vatican II religion…– *Pages 606-607*
▶ The form of baptism and conditional baptism; anyone can baptize in a state of necessity…– *Page 608*
▶ Practicing true devotion to Our Lady and the Rosary…– *Page 609*
▶ A few books we recommend people to obtain…– *Page 610*

The Truth about What Really Happened to the Catholic Church after Vatican II

John Paul II during a syncretist prayer gathering with various false religious leaders at Assisi in 1986 - This "ecumenical" activity was always condemned by the Catholic Church, and specifically labeled as a complete rejection of the Catholic Faith by Pope Pius XI in 1928. This is a revolution against the Faith – a new Gospel. What's going on here? Read this book to find out.

1. The Great Apostasy and a counterfeit Church predicted in the New Testament and in Catholic Prophecy

Luke 18:8- "But yet the Son of man, when he cometh, shall he find, think you, faith on earth?"

In the Gospel, Our Lord Jesus Christ informs us that in the last days the true Faith would hardly be found on the earth. He tells us that "in the holy place" itself there will be "the abomination of desolation" (Mt. 24:15), and a deception so profound that, if it were possible, even the elect would be deceived (Mt. 24:24).

Matthew 24:15- "**When therefore you shall see the abomination of desolation, which was spoken of by Daniel the prophet, <u>standing in the holy place</u>**: he that readeth let him understand."

Matthew 24:24-25- "For there shall arise false Christs and false prophets, and shall show great signs and wonders, **insomuch as to deceive (if possible) even the elect**. Behold I have told it to you, beforehand."

The Great Apostasy and a counterfeit Church predicted

> 2 Thess. 2:3-5- "Let no man deceive you by any means, for unless there come *a revolt* [apostasy] first, and the man of sin be revealed, the son of perdition, Who opposeth, and is lifted up above all that is called God, or that is worshipped, <u>so that he sitteth in the temple of God</u>, shewing himself as if he were God. Remember you not, that when I was yet with you, I told you these things?"

In 1903, Pope St. Pius X thought that he might be seeing the beginning of the evils which will fully come to pass in the last days.

> Pope St. Pius X, *E Supremi* (# 5), Oct. 4, 1903: "… **there is good reason to fear lest this great perversity may be as it were a foretaste, and perhaps the beginning of those evils which are reserved for the last days; and that there may already be in the world the 'Son of Perdition' of whom the Apostle speaks** (2 Thess. 2:3)."[1]

The New Testament tells us that this deception will happen in the very heart of the Church's physical structures, in "the Temple of God" (2 Thess. 2:4) and "in the holy place" (Mt. 24:15). It will arise because people receive not the love of the truth (2 Thessalonians 2:10).

In 2 Thessalonians 2, St. Paul speaks of the last days being characterized by a great apostasy that will be the worst ever – even worse than was experienced in the Arian crisis in the 4th century, in which an authentically Catholic priest was hardly to be found.

> Fr. William Jurgens: "At one point in the Church's history, only a few years before Gregory's [Nazianz] present preaching (A.D. 380), **perhaps the number of Catholic bishops in possession of sees, as opposed to Arian bishops in possession of sees, was no greater than something between 1% and 3% of the total.** Had doctrine been determined by popularity, today we should all be deniers of Christ and opponents of the Spirit."[2]

> Fr. William Jurgens: "**In the time of the Emperor Valens (4th century), Basil was virtually the only orthodox Bishop in all the East who succeeded in retaining charge of his see**… If it has no other importance for modern man, a knowledge of the history of Arianism should demonstrate at least that the Catholic Church takes no account of popularity and numbers in shaping and maintaining doctrine: else, we should long since have had to abandon Basil and Hilary and Athanasius and Liberius and Ossius and call ourselves after Arius."[3]

> St. Gregory Nazianz (+380), *Against the Arians*: "Where are they who revile us for our poverty and pride themselves in their riches? **They who define the Church by numbers and scorn the little flock?**"[4]

If the Arian crisis – just a prelude to the Great Apostasy – was this extensive, how extensive will the Great Apostasy foretold by Our Lord and Saint Paul be?

> Prophecy of St. Nicholas of Fluh (1417-1487): "The Church will be punished because the majority of her members, high and low, will become so perverted. **The Church will sink deeper and deeper until she will at last seem to be extinguished, and the succession of Peter and the other Apostles to have expired.** But, after this, she will be victoriously exalted in the sight of all doubters."[5]

The Great Apostasy and a counterfeit Church predicted

St. Paul further says that this apostasy will result in a man sitting in the temple of God and "shewing himself as if he were God." Later in this book, we prove that this is exactly what has happened by a man sitting in St. Peter's Basilica declaring that he and everyone else is God.

Fr. Herman Kramer was a Catholic priest who spent 30 years studying and writing a book on the Apocalypse. In his book, he wrote the following about St. Paul's prophecy concerning the Antichrist sitting in the Temple of God.

> "St. Paul says that Antichrist 'sitteth in the temple of God'... This is <u>not</u> the ancient Temple of Jerusalem, nor a temple like it built by Antichrist, as some have thought, for then it would be his own temple... this temple is shown to be a Catholic Church, possibly one of the churches in Jerusalem or **<u>St. Peter's in Rome, which is the largest church in the world and is in the full sense 'The Temple of God.'</u>**"[6]

Notice that Kramer says that "the Temple of God" probably refers to St. Peter's Basilica in Rome.

> Pope Pius XI, *Quinquagesimo ante* (#30), Dec. 23, 1929: "... such a great number of them <u>came to the Basilica of St. Peter's</u> for the jubilee of indulgence that We have probably **never seen that great temple** so crowded."[7]

The Catholic Encyclopedia article on "Antichrist" indicates that St. Bernard believed that the Antichrist would be an antipope:

> "...St. Bernard speaks in the passage of the Antipope [as the Beast of the Apocalypse]."[8]

> Bl. Joachim (d. 1202): "Towards the end of the world, Antichrist will overthrow the pope and usurp his see."[9]

But whether or not one believes that the Antichrist will be an antipope, it has definitely been prophesied that the forces of Antichrist will overtake Rome in the final days. On Sept. 19, 1846, Our Lady of La Salette prophesied that Rome would lose the Faith and become the Seat of the Antichrist in a final days apostasy from the one true Catholic Faith.

Our Lady of La Salette, Sept. 19, 1846: "Rome will lose the Faith and become the seat of the Anti-Christ... the Church will be in eclipse."

The Great Apostasy and a counterfeit Church predicted 4

This startling prophecy coincides with the prophecies in Sacred Scripture (Apocalypse 17 and 18), which inform us that the city of seven hills (Rome) will become a harlot (a counterfeit Bride of Christ), which will commit spiritual fornication (idolatry) and tread upon the blood of the saints (false ecumenism). The great harlot prophesied in the Bible is not the Catholic Church; it is a counterfeit Catholic Church, an apostate, phony Bride which arises in the last days to deceive Catholics and eclipse the true Church which has been reduced to a remnant. In this book we will bring forward the overwhelming, undeniable, irrefutable evidence from doctrinal grounds and unassailable facts that the "Church" which has arisen with the Second Vatican Council (1962-1965) is not the Catholic Church at all, but rather a massively fraudulent Counter-Church which denies the fundamental teachings of the Catholic Church.

We will show that the men who imposed this new Vatican II religion and the New Mass were not Catholics at all, but manifest heretics preaching a new religion.

In fact, any doubts about the authenticity of Our Lady's message at La Salette will be obliterated by a careful examination of the evidence in this book. Among other things, this book will document that the Vatican now teaches that Jews are perfectly free <u>not</u> to believe in Jesus Christ.

The Great Apostasy and a counterfeit Church predicted 5

This may startle some, but this is a fact. Without even considering all of the other apostasy which we will cover in this book, this fact proves that Our Lady's words have come true: Rome (not the Catholic Church) has lost the Faith (given way to a non-Catholic, counterfeit sect) and become the seat of the Antichrist.

In late 2001, the Pontifical Biblical Commission released a book entitled *The Jewish People and the Holy Scriptures in the Christian Bible*. The book **argues that the Jews' continued wait for the Messiah is validated and justified by the Old Testament**. "The expectancy of the Messiah was justified in the Old Testament," papal spokesman Joaquin Navarro-Valls explained, "and if the Old Testament keeps its value, then it keeps that as a value, too. <u>It says you cannot just say all the Jews are wrong and we are right</u>." Asked by reporters whether his statements might be taken to suggest that the Messiah may not in fact have come, Navarro-Valls replied, "It means it would be wrong for a Catholic to wait for the Messiah, <u>but not for a Jew</u>." This means that the Vatican now holds that the Jews are perfectly free to reject Christ; this is the teaching of the Vatican II "popes."

Rome has lost the Faith and become the seat of the Antichrist.

> 1 John 2:22 – "Who is a liar, but **he who denieth that Jesus is the Christ? He is antichrist,** who denieth the Father, and the Son."

But how did this come about, and what are Catholics to do about it? This book will endeavor to answer both of those questions in detail.

Endnotes for Section 1 :

[1] *The Papal Encyclicals*, by Claudia Carlen, Raleigh: The Pierian Press, 1990, Vol. 3 (1903-1939), p. 6.
[2] William Jurgens, *The Faith of the Early Fathers,* Collegeville, MN: The Liturgical Press, Vol. 2, p. 39.
[3] William Jurgens, *The Faith of the Early Fathers,* Vol. 2, p. 3.
[4] William Jurgens, *The Faith of the Early Fathers,* Vol. 2, p. 33.
[5] Yves Dupont, *Catholic Prophecy* by Yves Dupont, Rockford, IL: Tan Books, 1973, p. 30.
[6] Fr. Herman Kramer, *The Book of Destiny*, Tan Books, 1975, p. 321.
[7] *The Papal Encyclicals*, Vol. 3 (1903-1939), p. 351.
[8] *The Catholic Encyclopedia*, Volume 1, "Antichrist," Robert Appleton Co. 1907, p. 561.
[9] Rev. Culleton, *The Reign of Antichrist*, Tan Books, 1974, p. 130.

2. Pope Leo XIII's Original Prayer to St. Michael – a Prophecy about the Future Apostasy in Rome

Pope Leo XIII

Pope Leo XIII's original *Prayer to St. Michael* the Archangel is prophetic. Composed over 100 years ago, and then suppressed due to its startling content, Pope Leo XIII's original *Prayer to St. Michael* is one of the most interesting and controversial prayers relating to the present situation in which the true Catholic Church finds itself. On September 25, 1888, following his morning Mass, Pope Leo XIII became traumatized to the point that he collapsed. Those in attendance thought that he was dead. After coming to consciousness, the pope described a frightful conversation that he had heard coming from near the tabernacle. The conversation consisted of two voices – voices which Pope Leo XIII clearly understood to be the voices of Jesus Christ and the Devil. The Devil boasted that he could destroy the Church, if he were granted 75 years to carry out his plan (or 100 years, according to some accounts). The Devil also asked permission for "a greater influence over those who will give themselves to my service." To the Devil's requests, Our Lord reportedly replied: "you will be given the time and the power."

Shaken deeply by what he had heard, Pope Leo XIII composed the following original *Prayer to St. Michael* (which is also a prophecy) and ordered it to be recited after all Low Masses as a protection for the Church against the attacks from Hell. What follows is the original prayer (note especially the bolded portions), followed by some of our comments. **The Original Prayer was taken from *The Raccolta*, 1930, Benziger Bros., pp. 314-315.** *The Raccolta* is an imprimatured collection of the official and indulgenced prayers of the Catholic Church.

The Prayer:

O Glorious Archangel St. Michael, Prince of the heavenly host, be our defense in the terrible warfare which we carry on against principalities and Powers, against the rulers of this world of darkness, spirits of evil. Come to the aid of man, whom God created immortal, made in his own image and likeness, and redeemed at a great price from the tyranny of the devil.

Fight this day the battle of the Lord, together with the holy angels, as already thou hast fought the leader of the proud angels, Lucifer, and his apostate host, who were powerless to resist thee, nor was there place for them any longer in Heaven.

That cruel, that ancient serpent, who is called the devil or Satan, who seduces the whole world, was cast into the abyss with his angels. Behold, this primeval enemy and slayer of men has taken courage. Transformed into an angel of light, he wanders about with all the multitude of wicked spirits, invading the earth in order to blot out the name of God and of his Christ, to seize upon, slay and cast into eternal perdition souls destined for the crown of eternal glory. This wicked dragon pours out, as a most impure flood, the venom of his malice on men of depraved mind and corrupt heart, the spirit of lying, of impiety, of blasphemy, and the pestilent breath of impurity, and of every vice and iniquity.

These most crafty enemies have filled and inebriated with gall and bitterness the Church, the spouse of the immaculate Lamb, and have laid impious hands on her most sacred possessions. <u>In the Holy Place itself, where has been set up the See of the most holy Peter and the Chair of Truth for the light of the world, they have raised the throne of their abominable impiety, with the iniquitous design that when the Pastor has been struck, the sheep may be scattered</u>.

Arise then, O invincible Prince, bring help against the attacks of the lost spirits to the people of God, and give them the victory. They venerate thee as their protector and Patron; in thee holy Church glories as her defense against the malicious power of hell; to thee has God entrusted the souls of men to be established in heavenly beatitude. Oh, pray to the God of peace that He may put Satan under our feet, so far conquered that he may no longer be able to hold men in captivity and harm the Church. Offer our prayers in the sight of the Most High, so that they may quickly conciliate the mercies of the Lord; and beating down the dragon, the ancient serpent, who is the devil and Satan, do thou again make him captive in the abyss, that he may no longer seduce the nations. Amen.

Behold the Cross of the Lord; be scattered ye hostile powers.
The Lion of the tribe of Judah has conquered, the root of David.
Let thy mercies be upon us, O Lord.
As we have hoped in thee.
O Lord, hear my prayer.
And let my cry come unto thee.

Let us pray.
O God, the Father of our Lord Jesus Christ, we call upon thy holy name, and as suppliants we implore thy clemency, that by the intercession of Mary, ever Virgin immaculate and our Mother, and of the glorious Archangel St. Michael, thou wouldst deign to help us against Satan and all other unclean spirits, who wander about the world for the injury of the human race and the ruin of souls. Amen.

As one who reads the prayer (especially the bolded portion) can see, Pope Leo XIII foresaw and predicted the great apostasy; and he pinpointed that this apostasy would be led from Rome – Rome which alone is *"the Holy Place itself, <u>where</u> has been set up the See of the most holy Peter and the Chair of Truth for the light of the world."* **Pope Leo clearly foresaw that this place (Vatican City in Rome), where had been set up the Chair of Peter by the first Pope, St. Peter himself, would become the throne of Satan's abominable impiety**, with the *"iniquitous design that when the Pastor (the true Pope) has been struck, the sheep (the Catholic faithful) may be scattered."* These are Pope Leo XIII's words.

Pope Leo XIII was not predicting the defection of the Catholic Church (which is impossible, as the gates of Hell can never prevail against the Church [Mt. 16]), nor the defection of the Chair of Peter (which is also impossible), <u>but rather he was predicting the implementation of an apostate, counterfeit Catholic religion from Rome</u>, in which "the pastor" (the true pope) **is replaced by a usurping antipope** (as has occurred at times in Church history), with the iniquitous design that "the sheep may be scattered."

Pope Leo's prayer also foresaw that Satan's impure apostates would lay impious hands *"on the Church's most sacred possessions."* What are the Church's most sacred possessions? The most sacred possessions of the Church are those things which Christ entrusted to Her: namely, the deposit of faith (with all of its dogmas) and the seven sacraments instituted by Our Lord Jesus Christ Himself. Therefore, Pope Leo's prayer foresaw the attempted destruction of the deposit of faith with Vatican II and the new sacramental rites of the Vatican II Church. Both of these will be covered in detail in this book. We will see that Paul VI's laying of impious hands on the Church's seven sacramental rites beginning in April of 1969, which produced an invalid New Mass, an invalid New Rite of Ordination, and gravely doubtful rites of Confirmation and Extreme Unction, fulfilled Pope Leo's prediction to the letter.

In 1934, Pope Leo's striking prayer (given above) was changed without explanation. **<u>The key phrase referring to the apostasy in Rome (the Holy Place, where the See of Peter has been set up for the light of the world) was removed</u>**. Around the same time (now that Pope Leo had been dead), the use of Pope Leo XIII's original *Prayer to St. Michael* after each Low Mass was replaced by a totally new concoction, the now famous abbreviated *Prayer to St. Michael*, which still bears Pope Leo's name, but obviously was not written by the pope. This prayer goes as follows:

> "St. Michael the Archangel, defend us in battle, be our protection against the wickedness and snares of the devil; may God rebuke him, we humbly pray; and do thou, O Prince of the heavenly host, by the power of God, thrust into hell Satan and all evil spirits who wander through the world for the ruin of souls. Amen."

There is nothing wrong with this prayer to St. Michael; in fact, it is very good and efficacious. However, the point is that it's not the original *Prayer to St. Michael* that Pope Leo XIII composed and ordered to be recited at the end of every Low Mass. It was promoted as a substitute, so that the faithful would be unaware of the incredible content of the original prayer, as described above. If the original *Prayer to St. Michael* had been recited at the end of every Low Mass and not suppressed in 1934, how many millions more would have been stirred to a resistance when they encountered the attempted new post-Vatican II religion that we will cover in this book? How many would have seen through the systematic dismantling of the traditional Catholic Faith after Vatican II?

Pope Leo XIII's prophecy about the future apostasy in Rome

Pope Leo XIII's original *Prayer to St. Michael* also fits perfectly with Our Lady of La Salette's famous appearance and prediction in 1846: *"Rome will lose the faith and become the Seat of the Antichrist... the Church will be in eclipse."* Pope Leo's words suggest that Antichrist himself, or at least the forces of Antichrist, would set up their seat in Rome: *"In the Holy Place itself, where has been set up the See of the most holy Peter... they have raised **the throne of their abominable impiety**..."*

Another photo of John Paul II at his 1986 interreligious prayer service in Assisi, Italy – something totally condemned by the Catholic Church (more on this in the section on John Paul II)

3. The Message of Fatima: a heavenly sign marking the beginning of the end times and a prediction of apostasy from the Church

Lucia, Francisco and Jacinta of Fatima

> Fr. Mario Luigi Ciappi, papal theologian to Pope Pius XII: "In the Third Secret [of Fatima] it is foretold, among other things, that the great apostasy in the Church will begin at the top."[1]

The message and miracle of Our Lady of Fatima in 1917 is one of the greatest events in the history of the Catholic Church. Since the miracle at Fatima, which occurred on Oct. 13, 1917, was predicted to take place in advance, and was fulfilled in the presence of almost 100,000 people, it's probably the greatest miracle in Catholic history outside the Resurrection. The Fatima miracle and message also bear tremendous significance for our topic: *The Truth about What Really Happened to the Catholic Church after Vatican II.* Beginning on May 13, 1917, the Mother of God appeared six times to Jacinta (age 7), Francisco (age 9) and Lucia (age 10) in Fatima, Portugal. The Blessed Virgin told the children to pray the Rosary every day; she showed them a vision of Hell; and she made prophecies about World War II and the expansion of Communism ("the errors of Russia"), among other things.

> The Vision of Hell shown by Our Lady of Fatima to the children: "As the Lady spoke the last words, she opened Her hands once more, as She had done the two previous months. **The rays [of light] appeared to penetrate the earth, and we saw, as it were, a vast sea of fire. Plunged in this fire, we saw the demons and the souls [of the damned]. The latter were like transparent burning embers, all blackened or burnished bronze, having human forms**. They were floating about in that conflagration, now raised into the air by the flames which issued from within themselves, together with great clouds of smoke. **Now they fell back on every side like sparks in huge fires, without weight or equilibrium, amid shrieks and groans of pain and despair, which horrified us and made us tremble with fright (it must have been this sight which caused me to cry out, as people say they heard me).** The

demons were distinguished [from the souls of the damned] by their terrifying and repellent likeness to frightful and unknown animals, black and transparent like burning coals. **That vision only lasted for a moment, thanks to our good Heavenly Mother, Who at the first apparition had promised to take us to Heaven. Without that, I think that we would have died of terror and fear."[2]**

"You see Hell, where the souls of poor sinners go. To save them God wishes to establish in the world the devotion to my Immaculate Heart," Our Lady said.

The Fatima children shortly after the vision of Hell… one can see in their terrified countenances the truth of their words: that they would have died of fright at the vision of Hell if they had not been promised Heaven

On July 13, 1917, Our Lady also told the children that on Oct. 13, 1917 she would work a miracle that all would have to believe:

> "Lucia said, 'I wish to ask you to tell us who you are, and to perform a miracle so that everyone will believe that you have appeared to us!'
> 'Continue to come here every month,' answered the Lady. **'In October I will tell you who I am and what I wish, <u>and will perform a miracle that everyone will have to believe</u>**.'"[3] (Our Lady of Fatima, July 13, 1917)

Since the children had announced months in advance of Oct. 13 that the Lady would work a miracle, 70,000 to 100,000 people gathered at Fatima on Oct. 13 to see the miracle that was predicted to take place. There were also many nonbelievers who came to scoff when the predicted miracle didn't occur. However, as even the secular press confirmed, the Miracle of the Sun – as it's now known – did occur, just as it was predicted by the children and by Our Lady of Fatima. It stunned the gathered multitude, converted hardened unbelievers, including atheists and Freemasons, and confirmed thousands in the Catholic Faith.

Above: two pictures of the stunned crowd at Fatima on Oct. 13, 1917 witnessing the predicted miracle by Our Lady of Fatima

What was the Miracle of the Sun that so stunned and converted the enraptured audience of 70,000-plus at Fatima on Oct. 13, 1917? A brief examination of the miracle and its significance will go a long way in revealing: *The Truth about What Really Happened to the Catholic Church after Vatican II.*

> "The sun stood forth in the clear zenith like a great silver disk which, though bright as any sun they had ever seen, they could look straight at without blinking, and with a unique and delightful satisfaction. This lasted but a moment. While they gazed, the huge ball began to 'dance' – that was the word all the beholders applied to it. Now it was whirling rapidly like a gigantic fire-wheel. After doing this for some time, it stopped. Then it rotated again, with dizzy, sickening speed. Finally there appeared on the rim a border of crimson, which flung across the sky, as from a hellish vortex, blood-red streamers of flame, reflecting to the earth, to the trees and shrubs, to the upturned faces and the clothes all sorts of brilliant colors in succession: green, red, orange, blue, violet, the whole spectrum in fact. Madly gyrating in this manner three times, **the fiery orb seemed to tremble, to shudder, and then to plunge precipitately, in a mighty zigzag, toward the crowd**.
>
> "<u>**A fearful cry broke from the lips of thousands of terrified persons as they fell upon their knees, thinking the end of the world had come**</u>. Some said that the air became warmer at that instant; they

would not have been surprised if everything about them had burst into flames, enveloping and consuming them."[4]

"All over Portugal, in fact, the anti-clerical press was compelled to bear witness of the same sort. There was general agreement on the essentials. As Dr. Domingos Pinto Coelho wrote in *O Ordem*, 'The sun, sometimes surrounded with crimson flames, at other times aureoled with yellow and red, at still other times seemed to revolve with a very rapid movement of rotation, **still again seeming to detach itself from the sky, to approach the earth…**'"[5]

During the miracle the sun was seen to be speeding toward the earth **and the people thought the end of the world had come**. The significance should be obvious: **Fatima was an apocalyptic sign; it was a sign that the end was near, that the events which would precede the culmination of the world and the Second Coming of Jesus Christ were to begin**. Men must amend their lives before the end of the world really came.

Based on some of these considerations, many have concluded that Our Lady of Fatima is the woman clothed with the sun described in chapter 12:1 of the Apocalypse:

> "And **a great sign appeared in heaven**: **A woman clothed with the sun**, and the moon under her feet, and on her head a crown of twelve stars." (Apocalypse 12:1)

The Fatima seers also reported that Our Lady was made all of light – she was more brilliant than the sun. The evidence is very strong that Our Lady of Fatima was the woman clothed with the sun prophesied in the Apocalypse, chapter 12. In fact, there is a stunning confirmation that Our Lady's appearance at Fatima was the fulfillment of the prophecy in the Apocalypse about the woman clothed with the sun.

The Masonic Daily Paper, *O Seculo*, stunningly confirms without even knowing it that Our Lady was the woman clothed with the sun of the Apocalypse 12:1

The Miracle of the Sun worked by Our Lady of Fatima was reported by anti-Catholic papers throughout Portugal. The liberal, Masonic and anti-clerical daily of Lisbon, *O Seculo*, had its Editor in Chief, Avelino de Almeida, on hand to report on the event. To his credit, he honestly reported on the solar prodigy. What we want to draw to your attention is the title of his article which was published in *O Seculo* on Oct. 15, 1917. Giving an account of the extraordinary event at Fatima on Oct. 13, his article in *O Seculo* of October 15 was entitled:

> "How the sun danced in broad daylight at Fatima. The apparitions of the Virgin. – **The sign of Heaven**. – Thousands declare it a miracle. – War and peace."[6]

Please notice that the Masonic, anti-clerical daily of Lisbon described the event of Fatima and the Miracle of the Sun as **"The sign of Heaven."** Does that sound familiar?

> Apocalypse 12:1- "And **a great sign appeared in Heaven**: **A woman clothed with the sun**, and the moon under her feet, and on her head a crown of twelve stars."

Are we to believe that the Masonic newspaper of Lisbon had Apocalypse 12:1 in mind when publishing this article shortly after the solar prodigy in 1917? Were the anti-clericals considering the possibility that Our Lady's appearance constituted the woman clothed with the sun and the "sign of Heaven" described in the Bible? Of course not; not even Catholics at that time had connected Fatima with the woman clothed with the sun, let alone the anti-clericals who didn't even believe in Sacred Scripture or probably didn't even know about the prophecy in Apoc. 12:1! This headline, therefore, **is an unknowing confirmation,** *by a public and anti-Catholic source,* **that Our Lady of Fatima and her miracle on Oct. 13 were indeed the sign prophesied in Apocalypse 12:1**!

It's almost as if one were to ask God the question: Lord, how will we know when the great "sign of heaven," which you predicted in Apocalypse 12:1, will occur? And the Lord responded: just read the headline in the Masonic newspaper, for when this sign will occur it will be reported even in it.

This stunning fact not only serves to confirm that Our Lady of Fatima is the woman clothed with the sun of Apoc. 12:1, but also further confirms the authenticity of the Catholic Faith and Sacred Scripture.

Therefore, to finally round out our point about Fatima and its relevance to what has happened to the Catholic Church after Vatican II, we can say: since Fatima was the sign prophesied in Apoc. 12:1, this means that we are in the Apocalyptic era, the last days of the world.

Fatima, the sign of Apoc. 12:1, and the great red dragon (Communism), the sign of Apoc. 12:3, both come on the scene in 1917

Lending further support to the idea that Fatima was the "sign" of Apocalypse 12:1 is the fact that the Apocalypse speaks of the "great red dragon" just two verses later. Scripture seems to indicate that the two will come on the scene at the same time.

> Apocalypse 12:3- "And there was seen another sign in Heaven: **and behold a great red dragon**, having seven heads and ten horns: and on his heads seven diadems: **And his tail drew the third part of the stars of Heaven**, and cast them to the Earth…"

Many commentators consider the "great red dragon" to be Communism, since Communism is undeniably associated with red, and was responsible for the murder of over 20 million people in Russia alone. Under Vladimir Lenin, **the Bolsheviks took over Russia for Communism – gaining the significant victory which would make Communism a world power – on Nov. 7, 1917, immediately after the appearances of Our Lady in Fatima,** which had warned of the spread of "the errors of Russia."[7] Even today we speak of Communist China as "Red China." The Communist revolution in China was launched in celebratory fashion by men with "Enormous red banners, tens of thousands of red flags, and masses of red balloons flew over them."[8] The evidence that the "great red dragon" describes the Communist Empire is quite strong.

It's also very interesting that the great red dragon drew the third part of the stars of Heaven:

> Apocalypse 12:3- "And there was seen another sign in Heaven: **and behold a great red dragon**… **And his tail drew the third part of the stars of Heaven**, and cast them to the Earth…"

Is it just a coincidence that Communism, at its height, **held a third of the world in its grasp?**

> Warren H. Carroll, *The Rise and Fall of the Communist Revolution*, p. 418: "As Joseph Stalin walked into the Valley of the Shadow of Death, **the international communist movement which he led held a third of the world in its grasp**."9

Sister Lucia of Fatima told Fr. Fuentes in 1957 that we are in the last times

One of the three visionaries of Fatima, Sr. Lucia, told Fr. Fuentes in 1957:

> "Father, **the Most Holy Virgin did not tell me that we are in the last times of the world but she made me understand this for three reasons**. The first reason is because she told me that the Devil is in the mood for engaging in a decisive battle against the Virgin. And a decisive battle is the final battle where one side will be victorious and the other side will suffer defeat. Hence from now on we must choose sides. Either we are for God or we are for the Devil. There is no other possibility.
> "The second reason is because she said to my cousins as well as to myself that God is giving two last remedies to the world. These are the Holy Rosary and Devotion to the Immaculate Heart of Mary. **These are the last two remedies which signify that there will be no others.**
> "The third reason is because in the plans of Divine Providence, God always, before He is about to chastise the world, exhausts all other remedies. Now, when He sees that the world pays no attention whatsoever then, as we say in our imperfect manner of speaking, He offers us with a certain trepidation the last means of salvation, His Most Holy Mother. It is with a certain trepidation because if you despise and repulse this ultimate means we will not have any more forgiveness from Heaven because we will have committed a sin which the Gospel calls the sin against the Holy Spirit. This sin consists of openly rejecting with full knowledge and consent, the salvation which He offers. Let us remember that Jesus Christ is a very good Son and that He does not permit that we offend and despise His Most Holy Mother. We have recorded through many centuries of Church history the obvious testimony which demonstrates, by the terrible chastisements which have befallen those who have attacked the honor of His Most Holy Mother, how Our Lord Jesus Christ has always defended the honor of His Mother."10

As discussed already, the main feature of the end times is an apostasy from the Catholic Faith. In "the holy place" itself (Rome) there will be "the abomination of desolation" (Mt. 24:15), and a deception so profound that, if it were possible, even the elect would be deceived (Mt. 24:24). **The New Testament tells us that this deception will happen in the very heart of the Church's physical structures, in "the Temple of God" (2 Thess. 2:4).** It will arise because people receive not the love of the truth (2 Thessalonians 2:10). That is precisely why the very last words that Our Lady of Fatima gives us in the great secret of July 13, 1917 are:

> **"In Portugal the dogma of Faith will always be preserved**, etc."

These are the last words given before the undisclosed third secret of Fatima. From this scholars of Fatima have concluded that the third secret undoubtedly deals with a massive spiritual crisis and apostasy from the Catholic Faith among those who purport to hold positions of authority in the Church.

Since we don't have the complete sentence of Our Lady's last words of the July message, we cannot say for sure what they mean; but the sentence could be: "In Portugal the dogma of Faith will always be preserved *in a faithful remnant*…" Or: "In Portugal the dogma of Faith will always be preserved *until the Great Apostasy*…" Or: "In Portugal the dogma of Faith will always be preserved *among those who heed my warnings*…" The third secret undoubtedly deals with the present apostasy of the Vatican II sect. We will document this apostasy in great detail in this book.

As cited at the beginning of this section,"Fr." Mario Luigi Ciappi, the papal theologian to Pope Pius XII, stated:

> "In the Third Secret it is foretold, among other things, that the great apostasy in the Church will begin *at the top*."[11]

Another "cardinal" of the Vatican II Church incredibly admitted that the Third Secret deals with the post-Vatican II apostasy.

> "Cardinal" Silvio Oddi:"… the Third Secret [of Fatima]… is not about a supposed conversion of Russia…. but regards the 'revolution' in the Catholic Church."[12]

Testimonies that Heaven asked that the third secret of Fatima be revealed by 1960 at the latest[13]

- **Canon Galamba:** "When the bishop refused to open the letter, Lucy made him promise that it would definitely be opened and read to the world **either at her death or in 1960**, whichever would come first." (*La Verdad sobre el Secreto de Fatima,* Fr. Joaquin Alonso, Spanish Edition, pp. 46-47)

- **John Haffert:** "At the bishop's house (in Leiria), I sat at the table on his right, with the four Canons. During that first dinner, Canon Jose Galamba de Oliveira turned to me when the bishop had left the room momentarily and asked: "Why don't you ask the bishop to open the Secret?" Endeavoring not to show my ignorance concerning Fatima—which at that time was almost complete—I simply looked at him without expression. He continued: "The bishop can open the Secret. He doesn't have to wait **until 1960**." (*Dear Bishop!* John Haffert, AMI 1981, pp. 3-4)

- **Cardinal Cerejeira**: In February 1960 the Patriarch of Lisbon reported the directions which the Bishop of Leiria "has passed on to him" on the subject of the Third Secret: "Bishop da Silva enclosed (the envelope sealed by Lucy) in another envelope on which he indicated that **the letter had to be opened in 1960** by himself, Bishop Jose Correia da Silva, if he was still alive, or if not, by the Cardinal Patriarch of Lisbon." (*Novidades*, February 24, 1960, quoted by *La Documentation catholique*, June 19, 1960, col. 751)

- **Canon Barthas**: During his conversations with Sister Lucy on October 17-18, 1946, he had the opportunity to question her on the Third Secret. He writes: "When will the third element of the Secret be revealed to us?" Already in 1946, to this question Lucy and the Bishop of Leiria answered me uniformly, without hesitation and without comment: "**In 1960.**" And when I pushed my audacity so far as to ask why it was necessary to wait until then, the only response I received from either one was: **"Because the Blessed Virgin wishes it so."** (Barthas, *Fatima, merveille du XXe siecle*, p. 83. Fatima-editions, 1952)

- **The Armstrongs**: On May 14, 1953, Lucy received a visit from the Armstrongs, who were able to question her on the third Secret. In their account published in 1955, they confirmed that the third

Fatima: an end times sign and prediction of apostasy　　　　　　　　　　　　　　　　17

- Secret "had to be opened and divulged in 1960." (A. O. Armstrong, *Fatima, pilgrimage to peace*, The World's Work, Kingswood, Surrey, 1955)

- **Cardinal Ottaviani**: On May 17, 1955, Cardinal Ottaviani, Pro-Prefect of the Holy Office, came to the Carmel of Saint Teresa at Coimbra. He interrogated Lucy on the third Secret; and in his conference of 1967 recalled: "The message was not to be opened before 1960. I asked Sister Lucy, **'Why this date?' She answered, 'Because then it will seem clearer** (mais claro).'" (*La Documentation catholique*, March 19, 1967, col. 542)

- **Father Joaquin Alonso, official archivist of Fatima**: "Other bishops also spoke—and with authority—about the year 1960 as the date indicated for opening the famous letter. Thus, when the then titular Bishop of Tiava, and Auxiliary Bishop of Lisbon asked Lucy when the Secret was to be opened, he always received the same answer: **in 1960.**" (*La Verdad sobre el Secreto de Fatima*, Fr. Joaquin Alonso, Spanish Edition, p. 46)

- **Father Joaquin Alonso**: "When Don Jose, the first Bishop of Leiria, and Sister Lucy agreed that the letter was to be opened in 1960, they obviously meant that its contents should be made public for the good of the Church and the world." (ibid., p. 54)

- **Bishop Venancio:** "I think that the letter will not be opened before 1960. Sister Lucy had asked that it should not be opened before her death, or not before 1960. We are now in 1959 and Sister Lucy is in good health." **(***La Verdad sobre el Secreto de Fatima,* Fr. Joaquin Alonso, Spanish Edition, p. 46)

- **Father Fuentes:** Father Fuentes interviewed Sister Lucy on December 26, 1957, who told him: "Father, the Most Holy Virgin is very sad because no one has paid attention to Her Message, neither the good nor the bad. The good continue on their way but without giving any importance to Her Message… I am still not able to give any other details because it is still a secret. According to the will of the Most Holy Virgin, only the Holy Father and the Bishop of Fatima are permitted to know the Secret, but they have chosen not to know it so that they would not be influenced. **This is the third part [third Secret] of the Message of Our Lady which will remain secret until 1960."** (*La Verdad sobre el Secreto de Fatima*, Fr. Joaquin Alonso, Spanish Edition, p. 103-104)

- **F. Stein:** "The testimonies which have announced the revelation of the Secret for 1960 are of such weight and so numerous that in our opinion, even if the ecclesiastical authorities of Fatima [in 1959 the experts themselves were still unaware that Rome had taken the Secret from the Bishop of Leiria over two years previously] had not yet resolved to publish the Secret in 1960, they would now see themselves forced to do so by the circumstances." (*Mensagem de Fatima,* July-August, 1959)

- **Father Dias Coelho:** "… we can use, as an unquestionable fact, this assertion of Dr. Galamba de Oliveira (in 1953) in *Fatima, Altar do Mundo*: 'The third part of the Secret was sealed in the hands of His Grace the Bishop of Leiria, and will be opened either after the seer's death or at the latest in 1960.'" (*L'Homme Nouveau*, No. 269, November 22, 1959)

All testimonies and statements reveal clearly that Heaven wanted the third secret of Fatima revealed to the whole world no later than 1960, because it would be clearer then.

Why would the third secret of Fatima be clearer in 1960?

It was **on Jan. 25, 1959 that John XXIII announced that he had a special inspiration to suddenly call a new ecumenical council.** (Jan. 25, by the way, was the same day on which the unknown light that illuminated the world prior to World War II lit up the skies of Europe. This unknown light that appeared on Jan. 25, 1938 was predicted by Our Lady of Fatima as a warning that God was going to punish the world with the things that were revealed in the second part of the secret.

Was the fact that John XXIII called Vatican II on a Jan. 25 a warning about the coming punishment described in the third secret?)

This council called by John XXIII in 1959 would turn out to be Vatican II, the disastrous results of which are the subject of this book. Is the calling of this council in 1959 the reason that Our Blessed Mother requested the third secret of Fatima to be revealed by 1960? Was she directly warning us of the apostasy that would result from this council, which truly gave birth to a new, phony Counter-Catholic Church, as we will see in this book? Truly, the only major sign that had occurred by 1960, in regard to the tremendous apostasy we are now living through that would makes things "clearer," was that John XXIII had announced his intention to call a new council in 1959. In our view, it's quite obvious that the third secret of Fatima deals with the apostasy resulting from a false council; otherwise the third secret wouldn't make more sense in 1960, as Our Blessed Mother said it would.

Endnotes for Section 3:

[1] Ciappi's personal communication to a Professor Baumgartner in Salzburg, cited in *The Devil's Final Battle*, compiled by Paul Kramer, Good Counsel Publications, 2002; also cited by Father Gerard Mura, "The Third Secret of Fatima: Has It Been Completely Revealed?", the periodical *Catholic* (published by the Transalpine Redemptorists, Orkney Isles, Scotland, Great Britain), March 2002.
[2] William Thomas Walsh, *Our Lady of Fatima*, Doubleday Reprint, 1990, p. 81.
[3] William Thomas Walsh, *Our Lady of Fatima*, p. 80.
[4] William Thomas Walsh, *Our Lady of Fatima*, pp. 145-146.
[5] William Thomas Walsh, *Our Lady of Fatima*, p. 148.
[6] Portuguese Newspaper, *O Seculo*, Oct. 15, 1917.
[7] Warren H. Carroll, *The Rise and Fall of the Communist Revolution*, Front Royal, Virginia: Christendom Press, p. 93.
[8] Warren H. Carroll, *The Rise and Fall of the Communist Revolution*, p. 538.
[9] Warren H. Carroll, *The Rise and Fall of the Communist Revolution*, p. 418.
[10] Sr. Lucy's interview with Fr. Fuentes, quoted in *The Whole Truth About Fatima* by Frere Michel de la Sainte Trinite, Buffalo, NY:Immaculate Heart Publications, Vol. 3, p. 503 ff.
[11] Ciappi's personal communication to a Professor Baumgartner in Salzburg, cited above.
[12] Silvio Oddi, *The Meek Watchdog of God*, Rome: *Progetto Museali Editore*, 1995, pp. 217-218.
[13] Quotes on this point compiled by: http://www.tldm.org/news/in_1960.htm

4. A complete list of the Antipopes in History

To understand what God might allow to transpire in the final days, we must understand Catholic teaching on the Papacy and look at some examples in Church history of things that God has allowed to occur with regard to the Papacy. It's a fact of history, Scripture and tradition that Our Lord Jesus Christ founded His universal Church (the Catholic Church) upon St. Peter.

> Matthew 16:17-18-"And I say to thee: **That thou are Peter: and upon this rock I will build my Church, and the gates of hell shall not prevail against it. And I will give to thee the keys of the kingdom of heaven.** And whatsoever thou shalt bind upon earth, it shall be bound also in heaven: and whatsoever thou shalt loose upon earth, it shall be loosed also in heaven."

Our Lord made St. Peter the first pope, entrusted to him His entire flock, and gave him supreme authority in the universal Church of Christ.

> John 21:15-17-"**Jesus saith to Simon Peter**: Simon, son of John, lovest thou me? He saith to him: Yea, Lord, thou knowest that I love thee. **He saith to him: Feed my lambs**. He saith to him again: Simon, son of John, lovest thou me? He saith to him: Yea, Lord, thou knowest that I love thee. **He saith to him: Feed my lambs**. He saith to him a third time: Simon, son of John, lovest thou me? Peter was grieved, because he had said to him the third time: Lovest thou me? And he said to him: Lord, thou knowest all things: thou knowest that I love thee. **He said to him: Feed my sheep**."

But in the 2000 year history of the Catholic Church, there have been more than 40 antipopes. An antipope is a bishop who claims to be the pope, but was not canonically elected as Bishop of Rome (i.e., supreme pontiff). Here is a list of the 42 antipopes that the Church had to contend with before Vatican II:

1. St. Hippolytus (reconciled with Pope St. Pontian and died as martyr to the church), 217–235
2. Novatian, 251–258
3. Felix II (confused with a martyr with the same name and thus considered an authentic pope until recently), 355–365
4. Ursicinus (Ursinus), 366–367
5. Eulalius, 418–419
6. Laurentius, 498–499, 501–506
7. Dioscorus (legitimate perhaps as opposed to Boniface II but died 22 days after election), 530
8. Theodore (II) (opposed to antipope Paschal), 687
9. Paschal (I) (opposed to antipope Theodore), 687
10. Theofylact, 757
11. Constantine II, 767–768
12. Philip (replaced antipope Constantine II briefly; reigned for a day and then returned to his monastery), 768
13. John VIII, 844
14. Anastasius III Bibliothecarius, 855
15. Christopher, 903–904
16. Boniface VII, 974, 984–985
17. John Filagatto (John XVI), 997–9

A list of antipopes in History

18. Gregory VI, 1012
19. Sylvester III, 1045
20. John Mincius (Benedict X), 1058–1059
21. Pietro Cadalus (Honorius II), 1061–1064
22. Guibert of Ravenna (Clement III), 1080 & 1084–1100
23. Theodoric, 1100–1101
24. Adalbert, 1101
25. Maginulf (Sylvester IV), 1105–1111
26. Maurice Burdanus (Gregory VIII), 1118–1121
27. Thebaldus Buccapecuc (Celestine II) (legitimate but submitted to opposing pope, Honorius II, and afterwards considered an antipope), 1124
28. Pietro Pierleoni (Anacletus II), 1130–1138
29. Gregorio Conti (Victor IV), 1138
30. Ottavio di Montecelio (Victor IV), 1159–1164
31. Guido di Crema (Paschal III), 1164–1168
32. Giovanni of Struma (Callixtus III), 1168–1178
33. Lanzo of Sezza (Innocent III), 1179–1180
34. Pietro Rainalducci (Nicholas V), antipope in Rome, 1328–1330
35. Robert of Geneva (Clement VII), antipope of the Avignon line, 20 September 1378 – 16 September 1394
36. Pedro de Luna (Benedict XIII), antipope of the Avignon line, 1394–1423
37. Pietro Philarghi Alexander V, antipope of the Pisan line, 1409–1410
38. Baldassare Cossa (John XXIII), antipope of the Pisan line, 1410–1415
39. Gil Sánchez Muñoz (Clement VIII), antipope of the Avignon line, 1423–1429
40. Bernard Garnier (the first Benedict XIV), antipope of the Avignon line, 1425–c. 1429
41. Jean Carrier (the second Benedict XIV), antipope of the Avignon line, 1430–1437
42. Duke Amadeus VIII of Savoy (Felix V), 5 November 1439 – 7 April 1449
(*Wikipedia*, The Free Encyclopedia)

One of the most notorious cases in Church history was that of the Antipope Anacletus II, who reigned in Rome from 1130 to 1138. Anacletus had been implanted in an uncanonical election after Innocent II, the true pope, had already been chosen. Despite his invalid and uncanonical election, Antipope Anacletus II gained control of Rome and the support of the majority of the College of Cardinals. Anacletus held the support of almost the entire populace of Rome, until the true pope regained control of the city in 1138. (*The Catholic Encyclopedia*, "Anacletus," Vol. 1, 1907, p. 447.)

We must also now take a look at the Great Western Schism to see what God allowed in Church history and therefore what he could allow in the Great Apostasy.

5. The Great Western Schism (1378-1417) and what it teaches us about the post-Vatican II apostasy

-Massive confusion, multiple antipopes, antipopes in Rome, an antipope recognized by all the cardinals; The Great Western Schism proves that a line of antipopes at the heart of the post-Vatican II crisis is absolutely possible-

The Breakdown of the Great Western Schism

The Popes	Avignon Line (antipopes)	Pisan Line (antipopes)
Urban VI (1378-1389) ▼ Boniface IX (1389-1404) ▼ Innocent VII (1404-1406) ▼ Gregory XII (1406-1415) **The least supported pope in history, least recognized of the three claimants, rejected by almost all of Christendom**	**Clement VII (1378-1394)** recognized by all the living cardinals who had elected Urban VI ▼ **Benedict XIII (1394-1417)** recognized by St. Vincent Ferrer for a time	*line favored by most theologians of the time, elected by cardinals from both camps* **Alexander V (elected by cardinals at Pisa) 1409-1410** ▼ **John XXIII (1410-1415)** reigned in Rome, had widest support of three claimants
	Resolved with the election of Pope Martin V, 1417 at the C. of Constance	

How it all happened

The conclave in the Vatican (1378) after Pope Gregory XI's death was the first to meet in Rome since 1303. The popes had resided in Avignon for approximately 70 years due to political turmoil. The conclave was held amid scenes of unprecedented uproar.[1] Since France had become the home of the popes for the last 70 years, the Roman mob surrounding the conclave was quite unruly and clamored for the cardinals to elect a Roman, or at least an Italian. At one point, when it was believed that a Frenchman had been elected instead of an Italian, the mob stormed the palace:

> "In a fury the mob now began throwing stones at the windows of the palace and attacking the doors with picks and axes. There was no effective defending force; the crowd stormed in."[2]

Eventually an Italian, Pope Urban VI, was elected by 16 cardinals. The new pope asked the cardinals if they had elected him freely and canonically; they said they had. Shortly after the election, the 16 who had elected Urban VI wrote to the six cardinals who had remained stubbornly in Avignon:

The Great Western Schism: antipopes in Rome

> "We have given our votes for Bartolomeo, the Archbishop of Bari [Urban VI], who is conspicuous for his great merits and whose manifold virtues make him a shining example; we have in full agreement elevated him to the summit of apostolic excellence and have announced our choice to the multitude of Christians."[3]

CARDINALS REJECT POPE URBAN VI UNDER PRETEXT OF THE UNRULY ROMAN MOB

Shortly after his election, however, Pope Urban VI began to alienate the cardinals.

> **"The French cardinals, who formed the majority in the Sacred College, were dissatisfied with the city and wished to return to Avignon**, where there were no dilapidated basilicas and ruined palaces, no tumultuous Roman mobs and deadly Roman fevers; where life was, in a word, more comfortable. **Urban VI refused to leave Rome, and his stern resolve, intimated to them in no mincing words, to reform the Papal court and break down the luxury of its life, gave deep offense to the cardinals."**[4]

One by one the cardinals went to Anagni in France to vacation. "The new pope, suspecting nothing, had given them permission to go there for the summer. In mid-July… **they agreed among themselves that the April election had been invalid due to duress by the surrounding mob and that, using this as a reason, they would withdraw recognition from Urban**."[5]

After the news of the cardinals' decision to repudiate Urban VI had been circulated, the canonist Baldus, considered the most famous jurist of the day, published a treatise disagreeing with their decision. In it, he stated:

> "…there were no grounds on which the cardinals could repudiate a pope once they had elected him, and *none on which the Church as a whole could depose him, **except persistent and open heresy**.*"[6]

Despite the imprecision in this statement by Baldus – for a true pope can never be deposed; a heretic deposes himself – **we can clearly see in his words the commonly acknowledged truth that a claimant to the Papacy who is openly and persistently heretical can be rejected as a non-pope,** since he is outside the Church.

ALL LIVING CARDINALS REJECT URBAN VI AND RECOGNIZE AN ANTIPOPE

On July 20, 1378, **15 of the 16 cardinals who had elected Pope Urban VI withdrew from his obedience on the grounds that the unruly Roman mob had made the election uncanonical**. The one cardinal who did not repudiate Pope Urban VI was Cardinal Tebaldeschi, but he died shortly thereafter, on Sept. 7 – **leaving a situation where not one of the cardinals of the Catholic Church recognized the true pope, Urban VI. All of the living cardinals now regarded his election as invalid.**[7]

After repudiating Urban VI, on Sept. 20, 1378, the cardinals proceeded to elect Clement VII as "pope," who set up his rival "Papacy" in Avignon. The Great Schism of the West had begun.

> "The rebel cardinals then wrote to the European courts explaining their action. Charles V of France and the whole French nation immediately acknowledged Clement VII, as did also Flanders, Spain, and Scotland. The Empire and England, with the northern and eastern nations and most of the Italian republics, adhered to Urban VI."[8]

The Great Western Schism: antipopes in Rome 23

Even though the validity of the election of Urban VI was ascertainable, <u>one can see why many were taken in by the argument that the Roman mob had unlawfully influenced his election</u>, thereby rendering it uncanonical. Moreover, one can see how the position of Antipope Clement VII was strengthened considerably and imposingly in the eyes of many by the fact that 15 out of the 16 cardinals who had elected Urban VI came to repudiate his election as invalid. The situation that resulted after Antipope Clement VII's acceptance by the cardinals was a nightmare, a nightmare from the very beginning – a nightmare which shows us *how bad and confusing God will sometimes allow things to get, without violating the essential promises He made to His Church*:

> "The schism was now an accomplished fact, and **for forty years Christendom was treated with the melancholy spectacle of two and even three rival popes claiming its allegiance**. It was the most perilous crisis through which the Church had ever passed. Both popes declared a crusade against each other. **Each of the popes claimed the right to create cardinals and to confirm archbishops, bishops, and abbots, so that there were two Colleges of Cardinals and in many places two claimants for the high positions in the Church**. Each pope attempted to collect all the ecclesiastical revenues, and each excommunicated the other with all his adherents."[9]

The spectacle continued as popes and antipopes alike died, only to be succeeded by more. Pope Urban VI died in 1389, and was succeeded by Pope Boniface IX who reigned from 1389 to 1404. After Boniface IX's election, he was promptly excommunicated by Antipope Clement VII, and he responded by excommunicating him.

During his reign, **Pope Boniface IX "was unable to enlarge his sphere of influence in Europe; Sicily and Genoa actually fell away from him**. To prevent the spread of Clementine support in Germany he showered favors on the German king Wenceslas…"[10]

CARDINALS OF BOTH CAMPS TAKE AN OATH TO WORK TO END THE SCHISM PRIOR TO PARTICIPATING IN NEW ELECTIONS, WHICH DEMONSTRATES HOW BAD THE SITUATION HAD BECOME

Meanwhile, at Avignon, Antipope Clement VII died in 1394. Before electing Antipope Clement VII's successor, all 21 cardinals "swore to work for the elimination of the schism, each undertaking, if elected, to abdicate if and when the majority judged it proper."[11] Keep this in mind, as it will become relevant when we cover why a third claimant to the Papacy came into the picture.

The cardinals at Avignon proceeded to elect Pedro de Luna, (Antipope) Benedict XIII, to succeed Antipope Clement VII. Benedict XIII reigned as the Avignon claimant for the rest of the schism. For some time, Benedict XIII had in his support none other than the miracle-working Dominican, St. Vincent Ferrer. St. Vincent actually served as his confessor for a time,[12] believing the Avignon line to be the valid line (until some time later on in the schism). St. Vincent had obviously been persuaded that Pope Urban VI's election was invalid due to the unruly Roman mob, in addition to the formidable acceptance of the Avignon line by 15 out of the 16 cardinals who had taken part in Urban VI's election.

As a cardinal, Antipope Benedict XIII had originally taken part himself in the election of Pope Urban VI, and then abandoned Urban and helped elect Clement (having, of course, been convinced that Urban's election was invalid). As a cardinal under Antipope Clement VII, Benedict XIII "went to the Iberian peninsula for eleven years as his legate, and by his diplomacy **swung Aragon, Castile, Navarre, and Portugal to his [Antipope Clement VII's] obedience**."[13]

After having sworn to pursue the path of abdication in order to end the schism if the majority of his cardinals agreed, Antipope Benedict XIII alienated many of his cardinals when he went back on his promise and showed himself unwilling to consider abdication, even though the majority of his cardinals wanted him to. His rival, Pope Boniface IX, was equally unwilling.

In 1404, Pope Boniface IX (the successor to Urban VI) died, and Pope Innocent VII was elected as his successor by the eight cardinals available. Pope Innocent VII didn't live long, however; he died just two years later, in 1406. During his short reign, Innocent VII had remained opposed to meeting with the Avignon claimant, Benedict XIII, despite having taken an oath before his election to do everything in his power to end the schism, including abdication if necessary.

As the schism persisted, members of both camps became increasingly frustrated with both claimants' unwillingness to take effective measures to end the schism.

> **"Voices were heard on all sides demanding that union be restored. The University of Paris, or rather, its two most prominent professors, John Gerson and Peter d'Ailly, proposed that a General Council should be summoned to decide between the rival claimants."**[14]

In accordance with this widespread sentiment to take effective action to end the schism, another oath was taken before the election of Pope Innocent VII's successor.

> "… **each of the fourteen cardinals at the conclave following [Pope] Innocent VII's death swore that**, if elected, he would abdicate provided Antipope Benedict XIII did the same or should die; also that he would not create new cardinals except to maintain parity of numbers with the Avignon cardinals, and that within three months he would enter into negotiations with his rival about a place of meeting."[15]

The very fact that the cardinals preparing to elect a true pope took an oath such as this – which included negotiations with an antipope – shows how horrible the situation was during the schism, and how much support the antipope had in Christendom.

The conclave proceeded to elect Pope Gregory XII on Nov. 30, 1406. Hope that the end of the schism would come was renewed by Pope Gregory XII's negotiations with Antipope Benedict XIII. The two even agreed on a place to meet, but Pope Gregory XII wavered; he feared (and rightly so) the sincerity of Antipope Benedict XIII's intentions. Pope Gregory XII was also influenced against the path of resignation by some of his close relatives, who painted a negative picture of what might happen if he resigned.

CARDINALS FROM BOTH CAMPS GET FED UP, GO TO PISA AND ELECT A NEW "POPE" IN AN IMPRESSIVE CEREMONY WITH CARDINALS FROM BOTH SIDES

> "**As the negotiations [between Pope Gregory XII and Antipope Benedict XIII] dragged on, Gregory's cardinals became increasingly restive.** An open break became inevitable when Gregory, suspicious of their loyalty, broke his pre-election promise and on 4 May announced the creation of four new cardinals… **All but three of his original college now left him and fled to Pisa**…"[16]

The 14 cardinals who left Pope Gregory XII's obedience and fled to Pisa were joined there by 10 cardinals who left Antipope Benedict XIII's obedience. The cardinals from the two camps had arranged a council, and were resolved to end the schism by means of a joint election at Pisa.

> "In the eyes of the world the Council of Pisa was indeed a glittering assembly, attended by 24 cardinals (fourteen formerly adhering to Pope Gregory XII, ten to de Luna [Benedict XIII]… four patriarchs, 80 bishops, 89 abbots, 41 priors, the heads of four religious orders, and representatives of virtually every university, crowned head, and great noble house in Catholic Europe."[17]

The Cardinal Archbishop of Milan gave the opening address at Pisa. He condemned both claimants, Gregory XII and (Antipope) Benedict XIII, and formally summoned them to appear at the council. They were declared contumacious when they did not appear.

It must be stressed that, at this point in the schism (1409), people were so exasperated with the enduring disunion and the broken promises of the two claimants that the assembly at Pisa was widely received and supported. *It was made all the more impressive and appealing by the fact that its 24 cardinals were comprised of a substantial number of cardinals who had been part of both camps [Gregory XII and Antipope Benedict XIII].* This gave it the *appearance* of a united action of the Church's cardinals. **On June 29, 1409, the 24 cardinals unanimously elected Alexander V. Now there were three claimants to the Papacy at the same time.**

> Fr. John Laux, *Church History*, p. 405: "There were now three popes, and three Colleges of Cardinals, <u>in some dioceses three rival bishops, and in some Religious Orders three rival superiors</u>."[18]

<u>THE THIRD CLAIMANT, THE PISAN ANTIPOPE, HELD THE WIDEST SUPPORT AND MOST OF THE THEOLOGIANS BECAUSE HE HAD THE APPEARANCE OF BEING THE UNITED CHOICE OF CARDINALS FROM BOTH CAMPS</u>

The newly elected Pisan antipope, Alexander V, had the widest support in Christendom among the three claimants. The true pope, Gregory XII, had the least.

> From the beginning Alexander V "had the support of England, most of France, the Low Countries, Bohemia… Poland… his own Milan, Venice, and Florence. De Luna [Antipope Benedict XIII] retained the support of his own Aragon, Castile, parts of southern France, and Scotland… **<u>Gregory XII was the weakest of the three</u>**, retaining the loyalty only of Naples, western Germany, some north Italian cities, and steel-true Carlo Malatesta of Rimini… **<u>The Great Western Schism had become a triangle of distorted loyalties, with the true Pope the weakest of the three</u>**… The Catholic Church seemed to be suffering the fate that would overtake later Protestantism:

repeated, irrepressible subdivision... **Worst of all, no rescue from this disaster seemed possible.**"[19]

Most of the learned theologians and canonists of the time favored the Pisan line of antipopes.

"Through the fall of 1408 and the winter of 1409 debate continued to rage among the theologians and canonists. Most of them, in varying degrees of desperation, now favored the council regardless of who the true pope might be or how it was to be authorized."[20]

<u>NO TRUE POPE IN HISTORY HAD AS LITTLE SUPPORT AS POPE GREGORY XII NEAR THE END OF THE GREAT WESTERN SCHISM</u>

In 1411, the newly elected Holy Roman Emperor Sigismund followed the general sentiment and abandoned the true pope, Gregory XII.

"Sigismund wanted unanimous electoral endorsement, and **in view of the widespread abandonment of Gregory XII by many of those who had previously obeyed him (notably in Italy and England)** Sigismund's own confidence in Gregory's legitimacy may have been sincerely shaken. **No true pope in the Church's history had so little support as Gregory XII following the Council of Pisa.**"[21]

The newly elected Pisan antipope, Alexander V, didn't live long. He died less than a year after his election, in May of 1410. To succeed him, on May 17, 1410, the Pisan cardinals unanimously elected Baldassare Cossa as **John XXIII**. Like his predecessor Antipope Alexander V, John XXIII also held the widest support among the three claimants.

"**While there were still three claimants to the papacy, John [XXIII] commanded the widest support**, with France, England, and several Italian and German states recognizing him. With the help of Louis of Anjou... **he was able to establish himself in Rome**."[22]

As we see, Antipope John XXIII was able to reign in Rome. John XXIII (1410-1415) would be the last antipope to reign from Rome, until the post-Vatican II apostasy, which began with a man who also called himself John XXIII (Angelo Roncalli, 1958-1963).

During the 4th year of his reign as antipope, Antipope John XXIII summoned the Council of Constance in 1414, at the insistence of the Emperor Sigismund. It's quite interesting to note that the recent John XXIII also called Vatican II in the 4th year of his reign, 1962. And like Vatican II, the Council of Constance began as a false council, having been called by an antipope.

At this point in the schism, the Emperor Sigismund was determined to unite Christendom by working for the abdication of all three claimants. When Antipope John XXIII realized that he would not be accepted as the true pope at the Council of Constance, he fled from the council. "That evening Cossa fled Constance, riding on a small dark horse (in contrast to the nine white horses behind which he had entered the city in October), huddled in a large gray cloak wrapped round and round him to hide most of his face and body..."[23]

Antipope John XXIII was then formally condemned by the council as deposed. An order was sent out by the Emperor for his arrest; he was apprehended and thrown into prison. In prison, Antipope John XXIII "surrendered his papal seal and the fisherman's ring, with tears, to representatives of the council." He accepted the verdict against him without protest.[24]

> "When the Council of Constance (reckoned in part or whole the Sixteenth General, 1414-1417)... had deposed John, <u>it entered into negotiations with Gregory, who conveyed to it his willingness to abdicate provided he was allowed formally to convoke the assembled prelates and dignitaries afresh as a general council</u>; as pope he could not recognize one called by John. <u>This procedure was accepted, and at the 14th solemn session, on 4 July 1415, his cardinal John Dominici read out his bull convoking the council</u>, whereupon Carlo Malatesta [Pope Gregory XII] announced his resignation. The two colleges of cardinals were united, Gregory's acts in his pontificate were ratified..."[25]

So, after Antipope John XXIII was deposed, Pope Gregory XII agreed to convoke the Council of Constance (in order to confer upon it Papal legitimacy, which Antipope John XXIII could not give it) and then resign in the hope of ending the schism.

Meanwhile, Antipope Benedict XIII (the Avignon claimant) had been approached by Emperor Sigismund and asked to resign. He obstinately refused to the end, but by now the general sentiment had gone so far against him that his following was greatly diminished.

> "Sigismund, who had done all in his power to induce Benedict XIII, of the Avignon line, to abdicate, succeeded in detaching the Spaniards from his cause. Thereupon the Council declared his deposition, July 16, 1417."[26]

Both antipopes having been disposed of, and the true pope having resigned, the Council of Constance proceeded to elect Pope Martin V on Nov. 11, 1417, bringing an official end to the Great Western Schism. (The Avignon line of antipopes did continue after the death of Antipope Benedict XIII with the election of Antipope Clement VIII as his successor by his four remaining cardinals. These cardinals then regarded that election of Antipope Clement VIII invalid and elected Antipope Benedict XIV; but by the time of the deposition of Antipope Benedict XIII by the Council of Constance the Avignon line had lost so much support that these final two successors to Antipope Benedict XIII are so insignificant as to merit only a footnote.)

CONCLUSION: WHAT THE GREAT WESTERN SCHISM TEACHES US FOR OUR TIME

In this article we have reviewed one of the important chapters in Church history. In the process we have seen a number of very important things – things quite relevant to our present situation.

- We've seen that antipopes can exist.
- We've seen that antipopes can reign from Rome.
- We've seen that all of the living cardinals, shortly after the election of Pope Urban VI, repudiated him (the true pope) and recognized Antipope Clement VII. This illustrates that it's not at all incompatible with indefectibility (i.e., the promises of Christ to be with His Church and the Papacy until the end of time) <u>for all the cardinals</u> to recognize an antipope.

- We've seen that most of the theologians of the time favored the third line, the Pisan line of antipopes. This line of antipopes must have been a tantalizing option for many because cardinals from both camps supported it. This shows us how deceptive God will sometimes allow things to get without violating the essential promises He made to His Church. Moreover, the majority of theologians' support for the Pisan line demonstrates clearly that the common teaching of theologians on a particular matter (e.g., salvation), no matter how learned they are, is not binding, contrary to what some are asserting today.

- We've also seen that the principle that an open heretic cannot be regarded as the pope is ancient and was expressed by the leading canonist of the time, Baldus.

- We've seen that things were so bad and so desperate during the Great Western Schism that people didn't see any way out of this disaster – a disaster in which people were offered, at one point, three rival bishops, three rival religious superiors, and three rival claimants to the Papacy excommunicating one another.

- **Learning this can help us see clearly that what we have proven on doctrinal grounds, namely, that there has been a line of antipopes since Vatican II that has foisted upon the world a new counterfeit religion, which has reduced the true Catholic Church to a remnant (in fulfillment of Scriptural and Catholic prophecies about the deception of the Great Apostasy and the last days), is not a PATENT ABSURDITY, as some have wrongly said.**

On the contrary, if God allowed the aforementioned disaster to occur during the Great Western Schism (which could have been, at worst, just a prelude to the Great Apostasy), <u>with multiple antipopes reigning at once and the true pope the weakest of the three</u>, what kind of disaster and deception would He allow with antipopes (without ever violating the essential promises He made to His Church) during the final spiritual tribulation, <u>which will be the most deceptive of them all</u>? It is a PATENT ABSURDITY, and directly refuted by Catholic teaching and the facts of Church history, to assert that a line of antipopes which has created a counterfeit sect to oppose the true Church is an impossibility. Further, it is outrageous in the extreme to assert that such a situation is "patently absurd" after having reviewed the undeniable facts we have put forward to prove it true.

We will end this review of The Great Western Schism by quoting Fr. Edmund James O'Reilly, S.J. He had some very interesting things to say about the Great Western Schism in his book *The Relations of the Church to Society – Theological Essays*, written in 1882. In the process he mentions the possibility of a papal interregnum (a period without a pope) covering the whole period of the Great Western Schism (almost 40 years).

We begin with a quote from Father O'Reilly's discussion of the Great Western Schism.

> "We may here stop to inquire what is to be said of the position, at that time, of the three claimants, and their rights with regard to the Papacy. In the first place, there was all through, from the death of Gregory XI in 1378, a Pope – with the exception, of course, of the intervals between deaths and elections to fill up the vacancies thereby created. There was, I say, at every given time a Pope, really invested with the dignity of the Vicar of Christ and Head of the Church, whatever opinions might exist among many as to his genuineness; <u>**not that an interregnum covering the whole period would have been impossible or inconsistent with the promises of Christ, for this is by no means manifest**</u>, but that, as a matter of fact, there was not such an interregnum."[27]

Fr. O'Reilly says that an interregnum (a period without a pope) covering the whole period of the Great Western Schism is by no means incompatible with the promises of Christ about His Church. The period Fr. O'Reilly is speaking of began in 1378 with the death of Pope Gregory XI and ended essentially in 1417 with the election of Pope Martin V. **That's a thirty-nine year interregnum!**

Writing after the *First Vatican Council*, it is obvious that Fr. O'Reilly is on the side of those who, in rejecting Antipopes John XXIII, Paul VI, John Paul I, John Paul II and Benedict XVI, hold the possibility of a long-term vacancy of the Holy See. In fact, on page 287 of his book Fr. O'Reilly gives this prophetic warning:

> "The great schism of the West suggests to me a reflection which I take the liberty of expressing here. *If this schism had not occurred, the hypothesis of such a thing happening would appear to many chimerical (absurd). They would say it could not be; God would not permit the Church to come into so unhappy a situation.* Heresies might spring up and spread and last painfully long, through the fault and to the perdition of their authors and abettors, to the great distress too of the faithful, increased by actual persecution in many places where the heretics were dominant. *But that the true Church should remain between thirty and forty years without a thoroughly ascertained Head, and representative of Christ on earth, this would not be.* <u>Yet it has been</u>; <u>and we have no guarantee that it will not be again</u>, though we may fervently hope otherwise. What I would infer is, that *we must not be too ready to pronounce on what God may permit. We know with absolute certainty that He will fulfill His promises*... We may also trust that He will do a great deal more than what He has bound Himself by his promises. We may look forward with cheering probability to exemption for the future from some of the trouble and misfortunes that have befallen in the past. *But we, or our successors in the future generations of Christians, shall perhaps see stranger evils than have yet been experienced,* even before the immediate approach of that great winding up of all things on earth that will precede the day of judgment. I am not setting up for a prophet, nor pretending to see unhappy wonders, of which I have no knowledge whatever. <u>*All I mean to convey is that contingencies regarding the Church, not excluded by the Divine promises, cannot be regarded as practically impossible, just because they would be terrible and distressing in a very high degree*</u>."[28]

Fr. O'Reilly is saying that if the Great Western Schism had never occurred people would say that such a situation is impossible and incompatible with the promises of Christ to His Church, and that we cannot dismiss the possibility of similar and perhaps worse things in the future because they would be distressing in a very high degree.

Endnotes for Section 5:

[1] J.N.D. Kelly, *Oxford Dictionary of Popes*, Oxford University Press, 1986, p. 227.
[2] Warren H. Carroll, *A History of Christendom*, Vol. 3 (*The Glory of Christendom*), Front Royal, VA: Christendom Press, p. 429.
[3] Warren H. Carroll, *A History of Christendom*, Vol. 3 (*The Glory of Christendom*), p. 431.
[4] Fr. John Laux, *Church History*, Rockford, IL: Tan Books, 1989, p. 404.
[5] Warren H. Carroll, *A History of Christendom*, Vol. 3 (*The Glory of Christendom*), pp. 432-433.
[6] Quoted by Warren H. Carroll, *A History of Christendom*, Vol. 3 (*The Glory of Christendom*), p. 433.
[7] Warren H. Carroll, *A History of Christendom*, Vol. 3 (*The Glory of Christendom*), pp. 432-434.
[8] Fr. John Laux, *Church History*, p. 404.
[9] Fr. John Laux, *Church History*, p. 405.
[10] J.N.D. Kelly, *Oxford Dictionary of Popes*, p. 231.
[11] J.N.D. Kelly, *Oxford Dictionary of Popes*, p. 232.
[12] Fr. Andrew Pradel, *St. Vincent Ferrer: The Angel of the Judgment*, Tan Books, 2000, p. 39.
[13] J.N.D. Kelly, *Oxford Dictionary of Popes*, p. 237.
[14] Fr. John Laux, *Church History*, p. 405.
[15] J.N.D. Kelly, *Oxford Dictionary of Popes*, p. 235.
[16] J.N.D. Kelly, *Oxford Dictionary of Popes*, p. 235.
[17] Warren H. Carroll, *A History of Christendom*, Vol. 3 (*The Glory of Christendom*), p. 472.
[18] Fr. John Laux, *Church History*, p. 405.
[19] Warren H. Carroll, *A History of Christendom*, Vol. 3 (*The Glory of Christendom*), pp. 473-474.
[20] Warren H. Carroll, *A History of Christendom*, Vol. 3 (*The Glory of Christendom*), p. 471.

[21] Warren H. Carroll, *A History of Christendom*, Vol. 3 (*The Glory of Christendom*), p. 479.
[22] J.N.D. Kelly, *Oxford Dictionary of Popes*, p. 238.
[23] Warren H. Carroll, *A History of Christendom*, Vol. 3 (*The Glory of Christendom*), p. 485.
[24] Warren H. Carroll, *A History of Christendom*, Vol. 3 (*The Glory of Christendom*), p. 487.
[25] J.N.D. Kelly, *Oxford Dictionary of Popes*, p. 236.
[26] Fr. John Laux, *Church History*, p. 408.
[27] Fr. James Edmund O'Reilly, *The Relations of the Church to Society – Theological Essays*.
[28] Fr. James Edmund O'Reilly, p. 287.

6. The Catholic Church teaches that a heretic would cease to be pope, and that a heretic couldn't be validly elected pope

The Catholic Encyclopedia, "Heresy," 1914, Vol. 7, p. 261: "**The pope himself, if notoriously guilty of heresy, would cease to be pope** because he would cease to be a member of the Church."[1]

Heresy is the obstinate denial or doubt by a baptized person of an article of divine and Catholic Faith. In other words, a baptized person who *deliberately* denies an authoritative teaching of the Catholic Church *is a heretic*.

Martin Luther, perhaps the most notorious heretic in Church history, taught the heresy of Justification by faith alone, among many others

Besides antipopes reigning from Rome due to uncanonical elections, the Catholic Church teaches that if a pope were to become a heretic he would automatically lose his office and cease to be the pope. This is the teaching of all the doctors and fathers of the Church who addressed the issue:

> St. Robert Bellarmine, Cardinal and Doctor of the Church, *De Romano Pontifice*, II, 30:
> "**A pope who is a manifest heretic automatically (*per se*) ceases to be pope and head**, just as he ceases automatically to be a Christian and a member of the Church. Wherefore, he can be judged and punished by the Church. *This is the teaching of all the ancient Fathers* who teach that manifest heretics immediately lose all jurisdiction."
>
> St. Robert Bellarmine, *De Romano Pontifice*, II, 30:
> "**This principle is most certain. The non-Christian cannot in any way be Pope, as Cajetan himself admits (ib. c. 26). The reason for this is that he cannot be head of what he is not a member;** now he who is not a Christian is not a member of the Church, **and a manifest heretic is not a Christian, as is clearly taught by St. Cyprian (lib. 4, epist. 2), St. Athanasius (Scr. 2 cont. Arian.), St. Augustine (lib. De great. Christ. Cap. 20), St. Jerome (contra Lucifer.) and others; therefore the manifest heretic cannot be Pope.**"
>
> St. Francis De Sales (17th century), Doctor of the Church, *The Catholic Controversy*, pp. 305-306: "**Now when he [the Pope] is explicitly a heretic, he falls ipso facto from his dignity and out of the Church**..."
>
> St. Antoninus (1459): "**In the case in which the pope would become a heretic, he would find himself, by that fact alone and without any other sentence, separated from the Church.** A head separated from a body cannot, as long as it remains separated, be head of the same body from which it was cut off. A pope who would be separated from the Church by heresy, therefore, would by that very fact itself cease to be head of the Church. **He could not be a heretic and remain pope, because, since he is outside of the Church, he cannot possess the keys of the Church.**" (*Summa Theologica*, cited in *Actes de Vatican I*. V. Frond pub.)

That a heretic cannot be a pope is rooted in the dogma that heretics are not members of the Catholic Church

It should be noted that the teaching from the saints and doctors of the Church, which is quoted above – that a pope who became a heretic would automatically cease to be pope – is rooted in the infallible dogma that a heretic is not a member of the Catholic Church.

> Pope Eugene IV, *Council of Florence*, "Cantate Domino," 1441:
> "The Holy Roman Church firmly believes, professes and preaches that **all those who are outside the Catholic Church**, not only pagans **but also** Jews or **heretics** and schismatics, cannot share in eternal life and will go into the everlasting fire which was prepared for the devil and his angels, unless they are joined to the Church before the end of their lives…"[2]
>
> Pope Pius XII, *Mystici Corporis Christi* (# 23), June 29, 1943:
> "For not every sin, however grave it may be, is such as of its own nature **to sever a man from the Body of the Church, as does schism or heresy or apostasy.**"[3]

A heretic cannot be the pope

We can see that it's the teaching of the Catholic Church that a man is severed from the Church by heresy, schism or apostasy.

> Pope Leo XIII, *Satis Cognitum* (# 9), June 29, 1896:
> "The practice of the Church has always been the same, as is shown by the unanimous teaching of the Fathers, **who were wont to hold as *outside Catholic communion*, and *alien* to the Church, whoever would recede in the least degree from any point of doctrine proposed by her authoritative Magisterium."**[4]

> Pope Leo XIII, *Satis Cognitum* (# 9):
> "No one who merely disbelieves in all (these heresies) can for that reason regard himself as a Catholic or call himself one. For there may be or arise some other heresies, which are not set out in this work of ours, and, **if any one holds to a single one of these he is not a Catholic.**"[5]

> Pope Innocent III, *Eius exemplo*, Dec. 18, 1208:
> "By the heart we believe and by the mouth we confess **the one Church, not of heretics**, but the Holy Roman, Catholic, and Apostolic Church outside of which we believe that no one is saved."[6]

Thus, it's not merely the opinion of certain saints and doctors of the Church that a heretic would cease to be pope; it's a fact inextricably bound up with a dogmatic teaching. A truth inextricably bound up with a dogma is called a *dogmatic fact*. It is, therefore, a dogmatic fact that a heretic cannot be the pope. A heretic cannot be the pope, since one who is outside cannot head that of which he is not even a member.

> Pope Leo XIII, *Satis Cognitum* (#15), June 29, 1896:
> "No one, therefore, unless in communion with Peter can share in his authority, since **it is absurd to imagine** that he who is outside can command in the Church."[7]

Pope Paul IV issued a Papal Bull solemnly declaring that the election of a heretic as pope is null and void

In 1559 Pope Paul IV issued an entire Papal Bull dealing with the subject and the possibility of a heretic being elected pope.

(Pope Paul IV)

At the time that Paul IV issued the Bull (quoted below) there were rumors that one of the cardinals was a secret Protestant. In order to prevent the election of such a heretic to the Papacy, Pope Paul IV solemnly declared that **a heretic cannot be validly elected pope**. Below are the pertinent portions of the Bull. For the entire Bull, see our website.

> Pope Paul IV, Bull *Cum ex Apostolatus Officio*, Feb. 15, 1559: "1… Remembering also that, where danger is greater, it must more fully and more diligently be counteracted, We have been concerned lest false prophets or others, even if they have only secular jurisdiction, should wretchedly ensnare the souls of the simple, and drag with them into perdition, destruction and damnation countless peoples committed to their care and rule, either in spiritual or in temporal matters; and We have been concerned also **lest it may befall Us to see the abomination of desolation, which was spoken of by the prophet Daniel, in the holy place**. In view of this, Our desire has been to fulfill our Pastoral duty, insofar as, with the help of God, We are able, so as to arrest the foxes who are occupying themselves in the destruction of the vineyard of the Lord and to keep the wolves from the sheepfolds, lest We seem to be dumb watchdogs that cannot bark and lest We perish with the wicked husbandman and be compared with the hireling…
>
> 6. In addition, [by this Our Constitution, which is to remain valid in perpetuity We enact, determine, decree and define:-] **that if ever at any time it shall appear that any Bishop, even if he be acting as an Archbishop, Patriarch or Primate; or any Cardinal of the aforesaid Roman Church, or, as has already been mentioned, any legate, or even the Roman Pontiff, prior to his promotion or his elevation as Cardinal or Roman Pontiff, has deviated from the Catholic Faith or fallen into some heresy:**
>
> (i) **the promotion or elevation, even if it shall have been uncontested and by the unanimous assent of all the Cardinals, shall be null, void and worthless**;
> (ii) it shall not be possible for it to acquire validity (nor for it to be said that it has thus acquired validity) through the acceptance of the office, of consecration, of subsequent authority, nor through possession of administration, nor through the putative enthronement of a Roman Pontiff, or Veneration, or obedience accorded to such by all, nor through the lapse of any period of time in the foregoing situation;
> (iii) it shall not be held as partially legitimate in any way…
> (vi) **those thus promoted or elevated shall be deprived automatically, and without need for any further declaration, of all dignity, position, honour, title, authority, office and power**…
>
> 10. No one at all, therefore, may infringe this document of our approbation, re-introduction, sanction, statute and derogation of wills and decrees, or by rash presumption contradict it. **If anyone, however, should presume to attempt this, let him know that he is destined to incur the wrath of Almighty God and of the blessed Apostles, Peter and Paul.**
>
> Given in Rome at Saint Peter's in the year of the Incarnation of the Lord 1559, 15th February, in the fourth year of our Pontificate.
>
> + I, Paul, Bishop of the Catholic Church…"

With the fullness of his papal authority, Pope Paul IV declared that the election of a heretic is invalid, even if it takes place with the unanimous consent of the cardinals and is accepted by all.

A heretic cannot be the pope

Pope Paul IV also declared that he was making this declaration in order **to combat the arrival of the abomination of desolation, spoken of by Daniel, in the holy place. This is astounding, and it seems to indicate that the Magisterium itself is connecting the eventual arrival of the abomination of desolation in the holy place (Matthew 24:15) with a heretic posing as the pope** – perhaps because the heretic posing as the pope will give us the abomination of desolation in the holy place (the New Mass), as we believe is the case, or because the heretical antipope will himself constitute the abomination of desolation in the holy place.

The Catholic Encyclopedia repeats this truth declared by Pope Paul IV by asserting that the election of a heretic as pope would, of course, be completely null and void.

> *The Catholic Encyclopedia*, "Papal Elections," 1914, Vol. 11, p. 456: "**Of course, the election of a heretic, schismatic, or female [as Pope] would be null and void.**"[8]

In line with the truth that a heretic cannot be the pope, the Church teaches that heretics cannot be prayed for in the canon of the Mass

A pope is prayed for in the *Te Igitur* prayer of the canon of the Mass. But the Church also teaches that heretics cannot be prayed for in the canon of the Mass. If a heretic could be a true pope, there would be an insoluble dilemma. But it's actually not a dilemma because a heretic cannot be a valid pope:

> *Libellus professionis fidei*, April 2, 517, profession of faith prescribed under Pope St. Hormisdas: "And, therefore, I hope that I may merit to be in the one communion with you, which the Apostolic See proclaims, in which there is the whole and the true solidity of the Christian religion, **promising that in the future the names of those separated from the communion of the Catholic Church, that is, those not agreeing with the Apostolic See, shall not be read during the sacred mysteries**. But if I shall attempt in any way to deviate from my profession, I confess that I am a confederate in my opinion with those whom I have condemned. However, I have with my own hand signed this profession of mine, and to you, HORMISDAS, the holy and venerable Pope of the City of Rome, I have directed it."[9]

> Pope Benedict XIV, *Ex Quo Primum* (# 23), March 1, 1756:
> "***Moreover heretics and schismatics** are subject to the censure of major excommunication by the law of Can. de Ligu. 23, quest. 5, and Can. Nulli, 5, dist. 19.* **But the sacred canons of the Church forbid public prayer for the excommunicated as can be seen in chap. A nobis, 2, and chap.** *Sacris* **on the sentence of excommunication.** Though this does not forbid prayer for their conversion, **still such prayer must not take the form of proclaiming their names in the solemn prayer during the sacrifice of the Mass.**"[10]

Pope Pius IX, *Quartus Supra* (# 9), January 6, 1873:
"For this reason John, Bishop of Constantinople, **solemnly declared – and the entire Eighth Ecumenical Council did so later – 'that the names of those who were separated from communion with the Catholic Church, that is of those who did not agree in all matters with the Apostolic See, are not to be read out during the sacred mysteries.'"**[11]

Endnotes for Section 6:

[1] *The Catholic Encyclopedia*, "Heresy," New York: Robert Appleton Co., 1914, Vol. 7, p. 261.
[2] *Decrees of the Ecumenical Councils*, Sheed & Ward and Georgetown University Press, 1990, Vol. 1, p. 578; Denzinger, *The Sources of Catholic Dogma*, B. Herder Book. Co., Thirtieth Edition, 1957, no. 714.
[3] *The Papal Encyclicals*, by Claudia Carlen, Raleigh: The Pierian Press, 1990, Vol. 4 (1939-1958), p. 41.
[4] *The Papal Encyclicals*, Vol. 2 (1878-1903), p. 393.
[5] *The Papal Encyclicals*, Vol. 2 (1878-1903), p. 393.
[6] Denzinger 423.
[7] *The Papal Encyclicals*, Vol. 2 (1878-1903), p. 401.
[8] *The Catholic Encyclopedia*, "Papal Elections," 1914, Vol. 11, p. 456.
[9] Denzinger 172.
[10] *The Papal Encyclicals*, Vol. 1 (1740-1878), p. 84.
[11] *The Papal Encyclicals*, Vol. 1 (1740-1878), p. 415.

7. The Church's enemies, Communists and Freemasons, made an organized effort to infiltrate the Catholic Church

(END NOTES – PAGE 39)

> Pope Leo XIII, *Dall'Alto* (# 2), Oct. 15, 1890: "**It is needless now to put the Masonic sects upon their trial**. They are already judged; their ends, their means, their doctrines, and their action, are all known with indisputable certainty. **Possessed by the spirit of Satan, whose instrument they are, they burn like him with a deadly and implacable hatred of Jesus Christ and of His work; and they endeavor by every means to overthrow and fetter it.**"[1]

> Pope Leo XIII, *In Ipso* (# 1), March 3, 1891: "Nevertheless, it grieves us to think that **the enemies of the Church, joined in most wicked conspiracy, scheme to weaken and even, if possible, utterly wipe out** that wondrous edifice which God Himself has erected as a refuge for the human race."[2]

It's a well known fact that Communists and Freemasons made organized efforts to infiltrate the Catholic Church. They sent large numbers of their own men into the priesthood hoping to weaken and attack her by moving these men to high positions.

Mrs. Bella Dodd spent most of her life in the Communist Party of America and was Attorney General designate had the Party won the White House. After her defection, she revealed that one of her jobs as a Communist agent was to encourage young radicals (not always card-carrying Communists) to enter Catholic seminaries. She said that before she had left the Party in the U.S. she had encouraged almost 1,000 young radicals to infiltrate the seminaries and religious orders; she was only one Communist.

Brother Joseph Natale, the founder of Most Holy Family Monastery, was present at one of Bella Dodd's lectures in the early 1950's. He stated:

> "I listened to that woman for four hours and she had my hair standing on end. Everything she said has been fulfilled to the letter. You would think she was the world's greatest prophet, but she was no prophet. She was merely exposing the step-by-step battle plan of Communist subversion of the Catholic Church. She explained that of all the world's religions, the Catholic Church was the only one feared by the Communists, for it was its only effective opponent."[3]

Bella Dodd converted to Catholicism at the end of her life. Speaking as an ex-Communist, she said: "**In the 1930's, we put eleven hundred men into the priesthood in order to destroy the Church from within.**" The idea was for these men to be ordained, and then climb the ladder of influence and authority as monsignors and bishops. Back then, she said: "Right now they are in the highest places in the Church. They are working to bring about change in order that the Catholic Church would not be effective against Communism." She also said that these changes would be so drastic that "you will not recognize the Catholic Church." (This was 10 to 12 years before Vatican II.)

Brother Joseph went on relating what Bella Dodd had said: "**The whole idea was to destroy, not the institution of the Church, but rather the Faith of the people, and even use the institution of the Church, if possible, to destroy the Faith through the promotion of a pseudo-religion:**

something that resembled Catholicism but was not the real thing. Once the Faith was destroyed, she explained that there would be a guilt complex introduced into the Church… to label the 'Church of the past' as being oppressive, authoritarian, full of predjudices, arrogant in claiming to be the sole possessor of truth, and responsible for the divisions of religious bodies throughout the centuries. This would be necessary in order to shame Church leaders into an 'openness to the world,' and to a more flexible attitude toward all religions and philosophies. The Communists would then exploit this openness in order to undermine the Church."[4]

Freemasons made similar attempts to infiltrate the Catholic Church and elevate their own to the highest levels. The Luciferian secret society, the Carbonari, known as the *Alta Vendita*, wrote a set of *Permanent Instructions*, or Code of Rules, which appeared in Italy in 1818. It stated:

> "…It becomes the duty of the secret societies to make the first advance to the Church, and to the pope, with the object of conquering both. The work for which we gird ourselves is not the work of a day, nor of a month, nor a year. It may last for many years, perhaps a century… **What we must ask for, what we should look for and wait for, as the Jews wait for the Messiah, is a pope according to our wants**. We require a pope for ourselves, if such a pope were possible. With such a one we shall march more securely to the storming of the Church, than with all the little books of our French and English brothers."[5]

The same Freemasonic document made this striking prediction:

> "In a hundred years time… **bishops and priests will think they are marching behind the banner of the keys of Peter, when in fact they will be following our flag**… The reforms will have to be brought about in the name of obedience."[6]

These organizations and the individuals who belong to them are agents which the Devil uses to attack the true Church of Christ.

> Ephesians 6:12- "For our wrestling is not against flesh and blood; but against principalities and powers, against the rulers of the world of this darkness, against the spirits of wickedness in high places."

On April 3, 1844, a leader of the *AltaVendita* named Nubius wrote a letter to another highly-placed mason. **The letter spoke again about the plan to infiltrate the Catholic Church, and the attempt to insert a masonic "pope,"** who would promote the religion of Freemasonry. "Now then, in order to ensure a pope in the required proportions, we must first of all prepare a generation worthy of the kingdom of which we dream… **Let the clergy move forward under your banner (the masonic banner) always believing they are advancing under the banner of the apostolic keys**. Cast your net like Simon Bar Jonas; spread it to the bottom of sacristies, seminaries, and convents … You will have finished a revolution dressed in the pope's triple crown and cape, carrying the cross and the flag, a revolution that will need only a small stimulus to set fire to the four corners of the earth."[7]

Freemason Eliph Levi said in 1862: "**A day will come when the pope… will declare that all the excommunications are lifted and all the anathemas are retracted**, when all the Christians will be united within the Church, when the Jews and Moslems will be blessed and called back to her . . . she will permit all sects to approach her by degrees and will embrace all mankind in the communion of her love and prayers. Then, Protestants will no longer exist. Against what will they be able to protest? The sovereign pontiff will then be truly king of the religious world, and he will do whatever he wishes with all the nations of the earth."[8]

An apostate priest and former canon-lawyer,[9] named Fr. Roca (1830-1893), after being excommunicated said: "The papacy will fall; it will die under the hallowed knife which the fathers of the last council will forge."[10] Roca also said: "You must have a new dogma, a new religion, a new ministry, and new rituals that very closely resemble those of the surrendered Church. **The divine cult directed by the liturgy, ceremonial, ritual and regulations of the Roman Catholic Church will shortly undergo transformation at an ecumenical Council.**"[11]

Endnotes for Section 7:

[1] *The Papal Encyclicals*, by Claudia Carlen, Raleigh: The Pierian Press, 1990, Vol. 2 (1878-1903), p. 226.
[2] *The Papal Encyclicals*, Vol. 2 (1878-1903), p. 237.
[3] Statements of Bro. Joseph Natale relating what former Communist Bella Dodd said.
[4] Statements of Bro. Joseph Natale relating what former Communist Bella Dodd said.
[5] *The Permanent Instruction of the Alta Vendita*.
[6] *The Permanent Instruction of the Alta Vendita*.
[7] NUBIUS, Secret Instructions on the Conquest of the Church, in Emmanuel Barbier, *Les infiltrations maconiques dans i'Eglise*, Paris/Brussels: Desclee de Brouwer, 1901, p.5).part of this also in Piers Compton, *The Broken Cross*, Cranbrook, Western Australia: Veritas Pub. Co. Ptd Ltd, 1984, p. 15-16.
[8] Dr. Rara Coomaraswamy, *The Destruction of the Christian Tradition*, p. 133.
[9] Piers Compton, *The Broken Cross*, Cranbrook, Western Australia: Veritas Pub. Co. Ptd Ltd, 1984, p. 42.
[10] Dr. Rudolf Graber, *Athanasius and the Church of Our Time*.
[11] Piers Compton, *The Broken Cross*, p. 42.

END NOTES - PAGE 78

8. The Vatican II Revolution (1962-1965)

Yves Marsaudon, 33rd degree Scottish Rite Freemason, 1965: "… the courageous idea of liberty of thought… – **one can speak truly here of a revolution that has come from our Masonic lodges – has magnificently spread its wings over the dome of St. Peter's.**"[1]

(A session of Vatican II)

Vatican II was a council that took place from 1962-1965. Vatican II was a false council that constituted a revolution against 2000 years of Catholic teaching and Tradition. Vatican II contains many heresies that were directly condemned by past popes and infallible councils, as we will see. Vatican II attempted to give Catholics a new religion. In the period following Vatican II, massive changes in every aspect of Catholic Faith ensued, including the implementation of a New Mass.

(Before Vatican II)   (After Vatican II)

Vatican II also came out with new practices and views toward other religions. The Catholic Church cannot change its teaching on other religions and how it views the members of other religions, since these are truths of Faith delivered by Jesus Christ. Vatican II attempted to change those truths of the Catholic Church.

Vatican II was called by John XXIII, and it was solemnly promulgated and confirmed by Paul VI on Dec. 8, 1965. Vatican II was not a true general or ecumenical council of the Catholic Church because, as we will see in detail, it was called and confirmed by manifest heretics (John XXIII and Paul VI) who were not eligible for the papal election (see Paul IV's Apostolic Constitution above). The fruits of Vatican II are plain for all to see. Any honest Catholic who lived before the council and compares it with the religion in the dioceses today can attest to the fact that Vatican II inaugurated a new religion.

– The Most Specific Heresy in Vatican II –

Vatican II uses the same verb as the Council of Florence to teach just the opposite

The Council of Florence dogmatically defined that any individual who has a view contrary to the Catholic Church's teaching on Our Lord Jesus Christ or the Trinity, or any one of the truths about Our Lord or the Trinity, is rejected by God.

> Pope Eugene IV, Council of Florence, Bull *Cantate Domino*, 1442, *ex cathedra*: "…the holy Roman Church, founded on the words of our Lord and Savior, firmly believes, professes and preaches one true God, almighty, immutable and eternal, **Father, Son and Holy Spirit**… **Therefore it [the Holy Roman Church] condemns, <u>rejects</u>, anathematizes and declares to be outside the Body of Christ, which is the Church, <u>whoever holds opposing or contrary views</u>**."[2]

This is an infallible dogmatic definition of the Catholic Church on <u>individuals</u> who have a view on Our Lord Jesus Christ or the Holy Trinity that is contrary to that of the Church (e.g., Jews, Muslims, etc.). The Council of Florence solemnly defines that whoever has a view contrary to the Church's teaching on Our Lord and the Trinity (e.g., the Jews) is condemned and <u>rejected</u>! Note: the Council is not merely saying that *the view contrary to Our Lord* is rejected, but that <u>the individual</u> (e.g., the Jew) is <u>rejected</u>. This dogma is rooted in the truth that Our Lord specifically revealed in Sacred Scripture.

> Matthew 10:33- "But **he that shall deny me before men, I will also deny before my Father who is in heaven**."

The word "deny" means to reject or to repudiate. He who denies Our Lord is rejected by Him. But in its *Decree on Non-Christian religions*, Vatican II taught just the opposite.

> **Vatican II Declaration, *Nostra Aetate* (#4): "Although the Church is the new people of God, <u>the Jews should not be presented as rejected</u> or cursed by God, as if such views followed from the holy scriptures."**[3]

Vatican II denied the divinely revealed truth of Matthew 10:33, which was solemnly defined by the Council of Florence. The teaching of Vatican II is blatantly heretical.

But it gets even worse when one considers this in more detail. In case you have any doubt about this heresy, please consider the following:

Vatican II vs. The Dogmatic Council of Florence

Nostra Aetate #4 of Vatican II: "…<u>the Jews should not be presented as rejected</u> or cursed by God…"	Dogmatic Council of Florence: "Therefore it [<u>the Church</u>] condemns, <u>rejects</u>, anathematizes and declares to be outside the Body of Christ, which is the Church, <u>whoever holds opposing or contrary views</u>."
Vatican II, *Nostra Aetate* #4, Original Latin: "…Iudaei tamen neque ut a Deo **reprobati** neque ut maledicti exhibeantur…"[4]	The Latin of the Council of Florence: "Quoscunque ergo adversa et contraria sentientes damnat, **reprobat** et anathematizat et a Christi corpore, quod est ecclesia, alienos esse denuntiat."[5]

In making the infallible dogmatic declaration that all who have a view contrary to faith in Our Lord or the Trinity are rejected, **the original Latin of the Council of Florence uses the word "reprobat," which means "rejects."** It is from the Latin verb *reprobo*, which means "I reject" or "condemn."

But here's the bombshell: In *Nostra Aetate* #4 (Vatican II's Decree on Non-Christian Religions) to declare exactly the opposite, Vatican II uses the same verb! Vatican II uses "reprobati," **which is the past participle passive of *reprobo* – the very same verb that the Council of Florence used! This means that Vatican II and the Council of Florence are talking about the exact same thing – they use the exact same verb – <u>and they teach exactly the opposite</u>!** The Catholic Church defines that all individuals (Jews, etc.) who have a view contrary to Faith in Christ or the Trinity the Church "*reprobat*" (rejects). Vatican II tells us that the Jews should not be considered as "*reprobati*" (as having been rejected). Vatican II could hardly contradict Catholic dogma any more precisely!

There can be absolutely no doubt that Vatican II denies the dogmatic teaching of the Council of Florence. Although there are many blatant heresies in Vatican II, as we will see, this is the most specific one. Anyone who would deny that Vatican II teaches heresy, in light of these facts, is simply a liar.

This heresy in Vatican II's Declaration *Nostra Aetate* is the theological foundation for the Vatican II sect's current teaching on the Jews. It is the reason that the Vatican currently publishes books which teach that the Jews are perfectly free to live as if Christ had not come. It is the reason that the Vatican II sect teaches that the Old Covenant is valid. It is the reason why John Paul II and Benedict XVI both made trips to the Synagogue to attempt to validate the Jewish religion, as we will see.

> # The Other Principal Heresies of Vatican II
>
> We will now cover the other heresies found in the following documents of Vatican II:
>
> 1. *Unitatis Redintegratio* – Decree on Ecumenism
> 2. *Orientalium Ecclesiarum* – Decree on Eastern Catholic Churches
> 3. *Lumen Gentium* – "Dogmatic" Constitution on the Church
> 4. *Dignitatis Humanae* – Declaration on Religious Liberty
> 5. *Ad Gentes* – Decree on Missionary Activity
> 6. *Nostra Aetate* – Decree on Non-Christian Religions
> 7. *Gaudium et Spes* – Constitution on the Church in the Modern World
> 8. *Sacrosanctum Concilium* – Constitution on the Sacred Liturgy

Heresies by Document

1. *Unitatis Redintegratio* – Vatican II's Decree on Ecumenism.

> Vatican II document, *Unitatis Redintegratio* # 1:
> "Yet almost all, though in different ways, <u>long for</u> the one visible Church of God, <u>that truly universal Church</u> whose mission is to convert the whole world to the gospel, so that the world may be saved, to the glory of God."[6]

At the very beginning of its *Decree on Ecumenism*, Vatican II teaches that almost everyone longs for a truly universal Church, whose mission is to convert the world to the Gospel. What is the truly universal Church whose mission is to convert the world to the Gospel? It's the Catholic Church, of course, which alone is the one true Church of Christ. So what is Vatican II talking about, then? Why is Vatican II teaching that almost everyone *longs* for the truly universal Church of Christ when we already have it? The answer is that Vatican II teaches that people must *long* for the true Catholic Church because it teaches that it does not yet exist! For those who doubt that Vatican II was here denying that the Catholic Church exists, we will quote John Paul II's own interpretation of this passage.

> John Paul II, *Homily*, Dec. 5, 1996, <u>speaking of prayer with non-Catholics</u>: "**When we pray together, we do so with the longing 'that there may be one visible Church of God, <u>a Church truly universal</u> and sent forth to the whole world that the world may be converted to the Gospel and so be saved, to the glory of God'** (*Unitatis Redintegratio*, 1.)."

Here we see that John Paul II himself confirmed that the longing for the one visible Church of Christ is a longing on both sides – Catholic and non-Catholic, which means that in its *Decree on Ecumenism* (from which John Paul II was quoting), Vatican II was indeed longing for the one universal Church of Christ. Vatican II was therefore denying that the Catholic Church is the one universal Church of Christ.

The Heresies in Vatican II

Unitatis Redintegratio also affirmed that all baptized professing "Christians" are in communion with the Church and have a right to the name Christian, while not mentioning anything about the necessity for them to convert to the Catholic faith for salvation.

> Vatican II, *Unitatis Redintegratio #3:* "**For men who believe in Christ and have been truly baptized are in communion with the Catholic Church** even though this communion is imperfect. The differences that exist in varying degrees between them and the Catholic Church- whether in doctrine and sometimes in discipline, or concerning the structure of the Church- do indeed create many obstacles, sometimes serious ones, to full ecclesiastical communion. The ecumenical movement is striving to overcome these obstacles. **But even in spite of them it remains true that all who have been justified by faith in Baptism are incorporated into Christ, and have a right to be called Christian, and so are correctly accepted as brothers by the children of the Catholic Church.**"[7]

Notice that Vatican II teaches that these Protestant and schismatic sect members are in communion with the Catholic Church (albeit partial), and brothers of the same Church, with a right to the name Christian. The Catholic Church, on the other hand, teaches that they are outside the communion of the Church and *alien* to its faithful. This directly contradicts the teaching of Vatican II:

> Pope Leo XIII, *Satis Cognitum* (# 9), June 29, 1896: "The practice of the Church has always been the same, as is shown by the unanimous teaching of the Fathers, **who were wont to hold as *outside Catholic communion*, and *alien* to the Church, whoever would recede in the least degree** from any point of doctrine proposed by her authoritative Magisterium."[8]

The following quotation is from an article that appeared in a publication that is widely read and fully approved by the Vatican II sect, *St. Anthony Messenger*. We can see how this "approved" publication understood the teaching of Vatican II's *Decree on Ecumenism*.

> Renee M. Lareau, "Vatican II for Gen-Xers," *St. Anthony Messenger*, November 2005, p. 25: "***Unitatis Redintegratio* (Decree on ecumenism) and *Nostra Aetate* (Declaration on the Relationship of the Church to Non-Christian Religions) showed marked changes in the Church's attitudes toward other faiths**. Coming from a once insular institution that *had* insisted that there was no salvation outside the Church and that the Catholic Church was the one true Church of Christ, **the open-mindedness that characterized these teachings was remarkable. *Unitatis Redintegratio* affirmed that the Church includes all Christians and is not limited exclusively to the Catholic Church**, while *Nostra Aetate* acknowledged that the truth and holiness of non-Christian religions was the work of the same one true God."[9]

Has Renee misunderstood Vatican II? No, we just showed that *Unitatis Redintegratio* does indeed teach this very thing. Now we will see that it denies that the Church is fully Catholic and affirms that the aforementioned sects have salvation.

> Vatican II document, *Unitatis redintegratio* (# 4):
> "Nevertheless, the divisions among Christians prevent the Church from realizing in practice the fullness of Catholicity proper to her, in those of her sons and daughters who, though attached to her by baptism, are yet separated from full communion with her. Furthermore, the Church herself finds it more difficult to express in actual life her full Catholicity in all its bearings."[10]

The Heresies in Vatican II

Here, in #4 of the same *Decree on Ecumenism*, Vatican II denies that the Church of Christ is fully Catholic! If you believe this you cannot even say the Apostles' Creed: "I believe in… the holy Catholic Church." You would have to say, "*I believe in the not fully Catholic Church.*" But why would Vatican II assert such a ridiculous heresy? There is a reason. The word Catholic means "universal." As we saw already, Vatican II rejects that the Catholic Church is the universal Church of Christ by teaching that almost everyone *longs* for the universal Church, as if it doesn't exist.

> "Cardinal" Ratzinger, *Dominus Iesus* #17, approved by Antipope John Paul II, Aug. 6, 2000: "Therefore, **the Church of Christ is present and operative also in these Churches, even though they lack full communion with the Catholic Church** since they do not accept the Catholic doctrine of the Primacy, which, according to the will of God, the Bishop of Rome objectively has and exercises over the entire Church."[11]

The Vatican II religion holds that the Church of Christ is bigger than the Catholic Church. Since Vatican II's *Decree on Ecumenism* denies that the Catholic Church is the universal Church of Christ by *longing* for such a Church to exist, **it follows logically that Vatican II would teach that "the Church" (i.e., the universal Catholic Church) is not able to fully realize its catholicity/universality, due to "divisions among Christians."** In other words, according to the clear teaching of Vatican II, divisions among the countless Protestant sects, Eastern Schismatic sects and the Catholic Church prevent *the universal Church (of which we are all members according to Vatican II)* from fully realizing its true catholicity (universality).

All of this is a definite confirmation that Vatican II taught that heretical and schismatic sects make up the Church of Christ. **Vatican II's words about the universality of the Church of Christ being impaired by divisions among these sects would not make sense unless it held that these sects make up part of the Church of Christ**. With that explained, we will quote Pope Clement VI and Pope Leo XIII to contradict this awful heresy of Vatican II.

> Pope Clement VI, *Super quibusdam*, Sept. 20, 1351:
> "We ask: In the first place, whether you and the Church of the Armenians which is obedient to you, believe that all those who in baptism have received the same Catholic faith, and afterwards have withdrawn and will withdraw in the future from the communion of **THIS SAME ROMAN CHURCH, WHICH ONE ALONE IS CATHOLIC**, are schismatic and heretical, if they remain obstinately separated from the faith of this Roman Church."[12]

> Pope Leo XIII, *Satis Cognitum* (# 9), June 29, 1896:
> "The practice of the Church has always been the same, as is shown by the unanimous teaching of the Fathers, **who were wont to hold as outside Catholic communion, AND ALIEN TO THE CHURCH, WHOEVER WOULD RECEDE IN THE LEAST DEGREE FROM ANY POINT OF DOCTRINE PROPOSED BY HER AUTHORITATIVE MAGISTERIUM.**"[13]

As we can see, when heretics leave the Catholic Church they don't break its universality or catholicity. They simply leave the Church. But not according to the *Decree on Ecumenism* of Vatican II:

> Michael J. Daley, "The Council's 16 Documents," *St. Anthony Messenger*, Nov. 2005, p. 15: "Decree on Ecumenism (Unitatis Redintegratio) desires the restoration of union, not simply a return to Rome, among all Christians. **It admits that both sides were to blame for historical divisions** and gives guidelines for ecumenical activities."[14]

The Heresies in Vatican II

According to this commentator, Vatican II taught that the Protestants and schismatics weren't at fault for leaving the Catholic Church; both sides were to blame. Has Daley misunderstood Vatican II? No, Vatican II indeed teaches this very thing by this astounding statement:

> Vatican II, *Unitatis Redintegratio* #3: "**The children <u>who are born into these Communities and who grow up believing in Christ cannot be accused of the sin involved in the separation</u>**, and the Catholic Church embraces them as brothers, with respect and affection."
> (http://www.vatican.va/archive/hist_councils/ii_vatican_council/documents/vat-ii_decree_19641121_unitatis-redintegratio_en.html)
>
> **One must carefully consider this statement to get the full impact of its malice.** Without any clarification or qualification given, <u>Vatican II issues a general statement and excuses of the sin of separation (i.e. heresy and schism) all</u> who, having been born into Protestant and schismatic communities, grow up in them "believing in Christ." This is incredibly heretical. **It would mean that <u>one could not accuse any Protestant of being a heretic, no matter how anti-Catholic he is, if he had been born into such a sect</u>!** This directly contradicts Catholic teaching, as we saw (e.g. Leo XIII). All who reject even one dogma of the Catholic Faith are heretics and are guilty of severing themselves from the true Church.

Moving along, we come to # 3 of Vatican II's *Decree on Ecumenism*:

> Vatican II document, *Unitatis redintegratio* # 3:
> "Moreover some, and even most, of the significant elements and endowments which together go to build up and give life to the Church itself, <u>can exist outside the visible boundaries of the Catholic Church</u>: the written word of God; <u>the life of grace</u>; faith, hope and charity, with the other interior gifts of the Holy Spirit, and visible elements too."[15]

Here we discover more heresy in # 3 of the *Decree on Ecumenism*. It asserts that "the life of grace" (sanctifying grace/justification) exists outside the visible boundaries of the Catholic Church. This is directly contrary to the solemn teaching of Pope Boniface VIII in the Bull *Unam Sanctam*.

> Pope Boniface VIII, *Unam Sanctam*, Nov. 18, 1302:
> "With Faith urging us we are forced to believe and to hold the one, holy, Catholic Church and that, apostolic, and we firmly believe and simply confess **this Church outside of which there is no salvation <u>nor remission of sin</u>**, the Spouse in the Canticle proclaiming: 'One is my dove, my perfect one.'"[16]

Vatican II contradicted the dogma that there is no remission of sin outside the Catholic Church by asserting that one can possess the life of grace (which includes the remission of sins) outside the Catholic Church. And there is more heresy in the same section of the *Decree on Ecumenism*. Vatican II bluntly asserts that these communities it has been describing are means of salvation.

> Vatican II document, *Unitatis redintegratio* (# 3):
> "It follows that these separated churches and communities as such, though we believe them to be deficient in some respects, have by no means been deprived of significance

The Heresies in Vatican II 47

and importance in the mystery of salvation. <u>For the Spirit of Christ has not refrained from using them as means of salvation</u> whose efficacy comes from that fullness of grace and truth which has been entrusted to the Catholic Church."[17]

This is one of Vatican II's worst heresies. It constitutes a rejection of the dogma Outside the Catholic Church There is No Salvation.

> Pope St. Pius X, *Editae saepe* (# 29), May 26, 1910: **"The Church alone** possesses together with her magisterium the power of governing and sanctifying human society. Through her ministers and servants (each in his own station and office), **she confers on mankind suitable and necessary means of salvation."**[18]

> Pope Eugene IV, *Council of Florence*, "Cantate Domino," 1441, *ex cathedra*:
> "The Holy Roman Church firmly believes, professes and preaches that **all those who are outside the Catholic Church, not only pagans but also Jews or heretics and schismatics, cannot share in eternal life** and will go into the everlasting fire which was prepared for the devil and his angels, unless they are joined to the Church before the end of their lives ..."[19]

In its *Decree on Ecumenism* Vatican II also teaches that non-Catholics bear witness to Christ by shedding their blood. The following paragraph implies that there are saints and martyrs for Christ in non-Catholic Churches, which is a heresy.

> Vatican II document, *Unitatis redintegratio* # 4:
> "On the other hand, Catholics must gladly acknowledge and esteem the truly Christian endowments which derive from our common heritage and which are to be found among <u>our separated brothers and sisters</u>. It is right and salutary to recognize the riches of Christ and the virtuous deeds in the lives of others <u>who bear witness to Christ, even at times to the shedding of their blood</u>."[20]

Basing himself on this teaching, John Paul II repeated and expanded upon this heresy many times.

> John Paul II, *Ut Unum Sint* (# 1), May 25, 1995:
> "The courageous witness of <u>**so many martyrs of our century, including members of Churches and Ecclesial Communities not in full communion with the Catholic Church**</u>, gives new vigor to the Council's call and reminds us of our duty to listen to and put into practice its exhortation."[21]

> John Paul II, *Ut Unum Sint* (# 84), May 25, 1995:
> "Albeit in an invisible way, the communion between our Communities, even if still incomplete, is truly and solidly grounded in the full communion of the saints - those who, at the end of a life faithful to grace, are in communion with Christ in glory. **These *saints* come from all the Churches and Ecclesial Communities which gave them entrance into the communion of salvation."**[22]

The Catholic Church teaches dogmatically that outside the Church there are no Christian martyrs.

> Pope Pelagius II, epistle (2) *Dilectionis vestrae*, 585:
> "Those who were not willing to be at agreement in the Church of God, cannot remain with God; although given over to flames and fires, they burn, or thrown to wild beasts,

The Heresies in Vatican II

> they lay down their lives, **there will not be for them that crown of faith, but the punishment of faithlessness**, not a glorious result (of religious virtue), but the ruin of despair. Such a one can be slain; he cannot be crowned."[23]

> Pope Eugene IV, *Council of Florence*, Cantate Domino, Session 11, Feb. 4, 1442:
> "… **no one**, whatever almsgiving he has practiced, **even if he has shed blood for the name of Christ**, can be saved, unless he has remained within the bosom and unity of the Catholic Church."[24]

In its *Decree on Ecumenism*, Vatican II also teaches that Eastern heretics and schismatics help the Church to grow.

> Vatican II document, *Unitatis redintegratio* (#'s 13-15):
> "We now turn our attention to the two chief types of division as they affect the seamless robe of Christ. <u>The first division occurred in the east</u>, when the dogmatic formulas of the councils of Ephesus and Chalcedon were challenged, and later when ecclesiastical communion between the eastern patriarchates and the Roman See was dissolved… Everyone knows with what great love <u>the Christians of the east</u> celebrate the sacred liturgy… <u>Hence, through the celebration of the Holy Eucharist in each of these Churches, the Church of God is built up and grows</u>, and through concelebration their communion with one another is made manifest."[25]

The Catholic Church teaches that heretics are the gates of Hell.

> Pope Vigilius, *Second Council of Constantinople*, 553:
> "These matters having been treated with thorough-going exactness, we bear in mind what was promised about the holy Church and Him who said *the gates of hell will not prevail against it* **(by these we understand the death-dealing tongues of heretics)**… and so we count along with the devil, the father of lies, the uncontrolled tongues of heretics and their heretical writings, together with the heretics themselves who have persisted in their heresy even to death."[26]

> Pope St. Leo IX, *In terra pax hominibus*, Sept. 2, 1053, to the "Father" of the Eastern Orthodox, Michael Cerularius, Chap. 7: "The holy Church built upon a rock, that is Christ, and upon *Peter* or Cephas, the son of John who first was called Simon, because by **the gates of Hell, that is, by the disputations of heretics** which lead the vain to destruction, it would never be overcome."[27]

Another heresy which holds a prominent place in Vatican II's *Decree on Ecumenism* is the constant expression of respect for the members of non-Catholic religions.

> Vatican II document, *Unitatis redintegratio* # 3:
> "But in subsequent centuries much more extensive dissensions made their appearance and large communities came to be separated from the full communion of the Catholic Church – for which, often enough, both sides were to blame. **The children <u>who are born into these Communities and who grow up believing in Christ cannot be accused of the sin involved in the separation</u>**, and the Catholic Church embraces them as brothers, with <u>respect</u> and affection."[28]

The Catholic Church does not look upon the members of non-Catholic religions with respect. The Church works and hopes for their conversion, but denounces and anathematizes as heretical sect members those who reject Catholic teaching:

> Pope Innocent III, *Fourth Lateran Council*, 1215, Constitution 3, On Heretics:
> "**We excommunicate and anathematize every heresy raising itself up against this holy, orthodox and Catholic faith** which we have expounded above. <u>**We condemn all heretics, whatever names they may go under**</u>. They have different faces indeed but their tails are tied together in as much as they are alike in their pride."[29]

> Pope Pelagius II, epistle (1) *Quod ad dilectionem*, 585:
> "**If anyone, however, either suggests or believes or presumes to teach contrary to this faith, let him know that he is condemned and also anathematized** according to the opinion of the same Fathers."[30]

> *First Council of Constantinople*, 381, Can. 1:
> "<u>**Every heresy is to be anathematized**</u> **and in particular that of the Eunomians** or Anomoeans, that of the Arians or Eudoxians, that of the Semi-Arians or Pneumatomachi, that of the Sabellians, that of the Marcellians, that of the Photinians and that of the Apollinarians."[31]

Vatican II's *Decree on Ecumenism* also teaches that in theological matters we must treat with non-Catholics on an equal footing.

> Vatican II document, *Unitatis redintegratio* # 9:
> "We must get to know the outlook of our separated fellow Christians… Most valuable for this purpose are meetings of the two sides – especially for discussion of theological problems – <u>where each side can treat with the other on an equal footing</u>, provided that those who take part in them under the guidance of their authorities are truly competent."[32]

Please notice how specifically the wording of Vatican II's *Decree on Ecumenism* is condemned by Pope Pius XI's encyclical against ecumenism. Vatican II recommends that we "treat" with heretics on an equal footing, while Pope Pius XI describes the heretics as willing to "treat" with the Church of Rome, but only as "equals with an equal"! When one reads the incredible specificity with which Vatican II contradicted the past teaching of the Magisterium, one can only ask: was Satan himself writing the documents of Vatican II?

> Pope Pius XI, *Mortalium Animos* (# 7), Jan. 6, 1928, speaking of heretics:
> "Meanwhile they affirm that they would willingly <u>treat</u> with the Church of Rome, <u>**but on equal terms, that is as equals with an equal**</u>…"[33]

2. *Orientalium ecclesiarum* – Vatican II's Decree on Eastern Catholic Churches

The Vatican II Decree *Orientalium ecclesiarum* deals with eastern Catholic churches. It also deals with the Eastern Schismatic sects, the so-called "Orthodox" non-Catholic churches. In dealing with the so-called Orthodox in # 27 of this decree, Vatican II provides us with one of its most significant heresies.

> Vatican II document, *Orientalium Ecclesiarum* # 27:
> "Given the above-mentioned principles, <u>the sacraments of Penance, Holy Eucharist, and the anointing of the sick may be conferred on eastern Christians who in good faith are separated from the Catholic Church</u>, if they make the request of their own accord and are properly disposed."[34]

> For 20 centuries the Catholic Church consistently taught that heretics cannot receive the sacraments. This teaching is rooted in the dogma that outside the Catholic Church there is no remission of sins, defined by Pope Boniface VIII. It is also rooted in the dogma that sacraments only profit unto salvation those inside the Catholic Church, as defined by Pope Eugene IV.

Pope Boniface VIII, *Unam Sanctam*, Nov. 18, 1302:
"With Faith urging us we are forced to believe and to hold the one, holy, Catholic Church and that, apostolic, and we firmly believe and simply confess **this Church outside of which there is no salvation nor remission of sin**, the Spouse in the Canticle proclaiming: 'One is my dove, my perfect one.'"[35]

Pope Eugene IV, *Council of Florence*, "Cantate Domino," 1441, *ex cathedra*: "The Holy Roman Church firmly believes, professes and preaches that all those who are outside the Catholic Church, not only pagans but also Jews or heretics and schismatics, cannot share in eternal life and will go into the everlasting fire which was prepared for the devil and his angels, unless they are joined to the Church before the end of their lives; **that the unity of this ecclesiastical body is of such importance that only for those who abide in it do the Church's sacraments contribute to salvation** and do fasts, almsgiving and other works of piety and practices of the Christian militia produce eternal rewards; and that nobody can be saved, no matter how much he has given away in alms and even if he has shed blood in the name of Christ, unless he has persevered in the bosom and unity of the Catholic Church."[36]

Only for those who abide in the Catholic Church do the Church's sacraments contribute to salvation. This is a dogma! But this dogma is repudiated by Vatican II's outrageous teaching that it is lawful to give Holy Communion to those who do not abide in the Catholic Church. Popes throughout the ages have proclaimed that non-Catholics who receive the Holy Eucharist outside the Catholic Church receive it to their own damnation.

Pope Pius VIII, *Traditi Humilitati* (# 4), May 24, 1829:
"Jerome used to say it this way: **he who eats the Lamb outside this house will perish as did those during the flood who were not with Noah in the ark**."[37]

Pope Gregory XVI, *Commissum divinitus* (# 11), May 17, 1835:
"… whoever dares to depart from the unity of Peter might understand that he no longer shares in the divine mystery…'**Whoever eats the Lamb outside of this house is unholy**.'"[38]

Pope Pius IX, *Amantissimus* (# 3), April 8, 1862:
"… **whoever eats of the Lamb and is not a member of the Church, has profaned.**"[39]

John Paul II and Benedict XVI repeated and expanded upon this heresy of Vatican II many times. In the case of John Paul II, it is taught clearly in his new Code of Canon Law (Canon 844.3-4), in his *Directory for the Application of the Principles and Norms of Ecumenism* (#'s 122-125) and in his new catechism (#1401). He also made many references to this heresy in his speeches.

John Paul II, *General Audience,* Aug. 9, 1995:
"**Concerning aspects of intercommunion**, the recent Ecumenical Directory confirms and states precisely all that the Council said: that is, **a certain intercommunion is possible, since the Eastern Churches possess true sacraments**, especially the priesthood and the Eucharist.

"On this sensitive point, specific instructions have been issued, stating that, whenever it is impossible for a Catholic to have recourse to a Catholic priest, he may receive the sacraments of Penance, the Eucharist and the Anointing of the Sick from the minister of an Eastern Church (Directory, n. 123). Reciprocally, **Catholic ministers may licitly administer the sacraments of Penance, the Eucharist and the Anointing of the Sick to Eastern Christians who ask for them.**"

John Paul II, *Ut Unum Sint* (# 48), May 25, 1995:
"Pastoral experience shows that with respect to our Eastern brethren there should be and can be taken into consideration various circumstances affecting individuals, wherein the unity of the Church is not jeopardized nor are intolerable risks involved, **but in which salvation itself and the spiritual profit of souls are urgently at issue**. Hence, in view of special circumstances of time, place and personage, the Catholic Church has often adopted and now adopts a milder policy, offering to all the means of salvation and an example of charity among Christians **through participation in the sacraments and in other sacred functions and objects**… <u>**There must never be a loss of appreciation for the ecclesiological implication of sharing in the sacraments, especially the Holy Eucharist.**</u>"[40]

Three things are striking in this paragraph: 1) John Paul II calls for sharing in the sacraments, especially the Holy Eucharist; 2) he attempts to justify this by invoking "the spiritual profit of souls," which means that he is directly denying the definition of Eugene IV on how reception of the sacraments outside the Church does not profit one unto salvation; 3) **John Paul II reminds us never to forget the "ecclesiological implication" of sharing in the sacraments** – which implication is that these heretics and schismatics with whom they are sharing the sacraments are also in the same Church of Christ! Does the reader see what this heresy means? It means that the Vatican II Church, now headed by Benedict XVI, considers itself in the same Church of Christ with those to whom it gives Holy Communion, the Protestants and the Eastern Schismatics!

Besides its horrible teaching on giving the sacraments to non-Catholics, the Vatican II document *Orientalium ecclesiarum* spreads more of the heresy of indifferentism: the idea that God approves of all heretical sects.

Vatican II document, *Orientalium Ecclesiarum* # 30:
"They should also pray that the fullness of the strength and solace of <u>the holy Spirit, the Paraclete, may flow out upon those many Christians of any Church whatsoever</u> who, fearlessly confessing Christ, are undergoing suffering and distress."[41]

Contrary to the heresy of Vatican II, the Holy Spirit does not flow out upon members of any sect whatsoever.

> Pope Leo XII, *Ubi Primum* (# 14), May 5, 1824:
> "**It is impossible for the most true God**, who is Truth itself, the best, the wisest Provider, and the Rewarder of good men, **to approve all sects who profess false teachings** which are often inconsistent with one another and contradictory, **and to confer eternal salvation on their members**… by divine faith we hold one Lord, one faith, one baptism… **This is why we profess that there is no salvation outside the Church.**"[42]

> Pope St. Celestine I, *Council of Ephesus*, 431:
> "… remember that the followers of every heresy extract from inspired scripture the occasion of their error, and that <u>all heretics corrupt the true expressions of the holy Spirit</u> with their own evil minds and they draw down on their heads an inextinguishable flame."[43]

Finally, operating on the principle that all heretical sects are as good as the Catholic Church, and that the Holy Ghost approves of all heretical sects, *Orientalium ecclesiarum* calls for Catholics to share their churches with heretics and schismatics.

> Vatican II document, *Orientalium Ecclesiarum* # 28:
> "With the same principles in mind, <u>sharing in sacred functions and things and places is allowed among Catholics and their separated eastern brothers and sisters</u>…"[44]

3. *Lumen Gentium* – Vatican II's Constitution on the Church

Lumen Gentium, Vatican II's constitution on the Church, became famous (or rather, notorious) for its heretical teaching of collegiality. This is the idea that the bishops, taken as a whole, also possess supreme authority in the Catholic Church.

> Vatican II document, *Lumen Gentium* # 22:
> "However, <u>the order of Bishops</u>, which succeeds the college of apostles in teaching authority and pastoral government, and indeed in which the apostolic body continues to exist without interruption, <u>is also the subject of supreme and full power over the universal Church</u>, provided it remains united with its head …"[45]

We see that *Lumen Gentium* explicitly teaches that the College of Bishops possesses supreme and full power over the universal Church. If this were true, it would mean that Christ did not institute a single head in the Catholic Church in the person of St. Peter, but two supreme heads, the College of Bishops and Peter, which would make the Church a monster with two heads.

> Pope Boniface VIII, *Unam Sanctam*, Nov. 18, 1302:
> "… Of the one and only Church there is one body, **one head**, not two heads as a monster…"[46]

The pope alone possesses the supreme authority in the Church. The bishops do not.

> Pope Leo XIII, *Satis Cognitum* (# 14), June 29, 1896:
> "For He who made Peter the foundation of the Church also 'chose, twelve, whom He called apostles' (Luke 6:13); and just as it is necessary that the authority of Peter should be perpetuated in the Roman Pontiff, by the fact that the **bishops succeed the Apostles**,

they inherit their ordinary power, and thus the episcopal order necessarily belongs to the essential constitution of the Church. Although **they do not receive plenary, or universal, or supreme authority**, they are not to be looked upon as vicars of the Roman Pontiffs; because they exercise a power really their own, and are most truly called ordinary pastors of the peoples over whom they rule."[47]

Pope Leo XIII, *Satis Cognitum* (# 15):
"But the power of the Roman Pontiff is supreme, universal, and definitely peculiar to itself; but that of the bishops is circumscribed by definite limits, and definitely peculiar to themselves."[48]

Vatican II teaches that Catholics worship the same God as the Muslims

Besides the heresy of collegiality, there are others in *Lumen Gentium* that cannot be overlooked. Perhaps the most striking is found in *Lumen Gentium* 16.

Vatican II document, *Lumen Gentium* # 16:
"But the plan of salvation also embraces those who acknowledge the Creator, and among these the MOSLEMS are first; they profess to hold the faith of **Abraham AND ALONG WITH US THEY WORSHIP THE ONE MERCIFUL GOD WHO WILL JUDGE HUMANITY ON THE LAST DAY**."[49]

This is an amazing blasphemy! Catholics are worshippers of Jesus Christ and the Most Holy Trinity; the Muslims are not!

(Muslims reject the Divinity of Jesus Christ)

(Christians worship Jesus as God)

A child can understand that **we don't have the same God.**

Pope Gregory XVI, *Summo Iugiter Studio* (# 6), May 27, 1832:
"Therefore, they must instruct them in **the true worship of God, which is unique to the Catholic religion.**"[50]

Pope St. Gregory the Great: **"The holy universal Church teaches that it is not possible to worship God truly except in Her...**"[51]

Some people attempt to defend this awful heresy of Vatican II by asserting that Muslims acknowledge and worship one all-powerful God. They argue thus: There is only one God. And since Muslims worship one all-powerful God – not many deities, as the polytheists – they worship the same all-powerful God that we Catholics do.

> If it were true that Muslims worship the same God as Catholics because they worship one, all-powerful God, **then anyone who professes to worship one, all-powerful God worships the one true God together with Catholics**. There is no way around that. That would mean that those who worship Lucifer as the one true and all-powerful God worship the same God as Catholics! But this is clearly absurd. This should prove to anyone that the teaching of Vatican II is heretical. Those who reject the Holy Trinity don't worship the same God as those who worship the Holy Trinity!

It's clearly a denial of the Most Holy Trinity to assert that Muslims worship the true God without worshipping the Trinity. Secondly, and even worse when considered carefully, is the astounding statement that Muslims worship the One Merciful God Who **will judge humanity on the last day**! This is an incredible heresy. Muslims don't worship Jesus Christ, who is humanity's supreme judge on the last day. Therefore, they don't worship God who will judge mankind on the last day! To say that Muslims do worship God *who will judge mankind on the last day*, as Vatican II does in *Lumen Gentium 16*, is to deny that Jesus Christ will judge mankind on the last day.

> Pope St. Damasus I, *Council of Rome*, Can. 15:
> "If anyone does not say that HE **(JESUS CHRIST)** …**WILL COME TO JUDGE THE LIVING AND THE DEAD, HE IS A HERETIC."**[52]

In addition to this astounding heresy, in *Lumen Gentium 16* we find another prominent heresy.

Vatican II teaches that one can be an atheist through no fault of his own

> Vatican II document, *Lumen Gentium* # 16:
> "Nor does divine providence deny the helps that are necessary for salvation to those who, through no fault of their own, have not yet attained to the express recognition of God yet who strive, not without divine grace, to lead an upright life."[53]

Vatican II is teaching here that there are some people who, **THROUGH NO FAULT OF THEIR OWN, have not yet attained to the express recognition of God**. In other words, there are people who, through no fault of their own, don't believe in God (i.e., are atheists). This is heresy.

It is infallibly taught in Sacred Scripture that everyone above the age of reason can know with certainty that there is a God. They know this by the things that are made: the trees, the grass, the sun, the moon, the stars, etc. Anyone who is an atheist (who believes that there is no God) is without excuse. The natural law convicts him. This is a revealed truth of Sacred Scripture.

> Romans 1:19-21: "Because that which is known of God is manifest in them. For God hath manifested it unto them. For the invisible things of Him, from the creation of the world, are clearly seen, being understood by the things that are made; His eternal power also, and divinity: **SO THAT THEY ARE INEXCUSABLE.**"

St. Paul teaches that atheists are inexcusable because God's creation proves His existence. Vatican II, on the contrary, teaches that atheists can be excused. This causes us to ask, "What bible was Vatican II using?" It must have been the revised satanic edition. Vatican II's statement about those who don't acknowledge God is not only condemned by St. Paul, but also by Vatican Council I. **Vatican I dogmatically defined the principle set forth in Romans 1 – which directly contradicts the teaching of Vatican II.**

> Pope Pius IX, *First Vatican Council*, Session 3, On Revelation, Can. 1:
> "If anyone shall have said that the one true God, our Creator and Lord, **cannot be known with certitude by those things which have been made, by the natural light of human reason: let him be anathema.**"[54]

> Pope Pius IX, *First Vatican Council*, Session 3, On God the Creator, Can. 1:
> "If <u>anyone shall have denied</u> the one true God, Creator and Lord of visible and invisible things: let him be anathema."[55]

Vatican II falls directly under these anathemas by its heretical teaching above.

Vatican II teaches that the Church is united with those who don't accept the Faith or the Papacy

In *Lumen Gentium* 15, Vatican II teaches heresy on the issue of those who are united with the Church. If one were to sum up the characteristics of the unity of the Catholic Church, it would be that the Church is united with those baptized persons who accept the Catholic Faith in its entirety and remain under the unifying factor of the Papacy. To put it another way: **those people with whom the Catholic Church is surely <u>not</u> united are those who don't accept the Catholic Faith in its entirety or the Papacy**. But Vatican II lists those two criteria for unity and teaches just the opposite!

> **Vatican II document, *Lumen Gentium* # 15:**
> "<u>For several reasons the Church recognizes that it is joined to those who</u>, though baptized and so honoured with the Christian name, <u>do not profess the faith in its entirety or do not preserve communion under the successor of St. Peter.</u>"[56]

Vatican II says that the Church is united with those who <u>don't accept the Faith and the Papacy</u>. This is totally heretical. It's the opposite of the teaching of the Church. As we see below, it's a dogma that those who reject the Papacy, or any portion of the Faith, are not joined to the Catholic Church.

> Pope Pius IX, *Amantissimus* (# 3), April 8, 1862:
> "There are other, almost countless, proofs drawn from the most trustworthy witnesses which clearly and openly testify with great faith, exactitude, respect and obedience that **all who want to belong to the true and only Church of Christ must honor and obey this Apostolic See and the Roman Pontiff.**"[57]

> Pope Pius VI, *Charitas* (# 32), April 13, 1791:
> "Finally, in one word, stay close to Us. **For no one can be in the Church of Christ without being in unity with its visible head and founded on the See of Peter.**"[58]

> Pope Leo XIII, *Satis Cognitum* (# 9), June 29, 1896:
> "The practice of the Church has always been the same, as is shown by the unanimous teaching of the Fathers, WHO WERE WONT TO HOLD AS *OUTSIDE CATHOLIC COMMUNION*, AND ALIEN TO THE CHURCH, WHOEVER WOULD RECEDE IN THE LEAST DEGREE FROM ANY POINT OF DOCTRINE PROPOSED BY HER AUTHORITATIVE MAGISTERIUM."[59]

Vatican II also teaches that heretics honor Holy Scripture with a true religious zeal.

> Vatican II document, *Lumen Gentium* # 15, speaking of non-Catholics:
> "For there are many who hold the sacred scripture in honor as the norm for believing and living, displaying a sincere religious zeal... They are marked in baptism... and indeed there are other sacraments that they recognize and accept in their own Churches or ecclesiastical communities."[60]

The Catholic Church teaches that heretics repudiate the traditional Word of God.

> Pope Gregory XVI, *Inter Praecipuas* (# 2), May 8, 1844: "Indeed, you are aware that from the first ages called Christian, it has **been the peculiar artifice of heretics that, repudiating the traditional Word of God**, and rejecting the authority of the Catholic Church, they either falsify the Scriptures at hand, or alter the explanation of the meaning."[61]

4. *Dignitatis Humanae* – Vatican II's Declaration on Religious liberty

Vatican II's *Declaration on Religious Liberty* was without question the most notorious of all the documents of Vatican II. In order to understand why Vatican II's teaching on religious liberty is heretical one must understand the Catholic Church's infallible teaching on the issue.

It's a dogma of the Catholic Church that States have a right, and indeed a duty, to prevent the members of false religions from publicly propagating and practicing their false faiths. States must do this to protect the common good – the good of souls – which is harmed by the public dissemination of evil. This is why the Catholic Church has always taught that Catholicism should be the only religion of the State, and that the State should exclude and forbid the *public* profession and propagation of any other.

The Heresies in Vatican II

We will now look at three propositions that were condemned by Pope Pius IX in his authoritative Syllabus of Errors.

> Pope Pius IX, *Syllabus of Errors*, Dec. 8, 1864, # 77:
> "In this age of ours <u>it is no longer expedient</u> that the Catholic religion should be the only religion of the state, <u>to the exclusion of all other cults whatsoever</u>." – Condemned.[62]

Notice, the idea that the Catholic religion should <u>not</u> be the only religion of the State, to the exclusion of other religions, is condemned. That means that the Catholic religion should be the only religion of the State and that the others should be excluded from public worship, profession, practice and propagation. The Catholic Church doesn't force nonbelievers to believe in the Catholic Faith, since belief (by definition) is a free act of the will.

> Pope Leo XIII, *Immortale Dei* (#36), Nov. 1, 1885: "And, in fact, the Church is wont to take earnest heed that no one shall be forced to embrace the Catholic faith against his will, for, as St. Augustine wisely reminds us, 'Man cannot believe otherwise than of his own will.'"[63]

However, it teaches that States should forbid the propagation and public profession of false religions which lead souls to Hell.

> Pope Pius IX, *Syllabus of Errors*, # 78:
> "Hence in certain regions of Catholic name, it has been laudably sanctioned by law that **men immigrating there be allowed to have public exercises of any form of worship of their own**." – Condemned.[64]

> Pope Pius IX, *Syllabus of Errors*, Dec. 8, 1864, # 55:
> "**The Church is to be separated from the state, and the state from the Church**." – Condemned.[65]

In *Quanta Cura*, Pope Pius IX also condemned the idea that every man should be granted the civil right to religious liberty.

> Pope Pius IX, *Quanta Cura* (# 3), Dec. 8, 1864:
> "From which totally false idea of social government they do not fear to foster **<u>THAT ERRONEOUS OPINION</u>**, most fatal in its effects on the Catholic Church and the salvation of souls, called by Our predecessor, Gregory XVI, an insanity, **<u>NAMELY, THAT 'LIBERTY OF CONSCIENCE AND WORSHIP IS EACH MAN'S PERSONAL RIGHT, WHICH OUGHT TO BE LEGALLY PROCLAIMED AND ASSERTED IN EVERY RIGHTLY CONSTITUTED SOCIETY</u>**…"[66]

But Vatican II teaches just the opposite:

> Vatican II document, *Dignitatis humanae* # 2:
> "<u>This Vatican synod declares that the human person has a right to religious freedom</u>. Such freedom consists in this, that all should have such immunity from coercion by individuals, or by groups, or by any human power, that <u>no one should be forced to act against his conscience in religious matters, nor prevented from acting according to his conscience, whether in private or in public</u>, within due limits… <u>This right of the human person to religious freedom should have such recognition in the regulation of society **as to become a civil right**</u>."[67]

> Vatican II document, *Dignitatis humanae* # 2:
> "Therefore <u>this right to non-interference persists even in those who do not carry out their obligations of seeking the truth and standing by it; and the exercise of this right should not be curtailed</u>, as long as due public order is preserved."[68]

Vatican II teaches that religious liberty should be a civil right, which is directly condemned by Pope Pius IX. Vatican II also says that this right to religious liberty applies to public, as well as private, expression; and that no one should be prevented from the public expression or practice of his religion. The teaching of Vatican II is *direct* heresy against the infallible teaching of Pope Pius IX and a host of other popes. The teaching of Vatican II on religious liberty could literally have been added to the errors of the Syllabus of Errors condemned by Pope Pius IX.

Benedict XVI admits that Vatican II's teaching on Religious Liberty contradicts the teaching of the Syllabus of Errors of Pope Pius IX!

What's amazing is that Benedict XVI admits what we just proved above!

> Benedict XVI, *Principles of Catholic Theology*, 1982, p. 381: "If it is desirable to offer a **diagnosis of the text [of the Vatican II document, Gaudium et Spes] as a whole, <u>we might say that (in conjunction with the texts on religious liberty and world religions) it is a revision of the Syllabus of Pius IX, a kind of counter syllabus</u>**... As a result, <u>the one-sidedness of the position adopted by the Church under Pius IX</u> and Pius X in response to the situation created by the new phase of history inaugurated by the French Revolution, <u>was, to a large extent, corrected</u>..."[69]

Benedict XVI admits here that Vatican II's teaching (which he adheres to) is directly contrary to the teaching of the Syllabus of Errors of Pope Pius IX. In other words, he just admitted that Vatican II's teaching is contrary to the teaching of the Catholic Magisterium. One could hardly ask for more of a confirmation that the teaching of Vatican II is heretical. In his book, Benedict XVI repeats this again and again, calling the teaching of Vatican II "the countersyllabus," and saying that there can be no return to the Syllabus of Errors!

> Benedict XVI, *Principles of Catholic Theology*, 1982, p. 385: "By a kind of inner necessity, therefore, the optimism of **the countersyllabus gave way** to a new cry that was far more intense and more dramatic than the former one."[70]

> Benedict XVI, *Principles of Catholic Theology*, 1982, p. 391: " The task is not, therefore, to suppress the Council but to discover the real Council and to deepen its true intention in the light of present experience. **That means that there can be no return to the *Syllabus*,** which may have marked the first stage in the confrontation with liberalism and a newly conceived Marxism but cannot be the last stage."[71]

Vatican II's heresy is perhaps most clearly expressed in the next quote:

> Vatican II document, *Dignitatis humanae* # 3:
> "<u>So the state</u>, whose proper purpose it is to provide for the temporal common good, should certainly recognize and promote the religious life of its citizens. With equal certainty it <u>exceeds the limits of its authority, if it takes upon itself to direct or to prevent religious activity</u>."[72]

Vatican II says that the State exceeds its authority if it dares to prevent religious activity. This is totally heretical.

> Pope Leo XIII, *Libertas* (# 21-23), June 20, 1888:
> "**Justice therefore forbids, and reason itself forbids, the State to be godless**; or to adopt a line of action which would end in godlessness – **namely, to treat the various religions (as they call them) alike, and to bestow upon them promiscuously equal rights and privileges**. Since, then, the profession of one religion is necessary in the State, that religion must be professed which alone is true, and which can be recognized without difficulty, especially in the Catholic States, because the marks of truth are, as it were, engraven upon it… Men have a right freely and prudently to propagate throughout the State what things soever are true and honorable, so that as many as possible may possess them; but **lying opinions**, than which no mental plague is greater, **and vices which corrupt the heart and moral life should be diligently repressed by public authority**, lest they insidiously work the ruin of the State."[73]

Here we see Pope Leo XIII (simply reiterating the consistent teaching of pope after pope) teaching that **the State not only can, but should curtail and forbid the rights and privileges of other religions** to perform religious acts – exactly the opposite of what Vatican II declared. Such public acts, false opinions and false teachings should be repressed by public authority (the State), according to the teaching of the Catholic Church, so that souls are not scandalized or enticed by them.

The heresy of Vatican II on this issue is very clear, but there are always heretics who attempt to defend the indefensible.

Refuting attempted defenses of Vatican II's teaching on Religious Liberty

Some defenders of Vatican II's teaching on religious liberty argue that Vatican II simply taught that we shouldn't coerce people to believe.

> Patrick Madrid, *Pope Fiction*, p. 277: "Notice the Declaration [on religious liberty] endorses not a general freedom to believe whatever you want, but rather, a freedom from being coerced into believing something. **In other words, no one is to be forced to submit to the Catholic Faith.**"[74]

As we saw already, this is completely false. Vatican II didn't merely teach that the Catholic Church doesn't force or coerce an unbeliever to be a Catholic. Rather, Vatican II taught that States don't have the right to put down the public expression and propagation and practice of false religions (because the civil right to religious liberty should be universally recognized). Again, **we must understand the distinction between the two different issues** which the dishonest defenders of Vatican II sometimes attempt to conflate: First issue) the Catholic Church doesn't force or coerce a nonbeliever to believe, since belief is free – true; Second issue) the State cannot repress the public expression of these false religions – this is where Vatican II contradicts the Catholic Church on religious liberty. The second issue is the key.

To understand this better let's give an example: If a State were presented, for instance, with Muslims and Jews holding their religious services and celebrations in a public place (*even if they were not disturbing the peace or infringing on any private property or upsetting the public order at all*), the State could and should (according to Catholic teaching) repress these services and celebrations and send the Jews and Muslims home (or would arrest them, if the law were well established) since they scandalize others and could cause others to join these false religions. The State would tell them their obligation to be Catholic before God and try to convert them by directing them to the Catholic priests, but it wouldn't force them to do so. This is an example of the clear distinction between 1) forcing one to be Catholic, something the Church condemns, since belief is free and 2) the State's right to repress false religious activity, something the Church teaches.

> Pope Pius IX, *Syllabus of Errors*, # 78:
> "Hence in certain regions of Catholic name, it has been laudably sanctioned by law that **men immigrating there be allowed to have public exercises of any form of worship of their own**." – Condemned. [75]

But Vatican II teaches just the opposite. The passage quoted below is the clearest heresy of Vatican II on religious liberty. **We quote it again because this passage** is utterly indefensible and cuts through all attempted distortions, such as the distortion from Patrick Madrid above.

> ## Vatican II Document, *Dignitatis humanae* # 3:
> "**So the state**, whose proper purpose it is to provide for the temporal common good, should certainly recognize and promote the religious life of its citizens. With equal certainty it **exceeds the limits of its authority, if it takes upon itself to direct or to prevent religious activity**." [76]

Here Vatican II says that the State exceeds its authority if it dares to direct **or prevent** religious activity. We just saw above that the Syllabus of errors condemned the idea that the State cannot prevent the activity of other religions. This proves that Vatican II's teaching on religious liberty was clearly false and heretical, and that Vatican II wasn't merely teaching that one should not be coerced to become Catholic.

The "Within Due Limits" Subterfuge

Attempting to defend the heretical teaching of Vatican II on religious liberty by any means, the defenders of Vatican II will engage in tremendous distortions. They will quote the passage below from Vatican II and distort its teaching in the hope that the passage can (being thus distorted) somehow conform to traditional teaching against religious liberty. They assert that Vatican II didn't allow unconditional freedom of public worship, but mentioned certain "limits."

> Vatican II document, *Dignitatis humanae* # 2:
> "This Vatican synod declares that the human person has a right to religious freedom. Such freedom consists in this, that all should have such immunity from coercion by individuals, or by groups, or by any human power, that <u>no one should be forced to act against his conscience in religious matters, nor prevented from acting according to his conscience, whether in private or in public</u>, **within due limits**… This right of the human person to religious freedom should have such recognition in the regulation of society as to become a civil right." [77]

"See," they say, *"Vatican II taught that States could put limits on this religious expression; and this is in conformity with traditional teaching."* This is such a dishonest argument, such a distortion of the text, that Catholics should be outraged by it. In the passage above, **while teaching that no one (no matter what his religion) can be prevented from expressing his religion publicly, <u>Vatican II is simply covering all its bases and making sure that it doesn't go on the record as allowing anarchy in the State</u>**.

Vatican II had to add the clause "within due limits" so that it didn't go on the record endorsing, for instance, a religious group blocking traffic during rush hour or religious services being held in the middle of busy highways. Thus, it taught that *"no one... shall be prevented from acting according to his conscience, whether in private or in public, <u>within due limits</u>."* Vatican II is not in any way saying that a Catholic State could curtail the right of religious liberty of non-Catholic citizens; Vatican II is still teaching undeniable heresy on religious liberty: that religious liberty should be a civil right and that no one shall be prevented by the State from acting according to his conscience in public; *but it was simply indicating that <u>due public order cannot be violated by those exercising this right</u>*.

To prove that this is the meaning – which, of course, is obvious to any honest assessor of this issue – we can simply quote the very same #2 in that Declaration:

> Vatican II document, *Dignitatis humanae* # 2:
> "Therefore <u>this right to non-interference persists even in those who do not carry out their obligations of seeking the truth and standing by it; and the exercise of this right should not be curtailed, **as long as due public order is preserved**</u>."[78]

We can see that the "within due limits" phrase simply means *"as long as due public order is preserved."* Thus, *according to Vatican II, every man has the right to religious liberty, including the public expression and practice of his religion, which the State cannot curtail as long as due public order is preserved.* This is heretical. Vatican II did not conform to traditional teaching, no matter how hard heretics such as "Fr." Brian Harrison dishonestly attempt to use this clause to argue such. Vatican II taught that the State cannot prevent the public expression of false religions, as we see very clearly in this quote we've already discussed.

> Vatican II Document, *Dignitatis humanae* # 3:
> "<u>**So the state**</u>, whose proper purpose it is to provide for the temporal common good, should certainly recognize and promote the religious life of its citizens. With equal certainty it <u>**exceeds the limits of its authority, if it takes upon itself to direct or to prevent religious activity**</u>."[79]

There is no way at all to defend the indefensibly heretical teaching of Vatican II on religious liberty.

The "Religious Liberty teaching is not a dogma" Objection

In view of the clear contradiction between Vatican II's teaching on religious liberty and the traditional teaching, other defenders of the post-Vatican II apostasy have insisted that, despite the contradiction, the teaching of Vatican II doesn't involve heresy because the traditional teaching on religious liberty was not infallibly taught as a dogma.

> Chris Ferrara, *Catholic Family News*, "Opposing the Sedevacantist Enterprise, Part II," Oct. 2005, pp. 24-25: "The [Sedevacantist] Enterprise asserts that there is a flat contradiction

between DH [Vatican II's document *Dignitatis Humanae* on religious liberty] and the traditional teaching: DH affirms a natural right [sic] religious liberty in the public manifestations of false religions by members of non-Catholic sects, while the traditional teaching condemns this notion… **But let's assume for argument's sake that a flat contradiction exists between DH [*Dignitatis Humanae*] and the prior teaching**, and that this contradiction is manifest – i.e., no explanation is required to demonstrate it. **Even so, the contradiction would not involve manifest heresy as such**, since the Church's traditional teaching on the right and duty of the State to repress external violations of the Catholic religion is not a defined dogma of the Catholic Faith, nor is the teaching that there is no right as such publicly to manifest a false religion in Catholic states."[80]

This is <u>completely wrong</u>, and easily refuted. The idea taught by Vatican II, that every man should be granted the civil right to religious liberty, so that he is ensured by law the right to publicly practice and spread his false religion, was dogmatically, solemnly and infallibly condemned by Pope Pius IX in *Quanta Cura*. The language that Pius IX uses more than fulfills the requirements for a <u>dogmatic</u> definition. Please note especially the bolded and underlined portions.

> Pope Pius IX, *Quanta Cura* (#'s 3-6), Dec. 8, 1864, *ex cathedra*: "From which totally false idea of social government they do not fear to foster that erroneous opinion, most fatal in its effects on the Catholic Church and the salvation of souls, called by Our predecessor, Gregory XVI, an insanity, **NAMELY, THAT 'LIBERTY OF CONSCIENCE AND WORSHIP IS EACH MAN'S PERSONAL RIGHT, WHICH OUGHT TO BE LEGALLY PROCLAIMED AND ASSERTED IN EVERY RIGHTLY CONSTITUTED SOCIETY**; and that a right resides in the citizens to an absolute liberty, which should be restrained by no authority whether ecclesiastical or civil, **WHEREBY THEY MAY BE ABLE OPENLY AND PUBLICLY TO MANIFEST AND DECLARE ANY OF THEIR IDEAS WHATEVER, EITHER BY WORD OF MOUTH, BY THE PRESS, OR IN ANY OTHER WAY.**' But while they rashly affirm this, they do not understand and note that they are preaching liberty of perdition… Therefore, **BY OUR APOSTOLIC AUTHORITY, WE REPROBATE, PROSCRIBE, AND CONDEMN ALL THE SINGULAR AND EVIL OPINIONS AND DOCTRINES SPECIALLY MENTIONED IN THIS LETTER, AND WILL AND COMMAND THAT THEY BE THOROUGHLY HELD BY ALL THE SONS OF THE CATHOLIC CHURCH AS REPROBATED, PROSCRIBED AND CONDEMNED.**"[81]

Pope Pius IX solemnly condemns, reprobates and proscribes (outlaws) this evil opinion by his apostolic authority, and solemnly declares that all the sons of the Catholic Church must hold this evil opinion as condemned. This is solemn language and infallible teaching of the highest order. There is no doubt that *Quanta Cura* constitutes a dogmatic condemnation of the idea that religious liberty should be a civil right given to each man. Vatican II's teaching was, therefore, direct heresy against infallible dogmatic teaching on the issue.

Vatican II's teaching on Religious Liberty rejects the entire History of Christendom and destroys Catholic Society

We've shown that Vatican II's teaching on religious liberty is heretical. Many other examples could be given to illustrate that Vatican II's teaching on religious liberty is false, evil and uncatholic. For instance, the dogmatic *Council of Vienne* specifically enjoined on Catholic <u>leaders of States that they must publicly control (i.e. publicly suppress) the public practice</u> of Islamic worship. Pope Clement V was reminding the State of its duty to prohibit the public profession of false religions.

> Pope Clement V, *Council of Vienne*, 1311-1312:
> "**It is an insult to the holy name and a disgrace to the Christian faith** that in certain parts of the world subject to Christian princes where Saracens [i.e., the followers of Islam, also called Muslims] live, sometimes apart, sometimes intermingled with Christians, the Saracen priests, commonly called Zabazala, in their temples or mosques, in which the Saracens meet to adore **the infidel Mahomet**, loudly invoke and extol his name each day at certain hours from a high place… **This brings disrepute on our faith and gives great scandal to the faithful. These practices cannot be tolerated without displeasing the divine majesty**. We therefore, with the sacred council's approval, strictly forbid such practices henceforth in Christian lands. **We enjoin on Catholic princes, one and all**… **They are to forbid expressly the public invocation of the sacrilegious name of Mahomet**… Those who presume to act otherwise are to be so chastised by the princes for their irreverence, that others may be deterred from such boldness."[82]

According to Vatican II, this teaching of the *Council of Vienne* is wrong. It was also wrong, according to the teaching of Vatican II, that the Christian religion was declared to be the religion of the Roman Empire by Theodosius in 392 A.D. and all pagan temples were closed.[83] This shows us again that Vatican II's teaching on religious liberty was evil and heretical.

Vatican II's heretical teaching on religious liberty is precisely the reason why, following Vatican II, **a number of Catholic nations changed their Catholic constitutions in favor of secular ones**! The Catholic constitutions of Spain and Colombia were actually suppressed at the express direction of the Vatican, and the laws of those countries changed to permit the public practice of non-Catholic religions.

Changes to the Spanish Catholic Law as a result of the teaching of Vatican II

> The "Fuero de los Espanoles," the fundamental law of the Spanish State adopted on July 17, 1945, **only authorized the exercise of non-Catholic cults [religions] privately and forbade all propaganda activities on the part of false religions**.
>
> > Article 6, 1: "The profession and practice of the Catholic Religion, which is that of the Spanish State, will enjoy official protection."
> >
> > Article 6, 2: "… the only ceremonies and other open manifestations of religion allowed will be Catholic."
>
> We can see that, in conformity with traditional Catholic teaching, the Spanish law decreed that the only ceremonies *and public manifestations of religion would be Catholic*. **After Vatican II, however, the "Ley Organica del Estado" (Jan. 10, 1967) replaced this second paragraph of article 6 with the following:**
>
> > "The State will assume the protection of religious liberty which will be under the protection of the Judiciary responsible for safeguarding morals and public order."

> Moreover, the preamble to the Constitution of Spain, modified by this same "Ley Organica del Estado" after Vatican II, explicitly declared:
>
>> "... **Given the modification introduced in Article 6** by the `Ley Organica del Estado,' ratified by referendum of the nation, <u>in order to adapt its text to the conciliar Declaration on religious liberty promulgated Dec. 7, 1965 [by Vatican II]</u>, which demands the explicit recognition of this right [religious liberty], and conforms moreover to the second fundamental Principle of the Movement according to which the teaching of the Church ought to inspire our laws ..."
>
> We can see that the second section of Article 6 of the 1945 Constitution was replaced by that of the 1967 <u>**precisely in order to bring the laws of Spain into agreement with the declaration of Vatican II**</u>! Perhaps this revision of Catholic laws in a Catholic country, which was made in order to conform to the new religion of Vatican II, illustrates more than anything else the forces at work here. **Spain went from a Catholic nation to godless one, which now gives legal protection to divorce, sodomy, pornography and contraception, all thanks to Vatican II.**

Pope St. Pius X, *Vehementer Nos*, Feb. 11, 1906:
"We, in accord with the supreme authority which We hold from God, disapprove and condemn the established law which separates the French state from the Church, for those reasons which We have set forth: **because it inflicts the greatest injury upon God whom it solemnly rejects, declaring in the beginning that the state is devoid of any religious worship…"**[84]

Pope Gregory XVI, *Inter Praecipuas* (# 14), May 8, 1844:
"Experience shows that there is no more direct way of alienating the populace from fidelity and obedience to their leaders than through **<u>that indifference to religion propagated by the sect members under the name of religious liberty</u>.**"[85]

In line with its heretical teaching on religious liberty, Vatican II teaches the heresy that all religions have liberty of speech and liberty of the press.

Vatican II document, *Dignitatis Humanae* # 4:
"<u>In addition, religious communities are entitled to teach and give witness to their faith publicly **in speech and writing** without hindrance</u>."[86]

The idea that everyone has the right to liberty of speech and the press has been condemned by many popes. We will only quote Pope Gregory XVI and Pope Leo XIII. Notice that Pope Gregory XVI called this idea (*the very thing taught by Vatican II*) harmful and "never sufficiently denounced."

Pope Gregory XVI, *Mirari Vos* (# 15), Aug. 15, 1832:
"Here We must include **that harmful and never sufficiently denounced freedom to publish any writings whatever** and disseminate them to the people, which some dare to demand and promote with so great a clamor. **We are <u>horrified</u>** to see what **monstrous** doctrines and prodigious errors are disseminated far and wide in countless books, pamphlets, and other writings which, though small in weight, are very great in malice."[87]

Pope Leo XIII, *Libertas* (# 42), June 20, 1888:
"From what has been said it follows that it is quite unlawful to demand, to defend, or to grant unconditional freedom of thought, of speech, or writing, or of worship, as if these were so many rights given by nature to man."[88]

Pope Leo XIII, *Immortale Dei* (# 34), Nov. 1, 1885:
"**Thus, Gregory XVI in his encyclical letter *Mirari Vos*, dated August 15, 1832, inveighed with weighty words against the sophisms which even at his time were being publicly inculcated – namely, that no preference should be shown for any particular form of worship**; that it is right for individuals to form their own personal judgments about religion; that each man's conscience is his sole and all-sufficing guide; and **that it is lawful for every man to publish his own views, whatever they may be**, and even to conspire against the state."[89]

All of this Catholic teaching directly contradicts the heretical teaching of Vatican II.

5. *Ad Gentes* – Vatican II's Decree on Missionary Activity

Not surprisingly, we also find heresy in Vatican II's *Decree on Missionary Activity*.

Vatican II document, *Ad Gentes* # 6:
"For although the Church possesses totally and fully the means of salvation, it neither always nor at once puts or can put them all into operation, but is subject to beginnings and stages in the activity by which it strives to bring God's plan into effect. Indeed, at times, after a successful start and advance, it has to grieve at another reverse, or at least it halts in a certain state of semi-fulfillment and insufficiency."[90]

Vatican II asserts that the Catholic Church is insufficient as a means of salvation. This is a rejection of the dogma Outside the Church There is No Salvation. If there is no salvation outside the Church (a dogma), that necessarily means that the Church is sufficient for man's salvation!

Pope Innocent III, *Eius exemplo*, Dec. 18, 1208:
"By the heart we believe and by the mouth we confess the one Church, not of heretics, but **the Holy Roman, Catholic, and Apostolic Church outside of which we believe that no one is saved**."[91]

Pope Clement VI, *Super quibusdam*, Sept. 20, 1351:
"In the second place, we ask whether you and the Armenians obedient to you believe that **no man of the wayfarers outside the faith of this Church**, and outside the obedience to the Pope of Rome, **can finally be saved**."[92]

Vatican II document, *Ad Gentes* # 29:
"Together with the Secretariat for the promotion of Christian unity, it should search out ways and means for bringing about and organizing cooperation and harmonious relationships with other communities of Christians in their missionary projects, so that as far as possible the scandal of division may be removed."[93]

Ad Gentes 29 teaches that Catholics should work with Protestant sects in their missionary projects. This means that Vatican II considers a conversion to Protestantism a true conversion. This is heresy. There is no salvation outside the Catholic Church. A conversion to Protestantism is not a true conversion.

Pope Leo X, *Fifth Lateran Council*, Session 8, Dec. 19, 1513:
"And since truth cannot contradict truth, we define that every statement contrary to the enlightened truth of the faith is totally false and we strictly forbid teaching otherwise to be permitted. **We decree that all those who cling to erroneous statements of this kind, thus sowing heresies which are wholly condemned, should be avoided in every way and punished as detestable and odious heretics and infidels who are undermining the Catholic faith."**[94]

6. *Nostra Aetate* – Vatican II's Decree on Non-Christian Religions

Vatican II document, *Nostra aetate* # 3:
"The Church also looks upon Muslims with respect. They worship the one God living and subsistent, merciful and almighty, creator of heaven and earth, who has spoken to humanity and to whose decrees, even the hidden ones, they seek to submit themselves wholeheartedly, just as Abraham, to whom the Islamic faith readily relates itself, submitted to God… Hence they have regard for the moral life and worship God in prayer, almsgiving and fasting."[95]

Here we find Vatican II teaching that Muslims worship the one God, the Creator of Heaven and Earth. This is similar to, but slightly different from, the heresy that we have already exposed in *Lumen Gentium*. The false god of the Muslims (which is not the Trinity) didn't create Heaven and Earth. The Most Holy Trinity created Heaven and Earth.

Pope St. Leo IX, *Congratulamur vehementer*, April 13, 1053:
"**For I firmly believe that the Holy Trinity, the Father and the Son and the Holy Spirit**, is one omnipotent God, and in the Trinity the whole Godhead is co-essential and consubstantial, co-eternal and co-omnipotent, and of one will, power, majesty; **the creator of all creation, from whom all things, through whom all things, in whom all things which are in heaven or on earth, visible or invisible**. Likewise I believe that each person in the Holy Trinity is the one true God, complete and perfect."[96]

Interesting comparison of language between Vatican II and the Council of Florence

Vatican II document, *Nostra aetate* # 3: "The Church also looks upon Muslims with respect. They worship the one God living and subsistent, merciful and almighty, creator of heaven and earth, who has spoken to humanity and to whose decrees, even the hidden ones, they seek to submit themselves wholeheartedly, just as Abraham, to whom the Islamic faith readily relates itself, submitted to God… Hence they have regard for the moral life and **worship God in prayer, almsgiving and fasting**."	Pope Eugene IV, *Council of Florence*, 1441, *ex cathedra*:"The… Church firmly believes, professes and preaches that all those who are outside the Catholic Church, not only pagans but also Jews or heretics and schismatics, cannot share in eternal life and will go into the everlasting fire which was prepared for the Devil and his angels, unless they are joined to the Church before the end of their lives; that the unity of this ecclesiastical body is of such importance that only for those who abide in it do the Church's sacraments contribute to salvation and do **fasts, almsgiving and other works of piety** and practices of the Christian militia produce eternal rewards; and that nobody can be saved, no matter how much he has given away in alms and even if he has shed blood in the name of Christ, unless he has persevered in the bosom and unity of the Catholic Church."

The Heresies in Vatican II

Please notice that as the Council of Florence was dogmatically defining the necessity of the Catholic Faith for salvation, it emphasized the prayers, almsgiving and fasts of those inside the bosom of the Church. It stated that such almsgiving will not profit one who is outside the Church. It's interesting that Vatican II, in praising the Muslims and their false religion, uses almost the exact same language as the Council of Florence, but again with a contrary meaning: Vatican II **praises** the fasts, almsgiving and prayers of members of a false non-Catholic religion.

Nostra aetate 3 also says that the Catholic Church looks upon Muslims with respect, who seek to submit themselves to God wholeheartedly, just as Abraham did. But Vatican II's admiration for the infidel Muslims is not shared by the Catholic Church. The Church desires the *conversion* and eternal happiness of all the Muslims, but she recognizes that Islam is a horrible and false religion. She doesn't pretend that they submit themselves to God. She knows that they belong to a false religion.

> Pope Eugene IV, *Council of Basel*, Session 19, Sept. 7, 1434:
> "… there is hope that very many from **the abominable sect of Mahomet** will be converted to the Catholic faith."[97]

Pope Benedict strictly forbade Catholics to even give Muslim names to their children under pain of damnation.

> Pope Benedict XIV, *Quod Provinciale*, Aug. 1, 1754:
> "The Provincial Council of your province of Albania… decreed most solemnly in its third canon, among other matters, as you know, that **Turkish or Mohammedan names should not be given either to children or adults in baptism… This should not be hard for any one of you, venerable brothers, for none of the schismatics and heretics has been rash enough to take a Mohammedan name, and unless your justice abounds more than theirs, you shall not enter the kingdom of God.**"[98]

In the section on the most specific heresy in Vatican II (earlier), we covered that *Nostra Aetate* #4 teaches the heresy that the Jews should not be considered as rejected by God. We will not repeat that here.

Nostra aetate also made sure to remind the world how great Buddhism is, and how this false religion leads to the highest illumination.

Buddhists acknowledge many false gods

> Vatican II document, *Nostra aetate* # 2:
> "<u>In Buddhism</u>, according to its various forms, the radical inadequacy of this changeable world is acknowledged and <u>a way is taught whereby those with a devout and trustful spirit may be able to reach</u> either a state of perfect freedom or, relying on their own efforts or on help from a higher source, <u>the highest illumination</u>."[99]

Vatican II says that in Buddhism "a way is taught" whereby men can reach the highest illumination! This is apostasy. This is one of the worst heresies in Vatican II. Further, read how Paul VI (the man who solemnly promulgated Vatican II) understood its teaching on Buddhism.

> Paul VI, *General Audience to Japanese Buddhists*, Sept. 5, 1973: "**It is a great pleasure for us to welcome the members of the Japanese Buddhists Europe Tour, honored followers of the Soto-shu sect of Buddhism**… **At the Second Vatican Council** the Catholic Church exhorted her sons and daughters to study and evaluate the religious traditions of mankind and to 'learn by sincere and patient dialogue what treasures a bountiful God has distributed among the nations of the earth' (*Ad Gentes*, 11)… **Buddhism is one of the riches of Asia**…"[100]

<u>Basing himself on Vatican II</u> (which he solemnly promulgated), Paul VI says that this false and pagan religion is one of the "riches of Asia"!

Vatican II also praises the false religion of Hinduism for its inexhaustible wealth of "penetrating philosophical investigations," as well as its ascetical life and deep meditation.

> Vatican II document, *Nostra aetate* # 2: "<u>Thus in Hinduism the divine mystery is explored</u> and propounded with an inexhaustible wealth of myths and <u>penetrating philosophical investigations</u>, and liberation is sought from the distresses of our state either <u>through various forms of ascetical life or deep meditation or taking refuge in God</u> with loving confidence."[101]

Vatican II

The Heresies in Vatican II 69

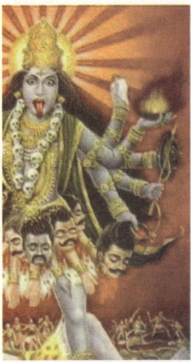

Kali, one of the approximately 330,000 false gods worshipped by the Hindus – a religion not condemned, but praised by Vatican II

Notice how specifically Vatican II's praise for the false religion of Hinduism is contradicted by Pope Leo XIII:

> Pope Leo XIII, *Ad Extremas* (#1), June 24, 1893: "Our thoughts turn first of all to the **blessed Apostle Thomas who is rightly called the founder of preaching the Gospel to the Hindus**. Then, there is Francis Xavier… Through his extraordinary perseverance, **he converted <u>hundreds of thousands of Hindus from the myths and vile superstitions of the Brahmans to the true religion</u>**. In the footsteps of this holy man followed numerous priests… they are continuing these noble efforts; nevertheless, in the vast reaches of the Earth, **many are still deprived of the truth, <u>miserably imprisoned in the darkness of superstition</u>**."[102]

Truly Two Different Religions

Pope Leo XIII, *Ad Extremas* (#1), June 24, 1893: "… Through his extraordinary perseverance, <u>he converted hundreds of thousands of Hindus from the **myths and vile superstitions** of the Brahmans to the true religion</u>. In the footsteps of this holy man followed numerous priests… they are continuing these noble efforts; nevertheless, in the vast reaches of the Earth, **many are still deprived of the truth, miserably imprisoned in the darkness of superstition**."	Vatican II document, *Nostra aetate* (# 2): "<u>Thus in Hinduism **the divine mystery is explored and propounded with an inexhaustible wealth of myths** and **penetrating philosophical investigations**</u>, and liberation is sought from the distresses of our state either <u>through various forms of ascetical life or deep meditation or taking refuge in God with loving confidence</u>."

Amid all of this blasphemy in Vatican II, no mention is made that these infidels must be converted to Christ; no prayer is offered that the Faith may be granted to them; and no admonition that these idolaters must be delivered from their impiety and the darkness of their superstitions. What we see is praise and esteem for these religions of the Devil. What we see is an unequivocal syncretism, which treats all religions as if they are paths to God.

> Pope Pius XI, *Mortalium Animos* (# 2), Jan. 6, 1928:
> "… that false opinion which considers all religions to be more or less good and praiseworthy, … Not only are those who hold this opinion in error and deceived, but also in distorting the idea of true religion they reject it…"[103]

> Pope Pius IX, *Qui Pluribus* (# 15), Nov. 9, 1846:
> "Also perverse is that shocking theory that it makes no difference to which religion one belongs, a theory greatly at variance even with reason. By means of this theory, those crafty men remove all distinction between virtue and vice, truth and error, honorable and vile action. They pretend that men can gain eternal salvation by the practice of any religion, **as if there could ever be any sharing between justice and iniquity, any collaboration between light and darkness, or any agreement between Christ and Belial.**"[104]

7. *Gaudium et Spes* – Vatican II's Constitution on the Church in the Modern World

> Vatican II document, *Gaudium et Spes* # 22:
> "<u>For by His incarnation the Son of God united Himself in some way with every human being</u>. He labored with human hands, thought with a human mind, acted with a human will, and loved with a human heart."[105]

One of the most frequently repeated heresies of the Vatican II sect is the idea that, by His Incarnation, Christ united Himself with each man. Vatican II speaks of a union between Christ and each man which results from the Incarnation itself. John Paul II took the baton of this heresy and ran with it full speed ahead to its logical consequence – universal salvation.

> John Paul II, *Redemptor Hominis* (# 13), March 4, 1979:
> "Christ the Lord indicated this way especially, when, as the Council teaches, '<u>by his Incarnation, He, the Son of God, in a certain way united Himself with each man</u>.' (*Gaudium et Spes*, 22.)."[106]

> John Paul II, *Redemptor Hominis* (# 13), March 4, 1979:
> "We are dealing with each man, for each one is included in the mystery of the Redemption and **with each one Christ has united Himself forever** through this mystery."[107]

We will cover more of John Paul II's teaching in this regard in the section on his heresies. The idea that God united himself to every man in the Incarnation is false and heretical. There is no union between Jesus Christ and each man that results from the incarnation itself.

The whole point of the Catholic Church is to unite mankind to Jesus Christ. This is done through faith and baptism. If the union between all of mankind and Jesus Christ occurred at the Incarnation, then the Church has no value and is in fact pointless. The same would have to be said of the Crucifixion, the Resurrection, the seven sacraments, etc., which are all of no importance in uniting mankind to Jesus Christ according to Vatican II and John Paul II. In this system, the Crucifixion of Christ by which the world was truly redeemed and given a chance to be saved becomes instead *merely a sign* of the union between Christ and each man that already exists and has existed since the Incarnation. The Redemption, then, has no saving value. One can see that in this system all of Catholic doctrine is simultaneously flushed down the toilet.

In fact, **this doctrine of Vatican II, which has been repeated and expanded upon countless times by John Paul II, is actually worse than the heretical doctrine of Martin Luther**. Luther, heretic that he was, at least believed that to be united with Christ one had to possess faith in the Cross of Jesus Christ. But according to the doctrine of Vatican II and John Paul II, faith in the Cross of Jesus Christ is superfluous since all of humanity has already been united to Christ "forever" (John Paul II, *Redemptor Hominis*, 13). We hope that the reader can see the incredible malice that lies behind the statement of Vatican II's Constitution *Gaudium et Spes* #22.

We will now quote the Catholic dogmas which reveal that union between sinful mankind and Christ only comes from faith and baptism; original sin is not remitted in any other way.

> Pope Eugene IV, *Council of Florence*, Session 11, Feb. 4, 1442, "Cantate Domino":
> "**With regard to children**, since the danger of death is often present and **the only remedy available to them is the sacrament of baptism by which they are snatched away from the dominion of the devil** and adopted as children of God …"[108]

> Pope Pius XI, *Quas Primas* (# 15), Dec. 11, 1925: "Indeed this kingdom is presented in the Gospels as such, into which men prepare to enter by doing penance; **moreover, they cannot enter it except through faith and baptism**, which, although **an external rite**, yet signifies and effects an interior regeneration."[109]

Union with Christ is also lost by separation from the Church, something Vatican II doesn't bother to mention.

> Pope Leo XIII, *Satis Cognitum* (# 5), June 29, 1896:
> "**Whoever is separated from the Church is united to an adulteress**. He has cut himself off from the promises of the Church, and he who leaves the Church of Christ cannot arrive at the rewards of Christ."[110]

Besides the heresy in *Gaudium et Spes* #22, there are a number of others in *Gaudium et Spes* that are worthy of note. *Gaudium et Spes* teaches that birth control is virtuous.

> Vatican II document, *Gaudium et spes* # 51:
> "The council is aware that in living their married life harmoniously, couples can often be restricted by modern living conditions and find themselves in circumstances in which the number of children cannot be increased, at least for a time, and the constant expression of love and the full sharing of life are maintained only with difficulty."[111]

> Vatican II document, *Gaudium et Spes* # 52:
> "Those who are learned in the sciences, especially in the biological, medical, social and psychological fields, can be of considerable service to the good of marriage and the family, and to the peace of conscience, if they collaborate in trying to throw more light on the various conditions which favor the virtuous control of procreation."[112]

> Vatican II document, *Gaudium et Spes* # 87:
> "For, according to the inalienable human right to marriage and parenthood, the decision about the number of children to have lies with the right judgment of the parents, and cannot in any way be entrusted to the judgment of public authority… In exploring

The Heresies in Vatican II

methods **to help couples regulate the number of their children**, appropriate information should be given on scientific advances that are well proven and are found to be in accordance with the moral order."[113]

Here we have Vatican II teaching that birth control can be virtuous and that couples can choose the number of children that are to be born. This is contrary to the natural law. God is the author of life. No human being is permitted to infringe upon God's will to bring new life into the world by controlling birth or limiting his family. Birth control is never allowed, regardless of whether it is performed by so-called "natural" or artificial methods. For more on this issue, see the section of this book dealing with Natural Family Planning.

Moving on, we must cover Vatican II's adoration of man.

> Vatican II document, *Gaudium et Spes* # 26:
> "There is also increasing awareness of the exceptional dignity which belongs to the human person, who is superior to everything and whose rights and duties are universal and inviolable."[114]

> Vatican II document, *Gaudium et Spes* # 12:
> "According to the almost unanimous opinion of believers and unbelievers alike, all things on earth should be related to man as their center and crown."[115]

This is blasphemy. If all things on earth should be related to man as their center and crown, this means that everything should be measured by man's law, not God's. This means that for all intents and purposes man is actually God – everything is to be related to him. Man has been put in the place of God.

Vatican II

8. *Sacrosanctum Concilium* – Vatican II's Constitution on the Sacred Liturgy

Sacrosanctum Concilium was Vatican II's constitution on the sacred liturgy. It was responsible for the incredible changes to the Mass and the other sacraments following Vatican II.

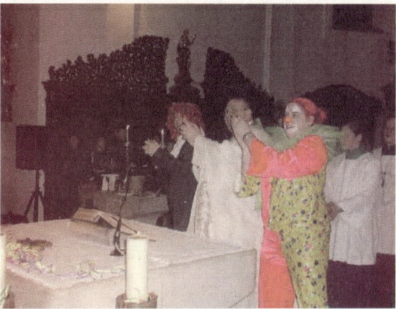
A post-Vatican II "Mass"

These incredible changes will be covered in more detail in the next section of this book dealing with "The Liturgical Revolution." What *Sacrosanctum Concilium* started, Paul VI finished by suppressing the traditional Latin Mass and replacing it with an invalid Protestant service that is referred to as the New Mass or *the Novus Ordo Missae* (the New Order of the Mass). The "New Mass" alone has been responsible for the departure of millions from the Catholic Church.

Another post-Vatican II "Mass"

Paul VI also changed the rites of all seven sacraments of the Church, making grave and possibly invalidating changes to the sacraments of Extreme Unction, Confirmation and Holy Orders. But it all began with Vatican II's Constitution, *Sacrosanctum Concilium*.

The revolutionary intentions of Vatican II are clear in *Sacrosanctum Concilium*.

> *Sacrosanctum Concilium #63b:* "There is to be a new edition of the Roman book of rites, and, following this as a model, each competent local church authority (see article 22.2) should prepare its own, adapted to the needs of individual areas, including those to do with language, as soon as possible."[116]

> *Sacrosanctum Concilium #66:* "Both rites of adult baptism are to be revised, the simpler one and the more elaborate one, the latter with reference to the renewed catechumenate."[117]

> *Sacrosanctum Concilium #67:* "The rite of infant baptism is to be revised, and adapted to the reality of the situation with babies."[118]

> *Sacrosanctum Concilium #71:* "The rite of confirmation is also to be revised."[119]

> *Sacrosanctum Concilium #72:* "The rites and formulas of penance are also to be revised in such a way that they express more clearly what the sacrament is and what it brings about."[120]

> *Sacrosanctum Concilium #76:* "The rites for different kinds of ordination are to be revised – both the ceremonies and the texts."[121]

> *Sacrosanctum Concilium #77:* "The rite of celebrating marriage in the Roman book of rites is to be revised, and made richer, in such a way that it will express the grace of the sacrament more clearly…"[122]

> *Sacrosanctum Concilium #79:* "The sacramentals should be revised… the revision should also pay attention to the needs of our time."[123]

> *Sacrosanctum Concilium #80:* "The rite of consecration of virgins found in the Roman pontifical is to be subjected to review."[124]

> *Sacrosanctum Concilium #82:* "The rite of burying little children should be revised, and a special mass provided."[125]

> *Sacrosanctum Concilium #89d:* "The hour of prime is to be suppressed."[126]

> *Sacrosanctum Concilium #93:* "… the hymns are to be restored to their original form. Things which smack of mythology or which are less suited to Christian holiness are to be removed or changed."[127]

> *Sacrosanctum Concilium #107:* "The liturgical year is to be revised."[128]

> *Sacrosanctum Concilium #128:* "The ecclesiastical canons and statutes which deal with the provision of visible things for worship are to be revised **AS SOON AS POSSIBLE**…"[129]

The Heresies in Vatican II   75

Yes, the Devil could not wait to destroy the precious liturgical heritage of the Catholic Church by means of the heretics at Vatican II. His goal was to leave as little of Tradition remaining as he could. And, as we will continue to document, that's exactly what he did.

Another post-Vatican II "Mass"

In *Sacrosanctum Concilium* #37 and #40.1, the Council falls into heresy against the teaching of Pope Pius X in *Pascendi* on Modernist Worship.

> *Sacrosanctum Concilium* # 37: "… (the Church) cultivates and encourages <u>the gifts and endowments of mind and heart possessed by various races and peoples</u>… Indeed, <u>**it sometimes allows them into the liturgy itself**</u>, provided they are consistent with the thinking behind the true spirit of the liturgy."[130]

Please notice: Vatican II is allowing the customs of various peoples into liturgical worship.

> *Sacrosanctum Concilium* # 40.1: "The competent local Church authority should carefully and conscientiously consider, in this regard, <u>**which elements from the traditions and particular talents of individual peoples can be brought into divine worship**</u>. <u>Adaptations which are adjudged useful or necessary should be proposed</u> to the apostolic see, and introduced with its consent."[131]

Notice again that Vatican II is calling for the customs and traditions of various peoples to be incorporated into the liturgy.

What Vatican II taught above (and what has been implemented all over the Vatican II Church in the decades following the promulgation of Vatican II) is exactly what Pope Pius X solemnly condemned in *Pascendi* as Modernist worship!

> Pope Pius X, *Pascendi Dominici Gregis* (# 26), Sept. 8, 1907, On the Worship of Modernists: **"THE CHIEF STIMULUS IN THE DOMAIN OF WORSHIP CONSISTS IN THE NEED OF ADAPTING ITSELF TO THE USES AND CUSTOMS OF PEOPLES**, as well as the need of availing itself of the value which certain acts have acquired by long usage."[132]

Vatican II's teaching was condemned word for word by Pope Pius X in 1907!

The Heresies in Vatican II

In *Sacrosanctum Concilium* #34 and #50, Vatican II again contradicted a dogmatic constitution of the Church word for word.

> *Sacrosanctum Concilium* # 34: "<u>The rites should radiate a rich simplicity</u>; they should be brief and lucid, avoiding pointless repetitions; they should be intelligible for the people, and should not in general require much explanation."[133]

> *Sacrosanctum Concilium* # 50: "<u>Therefore the rites</u>, in a way that carefully preserves what really matters, <u>should become simpler</u>. Duplications which have come in over the course of time should be discontinued, as should the less useful accretions."[134]

We can see just how "simple" they have become

Pope Pius VI explicitly condemned the idea that the traditional liturgical rites of the Church should be simplified in his dogmatic Constitution *Auctorem fidei*!

> Pope Pius VI, *Auctorem fidei*, Aug. 28. 1794, # 33:
> "The proposition of the synod by which it shows itself eager to remove the cause through which, in part, there has been induced a forgetfulness of the principles relating to the order of the liturgy, '**<u>by recalling it (the liturgy) to a greater simplicity of rites</u>**, by expressing it in the vernacular language, by uttering it in a loud voice…'" – **Condemned as rash, offensive to pious ears, insulting to the Church, favorable to the charges of heretics against it**.[135]

Sacrosanctum Concilium also called for changing the rite of every sacrament, in addition to calling for "bodily self expression" in the liturgy (# 30):

> *Sacrosanctum Concilium* # 30:
> "In order to encourage their taking an active share, <u>acclamations for the people</u>, together with responses, psalmody, antiphons and hymns, <u>should be developed, as well as actions, movements and **bodily self-expression**</u>."[136]

Vatican II also called for "radical adaptation" to the liturgy (#40):

Sacrosanctum Concilium # 40:
"However, in some places or in some situations, <u>there may arise a pressing need for a more **radical adaptation** of the liturgy</u>."[137]

These passages of Vatican II may form part of the reason why the modern churches of the Vatican II sect frequently conduct "Masses" at which one finds polka bands, electric guitars, balloons, drums, native American ceremonies, topless dancers and rock music (see our section on "The Liturgical Revolution"). One might also find the "priests" celebrating such "Masses" dressed in anything from football jerseys to clown costumes. Yes, the "spirit of Vatican II" has truly touched the modern-day churches of the Vatican II sect. However, true Catholics who have maintained their resistance to the Vatican II apostasy can take heart in the fact that Pope Gregory X at the *Second Council of Lyons,* and Pope Clement V at the *Council of Vienne*, authoritatively condemned all such abominations!

Pope Gregory X, *Second Council of Lyons*, 1274, Constitution 25:
"Churches, then, should be entered humbly and devoutly; **behavior inside should be calm, pleasing to God, bringing peace to the beholders, a source not only of instruction but of mental refreshment**… In churches the sacred solemnities should possess the whole heart and mind; the whole attention should be given to prayer. Hence where it is proper to offer heavenly desires with peace and calm, let nobody arouse rebellion, provoke clamor or be guilty of violence… **Idle and, even more, foul and profane talk must stop; chatter in all its forms must cease. Everything, in short, that may disturb divine worship or offend the eyes of the divine majesty should be absolutely foreign to the churches**, lest where pardon should be asked for our sins, occasion is given for sin, or sin is found to be committed… Those indeed who impudently defy the above prohibitions… will have to fear the sternness of divine retribution and our own, until having confessed their guilt, they have firmly resolved to avoid such conduct in the future."[138]

Pope Clement V, *Council of Vienne*, Decree # 22, 1311-1312:
"There are some, both clergy and laity, especially on the vigil of certain feasts when they ought to be in church persevering in prayer, **who are not afraid to hold licentious dances in the cemeteries of the churches and occasionally to sing ballads** and perpetrate many excesses. **From this sometimes there follows the violation of churches and cemeteries, disgraceful conduct and various crimes**; and the liturgical office is greatly disturbed, **to the offense of the divine majesty and the scandal of the people nearby.**"[139]

Finally, not wishing to leave anything untouched, *Sacrosanctum Concilium* made sure to call for pagan musical traditions in acts of Catholic worship (#119):

Sacrosanctum Concilium # 119:
"In some parts of the world, <u>especially in mission areas, peoples are found who have a musical tradition of their own</u>, a tradition which has great importance for their religious and cultural way of life… For this reason, special care should be taken in the musical training of missionaries, <u>so that, as far as possible, they will be able to encourage the traditional music of these peoples</u> in schools, in choirs, and <u>in acts of worship</u>."[140]

Thankfully, Pope Pius XII and the Council of Trent had already condemned any insertion of pagan musical tradition into the churches.

> Pope Pius IV, *Council of Trent*, Session 22, Decree on things to be observed and avoided at Mass: " And <u>**they should keep out of their churches the kind of music in which a base and suggestive element is introduced**</u> into the organ playing or singing, **and similarly all worldly activities**, empty and secular conversations, walking about, noises and cries, so that the house of God may truly be called and be seen to be a house of prayer."[141]

> Pope Pius XII, *Musicae sacrae* (# 42), Dec. 25, 1955: "**[On Liturgical Music] It must be *holy*. It must not allow within itself anything that savors of the profane** nor allow any such thing to slip into the melodies in which it is expressed."[142]

Is there any doubt that Vatican II tried to bring about a new apostate liturgy for its new apostate Church? Vatican II brings down the anathema of the Church on its head!

> Pope Paul III, *Council of Trent*, Session 7, Can. 13, *ex cathedra*:
> "**If anyone shall say that the received and approved rites of the Catholic Church** accustomed to be used in the solemn administration of the sacraments **may be disdained or omitted by the minister without sin** and at pleasure, <u>**or may be changed by any pastor of the churches to other new ones: let him be anathema.**</u>"[143]

There are other heresies in the documents of Vatican II. However, what has been covered should be enough to convince anyone of good will that no Catholic can accept this heretical council without denying the Faith. And it is not sufficient merely to resist the heresies of Vatican II; **one must entirely condemn this non-Catholic council and all who would obstinately adhere to its teachings.** For if a person rejects the heresies of Vatican II, yet still considers himself in communion with those who accept the heresies of Vatican II, then such a person is still actually in communion with heretics and is therefore a heretic.

Endnotes for Section 8:

[1] Yves Marsaudon in his book *Ecumenism Viewed by a Traditional Freemason*, Paris: Ed. Vitiano, 121; quoted by *Permanences*, no. 21 (July 1965), 87; also quoted by Bishop Tissier De Mallerais, *The Biography of Marcel Lefebvre*, Kansas City, MO: Angelus Press, 2004, p. 328.
[2] Denzinger, *The Sources of Catholic Dogma*, B. Herder Book. Co., Thirtieth Edition, 1957, no. 703-705.
[3] Walter M. Abbott, *The Documents of Vatican II*, The America Press, 1966, p. 666.
[4] *Decrees of the Ecumenical Councils*, Sheed & Ward and Georgetown University Press, 1990, Vol. 1, p. 970.
[5] *1937 Latin Version of Denzinger, Enchiridion Symbolorum*, Herder & Co.., no. 705.
[6] *Decrees of the Ecumenical Councils*, 1990, Vol. 2, p. 908.
[7] http://www.vatican.va/archive/hist_councils/ii_vatican_council/documents/vat-ii_decree_19641121_unitatis-redintegratio_en.html)
[8] *The Papal Encyclicals*, by Claudia Carlen, Raleigh: The Pierian Press, 1990, Vol. 2 (1878-1903), p. 393.
[9] Renee M. Lareau, " Vatican II for Gen-Xers," *St. Anthony Messenger*, November 2005, p. 25.
[10] *Decrees of the Ecumenical Councils*, Vol. 2, p. 912.
[11] "Cardinal" Ratzinger, *Dominus Iesus* #17, approved by John Paul II, Aug. 6, 2000.
[12] Denzinger 570a.
[13] *The Papal Encyclicals*, Vol. 2 (1878-1903), p. 393.
[14] Michael J. Daley, "The Council's 16 Documents" *St. Anthony Messenger*, Nov. 2005, p. 15.
[15] *Decrees of the Ecumenical Councils*, Vol. 2, p. 910.
[16] Denzinger 468.
[17] *Decrees of the Ecumenical Councils*, Vol. 2, p. 910.
[18] *The Papal Encyclicals*, Vol. 3 (1903-1939), pp. 121-122.
[19] *Decrees of the Ecumenical Councils*, Vol. 1, p. 578; Denzinger 714.
[20] *Decrees of the Ecumenical Councils*, Vol. 2, p. 912.
[21] *The Encyclicals of John Paul II*, Huntington, IN: Our Sunday Visitor Publishing Division, 1996, p. 914.
[22] *The Encyclicals of John Paul II*, p. 965.

23 Denzinger 247.
24 Denzinger 714.
25 *Decrees of the Ecumenical Councils*, Vol. 2, pp. 915-916.
26 *Decrees of the Ecumenical Councils*, Vol. 1, p. 113.
27 Denzinger 351.
28 http://www.vatican.va/archive/hist_councils/ii_vatican_council/documents/vat-ii_decree_19641121_unitatis-redintegratio_en.html
29 *Decrees of the Ecumenical Councils*, Vol. 1, p. 233.
30 Denzinger 246.
31 *Decrees of the Ecumenical Councils*, Vol. 1, p. 31.
32 *Decrees of the Ecumenical Councils*, Vol. 2, p. 914.
33 *The Papal Encyclicals*, Vol. 3 (1903-1939), p. 315.
34 *Decrees of the Ecumenical Councils*, Vol. 2, p. 907.
35 Denzinger 468.
36 *Decrees of the Ecumenical Councils*, Vol. 1, p. 578; Denzinger 714.
37 *The Papal Encyclicals*, Vol. 1 (1740-1878), p. 222.
38 *The Papal Encyclicals*, Vol. 1 (1740-1878), p. 256.
39 *The Papal Encyclicals*, Vol. 1 (1740-1878), p. 364.
40 *The Encyclicals of John Paul II*, p. 950.
41 *Decrees of the Ecumenical Councils*, Vol. 2, p. 907.
42 *The Papal Encyclicals*, Vol. 1 (1740-1878), p. 201.
43 *Decrees of the Ecumenical Councils*, Vol. 1, p. 74.
44 *Decrees of the Ecumenical Councils*, Vol. 2, p. 907.
45 *Decrees of the Ecumenical Councils*, Vol. 2, p. 866.
46 Denzinger 468.
47 *The Papal Encyclicals*, Vol. 2 (1878-1903), p. 400.
48 Denzinger 1961.
49 *Decrees of the Ecumenical Councils*, Vol. 2, p. 861.
50 *The Papal Encyclicals*, Vol. 1 (1740-1878), p. 231.
51 *The Papal Encyclicals*, Vol. 1 (1740-1878), p. 230.
52 Denzinger 73.
53 *Decrees of the Ecumenical Councils*, Vol. 2, p. 861.
54 Denzinger 1806.
55 Denzinger 1801.
56 *Decrees of the Ecumenical Councils*, Vol. 2, p. 860.
57 *The Papal Encyclicals*, Vol. 1 (1740-1878), p. 364.
58 *The Papal Encyclicals*, Vol. 1 (1740-1878), p. 184.
59 *The Papal Encyclicals*, Vol. 2 (1878-1903), p. 399.
60 *Decrees of the Ecumenical Councils*, Vol. 2, pp. 860-861.
61 Denzinger 1630.
62 Denzinger 1777.
63 *The Papal Encyclicals*, Vol. 2 (1878-1903), p. 115.
64 Denzinger 1778.
65 Denzinger 1755.
66 Denzinger 1690.
67 *Decrees of the Ecumenical Councils*, Vol. 2, p. 1002.
68 *Decrees of the Ecumenical Councils*, Vol. 2, p. 1003.
69 Benedict XVI, *Principles of Catholic Theology*, San Francisco, CA: Ignatius Press, 1982, p. 381.
70 Benedict XVI, *Principles of Catholic Theology*, p. 385.
71 Benedict XVI, *Principles of Catholic Theology*, p. 391.
72 *Decrees of the Ecumenical Councils*, Vol. 2, p. 1004.
73 *The Papal Encyclicals*, Vol. 2 (1878-1903), pp. 175-176.
74 Patrick Madrid, *Pope Fiction*, San Diego: Basilica Press, 1999, p. 277
75 Denzinger 1778.
76 *Decrees of the Ecumenical Councils*, Vol. 2, p. 1004.
77 *Decrees of the Ecumenical Councils*, Vol. 2, p. 1002.

78 *Decrees of the Ecumenical Councils*, Vol. 2, p. 1003.
79 *Decrees of the Ecumenical Councils*, Vol. 2, p. 1004.
80 Chris Ferrara, *Catholic Family News*, "Opposing the Sedevacantist Enterprise, Part II," Oct. 2005, pp. 24-25.
81 Denzinger 1690; 1699.
82 *Decrees of the Ecumenical Councils*, Vol. 1, p. 380.
83 Fr. John Laux, *Church History*, p. 98.
84 Denzinger 1995.
85 *The Papal Encyclicals*, Vol. 1 (1740-1878), p. 271.
86 *Decrees of the Ecumenical Councils*, Vol. 2, p. 1004.
87 *The Papal Encyclicals*, Vol. 1 (1740-1878), p. 238.
88 *The Papal Encyclicals*, Vol. 2 (1878-1903), p. 180.
89 *The Papal Encyclicals*, Vol. 2 (1878-1903), p. 114.
90 *Decrees of the Ecumenical Councils*, Vol. 2, p. 1015.
91 Denzinger 423.
92 Denzinger 570b.
93 *Decrees of the Ecumenical Councils*, Vol. 2, p. 1035.
94 *Decrees of the Ecumenical Councils*, Vol. 1, pp. 605-606.
95 *Decrees of the Ecumenical Councils*, Vol. 2, p. 969.
96 Denzinger 343.
97 *Decrees of the Ecumenical Councils*, Vol. 1, p. 479.
98 *The Papal Encyclicals*, Vol. 1 (1740-1878), pp. 49-50.
99 *Decrees of the Ecumenical Councils*, Vol. 2, p. 969.
100 *L'Osservatore Romano*, Sept. 13, 1973, p. 8.
101 *Decrees of the Ecumenical Councils*, Vol. 2, p. 969.
102 *The Papal Encyclicals*, Vol. 2 (1878-1903), p. 307.
103 *The Papal Encyclicals*, Vol. 3 (1903-1939), pp. 313-314.
104 *The Papal Encyclicals*, Vol. 1 (1740-1878), p. 280.
105 *Decrees of the Ecumenical Councils*, Vol. 2, p. 1082.
106 *The Papal Encyclicals*, Vol. 5 (1958-1981), p. 255.
107 *The Papal Encyclicals*, Vol. 5 (1958-1981), p. 255.
108 *Decrees of the Ecumenical Councils*, Vol. 1, p. 576.
109 Denzinger 2195; *The Papal Encyclicals*, Vol. 3 (1903-1939), p. 274.
110 *The Papal Encyclicals*, Vol. 2 (1878-1903), p. 391.
111 *Decrees of the Ecumenical Councils*, Vol. 2, pp. 1103-1104.
112 *Decrees of the Ecumenical Councils*, Vol. 2, p. 1105.
113 *Decrees of the Ecumenical Councils*, Vol. 2, p. 1132.
114 *Decrees of the Ecumenical Councils*, Vol. 2, p. 1085.
115 *Decrees of the Ecumenical Councils*, Vol. 2, p. 1075.
116 *Decrees of the Ecumenical Councils*, Vol. 2, p. 833.
117 *Decrees of the Ecumenical Councils*, Vol. 2, p. 833.
118 *Decrees of the Ecumenical Councils*, Vol. 2, p. 833.
119 *Decrees of the Ecumenical Councils*, Vol. 2, p. 833.
120 *Decrees of the Ecumenical Councils*, Vol. 2, p. 834.
121 *Decrees of the Ecumenical Councils*, Vol. 2, p. 834.
122 *Decrees of the Ecumenical Councils*, Vol. 2, p. 834.
123 *Decrees of the Ecumenical Councils*, Vol. 2, p. 834.
124 *Decrees of the Ecumenical Councils*, Vol. 2, p. 835.
125 *Decrees of the Ecumenical Councils*, Vol. 2, p. 835.
126 *Decrees of the Ecumenical Councils*, Vol. 2, p. 836.
127 *Decrees of the Ecumenical Councils*, Vol. 2, p. 836.
128 *Decrees of the Ecumenical Councils*, Vol. 2, p. 838.
129 *Decrees of the Ecumenical Councils*, Vol. 2, p. 838.
130 *Decrees of the Ecumenical Councils*, Vol. 2, p. 828.
131 *Decrees of the Ecumenical Councils*, Vol. 2, p. 829.
132 *The Papal Encyclicals*, Vol. 3 (1903-1939), p. 83.
133 *Decrees of the Ecumenical Councils*, Vol. 2, p. 827.

[134] *Decrees of the Ecumenical Councils*, Vol. 2, p. 831.
[135] Denzinger 1533.
[136] *Decrees of the Ecumenical Councils*, Vol. 2, p. 827.
[137] *Decrees of the Ecumenical Councils*, Vol. 2, p. 828.
[138] *Decrees of the Ecumenical Councils*, Vol. 1, p. 328.
[139] *Decrees of the Ecumenical Councils*, Vol. 1, p. 378.
[140] *Decrees of the Ecumenical Councils*, Vol. 2, p. 841.
[141] *Decrees of the Ecumenical Councils*, Vol. 2, p. 737.
[142] *The Papal Encyclicals*, Vol. 4 (1939-1958), pp. 283-284.
[143] Denzinger 856.

9. The Liturgical Revolution – A New Mass

END NOTES – PAGE 111

"Truly, if one of the devils in C.S. Lewis' *The Screwtape Letters* had been entrusted with the ruin of the liturgy he could not have done it better."[1]

THE NEW MASS VS. THE TRADITIONAL MASS

The Traditional Latin Mass, the most holy act of worship of the Roman Rite of the Catholic Church, was codified by Pope St. Pius V in his Bull *Quo Primum* in 1570.

In his famous Bull *Quo Primum*, Pope St. Pius V forbade changing the traditional Latin Mass.

> Pope St. Pius V, *Quo Primum Tempore,* July 14, 1570:
> "Now, therefore, in order that all everywhere may adopt and observe what has been delivered to them by the Holy Roman Church, Mother and Mistress of the other churches, *it shall be unlawful henceforth and forever throughout the Christian world to sing or to read Masses according to any formula other than this Missal published by Us…* **Accordingly, no one whosoever is permitted to infringe or rashly contravene this notice of Our permission, statute, ordinance, command, direction, grant, indult, declaration, will, decree, and prohibition. Should any venture to do so, let him understand that he will incur the wrath of Almighty God and of the blessed Apostles Peter and Paul."**[2]

On April 3, 1969, Paul VI replaced the Traditional Latin Mass in the Vatican II churches with his own creation, the New Mass or *Novus Ordo*. Since that time, the world has seen the following in the Vatican II churches which celebrate the New Mass or Novus Ordo:

The world has seen Clown Masses, in which the "priest" dresses as a clown in utter mockery of God.

The world has seen a priest dressed as Dracula; in a football jersey accompanied by cheerleaders; as a cheese-head…

…driving a Volkswagen down the aisle of church as the people sing hosanna. There have been disco Masses…

The invalid New Mass 84

...gymnastic performances during the New Mass; balloon Masses; Carnival Masses;

...nude Masses, at which scantily clad or nude people take part. The world has seen juggling Masses, at which a juggler performs during the New Mass.

The invalid New Mass 85

The world has seen priests celebrate the New Mass with Dorito Chips;

…with Mountain Dew; on a cardboard box; with cookies; with Chinese tea accompanied by ancestor worship; with a basketball as the priest bounces it all over the altar; with a guitar as the priest plays a solo performance. The world has witnessed the New Mass with a priest almost totally nude as he dances around the altar or with other high-wire abominations…

The world has seen New Masses with priests dressed in native pagan costumes;

The invalid New Mass 86

...with a Jewish Menorah placed on the altar;

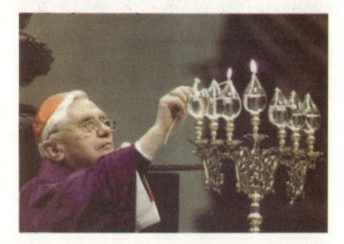

...with a statue of Buddha on the altar; with nuns making offerings to female goddesses; with lectors and gift bearers dressed up as voodoo Satanists. The world has seen the New Mass at

The invalid New Mass 87

which the performer is dressed in a tuxedo and tells jokes. The world has seen rock concerts at the New Mass;

…guitar and polka New Masses;

The invalid New Mass 88

…a puppet New Mass; a New Mass where the people gather round the altar dressed as devils;

…a New Mass where people perform lewd dances to the beat of a steel drum band. The world has seen a New Mass where nuns dressed as pagan vestal virgins make pagan offerings.

The invalid New Mass 89

The world has also seen New Masses incorporating every false religion. There have been Buddhist New masses;

The invalid New Mass

...Hindu and Muslim New Masses;

…New Masses where Jews and Unitarians offer candles to false gods. There are churches where the entire congregation says Mass with the priest;

…where the priest sometimes talks to the people instead of saying Mass.

What we have catalogued is just a tiny sampling of the kind of thing that occurs in every diocese in the world where the New Mass is celebrated, to one degree or another. Our Lord tells us, "By their fruits you shall know them" (Mt. 7:16). The fruits of the New Mass are incalculably scandalous, sacrilegious and idolatrous. This is because the New Mass itself, even in its most pure form, is a false, invalid Mass and an abomination.

The invalid New Mass 92

Even *an organization which defends the New Mass was forced to admit* the following about the typical New Mass – i.e., the New Mass normally offered in the churches (without even necessarily considering the aforementioned abominations and sacrileges that are commonplace): "Most of the New Masses we've attended… are happy-clappy festivities, the music is atrocious, the sermons are vacuous, and they are irreverent…"[3]

When the New Mass came out in 1969, Cardinals Ottaviani, Bacci, and some other theologians wrote to Paul VI about it. Keep in mind that what they said about the New Mass concerns the Latin Version, the so-called "most pure" version of the New Mass. Their study is popularly known as *The Ottaviani Intervention*. It states:

> "The Novus Ordo [the New Order of Mass] represents, both as a whole and in its details, a striking departure from the Catholic theology of the Mass as it was formulated in Session 22 of the Council of Trent."[4]

They could clearly see that the Latin version of the New Mass was a striking departure from the teaching of the Council of Trent. Of the twelve offertory prayers in the Traditional Mass, only two are retained in the New Mass. The deleted offertory prayers are the same ones that the Protestant heretics Martin Luther and Thomas Cranmer eliminated. The New Mass was promulgated by Paul VI with the help of six Protestant Ministers.

The invalid New Mass   93

The six Protestant Ministers who helped design the New Mass were: Drs. George, Jasper, Shepherd, Kunneth, Smith and Thurian.

Paul VI even admitted to his good friend Jean Guitton that his intention in changing the Mass <u>was to make it Protestant</u>.

> Jean Guitton (an intimate friend of Paul VI) wrote: "The intention of Pope Paul VI with regard to what is commonly called the [New] Mass, was to reform the Catholic liturgy in such a way that it should almost coincide with the Protestant liturgy. There was with Pope Paul VI an ecumenical intention to remove, or, at least to correct, or, at least to relax, what was too Catholic in the traditional sense in the Mass and, I repeat, to get the Catholic Mass closer to the Calvinist Mass."[5]

Paul VI removed what was too Catholic in the Mass in order to make the Mass a Protestant service.

A study of the propers and orations of the Traditional Mass versus the New Mass reveals a massacre of the Traditional Faith. The traditional Missal contains 1182 orations. About 760 of those were dropped entirely from the New Mass. Of the approximately 36% which remained, the revisers altered over half of them before introducing them into the new Missal. Thus, **<u>only some 17% of the orations from the Traditional Mass made it untouched into the New Mass</u>**. What's also striking is the content of the revisions that were made to the orations. The Traditional Orations which described the following concepts were specifically abolished from the New Missal: the depravity of sin; the snares of wickedness; the grave offense of sin; the way to perdition; terror in the face of God's fury; God's indignation; the blows of His wrath; the burden of evil; temptations; wicked thoughts; dangers to the soul; enemies of soul and body. Also eliminated were orations which described: the hour of death; the loss of heaven; everlasting death; eternal punishment; the pains of Hell and its fire. Special emphasis was made to abolish from the New Mass the orations which described detachment from the world; prayers for the departed; the true Faith and the existence of heresy; the references to the Church militant, the

The invalid New Mass 94

merits of the saints, miracles and Hell.[6] One can see the results of this massacre of the Traditional Faith from the propers of the New Mass.

The New Mass is fraught with sacrileges, profanations and the most ridiculous abominations imaginable because it reflects a false religion which has abandoned the traditional Catholic Faith.

The false religion the New Mass reflects is one reason why it is completely empty; it is why the fruits are utterly desolate, barren and almost unspeakably bad. The religion practiced at the churches where the New Mass is said, simply put, is a complete sacrilege and an empty celebration of man.

Even Dietrich von Hildebrand, a supporter of the Vatican II religion, said about the New Mass:

"Truly, if one of the devils in C.S. Lewis' *The Screwtape Letters* had been entrusted with the ruin of the liturgy he could not have done it better."[7]

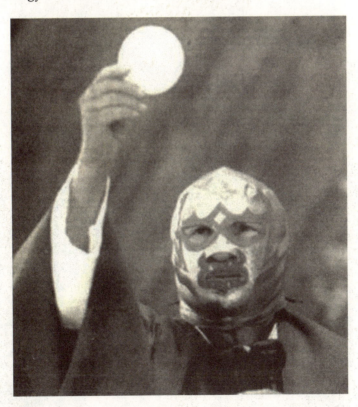

With the exception of a single genuflection by the celebrant after the consecration, virtually every sign of respect for the Body and Blood of Christ which characterized the Traditional Mass has either been abolished or made optional for the New Mass.

It's no longer obligatory for the sacred vessels to be gilded if they are not made of precious metals. Sacred vessels, which only the anointed hands of a priest could touch, are now handled by all.

The invalid New Mass

The priest frequently shakes hands before distributing the host.[8] The General Instruction for the New Mass also declares that altars no longer need to be of natural stone; that an altar stone containing the relics of martyrs is no longer required; that only one cloth is required on the altar; that it is not necessary to have a crucifix or even candles upon the altar.[9]

Not even one of the mandatory requirements developed over 2,000 years to ensure that the altar is of fitting dignity has been retained in the New Mass.

When the Protestants split from the Catholic Church in England in the 16th century, they changed the Mass to reflect their heretical beliefs. The altars were replaced by tables. Latin was replaced by English. Statues and icons were removed from the churches. The Last Gospel and the Confiteor were abolished. "Communion" was distributed in the hand. Mass was said out loud and facing the Congregation. Traditional music was discarded and replaced with new music. Three-fourths of the priests in England went along with the New Service.

This is also precisely what happened in 1969, when Paul VI promulgated the New Mass, the *Novus Ordo Missae*. The similarities between the 1549 Anglican Prayer Book and the New Mass are striking. One expert noted:

> "The extent to which the Novus Ordo Mass departs from the theology of the Council of Trent can best be gauged by comparing the prayers which the Consilium removed from the liturgy to those removed by the heretic Thomas Cranmer. **The coincidence is not simply striking – it is horrifying**. It cannot, in fact, be a coincidence."[10]

In order to emphasize their heretical belief that the Mass is not a sacrifice, but just a meal, the Protestants removed the altar and put a table in its place. In Protestant England, for example, "On November 23, 1550 the Privy Council ordered all altars in England destroyed and replaced by communion tables."[11]

The invalid New Mass　　　　　　　　　　　　　　　　　　　　　　　　　　　　　　　　98

A Vatican II church with a Protestant-like table for its new Protestant "Mass"

The chief Protestant heretics declared: "**The form of a table** shall more move the simple from the superstitious opinions of the popish Mass unto the right use of the Lord's Supper. For the use of an altar is to make sacrifice upon it: the use of a table is to serve men to eat upon."[12] The Welsh Catholic martyr, Richard Gwyn, declared in protest against this change: "**In place of an altar there is a miserable table**, in place of Christ there is bread."[13]

And St. Robert Bellarmine noted: "…**when we enter the temples of the heretics, where there is nothing except a chair for preaching and a table** for making a meal, we feel ourselves to be entering a profane hall and not the house of God."[14]

Just like the new services of the Protestant revolutionaries, the New Mass is celebrated on a table.

The invalid New Mass

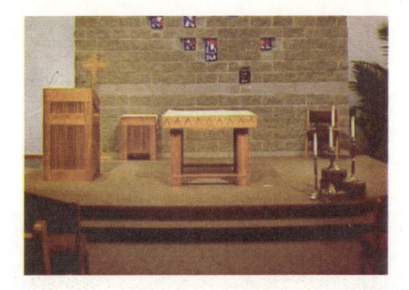

The 1549 Anglican Prayer Book was also called "The Supper of the Lord, and the holy Communion, commonly called the Mass."[15] This title emphasized the Protestant belief that the Mass is just a meal, a supper – and not a sacrifice. When Paul VI promulgated the General Instruction for the New Mass, it was entitled exactly the same way. Its title was: "The Lord's Supper or Mass."[16]

The 1549 Anglican Prayer Book removed from the Mass the psalm *Give Judgment for me, O God*, because of its reference to the altar of God. This psalm was also suppressed in the New Mass.

The 1549 Anglican Prayer Book removed from the Mass the prayer which begins *Take away from us our sins*, because it evokes sacrifice. This was also suppressed in the New Mass.

The prayer which begins *We beseech Thee, O Lord,* refers to relics in the altar stone. This prayer has been suppressed in the New Mass.

The invalid New Mass

> In the 1549 Anglican Prayer Book the *Introit, Kyrie, Gloria, Collect, Epistle, Gospel and Creed* were all retained. They have all been retained in the New Mass.
>
> The equivalent to the Offertory Prayers: *Accept, O holy Father…O God, Who has established the nature of man…We offer unto Thee, O Lord…In a humble spirit…Come, Thou Sanctifier, almighty… and Accept, most holy Trinity*, were all suppressed in the 1549 Anglican Prayer Book. They have all been suppressed in the New Mass, except for two excerpts.
>
> In the 1549 Anglican Prayer Book, the *Lift up your hearts* dialogue, *Preface* and *Sanctus* were all retained. They have been retained in the New Mass.

The Roman Canon was abolished by the 1549 Anglican Prayer Book. It has been retained only as an option in the New Mass.

Arch-heretics of the Protestant revolution: Thomas Cranmer (left) and Martin Luther (right)

Thomas Cranmer (the author of the 1549 Anglican Prayer Book) and Martin Luther both abolished the prayer *Deliver us, O Lord* – probably because it mentions the intercession of Our Lady and the saints. Only a modified version of this prayer has been retained in the New Mass, with no invocation of saints. It should also be noted that the Offertory prayer in the New Mass which begins *Blessed are you, Lord, God of all Creation* is taken from a Jewish Table Prayer.[17]

In fact, the Novus Ordo Mass also removed the traditional Good Friday prayer for the conversion of the Jews. This prayer has been replaced with a prayer, not that the Jews convert, but that they "grow" in faithfulness to His covenant! Thus, there is an expression of apostasy right in the official Good Friday prayer of the New Mass. It's a promotion of Judaism and the heresy that the Old Covenant is still valid.

Two different Good Friday prayers for the Jews for two different religions

On Good Friday, the Novus Ordo religion prays: "*for the Jewish people, the first to hear the word of God, **that they may continue to grow in the love of his name and in faithfulness to His covenant**.*"	But the Catholic Church prays on Good Friday: "for the perfidious Jews: that Our Lord and God may lift the covering off their hearts, so that they may acknowledge Jesus Christ Our Lord."

In the 1549 Anglican Prayer Book, the equivalent of the prayer which begins, *May the Mingling and Consecration of the Body and Blood*, was abolished. It's very interesting that only a modified version of this prayer has been kept in the New Mass with the important word "consecration" removed.

The 1549 Anglican Prayer Book abandoned the discipline of the Roman Rite in distributing Communion under one kind and gave Communion under both kinds. At the New Mass Communion under both kinds is distributed in many places in the world.

The 1552 version of the Anglican Prayer Book instructed that Communion was to be given in the hand to signify that the bread was ordinary bread and that the priest did not differ in essence from a layman.[18]

The New Mass implements Communion in the hand in almost every place in the world, and it even goes farther than Cranmer by allowing communicants to stand and receive from a lay minister.

The prayers in the Traditional Mass which begin with: *What has passed our lips as food* and *May Thy Body, O Lord, which I have eaten* both make explicit reference to the Real Presence of Christ in the Eucharist. Both have been suppressed in the New Mass.

The prayer which begins *May the tribute of my worship be pleasing to thee, most holy Trinity*, was the least acceptable prayer after Communion to all the Protestants, because of its reference to

The invalid New Mass   103

propitiatory sacrifice. Martin Luther, and Cranmer in his Anglican Prayer Book, suppressed it. Following their lead, it was suppressed in the New Mass.

Now to the Last Gospel. If the Last Gospel, which closes the Traditional Mass, had been included in the New Mass, then the New Mass would have clashed with the pattern of Protestant services, which conclude with a blessing. So it was not included in the New Mass.

The prayers after the Traditional Mass, the Leonine Prayers, including the *Hail Mary;* the *Hail Holy Queen;* the *O God our refuge;* the prayer to St. Michael; and the appeal to the Sacred Heart, formed, in practice, an important part of the liturgy. Five prayers less compatible with Protestantism could hardly be imagined. They have all been suppressed in the New Mass.

Considering all of this, even Michael Davies agreed: **"It is beyond dispute that… the Roman Rite has been destroyed."**[19]

Besides the fact that the New Mass is a Protestant service, there is also the fact that the Novus Ordo churches bear a striking and undeniable resemblance to Freemasonic lodges. Look at the pictures. Here is a Freemasonic lodge:

And here is a Novus Ordo church:

The invalid New Mass 104

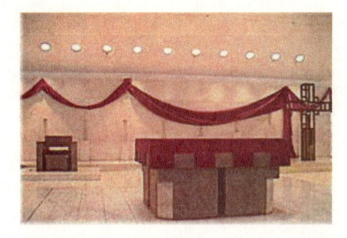

The two are almost indistinguishable; the focus of both is on man, with the Presider's Chair in the middle and a circular emphasis. Perhaps this is because the primary architect of Paul VI's New Mass was Cardinal Annibale Bugnini, who was a Freemason.

Annibale Bugnini, primary architect of the New Mass and a Freemason

"Cardinal" Annibale Bugnini was Chairman of the Consilium which drafted Paul VI's New Mass. Bugnini was initiated into the Masonic Lodge on April 23, 1963, according to the Masonic Register in 1976.[20]

In addition to all of these problems with the New Mass, there is one that looms even larger. The biggest problem with the New Mass is that it is not valid. Jesus Christ is not present in the New Mass because the New Mass has altered the very words of consecration.

PROOF THAT THE NEW MASS IS NOT VALID – THE WORDS OF CONSECRATION HAVE BEEN CHANGED

A sacrament is said to be valid if it takes place. The Sacrament of the Eucharist is valid if the bread and wine become the actual Body, Blood, Soul and Divinity of Jesus Christ. In order for any sacrament to be valid, matter, form, minister and intention must be present.

> **Pope Eugene IV**, *Council of Florence*, 1439: "All these sacraments are made up of three elements: namely, things as the <u>matter</u>, words as the <u>form</u>, and the person of the <u>minister</u> who confers the sacrament with the <u>intention</u> of doing what the Church does. **If any of these is lacking, the sacrament is not effected.**"[21]

The problem with the validity of the New Mass comes with the form, those <u>words</u> necessary to confect the Sacrament of the Eucharist. The form necessary to confect the Eucharist in the Roman Rite was declared by Pope Eugene IV at the Council of Florence.

> **Pope Eugene IV**, *Council of Florence*, Cantate Domino, 1441: "…the holy Roman Church, relying on the teaching and authority of the apostles Peter and Paul… uses this form of words in the consecration of the Lord's Body: *FOR THIS IS MY BODY*. And of His blood: *FOR THIS IS THE CHALICE OF MY BLOOD, OF THE NEW AND ETERNAL TESTAMENT: THE MYSTERY OF FAITH, WHICH SHALL BE SHED FOR YOU AND FOR MANY UNTO THE REMISSION OF SINS.*"[22]

In Pope St. Pius V's Decree *De Defectibus*, we find the same words repeated:

> **Pope St. Pius V**, *De Defectibus*, chapter 5, Part 1:
> "The words of Consecration, which are the FORM of this Sacrament, are these: *FOR THIS IS MY BODY*. And: *FOR THIS IS THE CHALICE OF MY BLOOD, OF THE NEW AND ETERNAL TESTAMENT: THE MYSTERY OF FAITH, <u>WHICH SHALL BE SHED FOR YOU AND FOR MANY UNTO THE REMISSION OF SINS</u>*. Now if one were to remove, or change anything in the FORM of the consecration of the Body and Blood, and in that very change of words the [new] wording would fail to mean the same thing, he would not consecrate the sacrament."[23]

This teaching appeared in the front of every Roman Altar Missal from 1570 to 1962. We can see that the same words mentioned by the Council of Florence are declared to be necessary by Pope St. Pius V. This is why all of these words of consecration are bolded in Traditional Roman Altar Missals, and why the Roman Missal instructs priests to hold the chalice until the completion of all these words.

Pope St. Pius V's teaching states that if the words of consecration are changed so that the meaning is altered, the priest does not confect the Sacrament. In the New Mass the words of consecration have been drastically changed, and the meaning has been altered.

First, the original Latin version of the New Mass has removed the words *mysterium fidei* – "the mystery of Faith" – from the words of consecration. This causes a grave doubt, because "*mysterium fidei*" is part of the form in the Roman Rite. Though the words "*mysterium fidei*" are not part of some of the Eastern Rite formulas of consecration, they have been declared to be part of the Roman Rite. They are also found in some Eastern Rites. Pope Innocent III and the Canon of the Mass also tell us that the words "*mysterium fidei*" were given by Jesus Christ Himself.

> Pope Innocent III, *Cum Marthae circa*, Nov. 29, 1202, in response to a question about the form of the Eucharist and the inclusion of 'mysterium fidei': "You have asked (indeed) who has added to the form of words which Christ Himself expressed when He changed the bread and wine into the Body and Blood, that in the Canon of the Mass which the general Church uses, which none of the Evangelists is read to have expressed… **In the Canon of the Mass that expression, 'mysterium fidei,' is found interposed among His words… Surely we find many such things omitted from the words as well as from the deeds of the Lord by the Evangelists**, which the Apostles are read to have supplied by word or to have expressed by deed… Therefore, **we believe that the form of words, as they are found in the Canon, the Apostles received from Christ**, and their successors from them."[24]

The words "the mystery of faith" in the consecration are a clear reference to the Real Presence of Christ in the Eucharist. These words were also removed by the heretic Thomas Cranmer in his 1549 Anglican Prayer book because of their clear reference to the Real Presence of Christ in the Eucharist.[25] When words are removed from a rite because the meaning they express contradicts the intended meaning of the rite, a doubt is caused. More could be said on this matter, but we must now move to the crushing blow to the validity of the New Mass.

In almost all vernacular translations of the New Mass in the world, the words of consecration read as follows:

FORM OF CONSECRATION IN THE NEW MASS

> "For this is my body. For this is the chalice of my blood, of the new and eternal testament. It shall be shed for you and FOR ALL SO THAT SINS MAY BE FORGIVEN."

The words "for you and for many unto the remission of sins" have been changed to *for you and for all so that sins may be forgiven*. The word "many" has been removed and replaced with the word "all." This huge change invalidates all the New Masses. First, the word *many* was used by Jesus to institute the sacrament of the Eucharist, as we see in Matthew 26:28: "For this is my blood of the new testament, which shall be shed for **many** unto remission of sins." The words used by Our Lord, "*for many unto remission of sins,*" represent the efficacy of the blood that Jesus shed. Jesus's blood is effective for the salvation of *many*, not all men. In the process of explaining this, *The Catechism of the Council of Trent* specifically states that Our Lord did not mean "all" and therefore didn't say it!

> *The Catechism of the Council of Trent*, On the Form of the Eucharist, p. 227:
> "The additional words *for you and for many*, are taken, some from Matthew, some from Luke, but were joined together by the Catholic Church under the guidance of the Spirit of God. **They serve to declare the fruit and advantage of His Passion**. For if we look to its

The invalid New Mass 107

value, we must confess that the Redeemer shed His Blood for the salvation of all; but if we look to the fruit which mankind has received from it, **we shall easily find that it pertains not unto all, but to many** of the human race. When therefore (our Lord) said: *For you,* He meant either those who were present, or those chosen from among the Jewish people, such as were, with the exception of Judas, the disciples with whom He was speaking. **When He added,** *And for many,* **He wished to be understood to mean the remainder of the elect** from among the Jews and Gentiles. <u>**WITH REASON, THEREFORE, WERE THE WORDS *FOR ALL* NOT USED**</u>, as in this place the fruits of the Passion are alone spoken of, and to the elect only did His Passion bring the fruit of salvation."[26]

As we can see, according to *The Catechism of the Council of Trent* the words "for all" were specifically not used by Our Lord because they would give a false meaning.

St. Alphonsus De Liguori, *Treatise on the Holy Eucharist*:
"The words *for you and for many* are used to distinguish the virtue of the Blood of Christ from its fruits: for the Blood of Our Savior is of sufficient value to save all men but its fruits are applied only to a certain number <u>and not to all</u>, and this is their own fault..."[27]

The use of "all" changes the meaning of the form of consecration. No one, not even a pope, can change the words that Jesus Christ specifically instituted for a sacrament of the Church.

Pope Pius XII, *Sacramentum Ordinis* (# 1), Nov. 30, 1947:
"...the Church has no power over the 'substance of the sacraments,' that is, over those things which, with the sources of divine revelation as witnesses, Christ the Lord Himself decreed to be preserved in a sacramental sign..."[28]

Since "all" doesn't mean the same thing as "many," the sacrament is not confected in the New Mass.

Pope St. Pius V, *De Defectibus*, chapter 5, Part 1:
"The words of Consecration, which are the FORM of this Sacrament, are these: FOR THIS IS MY BODY. And: FOR THIS IS THE CHALICE OF MY BLOOD, OF THE NEW AND ETERNAL TESTAMENT: THE MYSTERY OF FAITH, WHICH SHALL BE SHED FOR YOU AND FOR MANY UNTO THE REMISSION OF SINS. **Now if one were to remove, or change anything in the FORM of the consecration of the Body and Blood, and in that very change of words the [new] wording would fail to mean the same thing, he would not consecrate the sacrament.**" [29]

ANOTHER ANGLE TO THIS ISSUE ABSOLUTELY PROVES THAT THE NEW MASS IS INVALID

There is another angle to this issue that we must now examine. In his famous Bull, *Apostolicae Curae* in 1896, Pope Leo XIII teaches:

Pope Leo XIII, *Apostolicae Curae*, Sept. 13, 1896: "All know that **the sacraments of the New Law**, as sensible and efficient signs of invisible grace, **must both signify the grace which they effect and effect the grace which they signify.**"[30]

The invalid New Mass

If it does not signify the grace which it effects and effect the grace which it signifies it is not a sacrament – period. So, what is the grace effected by the Sacrament of the Holy Eucharist?

> Pope Eugene IV, *Council of Florence*, "Exultate Deo," **On the Eucharist**, 1439: "Finally, **this is a fitting way to signify <u>the effect of this sacrament, that is, the union of the Christian people with Christ</u>**."[31]

> St. Thomas Aquinas, *Summa Theologica*, Pt. III, Q. 73, A. 3: "Now it was stated above that <u>**the reality of the sacrament [of the Eucharist] is the unity of the mystical body,**</u> without which there is no salvation…"[32]

As the Council of Florence, St. Thomas Aquinas, and many other theologians teach, the grace effected by the Eucharist is the union of the faithful with Christ. St. Thomas calls this grace "the unity of the Mystical Body." The *grace effected* by the Eucharist (**the union of the faithful with Christ or the unity of the Mystical Body**) must be carefully distinguished from the Eucharist itself: the Body, Blood, Soul and Divinity of Christ.

Since *the union of the faithful with Christ is the grace effected by the Sacrament of the Eucharist* – or what is also called the reality of the Sacrament or the grace proper to the Sacrament of the Eucharist – this grace must be signified in the form of the consecration for it to be valid, as Pope Leo XIII teaches. Okay, so we must look at the traditional form of consecration and find where this grace – the union of the faithful with Christ – is signified.

The traditional form of consecration, as declared by Pope Eugene IV at the *Council of Florence* and Pope St. Pius V in *De Defectibus*, is as follows:

> "FOR THIS IS MY BODY. FOR THIS IS THE CHALICE OF MY BLOOD, OF THE NEW AND ETERNAL TESTAMENT: THE MYSTERY OF FAITH, WHICH SHALL BE SHED FOR YOU AND FOR MANY UNTO THE REMISSION OF SINS."

Note again: we are looking for that part of the form which signifies that the person who receives this sacrament worthily becomes united or more strongly united with Jesus Christ and His Mystical Body.

Do the words "*OF THE NEW AND ETERNAL TESTAMENT*" signify the union of the faithful with Christ/the Mystical Body? No. These words do not signify the Mystical Body, but rather they contrast the temporary and prefiguring sacrifices of the Old Law with the eternal and propitiatory sacrifice of Jesus Christ.

Do the words "*THE MYSTERY OF FAITH*" signify the union of the faithful with Christ/the Mystical Body? No. These words signify the real presence of Christ in the Eucharist, as Innocent III teaches; they do not signify the Mystical Body of Jesus Christ.

Do the words "*WHICH SHALL BE SHED*" signify the union of the faithful with Christ/the Mystical Body? No. These words denote true sacrifice.

The only words left in the form of consecration are: "<u>***FOR YOU AND FOR MANY UNTO THE REMISSION OF SINS.***</u>"

The *remission of sins* is necessary for **incorporation into the Mystical Body**, and remission of sins is an indispensable component of true justification, <u>by which one is fruitfully united to Jesus</u>

The invalid New Mass

Christ. The words **"for you and for many"** denote **the members** of the Mystical Body who have received such remission.

The words "**FOR YOU AND FOR MANY UNTO THE REMISSION OF SINS**" are the words in the form of Consecration which signify the union of the faithful with Christ/the union of the Mystical Body of Christ, which is the grace proper to the Sacrament of the Eucharist.

Now, if we look to the Novus Ordo form of consecration, do we find the Mystical Body/the union of the faithful with Christ (the grace proper to the Sacrament of the Eucharist) signified? Here is the form of consecration in the New Mass or Novus Ordo:

> New Mass form: "This is my body. This is the cup of my blood, of the new and eternal testament. It shall be shed for you and for all so that sins may be forgiven."

Is the union of the Mystical Body of Jesus Christ signified by the words "*for you and for all so that sins may be forgiven*"? No. Are all men part of the Mystical Body? No. Are all men part of the faithful united with Christ? No. We can see very clearly that the New Mass or Novus Ordo most certainly does not signify the union of the Mystical Body (the grace proper to the Sacrament of the Eucharist), and therefore it is not a valid sacrament!

One does not have to say anything more… the New Mass is not valid!

> Pope Leo XIII, *Apostolicae Curae*, 1896: "All know that the Sacraments of the New Law, as sensible and efficient signs of invisible grace, must both signify the grace which they effect and effect the grace which they signify."[33]

> Pope Leo XIII, *Apostolicae Curae*, 1896: "That form cannot be considered apt or sufficient for a Sacrament which omits that which it must essentially signify."[34]

> Pope Eugene IV, *Council of Florence*, "Exultate Deo," 1438: "…this is a fitting way to signify the effect of this sacrament, that is, the union of the Christian people with Christ."[35]

To further prove the point, we should note that in all the formulas of consecration in the liturgical rites of the Catholic Church, whether it is the Armenian Liturgy, the Coptic Liturgy, the Ethiopic Liturgy, the Syrian Liturgy, the Chaldean Liturgy, etc. the union of the faithful with Christ/the Mystical Body is signified in the form of consecration. No liturgy that has ever been approved by the Church fails to signify the union of the faithful with Christ.

Here are the portions of the forms of consecration of the Wine used in Eastern Rites which signify what the Traditional Mass does and what the New Mass doesn't: the union and members of the Church

> THE ARMENIAN LITURGY: "….shed *for you and for many for the expiation and forgiveness of sins.*"

Note that the union and members of the Mystical Body are signified by the words "*for you and for many for the expiation and forgiveness of sins.*"

The invalid New Mass

> THE BYZANTINE LITURGY: "… shed *for you and for many for the forgiveness of sins.*"

Note that the union and members of the Mystical Body are signified.

> THE CHALDEAN LITURGY: "…shed *for you and for many for the forgiveness of sins.*"

Note that the union and members of the Mystical Body are signified.

> THE COPTIC LITURGY: "…shed *for you and for many unto the forgiveness of sins.*"

Note that the union and members of the Mystical Body are signified.

> THE ETHIOPIC LITURGY: "… shed *for you and for many for the forgiveness of sin.*"

Note that the union and members of the Mystical Body are signified.

> THE LITURGY OF MALABAR: "… shed *for you and for many for the remission of sins.*"

Note that the union and members of the Mystical Body are signified.

> THE MARONITE LITURGY: (this form is identical to that which was always used in the Roman Rite)

> THE SYRIAN LITURGY: "This is my Blood, of the New Covenant, which shall be poured out and offered *for the forgiveness of the sins and eternal life of you and of many.*"

Note that the union and members of the Mystical Body are signified by the words "*for the forgiveness of the sins and eternal life of you and of many.*"

The formula of consecration in all Catholic liturgies signifies the union of the faithful with Christ/the Mystical Body of Christ, as we can see. The New Mass, which says, "for you and for all so that sins may be forgiven," does not signify the Mystical Body, since all do not belong to the Mystical Body. Thus, the New Mass does not signify the grace which the Eucharist effects. It is not valid.

Therefore, a Catholic cannot attend the New "Mass" under pain of mortal sin. Those who persist in doing so are committing idolatry (worshipping a piece of bread). Jesus Christ is not present there. The host is merely a piece of bread, not Our Lord's Body, Blood, Soul and Divinity. The Church has always taught that to approach a doubtful sacrament (which employs doubtful matter or form) is mortally sinful. In fact, Pope Innocent XI, *Decree of the Holy Office*, March 4, 1679,[36] even condemns the idea that Catholics can receive "*probable*" sacraments. And the New Mass is not merely doubtful, it is invalid, since it does not signify the grace it is supposed to effect. It is actually worse than a Protestant service; it is an abomination, which falsifies the words of Jesus Christ and the Catholic Faith.

Note: At the time we are writing this there is some talk that the Vatican, in order to deceive traditionalists back into the Counter Church and the false New Mass, is planning to correct the "for all" error in the form of consecration. The fact that the Vatican is going to do this proves that "for all" gives, as we've said, a false signification. Even if they do this, a Catholic would still have to avoid all New Masses under pain of mortal sin because the New Mass itself is a non-

Catholic service, it would still be missing the words "mysterium fidei" in the consecration, and most of the "priests" celebrating it are invalid anyway (as the next section proves).

Endnotes for Section 9:

[1] The words of Dietrich Von Hildebrand, who was, nevertheless, a supporter of the Vatican II religion but felt compelled to make such a statement about the New Mass. Quoted by Michael Davies, *Pope Paul's New Mass*, Kansas City, MO: Angelus Press, 1980, p. 80.
[2] Pope St. Pius V, *Bull Quo Primum*, July 14, 1570.
[3] *New Oxford Review*, Berkeley, CA, November, 2006, "Notes."
[4] *The Ottaviani Intervention*, Rockford, IL: Tan Books.
[5] Rama Coomeraswamy, *The Problems with the New Mass*, Tan Books, p. 34.
[6] Fr. Anthony Cekada, *The Problems With the Prayers of the Modern Mass*, Tan Books, 1991, pp. 9-13.
[7] Michael Davies, *Pope Paul's New Mass*, Kansas City, MO: Angelus Press, p. 80.
[8] Michael Davies, *Pope Paul's New Mass*, p. 126.
[9] Michael Davies, *Pope Paul's New Mass*, p. 395.
[10] Michael Davies, *Pope Paul's New Mass*.
[11] Warren H. Carroll, *A History of Christendom*, Vol. 4 (*The Cleaving of Christendom*), Front Royal, VA: Christendom Press, 2000, p. 229.
[12] Michael Davies, *Cranmer's Godly Order*, Fort Collins, CO: Roman Catholic Books, 1995, p. 183.
[13] Michael Davies, *Pope Paul's New Mass*, p. 398.
[14] *Octava Controversia Generalis. Liber Ii. Controversia Quinta. Caput XXXI.*
[15] Michael Davies, *Cranmer's Godly Order*, p. 65.
[16] Michael Davies, *Pope Paul's New Mass*, p. 285.
[17] Michael Davies, *Pope Paul's New Mass*, p. 320.
[18] Michael Davies, *Cranmer's Godly Order*, p. 210.
[19] Michael Davies, *Pope Paul's New Mass*, p. 504.
[20] Also discussed in *Pope Paul's New Mass*, pp. 102; 504-505.
[21] Denzinger, *The Sources of Catholic Dogma*, B. Herder Book. Co., Thirtieth Edition, 1957, 695.
[22] *Decrees of the Ecumenical Councils*, Vol. 1, p. 581; Denzinger 715.
[23] A common translation, found in many publications, of the Latin words from the Roman Altar Missal, in *De Defectibus*, Chap. 5, Part 1.
[24] Denzinger 414-415.
[25] Michael Davies, *Cranmer's Godly Order*, p. 306.
[26] *The Catechism of the Council of Trent*, Tan Books, 1982, p. 227.
[27] St. Alphonsus De Liguori, Treatise on *The Holy Eucharist*, Redemptorist Fathers, 1934, p. 44.
[28] Denzinger 2301.
[29] A common translation, found in many publications, of the Latin words from the Roman Altar Missal, in *De Defectibus*, Chap. 5, Part 1.
[30] Denzinger 1963.
[31] Denzinger 698.
[32] St. Thomas Aquinas, *Summa Theologica*, Allen, TX: Christian Classics, Pt. III, Q. 73, A. 3.
[33] Denzinger 1963.
[34] *The Great Encyclical Letters of Pope Leo XIII*, Tan Books, 1995, p. 401.
[35] Denzinger 698.
[36] Denzinger 1151.

10. The New Rite of Ordination

(handwritten note: END NOTES - PAGE 119)

Michael Davies: "... **every prayer in the traditional rite [of Ordination] which stated specifically the essential role of a priest as a man ordained to offer propitiatory sacrifice for the living and dead has been removed [from the New Rite of Paul VI]**. In most cases **these were the precise prayers removed by the Protestant reformers**, or if not precisely the same there are clear parallels."[1]

In addition to having invalidating changes made to the Mass, the Devil knew that he had to tamper with the rite of ordination so that the priests of the New Church would be invalid as well.

The New Rite of Holy Orders (bishops, priests, deacons) was approved and imposed by Paul VI on June 18, 1968. The following information is crucial for all Catholics to know, since it concerns the validity of essentially every "priest" ordained within the diocesan structure since approximately 1968; and consequently, it concerns the validity of countless confessions, indult Masses, etc.

On Nov. 30, 1947, Pope Pius XII issued an apostolic Constitution called "Sacramentum Ordinis." In this Constitution, Pope Pius XII declared, in virtue of his supreme apostolic authority, the words that are necessary for a valid ordination to the priesthood.

TRADITIONAL FORM FOR ORDINATION OF PRIESTS

Pope Pius XII, *Sacramentum Ordinis*, Nov. 30, 1947: "But regarding the matter and form in the conferring of every order, **by Our same supreme apostolic authority We decree and establish the following**: ... In the ordination of priests, the matter is the first imposition of the bishop's hands which is done in silence... **But the form [of Ordination] consists of the words of the preface of which the following are essential and so required for validity:**

▶ "Grant, we beseech You, Almighty Father, to these Your servants, the dignity of the Priesthood (presbyterii dignitatem); renew the spirit of holiness within them, **so that** they may hold from You, O God, the office of the second rank in Your service and by the example of their behavior afford a pattern of holy living."[2]

THE NEW FORM FOR ORDINATION OF PRIESTS

Here is the form of the New Rite of Ordination of Priests:

• "Grant, we beseech You, Almighty Father, to these Your servants, the dignity of the Priesthood; renew within them the spirit of holiness. May they hold from You, the office of the second rank in Your service and by the example of their behavior afford a pattern of holy living."[3]

The difference between the two forms is that the Latin word "*ut*" (which means "so that") has been omitted in the New Rite. This may seem insignificant, but in *Sacramentum Ordinis* Pius XII declared that this word was essential for validity. Further, the omission of "so that" gives rise to a relaxation of the naming of the sacramental effect (conferring the office of the second rank). In other words, removing "so that" *presupposes an ordination which has already taken place*, but is *not taking place as the words are being pronounced*.

The New Rite of Ordination 113

Since the new rite purports to be the Roman Rite, this removal of "ut" (so that) renders the new rite of *questionable validity*. However, there is a much bigger problem which proves that the New Rite is invalid.

THE BIGGEST PROBLEM WITH THE NEW RITE OF ORDINATION IS NOT THE FORM, BUT THE SURROUNDING CEREMONIES WHICH HAVE BEEN REMOVED

The change to the essential form is not the only problem with the New Rite of Ordination promulgated by Paul VI. The following points are just as significant because the Sacrament of Order, although instituted by Our Lord Jesus Christ, was not instituted by Our Lord *with a specific sacramental form* – unlike the Sacraments of the Eucharist and Baptism, which were instituted by Our Lord *with a specific sacramental form* – **so that the form of words in Ordination is given its meaning and significance by the surrounding rite and ceremonies.**

In his famous Bull, *Apostolicae Curae*, Sept. 13, 1896, Pope Leo XIII solemnly declared that Anglican Ordinations are invalid. This means that the Anglican sect doesn't have valid priests or bishops.

> Pope Leo XIII, *Apostolicae Curae*, Sept. 13, 1896: "… **of Our own motion and certain knowledge We pronounce and declare that Ordinations carried out according to the Anglican rite have been and are absolutely null and utterly void.**"[4]

In making this solemn pronouncement, it must be understood that Pope Leo XIII was not *making* Anglican Ordinations invalid, but rather he was declaring that they were invalid due to defects in the rite. **But what were those defects or problems which Leo XIII saw with the Anglican Rite, which contributed to its invalidity?**

> Pope Leo XIII, *Apostolicae Curae*, Sept. 13, 1896: "When anyone has rightly and seriously made use of the due form and the matter requisite for effecting or conferring the sacrament he is considered by that very fact to do what the Church does. On this principle rests the doctrine that a sacrament is truly conferred by the ministry of one who is a heretic or unbaptized, provided the Catholic rite be employed. **On the other hand, if the rite be changed, with the manifest intention of introducing another rite not approved by the Church, and of rejecting what the Church does, and what by the institution of Christ belongs to the nature of the sacrament, then it is clear that not only is the necessary intention wanting to the sacrament, but that the intention is adverse to and destructive of the sacrament.**"[5]

Here we see Pope Leo XIII teaching that if a minister uses the Catholic rite in conferring the Sacrament of Order, with the correct matter and form, he is considered for that very reason to have intended to do what the Church does – intending to do what the Church does is necessary for the validity of any sacrament. On the other hand, he tells us, **if the rite is changed with the manifest intention of introducing a new rite not approved by the Church, and of rejecting what the Church does, then the intention is not only insufficient, but is destructive of the Sacrament.**

And what were the things that Pope Leo XIII described as showing the destructive intention of the Anglican rite of Ordination?

Pope Leo XIII, *Apostolicae Curae*, Sept. 13, 1896: "For, to put aside other reasons which show this to be insufficient for the purpose in the Anglican rite, **let this argument suffice for all: from them has been deliberately removed whatever sets forth the dignity and office of the priesthood in the Catholic rite.** That form consequently cannot be considered apt or sufficient for the sacrament which omits what it ought essentially to signify."[6]

Pope Leo XIII, *Apostolicae Curae*, Sept. 13, 1896: "So it comes to pass that, **as the Sacrament of Orders and the true *sacerdotium* [sacrificing priesthood] of Christ were utterly eliminated from the Anglican rite, and hence the *sacerdotium* [priesthood] is in no wise conferred truly and validly** in the Episcopal consecration of the same rite, for the like reason, therefore, the Episcopate can in no wise be truly and validly conferred by it; and this the more so because among the first duties of the Episcopate is that of ordaining ministers for the Holy Eucharist and sacrifice."[7]

Pope Leo XIII, *Apostolicae Curae*, Sept. 13, 1896: "Being fully cognizant of the necessary connection between faith and worship, between '*the law of believing and the law of praying,*' under a pretext of returning to the primitive form, they corrupted the liturgical order in many ways to suit the errors of the reformers. **For this reason in the whole Ordinal not only is there no clear mention of the sacrifice, of consecration, of the sacerdotium [sacrificing priesthood], but, as we have just stated, every trace of these things, which had been in such prayers of the Catholic rite as they had not entirely rejected, was deliberately removed and struck out. In this way the native character – or spirit as it is called – of the Ordinal clearly manifests itself.** Hence, if vitiated in its origin it was wholly insufficient to confer Orders, it was impossible that in the course of time it could become sufficient since no change had taken place."[8]

> **Dear reader, these things described above by Pope Leo XIII as the downfall of the Anglican Rite of Ordination** – the systematic removal of every reference to the sacrifice of the Mass, consecration and the true sacrificing priesthood – **are exactly the things that occurred in the New Rite of Ordination promulgated by Paul VI!** In his book *The Order of Melchisedech*, despite his false conclusions on this and other matters, Michael Davies is forced to admit the following stunning facts:

Michael Davies: "As the previous section made clear, **every prayer in the traditional rite [of Ordination] which stated specifically the essential role of a priest as a man ordained to offer propitiatory sacrifice for the living and dead has been removed [from the New Rite of Paul VI]**. In most cases **these were the precise prayers removed by the Protestant reformers,** or if not precisely the same there are clear parallels."[9]

Michael Davies: "…**there is not one mandatory prayer in the new rite of ordination itself which makes clear that the essence of the Catholic priesthood is the conferral of the powers to offer the sacrifice of the Mass and to absolve men of their sins**, and that the sacrament imparts a character which differentiates a priest not simply in degree but in

The New Rite of Ordination   115

essence from a layman... There is not a word in it that is incompatible with Protestant belief."[10]

Here are some of the specific prayers and ceremonies which set forth the true nature of the priesthood in the Traditional Rite which have been specifically eliminated from the New Rite of Ordination of Paul VI. The following information is found in Michael Davies, *The Order of Melchisedech*, pp. 79 and following.

In the Traditional Rite, the bishop addresses the ordinands and says:

> ▶ **"For it is a priest's duty to offer sacrifice**, to bless, to lead, to preach and to baptize."

This admonition has been abolished.

The Litany of the Saints then follows in the Traditional Rite. It has been cut short in the New Rite. The New Rite abolishes the following unecumenical assertion:

> ▶ **"That Thou wouldst recall all who have wandered from the unity of the Church, and lead all believers to the light of the Gospel."**

Later on in the Traditional Rite, after pronouncing the essential form, which has been changed in the New Rite (see above), the bishop says another prayer, which includes the following:

> ▶ **"Theirs be the task to change with blessing undefiled, for the service of thy people, bread and wine into the Body and Blood of Thy Son."**

This prayer has been abolished.

In the Traditional Rite, the bishop then intones the *Veni Creator Spiritus*. While anointing each priest he says:

> ▶ **"Be pleased, Lord, to consecrate and sanctify these hands by this anointing, and our blessing. That whatsoever they bless may be blessed, and whatsoever they consecrate may be consecrated and sanctified in the name of Our Lord Jesus Christ."**

This prayer has been abolished. And this prayer was so significant that it was even mentioned by Pius XII in *Mediator Dei* #43:

> Pope Pius XII, *Mediator Dei* (# 43), Nov. 20, 1947: "... they alone [priests] have been marked with the indelible sign 'conforming' them to Christ the Priest, and that their hands alone have been consecrated, '*in order that **whatever they bless may be blessed, whatever they consecrate may become sacred and holy**, in the name of Our Lord Jesus Christ.*'"[11]

Notice that Pius XII, in speaking of how the priests have been marked in ordination, makes reference to this very important prayer which was specifically abolished by Paul VI's new 1968 Rite.

Shortly after this prayer in the Traditional Rite, the bishop says to each ordinand:

The New Rite of Ordination   116

> ▶ "Receive the power to offer sacrifice to God, and to celebrate Mass, both for the living and the dead, in the name of the Lord."

This exceptionally important prayer has been abolished in the New Rite.

In the Traditional Rite, the new priests then concelebrate Mass with the bishop. At the end, each new priest kneels before the bishop who lays both hands upon the head of each and says:

> ▶ "Receive the Holy Ghost. Whose sins you shall forgive, they are forgiven them; and whose sins you shall retain, they are retained."

This ceremony and prayer has been abolished.

In the Traditional Rite:

> ▶ "…the new priests then promise obedience to **their bishop who 'charges' them to bear in mind that offering Holy Mass is not free from risk** and that they should learn everything necessary from diligent priests before undertaking so fearful a responsibility."

This admonition has been abolished.

Finally, before completing the Mass, the bishop imparts a blessing:

> ▶ "The blessing of God Almighty, the Father, the Son, and the Holy Ghost, come down upon you, and make you blessed in the priestly Order, **enabling you to offer propitiatory sacrifices for the sins of the people** to Almighty God."

This blessing has been abolished.

> **Conclusion:** It is totally obvious from these facts that there is no intention in the New Rite of ordaining a true sacrificing priest. **Every single mandatory reference to the true sacrificing priesthood <u>was deliberately removed</u>, just like in the Anglican Rite** – which was declared invalid for that very reason by Pope Leo XIII.

Thus, the following words declared by Pope Leo XIII <u>apply exactly</u> to the New Rite of Paul VI.

> Pope Leo XIII, *Apostolicae Curae*, Sept. 13, 1896: "For this reason **in the whole Ordinal not only is there no clear mention of the sacrifice, of consecration, of the sacerdotium** [sacrificing priesthood], **but, as we have just stated, every trace of these things, which had been in such prayers of the Catholic rite as they had not entirely rejected, was deliberately removed and struck out**. In this way the native character – or spirit as it is called – of the Ordinal clearly manifests itself."[12]

The New Rite fits this description precisely. Could anyone deny this fact? No, to do so one would have to bear false witness. The New Rite of Ordination specifically eliminated the sacrificing priesthood. The intention it manifests is therefore contrary to the intention of the Church and cannot suffice for validity.

> Pope Leo XIII, *Apostolicae Curae*, Sept. 13, 1896: "For, <u>to put aside other reasons</u> which show this to be insufficient for the purpose in the Anglican rite, **let this argument suffice for all: <u>from them has been deliberately removed whatever sets forth the dignity and office of the priesthood in the Catholic rite</u>**. That form consequently cannot be

considered apt or sufficient for the sacrament which omits what it ought essentially to signify." [13]

Michael Davies proves the New Rite is invalid

In his book, *The Order of Melchisedech*, Michael Davies (a man who actually defended the validity of the New Rite of Ordination) is forced to make, in the face of the undeniable evidence, statement after statement which *proves* that the New Rite of Ordination must be considered invalid, just as the Anglican Rite. Here are a few:

> Michael Davies, *The Order of Melchisedech*, p. 97: "**If the new Catholic rite is considered satisfactory, then the entire case put by *Apostolicae Curae* [of Leo XIII] is undermined… If the new Catholic rite, shorn of any mandatory prayer signifying the essential powers of the priesthood, is valid, then there seems no reason why the 1662 Anglican rite should not be valid too,** and still less can there be any possible objection to the 1977 Anglican Series III Ordinal."
>
> Michael Davies, *The Order of Melchisedech*, p. 99: "As a final comment on the new Catholic ordinal, **I would like to quote a passage from *Apostolicae Curae* and to ask any reader to demonstrate to me how the words which Pope Leo XIII wrote of Cranmer's rite cannot be said to apply to the new Catholic Ordinal**, at least where mandatory prayers are concerned."
>
> Michael Davies, *The Order of Melchisedech*, p. 109: "… **the differences between the 1968 Catholic rite and the new Anglican Ordinal are so minimal that it is hard to believe that they are not intended for the same purpose**… It will be found that **every imperative formula which could be interpreted as conferring any specifically sacerdotal power denied to the faithful at large has been carefully excluded** from the new rite."

> Michael Davies, *The Order of Melchisedech*, pp. 94-95: "**When the changes [to the Rite of Ordination] are considered as a whole it seems impossible to believe that any Catholic of integrity could deny that the parallel with Cranmer's reform [the Anglican reform] is evident and alarming.** It is quite obvious that there are powerful forces within the Catholic Church and the various Protestant denominations determined to achieve a common Ordinal at all costs… The sixteenth century Protestants changed the traditional Pontificals because they rejected the Catholic doctrine of the priesthood. **Archbishop Bugnini and his *Consilium* changed the Roman Pontifical in a manner which makes it appear that there is little or no difference between Catholic and Protestant belief, thus undermining *Apostolicae Curae* [of Leo XIII]**."[14]
>
> St. Thomas Aquinas, *Summa Theologica*, Pt. III, Q. 60, A. 8: "… intention is essential to the sacrament, as will be explained further on. **Wherefore if he intends by such addition or suppression to perform a rite other than that which is recognized by the Church, it seems that the sacrament is invalid**; because he seems not to intend to do what the Church does."

It's also worth noting that Cranmer, in creating the invalid Anglican Rite, abolished the subdiaconate and minor orders and replaced them with a ministry in three degrees – bishops, priests, and deacons. This is exactly what Paul VI did in changing the Catholic rites.

The New Rite of Ordination   118

The New Rite does mention that the candidates for ordination are to be elevated to the "priesthood" – but so does the invalid Anglican. The fact is that Pope Leo XIII explained in *Apostolicae Curae* that if an ordination rite implies the exclusion of the power to offer propitiatory sacrifices, as the New Rite does, then it is necessarily invalid, although it may express or mention the word "priest."

The Congregation for Divine Worship and the Discipline of the Sacraments admitted that the Catholic theology of the priesthood was not made explicit in the 1968 rite.[15]

The fact is that the New Rite of Paul VI is an entirely new rite, which rejects what the Church does, by rejecting what by the institution of Christ belongs to the nature of the sacrament [the sacrificing priesthood], *so it is clear that the necessary intention manifested by this rite is insufficient, and even adverse to and destructive of the Sacrament of Holy Orders* (Leo XIII). These facts prove that the New Rite of Ordination of Paul VI cannot be considered valid, but must be considered invalid.

> Conclusion: This means that any Confessions made of grave sins to "priests" ordained in the New Rite must be made again to a validly ordained priest who was ordained in the Traditional Rite of Ordination by a bishop consecrated in the Traditional Rite of Episcopal Consecration. If one cannot remember which sins were confessed to New Rite "priests," and which were forgiven by a priest ordained in the Traditional Rite, then a Catholic must make a general confession mentioning all grave sins (if there were any) that may have been confessed to a "priest" ordained in the rite of Paul VI (the New Rite).

Obviously, no Catholic may lawfully approach "priests" ordained in the New Rite of Paul VI for either "Communion" or confession or any other sacrament requiring a valid priesthood <u>under pain of grave sin</u>, since they are not valid priests.

As mentioned already, Pope Innocent XI, *Decree of the Holy Office*, March 4, 1679,[16] condemns the idea that Catholics can receive "*probable*" sacraments. In other words, even if one believed that the New Rite of Ordination is probably valid (which is clearly false, since it is *clearly invalid*), one is still forbidden to receive sacraments from those "ordained" in it under pain of mortal sin. Sacraments may only be received when matter and form are certainly valid.

These facts mean that all indult Masses celebrated by "priests" ordained in the New Rite of Paul VI (1968 Rite) are invalid and cannot be attended.

The Society of St. Pius X occasionally has men join their society who were "ordained" in the New Rite of Ordination, and they don't always have them conditionally ordained – or at least they don't publicly admit it. The "Masses" offered by such "priests" would be invalid.

Those priests who were "ordained" in this New Rite of Paul VI who are open to the truth must be re-ordained by a validly consecrated bishop in the Traditional Rite. This also necessarily means that the *Novus Ordo Missae* (the New Mass), without even considering its own problems which render it invalid, is of course invalid if celebrated by any "priest" ordained in the New Rite of Ordination.

Endnotes for Section 10:

[1] Michael Davies, *The Order of Melchisedech*, Harrison, NY: Roman Catholic Books, 1993, p. 83.
[2] Denzinger, *The Sources of Catholic Dogma*, B. Herder Book. Co., Thirtieth Edition, 1957, no. 2301.
[3] *The Oratory Catechism*, Published by the Oratory of Divine Truth, 2000, p. 340; also *The Rites of the Catholic Church*, The Liturgical Press, Vol. 2, 1991, pp. 44-45.
[4] *The Great Encyclical Letters of Pope Leo XIII*, Rockford, IL: Tan Books, 1995, p. 405; Denzinger 1966.
[5] *The Great Encyclical Letters of Pope Leo XIII*, p. 404.
[6] *The Great Encyclical Letters of Pope Leo XIII*, p. 401.
[7] *The Great Encyclical Letters of Pope Leo XIII*, p. 402.
[8] *The Great Encyclical Letters of Pope Leo XIII*, pp. 402-403.
[9] Michael Davies, *The Order of Melchisedech*, Harrison, NY: Roman Catholic Books, 1993, p. 83.
[10] Michael Davies, *The Order of Melchisedech*, p. xix.
[11] *The Papal Encyclicals*, by Claudia Carlen, Raleigh: The Pierian Press, 1990, Vol. 4 (1939-1958), p. 127.
[12] *The Great Encyclical Letters of Pope Leo XIII*, pp. 402-403.
[13] *The Great Encyclical Letters of Pope Leo XIII*, p. 401.
[14] Michael Davies, *The Order of Melchisedech*, pp. 94-95.
[15] Michael Davies, *The Order of Melchisedech*, p. xxii.
[16] Denzinger 1151.

11. The New Rite of Consecration of Bishops

[handwritten: END NOTES – PAGE 121]

Paul VI also changed the rite for consecrating bishops. This is very significant because groups such as the Fraternity of St. Peter and the Institute of Christ the King (indult groups who offer the traditional Latin Mass) ordain their men in the Traditional Rite of Ordination, <u>but have the ordinations done by "bishops" who were made "bishops" in the New Rite of Episcopal Consecration</u>.

This issue is also significant because Benedict XVI, the man who currently purports to be the Bishop of Rome, was "consecrated" in this New Rite of Episcopal Consecration on May 28, 1977.[1] If he is not a validly consecrated bishop, he cannot be the Bishop of Rome.

In *Sacramentum Ordinis*, Nov. 30, 1947, Pope Pius XII declared what is the essential form for the Consecration of Bishops:

TRADITIONAL FORM FOR CONSECRATION OF BISHOPS

Pope Pius XII, *Sacramentum Ordinis*, Nov. 30, 1947: "But regarding the matter and form in the conferring of every order, **by Our same supreme apostolic authority We decree and establish the following**: …in the Episcopal ordination or consecration… the form consists of the words of the 'Preface,' of which the following are essential and so required for validity:

> ▶ "Complete in Thy priest the fullness of Thy ministry, and adorned in the raiment of all glory, sanctify him with the dew of heavenly anointing."[2]

With its mention of "*<u>the fullness of Thy ministry</u>… raiment of all glory*" this traditional form unequivocally signifies the power of the episcopacy, which is the "fullness of the priesthood." Paul VI's new form in the 1968 rite is given below. The two forms only have one thing in common, the single word "et," which means "and."

PAUL VI'S NEW FORM FOR CONSECRATION OF BISHOPS

> • "So now pour out upon this chosen one that power which is from you, the governing Spirit whom you gave to your beloved Son, Jesus Christ, the Spirit given by Him to the holy apostles, who founded the Church in every place to be your temple for the unceasing glory and praise of your name."[3]

This new form does not unequivocally signify the power of the episcopacy. The phrase "governing Spirit" is used to refer to many things in scripture or tradition (e.g. Psalm 5:14), but it doesn't unequivocally signify the powers of the episcopacy. Therefore, the new form is of gravely doubtful validity.

In addition to the devastating change to the essential form, many other things have been deleted. In fact, there is not one unambiguous statement about the intended sacramental effect of

Episcopal Consecration that can be found. In the Traditional Rite of Consecration, the consecrator instructs the bishop elect in the following terms:

> ▶ "**A bishop** judges, interprets, **consecrates, ordains**, offers, baptizes and confirms."

This has been abolished.

> ▶ In the Traditional Rite, the bishop-to-be is asked to confirm his belief in each and every article of the Creed.

This has been abolished.

> ▶ In the Traditional Rite, the bishop-to-be is asked if he will "anathematize every heresy that shall arise against the Holy Catholic Church."

This has been abolished. The deletion of this requirement to anathematize heresy is significant, for this is indeed one of the functions of a bishop.

In the Traditional Rite, after the consecratory prayer, the functions of a bishop are once again specified in these words:

> ▶ "Give him, O Lord, the keys of the Kingdom of Heaven... Whatsoever he shall bind upon earth, let it be bound likewise in Heaven, and whatsoever he shall loose upon earth, let it likewise be loosed in Heaven. Whose sins he shall retain, let them be retained, and do Thou remit the sins of whomsoever he shall remit... Grant him, O Lord, an Episcopal chair..."

This entire prayer has been abolished in the New Rite.

> **Conclusion:** Paul VI's New Rite of Episcopal Consecration has a radically different form from what Pius XII declared was necessary for validity. The new form does not unequivocally signify the powers of the episcopacy. The New Rite of Episcopal Consecration cannot be considered valid, since doubtful matter or form is considered invalid.

All "priests" ordained by "bishops" consecrated in this rite, even if the Traditional Rite of Ordination was used, such as with most of the Fraternity of St. Peter priests, Institute of Christ the King priests, etc. cannot be considered valid priests. Their "Masses" must be avoided.

Endnotes for Section 11:

---

[1] Biography of Benedict XVI, Vatican website: www.vatican.va
[2] Denzinger, *The Sources of Catholic Dogma*, B. Herder Book. Co., Thirtieth Edition, 1957, no. 2301.
[3] *The Rites of the Catholic Church*, Collegeville, MN: The Liturgical Press, 1991, Vol. 2, p. 73.

12. New Sacraments: the Changes to the Other Sacraments

"These most crafty enemies have filled and inebriated with gall and bitterness the Church, the spouse of the immaculate Lamb, *and have laid impious hands on her most sacred possessions*. In the Holy Place itself, where has been set up the See of the most holy Peter and the Chair of Truth for the light of the world, they have raised the throne of their abominable impiety, with the iniquitous design that when the Pastor has been struck, the sheep may be scattered." (Prophecy of Pope Leo XIII about a future apostasy, 1888)

Besides making invalidating changes to the Mass, the Rites of Ordination and Episcopal Consecration, as we covered already, Paul VI changed the rites of all five other sacraments.

BAPTISM

The New Order of Baptism was promulgated on May 15, 1969. The questions "Do you renounce Satan?" and "Do you believe…?" are now directed toward the "parents and godparents"; they are no longer directed toward the candidate for baptism. In the new rite, the candidate for baptism is not even asked if he believes.

In the new rite, the newly baptized child no longer receives the lighted candle – instead it is given to a parent or godparent. Also, the newly baptized child no longer receives a white garment – it is only mentioned symbolically. **The candidate for baptism is no longer required to make a baptismal vow**.

In addition, **all the exorcisms of the Devil are omitted in Paul VI's new rite of Baptism!** Why would one remove the exorcism prayers? Although Satan is mentioned in the texts, **he is not banished**.

Conclusion: As long as the person baptizing in the Novus Ordo Church pours water and uses the essential form – "*I baptize thee, in the name of the Father, and of the Son, and of the Holy Ghost*" – with the intention to do what the Church does, then the baptism is valid, despite these other problems in the surrounding rite. But these changes to the rite of Baptism, although not essential to validity, serve to reveal the true character and intentions of the men who have implemented the Vatican II revolution.

CONFIRMATION

The New Order of Confirmation was promulgated on Aug. 15, 1971. The form and the matter of the sacrament have been changed.

The traditional form for the sacrament of confirmation is:

> ▶ "I sign you with the Sign of the Cross, and I confirm you with the Chrism of salvation. In the name of the Father, and of the Son, and of the Holy Spirit. Amen."

The Other New Sacraments 123

<u>The new form in the New Rite for the sacrament of confirmation:</u>

- "N., receive the seal of the Gift of the Holy Spirit."

As we can see, **the traditional form of Confirmation has been fundamentally changed.** The new form actually uses the form that is used in the Eastern Rites. Why would Paul VI replace the traditional form in the Roman Rite with the form of the Eastern Rite? We will see the significance of this change when we look at the matter of Confirmation, which has also been changed. Most theologians traditionally regard the imposition of hands and the signing and anointing of the forehead as the proximate matter of Confirmation, and the chrism of olive oil and balm consecrated by the bishop as the remote matter. In Paul VI's New Rite of Confirmation, **the imposition of hands has been abolished, and other vegetable oils may replace olive oil, and any spice may be used instead of balm!**

In the New Testament, the imposition of hands was always present in confirmation (see Acts 8:17, Acts 19:6). But there is no imposition of hands in the New Rite of Confirmation. It has been abolished. This alone renders Paul VI's New Rite of Confirmation highly doubtful. Further, in the Eastern Rite of Confirmation, when the form is pronounced by the bishop, he imposes his hands, *thus completing by his action the words of the form*. In the new rite, however, even though the Eastern Rite form is used, the words are not completed by the action of imposition of hands, as in the Eastern Rite, thus rendering it highly doubtful.

Conclusion: All the changes considered, **the validity of the new Confirmation is highly doubtful.**

CONFESSION

The Sacrament of Penance has been changed into a "Celebration of Reconciliation." The New Order of Penance or Confession was promulgated by Paul VI on Dec. 2, 1973. The essential form necessary for a validly ordained priest to absolve someone are the following words:

> "I absolve you from your sins in the name of the Father, and of the Son, and of the Holy Spirit." (Council of Florence, "Exultate Deo," Denzinger 696.)

Perhaps this will come as a surprise, but this essential form has <u>not</u> been changed in the New Rite of Confession. There are some Novus Ordo priests who do not say "I absolve you from your sins in the name of the Father, and of the Son, and of the Holy Spirit," but use new forms such as: "I free you from every bond of sin that you are under." If one of these different forms is used, then the confession would be doubtful.

As we've shown, however, the "priests" at the Novus Ordo/Vatican II churches that have been ordained in the New Rite of Ordination (promulgated on June 18, 1968) **are not validly ordained**. This means that even if Novus Ordo "priests" use the essential form, "*I absolve you from your sins in the name of the Father, and of the Son, and of the Holy Spirit,*" if they were ordained in the New Rite they are not valid priests and it makes no difference.

Conclusion: The New Rite of Confession is valid, but only if the priest was ordained in the Traditional Rite by a bishop consecrated in the Traditional Rite – and if he adheres to the words "I absolve you of your sins in the name of the Father and of the Son and of the Holy Ghost."

The Other New Sacraments

EXTREME UNCTION

The New Rite of Extreme Unction was promulgated on November 30, 1972. The New Rite of Extreme Unction is now called the "Anointing of the Sick," which is to be administered to those who are seriously ill. The term "in danger of death" is avoided. The new rite addresses itself much more to the healing of illness rather than to the preparation for the hour of death. The new consecration of the oil and the thanksgiving for the oil contain many passages concerning physical recovery. **The prayer for Satan's expulsion is abolished. And no longer are the angels, Guardian Angles, the Mother of God and St. Joseph invoked.**

THE TRADITIONAL FORM OF EXTREME UNCTION

The traditional form of Extreme Unction is:

> ▶May the Lord forgive you by this holy anointing and His most loving mercy whatever sins you have committed by the use of your sight (hearing, sense of smell, sense of taste and power of speech, sense of touch, power to walk).

THE NEW FORM OF "ANOINTING OF THE SICK" (CALLED EXTREME UNCTION IN THE CATHOLIC CHURCH)

> • Through this holy anointing and His most loving mercy, may the Lord help you by the grace of the Holy Spirit (Penitent: Amen) so that when you have been freed from your sins, He may save you and in His goodness raise you up.

One can see that after the change the new form has acquired a considerably different emphasis. The emphasis is now on deliverance from illness. The fact that the new rite is called only "Anointing of the Sick" already suggests that one is to think of physical recovery. Consequently, the new rite is administered many times to the sick and elderly who are not in danger of death.

The new form is also ambiguous about when the forgiveness of sins is granted. The old form clearly indicated that the Lord is forgiving sins by this anointing. The new form mentions "when you have been freed of your sins," which could mean sometime in the future.

The matter in the new rite has also been changed. Throughout the history of the Church, olive oil was the matter of the Sacrament of Extreme Unction. In the new rite, however, instead of olive oil any other vegetable oil may be used. Instead of six anointings, only two are prescribed.

According to most theologians, the use of whatever vegetable oils one chooses renders the sacrament invalid. Not knowing whether the matter used in the New Rite is olive oil is enough to cause doubt.

Conclusion: The new rite of Extreme Unction is of doubtful validity.

MARRIAGE

The new order of marriage was promulgated on March 19, 1969. With the new celebration of marriage, almost all the prayers have been changed. In the traditional rite of marriage a reading from Ephesians (5:22-33) was prescribed, stipulating the subordination of the wife to the husband. In the new rite, a selection can be made from ten different readings, **one of which is the Ephesians verse, but the reading specifically omits the verses that address the subordination of the wife to the husband**! In the questioning of the bride and groom on their commitment to lead a true Christian marriage, they are not questioned separately, but together.

The nuptial Blessing has been changed; the wording has been altered. Also, mixed marriages are now very prevalent, many of which are invalid.

Despite these problems, the form and matter of the Sacrament of Matrimony cannot be changed, because the matter is constituted by the people getting married, and the form is their mutual consent. However, the changes to the rite of the Sacrament of Matrimony show again the character and intention of those who have implemented the Vatican II revolution.

Conclusion: The new rite of marriage is valid, but a traditional Catholic cannot be married according to the new rite. Many of the mixed marriages which are allowed are invalid. The new rite of marriage doesn't invoke God. The new rite of marriage is used to corrupt Catholic teachings and enforce a false understanding to the married couple. Since a priest is the witness of the church in marriage, a Catholic should not get married in front of any priest, even validly ordained, who is not 100% Catholic.

SUMMARY OF THE NEW SACRAMENTAL RITES CREATED BY PAUL VI FOR THE COUNTER-CHURCH

New Mass – invalid
New Rite of Ordination – invalid
New Rite of Episcopal Consecration – gravely doubtful
New Rite of Baptism – valid
New Rite of Confession – valid, if adhered to and used by a validly ordained priest
New Rite of Confirmation – gravely doubtful
New Rite of Extreme Unction – doubtful
New Rite of Marriage – valid

13. The Scandals and Heresies of John XXIII

> Yves Marsaudon, 33rd degree Scottish Rite Freemason: "The sense of universalism that is rampant in Rome these days is very close to our purpose for existence... **with all our hearts we support the revolution of John XXIII.**"[1]

John XXIII (Angelo Roncalli) - The man who called Vatican II and claimed to be pope from 1958-1963

Let's examine some of the facts about Angelo Roncalli (John XXIII). Angelo Roncalli was born in 1881 and held diplomatic posts in Bulgaria, Turkey and France. Roncalli was also "Patriarch" of Venice.

SOME OF JOHN XXIII'S ACTIVITIES BEFORE HIS "ELECTION" AS "POPE" IN 1958

For years the Holy Office had maintained a dossier on Angelo Roncalli (John XXIII) which read "suspected of Modernism." The file dated back to 1925, when Roncalli, who was known for his unorthodox teachings, was abruptly removed from his Professorship at the Lateran Seminary in mid-semester (he was accused of modernism) and shipped off to Bulgaria. This transfer to Bulgaria began his diplomatic career. Of particular concern to Rome was Roncalli's continuing, close association with the defrocked priest, Ernesto Buonaiuti, who was excommunicated for heresy in 1926.[2]

As early as 1926, Angelo Roncalli (John XXIII) wrote to one Orthodox Schismatic:

> "**Catholics and Orthodox are** not enemies, but **brothers. We have the same faith**; we share the same sacraments, and especially the Eucharist. We are divided by some disagreements concerning the divine constitution of the Church of Jesus Christ. The persons who were the cause of these disagreements have been dead for centuries. Let us abandon the old disputes and, each in his own domain, let us work to make our brothers good, by giving them good example. **Later on**, though traveling along different paths, **we shall achieve union among the churches to form together the true and unique Church of our Lord Jesus Christ**."[3]

This statement means that the one true Church has not yet been established.

In 1935, Angelo Roncalli arrived in Turkey and became friends with the Under Secretary of the Foreign Office, Naman Rifat Menemengioglu.[4] Menemengioglu said to Roncalli:

"The secularity of the State is our fundamental principle and the guarantee of our liberty." Roncalli responded: "The Church will be careful not to infringe your liberty."[5]

While in Turkey, Roncalli also stated: "You Irish are impossible. The moment you come into the world, even before you are baptized, **you begin damning everybody who doesn't belong to the Church, especially Protestants!**"[6]

Here is another quote which demonstrates Roncalli's heretical views: "The extreme anti-Catholic faction of the Greek Orthodox Church gleefully announced an agreement with the Church of England by which each recognized the validity of the other's Holy Orders. But Roncalli was genuinely pleased. To the Greeks who slyly asked him what he thought of the arrangement, he said sincerely, 'I have nothing but praise for our separated brothers for their zeal in taking a step toward the union of all Christians.'"[7]

Desmond O'Grady, former Vatican correspondent for the *Washington Post*, reported that while stationed in Istanbul in 1944 Roncalli "**gave a sermon on a council to be held in the postwar period.**"[8] When Roncalli was Nuncio to France, he was appointed Observer for the Holy See to the United Nations cultural agency, UNESCO. In July 1951, he gave a speech "lavishly praising UNESCO…"[9] Roncalli called UNESCO "this great international organization…"[10]

When Angelo Roncalli was the nuncio to France, **he appointed a thirty-third degree Freemason and close friend, the Baron Yves Marsaudon**, as head of the French branch of the Knights of Malta, a Catholic lay order.[11]

JOHN XXIII SAID TO BE A FREEMASON

Yves Marsaudon, the aforementioned French Freemason and author, **also claims that Roncalli [John XXIII] became a thirty-third degree Mason while a nuncio at France**. Mary Ball Martinez wrote that the **French Republican Guards from their posts observed: "…the Nuncio [Roncalli] in civilian clothes leaving his residence to attend the Thursday evening meetings of the Grand Orient [Masonic Lodge] of France**. Whereas exposure to such a dramatic conflict of loyalties would unnerve the average man, be he Catholic or Freemason, Angelo Roncalli seems to have taken it in his stride."[12]

The Magazine *30 Days* also held an interview several years ago with the head of the Italian Freemasons. The Grand Master of the Grand Orient of Italy stated: "As for that, **it seems that John XXIII was initiated (into a Masonic Lodge) in Paris and participated in the work of the Istanbul Workshops.**"[13]

One time in Paris, "Msgr." Roncalli attended a banquet and was seated next to a woman who was dressed in a very immodest low-cut gown. The company with Roncalli felt slightly ill at ease. The guests shot looks at the "Papal Nuncio." Roncalli broke the silence by stating with humor:

> "**I can't imagine why all the guests keep looking at me, a poor old sinner, when my neighbor, our charming hostess, is so much younger and more attractive.**"[14]

When John XXIII was later "elevated" to the College of Cardinals, he insisted upon receiving the red hat from the atheist and notoriously anti-clerical socialist Vincent Auriol, President of the country of France, whom he had described as "an honest socialist."[15]

John XXIII, as a cardinal, choosing to receive his cardinal's hat from notorious **Anti-Catholic Vincent Auriol**

Roncalli knelt before Auriol, and Auriol placed the cardinal's biretta on Roncalli's head. Auriol then hung a "broad red ribbon around the cardinal's neck embracing him on each cheek with a little bear-hug that imparted personal warmth to formal protocol."[16] Auriol had to wipe away his tears with a handkerchief when Roncalli left to assume his new dignity as "cardinal."[17]

At social functions in Paris, Roncalli (John XXIII) was also frequently seen socializing with the Soviet ambassador, M. Bogomolov, even though Bogomolov's government had resumed its pre-war policy of brutal extermination of Catholics in Russia.

Angelo Roncalli (John XXIII) socializing with Catholic killer

John XXIII was also known as a "good friend and confidant" of Edouard Herriot, Secretary of the Anti-Catholic Radical Socialists (of France).[18] "Perhaps Roncalli's greatest friend was the grand old socialist and anti-clerical, Edouard Herriot."[19]

The Scandals and Heresies of John XXIII   129

John XXIII with Ed Herriot and other radicals

Before Roncalli left Paris, he gave a farewell dinner for his friends. "The guests included politicians on the Right, the Left, and the Center united on this one occasion in their affection for their genial host."[20] When Roncalli was "Cardinal" of Venice, he "offered the Communists no grounds on which to criticize him. Habitual anti-clerical insults gave way to respectful silence."[21] While in Venice, "Cardinal" Roncalli **exhorted the faithful to welcome the Socialists** of all Italy, who were holding their thirty-second party" in Venice.[22]

"The Patriarch (John XXIII) had notices placed on the walls all over Venice for the opening of the thirty-second Congress of the Socialist Party of Italy (PSI) in February, 1957. They read as follows: 'I welcome the exceptional significance of this event, which is so important for the future of our country.'"[23]

> Pope Pius XI, *Quadragesimo Anno* (#120), May 15, 1931: "**No one can be at the same time a good Catholic and a true socialist**."[24]

Roncalli once spoke at the Venice town hall. He stated:

> "...I am happy to be here, even though there may be some present who do not call themselves Christians, but who can be acknowledged as such because of their good deeds."[25]

This is blatantly heretical.

JOHN XXIII'S ACTIVITIES AND STATEMENTS AFTER HIS "ELECTION" AS "POPE" IN 1958

Shortly after being "elected" and moving into the Vatican, "John XXIII found an ancient statue of Hippolytus, an antipope of the Third Century. He had the statue restored and placed at the entrance of the Vatican Library."[26] "Disappointed faces appeared everywhere in St. Peter's Square when John XXIII began his first papal blessing, for he hardly raised his arms. His sign of the cross seemed to the Romans a pitiful gesture, for he appeared to be moving his wrist at about hip level."[27]

"John XXIII pronounced himself embarrassed at being addressed as 'Holiness' [or] 'Holy Father'…"[28] "For a long time, John XXIII said 'I' instead of 'we' in his official talks. Popes are expected to use 'we' and 'us' at least on official occasions."[29]

When John XXIII published an encyclical on penance, it proclaimed no fast nor even any obligatory day of abstinence from food or secular pleasures.[30] John XXIII said of himself: **"I'm the Pope who keeps stepping on the accelerator."**[31]

John XXIII's father was a winegrower. Speaking of his father, John XXIII said:

> "There are only three ways a man can be ruined: women, gambling, and … farming. My father chose the most boring of the three."[32]

JOHN XXIII ON HERETICS, SCHISMATICS AND NON-CATHOLICS

John XXIII described what he thought the Second Vatican Council's attitude toward the non-Catholic sects should be with these words: "We do not intend to conduct a trial of the past. **We do not want to prove who was right or who was wrong**. All we want to say is, 'Let us come together; let us make an end of our divisions.'"[33] His instructions to "Cardinal" Bea, head of the Council's Secretariat for the Union of Christians, were, **"We must leave aside, for the moment, those elements on which we differ."**[34]

One time a "congressman suddenly blurted out: 'I'm a Baptist.' Smiling John XXIII said, 'Well, I'm John.'"[35] **John XXIII said to the non-Catholic Roger Schutz, founder of the ecumenical community at Taize (a non-Catholic, ecumenical monastery): "You are in the Church, be at peace."** Schutz exclaimed: "But then, we are Catholics!" John XXIII said: "Yes; we are no longer separated."[36]

This is blatantly heretical.

> Pope Eugene IV, Council of Florence, "Cantate Domino," 1441: "Therefore it [the Church] condemns, <u>rejects</u>, anathematizes and declares to be outside the Body of Christ, which is the Church, <u>whoever holds opposing or contrary views</u>."[37]

John XXIII received at the Vatican the first "Archbishop" of Canterbury, the first "prelate" of the U.S. Episcopal Church, and the first Shinto high priest.[38] John XXIII once remarked: **"If I were born a Muslim, I believe that I would have always stayed a good Muslim, faithful to my religion."**[39]

The Scandals and Heresies of John XXIII

One of John XXIII's first acts was to receive the Muslim Shah of Iran in audience. When the Shah of Iran was about to leave, "**John XXIII gave him his benediction which he had rephrased delicately to avoid offending the Mohammedan's religious principles**: 'May the most abundant favor of Almighty God be with you.'"[40]

By re-phrasing the blessing, John XXIII: 1) removed the Most Holy Trinity who is invoked in the blessing, so that he wouldn't offend the unbeliever; and 2) he gave a blessing to a member of a false religion. This is contrary to the scriptural teaching which forbids giving blessing to non-believers, as repeated by Pope Pius XI.

> Pope Pius XI, *Mortalium Animos* (#9), Jan. 6, 1928: "Everyone knows that John himself, <u>the Apostle of love</u>, who seems to reveal in his Gospel the secrets of the Sacred Heart of Jesus, and who never ceased to impress on the memories of his followers the new commandment 'Love one another,' **altogether forbade any intercourse with those who professed a mutilated and corrupt form of Christ's teaching**: 'If any man come to you and bring not this doctrine, receive him not into the house nor say to him: God speed you.' (II John 10)."[41]

On July 18, 1959, John XXIII suppressed the following prayer: "**Be Thou King of all those who are still involved in the darkness of idolatry or Islam.**"[42] In his Apostolic Brief on October 17, 1925, Pope Pius XI ordered that this prayer be publicly recited on the feast of Christ the King.[43] John XXIII removed from the Calendar of Saints the Fourteen Holy Helpers and a number of other saints, including St. Philomena.

St. Philomena, just one of the saints removed from the Calendar of the Saints by John XXIII and Paul VI

Under Pope Gregory XVI, the Sacred Congregation of Rites gave a full and favorable decision in favor of the veneration of St. Philomena; in addition, Pope Gregory XVI gave Saint Philomena the titles of: "Great Wonder Worker of the 19th century" and "Patroness of the Living Rosary."[44] She was canonized by the same Pope in 1837. **A canonization of a saint** is "a public and official declaration of the heroic virtue of a person and the inclusion of his or her name in the canon (roll or register) of the saints... This judgment of the Church **is infallible and irreformable**."[45]

John XXIII stated: "…whoever shouts is unjust! We must always respect the dignity of man standing before us, and above all the freedom of every man."[46]

Below is a picture of John XXIII meeting with Eastern Schismatics at Vatican II. John XXIII wanted the clergy of "Orthodox" Churches of Russia (many of whom were KGB agents) to participate at Vatican II. The "Orthodox" said that some of their clergy would attend, provided that there was no condemnation of Communism at Vatican II. Hence, John XXIII – the initiator of the Vatican II apostasy – brokered the "great deal" that was the Vatican-Moscow Agreement. The Vatican agreed not to condemn Communism at Vatican II, in exchange for, get this, Eastern Schismatics to be able to observe the proceedings!47 That's some deal, isn't it! John XXIII was clearly a Freemason and probably a Communist; he was the man who began the massive conspiracy and apostasy that is the Vatican II sect.

John XXIII with Eastern Schismatics at Vatican II

John XXIII saw where the non-Catholic observers at Vatican II were going to be seated and stated: **"That won't do! Put our separated brothers close to me."** As one pleased Anglican put it: "So, there we were – bang in the front row."48

On October 11, 1962, John XXIII gave his opening speech to the Council:

> "They say that our era, in comparison with past eras, is getting worse, and **they behave as though at the time of former councils everything was a full triumph for the Christian idea and life and for proper religious liberty. We feel we must disagree** with those prophets of gloom, who are always forecasting disaster, as though the end of the world were at hand. In the present order of things, Divine Providence is leading us to **a new order** of human relations…"

> "…errors vanish as quickly as they arise, like fog before the sun. The Church has always opposed these errors. Frequently she has condemned them with the greatest severity. **Nowadays, however, the Spouse of Christ prefers to make use of the medicine of mercy rather than that of severity**. She (the Church) considers that she meets the needs of the present day by demonstrating the validity of her teaching **rather than by condemnations**. …**Unfortunately, the entire Christian family has not yet fully attained this visible unity in truth.**"49

As we see above, in his opening speech at Vatican II, John XXIII stated that the Church had historically opposed and condemned errors, but today it wasn't going to issue any condemnations. He also uttered the heresy that the "entire Christian family has not yet fully attained this visible unity in truth." First, the **"entire Christian family" is only made up of Catholics**. To say that the "entire Christian family" includes non-Catholics, as John XXIII did, is heresy. Second, John XXIII said the Christian family (which is the Catholic Church) "has not yet fully attained this visible unity in truth." This is heresy. It's a denial of the unity of the true

Church of Christ, the Catholic Church. The true Church (the Catholic Church) is one in faith. The Catholic Church has already attained and will always maintain a "visible unity in truth."

> Pope Leo XIII, *Satis Cognitum* (# 4), June 29, 1896:
> "The Church in respect of its unity belongs to the category of things indivisible by nature, though heretics try to divide it into many parts."[50]

> Pope Leo XIII, *Satis Cognitum* (# 5):
> "'There is one God, and one Christ; and His Church is one and the faith is one; and one people, joined together in the solid unity of the body in the bond of concord. **This unity cannot be broken, nor the one body divided by the separation of its constituent parts.**'"[51]

John XXIII also changed the rubrics for the Breviary and Missal. He ordered the suppression of the Leonine Prayers, the prayers prescribed by Pope Leo XIII to be recited after Mass. These prayers were also prescribed by Pope St. Pius X and Pope Pius XI.[52] This included the Prayer to St. Michael the Archangel, a prayer that specifically makes mention of the battle that the Church wages against the Devil. John XXIII removed the Psalm *Judica me* from the Mass. John XXIII then suppressed the Last Gospel, the Gospel of St. John. This Gospel is also used in exorcisms.[53]

Next, John XXIII eliminated the second Confiteor in the Mass. **Only after all these changes did he introduce a change into the Canon of the Mass by inserting the name of St. Joseph.**[54] The request to have St. Joseph's name placed in the canon was officially rejected by Pope Pius VII on September 16, 1815,[55] and by Pope Leo XIII on August 15, 1892.[56] The other major changes regarding the Holy Sacrifice of the Mass (which preceded Paul VI's entirely new Mass in 1969) came into effect the first Sunday in Advent, 1964.

JOHN XXIII ON SOCIALISM AND COMMUNISM

John XXIII wrote a letter praising Marc Sangnier, the founder of the Sillon. The Sillon was an organization which was condemned by Pope Pius X. John XXIII wrote about Sangnier: "The powerful fascination of his (Sangnier's) words, of his soul, had thrilled me, **and the liveliest memories of my entire priestly youth are for his person and his political and social activity…**"[57]

In John XXIII's encyclical *Mater et Magistra* (on Christianity and social progress), he promoted socialist ideals and didn't condemn contraception or Communism even once. Being asked why he would reply to the greeting of a Communist dictator, John XXIII answered: "I am Pope John, not because of any personal merit, but because of an act of God, and **God is in every one of us**."[58] "John enjoyed himself thoroughly with the Communists; one might have thought they were his own brothers."[59] Communism was condemned 35 times by Pope Pius XI and 123 times by Pope Pius XII.[60]

On March 6, 1963, John XXIII received Aleksei Adzhubei and his wife, Rada, in a special audience. Rada was USSR Premier Khrushchev's daughter. Rada (Khrushchev's daughter) spoke about her meeting with John XXIII: "…he handed Aleksei and me a pair of symbolic gifts, which were intended for my father, too and he said: '…**That's for your Papa.**'"[61]

On the occasion of his eightieth birthday (Nov. 25, 1961), John XXIII received a telegram from Khrushchev offering his "congratulations and sincere wishes for good health and success in his noble aspirations to contribute to … peace on earth."[62]

General Secretary of the British Communist Party, John Gollan, before television cameras on April 21, 1963, **said the "encyclical (*Pacem in Terris*) [of John XXIII] had surprised and gladdened"** him and, therefore, he had externalized his "most sincere satisfaction at the recent 28th Party Congress."[63]

One of John XXIII's good friends was the Communist and Lenin Peace Prize winner Giacomo Manzu.[64] John XXIII said: "I see no reason why a Christian could not vote for a Marxist if he finds the latter to be more fit to follow such a political line and historical destiny."[65]

The Catholic Church has condemned Communism on more than 200 occasions.[66]

JOHN XXIII PRAISED BY FREEMASONS AND COMMUNISTS DURING HIS "PONTIFICATE"

John XXIII, *Pacem in terris* #14, April 11, 1963: "Also among man's rights is that of being able to worship God in accordance with the right dictates of his own conscience, and to profess his religion both in private and in public."

This is heresy. It's not man's right to worship false gods in public. This has been condemned by many popes, as we covered in the section on Vatican II. When the theologian of the Holy Office, Fr. Ciappi, told John XXIII that his encyclical *Pacem in Terris* contradicted the teaching of Popes Gregory XVI and Pius IX on religious liberty, John XXIII responded: **"I won't be offended by a few spots if most of it shines."**[67]

John XXIII's encyclical *Pacem in Terris* was praised by Masonic leaders themselves as a Masonic document. Here are just a few examples:

This is a quote from the *Masonic Bulletin*, the official organ of the Supreme Council of the 33rd Degree of the Ancient and Accepted Scottish Rite of Masons, for the Masonic District of the United States of Mexico, located at 56 Lucerna St., Mexico, D.F. (Year 18, No. 220, May 1963):

"THE LIGHT OF THE
GREAT ARCHITECT OF THE UNIVERSE
ENLIGHTENS THE VATICAN

"Generally speaking, the encyclical *Pacem in Terris,* addressed to all men of goodwill, has inspired comfort and hope. **Both in democratic and Communist countries it has been universally praised**. Only the Catholic dictatorships have frowned upon it and distorted its spirit.

"To us many concepts and doctrines it contains are familiar. We have heard them from illustrious rationalist, liberal, and **socialist** brothers. After having carefully weighed the meaning of each word, we might say that, the proverbial and typical Vatican literary rubbish notwithstanding, **the encyclical *Pacem in Terris* is a vigorous statement of Masonic doctrine… we do not hesitate to recommend its thoughtful reading.**"[68]

In the book *Resurgence du Temple,* published and edited by the Knights Templar (Freemasons), 1975:149, the following quote is of interest: "**The direction of our action: Continuation of the**

Work of John XXIII and all those who have followed him on the way to Templar Universalism."[69]

JOHN XXIII AND THE JEWS

John XXIII also did things like stopping his car so that he could bless Jews leaving their "Sabbath" worship.[70]

JOHN XXIII REVEALED THAT HE WAS A JEW?

John XXIII once greeted some Jewish visitors with the words, "I am Joseph, your brother."[71] Even though this very mysterious statement of John XXIII to Jews has been quoted frequently, the significance has not yet been explained. We believe there is a good explanation of its significance: This statement by John XXIII, "I am Joseph, your brother," **is a quotation from Genesis 45:4**. It was made by the patriarch Joseph, the son of Jacob, to his brothers when they came into Egypt during the time of famine. Those familiar with the Biblical account know that Joseph had been sold into slavery by his brothers many years before, **but had risen to the highest position in the kingdom of Egypt (even though he wasn't one of them)** because he had successfully interpreted Pharao's dream. Since he had risen to the highest position in the kingdom of the Egyptians, he was free to dispense the treasures of the kingdom at his pleasure – e.g., to his brothers. He gave plentifully to his brothers at no charge.

When we consider the evidence that John XXIII was a Freemason, that John XXIII began the process of revolution against the Catholic Church at Vatican II, and that John XXIII's "pontificate" initiated the new revolutionary attitude *toward Jews*, among other things, the meaning of his statement *to the Jews* becomes clear. **Just as Joseph, who was not one of the Egyptians, found himself entrenched at the very pinnacle of the hierarchy** of the Egyptians and revealed this to his brothers with the statement "I am Joseph, your brother," John XXIII told the Jews that he is "Joseph, your brother" **because he was actually a Jewish infiltrator entrenched at the very highest position in the hierarchy of the Christians** (or so it appeared). It was John XXIII's cryptic way of revealing what he really was: a conspiratorial antipope at the service of the Church's enemies.

Just prior to his death, John XXIII composed the following prayer for the Jews. This prayer was confirmed by the Vatican as being the work of John XXIII.[72]

> **"We realize today how blind we have been throughout the centuries and how we did not appreciate the beauty of the Chosen People** or the features of our favored brothers. **We are aware of the divine mark of Cain placed upon our forehead**. In the course of centuries our brother, Abel, has been lying bleeding and in tears on the ground through our fault, only because we had forgotten Thy love. Forgive us our unjustified condemnation of the Jews. **Forgive us that by crucifying them we have crucified You** for the second time. Forgive us. We did not know what we were doing."[73]

John XXIII says that the Jews are still the chosen people, which is heretical. The phrase "perfidious Jews" was the expression used by Catholics in the Good Friday Liturgy until John XXIII removed it in 1960.[74] The word perfidious means "unfaithful." "On Good Friday, 1963, the cardinal who was the celebrant in St. Peter's said the old words (perfidious Jews) from force of habit. **John XXIII stunned the worshippers by stopping him in midstream with the words, 'Say it over the new way.'**"[75]

The Scandals and Heresies of John XXIII

> Pope Benedict XIV, *A Quo Primum*, June 14, 1751:
> "Another threat to Christians has been the influence of **Jewish faithlessness... Surely it is not in vain that the Church has established the universal prayer which is offered up for the faithless Jews** from the rising of the sun to its setting, that they may be rescued from their darkness into the light of truth."[76]

To a recently baptized Jewish boy, John XXIII said: "By becoming a Catholic you do not become less a Jew."[77] On the night of John XXIII's death, the Chief Rabbi of Rome and other leaders of the Jewish community gathered with hundreds of thousands in Saint Peter's Square to mourn.[78]

Alden Hatch, author of *A Man Named John: The Life of John XXIII*, stated about John XXIII: "...surely none (of the previous popes) had so touched the hearts of people of all faiths – and of no faith. For they knew he loved them no matter what they were or what they believed."[79]

THE DEATH OF JOHN XXIII

After his death, the Vatican sent for Gennar Goglia, who with his colleagues embalmed John XXIII. Goglia injected ten liters of embalming fluid into John XXIII's wrist and stomach to neutralize any putrefaction.[80] This explains why John XXIII's body didn't decompose like normal bodies. In January 2001, John XXIII's body was exhumed and placed in a new bullet-proof crystal coffin now on display in St. Peter's basilica. John XXIII's face and hands were also covered in wax.[81]

STATEMENTS FROM FREEMASONS, COMMUNISTS AND NON-CATHOLICS PRAISING JOHN XXIII AFTER HIS DEATH

After the death of John XXIII, numerous documents from Communists, Masons, and Jews were sent to the Vatican expressing their sorrow for the death of John XXIII. People like "Fidel Castro and Nikita Khrushchev sent messages of praise and sorrow."[82]

From the June 4, 1963, edition of *The Reporter (El Informador)*:

> "**The Great Western Mexican Lodge of Free and Accepted Masons, on the occasion of the death of John XXIII, makes known its sorrow for the disappearance of <u>this great man who revolutionized the ideas, thoughts, and forms of the Roman Catholic liturgy</u>**. His encyclicals *Mater et Magistra* and *Pacem in Terris* have revolutionized the concepts favoring human rights and liberty. **Mankind has lost a great man**, and we Masons acknowledge his high principles, his humanitarianism, and his being a great liberal.
>
> Guadalajara, Jal., Mexico, June 3, 1963
>
> *Dr. Jose Guadalupe Zuno Hernandez*"[83]

Charles Riandey, a sovereign Grand Master of secret societies, in his preface to a book by Yves Marsaudon (State Minister of the Supreme Council of French secret societies), stated:

> **"To the memory of Angelo Roncalli**, priest, Archbishop of Messamaris, Apostolic Nuncio in Paris, Cardinal of the Roman Church, Patriarch of Venice, **Pope under the name of John XXIII, who has deigned to give us his benediction, his understanding, and his protection."**[84]

A second preface to the book was addressed to "his august continuer, His Holiness Pope Paul VI."[85]

The high ranking Freemason, Carl Jacob Burckhardt, wrote in the *Journal de Geneve*: "I know Cardinal Roncalli very well. He was a Deist and a Rationalist whose strength did not lie in the ability to believe in miracles and to venerate the sacred."[86]

A HERETIC CANNOT BE A VALID POPE

As we saw already, the Catholic Church teaches that a heretic cannot be a validly elected pope, since a heretic is not a member of the Catholic Church. The facts presented here prove that John XXIII, **the man who called Vatican II and began the apostate Conciliar Church, was clearly a heretic**. He was not a valid pope. Angelo Roncalli (John XXIII) was a non-Catholic, conspiratorial antipope who started the Vatican II apostasy.

THE AMAZING PARALLELS BETWEEN ANTIPOPE JOHN XXIII OF THE GREAT WESTERN SCHISM AND ANTIPOPE JOHN XXIII OF VATICAN II

The name "John" had been avoided by popes for five hundred years because the last man to have it was the notorious Antipope John XXIII (Baldassare Cossa) of the Great Western Schism. The parallels between the first Antipope John XXIII (Baldassare Cossa) and the second (Angelo Roncalli) are striking:

> **The reign of the first Antipope John XXIII spanned five years, from 1410 to 1415, just like the reign of the recent Antipope John XXIII, which spanned five years, from 1958 to 1963.**
>
> **The first Antipope John XXIII called a phony council, the Council of Constance**. (The Council of Constance later became a true ecumenical council, with certain sessions approved by the true pope; but at the time that Antipope John XXIII opened it, it was a false council.) **Likewise, the recent Antipope John XXIII (Angelo Roncalli) also called a false council, Vatican Council II!**
>
> **The first Antipope John XXIII opened his false council at Constance in the 4th year of his reign, 1414. The recent Antipope John XXIII opened Vatican II in the 4th year of his reign, 1962.**
>
> **The first Antipope John XXIII's reign ended shortly before the 3rd Session of his false Council, in 1415. The recent Antipope John XXIII died shortly before the 3rd Session of Vatican II, in 1963, thus ending his reign.**

We believe that the similarities between the first Antipope John XXIII and the second are not merely coincidences. The first Antipope John XXIII was also the last antipope to reign from Rome. Was Angelo Roncalli, the recent Antipope John XXIII, *by taking that name*, indicating symbolically (in the cryptic way that Freemasons do things) that he is continuing in the line of antipopes to reign from Rome?

Cardinal Heenan, who was present at the 1958 conclave which gave us John XXIII, once mentioned: "There was no great mystery about Pope John's election. He was chosen because he was a very old man. His chief duty was to make Msgr. Montini (later Paul VI), the Archbishop of Milan, a cardinal so that he could be elected in the next conclave. That was the policy and it was carried out precisely."[87]

Endnotes for Section 13:

[1] Yves Marsaudon in his book *Ecumenism Viewed by a Traditional Freemason*, Paris: Ed. Vitiano; quoted by Dr. Rama Coomaraswamy, *The Destruction of the Christian Tradition*, p. 247.
[2] Lawrence Elliott, *I Will Be Called John*, 1973, pp. 90-92.
[3] Luigi Accattoli, *When A Pope Asks Forgiveness*, New York: Alba House and Daughters of St. Paul, 1998, pp. 18-19.
[4] Alden Hatch, *A Man Named John*, NY, NY: Hawthorn Books Inc., 1963, p. 93.
[5] Alden Hatch, *A Man Named John*, p. 94.
[6] Alden Hatch, *A Man Named John*, p. 96.
[7] Alden Hatch, *A Man Named John*, p. 98.
[8] *St. Anthony's Messenger*, Nov. 1996.
[9] Alden Hatch, *A Man Named John*, p. 117.
[10] Alden Hatch, *A Man Named John*, p. 118.
[11] Paul I. Murphy and R. Rene Arlington, *La Popessa*, 1983, pp. 332-333.
[12] Mary Ball Martinez, *The Undermining of the Catholic Church*, Hillmac, Mexico, 1999, p. 117.
[13] Giovanni Cubeddu, *30 Days*, Issue No. 2-1994., p. 25.
[14] Kurt Klinger, *A Pope Laughs, Stories of John XXIII*, NY, NY: Holt, Rinehart and Winston, 1964, p. 90.
[15] Alden Hatch, *A Man Named John*, p. 121.
[16] Alden Hatch, *A Man Named John*, p. 123.
[17] Kurt Klinger, *A Pope Laughs*, p. 99.
[18] Rev. Francis Murphy, *John XXIII Comes To The Vatican*, 1959, p. 139.
[19] Alden Hatch, *A Man Named John*, p. 114.
[20] Alden Hatch, *A Man Named John*, p. 125.
[21] Kurt Klinger, *A Pope Laughs, Stories of John XXIII*, p. 104.
[22] Mark Fellows, *Fatima in Twilight*, Niagra Falls, NY: Marmion Publications, 2003, p. 159.
[23] Kurt Klinger, *A Pope Laughs, Stories of John XXIII*, p. 105.
[24] *The Papal Encyclicals*, by Claudia Carlen, Raleigh: The Pierian Press, 1990, Vol. 4 (1903-1939), p. 434.
[25] Peter Hebblethwaite, *John XXIII, The Pope of the Council*, Doubleday, ed. Le Centurion, 1988, p. 271.
[26] Paul Johnson, *Pope John XXIII*, pp. 37, 114-115, 130.
[27] Kurt Klinger, *A Pope Laughs, Stories of John XXIII*, p. 24.
[28] *Time Magazine*, "1962 Man of the Year: Pope John XXIII," Jan. 4, 1963 issue.
[29] Kurt Klinger, *A Pope Laughs, Stories of John XXIII*, p. 49.
[30] Romano Amerio, *Iota Unum*, Angelus Press, 1998, p. 241.
[31] Kurt Klinger, *A Pope Laughs, Stories of John XXIII*, p. 134.
[32] Kurt Klinger, *A Pope Laughs, Stories of John XXIII*, p. 110.
[33] Alden Hatch, *A Man Named John*, p. 192.
[34] Alden Hatch, *A Man Named John*, p. 192.
[35] Alden Hatch, *A Man Named John*, p. 194.
[36] Luigi Accattoli, *When A Pope Asks Forgiveness*, p. 19.
[37] Denzinger, *The Sources of Catholic Dogma*, B. Herder Book. Co., Thirtieth Edition, 1957, no. 705.
[38] *Time Magazine*, "1962 Man of the Year: Pope John XXIII," Jan. 4, 1963 issue.
[39] Allegri, *Il Papa che ha cambiato il mondo*, ed., Reverdito, 1998, p. 120. Also quoted in *Sacerdotium*, Issue #11, 2899 East Big Beaver Rd., Suite 308, Troy, MI., p. 58.

40 Alden Hatch, *A Man Named John*, p. 193.
41 *The Papal Encyclicals*, Vol. 3 (1903-1939), p. 316.
42 Luigi Accattoli, *When A Pope Asks Forgiveness*, p. 20.
43 Fr. F.X. Lasance, *My Prayer Book*, 1938 ed., p. 520a.
44 Fr. Paul O'Sullivan, O.P., *Saint Philomena, The Wonder Worker*, Rockford, IL: Tan Books, 1993, pp. 69-70.
45 *A Catholic Dictionary*, edited by Donald Attwater, Tan Books, 1997, p. 72.
46 Kurt Klinger, *A Pope Laughs, Stories of John XXIII*, p. 135.
47 Mark Fellows, *Fatima in Twilight*, Niagra Falls, NY: Marmion Publications, 2003, p. 180.
48 Alden Hatch, *A Man Named John*, NY, p. 14.
49 Walter Abbott, *The Documents of Vatican II*, The America Press, 1966, pp. 712; 716; 717.
50 *The Papal Encyclicals*, Vol. 2 (1878-1903), p. 389.
51 *The Papal Encyclicals*, Vol. 2 (1878-1903), p. 390.
52 *The Reign of Mary*, Spokane, WA., Spring, 1986, p. 10.
53 *The Reign of Mary*, Vol. XXIX, No. 93, p. 16.
54 *The Reign of Mary*, Vol. XXIX, No. 93, p. 16.
55 *The Reign of Mary*, Vol. XXII, No. 64, p. 8.
56 *The Reign of Mary*, Spring, 1986, pp. 9-10.
57 Angelo Giuseppe Roncalli, *John XXIII, Mission to France*, 1944-1953, pp. 124-125.
58 *The Reign of Mary*, Spring, 1986, p. 9.
59 Kurt Klinger, *A Pope Laughs, Stories of John XXIII*, p. 57.
60 Piers Compton, *The Broken Cross*, Cranbrook, Western Australia: Veritas Pub. Co., 1984, p. 45.
61 Kurt Klinger, *A Pope Laughs, Stories of John XXIII*, p. 24.
62 Mark Fellows, *Fatima in Twilight*, p. 177; also Piers Compton, *The Broken Cross*, p. 44.
63 Fr. Joaquin Arriaga, *The New Montinian Church*, Brea, CA., p. 170.
64 Curtis Bill Pepper, *An Artist and the Pope*, London, England: Grosset & Dunlap, Inc. Front cover & inside slip cover of book; also look at p. 5.
65 Fr. Joaquin Arriaga, *The New Montinian Church*, Brea, Ca., p. 570.
66 Michael Davies, *Pope John's Council*, Kansas City, MO: Angelus Press, 1992, p. 150.
67 *Catholic Restoration*, March-April 1992, Madison Heights, MI, p. 29.
68 Fr. Joaquin Arriaga, *The New Montinian Church*, pp. 147-148.
69 A.D.O. Datus, "Ab Initio," p. 60.
70 George Weigel, *Witness to Hope*, New York, NY: Harper Collins Publishers, Inc., 1999, p. 484.
71 Bart McDowell, *Inside the Vatican*, Washington D.C.: National Geographic Society, 1991, p. 193; also can be seen in *Time Magazine*, Jan 4, 1963 issue; also quoted in *The Bible, The Jews and the Death of Jesus*, Bishops' Committee for Ecumenical and Interreligious Affairs, United States Conference of Catholic Bishops, 2004, p. 59.
72 *The Reign of Mary*, "John XXIII and the Jews," Spring, 1986, p. 11.
73 *B'nai B'rith Messenger*, Friday, November 4, 1964.
74 Luigi Accattoli, *When A Pope Asks Forgiveness*, p. 15.
75 Alden Hatch, *A Man Named John*, p. 192.
76 *The Papal Encyclicals*, Vol. 1 (1740-1878), pp. 41-42.
77 *Catholic Restoration*, May-June 1993, Madison Heights, MI, p. 24.
78 Darcy O' Brien, *The Hidden Pope*, New York, NY: Daybreak Books, 1998, p. 10.
79 Alden Hatch, *A Man Named John*, after p. 238 (1st page of insert).
80 Wendy Reardon, *The Deaths of the Popes*, Jefferson, NC., McFarland & Co., Inc., 2004, p. 244.
81 Wendy Reardon, *The Deaths of the Popes*, p. 244.
82 Alden Hatch, *A Man Named John*, after p. 238 (7th page of insert).
83 Fr. Joaquin Arriaga, *The New Montinian Church*, p. 147.
84 Piers Compton, *The Broken Cross*, Cranbrook, Western Australia: Veritas Pub. Co. Ptd Ltd, 1984, p. 50.
85 Piers Compton, *The Broken Cross*, Cranbrook, p. 50.
86 A.D.O Datus, "AB INITIO," p. 60.
87 Cardinal Heenan's biography, *Crown of Thorns*.

14. The Heresies of Paul VI (1963-1978), the man who gave the world the New Mass and the Teachings of Vatican II

"How could a successor of Peter have caused in so short a time more damage to the Church than the Revolution of 1789?... the deepest and most excessive in Her history... what no heresiarch has ever succeeded in doing?... Do we really have a pope or an intruder sitting on the Chair of Peter?"[1] (Archbishop Marcel Lefebvre, commenting on Paul VI's reign in 1976)

Paul VI

Paul VI was the man who claimed to be the head of the Catholic Church from June 21, 1963 to August 6, 1978. **He was the man who promulgated the Second Vatican Council and the New Mass**. We've already seen that the evidence indicates that the man who preceded and elevated Paul VI, John XXIII, was a Freemason and a manifest heretic. We've also seen that the documents of Vatican II contain many heresies, and that the New Mass, which Paul VI eventually promulgated, represented a liturgical revolution.

Paul VI solemnly ratified all 16 documents of Vatican II. It is not possible for a true pope of the Catholic Church to solemnly ratify teachings that are heretical. As we will show in more detail later in this book, the fact that Paul VI did solemnly ratify the heretical teachings of Vatican II proves that Paul VI was not a true pope, but an antipope.

It's important to keep in mind that Paul VI was the one who gave the world the New Mass, the other new "sacraments," and the heretical teachings of Vatican II. If you go to the New Mass or embrace the teachings of Vatican II, **the confidence that you have that these things are legitimate is directly connected to the confidence that you have that Paul VI was a true Catholic pope**.

We will now expose the amazing heresies of Paul VI. We will show, from his official speeches and writings, that Paul VI was a complete apostate who was not even remotely Catholic. All of the official speeches and writings of the men who claim to be pope are contained in the Vatican's weekly newspaper, *L' Osservatore Romano*. The Vatican has reprinted issues of their newspaper from April 4, 1968 to the present. From those speeches, we will now prove that Paul VI was not a true pope because of the irrefutable and undeniable evidence that he was a complete heretic and an apostate.

> Paul VI, *General Audience*, Dec. 6, 1972: "Does God exist? Who is God? And what knowledge can man have of him? What relationship must each of us have with him? To answer each of these questions would lead us to endless and complex discussions…"[2]

These questions don't lead us to endless and complex discussions. Does God exist? Yes. Who is God? The Holy Trinity. What knowledge can man have of him? The Catholic Faith. What relationship must each of us have with him? To belong to the Church He established. Paul VI is stating that these are endless and complex questions. No Catholic would assert such nonsense, which mocks and renders meaningless the Catholic Faith and the true God.

> Paul VI, *General Audience*, June 27, 1973: "…**everything must change, everything must progress. Evolution seems to be the law that brings liberation**. There must be a great deal that is true and good in this mentality…"[3]

Here Paul VI explicitly states and approves the Modernist blasphemy that everything is in a state of evolution. His heresy was explicitly condemned by Pope Pius X.

> Pope Pius X, *Pascendi* (# 26), Sept. 8, 1907, explaining the doctrine of the Modernists: **"To the laws of evolution everything is subject – dogma, Church, worship, the Books we revere as sacred, even faith itself…"**[4]

PAUL VI ON NON-CHRISTIAN RELIGIONS

The Catholic Church teaches that all non-Catholic religions are false. There is only one true Church, outside of which no one can be saved. This is Catholic dogma.

> Pope St. Gregory the Great, 590-604: "The holy universal Church teaches that it is not possible to worship God truly except in her **and asserts that all who are outside of her will not be saved.**"[5]

All of the other religions belong to the Devil. This is the teaching of Jesus Christ, the Catholic Church and Sacred Scripture. See 1 Cor. 10:20 and Psalm 95:5. Anyone who shows esteem for non-Christian religions, or regards them as good or deserving of respect, denies Jesus Christ and is an apostate.

> Paul VI, General Audience, Nov. 8, 1972: "Ecumenism began in this way; as respect for non-Christian religions…"[6]

> Pope Pius XI, *Mortalium Animos* (# 2), Jan. 6, 1928:
> "...that false opinion which considers all religions to be more or less good and praiseworthy... Not only are those who hold this opinion in error and deceived, but also in distorting the idea of true religion they reject it..."[7]

Here is more of what Paul VI thought about non-Christian religions of the Devil:

> Paul VI, *Address*, Sept. 22, 1973: "...**noble non-Christian religions**..."[8]

This is apostasy – a total rejection of Jesus Christ.

> Paul VI, *General Audience*, Jan. 12, 1972: "...a disconcerting picture opens up before our eyes: that of religions, **the religions invented by man; attempts that are sometimes extremely daring and noble**..."[9]

Here Paul VI says that religions **invented by man** are sometimes extremely noble! This is apostasy – a rejection of Jesus Christ and the Catholic Faith.

> Paul VI, *Message*, Dec. 6, 1977: "...non-Christian religions, which the Church respects and esteems..."[10]

He is saying that he <u>esteems</u> false religions.

> Paul VI, *Message*, Nov. 24, 1969: "...overcome divisions, by **developing a mutual respect between the different religious confessions**."[11]

> Paul VI, *Address*, Dec. 3, 1970: "We greet with **respect** the representatives of **all the other religions who have honored us by their presence**."[12]

> Paul VI, *General Audience*, July 6, 1977: "**We welcome with sincere respect** the Japanese delegation of **the Konko-kyo religion**."[13]

> In his *Address*, Aug. 22, 1969, Paul VI praised the Hindu Gandhi, and stated that he was: "Ever conscious of God's presence..."[14]

Hindus are pagans and idolaters who worship many different false gods. For Paul VI to praise the notorious Hindu Gandhi as "ever-conscious of God's presence" shows again that Paul VI was a complete religious indifferentist. Paul VI also officially praised the false religion of Hinduism in the official Vatican II document *Nostra Aetate* #2 (on non-Christian religions), as we quoted in the section on Vatican II.

> Paul VI, *Apostolic Exhortation*, Dec. 8, 1975: "The Church respects and esteems these non-Christian religions..."[15]

Notice again that Paul VI <u>esteems false religions</u>; this is satanic.

> Paul VI, *Address*, Aug. 24, 1974: "Religious and cultural differences in India, as you have said, are honored and respected... **We are pleased to see that this mutual honor and esteem is practiced**..."[16]

Paul VI says that <u>religious differences are honored</u> in India and that he is pleased to see this. This means that he honors the worship of false gods.

> Paul VI, *Address to Synod of Bishops*, Sept. 2, 1974: "Likewise we cannot omit a reference to **the non-Christian religions. These, in fact, must no longer be regarded as rivals, or obstacles to Evangelization...**"[17]

Here Paul VI boldly reveals that he is preaching a new Gospel. Non-Christian religions, he tells us, are no longer our obstacle to evangelization. This is an antichrist religion of apostasy.

> Pope Gregory XVI, *Mirari Vos* (# 13), Aug. 15, 1832: "They should consider the testimony of Christ Himself that 'those who are not with Christ are against Him,' (Lk. 11:23) and that they disperse unhappily who do not gather with Him. **Therefore, 'without a doubt, they will perish forever, unless they hold the Catholic faith whole and inviolate'** (Athanasian Creed)."[18]

> Paul VI, *Address to Dalai Lama*, Sept. 30, 1973: "We are happy to welcome Your Holiness today... You come to us from Asia, the cradle of **ancient religions and human traditions which are rightly held in deep veneration.**"[19]

Paul VI tells us that it is right to hold false religions which worship false gods in "deep veneration"! This may be the worst heresy that Paul VI uttered.

> Paul VI, Address, August, 1969: "...Uganda includes differing faiths which respect and esteem one another."[20]

The true religion esteems false religions? No, this again is blatantly heretical.

> Paul VI, *Message to Pagan Shinto Priests*, March 3, 1976: "**We know the fame of your temple, and the wisdom that is represented so vividly by the images contained therein.**"[21]

This is one of the most evil, revealing and heretical statements that Paul VI ever uttered. He is praising the wisdom contained in the images in the pagan Shinto Temple; in other words, he is praising the idols of the Shintoists!

PAUL VI ON BUDDHISM

Buddhism is a false, pagan religion of the East which teaches belief in re-incarnation and karma. Buddhists hold that life is not worth living, and that every form of conscious existence is an evil. Buddhists worship various false gods. Buddhism is an idolatrous and false religion of the Devil. Here's what Paul VI thought about Buddhism:

> Paul VI, *General Audience to Japanese Buddhists*, Sept. 5, 1973: "**It is a great pleasure for us to welcome the members of the Japanese Buddhists Europe Tour, honored followers of the Soto-shu sect of Buddhism**... At the Second Vatican Council the Catholic Church exhorted her sons and daughters to study

The Heresies of Paul VI

> and evaluate the religious traditions of mankind and to '**learn by sincere and patient dialogue what treasures** a bountiful God has distributed among the nations of the earth' (*Ad Gentes*, 11)… **Buddhism is one of the riches of Asia**…"22

According to Paul VI, the false, pagan and idolatrous religion of Buddhism is one of the "riches" of Asia!

> Paul VI, *General Audience to Japanese Buddhist Mission Tour*, Oct. 24, 1973: "Once again it is our pleasure to welcome a distinguished group of the Japan Buddhist Mission Tour. We are happy to reiterate the esteem we have for your country, **your noble traditions**…"23

> Paul VI, *Speech to Tibetan Buddhist Spiritual Leader*, Jan. 17, 1975: "The Second Vatican Council has expressed **sincere admiration for Buddhism in its various forms**… We wish Your Holiness and all your faithful an abundance of Prosperity and Peace."24

Notice his idolatry and apostasy in admiring, not only Buddhists, but the false religion of Buddhism.

> Paul VI, *Address to Buddhists*, June 5, 1972: "**It is with great** cordiality and **esteem that we greet** so distinguished a group of **Buddhist leaders** from Thailand… **We have a profound regard for… your precious traditions**."25

> Paul VI to a group of Buddhist Leaders, June 15, 1977: "To the distinguished group of Buddhist leaders from Japan we bid a warm welcome. **The Second Vatican Council declared that the Catholic Church looks with sincere respect on your way of life**… On this occasion we are happy to recall the words of St. John: 'The world, with all it craves for, is coming to an end; but anyone who does the will of God remains forever'."26

He first says that the Catholic Church looks with sincere respect upon the Buddhists' way of life. This is heresy. He then says that, on this occasion, he must recall the words of St. John: anyone who does the will of God remains forever. His meaning is clearly that Buddhists will live forever; that is, they will be saved. This is totally heretical.

> Paul VI, *Address to Buddhist Patriarch of Laos*, June 8, 1973: "… **Buddhism**… **the Catholic Church** considers its spiritual riches with esteem and respect and **wishes to collaborate with you, as religious men, to bring about real peace and the salvation of man**."27

Paul VI says that the Catholic Church considers with esteem the spiritual riches of the false religion of Buddhism. He then says that he wishes to collaborate with the Buddhist Patriarch to bring about the salvation of man! This is heresy and apostasy.

PAUL VI ON ISLAM

Islam is a false religion which denies the Divinity of Christ and rejects the Most Holy Trinity. Besides rejecting the true God, Islam allows polygamy up to four wives, and its followers (Muslims) spread this false religion with a zeal unequalled by the others. Islam is the most viciously anti-Christian major false religion in the world. To convert to Christianity in many Islamic countries means death. The propagation of the true Faith is strictly prohibited by the

Muslims. Islamic society is one of the most evil things in human history. Here is what Paul VI thought about this false religion which rejects Christ and the Trinity:

> Paul VI, *Speech*, Sept. 9, 1972: "We would also like you to know that the Church recognizes **the riches of the Islamic faith – a faith that binds us to the one God.**"[28]

Paul VI speaks about the "riches" of the Islamic Faith, a "Faith" that rejects Jesus Christ and the Trinity. He says this "Faith" binds us to the One God. This is apostasy.

> Paul VI, *Address*, Sept. 18, 1969: "…Moslems… along with us adore the one and merciful God, who on the last day will judge mankind."[29]

Moslems don't worship the one true God, the Holy Trinity, together with Catholics, as we covered in the section on the heresies of Vatican II. To assert that Muslims do worship the same God as Catholics is heresy. And Moslems certainly don't worship God who will judge mankind on the last day, Jesus Christ.

> Paul VI, *Address to Muslim Ambassador*, June 4, 1976: "… Moroccan Moslems … our brothers in faith in the one God. You will always be made very welcome and you will find esteem and understanding here."[30]

He says that Muslims are brothers in the Faith. This is apostasy. He then says that Muslims will always find *esteem* at the Vatican.

> Paul VI, *Address*, Dec. 2, 1977: "…the Moslems (who) profess to hold the faith of Abraham, and together with us they adore the one, merciful God, mankind's judge on the last day, as the Second Vatican Council solemnly declared." [31]

> Paul VI, *Address*, August, 1969: "…Our lively desire to greet, in your persons, the great Moslem communities spread throughout Africa? You thus enable Us to manifest here **Our high respect for the faith you profess**… In recalling the Catholic and Anglican Martyrs, **We gladly recall also those confessors of the Moslem faith** who were the first to suffer death…"[32]

He mentions his high respect for the false faith of Islam, and he commemorates Muslims who witnessed to this false religion through death. This is total apostasy.

> Paul VI, Angelus Address, Aug. 3, 1969: "**Twenty-two martyrs** were recognized, but there were many more, and not only Catholics. **There were also Anglicans and some Mohammedans.**"[33]

This is probably the most scandalous statement we've ever seen regarding the heresy that there are non-Catholic martyrs. Paul VI says that Muslims (who don't even believe in Christ or the Trinity) are martyrs, in addition to Anglicans. This is truly amazing and totally heretical.

> Pope Eugene IV, *Council of Florence*, 1441, *ex cathedra*:
> "….nobody can be saved, no matter how much he has given away in alms and even if he has shed blood in the name of Christ, unless he has persevered in the bosom and unity of the Catholic Church."[34]

> Pope Eugene IV, *Council of Florence*, dogmatic Athanasian Creed, 1439: "Whoever wishes to be saved, needs above all to hold the Catholic faith; unless each one preserves this whole and inviolate, he will without a doubt perish in eternity…"[35]

PAUL VI ON RELIGIOUS LIBERTY

> Paul VI, *Address,* July 9, 1969: "**She [the Church] has also affirmed, during Her long history, at the cost of oppression and persecution,** freedom for everyone to profess his own religion. No one, She says, is to be restrained from acting, no one is to be forced to act in a manner contrary to his own beliefs… As we said, the Council demanded a true and public religious freedom…"[36]

This is completely false and heretical. The Catholic Church has affirmed during her long history, at the cost of oppression and persecution, that the religion of Jesus Christ is the only one that is true; and that Christ is truly God and truly man. Paul VI would have us believe, however, that the martyrs were tortured horribly, not for their profession of faith in Christ, but in order for all to have freedom to profess their various false religions! This is an astoundingly heretical distortion of the truth!

> Paul VI, *Message*, Dec. 10, 1973: "… the repeated violations of the sacred right to religious liberty in its various aspects and the absence of an international agreement supporting this right…"[37]

> Paul VI, Letter, July 25, 1975: "…the Holy See rejoices to see specifically emphasized the right of religious liberty."[38]

Again, in the section on Vatican II we showed that the doctrine on religious liberty which was advocated by Paul VI was, in fact, condemned by Catholic popes.

PAUL VI ON THE "ORTHODOX"

Here we see Paul VI giving a clear Masonic handshake to the Eastern Schismatic Patriarch of Constantinople, Athenagoras, on Jan. 5, 1964. The two also mutually lifted the reciprocal excommunications of 1054. Translation: this means that Paul VI considered that the Eastern "Orthodox" are no longer excommunicated even though they deny the Papacy. Therefore, according to him, the Papacy is not a dogma binding under pain of excommunication.

The Heresies of Paul VI

The Eastern Orthodox are schismatics who reject Papal Infallibility and the last 13 General Councils of the Catholic Church. They reject that the Holy Ghost proceeds from the Second Person of the Trinity; they permit divorce and remarriage; and many of them reject the Immaculate Conception. Here's what Paul VI thought of these schismatics:

> Paul VI, *Speech*, April 19, 1970, speaking of the deceased schismatic Patriarch of Moscow: **"To the very end he was conscious and solicitous for his great ministry."**[39]

He says that leadership in a schismatic church is a great ministry.

> Paul VI, *Address*, Jan. 24, 1972: "...**greet among us an eminent representative of the venerable Orthodox Church... a man of great piety**..."[40]

> Paul VI, *Speech*, Jan. 23, 1972: "...the great, venerable and excellent Orthodox Patriarch..."[41]

> Paul VI, *Address to Schismatic Delegation*, June 27, 1977: "Then, ten years later, we paid a visit to your holy Church..."[42]

> Paul VI, *General Audience*, Jan. 20, 1971: "... the venerable Eastern Orthodox Churches..."[43]

He says that schismatic churches are venerable.

> Paul VI, speaking of the death of the Schismatic Patriarch Athenagoras, July 9, 1972: "...we recommend this great man to you, a man of a venerated Church..."[44]

> Paul VI, *Address*, May 25, 1968: "...the venerable Orthodox Church of Bulgaria."[45]

> Paul VI, *Common Declaration with Patriarch of Syrian Schismatic Sect*, Oct. 27, 1971: "This should be done with love, with openness to the promptings of the Holy Spirit, and with **mutual respect for each other and each other's Church.**"[46]

So Paul VI respects the rejection of the Papacy and Papal Infallibility.

> Paul VI, *Telegram upon election of new Schismatic Patriarch of Constantinople*, July, 1972: "At the moment when you assume a heavy charge in the service of the Church of Christ..."[47]

This means that the schismatic Church is the Church of Christ.

> Paul VI, *Address*, Dec. 14, 1976: "...very dear Brothers, sent by the venerable Church of Constantinople... **we carried out the solemn and sacred ecclesial act of lifting the ancient anathemas,** an act with which we wished to remove the memory of these events forever from the memory and the heart of the Church..."[48]

The schismatic "Orthodox" are anathematized by the Catholic Church for denying the Papacy, and not accepting dogmas of the Catholic Faith. But Paul VI solemnly lifted these anathemas against them, as we mentioned above. Like the statement above, this address of Paul VI means he attempted to overturn the Papacy as a dogma which must be believed under pain of anathema or condemnation.

> Paul VI, *Letter*, March 7, 1971, regarding the death of two schismatic patriarchs: "…moved by the death of His Holiness Patriarch Kyrillos VI we express our sincere sympathy with assurance of **our prayers for the eternal repose of your beloved pastor** and **for God's consoling blessing on the entire Coptic Orthodox Church**."[49]

Notice two things: First, Paul VI says that he will pray for the soul of the deceased schismatic, indicating that the deceased non-Catholic patriarch can be saved, which is heretical. Second, he calls for God's consoling blessing on the entire Coptic Orthodox Church. How about that there is only one true Church and that the Coptic Schismatic Church is not part of it? How about God's grace of conversion for the Coptic Orthodox to the true Church? Paul VI's statement shows again that he held heretical sects to be true Churches, and the Catholic Faith to be meaningless.

> Pope Gregory XVI, May 27, 1832: "Be not deceived, my brother; if anyone follows a schismatic, he will not attain the inheritance of the kingdom of God."[50]

> Paul VI, *Letter to Schismatic*, November, 1976: "…the first Pan-Orthodox Conference in preparation for **the Great Holy Council of the Orthodox Churches** is beginning its work… for the best service of **the venerable Orthodox Church**."[51]

He calls the schismatic council "holy" and the schismatic Church "venerable." Paul VI was a schismatic.

> Paul VI, *General Audience*, Jan. 24, 1973: "…**our brother of venerated memory**, the ecumenical Patriarch of Constantinople…"[52]

> Paul VI, *Message concerning deceased Russian schismatic*, April 7, 1972: "…we express to Your Eminence and the Holy Synod of the Georgian Orthodox Church our sincere condolences **with the assurance of our prayers for the eternal repose of your pastor**…"[53]

> Paul VI, *Message*, May 23, 1968, **to the Schismatic Patriarch of Moscow**: "…**Holiness**, on the occasion of the celebrations for the fiftieth anniversary for the day when the Synod of the whole Orthodox Church of Russia re-established the Patriarchal See of Moscow… we have delegated to participate in the solemn celebrations which will take place in your Patriarchal City **our very dear brothers in the Episcopate**…"[54]

He calls the schismatic Patriarch "Holiness" and celebrates the fiftieth anniversary of the schismatic Church.

> Paul VI, *Speech to Schismatic*, July 1, 1978: "We receive you with affection and *esteem*."[55]

> Paul VI, *General Audience*, Nov. 30, 1977: "We greet you joyfully, **beloved brothers, who represent here His Holiness** Patriarch Pimen and **the Russian Orthodox Church**… **all our esteem** and brotherly love **to His Holiness Patriarch Pimen, to his clergy and to the whole people of the faithful**."[56]

Paul VI went on to say in a letter about the schismatic Athenagoras (July, 1972): "…we pray the Lord to receive into His heavenly kingdom him…"[57]

> Paul VI, *Joint Declaration with the Schismatic "Pope" Shenouda III*, May 10, 1973: "Paul VI, Bishop of Rome and Pope of the Catholic Church, and **Shenouda III, Pope of Alexandria and Patriarch of the See of St. Mark**… In the name of this charity, **we reject all forms of proselytism… Let it cease, where it may exist**…"[58]

This is all one really needs to see to know that Paul VI was a schismatic and not a Catholic. He makes a Joint Declaration with a schismatic "pope." He acknowledges this schismatic as the holder of the See of St. Mark. This is a blasphemy against the Papacy, since this schismatic holds no authority whatsoever. He rejects all forms of proselytism – that is, trying to convert the schismatics – and he says "let it cease where it may exist"! Paul VI was a formal heretic and schismatic.

PAUL VI ON OTHER PROTESTANT SECTS

Protestantism began with the German priest Martin Luther, who left the Catholic Church and started the Protestant revolution in 1517. Luther denied free will, the Papacy, praying to the saints, Purgatory, Tradition, Transubstantiation and the Holy Sacrifice of the Mass. Luther replaced the Mass with a memorial service commemorating the Last Supper. All the sacraments except Baptism and the Holy Eucharist were rejected. Luther held that after the fall of Adam man cannot produce any good works. Most Protestants hold the same beliefs as Luther, but all of them reject numerous Catholic dogmas. Here's what Paul VI thought of these heretics and schismatics:

> Paul VI, *Angelus Address*, Jan. 17, 1971: "From polemical opposition among the various Christian denominations we have passed to mutual respect…"[59]

Here Paul VI reveals that the Vatican II agenda with regard to Protestant sects has gone from polemical opposition – in other words, an opposition to their false doctrines – to an attitude of acceptance of, and mutual respect for, their false religion.

> Paul VI, *Speech to Representatives of non-Catholic churches in Geneva*, June, 1969: "The spirit that animates us… This spirit lays down, as the first basis of every fruitful contact between different confessions, **that each profess his faith loyally**."[60]

Paul VI is saying that the Protestants should not become Catholic, but remain loyal to their own sects.

> Paul VI, *Homily*, Jan. 25, 1973: "…express a respectful and affectionate thought in Christ to Christians of other denominations residing in this city and assure them of our **esteem**…"[61]

This is an incredible homily. In it he's assuring the heretics of other denominations of his *esteem*. Consider that Paul VI didn't even personally know all the people he was esteeming. He didn't know anything about them <u>except that they belong to one of these sects</u>, and he assured them of his esteem *on that basis*!

> Paul VI, *Letter*, Aug. 6, 1973, to the World Council of Churches: "**The World Council of Churches has been created in order,** by the grace of God, to serve the Churches and Ecclesial Communities in their endeavors **to restore and to manifest to all that perfect communion in faith and love which is the gift of Christ to His Church.**"[62]

Paul VI says that the World Council of Churches has been created to restore and to manifest to all that perfect communion in faith and love which is the gift of Christ to His Church. Notice the astounding implication of this statement. The perfect communion in faith and charity which is the gift of Christ to His Church is the organization of the Catholic Church, the universal Church founded by Christ. **But Paul VI says that this is manifested by the World Council of Churches!** He has replaced the Catholic Church with the World Council of Churches. The World Council of Churches is an organization made up of many different sects and denominations. A traditional commentator would correctly label it a Communist front group – meant to water-down and liberalize the "Christian" churches of the world. But it is undoubtedly a very heretical ecumenical organization made of various man-made religions.

> Paul VI, Discourse, Dec. 12, 1968: "…our sons are on friendly terms with their Christian brothers, Lutheran Evangelicals…"[63]

> Pope Pius IV, profession of faith, *Council of Trent*, ex cathedra: "This true Catholic faith, outside of which no one can be saved… I now profess and truly hold…"[64]

> Paul VI, *Address,* April 28, 1977: "…relations between the Catholic Church and the Anglican Communion… **these words of hope, 'The Anglican Communion united not absorbed,' are no longer a mere dream."**[65]

This means that Paul VI **wants to unite with the Anglican sect without absorbing them; that is, without converting them**.

> Paul VI, *Speech*, Aug. 2, 1969: "We wished to meet the Anglican Church which flourishes in this country. We wished to pay homage to those sons of whom it is most proud, those who – together with our own Catholic martyrs – gave the generous witness of their lives to the Gospel…"[66]

> Paul VI, Speaking of the death of the Protestant Martin Luther King, Jr., April 7, 1968: "…we shall all share the hopes which his martyrdom inspires in us."[67]

> Pope Gregory XVI, May 27, 1832:
> "Finally some of these misguided people attempt to persuade themselves and others that men are not saved only in the Catholic religion, but that even heretics may attain eternal life."[68]

PAUL VI ON BIRTH CONTROL

Paul VI favored birth control.

> Paul VI, *Speech*, Nov. 16, 1970: "…this, among other effects, will undoubtedly favor **a rational control of birth by couples**…"[69]

> Paul VI, Address, Aug. 24, 1969: "…the liberty of husband and wife and does not forbid them a moral and reasonable **limitation of birth**…"[70]

> Paul VI, *Humanae Vitae* (No. 16), July 25, 1968: "It cannot be denied that in each case the married couple, for acceptable reasons, are both perfectly clear in their intention to avoid children and wish to make sure that none will result."[71]

Paul VI says in *Humanae Vitae* that couples are perfectly free to have zero children if they want to.

PAUL VI ON THE UNITED NATIONS

The United Nations is an evil organization that promotes contraception and abortion, and looks to take control of the decision-making for every country on the planet. Former UN Secretary General U Thant praised the Communist Lenin as a man whose "ideals were reflected in the United Nations Charter."[72] Here's what Paul VI thought of the UN:

> Paul VI, *Address*, Feb. 5, 1972: "…**we have faith in the UN**."[73]

> Paul VI, *Message*, April 26, 1968: "…may all men of heart join together peacefully in order **that the principles of the United Nations may be not only proclaimed, but put into effect**, and that not only the constitution of States may promulgate them, but public authorities apply them…"[74]

> Paul VI, *Address to Secretary General of the U.N.*, July 9, 1977: "We wish to listen to the voice of the authorized representative of the United Nations Organization… all this merely emphasizes more the beneficial and **irreplaceable role of the United Nations Organization**…"[75]

> Paul VI, *Message to U.N.*, Oct. 4, 1970: "Today we wish once more to repeat the words which we had the honor to pronounce on 4th October 1965 from the tribune of your assembly: '**This Organization represents the path that has to be taken for modern civilization and for world peace**… Where else, moreover, could these governments and peoples better find a bridge to link them, a table round which they can gather, and a tribunal where they may plead the cause of justice and peace?... **who better than the United Nations Organization and its specialized agencies will be able to take up the challenge presented to all mankind?... There exists in effect a common good of man, and it is up to your Organization, because of its dedication to universality**, which is its reason for being, to promote it untiringly."[76]

First, Paul VI says that the U.N. is the path that has to be taken. He says that the U.N., not the Catholic Church, is the best means for the cause of justice and peace for the world. Second, he says that the U.N. is the universal (that is, *Catholic*) body for mankind! He is replacing the Church with the UN.

PAUL VI PROMOTING THE NEW WORLD ORDER

> Paul VI, *Message to President of a U.N. Conference*, May, 1976: "…**this new international economic order that has to be ceaselessly built up**."[77]

> Paul VI, *Message*, Sept. 8, 1977: "Stress is legitimately laid nowadays on the necessity of **constructing a new world order**…"[78]

> Paul VI, *Message to United Nations*, May 24, 1978: "…we are aware that the path which must lead to the coming of a new international order… cannot in any case be as short as we would like it to be… **Disarmament, a new world order** and development are three obligations that are inseparably bound together…"[79]

PAUL VI ON THE WORSHIP OF MAN

Paul VI, *Address*, Feb. 7, 1971: "All honor then to man!"[80]

Paul VI, *Address*, Aug. 1, 1969: "…do not let yourselves become discouraged by the obstacles and difficulties that constantly arise; **do not lose faith in man**."[81]

Paul VI, *Message*, March 25, 1971: "…man, to whom all things on earth should be related as their center and crown."[82]

This is blasphemy. Paul VI was quoting the heresy of Vatican II here.

Paul VI, *Speech*, Nov. 18, 1971: "On our visit to Bombay we emphasized: 'Man must meet man.'"[83]

Paul VI, *Audience*, Jan. 10, 1972: "For the demands of justice, Gentlemen, can only be gathered in the light of truth, that truth which is man…"[84]

This means that man is the truth.

Paul VI, *Address*, April 11, 1973: "…always anxious to safeguard, above everything else, the primacy of man…"[85]

In his *Angelus Address*, Jan. 27, 1974, Paul VI spoke positively of: "…the cult of man for man's sake."[86]

Paul VI, *Address*, Feb. 15, 1974: "…as Your Excellency has rightly recalled – that the final aim is man…"[87]

Paul VI, *Address*, Dec. 29, 1968: "The Christian mystery which rests on Man…"[88]

Paul VI, *Audience*, April 28, 1969: "In the final analysis, there are no true riches but man…"[89]

Paul VI, *Angelus Address*, July 20, 1969: "We would do well to meditate on man…"[90]

Paul VI, *General Audience*, July 28, 1971: "The dignity of man! We will never be able to appreciate and honor it enough."[91]

Paul VI, *Discourse*, Sept. 4, 1968: "…the themes which today pre-occupy religion, be it Catholic or non-Catholic, **all these converge from different directions upon one central, dominant focus, namely: man**. 'According to the almost unanimous opinion of believers and unbelievers alike, all things on earth should be related to man as their center and crown.'"[92]

Paul VI, *Angelus Message*, July 13, 1975: "…the most precious science of all, the science of knowing oneself, of reflecting, almost dreaming, about one's own conscience… Long live the holiday free of other commitments, but occupied in exploring the secrets of one's own life."[93]

The Heresies of Paul VI

Think about this astounding message. He doesn't say that theology, the study of God, is the most precious science; he says it is the science of knowing oneself and dreaming about one's own conscience. He also says long live the holiday (that is, long live the holy day) free of other commitments (perhaps free of attending Mass?), a holy day occupied in exploring the secrets of one's own life. In other words, he wants a holy day about man with no other commitments. This is clearly the worship of man.

> Paul VI, *Angelus Message*, Sept. 26, 1976: "We are in ecstasy of admiration for the human countenance..."[94]

> Paul VI, *Address*, Oct. 16, 1976: "...if the Gospel is for man, we Christians are completely for the Gospel."[95]

Notice that he only says that we are for the Gospel if the Gospel is for man.

> Paul VI, *Address*, Dec. 4, 1976: "...above all ideological conditionings, the greatness and dignity of the human person must emerge as the only value to promote and defend."[96]

> Paul VI, *Christmas Message*, Dec. 25, 1976: "Let us honor fallen and sinful humanity."[97]

> Paul VI, *Speech*, June 10, 1969: "For in the final analysis there is no true riches but the riches of man."[98]

PAUL VI ON CHRISTMAS

> Paul VI, *General Audience*, Dec. 17, 1969: "...Christmas is the birthday of Life. Of our life."[99]

Christmas is the Birthday of Jesus Christ. It's not the Birthday of our life because we are not Jesus Christ. But this is what Paul VI was preaching.

> Paul VI, *Angelus Address*, Dec. 21, 1974: "A merry Christmas to you... It is the feast of human life..."[100]

> Paul VI, *Christmas Message*, Dec. 25, 1976: "Brethren, let us honor in the Birth of Christ the incipient life of man."[101]

The word *incipient* means "Beginning; in an initial stage."[102] So, Paul VI is saying that in the Birth of Christ we find in the beginning stages of the life of man. This implies, once again, that man is Christ.

> Paul VI, *Angelus Message*, Dec. 18, 1976: "Christmas is a feast of mankind... dedicated, as a happy effect, to honor human existence."[103]

> Paul VI, *Speech*, Sept. 12, 1970: "...the only word which explains Man is God himself made Man, the Word made Flesh."[104]

This clearly means that man is God Himself made man, Our Lord Jesus Christ.

> Pope Pius X, *E Supremi Apostolatus*, Oct. 4, 1903: "...**the distinguishing mark of Antichrist, man has with infinite temerity put himself in the place of God...**"[105]

Paul VI was a manifest heretic and a non-Catholic antipope.

OTHER CHANGES MADE BY PAUL VI

Paul VI giving away the Papal Tiara

On November 13, 1964, Paul VI gave away the triple-crowned papal tiara. Paul VI had the tiara auctioned at the New York World's Fair.[106] **The Papal Tiara is a sign of a true Pope's authority –** the three crowns representing the dogmatic, liturgical and disciplinary authority of a pope. By giving it away, Paul VI was symbolically giving away the authority of the Papacy (although he had none to give away since he was actually an antipope). But **it was a symbolic act of how he was a satanic infiltrator whose whole mission was to attempt to destroy the Catholic Church**. (Also notice "Cardinal" Ottaviani, whom many falsely think was a true conservative, standing right next to Antipope Paul VI as he does this).

PAUL VI WAS ALSO SEEN MANY TIMES WEARING THE BREAST-PLATE OF THE EPHOD, A.K.A., THE RATIONAL OF JUDGMENT OF A JEWISH HIGH-PRIEST

Paul VI wearing the breastplate of the ephod, a vestment used by Freemasons and Jewish High-Priests

Notice the twelve stones which represent the twelve tribes of Israel. **Not only is this the breast-plate of a Jewish High-Priest, but according to the *Encyclopedia of Freemasonry* by Mackey, the ephod is also "worn in the (Masonic) American Chapters of the Royal Arch, by the High-Priest as an official part of his official ornaments."** The ephod was the vestment that was worn by Caiphas, the High-Priest of the Jewish religion, who ordered Our Lord Jesus Christ to be put to death by crucifixion.

Antipope Paul VI wore the breast-plate of the Ephod, a.k.a. the Rational of Judgment of the High-Priest, numerous times. God allows things such as this to come out to show the people that these men are infiltrators and enemies of the Catholic Church.

In addition to all of the heresies we have covered in the speeches of Paul VI, he was the man who authoritatively implemented the false Second Vatican Council, changed the Catholic Mass into a Protestant service, and changed the rite of every single Sacrament. He changed the matter or form of the Eucharist, Extreme Unction, Holy Orders, and Confirmation. Paul VI wanted to put Christ to death in the Mass (by removing it and replacing it with a counterfeit), and wanted to kill His Catholic Church by attempting to change the Church completely.

Within two years of the close of Vatican II, Paul VI removed the index of forbidden books, a decision one commentator rightly called "incomprehensible."

Another shot of Paul VI wearing the breastplate of the ephod

Paul VI then abolished the oath against Modernism, at a time when Modernism was flourishing as never before. On Nov. 21, 1970,[107] Paul VI also excluded all cardinals over 80 years of age from participating in papal elections. Paul VI disestablished the papal court, disbanded the Noble Guard and the Palatine Guards.[108] Paul VI abolished the rite of Tonsure, all four Minor Orders, and the rank of Subdiaconate.[109]

"**Paul VI gave back to the Muslims the Standard of Lepanto**. The history of the flag was venerable. It was taken from a Turkish admiral during a great naval battle in 1571. While Pope St. Pius V fasted and prayed the Rosary, an out-numbered Christian fleet defeated a much larger Moslem navy, thus saving Christendom from the infidel. In honor of the miraculous victory, Pius V instituted the Feast of Our Lady of the Most Holy Rosary to commemorate her intercession. **In one dramatic act, Paul VI renounced not only a remarkable Christian victory, but the prayers and sacrifices of a great pope and saint.**"[110]

Under Paul VI, the Holy Office was reformed: its primary function now was research, not defending the Catholic Faith.[111] According to those who watched film of Paul VI's visit to Fatima, he did not pray one Hail Mary.[112]

In 1969, Paul VI removed forty saints from the official liturgical calendar.[113]

Paul VI removed solemn exorcisms from the baptismal rite. In the place of the solemn exorcisms, he substituted an optional prayer that makes only a passing reference to fighting the Devil.[114]

Another clear shot of Paul VI wearing the breastplate of the ephod

Paul VI granted more than 32,000 requests from priests who had asked to be released from their vows and returned to lay status – the greatest exodus from the priesthood since the Protestant revolution.[115]

Paul VI's disastrous influence was visible immediately. For example, in Holland not a single candidate applied for admission to the priesthood in 1970, and within 12 months every seminary there was closed.[116] Spiritual destruction was everywhere; countless millions left the Church; countless others ceased practicing their Faith and confessing their sins.

And while Paul VI was the cause of this unrelenting disaster and spiritual destruction, like the sly serpent he was, he calculatingly misdirected the attention away from himself. In perhaps his most famous quotation, he noted that Satan's smoke had made its way into the Temple of God.

> Paul VI, *Homily*, June 29, 1972: "**Satan's smoke has made its way into the Temple of God through some crack...**"[117]

When Paul VI made this statement, everyone looked at the cardinals, the bishops and the priests to discover where this smoke of Satan might be. They looked at everyone except the man who made the statement. But Paul VI was actually the smoke of Satan, and he made the statement to misdirect people away from himself; and in this he was successful. But what is perhaps most frightening is that Paul VI's famous statement is basically a direct reference to Apocalypse 9:1-3.

> Apoc. 9:1-3: "And there was given to him the key of the bottomless pit. And he opened the bottomless pit: <u>and the smoke of the pit arose</u>, as the smoke of a great furnace..."

In Apocalypse 9, we see a direct reference to the smoke of Satan, and to someone who is given the key to unleash it. Antipope Paul VI did not have the keys of Peter, but he was given the key to the bottomless pit. He was the one who brought in the smoke of Satan from the great furnace; as he says, from some crack.

> Jean Guitton, an intimate friend of Paul VI, related what Paul VI said at the final session of Vatican II: "It was the final session of the Council," Guitton wrote, "the most essential, in which Paul VI was to bestow on all humanity the teachings of the Council. He announced this to me on that day with these words, '**I am about to blow the seven trumpets of the Apocalypse.**'"[118]

> Paul VI, *Speech to Lombard Seminary*, Dec. 7, 1968: "The Church finds herself in an hour of disquiet, of self-criticism, **one might say even of self-destruction**... **The Church is wounding herself.**"[119]

Here Paul VI again mocks the people. He says the Church is in "self-destruction" and is "wounding herself." He is referring to himself again, for *he* was the one trying to destroy her and wound her at every turn!

PAUL VI ON "MAGIC"

The Oxford Illustrated Dictionary defines magic as: "Pretended art of influencing events by occult control of nature or of spirits, witchcraft..."[120]

Catholics are forbidden to practice magic. But Paul VI frequently spoke of magic.

> Paul VI, *Homily*, Nov. 12, 1972: "Where does it come from, this **interior magic** that banishes fear..."[121]

> Paul VI, *General Audience*, Dec. 30, 1970: "...**invisible but overpowering magic** of the flood of public opinion..."[122]

> Paul VI, *Message*, Jan. 1, 1975: "Reconciliation!... Could not **this magic word** find a place in the dictionary of your hopes..."[123]

> Paul VI, *Homily*, May 11, 1975: "You, artists of the theatre and the cinema... who possess **the magic art** of offering with voice and with music... the real-life scene of the event..."[124]

> Paul VI, *Speech*, May 18, 1969: "Everything is transformed under **the magical influence** of science..."[125]

> Paul VI, *Message to Brazilian People*, February, 1972: "Service: **a magic word** that galvanizes into action..."[126]

> Paul VI, *Address*, June 23, 1973: "…the religious root seems to have lost so much of its **magical power** of inspiration?"[127]

Why did Paul VI speak so much about magic? It was, in our opinion, precisely because he knew that it was Black Magic that allowed him, a satanic infiltrator, to fool the world into thinking that he was a pope so he could then destroy the Mass and almost the entire Catholic Church. He knew that it was his Black Magic that allowed him to get away with changing the rite to every sacrament and foisting his new Vatican II religion upon the world.

PAUL VI ADMITTED HIS CHURCH IS THE WHORE OF BABYLON

In the Apocalypse, chapters 17 and 18, there is predicted that a whore will arise in the last days from the city of seven hills, which is Rome. This whore will tread upon the blood of the martyrs and saints. This whore is clearly contrasted with the immaculate bride of Christ, the Catholic Church. In other words, the whore of Babylon will be a false church from Rome that will appear in the last days. Near the end of this book we bring forward the evidence that the Whore of Babylon is the Vatican II sect, a false bride which arises in Rome in the last days in order to deceive the Catholic Faithful.

> In her appearance at La Salette, France, Sept. 19, 1846, the Blessed Mother predicted: **"Rome will lose the Faith and become the seat of the Anti-Christ… the Church will be in eclipse."**

In the following quote, Antipope Paul VI essentially admits that his new Church is this false Church by admitting that his "Church" has thrown off its opposition to the world, which characterizes the true Church.

> Paul VI, *General Audience*, Oct. 1, 1969: "On the other hand, She [the Church] is also trying to adapt herself and assimilate herself to the world's ways; She is taking off her distinctive sacral garment, for She wants to feel more human and earthly.
> "She is tending to let herself be absorbed by the social and temporal milieu. She has almost been seized by human respect at the thought that She is different in some way and obliged to have a style of thought and life which is not that of the world. **She is undergoing the world's changes and degradations with conformist, almost *avante-garde* zeal.**"[128]

Here Paul VI admits that the post-Vatican II Church is a false Church which has adapted itself to the world and assimilated the world's ways with zeal. This is a stunning admission by Paul VI. He is admitting in so many words that the post-Vatican II Church is the Whore of Babylon.

When one combines the fact that Paul VI frequently wore the Jewish Ephod with all of his other systematic attempts to destroy all of Catholic Tradition, the evidence is strong that he was a satanic Jewish infiltrator.

In fact, Paul VI's ancestors were of Jewish origin. His actual name was Giovanni Montini. The Montini family is listed in the *Golden Book of Noble Italian Heritage* (1962-1964, p. 994): "A branch of the… noble family from Brescia… wherefrom their noble blazon comes and which avows as its sure trunk and founder, a Bartholomew (Bartolino) de Benedictis, said **Montini was of Hebrew origin.**"[129]

ANOTHER PICTURE OF ANTIPOPE PAUL VI WEARING THE RATIONAL OF A JEWISH HIGH-PRIEST

We have proven that Paul VI was a complete apostate who believed that false religions are true, that heresy and schism are fine, and that schismatics should not be converted, just to name a few.

If you accept Vatican II or the New Mass or the new sacramental rites – in short, if you accept the Vatican II religion – this is the man whose religion you are following, a manifestly heretical infiltrator, whose whole mission was to attempt to overturn and destroy as much of the Catholic Faith as possible.

Catholics must have no part with Antipope Paul VI's New Mass (the Novus Ordo) and must completely reject Vatican II and the new sacramental rites. Catholics must completely reject Antipope Paul VI for the non-Catholic antipope he was. Catholics must reject and not support any group which accepts this apostate as a valid pope, or which accepts the New Mass or Vatican II or the new sacramental rites of Paul VI.

The Heresies of Paul VI   161

ANTIPOPE PAUL VI'S SIGNATURE CONTAINING THREE 6'S

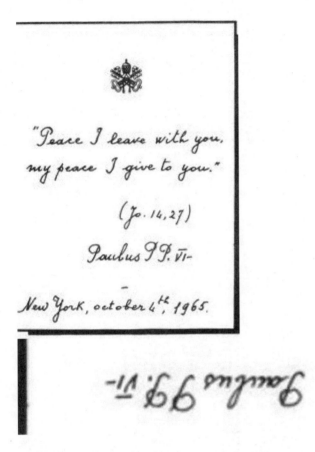

Here is a picture of Antipope Paul VI's signature. If you turn it upside-down, you see that there are three clear 6's. The shot below is a close-up of his name turned upside-down. The three 6's are clear. As far as we know, this is the way that Paul VI's signature always appeared.

Endnotes for Section 14:

[1] Declaration of Archbishop Marcel Lefebvre, August, 1976; partially quoted by Bishop Tissier De Mallerais, *The Biography of Marcel Lefebvre*, Kansas City, MO: Angelus Press, 2004, p. 505.
[2] *L'Osservatore Romano* (the Vatican's Newspaper), Dec. 14, 1972, p. 1.
[3] *L'Osservatore Romano*, July 5, 1973, p. 1.
[4] *The Papal Encyclicals*, by Claudia Carlen, Raleigh: The Pierian Press, 1990, Vol. 3 (1903-1939), p. 82.
[5] *The Papal Encyclicals*, Vol. 1 (1740-1878), p. 230.
[6] *L'Osservatore Romano*, Nov. 16, 1972, p. 1.
[7] *The Papal Encyclicals*, Vol. 3 (1903-1939), pp. 313-314.
[8] *L'Osservatore Romano*, Oct. 11, 1973, p. 10.
[9] *L'Osservatore Romano*, Jan. 20, 1972, p. 1.
[10] *L'Osservatore Romano*, Dec. 22, 1977, p. 2.
[11] *L'Osservatore Romano*, Dec. 18, 1969, p. 2.
[12] *L'Osservatore Romano*, Dec. 17, 1970, p. 7.
[13] *L'Osservatore Romano*, July 14, 1977, p. 12.
[14] *L'Osservatore Romano*, Oct. 9, 1969, p. 5.

[15] *L'Osservatore Romano*, Dec. 25, 1975, p. 5.
[16] *L'Osservatore Romano*, Sept. 12, 1974, p. 2.
[17] *L'Osservatore Romano*, Oct. 10, 1974, p. 7.
[18] *The Papal Encyclicals*, Vol. 1 (1740-1878), p. 238.
[19] *L'Osservatore Romano*, Oct. 11, 1973, p. 4.
[20] *L'Osservatore Romano*, Aug. 14, 1969, p. 12.
[21] *L'Osservatore Romano*, March 11, 1976, p. 12.
[22] *L'Osservatore Romano*, Sept. 13, 1973, p. 8.
[23] *L'Osservatore Romano*, Nov. 1, 1973, p. 1.
[24] *L'Osservatore Romano*, Jan. 30, 1975, p. 5.
[25] *L'Osservatore Romano*, June 15, 1972, p. 5.
[26] *L'Osservatore Romano*, June 23, 1977, p. 5.
[27] *L'Osservatore Romano*, June 21, 1973, p. 5.
[28] *L'Osservatore Romano*, Sept. 21, 1972, p. 2.
[29] *L'Osservatore Romano*, Oct. 2, 1969, p. 2.
[30] *L'Osservatore Romano*, June 24, 1976, p. 4.
[31] *L'Osservatore Romano*, Dec. 22, 1977, p. 2.
[32] *L'Osservatore Romano*, Aug. 14, 1969, p. 10.
[33] *L'Osservatore Romano*, Aug. 7, 1969, p. 1.
[34] Denzinger 714.
[35] *Decrees of the Ecumenical Councils*, Vol. 1, pp. 550-553; Denzinger, *The Sources of Catholic Dogma*, B. Herder Book. Co., Thirtieth Edition, 1957, no. 39-40.
[36] *L'Osservatore Romano*, July 17, 1969, p. 1.
[37] *L'Osservatore Romano*, Dec. 20, 1973, p. 3.
[38] *L'Osservatore Romano*, Aug. 14, 1975, p. 3.
[39] *L'Osservatore Romano*, April 23, 1970, p. 12.
[40] *L'Osservatore Romano*, Feb. 10, 1972, p. 3.
[41] *L'Osservatore Romano*, Jan. 27, 1972, p. 12.
[42] *L'Osservatore Romano*, July 14, 1977, p. 10.
[43] *L'Osservatore Romano*, Jan. 28, 1971, p. 1.
[44] *L'Osservatore Romano*, July 13, 1972, p. 12.
[45] *L'Osservatore Romano*, June 6, 1968, p. 5.
[46] *L'Osservatore Romano*, Nov. 4, 1971, p. 14.
[47] *L'Osservatore Romano*, July 27, 1972, p. 12.
[48] *L'Osservatore Romano*, Jan. 1, 1976, p. 6.
[49] *L'Osservatore Romano*, March 18, 1971, p. 12.
[50] *The Papal Encyclicals*, Vol. 1 (1740-1878), p. 230.
[51] *L'Osservatore Romano*, Dec. 30, 1976, p. 8.
[52] *L'Osservatore Romano*, Feb. 1, 1973, p. 12.
[53] *L'Osservatore Romano*, May 11, 1972, p. 4.
[54] *L'Osservatore Romano*, June 6, 1968, p. 4.
[55] *L'Osservatore Romano*, July 13, 1978, p. 3.
[56] *L'Osservatore Romano*, Dec. 15, 1977, p. 4.
[57] *L'Osservatore Romano*, July 13, 1972, p. 12.
[58] *L'Osservatore Romano*, May 24, 1973, p. 6.
[59] *L'Osservatore Romano*, Jan. 21, 1971, p. 12.
[60] *L'Osservatore Romano*, June 19, 1969, p. 9.
[61] *L'Osservatore Romano*, Feb. 8, 1973, p. 7.
[62] *L'Osservatore Romano*, Sept. 6, 1973, p. 8.
[63] *L'Osservatore Romano*, Dec. 26, 1968, p. 4.
[64] Denzinger 1000.
[65] *L'Osservatore Romano*, May 5, 1977, p. 1.
[66] *L'Osservatore Romano*, Aug. 14, 1969, p. 1.
[67] *L'Osservatore Romano*, April 18, 1968, p. 2.
[68] *The Papal Encyclicals*, Vol. 1 (1740-1878), p. 229.
[69] *L'Osservatore Romano*, Nov. 26, 1970, p. 7.
[70] *L'Osservatore Romano*, Sept. 5, 1968, p. 10.
[71] *The Papal Encyclicals*, Vol. 5 (1858-1981), p. 227.
[72] http://www.worldnetdaily.com/news/article.asp?ARTICLE_ID=16291
[73] *L'Osservatore Romano*, Feb. 17, 1972, p. 5.
[74] *L'Osservatore Romano*, May 2, 1968, p. 4.
[75] *L'Osservatore Romano*, July 21, 1977, p. 6.
[76] *L'Osservatore Romano*, Oct. 15, 1970, p. 3.

77 *L'Osservatore Romano*, June 17, 1976, p. 3.
78 *L'Osservatore Romano*, Sept. 22, 1977, p. 11.
79 *L'Osservatore Romano*, June 15, 1978, p. 3.
80 *L'Osservatore Romano*, Feb. 11, 1971, p. 12.
81 *L'Osservatore Romano*, Aug. 14, 1969, p. 8.
82 *L'Osservatore Romano*, May 27, 1971, p. 5.
83 *L'Osservatore Romano*, Dec. 2, 1971, p. 3.
84 *L'Osservatore Romano*, Jan. 20, 1972, p. 7.
85 *L'Osservatore Romano*, April 19, 1973, p. 9.
86 *L'Osservatore Romano*, Feb. 7, 1974, p. 6.
87 *L'Osservatore Romano*, Feb. 28, 1974, p. 3.
88 *L'Osservatore Romano*, Jan. 2, 1969, p. 12.
89 *L'Osservatore Romano*, May 8, 1969, p. 3.
90 *L'Osservatore Romano*, July 24, 1969, p. 12.
91 *L'Osservatore Romano*, Aug. 5, 1971, p. 12.
92 *L'Osservatore Romano*, Sept. 12, 1968, p. 1.
93 *L'Osservatore Romano*, July 24, 1975, p. 2.
94 *L'Osservatore Romano*, Oct. 7, 1976, p. 2.
95 *L'Osservatore Romano*, Oct. 28, 1976, p. 4.
96 *L'Osservatore Romano*, Dec. 16, 1976, p. 4.
97 *L'Osservatore Romano*, Dec. 30, 1976, p. 1.
98 *L'Osservatore Romano*, June 19, 1969, p. 6.
99 *L'Osservatore Romano*, Dec. 25, 1969, p. 3.
100 *L'Osservatore Romano*, Jan. 1, 1976, p. 11.
101 *L'Osservatore Romano*, Dec. 30, 1976, p. 1.
102 *The Oxford Illustrated Dictionary*, p. 425.
103 *L'Osservatore Romano*, Dec. 30, 1976, p. 5.
104 *L'Osservatore Romano*, Sept. 24, 1970, p. 2.
105 *The Papal Encyclicals*, Vol. 3 (1903-1939), p. 6.
106 Fr. Joaquin Arriaga, *The New Montinian Church*, pp. 394-395.
107 *L'Osservatore Romano*, Dec. 3, 1970, p. 10.
108 George Weigel, *Witness to Hope*, p. 238.
109 *The Reign of Mary*, Vol. XXVI, No. 81, p. 17.
110 Mark Fellows, *Fatima in Twilight*, Niagra Falls, NY: Marmion Publications, 2003, p. 193.
111 Mark Fellows, *Fatima in Twilight*, p. 193.
112 Mark Fellows, *Fatima in Twilight*, p. 206.
113 Nino Lo Bello, *The Incredible Book of Vatican Facts and Papal Curiosities*, Ligouri, MO: Liguori Pub., 1998, p. 195.
114 *The Reign of Mary*, Vol. XXVIII, No. 90, p. 8.
115 George Weigel, *Witness to Hope*, New York, NY: Harper Collins Publishers, Inc., 1999, p. 328.
116 Piers Compton, *The Broken Cross*, Cranbrook, Western Australia: Veritas Pub. Co. Ptd Ltd, 1984, p. 138.
117 *L'Osservatore Romano*, July. 13, 1972, p. 6.
118 Jean Guitton, "Nel segno dei Dodici," interview by Maurizio Blondet, *Avvenire*, Oct. 11, 1992.
119 *L'Osservatore Romano*, Dec. 19, 1968, p. 3.
120 *The Oxford Illustrated Dictionary*, Second Edition, p. 512.
121 *L'Osservatore Romano*, Nov. 23, 1972, p. 1.
122 *L'Osservatore Romano*, Jan. 7, 1971, p. 1.
123 *L'Osservatore Romano*, Sept. 26, 1974, p. 6.
124 *L'Osservatore Romano*, May 22, 1975, p. 3.
125 *L'Osservatore Romano*, May 18, 1969, p. 12.
126 *L'Osservatore Romano*, March 9, 1972, p. 2.
127 *L'Osservatore Romano*, July 12, 1973, p. 6.
128 *L'Osservatore Romano*, Oct. 9, 1969, p. 1.
129 Fr. Joaquin Arriaga, *The New Montinian Church*, p. 391.

15. The Scandals and Heresies of John Paul I

*"He could and did accept divorcees. **He also easily accepted others who were living in what the Church calls 'sin.'**"[1]* (Father Mario Senigaglia, secretary to John Paul I when he was "Patriarch" of Venice)

John Paul I (Albino Luciani)

The man who claimed to be pope between Paul VI and John Paul II for 33 days in 1978…

Albino Luciani (John Paul I) was born the son of a committed Socialist.[2] John XXIII personally consecrated Luciani a bishop on Dec. 27, 1958.[3] Luciani was named a "cardinal" by Paul VI.[4]

Luciani had formed friendships with many non-Catholics. Phillip Potter, Secretary of the World Council of Churches, had been his house guest. Other guests of his included Jews, Anglicans and Pentecostal "Christians." He had exchanged books and very friendly letters with Hans Kung.[5]

Luciani (John Paul I) had several times quoted Hans Kung favorably in his sermons.[6] (For those who don't know, Hans Kung denies the Divinity of Christ.) Luciani "was aware that a number of the lay Catholics he knew were members of various lodges (Masonic) – in much the same way that he had friends who were Communists."[7]

Luciani made a thorough study of "responsible parenthood" and consulted with many doctors and theologians. Like John XXIII and Paul VI, Luciani had studied the possibility of the "pill" being used as a "natural" method of regulating births.[8] Those who had fallen into using artificial contraception and then went to confession found Luciani "very compassionate."[9]

In April of 1968, Albino Luciani wrote and submitted a report to Paul VI recommending that the Catholic Church should approve the use of the anovulant pill developed by Professor Pincus. Luciani recommended that this pill should become the Catholic birth-control pill.[10] United Press International (UPI) discovered that Luciani had advocated a Vatican ruling in favor of artificial birth control. Italian newspapers also carried stories. To substantiate the story, these newspaper reports referred to the Luciani document which was sent to Paul VI by "Cardinal" Urbani of Venice, in which the strong recommendation in favor of the contraceptive pill had been made.[11]

Later on during his "papacy" – when he was "John Paul I" – Luciani often quoted from the pronouncements and encyclicals of Paul VI. Notably absent was any reference of John Paul I to *Humanae Vitae*.[12]

On April 13, 1968, Luciani talked to the people of Vittorio Veneto about this issue of birth control.[13] Luciani made the following observations:

> "It is easier today, given the confusion caused by the press, to find married persons who do not believe that they are sinning. If this should happen it may be opportune, under **the usual conditions, not to disturb them**...
>
> "Let us pray that the Lord may help the pope to resolve this question [whether Catholics should be able to use artificial birth control]. There has never perhaps been such a difficult question for the Church – both for the intrinsic difficulties and for the numerous implications affecting other problems, and for the acute way in which it is felt by the vast mass of the people."[14]

When Albino Luciani became "Patriarch" of Venice, his personal secretary was Father Mario Senigaglia. Senigaglia discussed with Luciani (with whom he had developed an almost father-son relationship) different moral cases involving parishioners. Luciani always approved the liberal view that Senigaglia took. Senigaglia said: "He was a very understanding man. Very many times I would hear him say to couples, 'We have made of sex the only sin, when in fact it is linked to human weakness and frailty and is therefore perhaps the least of sins.'"[15]

Senigaglia confirmed that Luciani's personal view on divorce would have surprised his critics: "He could and did accept divorcees. **He also easily accepted others who were living in what the Church calls 'sin.'**"[16]

He was also a promoter of false ecumenism. "**During his nine years there [as "Patriarch" of Venice] he hosted five ecumenical conferences, including the meeting of the Anglican-Roman Catholic International Commission** which introduced an agreed statement on authority in 1976..."[17]

LUCIANI ON A NEW INTERNATIONAL ORGANIZATION

> Luciani: "A gradual, controlled, and universal disarmament is possible only if an international organization with more efficient powers and possibilities for sanctions than the present United Nations comes into being..."[18]

LUCIANI ON CHRISTIANS

Quoting Gandhi, Luciani said: "I admire Christ but not Christians."[19] In an Easter sermon in 1976, Luciani made the following statement:

> "Thus Christian morality adopted the theory of the just war; thus the Church allowed the legalization of prostitution (even in the Papal States), while obviously it remained forbidden on a moral level."[20]

It is a blasphemy to assert that the Catholic Church would allow the legalization of prostitution.

As Patriarch of Venice, on December 24, 1977, Albino Luciani stated the following about the French Revolution: "...the intentions of those who had kindled insurrection and revolution at the beginning had been very good ones, and the slogan proclaimed was 'Liberty, Fraternity, Equality.'"[21]

Shortly before the 1978 conclave, Luciani was asked his opinion of the first test-tube baby, Louise Brown. Speaking of the test-tube baby and her parents, Luciani said: "Following the example of God, who desires and loves human life, I too send my best wishes to the baby. As for the parents, I have no right to judge them; subjectively, if they acted with good intentions and in good faith, **they may even have great merit before God for what they have decided and asked the doctors to do.**"[22]

Luciani had more than any other "cardinal" put into practice the spirit of John XXIII's Second Vatican Council.[23] John Paul I renounced the papal tiara and replaced the coronation ceremony with a simple celebration.[24] The tiara which was sold by Paul VI was now replaced by the pallium, a white woolen stole around the shoulders.[25]

John Paul I said the following in his first speech announcing the program for his "pontificate":

> 1) "The echo of its daily life gives witness that, despite all obstacles, it (the Church) lives in the heart of men, even those who do not share its truth or accept its message."[26]
> 2) "...**the Second Vatican Council (to whose teachings we wish to commit our total ministry**)..."[27]
> 3) "We wish to continue to put into effect the heritage of the Second Vatican Council. Its wise norms should be followed out and perfected."[28]
> 4) "...we place a priority on the revision of the two codes of canon law: that of the oriental tradition and that of the Latin tradition..."[29]
> 5) "**We wish to continue the ecumenical thrust**, which we consider a final directive from our immediate Predecessors."[30]

During the Inauguration of John Paul I, he said: "We greet also with reverence and affection <u>all the people in the world</u>. We regard them and love them as our brothers and sisters, since they are children of the same heavenly Father and <u>brothers and sisters in Christ Jesus</u>."[31]

Speaking to a friend about the schismatic Patriarch of Moscow, Nikodem, John Paul I called him "a real saint."[32]

In a letter to the new schismatic patriarch of Moscow about the death of the recently deceased schismatic patriarch of Moscow, John Paul I said:

> "...we express to Your Holiness and to the Holy Synod of the Russian Orthodox Church our feelings of keen sorrow. We assure you of our prayer for the repose of the soul of **this devoted servant of his Church** and constructor of the deepening relations between our Churches. **May God receive him into his joy and his peace.**"[33]

John Paul I calls the deceased Russian schismatic, who rejected Papal Infallibility and the last 13 dogmatic councils (among other Catholic teachings), a "devoted servant of his Church."

John Paul I "believed in greater power-sharing with the bishops throughout the world and planned to decentralize the Vatican structure."[34]

John Paul I said, "The Church should not have power nor possess wealth... **How beautiful it would have been if the pope had himself voluntarily renounced all temporal power!**"[35] John Paul I told the diplomatic corps that the Vatican renounced all claims to temporal power.[36]

> Pope Pius IX, *Nullis Certe Verbis* (# 1), Jan. 19, 1860:
> "...in kind letters sent to Us and by pastoral letters of other religious and learned writings,

you vehemently denounced the sacrilegious attacks made on the civil power of the Roman Church. And defending constantly this dominion, you proclaimed and taught that **God gave the civil power to the Roman Pontiff**, so that he, never subject to any power, might exercise in full liberty and without any impediment the supreme task of the apostolic ministry divinely committed to him by Christ our Lord."[37]

John Paul I often spoke of Paul VI with admiration and affection: "He was a great pope and suffered much. He was not understood…"[38]

John Paul I also spoke of God as "mother."

> John Paul I, *Angelus Message*, Sept. 10, 1978: "He (God) is our father; **even more he is our mother.**"[39]

In his *General Audience* on September 13, 1978, John Paul I spoke on the subject of immutable truths and said:

> "Those are the truths: we must walk along the way of these truths, understanding them more and more, bringing ourselves up-to-date, proposing them in a form suited to the times. Pope Paul too had the same thought."[40]

In September 1978, Luciani was heard in the papal apartments talking to his Secretary of State, "Cardinal" Villot: "I will be happy to talk to this United States delegation on the issue. To my mind we cannot leave the situation as it currently stands." The "issue" was world population. The "situation" was *Humanae Vitae*.[41]

At the top of his list of priorities of reform and change was radically altering the Vatican's relationship with capitalism and alleviating what he believed was the suffering that had stemmed directly from *Humanae Vitae*.[42] [We want to make it clear that we are not suggesting that *Humanae Vitae* was a good document. Not at all. *Humanae Vitae* taught that couples could use "natural" birth control and have no children at all, as is covered in this book. The point is that *Humanae Vitae* did denounce artificial contraception, and John Paul I was very opposed to it for that reason.]

In May of 1978, Luciani had been invited to attend and speak at an international congress being held in Milan on June 21-22. The main purpose of the congress was to celebrate the upcoming anniversary of the encyclical *Humanae Vitae*. Luciani had let it be known that he would not speak at the congress and that he would not attend.[43]

On September 19, 1978, John Paul I had a meeting with his Secretary of State "Cardinal" Villot. John Paul I stated:

> "Eminence, we have been discussing birth control for about forty-five minutes. If the information I have been given, the various statistics, if that information is accurate, then during the period of time we have been talking, over one thousand children under the age of five have died of malnutrition. During the next forty-five minutes while you and I look forward with anticipation to our next meal, a further thousand children will die of malnutrition. By this time tomorrow thirty thousand children who at this moment are alive, will be dead – of malnutrition. God does not always provide."[44]

The Vatican claimed that John Paul I died of a massive heart attack around 11p.m. on September 28, 1978.[45]

We have proven that John Paul I was a manifest heretic who, among other things, fully approved of the religious indifferentism and false ecumenism of the Second Vatican Council. Since he was a heretic, he could not have been a validly elected pope. He was a non-Catholic antipope.

Endnotes for Section 15:

[1] David Yallop, *In God's Name (An investigation into the Murder of John Paul I)*, Bantam Books, 1984, pp. 60-61.
[2] David Yallop, *In God's Name*, p. 60.
[3] Raymond and Lauretta Seabeck, *The Smiling Pope*, Huntington, IN: Our Sunday Visitor Publishing, 2004, p. 27.
[4] Raymond and Lauretta Seabeck, *The Smiling Pope*, p. 58.
[5] David Yallop, *In God's Name*, pp. 86, 190.
[6] David Yallop, *In God's Name*, p. 190.
[7] David Yallop, *In God's Name*, p. 201.
[8] Raymond and Lauretta Seabeck, *The Smiling Pope*, p. 35.
[9] Raymond and Lauretta Seabeck, *The Smiling Pope*, p. 36.
[10] David Yallop, *In God's Name*, p. 32.
[11] David Yallop, *In God's Name*, p. 191.
[12] David Yallop, *In God's Name*, p. 192.
[13] David Yallop, *In God's Name*, p. 32.
[14] David Yallop, *In God's Name*, p. 33.
[15] David Yallop, *In God's Name*, p. 61.
[16] David Yallop, *In God's Name*, pp. 60-61.
[17] J.N.D. Kelly, *Oxford Dictionary of Popes*, Oxford University Press, 2005, p. 325.
[18] David Yallop, *In God's Name*, p. 62.
[19] David Yallop, *In God's Name*, p. 65.
[20] David Yallop, *In God's Name*, p. 60.
[21] Raymond and Lauretta Seabeck, *The Smiling Pope*, p. 120.
[22] David Yallop, *In God's Name*, p. 233.
[23] David Yallop, *In God's Name*, p. 90.
[24] Luigi Accattoli, *When A Pope Asks Forgiveness*, New York: Alba House and Daughters of St. Paul, 1998, p. 37.
[25] David Yallop, *In God's Name*, p. 185.
[26] *L' Osservatore Romano* (The Vatican's Newspaper), Aug. 31, 1978, p. 6.
[27] *L' Osservatore Romano*, Aug. 31, 1978, p. 6.
[28] *L' Osservatore Romano*, Aug. 31, 1978, p. 6.
[29] *L' Osservatore Romano*, Aug. 31, 1978, p. 6.
[30] *L' Osservatore Romano*, Aug. 31, 1978, p. 6.
[31] *L' Osservatore Romano*, Sept. 7, 1978, p. 1.
[32] Raymond and Lauretta Seabeck, *The Smiling Pope*, p. 64.
[33] *L' Osservatore Romano*, Sept. 14, 1978, p. 2.
[34] David Yallop, *In God's Name*, p. 189.
[35] Luigi Accattoli, *When A Pope Asks Forgiveness*, p. 44.
[36] David Yallop, *In God's Name*, p. 210.
[37] *The Papal Encyclicals*, Vol. 1 (1740-1878), p. 359.
[38] Raymond and Lauretta Seabeck, *The Smiling Pope*, p. 44.
[39] *L' Osservatore Romano*, September 21, 1978, p. 2.
[40] *L' Osservatore Romano*, Sept. 21, 1978, p. 1.
[41] David Yallop, *In God's Name*, p. 192,193.
[42] David Yallop, *In God's Name*, p. 194.
[43] David Yallop, *In God's Name*, p. 192.
[44] David Yallop, *In God's Name*, p. 196.
[45] Raymond and Lauretta Seabeck, *The Smiling Pope*, p. 70.

END NOTES - PAGE 224

16. The Heresies of John Paul II, the most traveled man in history and perhaps the most heretical

Jewish maestro Gilbert Levine, telling CNN's Larry King about John Paul II:
"KING: **The pope congratulated your children's bar mitzvahs?**
"LEVINE: **Not only congratulate us, he sent us a menorah.**
"KING: **He sent you a menorah?**
"LEVINE: **He gave it to us,** actually, didn't send it. **Actually gave us a menorah.** I think it's from the 16th century in Prague. It's the most beautiful menorah. **He sent a letter on the occasion of each of my son's bar mitzvahs.** He also had the cardinal in charge of Catholic/Jewish relations send a letter that was read out in my Orthodox shul on the occasion of my son's recent bar mitzvah, and the rabbi read it as if it were from a rabbi."[1]

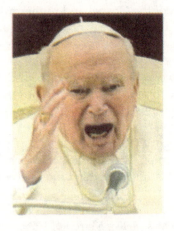

Karol Wojtyla (John Paul II) claimed to be the pope from 1978-2005

THE HERESIES OF JOHN PAUL II

John Paul II taught universal salvation, that all men will be saved

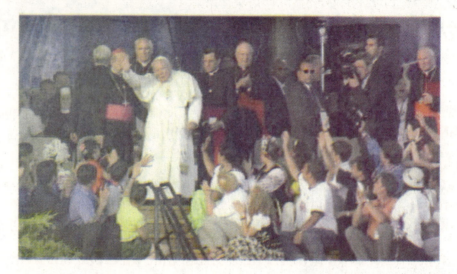

The only difficulty in discussing the heresies of John Paul II is deciding where to begin. His heresies are so numerous that one is almost overwhelmed with the decision of where to start. A good place to begin is his consistent teaching of universal salvation. The idea that all men are saved is contrary to the clear words of the Gospel and numerous Catholic dogmas, especially the dogmas that Outside the Catholic Church there is no salvation and that all who die in original sin or mortal sin cannot be saved.

> Pope Gregory X, *2nd Council of Lyons*, 1274, ex cathedra:
> "The souls of those who die in mortal sin or with original sin only... immediately descend into Hell, yet to be punished with different punishments."[2]

However, John Paul II held and taught that in the Incarnation, the Son of God united Himself with every man in an unbreakable union, which made it impossible, according to him, for anyone to go to Hell. John Paul II explicitly taught that this union between Christ and each man lasts forever.

> John Paul II, *Redemptor Hominis* (# 13), March 4, 1979:
> "We are dealing with each man, for each one is included in the mystery of the Redemption and with each one Christ has united Himself <u>forever</u> through this mystery."[3]

> John Paul II, *Redemptoris Missio* (# 4), Dec. 7, 1990:
> "The Redemption event brings salvation to all, 'for each one is included in the mystery of the Redemption and with each one *Christ has united himself <u>forever</u>* through this mystery.'"[4]

> John Paul II, *Centesimus Annus* (# 53):
> "We are not dealing here with man in the 'abstract,' but with the real, 'concrete,' 'historical' man. We are dealing with *each individual*, since each one is included in the mystery of the Redemption and *through this mystery Christ has united himself with each one <u>forever</u>*."[5]

Notice the word "forever" in all three of these quotations. Yes, in three different encyclicals, John Paul II bluntly asserts that every man is united with Christ <u>forever</u>. This means that all men are saved. Hell is eternal separation from God, but no one is ever separated from God according to John Paul II. Everyone is united with God forever. This is universal salvation.

There are many other quotations we could bring forward to prove that John Paul II taught that all men are saved. For example, in 1985, John Paul II explained how the redemptive Blood of Christ is not merely available to all (which is true), but that it actually reaches all and <u>saves all</u>.

> John Paul II, *Homily*, June 6, 1985:
> "The Eucharist is the sacrament of the covenant of the Body and Blood of Christ, of the covenant which is eternal. This is the covenant which embraces all. **This Blood reaches all and saves all**."[6]

In contrast with this, the dogmatic teaching of the Catholic Church affirms that the Blood of Christ does not reach all or save all.

> Pope Paul III, *Council of Trent*, Sess. 6, *ex cathedra*: "But although Christ died for all, yet not all receive the benefit of His death, but those <u>only</u> to whom <u>the merit of His Passion</u> is communicated."[7]

Only those who are freed from original sin by Baptism, and united to Him through the sacraments and the true faith, receive the benefit of Christ's death.

> John Paul II, *Homily*, April 27, 1980:
> "... Jesus makes us, in Himself, once more sons of His Eternal Father. **He obtains, once and for all, the salvation of man: of each man and of all**..."[8]

> John Paul II, *General Audience*, Dec. 27, 1978:
> "Jesus is the Second Person of the Holy Trinity become a man; and therefore in Jesus, human nature and therefore <u>**the whole of humanity, is redeemed, saved, ennobled to the extent of participating in 'divine life' by means of Grace**</u>."[9]

Here John Paul II explains that the whole of humanity has been saved and is participating in the divine life. The phrase "participating in the divine life" refers to the state of justification or the state of sanctifying grace. By saying that all of humanity participates in the divine life, John Paul II is saying that all of humanity is in the state of grace! **That means that no one is in mortal sin or original sin.**

With a doctrine such as this, who wouldn't be loved by the world? John Paul II appealed to, and was loved by the masses, because he accepted everyone's religion and taught that everyone is united with Christ no matter what they believed or did. This religious indifferentism characterized his anti-pontificate.

John Paul II taught that the Holy Ghost is responsible for non-Christian Religions

Besides his incredible doctrine of universal salvation and universal justification, there are many other heresies from John Paul II for us to examine. Of particular note is his teaching on the Third Person of the Blessed Trinity, the Holy Ghost. What John Paul II taught about the Holy Ghost was so blasphemous and heretical that it was arguably his worst heresy.

> John Paul II, *Redemptor Hominis* (# 6), March 4, 1979:
> "Does it not sometimes happen that ***the firm belief of the followers of the non-Christian religions – a belief that is also an effect of the Spirit of truth*** operating outside the visible confines of the Mystical Body…"[10]

John Paul II says that the firm belief of the followers of non-Christian religions proceeds from the Holy Spirit, the Spirit of Truth. Since we know from Sacred Scripture and Catholic teaching that Satan is the author of all non-Christian religions, what is being stated here by John Paul II is that the Holy Spirit, the Spirit of Truth, is actually the spirit of lies: Satan. This is an unbelievable blasphemy against God.

Scripture and Tradition teach us that non-Christian religions belong to the devil, and the "gods" they worship are actually demons.

> Psalm 95:5- "For all the gods of the Gentiles are devils…"

> 1 Cor. 10:20- "But the things which the heathens sacrifice, they sacrifice to devils, and not to God. And I would not that you should be made partakers with devils."

Since John Paul II taught that belief in these religions is a result of the Spirit of Truth, that is why he repeatedly praised, promoted and even prayed with the members and leaders of non-Christian religions.

John Paul II with African Animists (witch doctors), more on this later

John Paul II, *Redemptoris Missio* (# 29), Dec. 7, 1990: "**The Church's relationship with other religions is dictated by a twofold respect:** 'Respect for man in his quest for answers to the deepest questions of his life, **and respect for the action of the Spirit in man.**'"11

Here John Paul II says that respect for non-Christian religions is dictated by respect for the action of the Spirit in man. This clearly means that the Spirit is responsible for these non-Christian religions, which again means that the Holy Spirit is to be understood as the spirit of lies: Satan.

John Paul II, *Redemptoris Missio* (# 56), Dec. 7, 1990:
"**Other religions constitute a positive challenge for the Church: they stimulate her both to discover** and acknowledge **the signs of Christ's presence and of the working of the Spirit**."12

John Paul II states that other religions stimulate us to discover the presence and the working of the Spirit. This means that non-Christian religions are a work of the Spirit – the Holy Spirit – which again equates the Spirit of Truth with the spirit of lies: Satan.

John Paul II taught and practiced complete Religious Indifferentism

Pope Pius IX, *Qui Pluribus* (# 15), Nov. 9, 1846:
"**Also perverse is that shocking theory that it makes no difference to which religion one belongs, a theory greatly at variance even with reason**. By means of this theory, those crafty men remove all distinction between virtue and vice, truth and error, honorable and vile action. They pretend that men can gain eternal salvation by the practice of any religion, **as if there could ever be any sharing between justice and iniquity, any collaboration between light and darkness, or any agreement between Christ and Belial**."13

The Heresies of John Paul II   174

John Paul II's religious indifferentism was perhaps the most common characteristic of his volumes of writings and speeches. He constantly praised and esteemed non-Christian religions, thereby denying the Most Holy Trinity and the necessity of believing in the one true Catholic religion, while making a mockery of the deaths of the martyrs.

> John Paul II, *Address at Airport in Korea*, May 3, 1984: "**Yours is a proud and sturdy people**... <u>**bearing splendid fruits in art, religion**</u>, **and human living. Your ancestors embraced such overwhelming spiritual worlds as Confucianism and Buddhism, yet made them truly their own,** *enhanced them*, **lived them and <u>even</u> transmitted them to others.** Wonhyo and Sosan... eloquently express this *feat*."[14]

The word "feat" means an extraordinary act. So John Paul II says that the false religions Buddhism and Confucianism are <u>splendid fruits in religion</u>, and that it was an extraordinary act that the Koreans transmitted these religions of Satan to others!

> Pope Gregory XVI, *Probe Nostis* (# 6), Sept. 18, 1840:
> "We are thankful for the success of apostolic missions in America, the Indies, and other <u>faithless</u> lands... **They search out those who sit in darkness and the shadow of death** to summon them to the light and life of the Catholic religion... **At length they snatch them from the Devil's rule**, by the bath of regeneration and promote them to the freedom of God's adopted sons."[15]

John Paul II at the Buddhist Temple

In his second Asian journey in 1984, John Paul II visited the Buddhist Temple. Before reaching the Temple, he expressed how anxious he was to meet "His Holiness, the supreme Buddhist Patriarch in the Temple." A few days before going to the Buddhist Temple, John Paul II also said:

> John Paul II, May 6, 1984: "...the world looks to Korea with particular interest. For the Korean people throughout history have sought, in the great ethical and religious visions of Buddhism and Confucianism, the path to renewal of self... <u>**May I address a particular greeting to the members of the Buddhist tradition as they prepare to celebrate the festivity of the Coming of the Lord Buddha?**</u> May your rejoicing be complete and your joy fulfilled."[16]

John Paul II then went into the temple of idolatry and bowed to the Buddhist Patriarch who stood in front of a gigantic statue of Buddha. This constitutes an act of apostasy.

The Heresies of John Paul II

John Paul II in the Buddhist Temple

John Paul II, *General Audience*, Jan. 11, 1995:
"**I gladly take this occasion to <u>assure</u> those who follow the Buddhist religion of my *deep* respect and sincere esteem.**"[17]

Pope Leo XIII, Dec. 8, 1892:
"Everyone should avoid familiarity or friendship with anyone suspected of belonging to masonry or to affiliated groups. Know them by their fruits and avoid them. **Every familiarity should be avoided, not only with those impious libertines who openly promote the character of the sect, <u>but also with those who hide under the mask of universal tolerance, respect for all religions</u>**..."[18]

John Paul II, *Homily*, April 12, 1997:
"… the Church, which seeks only to be able freely to preach … **with <u>respect for… every religion</u>.**"[19]

John Paul II received the mark of the adorers of Shiva

On Feb. 2, 1986, John Paul II received on his forehead the *Tilac* or *Tika*, the red powdery paste of the Hindus, the sign of recognition of the adorers of Shiva. This is total idolatry and apostasy.

John Paul II venerated the Hindu Gandhi

In March of 1986, John Paul II went to New Delhi, India, the place where the Hindu Mahatma Gandhi was incinerated. Mahatma Gandhi was a pagan and an idolater who worshipped false gods.

John Paul II took off his shoes before Gandhi's monument and stated: "Today as a pilgrim of peace, I have come here to pay homage to Mahatma Gandhi, **hero of humanity**."[20]

An idolater and a pagan was a "hero of humanity," according to John Paul II.

The Heresies of John Paul II

As we see here, John Paul II also threw flowers on Gandhi's tomb to honor and commemorate this pagan. St. Thomas Aquinas explains that just as there are heretical statements, there are heretical and apostate actions.

> St. Thomas Aquinas, *Summa Theologica*, Pt. I-II, Q. 103, A. 4: "All ceremonies are professions of faith, in which the interior worship of God consists. **Now man can make profession of his inward faith, by deeds as well as by words**: and in either profession, if he make a false declaration, he sins mortally."[21]

St. Thomas even gives us an example:

> St. Thomas Aquinas, *Summa Thelogica*, Pt. II-II, Q. 12, A. 1, Obj. 2: "...if anyone were to... worship at the tomb of Mahomet, he would be deemed an apostate."[22]

One can manifest his apostasy by words or by deeds. By what he *did*, in addition to what he said, John Paul II manifested the equivalent of worshipping at the tomb of Mahomet. He venerated a Hindu.

John Paul II's Apostasy in Assisi

On Oct. 27, 1986, John Paul II invited the major leaders of all the false religions of the world to come to Assisi, Italy for a World Day of Prayer for Peace. John Paul II prayed with over 100 different religious leaders of various false religions, thereby repudiating the teaching of Scripture and the 2000-year teaching of the Catholic Church which outlaws such prayer with false religions.

The entire day of prayer with the pagans, infidels and heretics was John Paul II's idea. During this meeting the Dalai Lama placed a Buddhist statue on the tabernacle in the church of St. Francis.

The Statue of Buddha on the Tabernacle at Assisi

The Heresies of John Paul II

Among the various false religious leaders at Assisi there were rabbis, Islamic muftis, Buddhist monks, Shintoists, assorted Protestant ministers, Animists, Jainists and others.

During the meeting, a member of each false religion came forward and offered a prayer for peace – blasphemous prayers, for instance, as the Hindu prayer said: "*Peace be on all gods*." (The Animist leader prayed to the "Great Thumb.") But their gods are devils, as we saw above, **so peace was being prayed for all the devils** (who created these false religions) **at the Vatican-sponsored World Day of Prayer for Peace!** The Vatican II religion wants you to be in communion with devils.

In 1928, Pope Pius XI authoritatively condemned this inter-religious activity and denounced it as apostasy from the true Faith.

> Pope Pius XI, *Mortalium Animos* (# 2), Jan. 6, 1928: "For which reason conventions, meetings and addresses are frequently arranged by these persons, at which a large number of listeners are present, and at which all without distinction are invited to join in the discussion, both infidels of every kind, and Christians, even those who have unhappily fallen away from Christ or who with obstinacy and pertinacity deny His divine nature and mission. Certainly such attempts can nowise be approved by Catholics, founded as they are on that false opinion which considers all religions to be more or less good and praiseworthy, since they all in different ways manifest and signify that sense which is inborn in us all, and by which we are led to the obedient acknowledgment of His rule. **Not only are those who hold this opinion in error and deceived, but also in distorting the idea of true religion they reject it**, and little by little, turn aside to naturalism and atheism, as it is called; from which it clearly follows that one who supports those who hold these theories and attempt to realize them, is altogether abandoning the divinely revealed religion."

> Pope Pius XI, *Mortalium Animos* (# 10): "So, Venerable Brethren, it is clear why **this Apostolic See has never allowed its subjects to take part in the assemblies of non-Catholics…**"[23]

> John Paul II, *Angelus Address*, Oct. 12, 1986: "In a few days we shall go to Assisi, representatives of the Catholic Church, of other Christian Churches and ecclesial communities, and of the great religions of the world… I issued this invitation to 'believers of all religions.'"[24]

> John Paul II, *Redemptoris Missio* (# 55), Dec. 7, 1990:
> "God… **does not fail to make himself present in many ways**, not only to individuals but also to entire peoples through **their spiritual riches, of which their religions are the main and essential expression**…"[25]

Here again we find a clear expression of John Paul II's apostasy. He says that God makes Himself present through the **spiritual riches** of peoples, of which **their religions are the main expression**. This means that God makes Himself present to peoples through non-Christian religions, which means that non-Christian religions are true and inspired by God.

> Pope Pius VIII, May 24, 1829: "Against these experienced sophists **the people must be taught that the profession of the Catholic faith is uniquely true**, as the apostle proclaims: one Lord, one faith, one baptism."[26]

John Paul II, *Address*, May 22, 2002: "Praise to you, followers of Islam… Praise to you, Jewish people… Praise especially to you, Orthodox Church…"[27]

Pope Gregory XVI, *Mirari Vos* (# 13), Aug. 15, 1832: "They should consider the testimony of Christ Himself that 'those who are not with Christ are against Him,' and that they disperse unhappily who do not gather with Him. Therefore, '**without a doubt, they will perish forever, unless they hold the Catholic faith** whole and inviolate.'"[28]

John Paul II, *Redemptoris Missio* (#10), Dec. 7, 1990: "The universality of salvation means that it is granted not only to those who explicitly believe in Christ and have entered the Church."[29]

Pope Eugene IV, *Council of Florence*, dogmatic Athanasian Creed, 1439: "Whoever wishes to be saved, needs above all to hold the Catholic faith; unless each one preserves this whole and inviolate, he will without a doubt perish in eternity… **But it is necessary for eternal salvation that he faithfully believe also in the incarnation of our Lord Jesus Christ…**"[30]

John Paul II's other ecumenical meetings

John Paul II continued with his wild program of apostasy, totally condemned by the teaching of the Catholic Church, after the Assisi event. John Paul II sponsored pagan prayer meetings at Kyoto (1987), Rome (1988), Warsaw (1989), Bari (1990), and Malta (1991), as well as numerous meetings after 1991.

John Paul II being "blessed" in a pagan ritual by an Indian Shaman in 1987[31]

There was the outrageous pagan prayer meeting in 1999, which was officially dubbed "The Pan-Christian Encounter," at which a large gathering of false religions came to the Vatican at the request of John Paul II (more on this in a bit).

John Paul II prayed with African Animists

On August 8, 1985, John Paul II prayed with African Animists (witch doctors). John Paul II recalled the meeting:

> "Particularly noteworthy was the prayer meeting at the sanctuary of Our Lady of Mercy at Lake Togo **where, for the first time, I also prayed with a group of Animists**."[32]

It has been stated that while in Togo he actually paid homage to the sacred snakes.

In Cotonou, Africa on Feb. 4, 1993, chanting girls treated John Paul II to a "trance inducing" voodoo dance.

John Paul II has also taken part in many events, both in Rome and abroad, where a native pagan ritual is included. These rituals spring from cultures which are entirely demonic and satanic in every aspect of their organized religious practices, yet were included in many of John Paul II's liturgical events.

Above: John Paul II's "Mass" in 2002 in Mexico City, which incorporated the customs of the demonic Aztec culture. Indians danced before the altar wearing headdresses and breastplates and some left their midriffs exposed. As they performed, the snake-like hiss of rattles and the beating of tom-toms could be heard. John Paul II himself was actually the recipient of a pagan "purification" ritual which a woman performed.

The "Pan-Christian" Encounter: John Paul II's Apostate Prayer Meeting in 1999

Pictured above is John Paul II, surrounded by an assorted group of pagans and idolaters, including one half-dressed, on Nov. 7, 1999 – at another one of his countless apostate interreligious prayer meetings. Notice the masked pagan just behind John Paul II on our left and his right. John Paul II praised them for esteemed them their false religions of the Devil. This is nothing other than a general occultism.

This meeting was called the "Pan-Christian Encounter." This is interesting considering that, in his encyclical *Mortalium Animos*, Pope Pius XI described the heretics who promoted religious indifferentism as "*These Pan-Christians…*"[33] Some of the things that occurred during John Paul II's October 1999 pan-religious meeting included: an American Indian pivoting in the center of St. Peter's Square at sunset "blessing the four corners of the Earth," and Muslims who had spread out newspaper at the Vatican kneeling toward Mecca and praying.[34]

Pope Leo X, *Fifth Lateran Council*, Session 9, May 5, 1514:
"Sorcery, by means of enchantments, divinations, superstitions and the invoking of demons, is prohibited by both civil laws and the sanctions of the sacred canons."[35]

John Paul II's Assisi II Prayer-Meeting with False Religions– another apostate prayer meeting in 2002

Most recently there was the spectacle of Assisi 2002. On Jan. 24, 2002, John Paul II held another pagan prayer meeting in the city of Assisi, Italy, a repeat of the abominable event that took place in 1986. However, this Assisi meeting may have been even worse.

During the Assisi II prayer meeting, the representative of every false religion involved was allowed to come to the pulpit and give a sermon on world peace. In the presence of John Paul II, a voodoo high priest came to the pulpit outside the Basilica of St. Francis and gave the voodoo prescription for world peace. (Voodooists, remember, are witchdoctors.) Therefore, by John Paul II's arrangement, from a pulpit outside the historic Basilica of St. Francis, a witchdoctor was allowed to give a sermon and provide his prescription for world peace! This would involve slitting the throats of goats, chickens, doves and pigeons, and draining their blood from their arteries.

The Hindu woman told the entire crowd that everyone is God, as John Paul II looked on. After the Jew, the Buddhist, the Muslim, the Hindu, the witchdoctor and the rest were finished preaching, the various false religious leaders broke up into different rooms to pray to their false gods.

> **4. Invitation to Prayer:**
> The **Holy Father** invites all present to proceed to their respective places for prayer.
>
> ## II. Prayer in different places
>
> ### 1. Access to the different places of prayer:
>
> A. Lower Basilica: *Christians*
>
> B. Sacred Convent:
>
> Room A: *Islam*
> Room B: *Buddhism*
> Room C: *Sikhism*
> Room D: *African Traditional Religions*
> Room E: *Hinduism*
> Room F: *Tenrikyo*
> Room G: *Shintoism*
> Room H: *Judaism*
> Room I: *Zoroastrianism, Janinism, and Confucianism*

John Paul II had it arranged in advance that each false religion was given a separate room in which to worship the Devil.

All of the crucifixes were removed, and the crucifixes which could not be removed were covered. John Paul II made sure that the infidels, witchdoctors and pagans saw no sign of Jesus Christ.

The Muslims needed a room which faced East toward Mecca, and it was given to them. The Zoroastrians needed a room with a window, so that the smoke from the wood chips that they burned to the Devil could exit through it – and it was given to them. The Jews wanted a room that had never before been blessed; in other words, a room that had never been blessed in the name of Jesus Christ, and John Paul II provided them with one. Greater abomination, blasphemy and rejection of the true God almost cannot be imagined.

> *The Council of Elvira*, A.D. 305: "**It has been decreed that those who in adult age after receiving Baptism shall go into the pagan temples to worship idols, which is a deadly crime and the height of wickedness,** shall not be admitted to communion even at death."[36]

As we see from this regional council, in the early Church going into the pagan temple (which John Paul II did in Thailand) to worship idols was considered the height of wickedness. It represented such apostasy from the Faith that those *who even repented* of it were only admitted to confession (not Communion). If going into the pagan temple was considered such severe apostasy, **what would they say about a purported leader of the Church who turns the Catholic churches themselves into pagan temples so that the pagans can worship false gods in them?** They would undoubtedly consider it the height of apostasy.

Pope Pius XI, *Ad Salutem* (# 27), April 20, 1930: "...all the compulsion and folly, all the outrages and lust, introduced into man's life by the demons through the worship of false gods."[37]

John Paul II's Apostasy with the Muslims

On May 14, 1999, John Paul II bowed to and kissed the Koran. The Koran is the Muslims' holy book which blasphemes the Most Holy Trinity and denies the Divinity of Jesus Christ. To revere the holy book of a false religion has always been considered an act of apostasy – a complete rejection of the true religion. This act alone made John Paul II an apostate; for it is equivalent to worshipping at the tomb of Mahomet, which St. Thomas points out would make one an apostate.

St. Thomas Aquinas, *Summa Theologica*, Pt. II, Q. 12, A. 1, Obj. 2: "... if anyone were to... worship at the tomb of Mahomet, he would be deemed an apostate."

During his visit to Germany on Nov. 17, 1980, John Paul II encouraged the Muslims to "*Live your faith also in a foreign land...*"[38]

In Feb. of 2000, John Paul II met with the Islamic "Grand Sheikh" Mohammed. John Paul II committed another act of apostasy in his speech to the Muslims.

John Paul II, Message to "Grand Sheikh Mohammed," Feb. 24, 2000: "Islam is a religion. Christianity is a religion. Islam has become a culture. Christianity has become also a culture... I thank your university, the biggest center of Islamic culture. **I thank those who are developing Islamic culture**..."[39]

John Paul II thanked those who develop Islamic culture! He thanked the infidels for developing a culture which denies Jesus Christ, the Trinity and the Catholic Faith on a massive scale, and keeps hundreds of millions in the darkness of the Devil. Of all the evil things in the world that one can think of, Islamic culture probably ranks in the top five of the most evil.

Pope Callixtus III: "I vow to... exalt the true Faith, and to extirpate **the diabolical sect of the reprobate and faithless Mahomet** [Islam] in the East."[40]

The middle ages were a constant spiritual and physical battle between the Christian West and the Islamic hordes. This statement of John Paul II constitutes a rejection of Jesus Christ and formal apostasy. No Catholic would ever make such a statement even one time.

John Paul II asked St. John the Baptist to protect Islam!

On March 21st, 2000, John Paul II asked St. John the Baptist to protect Islam (the religion of the Muslims), which denies Christ and the Trinity, and keeps hundreds of millions of souls in the darkness of the Devil.

> John Paul II, March 21, 2000:
> "**May Saint John the Baptist protect Islam and all the people of Jordan...**"[41]

This is to ask St. John to protect the denial of Christ and the damnation of souls.

On April 12, 2000, John Paul II met with the King of Morocco, a descendant of the false prophet of Islam, Muhammad. John Paul II asked him, "You are a descendant of the Prophet, aren't you?"[42]

John Paul II's Apostasy in the Mosque

On May 6, 2001, John Paul II culminated his years-worth of apostasy with the Muslims by traveling to and attending the "Great Umayyad Mosque" of Damascus. While in the mosque, John Paul II actually took off his shoes out of reverence for the temple of infidelity.

The Heresies of John Paul II   188

In the upper left, we see John Paul II entering "Great Umayyad Mosque" of Damascus on May 6, 2001. In the other photos, we see him in the mosque with the infidel Grand Mufti, Sheikh Ahmad Kfutaro. While in the mosque, John Paul II was also seated in a chair identical to that of the infidel Grand Mufti. Here is the statement that John Paul II made to the Muslims that day:

> John Paul II, *Speech to the Muslims from the Mosque*, May 6, 2001: "It is in mosques and churches that the Muslim and Christian communities shape their religious identity... What sense of identity is instilled in young Christians and young Muslims in our churches and mosques? **It is my ardent hope that Muslim and Christian religious leaders and teachers will present <u>our two great communities in respectful dialogue</u>,** never more as communities in conflict."[43]

It's very interesting to note that the "Omayyad" caliphate (a line of Muslim rulers), after which that particular mosque that John Paul II attended is named, was a line of Muslim rulers that was hugely involved in waging war on Catholic Spain in the 700-year war of Muslims vs. Christians in Spain.

> "Abdurrahman **the last survivor of the Omayyads had become the ruler of Muslim Spain about the time that Fruela became the ruler of Christian Spain; by 759 the two kings clashed in Galicia.**"[44]

The fact that the mosque he attended was named after a group that is so representative of anti-Christianity just adds insult to his apostasy. The blood of all the faithful Catholics who died fighting the Omayyads for the very survival of Christian Spain cries out against him.

> Apocalypse 17:6- "**And I saw the woman drunk with the blood of the saints, and with the blood of the martyrs of Jesus.** And I wondered when I had seen her…"

John Paul II teaches that Muslims and Catholics Have the Same God

Earlier in the book, we covered Vatican II's heretical teaching that Catholics and Muslims together worship the one true God. John Paul II repeated this heresy of Vatican II countless times.

> John Paul II, *Encyclical On Social Concerns* (# 47), Dec. 30, 1987:
> "… **Muslims who, like us, believe in the just and merciful God.**"[45]

> John Paul II, *Homily*, Oct. 13, 1989:
> "… *the followers of Islam* who believe in the same good and just God."[46]

> John Paul II, *Homily*, Jan. 28, 1990:
> "… **our Muslim brothers** and sisters… **who worship as we do the one and merciful God.**"[47]

> John Paul II, *General Audience*, May 16, 2001:
> "… **the believers of Islam, to whom we are united by the adoration of the one God.**"[48]

> John Paul II, *General Audience*, May 5, 1999:
> "Today I would like to repeat what I said to young Muslims some years ago in Casablanca: '**We believe in the same God**…'"[49]

This is blasphemy and apostasy. Muslims reject the Most Holy Trinity. They don't worship the one true God. By asserting that Muslims and Catholics believe in the same God over and over again, John Paul II denied the Most Holy Trinity over and over again. Furthermore, one is struck by the specificity with which John Paul II (just like Vatican II) denied Jesus Christ in many of these quotations. For example:

> John Paul II, *New Catechism* (paragraph 841):
> "… Muslims; these profess to hold the faith of Abraham, and together with us they adore the one, merciful God, **mankind's judge on the last day**."[50]

Here we find John Paul II's catechism teaching that the Muslims' god (who is not Jesus Christ) will judge mankind on the last day. This means Jesus Christ will not judge mankind on the last day, but rather the god whom the Muslims worship will. This is a denial of the Second Coming of Jesus Christ to judge the living and the dead.

> Pope St. Damasus I, *Council of Rome*, 382, Can. 15:
> "If anyone does not say that **He** *Jesus Christ*… **will come to judge the living and the dead, he is a heretic.**"[51]

John Paul II's Apostasy with the Jews

On April 13, 1986, John Paul II traveled to the Jewish Synagogue in Rome.

John Paul II arriving at the Jewish Synagogue, April 13, 1986

Here we see John Paul II arriving at the Jewish Synagogue in Rome in 1986, where he took part in a Jewish worship service. In taking part in a Jewish worship service, John Paul II committed a public act of apostasy, and showed again that he was a manifest heretic and an apostate. Notice that John Paul II and the rabbi greeted each other as if they were long-lost best friends. During his stay at the synagogue, John Paul II bowed his head as the Jews prayed for the coming of their "Messiah."

The Heresies of John Paul II

John Paul II in the Synagogue of the Jews

This incredible act of apostasy by John Paul II was directly connected to his heretical teaching that the Old Covenant is still in force. The Catholic Church teaches that with the coming of Jesus Christ and the promulgation of the Gospel, the Old Covenant (that is, the agreement made between God and the Jews through the mediation of Moses) ceased, and was replaced with the New Covenant of Our Lord Jesus Christ. It's true that some aspects of the Old Covenant are still valid because they are included in the New and Eternal Covenant of Jesus Christ, such as the Ten Commandments; but the Old Covenant itself (the agreement between God and the Jewish people) ceased with the coming of the Messiah. Therefore, to say that the Old Covenant is still valid is to assert that Judaism is a true religion and that Jesus Christ is not really the Messiah. It is also to deny defined Catholic dogma, such as the teaching of the Council of Florence, which defined *ex cathedra* that the Old Law is now dead and that those who attempt to practice it (namely, the Jews) cannot be saved.

> Pope Eugene IV, *Council of Florence*, 1441, ex cathedra:
> "**The Holy Roman Church firmly believes, professes and teaches that the matter pertaining to the law of the Old Testament, the Mosaic law, which are divided into ceremonies, sacred rites, sacrifices, and sacraments...** after our Lord's coming... **ceased,** and the sacraments of the New Testament began... **All, therefore, who after that time (the promulgation of the Gospel) observe circumcision and the Sabbath and the other requirements of the law, the holy Roman Church declares alien to the Christian faith and not in the least fit to participate in eternal salvation.**"[52]

Pope Benedict XIV reiterated this dogma in his encyclical *Ex Quo Primum*.

> Pope Benedict XIV, *Ex Quo Primum* (# 61):
> "**The first consideration is that the ceremonies of the Mosaic Law were abrogated by the coming of Christ and that they can no longer be observed without sin after the promulgation of the Gospel.**"[53]

Pope Pius XII, *Mystici Corporis Christi* (#'s 29-30), June 29, 1943: "And first of all, by the death of our Redeemer, **the New Testament took the place of the Old Law which had been abolished**... on the gibbet of His death **Jesus made void the Law with its decrees**

The Heresies of John Paul II

> [Eph. 2:15]… establishing the New Testament in His blood shed for the whole human race. 'To such an extent, then,' says St. Leo the Great, speaking of the Cross of our Lord, 'was there effected a transfer from the Law to the Gospel, from the Synagogue to the Church, from many sacrifices to one Victim, that, as our Lord expired, that mystical veil which shut off **the innermost part of the temple and its sacred secret was rent violently from top to bottom.' On the Cross then the Old Law died**, soon to be buried and to be a bearer of death…"[54]

John Paul II repeatedly repudiated this dogma, in word and deed – a dogma taught by the Catholic Church for 2000 years, defined infallibly by the Council of Florence, and affirmed clearly by Popes Benedict XIV and Pius XII.

In an address to Jews in Mainz, West Germany, Nov. 17, 1980, John Paul II spoke of, "the Old Covenant, never revoked by God…"[55]

> Pope Benedict XIV, *Ex Quo Primum* (# 59), March 1, 1756:
> "However they are not attempting to observe **the precepts of the old Law which as everybody knows have been revoked by the coming of Christ**."[56]

We see here that Pope Benedict XIV condemns the heresy taught by John Paul II, that the Old Covenant has never been revoked by God! John Paul II repeated the same bold heresy in a 1997 speech:

> John Paul II, *Meeting on the Roots of Anti-Semitism*, 1997: **"This people [the Jewish people]** has been called and led by God, Creator of Heaven and Earth. Their existence then is not a mere natural or cultural happening… It is a supernatural one. **This people continues in spite of everything to be the people of the covenant**…"[57]

It's important to note that the Vatican II sect's "Archbishop" of Strasbourg, France, Joseph Dore, recalled with glee John Paul II's aforementioned heresy on the Old Covenant, which John Paul II uttered in the speech in Mainz, West Germany and elsewhere. Notice that "Archbishop" Dore admits that Vatican II changed the traditional teaching of the Church on the cessation of the Old Covenant.

> Archbishop Joseph Dore of Strasbourg, France, Speech to B'nai B'rith (Jewish Freemasons), August, 2003: "Whatever the depiction [of the Jews in traditional Catholic art]… **the theological message is the same – God's election has now passed to the Christian people; and the Church, the true Israel, may triumph, She who confesses the saving truth brought by Christ.**
> "**At Vatican II, the Catholic Church finally revised this teaching** and understood to what extent it contradicts the Bible itself… In 1973, the French episcopacy, particularly under the influence of Msgr. Elchinger, [past] Bishop of Strasbourg, published a document of unparalleled moral force on Judeo-Christian relations, while **Pope John Paul II recalled on numerous occasions the permanence of the First Covenant** [*Ed.* the Old Covenant], 'which was never revoked' by God [John Paul II, Mainz, W. Germany, 1980]. Today, we desire to work together with our elder brothers toward reconciliation and fraternal dialogue. Yet **we must have the humility to recognize that the doctrine of contempt and the 'theology of substitution' – making the Church to be the new and only Israel of God – still penetrate the minds of a large number.**"[58]

In fact, John Paul II teaches the same heresy on the Old Covenant in his new catechism, again directly opposed to Catholic dogma.

John Paul II, *New Catechism of the Catholic Church*, paragraph 121: "… **for the Old Covenant has never been revoked.**"[59]

John Paul II's Unbelievable Message in Commemoration of the Jewish Synagogue

John Paul II, *Message to Chief Rabbi of Rome*, May 23, 2004: "To the most distinguished Dr. Riccardo Di Segni, Chief Rabbi of Rome. Shalom! With deep joy **I join the Jewish Community of Rome which is celebrating the centenary [100th anniversary] of the Great Synagogue in Rome**, a symbol and a reminder of the millennial presence in this city of the people of the Covenant of Sinai. For more than 2000 years **your community** has been an integral part of life in the city; **it can boast of being the most ancient Jewish community in Western Europe and of having played an important role in spreading Judaism on this Continent**. Today's commemoration, therefore, acquires a special significance… Since I am unable to attend in person, I have asked my Vicar General Camillo Ruini, to represent me; he is accompanied by Cardinal Walter Kasper, President of the Holy See's Commission for Relations with the Jews. **They formally express my desire to be with you this day**.

"In offering you my respectful greeting, distinguished Dr. Riccardo Di Segni, I extend my cordial thoughts to all the Members of the Community, to their President, Mr. Leone Elio Paserman, and to all who are gathered to witness once again to **the importance and vigor** of the religious patrimony that is celebrated every Saturday in the Great Synagogue of Rome…

Today's celebration, **in whose joy we all readily join**, recalls the first century of this majestic Synagogue. It stands on the banks of the Tiber, witnessing with the harmony of its architectural lines to faith and to praise of the Almighty. **The Christian Community of Rome, through the Successor of Peter, joins you in thanking the Lord for this happy occasion** [the 100th anniversary of the Synagogue!]. As I said during the Visit I mentioned, **we greet you as our 'beloved brothers' in the faith of Abraham**, our Patriarch… **you continue to be the first-born people of the Covenant** (*Liturgy of Good Friday, General Intercessions, For the Jewish People*)…

[These friendly relations] **saw us united in commemorating the victims of the Shoah** [deceased Jews who did not accept Christ], **especially those who were wrenched from their families and from your beloved Jewish Community in Rome** in October 1943 and interned in Auschwitz. **May their memory be blessed** and induce us to work as brothers and sisters…

…**the Church has not hesitated to express deep sorrow** at the 'failures of her sons and daughters in every age' and, in an act of repentance, **has asked forgiveness for their responsibility connected in any way with the scourges of anti-Judaism** and anti-Semitism…

Today… we are addressing a fervent prayer to the Eternal One, to the God of Shalom, so that enmity and hatred may no longer overpower those who turn to **our father, Abraham – Jews, Christians and Muslims**…

"Our meeting today is, as it were, in preparation for your imminent solemnity of Shavu'ot and of our Pentecost which proclaim the fullness of our respective paschal celebrations. May these feasts see us united in praying David's paschal *Hallel*." (*L'Osservatore Romano*, June 2, 2004, p. 7.)

The Heresies of John Paul II   194

Here is a brief summary of John Paul II's 2004 message in commemoration of the synagogue:

1) He joins the Jewish community in commemorating the 100th anniversary of the synagogue – apostasy.

2) He says this Jewish community can <u>boast</u> of being the most ancient synagogue in Western Europe and of having spread Judaism – total apostasy.

3) He formally expresses his desire that he could have been with them, in the synagogue, commemorating it – apostasy.

4) He praises the importance and the <u>vigor</u> of the religion that is celebrated every Saturday in Rome – apostasy. The word "vigor" means "*Active physical strength or energy; **flourishing physical condition, vitality**; mental or moral strength, force or energy.*" Thus, he is telling them again that their Covenant with God is valid, flourishing, in force.

5) On behalf of the entire Christian Community in Rome, as supposed "successor of St. Peter," he formally thanks the Lord for the 100 years of the synagogue! – apostasy!

6) He greets the Jews as beloved brothers of the faith of Abraham, which is another total denial of Christ, as scripture teaches that only those who are <u>of Christ</u> have the faith of Abraham.

> Galatians 3:14- "*That the blessing of Abraham might come on the Gentiles <u>through Christ Jesus</u>: **that we may receive the promise of the spirit by faith.**"
>
> Galatians 3:29- "**<u>And if you be Christ's</u>; then you are the seed of Abraham.**"
>
> Pope St. Gregory the Great (+ c. 590): "*… <u>if you be Christ's then you are the seed of Abraham</u>* (Gal. 3:29). **If we because of our faith in Christ are deemed children of Abraham, <u>the Jews therefore because of their perfidy have ceased to be His seed</u>**."[60]
>
> Pope St. Leo the Great, Dogmatic Letter to Flavian (449), read at Council of Chalcedon (451), ex cathedra: "The promises were spoken to Abraham and his seed. <u>He does not say "to his seeds" – as if referring to multiplicity – but to a single one</u>, '**and to thy seed,' which is Christ** (Gal. 3:16)."[61]

7) He states that the Jews "continue to be the first-born people of the Covenant," quoting the Good Friday prayer of the New Mass, which prays that the Jews "continue" in faithfulness to God's Covenant. John Paul II is blatantly teaching, once gain, that the Jews' Covenant with God is still valid – bold heresy.

8) He commemorates those who died as Jews and says that their memory should be blessed – heresy.

9) On behalf of "the Church," he repents for <u>any anti-Judaism</u> – apostasy. This would include the Church's anti-Jewish dogma that Jews who die without conversion to Catholicism go to Hell, *and therefore need to be converted and saved.* He is just mocking Our Lord and the Church.

This speech ranks right near the top of John Paul II's blasphemies and heresies. John Paul II was totally in favor of the denial of Christ; he clearly taught that the Old Covenant is still valid; he totally denied Jesus Christ and the Catholic Faith; he put his apostasy right in the world's face. Those who hold that this manifest heretic and apostate was a Catholic, *while aware of these facts*, and refuse to denounce him as a heretic, are truly enemies of God.

> 1 John 2:22 – "Who is a liar, but he who denieth that Jesus is the Christ? He is antichrist, who denieth the Father, and the Son."

John Paul II's best-friend, Jerzy Kluger, was a Jew.

John Paul II embracing his best-friend, the Jew, Jerzy Kluger

Of course, John Paul II never tried to convert Kluger. Kluger explicitly stated that John Paul II never game him the slightest indication that he wanted to convert him. Rather, Kluger credits his life-long relationship with John Paul II with making him "feel more Jewish." As a youth, John Paul II played soccer goalie on the Jewish squad with Kluger; they played against the Catholics. In a letter to Kluger on March 30, 1989, regarding the destruction of a synagogue during World War II, John Paul II wrote the following:

> "I venerate… **also this place of worship [the synagogue]**, which the invaders destroyed."[62]

This is blunt apostasy. By venerating the synagogue, John Paul II is venerating the Jews' denial that Jesus Christ is the Messiah.

But Jerzy Kluger was not the only Jew who was made to feel more Jewish by John Paul II. There is the Jewish maestro, Gilbert Levine.

The Heresies of John Paul II

Jewish Maestro Gilbert Levine with John Paul II[63]

Levine noted that, in their many-year relationship, John Paul II never gave him the slightest indication that he wanted to convert him. Levine also noted publicly that, after getting to know John Paul II, he returned to the practice of Judaism.

John Paul II asked Levine to conduct a concert in the Vatican to commemorate the Holocaust. Levine agreed, and with Antipope John Paul II in attendance the concert took place in the Vatican. <u>All of the crucifixes were covered</u>.

John Paul II seated next to the Jewish Rabbi for the Holocaust Concert (a Jewish Prayer Service) in the Vatican

The concert began with "Kol Nidre," the prayer sung on the holiest day of the Jewish calendar. A few of the many Jews in attendance also lit candles during the ceremony, which quickly became a Jewish religious service in the Vatican. After the concert Levine remarked:

> **"It was like I was in a Jewish liturgical service in the Vatican. It was a night of prayer… of Jewish prayer."**[64]

After the concert John Paul II called for Levine to receive the Vatican Knighthood. Levine became a Knight Commander of the Equestrian Order of St. Gregory the Great. John Paul II chose "Cardinal" Lustiger of Paris to bestow the honor. Lustiger himself, who was raised a Jew,

The Heresies of John Paul II 197

stated in a 1981 interview: "*I am a Jew. For me the two religions are one.*"[65] The honor that John Paul II had bestowed on Levine is one of the very highest that can be received by laymen.

> ## Gilbert Levine revealed the full depths of John Paul II's apostasy in an interview on Larry King Live, April 4, 2005.
>
> During an interview on CNN's *Larry King Live*, April 4, 2005, Gilbert Levine revealed that John Paul II:
>
> - sent each of his sons letters to <u>congratulate</u> them for their bar mitzvahs;
> - that <u>John Paul II himself gave his family a Jewish menorah</u>;
> - that John Paul II had "Cardinal" Kasper send the Levines a letter on the occasion of the bar mitzvah that was "astounding," which told them to be proud of their Jewish heritage and <u>live it out to the full</u>, and that the letter was so Jewish that the rabbi said it was from a rabbi, when it was actually from Kasper at the behest of John Paul II.

This proves that John Paul II officially encouraged the practice of Judaism; that he officially encouraged the denial of Christ; that he officially helped people practice the Old Covenant; and that he celebrated their observance of the Jewish religion with them. In light of these facts, anyone who says that John Paul II was not a non-Catholic apostate simply denies Jesus Christ – period. Here is an excerpt from the interview on CNN's Larry King Live:

"KING: How much of music did he understand?

"LEVINE: Wonderfully. **So much so that I, as a Jewish conductor, suggested for that 1994 concert that I do a work of Mahler. And he said, "didn't Mahler convert to Catholicism to become the music director of the Vienna Philharmonic?" I as a musician didn't -- didn't think of that. It's not that I didn't know it, I didn't think of it. That's the kind of sensitivity he had to Jewish issues. And he wanted to broaden it out. And what happened was he felt like it was a -- music could be a vehicle for interfaith dialogue.**

"KING: **The pope congratulated your children's bar mitzvahs?**

"LEVINE: **Not only congratulate us, he sent us a menorah.**

"KING: **He sent you a menorah?**

"LEVINE: **He gave it to us,** actually, didn't send it. **Actually gave us a menorah.** I think it's from the 16th century in Prague. It's the most beautiful menorah. **He sent a letter on <u>the occasion of each of my son's bar mitzvahs</u>.** He also had the cardinal in charge of Catholic/Jewish relations send a letter that was read out in my Orthodox shul on the occasion of my son's recent bar mitzvah, and the rabbi read it as if it were from a rabbi. At the end, it said, "it's by Rabbi Joel Schwartz." He said, but it wasn't by Rabbi Joel Schwartz. It was by Rabbi -- by Cardinal Kasper. It was astounding. It was a letter that said, you should be proud of your Jewish heritage and live it out to its full.

"KING: Where have you been? Why have we just found you? You conduct all over?

The Heresies of John Paul II   198

"LEVINE: Yes. I conduct all over, and I conducted for him in the Vatican many times. I conducted also for him at World Youth Day in Denver. Me, conducting for Catholic youth? And on that occasion, he came over to me and disrupted the entire performance, put his arm around me and said, did I disturb you, Maestro? And he had in fact stopped the whole show.

"KING: Are you going to the funeral?

"LEVINE: Of course. I am leaving tomorrow morning. And I will be at the funeral. I couldn't not be there." – End of except from interview[66]

Notice that Gilbert Levine wanted to use the music of the former Jew, Mahler, for the concert, but John Paul II <u>discouraged it by pointing out that Mahler was a Jew who converted to Catholicism</u>!

John Paul II Praying at the Wailing Wall

On March 26, 2000, John Paul II prayed at the Western Wall in Jerusalem. The Western Wall is the stone remnant of the Jewish Temple in Jerusalem that was destroyed by the Romans in 70 A.D. The Jews pray at the Western Wall as the holiest site in Judaism.

John Paul II praying at the Wailing or Western Wall in Jerusalem

The destruction of the Temple in 70 A.D., leaving only the Western Wall, has always been understood by Catholics to signify God's judgment on the Jews. **The destruction of the Temple prevented Jews from being able to offer sacrifice, which meant that their religion had come to an end. The destruction of the Temple was God's powerful sign to the Jews that the Messiah had come, that the Old Covenant had ceased, and that the Temple had been replaced by the Catholic Church.**

So when a Jew prays at the Western Wall, or leaves a prayer there, it is a denial that Jesus is the Messiah; it is an affirmation that he holds that the Old Covenant is still in force; and it is a pitiful and sad attempt to ignore God's very obvious sign that the Jews must abandon the destroyed Temple and enter the Catholic Church.

So when John Paul II himself prayed at the Western Wall in March of 2000, it was an attempt to validate Judaism. It was a denial that Jesus Christ is the Messiah, an indication that he holds that the Old Covenant is still in force, and a mockery of God's clear sign that the Jews must abandon the destroyed Temple and enter the Catholic Church. One informed commentator pointed out that, when John Paul II prayed at the Western Wall, most of the nation of Israel was watching on television. This means that every Jew watching on television was given the impression by John Paul II that he doesn't need to convert to Jesus Christ because Christ is not the Messiah.

The prayer that John Paul II left at the Western Wall asked forgiveness for sins against the Jewish people.

Other Apostasy with the Jews during the Reign of John Paul II

In late 2001, a Vatican Commission under John Paul II released a book entitled *The Jewish People and the Holy Scriptures in the Christian Bible*. **The book argues that the Jews' wait for the coming of the Messiah is still valid.** There is more on this book in the section later on dealing with Benedict XVI.

On August 13, 2002, the American bishops in union with John Paul II issued a document on the Jews. Spearheaded by the notorious apostate William Keeler of Baltimore, and without a peep of objection from John Paul II, the document publicly declared: "… *campaigns that target Jews for conversion to Christianity are no longer theologically acceptable in the Catholic Church.*"[67]

All of this proves that John Paul II and his bishops were/are complete apostates from the Catholic Faith.

John Paul II's incredible Heresies regarding Baptized Non-Catholics (i.e., heretics and schismatics)

We have already examined and exposed in detail John Paul II's undeniable apostasy with paganism, Islam and Judaism. Besides the many statements and acts of heresy and apostasy that John Paul II committed with those false and non-Christian religions, there are also his incredible heresies regarding baptized non-Catholics and their heretical sects. For example:

John Paul II taught that schismatics don't need to be converted

John Paul II in the Syrian "Orthodox" Cathedral of St. George with schismatic Patriarchs Zakka I and Ignatius IV in 2001[68]

John Paul II taught that Eastern Schismatics (the so-called Orthodox) don't need to be converted to the Catholic Church. To provide a little background: The Eastern Schismatics (the so-called "Orthodox") reject the dogma of the Papacy, which means that they reject the supreme authority of all the true popes in history. They reject the dogma of Papal Infallibility: the truth that a pope teaches infallibly when speaking from the Chair of Peter. They reject the dogma of the Immaculate Conception, they refuse to accept the last 13 Councils of the Roman Catholic Church, and they allow divorce and re-marriage.

> John Paul II, Homily, May 23, 2002: "I wish to repeat once again, **honor also to you, the holy Orthodox Church**…"[69]

In his outrageous *Directory for the Application of the Principles and Norms of Ecumenism* (#125), John Paul II encouraged interfaith worship with these Eastern Schismatics and stated: "… **any suggestion of proselytism should be avoided.**"[70] As we cover later, John Paul II approved the Directory on Ecumenism in *Ut Unum Sint* # 58 and elsewhere.

To *proselytize* is to convert someone. So John Paul II held that any effort to convert the Eastern Schismatics should be avoided. Here are the words of a real Catholic pope, Pope Benedict XIV, on the exact same topic.

> Pope Benedict XIV, *Allatae Sunt* (# 19), July 26, 1755:
> "First, the missionary who is attempting with God's help to bring back Greek and eastern schismatics to unity **should devote all his effort to the single objective of delivering them from doctrines at variance with the Catholic faith.**"[71]

> Pope Benedict XIV, *Allatae Sunt* (# 19):
> "For **the only work entrusted to the missionary** is that of recalling the Oriental to the Catholic faith…"[72]

One can easily see the difference between the two religions: the Catholic religion teaches that all of its teachings must be accepted and that non-Catholics need to be converted. The non-Catholic religion of John Paul II (the Vatican II religion) teaches that the Catholic faith is meaningless and that non-Catholics should not be converted.

Walter Kasper, a high-ranking member of the Vatican II Church, understands this quite well. Kasper was made a "cardinal" and the head of the Vatican's Council for Promoting Christian Unity by John Paul II. Benedict XVI confirmed Kasper in his position as head of the Vatican's Council for Promoting Christian Unity. Expressing the view of both John Paul II and Benedict XVI, Kasper stated:

> "… today we no longer understand ecumenism in the sense of a return, by which the others would 'be converted' and return to being 'Catholics'. This was expressly abandoned by Vatican II."[73]

Catholics who were tortured and martyred because they refused to become Eastern Schismatics

In his 1945 encyclical *Orientales Omnes Ecclesias*, Pope Pius XII gives a few examples of Catholics in history who were tortured and killed because they wouldn't abandon fidelity to the Papacy and become Eastern "Orthodox" schismatics. St. Josaphat is one famous example, but there are many others. St. Josaphat converted many Eastern Schismatics back to the Catholic Faith until he was murdered by them for his efforts to bring people back into union with the Papacy.

> Pope Pius XII, *Orientales Omnes Ecclesias* (# 15), Dec. 23, 1945: "**Josaphat Kuntzevitch**… was famed for his holiness of life and apostolic zeal, and was an intrepid champion of Catholic unity. **He was hunted down with bitter hatred and murderous intent by the schismatics and on 12th November 1623 he was inhumanly wounded and slain with a halbred.**"[74]

There were many others who were fined, flogged, tortured, drowned and killed because they wouldn't become Eastern Schismatics.

> Pope Pius XII, *Orientales Omnes Ecclesias* (# 20), Dec. 23, 1945: "**Those of the faithful who would not depart from the true faith, and dutifully and undauntedly resisted the union with the dissident [schismatic] Church imposed in 1875, were shamefully punished with fines and flogging and exile.**"[75]

> Pope Pius XII, *Orientales Omnes Ecclesias* (# 46), Dec. 23, 1945: "The Ruthenian community received… a noble company of confessors and martyrs. **To preserve their faith unimpaired and to maintain their zealous loyalty to the Roman pontiffs, these did not hesitate to endure every kind of labor and hardship**, or even to go gladly to their death… Josaphat Kuntzevitch… **He was the outstanding martyr for Catholic faith and unity at that period, but not the only one; not a few of the clergy and the laity received the same palm of victory after him; some were slain with the sword, some atrociously flogged to death, some drowned in the Dneiper**, so passing from their triumph over death to Heaven."[76]

> Pope Pius XII, *Orientales Omnes Ecclesias* (# 49), Dec. 23, 1945: "Besides all of this a new and no less bitter persecution of Catholicism was begun a few years before the partition of Poland. At the time when the troops of the Russian emperor had invaded Poland many churches of the Ruthenian rite were taken away from Catholics by force of arms; **the priests who refused to abjure their faith [and become schismatics] were put in chains, insulted, scourged and cast into prison, where they suffered cruelly from hunger, thirst and cold.**"[77]

The Heresies of John Paul II

By its heretical teaching that the "Orthodox" schismatics are not outside the Church and don't need conversion for salvation, the Vatican II sect utterly mocks the saints and martyrs who suffered horribly not to become schismatics.

The Vatican's Balamand Statement with the Eastern Schismatics, approved by John Paul II, rejects converting these non-Catholics as "outdated ecclesiology"

On June 24, 1993, the Vatican signed the Balamand Statement with the Eastern Schismatics (the so-called "Orthodox Church"). In this Balamand Statement (quoted below), which was approved by John Paul II, any attempt to convert the Eastern Schismatics is rejected as "*the outdated ecclesiology of return to the Catholic Church*." Here are some passages from the amazingly heretical Balamand Statement:

> Vatican II Sect's Balamand Statement with the "Orthodox," 1993, #10: "The situation thus created resulted in fact in tensions and oppositions. Progressively, in the decades which followed these unions, **missionary activity tended to include among its priorities the effort to convert other Christians, individually or in groups, so as "to bring them back" to one's own Church**. In order to legitimize this tendency, a source of proselytism, **the Catholic Church developed the theological vision according to which she presented herself as the only one to whom salvation was entrusted**. As a reaction, the Orthodox Church, in turn, came to accept the same vision according to which only in her could salvation be found…"
>
> #'s 14-15: "…**According to the words of Pope John Paul II**, the ecumenical endeavor of the sister Churches of East and West, grounded in dialogue and prayer, is the search for perfect and total communion which **is neither absorption nor fusion** but a meeting in truth and love (cf. Slavorum Apostoli, 27). 15. While the inviolable freedom of persons and their obligation to follow the requirements of their conscience remain secure, **in the search for re-establishing unity there is no question of conversion of people from one Church to the other in order to ensure their salvation**."
>
> 22. "**Pastoral activity in the Catholic Church, Latin as well as Oriental, no longer aims at having the faithful of one Church pass over to the other; that is to say, it no longer aims at proselytizing among the Orthodox**. It aims at answering the spiritual needs of its own faithful **and it has no desire for expansion at the expense of the Orthodox Church**."
>
> 30. "To pave the way for future relations between the two Churches, **passing beyond the out-dated ecclesiology of return to the Catholic Church** connected with the problem which is the object of this document, special attention will be given to the preparation of future priests and of all those who, in any way, are involved in an apostolic activity carried on in a place where the other Church traditionally has its roots. Their education should be objectively positive with respect of the other Church." (http://www.cin.org/east/balamand.html)

This is incredibly bold heresy! This document, approved by the Vatican II antipopes, is definitely one of the worst heresies of the Vatican II sect. It bluntly mentions, and then totally rejects, the traditional dogma of the Catholic Church that the schismatics must be converted to the Catholic Faith for unity and salvation.

John Paul II called the Balamand Statement a "new step" that "should help all the local Orthodox Churches and all the local Catholic Churches, both Latin and Oriental, which live together in a single region, to continue their commitment to the dialogue of charity and to begin or to pursue relations of cooperation in the area of their pastoral activity."[78]

Please notice especially #'s 14-15, which state that "*in the search for re-establishing unity there is no question of conversion of people from one Church to the other in order to ensure their salvation…*" Please notice #22, which states that the Catholic Church "*has no desire for expansion at the expense of the Orthodox Church*" and #30, which rejects the "outdated *ecclesiology of return to the Catholic Church.*" Notice how all of this bluntly rejects the Catholic dogma that non-Catholics must return to the Catholic Church for salvation and Christian unity.

> Pope Pius XI, *Mortalium Animos* (# 10), Jan. 6, 1928:
> "… the union of Christians can only be promoted by promoting the **_return_** to the one true Church of Christ of those who are separated from it…"[79]

So it is a fact that John Paul II and his false sect reject word-for-word the dogma of the Catholic faith: Christian unity is only achieved by conversion to Catholicism. We see this rejection of Catholic dogma again in the next quote.

More of John Paul II's incredible heresies with the Eastern "Orthodox" Schismatics

> John Paul II, *Homily*, Jan. 25, 1993:
> "**The way to achieve Christian unity, in fact,' says the document of the Pontifical Commission for Russia, 'is not proselytism but fraternal dialogue…**"[80]

It is therefore a fact that John Paul II teaches that the faith of Rome is not to be held by non-Catholics; therefore, he cannot be looked upon as holding the true Catholic Faith.

> Pope Leo XIII, *Satis Cognitum* (# 13), June 29, 1896:
> "**You are not to be looked upon as holding the true Catholic faith if you do not teach that the faith of Rome is to be held.**"[81]

Those who assert, in the face of these facts, that John Paul II is to be looked upon as holding the true Catholic faith (in other words, that was a true Catholic pope) are denying this teaching of the Catholic Church.

In his encyclical on *Sts. Cyril and Methodius* (#27), John Paul II again indicated that Eastern Schismatics should not be converted to the Catholic Church. He stated that unity with the schismatics "**is neither absorption nor fusion**,"[82] which means not by conversion. As we saw above, *The Balamand Statement* with the Orthodox actually quoted this very phrase from John Paul II's encyclical on Sts. Cyril and Methodius to prove that Catholics should not convert the Orthodox.

John Paul II has confirmed his heresy in countless meeting with the schismatics. On Feb. 24, 2000, John Paul II met with the non-Catholic, schismatic Bishop of Alexandria, "Pope" Shenouda III.

The Heresies of John Paul II

John Paul II meeting with the schismatic Bishop of Alexandria, who calls himself "Pope" Shenouda III

In his message to the schismatic bishop, John Paul II called him "Your Holiness" and said:

> John Paul II, *Message to "Pope" Shenouda III*, Feb. 24, 2000: "I am grateful for all you have said, Your Holiness… **God bless the Church of Pope Shenouda**. Thank you."[83]

In other words, John Paul II said: "God bless the schismatic Church!" This is a rejection of the Catholic Faith. Scripture specifically tells us that we cannot say "God speed" (in other words, "God bless") to heretics.

> "If any man come to you and <u>bring not this doctrine</u>, receive him not into the house **nor say to him: God speed you**." (II John 10)

By saying "God bless" to a false Church, one is asking God to multiply and propagate that false sect.

WORLD NEWS
FRIDAY, NOVEMBER 17, 2000 • PITTSBURGH CATHOLIC

Pope backs new cathedral

BUCHAREST, Romania — The Romanian Orthodox Church has raised 40 percent of funding needed for construction of a cathedral in Bucharest, including a $100,000 contribution from Pope John Paul II, said an Orthodox official.

The Heresies of John Paul II 205

John Paul II and Teoctist (the schismatic Patriarch of Romania) jointly denouncing converting each other in a 2002 Joint Declaration

On October 12, 2002, John Paul II and the schismatic Patriarch of Romania jointly denounced trying to convert each other in a common declaration. They stated: "Our aim and our ardent desire is full communion, <u>*which is not absorption*</u>..."[84] This means not by conversion. John Paul II frequently used the phrase "neither absorption nor fusion" to indicate that unity with the schismatics is not by converting them. Remember, that phrase was used with this very meaning in the Balamand Statement (cited earlier) with the schismatic "Orthodox."

Teoctist, the schismatic Patriarch of Romania, **had already revealed in 1999 that John Paul II made a large donation to his non-Catholic Church**.[85] Zenit News Service and others (see previous page) reported that John Paul II's donation to the schismatic patriarch was $100,000!

> "Romanian Orthodox clergy said today that John Paul II has donated $100,000 toward the construction of an Orthodox Cathedral here that will accommodate up to 2,000 people, Agence France-Presse reported."[86]

> Pope Innocent III, *Fourth Lateran Council*, Constitution 3 on Heretics, 1215: "Moreover, we determine to subject to excommunication believers who receive, defend, or <u>support heretics</u>."[87]

In his address on the same day as their Joint Declaration, John Paul II told the schismatic Patriarch Teoctist: "*The goal is… to reach a unity which implies <u>neither absorption nor fusion</u>…*"[88]

So, John Paul II has publicly ensured his listeners over and over again that Catholics should not try to convert non-Catholics and that the Catholic Faith is not necessary for attaining salvation.

> Pope Pius IX, *Nostis et Nobiscum* (# 10), Dec. 8, 1849: "In particular, **ensure that the faithful are deeply and thoroughly convinced of the truth of the doctrine that the Catholic faith is necessary for attaining salvation.**"[89]

In fact, in the same address to the schismatic Patriarch of Romania, John Paul II made this incredible statement:

"For her part, the Catholic Church recognizes the mission which the Orthodox Churches are called to carry out in the countries where they have been rooted for centuries. **She desires <u>nothing else</u> than to help this mission…**"[90]

So much for the Papacy! So much for the last 1000 years of dogmatic statements that the schismatics reject! So much for divorce and re-marriage! And so much for the Catholic Church, according to John Paul II. According to this apostate, all of this means nothing and in fact should not be believed because "the Church" desires nothing else than to keep these people in schism and outside her teachings.

Pope Gregory XVI, May 27, 1832: "Be not deceived, my brother; if anyone follows a schismatic, he will not attain the inheritance of the kingdom of God."[91]

Pope Leo XII, *Encyclical*, May 24, 1824: "**We address all of you who are still removed from the true Church and the road to salvation**. In this universal rejoicing, one thing is lacking: that… you might sincerely agree with **the mother Church, outside of whose teachings there is no salvation.**"[92]

Pope Leo XII, *Ubi Primum* (# 14), May 5, 1824:
"It is impossible for the most true God, who is Truth itself, the best, the wisest Provider, and the Rewarder of good men, **to approve all sects who profess false teachings** which are often inconsistent with one another and contradictory, **and to confer eternal rewards on their members**… by divine faith we hold one Lord, one faith, one baptism… **This is why we profess that there is no salvation outside the Church.**"[93]

Pope Pius XI, *Mortalium Animos* (# 11), Jan. 6, 1928: "The Catholic Church is alone in keeping the true worship… **if any man enter not here, or if any man go forth from it, he is a stranger to the hope of life and salvation.**"[94]

Here we see John Paul II and the schismatic Patriarch Teoctist sitting on equal level chairs

The Heresies of John Paul II

This is another action by which John Paul II manifested that he accepted the "Orthodox" heresy that all bishops are equal. John Paul II held that it's fine to deny the Primacy of the Bishop of Rome.

In the Summer of 2003, John Paul II <u>again</u> repudiated the proselytism of the Eastern Schismatics.

> John Paul II, *Ecclesia in Europa*, Post-Synodal Apost. Exhortation, June 28, 2003: "At the same time **I wish to assure once more the pastors and our brothers and sisters of the Orthodox Churches that the new evangelization is in no way to be confused with proselytism**..."[95]

> Pope Pius IX, Vatican Council I, Sess. 4, Chap. 3, ex cathedra: "Furthermore We teach and declare that the Roman Church, by the disposition of the Lord, holds the sovereignty of ordinary power over all others... **This is the doctrine of Catholic truth from which no one can deviate and keep his faith and salvation**."[96]

This infallible definition of Vatican I declares that anyone who deviates from the dogma of the Papacy (that the Pope of Rome holds sovereign power in the Church of Christ), such as the "Orthodox" schismatics and the Protestants, cannot keep his faith and salvation. Yet, John Paul II tells us that the Orthodox schismatics and the Protestants not only can keep their faith and salvation while denying the Papacy, but *should not* believe in the Papacy. He was a complete heretic who rejected this dogma of Vatican I.

John Paul II Declaring a Communion and Unity of Faith with non-Catholic Sects

In his encyclical *Ut Unum Sint,* John Paul II declared that his "Church" is in communion with non-Catholic sects an incredible 16 times, and he declared that he has the same faith as non-Catholic sects 8 times.

> John Paul II, *Ut Unum Sint* (# 62), May 25, 1995, speaking about the non-Catholic and Schismatic Patriarch of Ethiopia: "When the Venerable Patriarch of the Ethiopian Church, Abuna Paulos, paid me a visit in Rome on June 11, 1993, together we emphasized **the deep communion existing between our two Churches**: 'We share the same faith handed down from the Apostles... moreover, we can affirm that **we have the one faith in Christ**...'"[97]

> Pope St. Leo the Great, *Sermon 129*:
> "Wherefore, since outside the Catholic Church there is nothing perfect, nothing undefiled... **we are in no way likened with those who are divided from the unity of the Body of Christ;** *we are joined in no communion*."[98]

When John Paul II asserts that he has the same faith and communion as non-Catholic sects, he is asserting that he is a non-Catholic.

John Paul II gave a relic to schismatic Karekin II, and he declared that his sect is the "Bride of Christ"

John Paul II also gave Karekin II, the head of the schismatic Church in Armenia, a relic of St. Gregory the Illuminator.

John Paul II gives a relic of St. Gregory the Illuminator to the head of the schismatic "Church" in Armenia

John Paul II, *Homily to <u>schismatic</u> Patriarch Karekin II*, Nov. 10, 2000: "… **I am delighted to return to Your Holiness a relic of St. Gregory the Illuminator**… The relic will be placed in the new cathedral now being built… **My hope is that the new cathedral will adorn with still greater beauty** *the Bride of Christ in Armenia*…"[99]

St. Gregory the Illuminator (c. 257-332 A.D.) was the "apostle of Armenia," the one who propagated the true Christian Faith (the Catholic Faith) in Armenia:

"Working very closely together, King Tiridates and St. Gregory the Illuminator destroyed all the old pagan shrines in Armenia, beginning with those of the goddess Anahit and the god Tir, for whom the King had been named. Crosses were erected in their place. Very large numbers of people were baptized."[100]

By giving the relic of this great Christian apostle of Armenia to the schismatics, John Paul II was clearly indicating that he considered the schismatics as possessors of the true Christian Faith – the true Faith that St. Gregory the Illuminator held. Further, in the homily above, we can see that John Paul II called the schismatic Orthodox Church "the Bride of Christ," a title reserved to the Catholic Church!

John Paul II's Heresy with the Anglican Sect

Because Margaret Clitherow refused to accept the Anglican sect and its "Mass" – but rather invited Catholic priests into her home against the penal laws – she was martyred by being crushed to death under a large door loaded with heavy weights. This style of execution is so painful that it is called "severe and harsh punishment." **She suffered it all because she wouldn't** accept **Anglicanism**. The Vatican II sect, however, teaches that Anglicans are fellow "Christians" who don't need conversion, and whose invalid "bishops" are actually true bishops of the Church of Christ. The Vatican II sect teaches that her martyrdom was pointless.

John Paul II goes to the Anglican Cathedral and takes part in the worship of the Anglican sect – formal heresy by deed

John Paul II speaking at the Anglican Cathedral of Canterbury in 1982[101]

John Paul II mocking the English Martyrs by his joint prayer with the Anglican "Archbishop" of Canterbury, 1982

John Paul II in common prayer with the schismatic and heretical "Archbishop" of Canterbury (an Anglican), who is just a layman posing as a bishop

On May 29, 1982, in the Anglican Cathedral John Paul II knelt in a "prayer of interfaith" with the "Archbishop" of Canterbury, Robert Runcie, thus mocking the martyrdoms of so many Catholic saints, who bravely shed their blood rather than accept the false Anglican sect or partake in false worship.

> Pope Pius IX, *Neminem vestrum* (# 5), Feb. 2, 1854: "We want you to know that those same monks sent Us a splendid profession of Catholic faith and doctrine… **They eloquently acknowledged and freely received <u>the regulations and decrees which the popes and the sacred congregations published</u> or would publish – <u>especially those which prohibit *communicatio in divinis* (communion in holy matters) with schismatics</u>**."[102]

John Paul II Bestowed the Pectoral Cross on the head of the Anglican Sect, a Layman

In 2003, John Paul II bestowed the pectoral cross upon Rowan Williams, the Anglican "Archbishop" of Canterbury.

John Paul II kissing the ring of Rowan Williams, the head of the Anglican sect, on whom he also bestowed a pectoral cross, even though Williams is just a layman

For those who don't know, the Anglican non-Catholic sect doesn't even have valid priests or valid bishops. Pope Leo XIII infallibly declared that Anglican ordinations are invalid.

> Pope Leo XIII, "Apostolicae Curae," Sept. 13, 1896, ex cathedra: "… by Our authority, of Our own inspiration and certain knowledge <u>We pronounce and declare that ordinations enacted according to the Anglican rite have hitherto been and are invalid and entirely void</u>…"[103]

Anglican "priests" and "bishops" are, therefore, laymen, besides being non-Catholic heretics and schismatics. Yet, after the election of the new Anglican "Archbishop" of Canterbury (Rowan Williams), **John Paul II dispatched the apostate Walter Kasper to give this non-Catholic layman a pectoral cross and a telegram of approval!** This is so heretical that there are almost no words to describe it.

> Anglican "Archbishop" of Canterbury Rowan Williams to John Paul II, Oct. 4, 2003: "In 1966 Pope Paul VI gave Archbishop Michael Ramsey his own Episcopal ring, which has been treasured by his successors and which I wear today. **I am glad to thank you for the personal gift of a pectoral cross, sent to me on the occasion of my enthronement earlier this year.** As I took on my new ministry I appreciated deeply that sign of a shared task..."[104]

The pectoral cross is a traditional Catholic symbol of episcopal authority. By bestowing the pectoral cross upon the apostate Rowan Williams – who is also in favor of women priests and homosexuals being ordained – **John Paul II not only flatly denied by his deed Pope Leo XIII's infallible definition that Anglican orders are invalid,** but he also made a complete mockery of the Catholic dogmas on the Papacy and the Church of Christ.

And what makes this action of John Paul II even more incredible is the fact that Williams himself has been banned from conducting "Communion" services in 350 Anglican parishes for his view in favor of women priests![105] But that didn't stop John Paul II; he just pushed ahead with the apostasy.

John Paul II even indicated that the non-Catholic layman Williams is the legitimate bishop of the "See of Canterbury."

> John Paul II, "To the Most Reverend and Right Honorable Rowan Williams, Archbishop of Canterbury," Oct. 4, 2003: "**These encounters have sought to renew the links between the See of Canterbury and the Apostolic See**... It is fidelity to Christ which compels us to continue to search for full visible unity and to find appropriate ways of engaging, whenever possible, in common witness and mission... I pray for a renewed outpouring of the Holy Spirit upon you... May God keep you safe, watch over you and always guide you in the exercise of your lofty responsibilities."[106]

As shown above, during a meeting with Rowan Williams, John Paul II also kissed his ring, which demonstrated again that John Paul II recognized this non-Catholic layman as a legitimate bishop in the Church of Christ. John Paul II mocked Jesus Christ, the Catholic Church and all the English martyrs who suffered horrible tortures for refusing to abandon Catholicism and become Anglican. With this action, John Paul II rejected the Catholic Church's teaching on the Episcopacy, Ordination, Apostolic Succession and Church Unity.

John Paul II went to the Lutheran Temple

John Paul II in the Lutheran temple in 1983

In 1983, John Paul II visited a Lutheran temple for the 500th anniversary of Martin Luther's birth. This is another heretical action – partaking of the worship ceremonies of a non-Catholic religion and celebrating a heresiarch – which absolutely proves that John Paul II was not a Catholic.

John Paul II praised Luther, Calvin, Zwingli and Hus

John Paul II also praised the greatest enemies that the Catholic Church has ever known, including the Protestant revolutionaries Luther and Calvin. In Oct. 1983, John Paul II, speaking of Martin Luther, stated: *"Our world even today experiences his great impact on history."*[107] And on June 14, 1984, John Paul II praised Calvin as one who was trying to "make the Church more faithful to the will of the Lord."[108] To patronize, support and defend heretics is to be a heretic. To praise the worst heretics in Church history, such as Luther and Calvin, is beyond heresy.

> Pope Gregory XVI, *Encyclical*, May 8, 1844:
> "But later even more care was required when *the Lutherans and Calvinists* **dared to oppose the changeless doctrine of the faith with an almost incredible variety of errors**. They left no means untried to deceive the faithful with perverse explanations of the sacred books..."[109]

John Paul II also praised the notorious heretics Zwingli and Hus. He even went so far as to say that John Hus, who was condemned as a heretic by the Council of Constance, was a man of "infallible personal integrity"![110]

John Paul II approved the Vatican-Lutheran Agreement on Justification

On Oct. 31, 1999, "Cardinal" Edward Cassidy and Lutheran "Bishop" Christian Krause shake hands at the signing of *The Joint Declaration on the Doctrine of Justification* in Augsburg, Germany. This agreement, **which was approved by John Paul II**, teaches: that Justification comes by "faith alone" (Annex, 2, C); that the Canons of the Council of Trent no longer apply to the Lutherans (#13); that none of the Lutheran teaching in the Joint Declaration, including the heresy of Justification by faith alone and numerous other Lutheran heresies, is condemned by Trent (#41). In short, this agreement between the "Church" of John Paul II and the Lutheran sect utterly rejects the dogmatic Council of Trent. It is a veritable declaration that the sect of John Paul II is a Protestant sect. (A little later in the book there is a section on this amazingly heretical agreement.)

> John Paul II, Jan. 19, 2004, *At a Meeting with Lutherans From Finland*: "… I wish to express my gratitude for the ecumenical progress made between Catholics and Lutherans in the five years **since the signing of the *Joint Declaration on the Doctrine of Justification*.**"[111]

John Paul II taught that non-Catholics can receive Communion

John Paul II also taught that non-Catholics may lawfully receive Holy Communion. Canon 844.3 of his 1983 Code of Canon Law states that:

> "Catholic ministers may licitly administer the sacraments of penance, Eucharist, and anointing of the sick to members of the oriental churches which do not have full communion with the Catholic Church..."[112]

The idea that non-Catholics may lawfully receive Holy Communion or the other sacraments is contrary to the 2000 year teaching of the Catholic Church.

> Pope Pius IX, *Encyclical*, April 8, 1862:
> "... 'whoever eats of the Lamb and is not a member of the Church, has profaned.'"[113]

What's particularly significant about this heresy of John Paul II (that it is lawful to give Holy Communion to non-Catholics) is the fact that it also appears in his new catechism, paragraph # 1401. This document was promulgated by the so-called supreme apostolic authority of John Paul II. In his constitution *Fidei Depositum*, John Paul II promulgated his new catechism using his "apostolic authority" to declare that it is a "sure norm for teaching the faith."

> John Paul II, *Fidei Depositum*, Oct. 11, 1992:
> "The *Catechism of the Catholic Church*, which I approved June 25th last and the publication of which **I today order by virtue of my Apostolic authority**, *is a statement of the Church's faith and of Catholic doctrine*... **I declare it to be a sure norm for teaching the faith**."[114]

John Paul II's catechism is not a sure norm for teaching the faith. It's a sure norm for teaching heresy. Therefore, since John Paul II has pretended to declare from the Chair of Peter that his catechism is a sure norm for teaching the faith when it is not, we know that he does not sit in the Chair of Peter. A pope cannot err when speaking from the Apostolic See, that is, with his apostolic authority from the Chair of Peter.

> Pope Pius IX, *Vatican Council I*, ex cathedra: "... in the Apostolic See the Catholic religion has always been preserved untainted, and holy doctrine celebrated."[115]

> Pope Pius IX, *Vatican Council I*, ex cathedra:
> "So, this gift of truth and a never failing faith was divinely conferred upon Peter and his successors in this chair..."[116]

This heresy on non-Catholics being allowed to receive Holy Communion was also taught in Vatican II, as we covered already. John Paul II also commented on this teaching with approval in *Ut Unum Sint*:

> John Paul II, *Ut Unum Sint* (# 58), May 25, 1995:
> "... By reason of the very close sacramental bonds between the Catholic Church and the Orthodox Church... the Catholic Church has often adopted and now adopts a milder policy, offering to all the means of salvation and an example of charity among Christians **through participation in the sacraments and in other sacred functions and objects**... **There must never be a loss of appreciation for the ecclesiological implication of sharing in the sacraments, especially the Holy Eucharist**."[117]

He notes the "ecclesiological implication" of sharing in the sacraments with the "Orthodox." His implication is that they are part of the same Church.

John Paul II taught that non-Catholic sects are a means of salvation

Following Vatican II, John Paul II also taught that non-Catholic sects are a means of salvation, which is heresy.

> John Paul II, *New Catechism, paragraph 819*, speaking of non-Catholic Churches: "**Christ's Spirit uses these Churches and ecclesial communities as means of salvation...**"[118]

> Pope Pius IV, profession of faith, Council of Trent, ex cathedra: "**This true Catholic faith, outside of which no one can be saved**... I now profess and truly hold..."[119]

John Paul II taught that non-Catholic sects have Saints and Martyrs

John Paul II repeatedly taught that non-Catholic sects have saints and martyrs.

> John Paul II, *Ut Unum Sint* (# 84), May 25, 1995, Speaking of non-Catholic "Churches": "Albeit in an invisible way, the communion between our Communities, even if still incomplete, is truly and solidly grounded in the full communion of the saints - those who, at end of a life faithful to grace, are in communion with Christ in glory. **These *saints* come from all the Churches and Ecclesial Communities WHICH GAVE THEM ENTRANCE INTO THE COMMUNION OF SALVATION.**"[120]

This is undeniable, clear-cut manifest heresy. It is an article of divine and Catholic Faith that those who are not in the Catholic Church, even if they shed blood in the name of Christ, cannot be saved.

> Pope Eugene IV, *Council of Florence, ex cathedra:*
> "**... no one, even if he has shed blood in the name of Christ, can be saved, unless he has remained in the bosom and unity of the Catholic Church.**"[121]

This solemnly defined dogma of the Council of Florence was repeated by Pope Pius XI:

> Pope Pius XI, *Rappresentanti in terra* (# 99), Dec. 31, 1929: "It stands out conspicuously in the lives of numerous **saints, whom the Church, and she alone, produces**, in whom is perfectly realized the purpose of Christian education..."[122]

It's hard to imagine a more specific and explicit denial of this particular dogma than *Ut Unum Sint* #84 of John Paul II (quoted above).

> Pope Gregory XVI, *Summo Iugiter Studio*, May 27, 1832:
> "**Finally some of these misguided people attempt to persuade themselves and others that men are not saved only in the Catholic religion, but that even heretics may attain eternal life.**"[123]

Also, please notice that not only does the manifest heretic John Paul II declare in *Ut Unum Sint* #84 that "saints" come from non-Catholic Churches (clear heresy), but he goes beyond that and declares that such **non-Catholic sects "gave them" their salvation**: "the Churches and Ecclesial Communities *which gave them entrance into* the communion of salvation."

John Paul II, *Ut Unum Sint* (# 83), May 25, 1995:
"**All Christian Communities** know that, thanks to the power given by the Spirit, obeying that will and overcoming those obstacles are not beyond their reach. <u>**All of them in fact have martyrs for the Christian faith.**</u>"[124]

John Paul II, *speech <u>to schismatic non-Catholic</u> Patriarch Karekin II*, Nov. 9, 2000:
"Again, I thank **Your Holiness** for your willingness to be part of that liturgy in the person of your representative. In effect, '**perhaps the most convincing form of ecumenism is <u>the ecumenism of the saints and of the martyrs</u>**. The *communio sanctorum* speaks louder than the things which divide us.'"[125]

John Paul II, *Ut Unum Sint* (# 1), May 25, 1995:
"The courageous witness <u>of so many martyrs of our century, including members of **Churches and Ecclesial Communities not in full communion with the Catholic Church**</u>, gives new vigor to the Council's call and reminds us of our duty to listen to and put into practice its exhortation."[126]

John Paul II, *Salvifici Doloris* (# 22), Feb. 11, 1984:
"**Christ's resurrection has revealed 'the glory of the future age' and, at the same time, has confirmed 'the boast of the cross':** *the glory that is hidden in the very suffering of Christ* **and which has been and is often mirrored in human suffering**, as an expression of man's spiritual greatness. **This glory must be acknowledged not only in the martyrs for the Faith but in many others also who, at times, <u>even without belief in Christ</u>, suffer and give their lives for the truth and for a just cause**. In the sufferings of all of these people the great dignity of man is strikingly confirmed."[127]

John Paul II, *Angelus Address,* Sept. 19, 1993:
"In the unbounded space of Eastern Europe, <u>**the Orthodox Church too can well say**</u> at the end of this century what the Fathers of the Church had proclaimed about the initial spread of the Gospel: 'Sanguis martyrum – semen Christianorum' [<u>the blood of martyrs is the seed of Christians</u>]."[128]

John Paul II, *Tertio Millennio Adveniente* (# 37), Nov. 10, 1994:
"**The witness to Christ borne even to the shedding of blood has become a common inheritance of <u>Catholics, Orthodox, Anglicans and Protestants</u>, as Pope Paul VI pointed out in his Homily for the Canonization of the Ugandan Martyrs.**"[129]

John Paul II, *Tertio Millennio Adveniente* (# 37), Nov. 10, 1994:
"… the local Churches should do everything possible to ensure that **the memory of those who have suffered martyrdom should be safeguarded, gathering the necessary documentation. This gesture cannot fail to have an ecumenical character and expression. <u>Perhaps the most convincing form of ecumenism is the ecumenism of the saints and martyrs</u>**. The *communio sanctorum* speaks louder than the things which divide us."[130]

John Paul II, *Ut Unum Sint* (# 84), May 25, 1995:
"In a theocentric vision, **<u>we Christians already have a common *martyrology*</u>**. This includes the martyrs of our own century, more numerous than one might think…"[131]

John Paul II, *Ut Unum Sint* (# 84), May 25, 1995:
"**In the radiance of <u>the 'heritage of the saints' belonging to all Communities</u>,** the 'dialogue of conversion' toward full and visible unity thus appears as a source of hope. The universal presence of the saints is in fact a proof of the transcendent power of the Spirit." [132]

John Paul II, *General Audience,* May 12, 1999: "The experience of **martyrdom** joined Christians of various denominations in Romania. **<u>The Orthodox, Catholics and Protestants</u>** gave a united witness to Christ by the sacrifice of their lives."[133]

All of this is **repeated, public and formal heresy**. And to think that some "traditionalists" have the audacity to assert that John Paul II never denied a dogma! What an outrage and a lie! This heresy alone, without even considering all the others, proves that he was not a Catholic. It proves that John Paul II directly rejected the solemnly defined dogma (from the Council of Florence above) that non-Catholics cannot be saved even if they shed their blood for Christ.

> Pope Pelagius II, epistle (2) *Dilectionis vestrae*, 585:
> "Those who were not willing to be at agreement in the Church of God, cannot remain with God; <u>**although given over to flames and fires**, they burn, or thrown to wild beasts, they lay down their lives, **there will not be for them that crown of faith**</u>, but the **punishment of faithlessness**, not a glorious result (of religious virtue), but the ruin of despair. Such a one can be slain; he cannot be crowned."[134]

John Paul II approved of the practice of Altar Girls

John Paul II with Altar Girls

John Paul II also approved of the practice of altar girls, a practice that is rampant in Vatican II churches. The practice of altar girls was condemned *as evil* by Pope Benedict XIV, Pope St. Gelasius and Pope Innocent IV.

> Pope Benedict XIV, *Encyclical,* July 26, 1755:
> "**Pope Gelasius** in his ninth letter to the bishops of Lucania <u>**condemned *the evil* practice which had been introduced of women serving the priest at the celebration of Mass**</u>. Since this abuse had spread to the Greeks, **Innocent IV strictly forbade it in his letter to the bishop of Tusculum:** 'Women should not dare to serve at the altar; they should be altogether refused this ministry.' **We too have forbidden this practice in the same words in Our oft-repeated constitution...**"[135]

John Paul II also "canonized" people who fully embraced the heresies of Vatican II, the New Mass and religious indifferentism. This is impossible for a true pope to do, since canonizations by true popes are infallible. This again serves to prove that John Paul II was not a true pope.

John Paul II also condemned the Crusades. The Crusades were solemnly approved by four councils and more than 10 popes, including Pope Urban II, Pope Callistus II, Pope Alexander III, Pope Callistus III, Pope Clement V and others.

John Paul II awarded by Freemasons

John Paul II receiving the B'nai B'rith (Freemasonic Lodge of New York) on March 22, 1982

In December of 1996, **the Grand Orient Lodge of Italian Freemasonry offered John Paul II its greatest honor, the Order of Galilee,** as an expression of thanks for the efforts that he made in support of Freemasonic ideals. The representative of Italian Freemasonry noted that John Paul II merited the honor because he had promoted "the values of universal Freemasonry: fraternity, respect for the dignity of man, and the spirit of tolerance, central points of the life of true masons."[136]

John Paul II apologized to Red China

On Oct. 24, 2001, John Paul II apologized to Red China. That's correct: John Paul II apologized to the satanic Communist regime in China for the supposed wrongs of Catholics! He even praised the social justice of Red China.

> John Paul II, Oct. 24, 2001: "The Catholic Church for her part regards with respect <u>this impressive thrust and far-sighted planning</u>… The Church has very much at heart the values and objectives which are of primary importance also to modern China: solidarity, peace, social justice…"[137]

Social justice in China includes a one-child-per-family policy, which is imposed by forced abortion and contraception. The Chinese Government slaughters millions of children every year, in addition to imprisoning, torturing and murdering Catholics.

John Paul II stated that the Catholic Church and China are two ancient institutions *"not in opposition to one another."*[138] To praise the social justice of Communist China is beyond heresy; it's satanic.

John Paul II promoted the theory of evolution

On Oct. 22, 1996, John Paul II declared that evolution is *"more than a mere hypothesis."*[139] This indicated that he considered evolution to be true.

John Paul II said that Heaven, Hell and Purgatory are not actual places

In a series of speeches in the summer of 1999, reported in the official Vatican newspaper, John Paul II said that Heaven, Hell and Purgatory are not actual places.

At his *general audience* on July 21, 1999, John Paul II said that Heaven is not an actual place.[140]

On July 28, 1999, John Paul II said:

> 1) "It is precisely this tragic situation that Christian doctrine explains when it speaks of eternal damnation of Hell. **It is not a punishment imposed externally by God but a development of premises already set by people in this life**."[141]

> 2) "By using images, the New Testament presents the place destined for evildoers as a fiery furnace, where people will 'weep and gnash their teeth'... **The images of Hell that Sacred Scripture presents to us must be correctly interpreted**. They show the complete frustration and emptiness of life without God. **Rather than a place**, Hell indicates the state of those who freely and definitively separate themselves from God, the source of all life and joy."[142]

> 3) "Eternal damnation remains a real possibility, but we are not granted, without special divine revelation, **the knowledge of whether or which human beings are effectively involved in it**. The thought of Hell - and even less **the improper use of biblical images** - must not create anxiety or despair, but is a necessary and healthy reminder of freedom within the proclamation that the risen Jesus has conquered Satan, giving us the Spirit of God who makes us cry 'Abba, Father!'"[143]

This speech of John Paul II in itself constitutes formal heresy. He says we don't know whether human beings are damned. It's a divinely revealed truth of the Gospel that human beings are involved in eternal damnation, as Jesus says repeatedly. For instance:

> Matthew 13:39-42- "Even as cockle therefore is gathered up, and burnt with fire: **so shall it be at the end of the world**. The Son of man shall send his angels, and they shall gather out of his kingdom all scandals, and them that work iniquity. **And shall cast them into the furnace of fire: there shall be weeping and gnashing of teeth**."

In a brief audience in Polish to fellow countrymen, John Paul II recalled the teaching of the heretic Hans Urs von Balthasar that, "There is a Hell, **but it could be empty**."[144]

On August 4, 1999, John Paul II said that Purgatory is not an actual place.[145]

> Pope Pius IV, *Council of Trent*, Session 25, Dec. 3-4, 1563: "As the Catholic Church, instructed by the Holy Spirit, has taught from holy scripture and the ancient tradition of the fathers in its councils and most recently in this ecumenical synod that **Purgatory exists**, and that **the souls detained there** are helped by the prayers of the faithful and most of all by the acceptable sacrifice of the altar."[146]

At the Assisi meeting of Jan. 24, 2002, John Paul II issued "the Decalogue of Assisi." The word *Decalogue* means "the ten commandments."

John Paul II, May 21, 2002: "To help create a world of greater justice and solidarity, take to heart the need to promote **the 'Decalogue of Assisi,'** proclaimed at the Day of Prayer for Peace last 24 January." [147]

So John Paul II was saying that people need to proclaim the new ten commandments that he issued at Assisi.

John Paul II changed the Rosary

John Paul II venerating a loaf of bread?!

John Paul II also changed the Rosary. In Oct. 2002, John Paul II added five new mysteries to the Rosary, called "the Mysteries of Light." In the document which promulgated the mysteries of light, John Paul II stated:

> "Anyone who contemplates Christ through the various stages of his life cannot fail to perceive in him *the truth about man.*"[148]

When we contemplate the mysteries of Christ, we don't perceive in Him the truth about man. John Paul II said this because he taught that man is God; and specifically, that the truth about man is that he is Jesus Christ.

John Paul II taught that man is Christ

John Paul II, Very First Homily, Forever Marking the Beginning of his Pastoral Ministry, Sunday, Oct. 22, 1978: "*'You are the Christ, the Son of the living God'* (Mt. 16:16). These words were spoken by Simon, son of Jonah, in the district of Caesarea Philippi... These words mark the beginning of Peter's mission in the history of salvation...

> "On this day and in this place these same words must again be uttered and listened to: *'You are the Christ, the Son of the living God.'* Yes, Brothers and sons and daughters, these words first of all… please listen once again, today, in this sacred place, to the words uttered by Simon Peter. In those words is the faith of the Church. ***In those same words is the new truth, indeed, the ultimate and definitive truth about man: the Son of the living God – 'You are the Christ, the Son of the living God.'***"[149]

In his first ever homily as "pope" in 1978, in the very speech which will forever mark the beginning of his pastoral ministry, Sunday, Oct. 22, 1978, John Paul II proclaimed to the world that MAN is the Christ, the Son of the Living God of Matthew 16:16! He even said that this is a "new truth" – a new truth which he was here to reveal. "Thou art the Christ, the Son of the Living God," spoken by St. Peter about Our Lord Jesus Christ, are the words which describe the truth about man, according to John Paul II. This is extremely significant, for it proves that Our Lady's words at La Salette have come true.

> Our Lady of La Salette, Sept. 19, 1846: "Rome will lose the Faith and become the seat of the Anti-Christ… the Church will be in eclipse."

In fact, John Paul II preached that man is Christ in many ways. Sometimes it was very subtle and clever, at other times it was very obvious and bold. This is covered in detail at the end of this book, but here are just a few quotes:

> John Paul II, *General Audience*, Feb. 22, 1984: "… **so that consciences can be freed in the full truth of man, who is Christ**, 'peace and mercy' for everyone."[150]

> John Paul II, *Homily*, Dec. 17, 1991: "Dear brothers and sisters, **look to Christ, the Truth about man**…"[151]

> John Paul II, *Homily*, Dec. 10, 1989: "… **make straight the way of the Lord and of man**…"[152]

> John Paul II, *Homily*, August 10, 1985: "**Today, in consecrating your cathedral, we ardently desire that it become a 'true temple of God and man…'**"[153]

> John Paul II, Dec. 25, 1978: "**Christmas is the feast of man.**"[154]

> John Paul II, Dec. 25, 2001: "… let us pause in adoration in the cave, and gaze upon the Newborn **Redeemer. In him we can recognize the face of every little child who is born**…"[155]

> John Paul II, Dec. 25, 1985: "What is grace? Grace is precisely the manifestation of God… Grace is God as "our Father." It is the Son of God… It is the Holy Spirit… **Grace is, also, man**…"[156]

John Paul II, March 31, 1991: "**Let respect for man be total... Every offense against the person is an offense against God...**"[157]

John Paul II, Jan. 24, 2002: "To offend against man is, most certainly, to offend against God."[158]

John Paul II, *Address to Ambassador of Tunisia*, May 27, 2004, p. 8: "...For its part, <u>the modest Catholic community that lives in Tunisia has no other ambition than to witness to the dignity of man</u>..."[159]

The "Catholic community" in Tunisia has no other ambition than to witness to the dignity of man? By such a statement **John Paul II was again indicating that the "Catholic" community in Tunisia has no desire to convert other non-Catholics**, but only to witness to the dignity of man.

John Paul II, *Homily*, June 24, 1988: "... **God wishes to encounter in man the whole of creation.**"[160]

This means that in man one can find the whole of creation.

Antipope John Paul II, *Address to Missionaries of Precious Blood*, September 14, 2001: "And at the moment of Easter this joy came to its fullness as the light of divine glory shone on the face of <u>the Risen Lord, whose wounds shine forever like the Sun. This is the truth of who you are</u>, dear Brothers..."[161]

John Paul II, *Redemptor Hominis*, March 4, 1979: "**IN REALITY, THE NAME FOR THAT DEEP AMAZEMENT AT MAN'S WORTH AND DIGNITY IS THE GOSPEL, THAT IS TO SAY: THE GOOD NEWS. IT IS ALSO CALLED CHRISTIANITY.**"[162]

The Gospel is Jesus Christ (His Life and Teaching); it's the religion of faith and morals He revealed to the world. To say that the Gospel, the Good News and Christianity are the "deep amazement at man" is to equate man with Jesus Christ; but this is exactly why John Paul II said it and what he was doing.

Galatians Chapter 1:8: "*But though we, or an angel from heaven, preach a gospel to you besides that which we have preached to you, let him be anathema.*"

John Paul II was anathema. He preached a new Gospel, not of Jesus Christ, but of man in the place of Christ – the Gospel of Antichrist.

Pope Pius X, *E Supremi Apostolatus*, Oct. 4, 1903: "... **the distinguishing mark of Antichrist, man has with infinite temerity put himself in the place of God...**"[163]

John Paul II carrying the "Broken Cross"

Paul VI, John Paul I, John Paul II and Benedict XVI have carried a cross that very few have understood – the sinister bent or broken cross on which the Body of Christ is displayed as a repulsive and distorted figure. This bent or broken cross was used by black magicians and sorcerers in the sixth century to represent the Biblical term "mark of the beast." Satanists in the fifth and sixth centuries, as well as black magicians and sorcerers of the Middle Ages (476-1453), used such figurines to represent their hatred for Christianity. The fact that the broken cross was used for occult purposes can be seen in the Museum of Witchcraft in Bayonne, France.[164]

Concluding Points about John Paul II

So the question that everyone professing to be Catholic must ask himself is this: was John Paul II the head of the Catholic Church? Or was John Paul II part of a different religion? If John Paul II was part of a different religion – *and who would dare deny this in light of the undeniable and overwhelming evidence we have just presented?* – then he could not have been the head of the Catholic Church.

> St. Francis De Sales, Doctor of the Church:
> "It would indeed be <u>one of the strangest monsters that could be seen</u> – if the head of the Church *were not of the Church*."[165]

We have proven beyond doubt that John Paul II was a manifest heretic. Since he was a heretic, he could not have been a validly elected pope. **He was a non-Catholic antipope**. As quoted already, Pope Paul IV solemnly taught in his Feb. 15, 1559 Bull, *Cum ex Apostolatus officio*, that it is impossible for a heretic to be a validly elected pope.

Endnotes for Section 16:

[1] www.cnn.com, archives of *Larry King Live* show, April 4, 2005.
[2] Denzinger, *The Sources of Catholic Dogma*, B. Herder Book. Co., Thirtieth Edition, 1957, no. 464.
[3] *The Papal Encyclicals*, by Claudia Carlen, Raleigh: The Pierian Press, 1990, Vol. 5 (1958-1981), p. 255.
[4] *The Encyclicals of John Paul II*, Huntington, IN: Our Sunday Visitor Publishing Division, 1996, p. 497.
[5] *The Encyclicals of John Paul II*, p. 643.
[6] *L' Osservatore Romano* (The Vatican's Newspaper), July 1, 1985, p. 3
[7] Denzinger 795.
[8] *L'Osservatore Romano*, June 23, 1980, p. 3.
[9] *L'Osservatore Romano*, Jan. 1, 1979, p. 8.
[10] *The Papal Encyclicals*, Vol. 5 (1958-1981), p. 249.
[11] *The Encyclicals of John Paul II*, p. 517.
[12] *The Encyclicals of John Paul II*, p. 542.
[13] *The Papal Encyclicals*, Vol. 1 (1740-1878), p. 280.
[14] *L'Osservatore Romano*, May 7, 1984, p. 3.
[15] *The Papal Encyclicals*, Vol. 1 (1740-1878), p. 260.
[16] *L'Osservatore Romano*, May 14, 1984, p. 7.
[17] *L'Osservatore Romano*, Jan. 18, 1995, p. 11.
[18] *The Papal Encyclicals*, Vol. 2 (1878-1903), p. 304.
[19] *L'Osservatore Romano*, April 16, 1997, p. 3.
[20] Quoted in Abbe Daniel Le Roux, *Peter, Lovest Thou Me?*, Angelus Press, 1988, p. 147.
[21] St. Thomas Aquinas, *Summa Theologica*, Pt. I-II, Q. 103., A. 4.
[22] St. Thomas Aquinas, *Summa Thelogica*, Pt. II-II, Q. 12, A. 1, Obj. 2.
[23] *The Papal Encyclicals*, Vol. 3 (1903-1939), p. 317.
[24] *L'Osservatore Romano CD-Rom*, Year 1986, Vatican City, Angelus Address of John Paul II, Oct. 12, 1986.
[25] *The Encyclicals of John Paul II*, p. 540.
[26] *The Papal Encyclicals*, Vol. 1 (1740-1878), p. 222.
[27] *L' Osservatore Romano*, May 29, 2002, p. 4.
[28] *The Papal Encyclicals*, Vol. 1 (1740-1878), pp. 237-238.
[29] *The Encyclicals of John Paul II*, p. 502.
[30] *Decrees of the Ecumenical Councils*, Sheed & Ward and Georgetown University Press, 1990, Vol. 1, pp. 550-553; Denzinger 39-40.
[31] *Our Sunday Visitor*, April 17, 2005.
[32] *L'Osservatore Romano*, August 26, 1985, p. 9.
[33] *The Papal Encyclicals*, Vol. 3 (1903-1939), p. 316.
[34] Associated Press, "Religious Leaders denounce Extremism," Oct. 29, 1999.
[35] *Decrees of the Ecumenical Councils*, Vol. 1, p. 625.
[36] Quoted by Amleto Giovanni Cicognani, *Canon Law*, Philadelphia, PA: The Dolphin Press, 1935, p. 177.
[37] *The Papal Encyclicals*, Vol. 3 (1903-1939), p. 381.
[38] *L'Osservatore Romano*, Dec. 9, 1980, p. 5.
[39] *L'Osservatore Romano*, March 1, 2000, p. 5.
[40] Von Pastor, *History of the Popes*, II, 346; quoted by Warren H. Carroll, *A History of Christendom*, Vol. 3 (*The Glory of Christendom*), Front Royal, VA: Christendom Press, 1993, p. 571.
[41] *L' Osservatore Romano*, March 29, 2000, p. 2.
[42] *The Catholic World Report*, "World Watch," June, 2000, p. 16.
[43] *L'Osservatore Romano CD-Rom*, Year 2001, Speech of John Paul II from the mosque, May 6, 2001.
[44] Warren H. Carroll, *A History of Christendom (The Building of Christendom)*, Vol. 2, p. 298.
[45] *The Encyclicals of John Paul II*, p. 474.
[46] *L'Osservatore Romano*, Oct. 23, 1989, p. 12.
[47] *L'Osservatore Romano*, Feb. 19, 1990, p. 12.
[48] *L'Osservatore Romano*, May 23, 2001, p. 11.
[49] *L'Osservatore Romano*, May 12, 1999, p. 11.
[50] *The Catechism of the Catholic Church*, by John Paul II, St. Paul Books & Media, 1994, p. 223.
[51] Denzinger 73.
[52] Denzinger 712.
[53] *The Papal Encyclicals*, Vol. 1 (1740-1878), p. 98.
[54] *The Papal Encyclicals*, Vol. 4 (1939-1958), p. 42.
[55] *L' Osservatore Romano*, Dec. 9, 1980, p. 6.
[56] *The Papal Encyclicals*, Vol. 1 (1740-1878), p. 98.
[57] *Documentation Catholique* 94 (1997), 1003; quoted in *The Bible, The Jews and the Death of Jesus*, Bishops' Committee for Ecumenical and Interreligious Affairs, United States Conference of Catholic Bishops, 2004, p. 31.
[58] *Bulletin du prieure Marie-Reine* [195 rue de Bale, 68100 Mulhouse]; also *The Angelus*, Feb-March 2004, p. 70.
[59] *The Catechism of the Catholic Church*, #121.

60 *The Sunday Sermons of the Great Fathers*, Chicago: Regnery Press, 1959, Vol. 1., p. 92.
61 *Decrees of the Ecumenical Councils*, Vol. 1, p. 78.
62 Darcy O' Brien, *The Hidden Pope*, New York, NY: Daybreak Books, 1998, pp. 368-369.
63 http://www.lehman.cuny.edu/lehman/enews/2005_09_26/feat_pac.html
64 Gilbert Levine, Interview with *CBS's 60 Minutes*.
65 Romano Amerio, *Iota Unum*, Kansas City, MO: Angelus Press, 1998, p. 578.
66 www.cnn.com, archives of *Larry King Live* show, April 4, 2005.
67 *Catholic Family News*, Niagra Falls, NY, September, 2002, p. 3.
68 *L' Osservatore Romano*, 2001.
69 *L' Osservatore Romano*, May 29, 2002, p. 5.
70 *Directory for the Application of the Principles and Norms of Ecumenism*, by the Pontifical Council for Promoting Christian Unity, Boston, MA: St. Paul Books & Media, pp. 78-79.
71 *The Papal Encyclicals*, Vol. 1 (1740-1878), p. 57.
72 *The Papal Encyclicals*, Vol. 1 (1740-1878), p. 58.
73 *Adista*, Feb. 26, 2001.
74 *The Papal Encyclicals*, Vol. 4 (1939-1958), p. 93.
75 *The Papal Encyclicals*, Vol. 4 (1939-1958), p. 95.
76 *The Papal Encyclicals*, Vol. 4 (1939-1958), p. 99.
77 *The Papal Encyclicals*, Vol. 4 (1939-1958), p. 100.
78 Information Service 84 (1993/III-IV) 145; http://www.cnewa.org/ecc-bodypg-us.aspx?eccpageID=82&IndexView=alpha#footnote45
79 *The Papal Encyclicals*, Vol. 3 (1903-1939), p. 317.
80 *L'Osservatore Romano*, Jan. 27, 1993, p. 2.
81 *The Papal Encyclicals*, Vol. 2 (1878-1903), p. 399.
82 *The Encyclicals of John Paul II*, p. 248.
83 *L' Osservatore Romano*, March 1, 2000, p. 5.
84 *L' Osservatore Romano*, Oct. 16, 2002, p. 5.
85 *America* Magazine, "A New Chapter in Catholic-Orthodox Relations," July 3-10, 1999, Vol. 181, No. 1
86 Zenit.org, November 2, 2000.
87 *Decrees of the Ecumenical Councils*, Vol. 1, p. 234.
88 *L' Osservatore Romano*, Oct. 16, 2002, p. 4.
89 *The Papal Encyclicals*, Vol. 1 (1740-1878), p. 297 and footnote 4.
90 *L' Osservatore Romano*, Oct. 16, 2002, p. 4.
91 *The Papal Encyclicals*, Vol. 1 (1740-1878), p. 230.
92 *The Papal Encyclicals*, Vol. 1 (1740-1878), p. 207.
93 *The Papal Encyclicals*, Vol. 1 (1740-1878), p. 201.
94 *The Papal Encyclicals*, Vol. 3 (1903-1939), p. 318.
95 *L'Osservatore Romano*, July 2, 2003, p. V.
96 Denzinger 1827.
97 *The Encyclicals of John Paul II*, p. 953.
98 Quoted in *Sacerdotium*, # 2, Instauratio Catholica, Madison Heights, WI, p. 64.
99 *L'Osservatore Romano*, Nov. 15, 2000, p. 6/7 – Joint Communique of John Paul II and Catholicos Karekin II.
100 Warren H. Carroll, *A History of Christendom*, Christendom Press, 1985, Vol. 1, p. 539.
101 *30 Days Magazine*, November, 1996.
102 *The Papal Encyclicals*, Vol. 1 (1740-1878), p. 321.
103 Denzinger 1966.
104 *L'Osservatore Romano*, 10/8/03, p. 9.
105 CWNews, Sept. 8, 2003.
106 *L'Osservatore Romano*, Oct. 8, 2003, p. 9.
107 *L'Osservatore Romano*, Nov. 14, 1983, p. 9.
108 *L'Osservatore Romano*, July 9, 1985, p. 5.
109 *The Papal Encyclicals*, Vol. 1 (1740-1878), p. 268.
110 *30 Days Magazine*, Issue No. 7-8, 1995, p. 19.
111 *L'Osservatore Romano*, Jan. 28, 2004, p. 4.
112 *The Code of Canon Law (1983), A Text and Commentary*, Commissioned by the Canon Law Society of America, Edited by James A. Coriden, Thomas J. Green, Donald E. Heintschel, Mahwah, NJ: Paulist Press, 1985, p. 609.
113 *The Papal Encyclicals*, Vol. 1 (1740-1878), p. 364.
114 *The Catechism of the Catholic Church*, p. 5.
115 Denzinger 1833.
116 Denzinger 1837.
117 *The Encyclicals of John Paul II*, p. 950.
118 *The Catechism of the Catholic Church*, p. 216.
119 Denzinger 1000.

[120] *The Encyclicals of John Paul II*, p. 965.
[121] Denzinger 714.
[122] *The Papal Encyclicals*, Vol. 3 (1903-1939), p. 368.
[123] *The Papal Encyclicals*, Vol. 1 (1740-1878), p. 229.
[124] *The Encyclicals of John Paul II*, p. 965.
[125] *L' Osservatore Romano*, Nov. 15, 2000, p. 5.
[126] *The Encyclicals of John Paul II*, p. 914.
[127] *Salvifici Doloris*, Apostolic Letter of John Paul II, Feb. 11, 1984, Pauline Books, p. 35.
[128] *L'Osservatore Romano CD-Rom*, Year 1993, Angelus Address of John Paul II, Sept. 9, 1993.
[129] *L'Osservatore Romano CD-Rom*, Year 1994, *Tertio Millennio Adveniente* of John Paul II, Nov. 10, 1994.
[130] *L'Osservatore Romano CD-Rom*, Year 1994, *Tertio Millennio Adveniente* of John Paul II, Nov. 10, 1994.
[131] *The Encyclicals of John Paul II*, p. 965.
[132] *The Encyclicals of John Paul II*, p. 965.
[133] *L' Osservatore Romano*, May 19, 1999, p. 11.
[134] Denzinger 247.
[135] *The Papal Encyclicals*, Vol. 1 (1740-1878), p. 64.
[136] *The Remnant*, St. Paul, MN, April 30, 2000, p. 6.
[137] *L' Osservatore Romano*, Oct. 31, 2001, p. 3.
[138] *L' Osservatore Romano*, Oct. 31, 2001, p. 4.
[139] Statement to the Pontifical Academy of Sciences, Oct. 22, 1996, Original French Version.
[140] *National Catholic Register*, Mt. Morris, IL, August 1-7, 1999, p. 4.
[141] *L' Osservatore Romano*, August 4, 1999, p. 7.
[142] *L' Osservatore Romano*, August 4, 1999, p. 7.
[143] *L' Osservatore Romano*, August 4, 1999, p. 7.
[144] *National Catholic Register*, August 8-14, 1999.
[145] *National Catholic Register*, August 15-21, 1999, p. 5.
[146] *Decrees of the Ecumenical Councils*, Vol. 2, p. 774.
[147] *L' Osservatore Romano*, June 19, 2002, p. 9.
[148] *L' Osservatore Romano*, Oct. 23, 2002, p. 5.
[149] *L'Osservatore Romano*, Nov. 2, 1978, p. 1.
[150] *L'Osservatore Romano*, Feb. 27, 1984, p. 1.
[151] *L'Osservatore Romano*, Jan. 8, 1992, p. 9.
[152] *L'Osservatore Romano*, Jan. 22, 1990, p. 6.
[153] *L'Osservatore Romano*, Sept. 2, 1985, p. 3.
[154] *L'Osservatore Romano*, Jan. 1, 1979, p. 1.
[155] *L' Osservatore Romano*, Jan. 2, 2002, p. 1.
[156] *L'Osservatore Romano*, Jan. 6, 1986, p. 1.
[157] *L'Osservatore Romano*, April 2, 1991, p. 1.
[158] *L'Osservatore Romano*, Jan. 30, 2002, p. 6/7.
[159] *L'Osservatore Romano*, June 16, 2004, p. 8.
[160] *L'Osservatore Romano*, Aug. 29, 1988, p. 10.
[161] *L'Osservatore Romano*, Sept. 19, 2001, p. 10.
[162] *The Papal Encyclicals*, Vol. 5 (1958-1981), pp. 251-252.
[163] *The Papal Encyclicals*, Vol. 3 (1903-1939), p. 6.
[164] Piers Compton, *The Broken Cross*, p. 72.
[165] St. Francis De Sales, *The Catholic Controversy*, Rockford, IL: Tan Books, 1989, p. 45.

17) The Vatican II sect's Protestant Revolution: the 1999 Joint Declaration with the Lutherans on Justification

Vatican-Lutheran Agreement on Justification, Oct. 31, 1999: "# 13. **IN LIGHT OF THIS CONSENSUS, THE CORRESPONDING DOCTRINAL CONDEMNATIONS OF THE 16TH CENTURY [the Council of Trent] DO NOT APPLY TO TODAY'S PARTNER."**[1]

With the approval of John Paul II, on Oct. 31, 1999 "Cardinal" Edward Cassidy and Lutheran "Bishop" Christian Krause sign *The Joint Declaration on the Doctrine of Justification* in Augsburg, Germany

On October 31, 1999, the Vatican under John Paul II approved a joint declaration with the Lutherans on the doctrine of Justification. The idea that Catholics could agree to a joint declaration with Lutherans on the doctrine of justification should immediately strike a Catholic as absurd because Catholics are required to believe in the dogmatic teaching of the Council of Trent, while Lutherans reject the dogmatic teaching of the Council of Trent.

> Pope Paul III, Council of Trent, Sess. 6, On Justification, Introduction: "...**the holy ecumenical and general synod of <u>Trent</u> lawfully assembled in the Holy Spirit... cardinals of the Holy Roman Church and apostolic legates *a latere*, presiding... purpose to expound to all the faithful of Christ <u>the true and salutary doctrine of justification, which the "son of justice" (Mal. 4:2), Christ Jesus, "the author and finisher of our faith" (Heb. 12:2) taught, the apostles transmitted and the Catholic Church, under the instigation of the Holy Spirit, has always retained</u>...**"[2]

> Pope Paul III, Council of Trent, Session 6, Chap. 16:
> "**After this Catholic doctrine of justification - <u>which, unless he faithfully and firmly accepts, no one can be justified</u>** - it seemed good to the holy Synod to add these canons,

so that all may know, not only what they must hold and follow, but also what they ought to shun and avoid."[3]

Obviously, the only agreement that could be reached is one where the Lutherans rejected their heresy and accepted Catholic dogma. However, this was not what the *Joint Declaration with the Lutherans* – which was approved by John Paul II and Benedict XVI – was about.

The *Joint Declaration with the Lutherans on the Doctrine of Justification* is so heretical that there are almost no words to describe it. It completely repudiates the Council of Trent. Since some of the defenders of the Vatican II sect and even some of the "traditionalists" have offered some of the most ridiculous and dishonest attempts to defend this agreement, we will briefly review why this document is heretical, why it is a complete repudiation of the Council of Trent, and why it actually constitutes an official declaration by John Paul II and Benedict XVI themselves that their sect is, in reality, a non-Catholic, Protestant "Church."

▶1) Joint Declaration With Lutherans on Justification, Oct. 31, 1999: "**# 5. THE PRESENT JOINT DECLARATION**… does not cover all that either church teaches about justification; it does encompass a consensus on basic truths of the doctrine of justification and **SHOWS THAT THE REMAINING DIFFERENCES ARE NO LONGER THE OCCASION FOR DOCTRINAL CONDEMNATIONS.**"[4]

This means that the remaining differences between Lutherans and Catholics on Justification – for example, *the fact that Lutherans don't accept the Council of Trent's Decree on Justification as dogmatic* – are no longer the occasion for doctrinal condemnations. This is blatantly HERETICAL. The very fact that the Lutherans don't accept the Council of Trent's Decree on Justification as dogmatic is an occasion for their doctrinal condemnation, as we just saw.

▶ (2) Joint Declaration With the Lutherans on Justification, Oct. 31, 1999: "41. Thus the doctrinal condemnations of the 16th century [i.e., the Council of Trent], in so far as they are related to the doctrine of justification, appear in a new light: **The teaching of the Lutheran churches presented in this Declaration does not fall under the condemnations from the Council of Trent**."[5]

This means that <u>none</u> of the teaching of the Lutherans in the Joint Declaration (JD) is condemned by the Council of Trent! But in the JD, besides the other heresies taught by the Lutherans (as we will see), <u>the Lutheran churches teach the heresy of Justification by "faith alone,"</u> which was condemned by the Council of Trent approximately 13 times!

▶Joint Declaration with the Lutherans on Justification: "26. <u>According to Lutheran understanding, God justifies sinners in **faith alone**</u> (sola fide)."[6]

Pope Paul III, *Council of Trent*, Session 6, Chap. 10, *ex cathedra*:
"'You see, that by works a man is justified **and not by faith alone**' (Jas. 2:24)."[7]

Thus, the statement in #41 of the JD means that the "Catholic" side agrees that <u>all the dogmatic canons and decrees in Trent condemning faith alone are overturned</u>, and that faith alone is no longer contrary to or condemned by Trent. It is not possible for heresy to be any more formal than this.

▶3) Joint Declaration With the Lutherans on Justification, Oct. 31, 1999: "**# 13. <u>IN LIGHT OF THIS CONSENSUS, THE CORRESPONDING DOCTRINAL CONDEMNATIONS OF THE 16TH CENTURY [the Council of Trent] DO NOT APPLY TO TODAY'S PARTNER."</u>**[8]

This again means that the fact that the Lutherans don't accept the Council of Trent's Decree on Justification *in totality* is not heretical, which is a denial of the Council of Trent. The Council of Trent condemned as heretical <u>anyone</u> who does not accept <u>all</u> of its teaching, as we saw above.

So, don't be misled by those <u>liars</u> who try to convince people that the JD didn't really deny the Council of Trent, or that *"it's much more complicated than that."* These people are used by the Devil to defend the apostate Vatican II sect. The *Joint Declaration with the Lutherans on the Doctrine of Justification* completely rejects the dogmatic Council of Trent. Anyone who denies this is simply a liar.

SOME OTHER HERESIES IN THE JOINT DECLARATION

In fact, besides "faith alone," there are <u>hordes of other heresies in the JD which were specifically condemned by Trent</u>. See the longer article on our website *Joint Declaration with the Lutherans on Justification* if you want all the gory details. The JD has heresy spilling out of it. Here are just a few others:

▶Joint Declaration with Lutherans: "21. According to the Lutheran teaching, **<u>human beings are incapable of cooperating in their salvation</u>**, because as sinners they actively oppose God and his saving action."[9] – HERESY CONDEMNED BY TRENT!

•Pope Paul III, *Council of Trent*, Session 6, Can. 4:
"**If anyone shall say that man's free will moved and aroused by God does not cooperate** by assenting to God who rouses and calls, whereby it disposes and prepares itself to obtain the grace of justification, and that it cannot dissent, if it wishes, but that like something inanimate it does nothing at all and is merely in a passive state: **let him be anathema.**"[10]

▶Joint Declaration with Lutherans: "23. …Lutherans… intend rather to express that <u>justification</u> remains free from human cooperation and <u>is not dependent upon the life-renewing effects of grace in human beings</u>." – HERESY CONDEMNED BY TRENT!

•Pope Paul III, *Council of Trent*, Session 6, Can. 1:
"**If anyone shall say that man can be justified** before God by his own works which are done either by his own natural powers, or through the teaching of the Law, and **without divine grace through Christ Jesus: let him be anathema.**"[11]

▶Joint Declaration with Lutherans: "29. <u>Lutherans understand this condition of the Christian as a being 'at the same time righteous and sinner.'</u> Believers are totally righteous, in that God forgives their sins through Word and Sacrament and grants the righteousness of Christ which they appropriate in faith. In Christ, they are made just before God. <u>Looking at themselves through the law, however, they recognize that they remain totally sinners."</u>[12] – HERESY CONDEMNED BY TRENT!

This heresy is also called *"simul justus et peccator"* (at the same time just and sinner) and was one of Martin Luther's favorites. It was vigorously condemned by Trent in the following two passages.

> • Pope Paul III, *Council of Trent*, Session 5:
> "If anyone denies that by the grace of our Lord Jesus Christ, which is conferred in baptism, the guilt of original sin is remitted, or **even asserts that the whole of that which has the true and proper nature of sin is not taken away**, but says that it is only touched in person or is not imputed, **let him be anathema.**"[13]

> Pope Paul III, *Council of Trent*, Session 5:
> "**For in those who are born again [Justified]**, God hates nothing, because '**there is no condemnation**, to those who are truly buried together with Christ by baptism unto death' (Rom. 6:4), who do not 'walk according to the flesh' (Rom. 8:1), but putting off 'the old man' and putting on the 'new, who is created according to God' (Eph. 4:22 ff.; Col. 3:9), **are made innocent, immaculate, pure, guiltless**, and beloved sons of God, 'heirs indeed of God, but co-heirs with Christ' (Rom. 8:17), so that there is nothing whatever to retard their entrance into Heaven."[14]

> ▶ Joint Declaration with Lutherans: "29. ...Lutherans say that justified persons are also sinners and that their opposition to God is truly sin, <u>they do not deny that, despite this sin, they are not separated from God</u> and that this is a 'ruled' sin."[15] – HERESY CONDEMNED BY TRENT

> Pope Paul III, *Council of Trent*, Session 6, Chap. 15:
> "... the doctrine of divine law which excludes from the kingdom of God not only the unbelievers, but also the faithful who are fornicators, adulterers, effeminate, liers with mankind, thieves, covetous, drunkards, railers, extortioners (1 Cor. 6:9), and all others who commit **deadly sins**, from which with the assistance of divine grace they can refrain and **for which they are separated from the grace of God.**"[16]

Remember, all of these teachings of the Lutherans in the Joint Declaration – which are blatantly heretical and clearly condemned by the Council of Trent – are declared to be not condemned by Trent in #41 of the Joint Declaration!

We could go on, but what has been covered above is sufficient to establish the point.

Some of the false teachers who have tried to belittle the significance of the JD have tried to deceive their readers and listeners by saying that the <u>two other documents</u> which go along with the JD actually clarify everything. THIS IS <u>PURE HOGWASH</u>! The two other documents that go along with the JD: 1) The *Official Common Statement by the Lutheran World Federation and the Catholic Church* and 2) the *Annex to the Official Common Statement* confirm everything in the JD. They don't contradict its heresies at all, but repeat them, as we see here:

> Official Common Statement, #1 (part of the Joint Declaration): "On the basis of this consensus <u>the Lutheran World Federation and the Catholic Church declare together</u>:
> "**The teaching of the Lutheran Churches presented in the Declaration does not fall**

under the condemnations from the Council of Trent. The condemnations in the Lutheran Confessions do not apply to the teaching of the Roman Catholic Church presented in this Declaration (JD # 41).'"[17]

Moreover, the *Annex to the Official Common Statement* actually goes farther than the JD itself and professes belief in justification by faith alone on the "Catholic" side!

> ►Annex to the Official Common Statement, #2, C ["Catholic" side and Lutheran side together]: "Justification takes place by grace alone, by **faith alone**, the person is justified apart from works."[18]

Please understand: this "Annex" is the part of the Joint Declaration which the defenders of the Vatican II sect say clarifies everything and "makes it okay"! They say the Annex makes everything in the JD completely conformable to Catholic teaching. What a lie! In the following quote, we see a defender of the Vatican II sect attempting to use this very argument. The Novus Ordo/Vatican II defenders who use this type of argument think or hope that the person with whom they are conversing is ignorant of the two accompanying documents (the Annex and the OCS) – so that they can pass off the false impression that these two documents mitigate or explain away the heresies in the Joint Declaration. They hope that the other person, being unfamiliar with them, will have no response. The argument doesn't work, however, with those who are familiar with what these other two documents actually say.

> Leon Suprenant, *President of Catholics United for the Faith*, to MHFM, attempting to defend the JD, Jan. 20, 2005: "...**one must read the OCS and the co-published "Catholic Annex" to get an adequate understanding of the Church's position on the JD**. (Please let me know if you need a copy of either of these documents)."[19]

As we see here, he attempted to respond to the heresies we quoted in the Joint Declaration by saying that the Annex and the OCS [Official Common Statement] make everything okay. But as we've shown, this is complete nonsense. The Annex and the Official Common Statement confirm what is in the JD. Further, the Annex declares that the "Catholics" *not only accept faith alone as not contrary to Trent* (as the JD says), but that Catholics believe in faith alone themselves! If, as he says, the Annex is required to get an understanding of what is taught by the JD, then he is admitting that he believes in Justification by faith alone.

In short, the attempts to defend the JD by making reference to the other two documents which accompanied it are utterly false, and for those familiar with the facts, they are <u>outrageous lies</u>.

Moreover, even if the Annex didn't assert this abominable heresy of Justification by faith alone *on the Catholic side*, it wouldn't matter because all of the heresies catalogued above – whether on the Lutheran side or the "Catholic" side of the JD – are accepted as not condemned by the Council of Trent. Furthermore, as proven in point 1 of this column, the JD specifically says that the Lutherans' remaining differences with Catholics on Justification are not an occasion for doctrinal condemnations. So don't be fooled by those liars who tell you that *"yeah, there are problems with the JD, but none of the heresies appear on the Catholic side, just on the Lutheran side."* It is simply not true and, more importantly, *it doesn't make a difference.*

The Vatican II sect, including John Paul II, Benedict XVI and the official Vatican newspaper all approve of the Joint Declaration. This proves that they are manifest heretics.

> John Paul II, Jan. 19, 2004, *At a Meeting with Lutherans From Finland*: "… I wish to express my gratitude for the ecumenical progress made between Catholics and Lutherans in the five years **since the signing of the *Joint Declaration on the Doctrine of Justification*.**"[20]
>
> Benedict XVI, *Address to Protestants at World Youth Day*, August 19, 2005: "… **the important Joint Declaration on the Doctrine of Justification (1999)** …"[21]
>
> Benedict XVI, *Address to Methodists*, Dec. 9, 2005: "**I have been encouraged by the initiative** which would bring the member churches of the World Methodist Council into association with the **Joint Declaration on the Doctrine of Justification, signed by the Catholic Church** and the Lutheran World Federation in 1999."[22]
>
> Mons. John A. Radano, *Pontifical Council for Promoting Christian Unity*: "This latter meeting [between Baptists and "Catholics"], 5-6 December, at the suggestion of the Baptists focused one day on **the *Joint Declaration on the Doctrine of Justification* (JD) signed by the Catholic Church** and the Lutheran World Federation in 1999…"[23]

This means that the "Church" of John Paul II **officially accepts** the *Joint Declaration with the Lutherans on the Doctrine of Justification* and rejects the Council of Trent. The Catholic Church, on the other hand, retains and **will always retain** the Council of Trent's Doctrine on Justification, which was delivered by Christ to the Apostles.

> Pope Paul III, Council of Trent, Sess. 6, On Justification, Introduction: "...**the holy ecumenical and general synod of Trent** lawfully assembled in the Holy Spirit... cardinals of the Holy Roman Church and apostolic legates *a latere*, presiding… **purpose to expound to all the faithful of Christ the true and salutary doctrine of justification, which the "son of justice" (Mal. 4:2), Christ Jesus, "the author and finisher of our faith" (Heb. 12:2) taught, the apostles transmitted and the Catholic Church, under the instigation of the Holy Spirit, has always retained**..."[24]

Thus, the "Church" of John Paul II is not the Catholic Church, and those who are aware of these facts and then affirm communion with it are simply affirming communion with manifest heretics and are sinning against the Faith.

Endnotes for Section 17:

[1] *L'Osservatore Romano* (The Vatican's Newspaper), Nov. 24, 1999.
[2] Denzinger, *The Sources of Catholic Dogma*, B. Herder Book. Co., Thirtieth Edition, 1957, no. 792a.
[3] Denzinger 810.
[4] *L'Osservatore Romano*, Nov. 24, 1999.
[5] *L'Osservatore Romano*, Nov. 24, 1999.
[6] *L'Osservatore Romano*, Nov. 24, 1999.
[7] Denzinger 803.
[8] *L'Osservatore Romano*, Nov. 24, 1999.
[9] *L'Osservatore Romano*, Nov. 24, 1999.
[10] Denzinger 814.
[11] Denzinger 811.
[12] *L'Osservatore Romano*, Nov. 24, 1999.
[13] Denzinger 792.
[14] Denzinger 792.
[15] *L'Osservatore Romano*, Nov. 24, 1999.
[16] Denzinger 808.
[17] *L'Osservatore Romano*, Nov. 24, 1999.

[18] *L'Osservatore Romano*, Nov. 24, 1999.
[19] Communication to MHFM.
[20] *L'Osservatore Romano*, Jan. 28, 2004, p. 4.
[21] *L'Osservatore Romano*, August 24, 2005, p. 8.
[22] *L'Osservatore Romano*, Dec. 21/28, p. 5.
[23] *L'Osservatore Romano*, Jan. 28, 2004, p. 4.
[24] Denzinger 792a.

18. The Vatican II sect vs. the Catholic Church on partaking in non-Catholic worship

Pope Pius XI, *Mortalium Animos* (# 10), Jan. 6, 1928: "… this Apostolic See has never allowed its subjects to take part in the assemblies of non-Catholics…"[1]

John Paul II in common prayer in 1982, in the Anglican Cathedral, with the schismatic and heretical "Archbishop" of Canterbury (an Anglican), who is just a layman posing as a bishop

We've already documented that the Vatican II antipopes repeatedly partake in non-Catholic religious ceremonies. This was condemned by Pope Pius XI. Expressing the universal Tradition of the Church on this matter, he stated:

Pope Pius XI, *Mortalium Animos* (# 10), Jan. 6, 1928: "… **this Apostolic See has never allowed its subjects to take part in the assemblies of non-Catholics**…"[2]

All Catholic moral theology manuals before Vatican II reiterated this truth. They taught that it's a mortal sin against the divine law for Catholics to partake in non-Catholic worship.

Pope Pius IX, *Neminem vestrum* (# 5), Feb. 2, 1854: "We want you to know that those same monks sent Us a splendid profession of Catholic faith and doctrine… **They eloquently acknowledged and freely received the regulations and decrees which the popes and the sacred congregations published or would publish – especially those which prohibit *communicatio in divinis* (communion in holy matters) with schismatics**… They acknowledge that they condemn the error of the schismatic Armenians and recognize that they are outside of the Church of Jesus Christ."[3]

Notice that the decrees and regulations of the popes prohibit communication in divine things with schismatics.

> Pope Pius VI, *Charitas* (# 31-32), April 13, 1791, speaking of priests who went along with the notoriously heretical civil constitution of the clergy in France: "Above all, avoid and condemn the sacrilegious intruders… **do not hold communion with them especially in divine worship.**"[4]

Speaking of priests who belong to the "Old Catholic" sect, which publicly rejects Vatican I and its definition on Papal Infallibility, Pope Pius IX declared:

> Pope Pius IX, *Graves ac diuturnae* (# 4), March 23, 1875: "**They [the faithful] should totally shun their religious celebrations, their buildings,** and their chairs of pestilence which they have with impunity established to transmit the sacred teachings. They should shun their writings and all contact with them. They should not have any dealings or meetings with usurping priests and apostates from the faith who dare to exercise the duties of an ecclesiastical minister without possessing a legitimate mission or any jurisdiction."[5]

> Canon 1258.1, 1917 Code of Canon Law: "It is not licit for the faithful by any manner to assist actively or to have a part in the sacred rites of non-Catholics."[6]

But the Vatican II sect and its "popes" officially teach just the opposite:

> Vatican II document, *Unitatis redintegratio* (# 15):
> "These churches [the schismatic "Orthodox"], though separated from us, yet possess true sacraments… Therefore **some worship in common**, given suitable circumstances and the approval of church authority, **is not merely possible but to be encouraged**."[7]

This is an attempt to overturn the divine law forbidding Catholics to partake in non-Catholic worship. It is heresy. This is why we have repeatedly seen the post-Vatican II antipopes partake in non-Catholic worship and pray with non-Catholics.

Benedict XVI praying ecumenical Vespers on Sept. 12, 2006.[8] Notice that Benedict XVI explicitly acknowledges that he is worshipping with them.

> Benedict XVI, *Address during ecumenical Vespers service*, Sept. 12, 2006: "Dear Brothers and Sisters in Christ! We are gathered, <u>Orthodox Christians, Catholics and Protestants – and together with us there are also some Jewish friends</u> – to sing together the evening praise of God… This is an hour of gratitude for the fact that **we can pray together in this way**…"[9]

In this book, we have given and will continue to give many other examples of this activity from the Vatican II antipopes.

The incredible Directory for the Application of the Principles and Norms of Ecumenism

Perhaps the clearest expression of the new religion in regard to participation in non-Catholic worship is the *Directory for the Application of the Principles and Norms of Ecumenism*, promulgated by John Paul II and the Pontifical Council for Promoting Christian Unity in 1993.

> In # 23, it encourages Episcopal Conferences to take "special measures" to <u>avoid the "danger of proselytism"</u> (trying to convert others).[10]

> In # 50c, it encourages Catholic religious to organize meetings among Protestants of "<u>various churches… for liturgical prayer</u>, for recollection, and spiritual exercises."[11]

> In # 85, the Directory explains how "it is useful" to encourage <u>exchanges between Catholic monasteries and those of other religions</u>.[12]

In # 118, the Directory says that <u>Catholics who attend non-Catholic churches are **"encouraged to take part in the psalms, responses, hymns and common actions of the Church in which they are guests**</u>**."**[13]

As we can see, #50c and #118 specifically encourage exactly what Pius XI said the Apostolic See has never allowed: participation in non-Catholic worship.

In # 119, it states: "<u>In a Catholic liturgical celebration, ministers of other Churches or ecclesial Communities may have the place and liturgical honors proper to their rank and their role</u>..."[14]

In # 137, it states, "<u>if priests, ministers or communities not in full communion with the Catholic Church do not have a place or the liturgical objects necessary for celebrating worthily their religious ceremonies, the diocesan bishop may allow them the use of a church or a Catholic building</u> and also lend them what may be necessary for their services. Under similar circumstances, permission may be given to them for interment or for the celebration of services at Catholic cemeteries."[15]

In # 158, the Directory says that when mixed marriages take place "the local Ordinary may permit the Catholic priest **to invite the minister of the party of the other Church or ecclesial Community to participate in the celebration of the marriage, to read from the Scriptures, give a brief exhortation, and bless the couple.**"[16]

In # 187, the Directory recommends that Catholics and non-Catholics work together in drawing up texts of common Creeds, psalms, scriptural readings, and hymnbooks to be used when they pray and witness together.[17]

This is a new religion. It is an official program of participation in non-Catholic worship, directly contrary to the divine law which teaches that Catholics are forbidden to partake in non-Catholic worship.

On March 25, 1993, Antipope John Paul II "approved this Directory, confirmed it by his authority and ordered that it be published. Anything to the contrary notwithstanding."[18] John Paul II also approved this incredibly heretical directory on ecumenism in his encyclical *Ut Unum Sint*:

> John Paul II, *Ut Unum Sint* (# 16), May 25, 1995: "More recently, **the *Directory for the Application of Principles and Norms of Ecumenism*, issued with my approval** by the Pontifical Council for Promoting Christian Unity, has applied them to the pastoral sphere."[19]

So, the question is: How can the Catholic Church now teach and recommend (participation in non-Catholic worship) exactly what the Catholic Church has always forbidden under pain of mortal sin? The answer is that it cannot overturn something that involves the Faith and is connected to the divine law. The answer is that such a new teaching is absolute proof that the Vatican II sect and its antipopes are formally heretical and hold no authority in the Catholic Church.

Endnotes for Section 18:

[1] *The Papal Encyclicals*, by Claudia Carlen, Raleigh: The Pierian Press, 1990, Vol. 3 (1903-1939), p. 317.
[2] *The Papal Encyclicals*, Vol. 3 (1903-1939), p. 317.
[3] *The Papal Encyclicals*, Vol. 1 (1740-1878), p. 321.
[4] *The Papal Encyclicals*, Vol. 1 (1740-1878), p. 184.
[5] *The Papal Encyclicals*, Vol. 1 (1740-1878), p. 452
[6] *The 1917 Pio-Benedictine Code of Canon Law*, translated by Dr. Edward Von Peters, San Francisco, CA: Ignatius Press, 2001, p. 83.
[7] *Decrees of the Ecumenical Councils*, , Sheed & Ward and Georgetown University Press, 1990, Vol. 2, pp. 915-916.
[8] *L'Osservatore Romano*, Sept. 20, 2006, p. 10.
[9] *L'Osservatore Romano*, Sept. 20, 2006, p. 10.
[10] *Directory for the Application of the Principles and Norms of Ecumenism*, by the Pontifical Council for Promoting Christian Unity, Boston, MA: St. Paul Books & Media, p. 21.
[11] *Directory for the Application of the Principles and Norms of Ecumenism*, p. 37.
[12] *Directory for the Application of the Principles and Norms of Ecumenism*, p. 59.
[13] *Directory for the Application of the Principles and Norms of Ecumenism*, p. 77.
[14] *Directory for the Application of the Principles and Norms of Ecumenism*, p. 77.
[15] *Directory for the Application of the Principles and Norms of Ecumenism*, p. 83.
[16] *Directory for the Application of the Principles and Norms of Ecumenism*, pp. 90-91.
[17] *Directory for the Application of the Principles and Norms of Ecumenism*, pp. 105-106.
[18] *Directory for the Application of the Principles and Norms of Ecumenism*, p. 124.
[19] *The Encyclicals of John Paul II*, Huntington, IN: Our Sunday Visitor Publishing Division, 1996, p. 924.

END NOTES - PAGE 242

19. The Vatican II sect vs. the Catholic Church on non-Catholics receiving Holy Communion

Pope Pius VIII, *Traditi Humilitati* (# 4), May 24, 1829:
"Jerome used to say it this way: **he who eats the Lamb outside this house will perish as did those during the flood who were not with Noah in the ark.**"[1]

Benedict XVI giving Communion to the public heretic, Bro. Roger Schutz,[2] the Protestant founder of Taize on April 8, 2005

In the preceding sections on the heresies of Vatican II and John Paul II, we covered that they both teach the heresy that non-Catholics may lawfully receive Holy Communion. It's important to summarize the Vatican II sect's official endorsement of this heretical teaching here for handy reference:

Vatican II

Vatican II document, *Orientalium Ecclesiarum* # 27:
"Given the above-mentioned principles, <u>the sacraments of Penance, Holy Eucharist, and the anointing of the sick may be conferred on eastern Christians who in good faith are separated from the Catholic Church</u>, if they make the request of their own accord and are properly disposed."[3]

Paul VI solemnly confirming Vatican II

Antipope Paul VI, at the end of every Vatican II document: "EACH AND EVERY ONE OF THE THINGS SET FORTH IN THIS DECREE HAS WON THE CONSENT OF THE FATHERS. WE, TOO, <u>BY THE APOSTOLIC AUTHORITY CONFERRED ON US BY CHRIST</u>, JOIN WITH THE VENERABLE FATHERS IN <u>APPROVING, DECREEING, AND ESTABLISHING</u> THESE THINGS IN THE HOLY SPIRIT, AND WE DIRECT THAT WHAT HAS THUS BEEN ENACTED IN SYNOD BE PUBLISHED TO GOD'S GLORY... I, PAUL, BISHOP OF THE CATHOLIC CHURCH."[4]

Their New Official Catechism

John Paul II, *Catechism of the Catholic Church* (# 1401):
"... **Catholic ministers may give the sacraments of Eucharist, Penance, and Anointing of the Sick to other Christians not in full communion with the Catholic Church**..."[5]

John Paul II solemnly confirming New Catechism

John Paul II, *Fidei Depositum,* Oct. 11, 1992:
"The *Catechism of the Catholic Church,* which I approved June 25th last and the publication of which **I today order by virtue of my Apostolic authority**, *is a statement of the Church's faith and of Catholic doctrine*... **I declare it to be a sure norm for teaching the faith**."[6]

Their New Code of Canon Law

Canon 844.4, 1983 Code of Canon Law:
"If the danger of death is present or other grave necessity, in the judgment of the diocesan bishop or the conference of bishops, <u>Catholic ministers may licitly administer these sacraments to other Christians who do not have full communion with the Catholic Church</u>, who cannot approach a minister of their own community and on their own ask for it, provided they manifest Catholic faith in these sacraments and are properly disposed."[7]

Canon 844.3, 1983 Code of Canon Law:
"<u>Catholic ministers may licitly administer the sacraments of penance, Eucharist, and anointing of the sick to members of the oriental churches which do not have full communion with the Catholic Church</u>, if they ask on their own for the sacraments and are properly disposed. This holds also for members of other churches, which in the judgment of the Apostolic See are in the same condition as the oriental churches as far as these sacraments are concerned."[8]

Encyclical

John Paul II, *Ut Unum Sint* (# 46), May 25, 1995: "... **Catholic ministers are able, in certain particular cases, to administer the Sacraments of the Eucharist, Penance and Anointing of the Sick to Christians who are not in full communion with the Catholic Church**..."

Speeches (this is just one of many quotes that could be given)

John Paul II, *General Audience*, Aug. 9, 1995:
"**Concerning aspects of intercommunion**, the recent Ecumenical Directory confirms and states precisely all that the Council said: that is, **a certain intercommunion is possible, since the Eastern Churches possess true sacraments**, especially the priesthood and the Eucharist.

"On this sensitive point, specific instructions have been issued, stating that, whenever it is impossible for a Catholic to have recourse to a Catholic priest, he may receive the sacraments of Penance, the Eucharist and the Anointing of the Sick from the minister of an Eastern Church (Directory, n. 123). Reciprocally, **Catholic ministers may licitly administer the sacraments of Penance, the Eucharist and the Anointing of the Sick to Eastern Christians who ask for them.**"

Encyclical commenting on this heresy

John Paul II, *Ut Unum Sint* (# 58), May 25, 1995:
"… By reason of the very close sacramental bonds between the Catholic Church and the Orthodox Church… the Catholic Church has often adopted and now adopts a milder policy, offering to all the means of salvation and an example of charity among Christians **through participation in the sacraments and in other sacred functions and objects… There must never be a loss of appreciation for the ecclesiological implication of sharing in the sacraments, especially the Holy Eucharist.**"[9]

He notes the "ecclesiological implication" of sharing in the sacraments with the "Orthodox." His implication is that they are part of the same Church.

There are other quotes we could have given. **This clearly proves that if the Vatican II antipopes are true popes, it's the official teaching of the Catholic Church that heretics and schismatics may be lawfully given Holy Communion. But that's impossible since the Catholic Church has infallibly taught the opposite.**

The Catholic Church and her popes teach just the opposite

For 20 centuries the Catholic Church consistently taught that heretics cannot receive the sacraments. This teaching is rooted in the dogma that outside the Catholic Church there is no remission of sins, defined by Pope Boniface VIII. It is also rooted in the dogma that sacraments only profit unto salvation those inside the Catholic Church, as defined by Pope Eugene IV.

Pope Boniface VIII, *Unam Sanctam*, Nov. 18, 1302: "With Faith urging us we are forced to believe and to hold the one, holy, Catholic Church and that, apostolic, and we firmly believe and simply confess **this Church outside of which there is no salvation nor remission of sin**, the Spouse in the Canticle proclaiming: 'One is my dove, my perfect one.'"[10]

Pope Eugene IV, *Council of Florence*, "Cantate Domino," 1441, *ex cathedra*: "The Holy Roman Church firmly believes, professes and preaches that all those who are outside the Catholic Church, not only pagans but also Jews or heretics and schismatics, cannot share in eternal life and will go into the everlasting fire which was prepared for the devil and his angels, unless they are joined to the Church before the end of their lives; **that the unity of this ecclesiastical body is of such importance that only for those who abide in it do the Church's sacraments contribute to salvation** and do fasts, almsgiving and other works of piety and practices of the Christian militia produce eternal rewards; and that nobody can be saved, no matter how much he has given away in alms and even if he has shed blood in the name of Christ, unless he has persevered in the bosom and unity of the Catholic Church."[11]

Only for those who abide in the Catholic Church do the Church's sacraments contribute to salvation. This is a dogma! But this dogma is repudiated by Vatican II's outrageous teaching that it is lawful to give Holy Communion to those who do not abide in the Catholic Church. Popes throughout the ages have proclaimed that non-Catholics who receive the Holy Eucharist outside the Catholic Church receive it to their own damnation.

> Pope Pius VIII, *Traditi Humilitati* (# 4), May 24, 1829:
> "Jerome used to say it this way: **he who eats the Lamb outside this house will perish as did those during the flood who were not with Noah in the ark.**"[12]

> Pope Gregory XVI, *Commissum divinitus* (# 11), May 17, 1835:
> "… whoever dares to depart from the unity of Peter might understand that he no longer shares in the divine mystery…'**Whoever eats the Lamb outside of this house is unholy.**'"[13]

> Pope Pius IX, *Amantissimus* (# 3), April 8, 1862:
> "… **whoever eats of the Lamb and is not a member of the Church, has profaned.**"[14]

As we can see, this is not a merely disciplinary matter which a pope could change; for it's connected with the dogma that heretics are outside the Church and in the state of sin. Being outside the Church and in a state of sin, they cannot receive the Eucharist unto salvation (Eugene IV), but only unto damnation. To change this law is to attempt to change dogma.

The fact is that the Catholic Church cannot authoritatively teach that it's lawful for non-Catholics to receive Holy Communion, just like it cannot authoritatively teach that it's lawful for people to get abortions. The idea that non-Catholics may lawfully receive Holy Communion is a heresy that has been repeatedly condemned. It is contradicted by the entire history of the Church. **This issue alone proves that the Vatican II antipopes are not true popes, and that we are dealing with two different religions** (the Catholic religion and all the popes vs. the religion of the Vatican II sect and its antipopes).

Endnotes for Section 19:

[1] *The Papal Encyclicals*, by Claudia Carlen, Raleigh: The Pierian Press, 1990, Vol. 1 (1740-1878), p. 222.
[2] *Catholic News Service*, 2005.
[3] *Decrees of the Ecumenical Councils*, Sheed & Ward and Georgetown University Press, 1990, Vol. 2, p. 907.
[4] Walter Abbott, *The Documents of Vatican II*, New York: The America Press, 1966, p. 386, etc.
[5] *Catechism of the Catholic Church*, by John Paul II, St. Paul Books & Media, 1994, #1401.
[6] *Catechism of the Catholic Church*, by John Paul II, p. 5.
[7] *The Code of Canon Law (1983), A Text and Commentary*, Commissioned by the Canon Law Society of America, Edited by James A. Coriden, Thomas J. Green, Donald E. Heintschel, Mahwah, NJ: Paulist Press, 1985, p. 609.
[8] *The Code of Canon Law (1983), A Text and Commentary*, p. 609.
[9] *The Encyclicals of John Paul II*, Huntington, IN: Our Sunday Visitor Publishing Division, 1996, p. 950.
[10] Denzinger, *The Sources of Catholic Dogma*, B. Herder Book. Co., Thirtieth Edition, 1957, no. 468.
[11] *Decrees of the Ecumenical Councils*, Vol. 1, p. 578; Denzinger 714.
[12] *The Papal Encyclicals*, Vol. 1 (1740-1878), p. 222.
[13] *The Papal Encyclicals*, Vol. 1 (1740-1878), p. 256.
[14] *The Papal Encyclicals*, Vol. 1 (1740-1878), p. 364.

END NOTES - PAGE 295

20. The Heresies of Benedict XVI (2005-)

Benedict XVI "Hailed for Praying like Muslims Toward Mecca," Dec 1, 2006 — ISTANBUL (Reuters) - "**Pope Benedict ended a sensitive, fence-mending visit to Turkey on Friday amid praise for visiting Istanbul's famed Blue Mosque and praying there facing toward Mecca 'like Muslims.'**… 'The Pope's dreaded visit was concluded with a wonderful surprise,' wrote daily Aksam on its front page. '**In Sultan Ahmet Mosque, he turned toward Mecca and prayed like Muslims,**'…'"[1]

Benedict XVI praying like Muslims toward Mecca in a mosque, with arms crossed in the Muslim prayer gesture called "the gesture of tranquility," on Nov. 30, 2006

Benedict XVI is Joseph Ratzinger. Joseph Ratzinger was one of the most radical theologians at Vatican II, where his ideas were influential in guiding the revolutionary course of the council.

Karl Rahner (left) with Fr. Joseph Ratzinger (right) at Vatican II[2]

At Vatican II, Ratzinger hung around with notorious heretics such as Karl Rahner. And even though he was a priest, Joseph Ratzinger showed up at Vatican II not in clerical garb, but in a suit and tie.

Ratzinger was named a "cardinal" by Paul VI in 1977, and became Prefect for the Congregation for the Doctrine of the Faith five years later.

During these years, Ratzinger wrote a staggering number of books. The heresies from Ratzinger that will be covered here come from having read many of his speeches and 24 books written by him.

> Many Catholics are familiar with the fact that in the year 2000 the Vatican allegedly revealed the Third Secret of Fatima. Most traditionalists immediately recognized that the so-called "Third Secret" which the Vatican released was not the real Third Secret of Fatima, but rather that a massive fraud had been perpetrated on the world. The primary author of the document which attempted to convince the world of this fraud against Our Lady's message at Fatima was Joseph Ratzinger, Benedict XVI.

The document on the so-called "Third Secret," entitled *The Message of Fatima*, was authored by Ratzinger and "Cardinal" Bertone. It was an attempt to "debunk" the Message of Fatima, as the *Los Angeles Times* was forced to admit. In the document, Ratzinger referred to only one Fatima scholar, Fr. Edouard Dhanis. Fr. Dhanis held that large portions of the Message of Fatima were fabrications of Lucy. By referring to Dhanis as his Fatima "expert," Ratzinger showed that he also holds that the Message of Fatima is a fabrication.

This reveals one of the primary characteristics of Ratzinger. He is a deceiver. He will give the appearance of devotion to something (e.g. Fatima), while trying to rip apart its meaning. He will give the appearance of conservatism, while inculcating the most abominable heresies. We will now cover the astounding heresies of Joseph Ratzinger, Benedict XVI.

BENEDICT XVI'S HERESIES ON THE JEWS

Based on Scripture and Tradition, the Catholic Church teaches infallibly that it is necessary for salvation to believe in Jesus Christ and the Catholic Faith.

> John 8:23-24-"… for if you believe not that I am He, you shall die in your sin."

> Pope Eugene IV, *Council of Florence*, 1439, *ex cathedra*: "Whoever wishes to be saved, needs above all to hold the Catholic faith… it is necessary for eternal salvation that he faithfully believe also in the incarnation of our Lord Jesus Christ… the Son of God is God and man…"[3]

The Catholic Church also teaches infallibly that the Old Covenant ceased with the coming of Christ, and was replaced with the New Covenant. The Council of Florence taught that those who practice the Old Law and the Jewish religion are sinning mortally and are "**alien to the Christian faith and not in the least fit to participate in eternal salvation**, unless someday they recover from these errors."[4]

> In 2001, however, the Pontifical Biblical Commission released a book entitled *The Jewish People and Their Sacred Scriptures in the Christian Bible.* This book rejects the dogma that the Old Covenant has ceased. It teaches that the Old Covenant is still valid, and that the Jews' wait for the Coming of the Messiah (which was part of the Old Covenant) is also still valid. It teaches that Jesus doesn't have to be seen as the prophesied Messiah; it is possible to see Him, as the Jews do, as not the Messiah and not the Son of God.

In section II, A, 5, *The Jewish People and their Sacred Scriptures in the Christian Bible* states:

"Jewish messianic expectation is not in vain…"[5]

In section II, A, 7, *The Jewish People and their Sacred Scriptures in the Christian Bible* states:

> "…to read the Bible as Judaism does necessarily involves **an implicit acceptance of all its presuppositions**, that is, the full acceptance of what Judaism is, in particular, the authority of its writings and rabbinic traditions, **which exclude faith in Jesus as Messiah and Son of God**… Christians can and ought to admit that **the Jewish reading of the Bible is a possible one**…"[6]

> So, according to this Vatican book, Christians can and ought to admit that the Jewish position that Jesus is not the Son of God and the prophesied Messiah is a possible one! **The preface for this totally heretical book was written by none other than Joseph Ratzinger, the now Benedict XVI.**

This is antichrist!

1 John 2:22 – "… he who denieth that Jesus is the Christ? He is antichrist…"

Heresy is a rejection of a dogma of the Catholic Faith; apostasy is a rejection of the entire Christian Faith. This book contains both heresy and apostasy, fully endorsed by Benedict XVI.

Benedict XVI teaches that Jesus doesn't have to be seen as the Messiah

Benedict XVI teaches the same denial of Jesus Christ in a number of his books:

> Benedict XVI, *God and the World*, 2000, p. 209: "**It is of course possible to read the Old Testament so that it is not directed toward Christ; it does not point quite unequivocally to Christ.** And if Jews cannot see the promises as being fulfilled in him, this is not just ill will on their part, but genuinely because of the obscurity of the texts… **There are perfectly good reasons, then, for denying that the Old Testament refers to Christ and for saying, No, that is not what he said.** And there are also

The Heresies of Benedict XVI

> **good reasons for referring it to him – that is what the dispute between Jews and Christians is about."**[7]

Benedict XVI says that there are perfectly good reasons for <u>not</u> believing that the Old Testament refers to Christ as the prophesied Messiah. He says that the Old Testament doesn't point unequivocally to Our Lord as the Messiah. This is another total denial of the Christian Faith.

What makes this apostasy all the more outrageous is the fact that the New Testament is filled with passages which declare that Our Lord is the fulfillment of Old Testament prophecy. To quote just *one passage of many*, in John 5 Our Lord specifically tells the Jews that what is written in the Old Testament concerning Him will convict them.

> John 5:39, 45-47 – "**Search the scriptures, for you think in them to have life everlasting; and the same are they that give testimony of me**… **the one who will accuse you is Moses**, in whom you have placed your hope. For if you had believed Moses, you would have believed me, **because he wrote about me**."

But, according to Benedict XVI, all of these Biblical declarations that Our Lord is the fulfillment of Old Testament prophecies, including Our Lord's own words, may be false. According to Benedict XVI, the Jewish reading that Our Lord is <u>not</u> the Messiah, not the Son of God, and not foretold in the Old Testament, is possible and valid. This is totally heretical, apostate and antichrist.

Benedict XVI also denies Jesus Christ in his book *Milestones*:

> Benedict XVI, *Milestones*, 1998, pages 53-54: "I have ever more come to the realization that <u>**Judaism**</u>… **<u>and the Christian faith</u>** described in the New Testament are two ways of appropriating Israel's Scriptures, **<u>two ways that, in the end, are both determined by the position one assumes with regard to the figure of Jesus of Nazareth. The Scripture we today call Old Testament is in itself open to both ways</u>**…"[8]

Benedict XVI again declares that Scripture is open to holding the Jewish view of Jesus, that Jesus is not the Son of God. This is precisely why Benedict XVI repeatedly teaches the heresy that Jews don't need to believe in Christ for salvation.

> Benedict XVI, *Zenit News story*, Sept. 5, 2000: "[W]e are in agreement that <u>a Jew</u>, and this is true for believers of other religions, <u>does not need to know or acknowledge Christ as the Son of God in order to be saved</u>…"[9]

> Benedict XVI, *God and the World*, 2000, pages 150-151: "…**their [the Jews] No to Christ brings the Israelites** into conflict with the subsequent acts of God, but at the same time we know that they are assured of the faithfulness of God. **<u>They are not excluded from salvation</u>**…"[10]

This is a total rejection of Catholic dogma.

Benedict XVI's Public Act of Apostasy at the German Synagogue

All of this is why on August 19, 2005 – a Friday at noon, the same day and hour that Jesus was crucified – Benedict XVI arrived at the Jewish Synagogue in Cologne, Germany and took active part in a Jewish worship service. To take active part in non-Catholic worship is a sin against the divine law and the First Commandment, as was always taught before Vatican II.

> St. Ambrose, *Sermo 37, The Two Ships*: "**The faithlessness of the Synagogue is an insult to the Savior**. Therefore He chose the bark of Peter, and deserted that of Moses; that is, **He rejected the faithless Synagogue, and adopts the believing Church**."[11]

Benedict XVI in the synagogue of the Jews, taking active part in Jewish worship on Aug. 19, 2005[12]

In taking part in a Jewish worship service, Benedict XVI committed a public act of apostasy. At the synagogue, Benedict XVI was seated prominently near the front. The synagogue was packed with Jews who were there to see him. Benedict XVI was not only an integral part of the Jewish worship service, he was its main feature. This is without any doubt *active participation* in the Jewish religion.

The Heresies of Benedict XVI 249

Very close to Benedict XVI, the cantor of the synagogue prayed and sang Jewish prayers *at the top of his lungs*. Benedict made gestures, such as bowing his head and clapping his hands, to show his approval and participation in the Jewish service. He joined the Jews in the *Kaddish prayer*, and Yiddish music blared in the background.

When Benedict XVI rose to speak (and eventually to pray) in the synagogue, the entire synagogue rose to its feet and applauded him – applauded him for his acceptance of their religion. **Everyone on earth who saw this event knows that it had one meaning: Benedict XVI has no problem with Jews who reject Jesus Christ, and (according to him) they have no obligation to accept Jesus Christ to be saved.**

Benedict XVI teaches that Jews can be saved, that the Old Covenant is valid, and that Jesus Christ is not necessarily the Messiah. He is a bold heretic against the Gospel and the Catholic Faith.

Pope Eugene IV, Council of Florence, "Cantate Domino," 1441, *ex cathedra*: "The Holy Roman Church firmly believes, professes and preaches that **all those who are outside the Catholic Church**, not only pagans **but also Jews** or heretics and schismatics, **cannot share in eternal life and will go into the everlasting fire** which was prepared for the devil and his angels, unless they are joined to the Church before the end of their lives…"[13]

Benedict XVI encourages the Chief Rabbi of Rome in his "mission"

Benedict XVI exchanges a gift with rabbis at Castelgandolfo, Sept. 15, 2005[14]

Benedict XVI, *Address to Chief Rabbi of Rome*, Jan. 16, 2006: "**Distinguished Chief Rabbi, you were recently entrusted with the spiritual guidance of Rome's Jewish Community**; you have taken on this responsibility enriched by your experience as a scholar and a doctor who has shared in the joys and sufferings of a great many people. **I offer you my heartfelt good wishes for your mission**, and I assure you of my own and my collaborators' cordial **esteem** and friendship."[15]

This is apostasy. Benedict XVI encourages the Chief Rabbi in his "mission"! He also expresses his esteem for the Rabbi and his Christ-rejecting apostolate.

Benedict XVI, *General Audience*, Jan. 17, 2007: "**For almost 20 years now the Italian Bishops' Conference has dedicated this Judaism Day to furthering knowledge and esteem for it** and for developing the relationship of reciprocal friendship between the Christian and Jewish communities, a relationship that has developed positively since the Second Vatican Council and **the historic visit of the Servant of God John Paul II to the Major Synagogue in Rome**…. **Today I invite you all to address an ardent prayer to the Lord that Jews and Christians may** respect and **esteem one another**…"[16]

He speaks positively of a day dedicated to Judaism. This day, according to Benedict XVI, is to further esteem for Judaism (a false religion which rejects Christ). This is an utter rejection of the Catholic Faith and Jesus Christ.

BENEDICT XVI TEACHES THAT PROTESTANTS AND SCHISMATICS DON'T NEED TO BE CONVERTED

Benedict XVI as a "cardinal" in 1984 meeting with Syrian schismatic Patriarch Zakka[17]

Heretics and schismatics, such as Protestants and the Eastern Orthodox, are outside the Catholic Church and must be converted to the Catholic Faith for unity and salvation. It's necessary for them to accept all the Catholic dogmas and councils, including the dogmatic definitions at Vatican I in 1870. This is infallible Catholic teaching.

However, Benedict XVI teaches that Protestants and Eastern Schismatics don't need to be converted, and don't need to accept Vatican Council I. We are providing extra context for this quotation, despite its length, since it's such a significant heresy.

> Benedict XVI, *Principles of Catholic Theology*, 1982, pp. 197-198: "Against this background we can now weigh the possibilities that are open to Christian ecumenism. The maximum demands on which the search for unity must certainly founder are immediately clear. **On the part of the West, the maximum demand would be that the East recognize the primacy of the bishop of Rome in the full scope of the definition of 1870** and in so doing submit in practice, to a primacy such as has been accepted by the Uniate churches. On the part of the East, the maximum demand would be that the West declare the 1870 doctrine of primacy erroneous and in so doing submit, in practice, to a primacy such as has been accepted with the removal of the Filioque from the Creed and including the Marian dogmas of the nineteenth and twentieth centuries. **As regards Protestantism, the maximum demand of the Catholic Church would be that the Protestant ecclesiological ministers be regarded as totally invalid and that Protestants be converted to Catholicism;** the maximum demand of Protestants, on the other hand, would be that the Catholic Church accept, along with the unconditional acknowledgement of all Protestant ministries, the Protestant concept of ministry and their understanding of the Church and thus, in practice, renounce the apostolic and sacramental structure of the Church, which would mean, in practice, the conversion of Catholics to Protestantism and their acceptance of a multiplicity of distinct community structures as the historical form of the Church. **While the first three maximum demands are today rather unanimously rejected by Christian consciousness**, the fourth exercises a kind of fascination for it – as it were, a certain conclusiveness that makes it appear to be the real solution to the

The Heresies of Benedict XVI

problem. This is all the more true since there is joined to it the expectation that a Parliament of Churches, a 'truly ecumenical council', could then harmonize this pluralism and promote a Christian unity of action. That no real union would result from this, but that its very impossibility would become a single common dogma, should convince anyone who examines the suggestion closely that such a way would not bring Church unity but only a final renunciation of it. As a result, **none of the maximum solutions offers any real hope of unity**." [18]

Notice that Benedict XVI specifically mentions, **and then bluntly rejects**, the traditional teaching of the Catholic Church that the Protestants and Eastern Schismatics must be converted to the Catholic Faith. He says that their conversion and acceptance of Vatican I and the Papacy is NOT the way for unity. This is a total rejection of the Catholic Faith.

He repeats the same heresy on the next page of his book, where he says that non-Catholics are not required to accept the Papal Primacy:

> Benedict XVI, *Principles of Catholic Theology* (1982), p. 198: "**Nor is it possible, on the other hand, for him to regard as the only possible form and, consequently, as binding on all Christians the form this primacy has taken in the nineteenth and twentieth centuries.** The symbolic gestures of Pope Paul VI and, in particular, his kneeling before the representative of the Ecumenical Patriarch [the schismatic Patriarch Athenagoras] were an attempt to express precisely this…"[19]

Benedict XVI is referring to the Papal Primacy here, and he says that all Christians are not bound to believe in the Papal Primacy as defined by Vatican I in 1870! This means that Benedict XVI claims to be a Catholic and the pope while he holds that heretics and schismatics are not bound to believe in the Papacy! This is one of the greatest frauds in human history. Further, **notice that Benedict XVI even admits that Paul VI's ecumenical gestures with the schismatics were meant to show precisely that the schismatics don't have to accept the Papal Primacy**. This is a blatant denial of Vatican Council I.

> Pope Pius IX, *Vatican Council I*, ex cathedra: "… all the faithful of Christ must believe that the Apostolic See and the Roman Pontiff hold primacy over the whole world… This is the doctrine of Catholic truth from which no one can deviate and keep his faith and salvation."[20]

The Church itself was founded by Our Lord upon the Papal Primacy, as the Gospel declares (Matthew 16:18-20) and as Catholic dogma defines:

> Pope Boniface VIII, *Unam Sanctam*, Nov. 18, 1302, *ex cathedra*:
> "…we declare, we proclaim, we define that it is absolutely necessary for salvation that every human creature be subject to the Roman Pontiff.."[21]

People need to seriously meditate on how bad this is that Benedict XVI holds that all Christians are not required to accept the primacy of the popes. It alone proves that he is a manifest heretic. But it gets even worse…

Benedict XVI not only denies the dogma that non-Catholics need to believe in the Papacy, but questions whether popes have supreme jurisdiction in the Church at all!

For long sections of his book, *Principles of Catholic Theology*, Benedict XVI engages in detailed discussions of issues dealing with the Eastern "Orthodox" (the schismatics), as well as Luther, the Protestants, etc. These discussions are fascinating for our purposes, since they constitute a veritable position paper of Benedict XVI on these topics. In his discussion concerning the "Orthodox," one discovers that Benedict XVI doesn't even believe in the dogma of the Papacy. **It is important to remember that the Eastern Schismatics (the so-called "Orthodox") often readily admit that the popes are the successors of St. Peter as Bishops of Rome. Many of the "Orthodox" also say that the pope, as the Bishop of Rome, is "the first among equals" with a "primacy of honor"**; but they deny – and in this consists their chief heresy and schism – that the popes have a primacy of <u>supreme jurisdiction</u> from Christ to rule the entire Church.

> Pope Pius XI, *Mortalium Animos* (# 7), Jan. 6, 1928, speaking of heretics and schismatics: **"Among them there indeed are some, though few, who grant to the Roman Pontiff a primacy of honor** or even a certain jurisdiction or power, but this, however, they consider not to arise from the divine law but from the consent of the faithful."[22]

Benedict XVI discusses the position of these schismatics, which rejects the primacy of supreme jurisdiction of the popes, and here's what he says:

> Benedict XVI, *Principles of Catholic Theology* (1982), pp. 216-217: "Patriarch Athenagoras [the non-Catholic, schismatic Patriarch] spoke even more strongly when he greeted the Pope [Paul VI] in Phanar: 'Against all expectation, **the bishop of Rome is among us, the first among us in honor,** 'he who presides in love'.' **It is clear that, in saying this, the Patriarch [the non-Catholic, schismatic Patriarch] did not abandon the claims of the Eastern Churches or acknowledge the primacy of the west**. Rather, he stated plainly what the East understood as the order, the rank and title, of the equal bishops in the Church – **and it would be worth our while to consider whether this archaic confession, which has nothing to do with the 'primacy of jurisdiction' but confesses a primacy of 'honor' and agape, might not be recognized as a formula that adequately reflects the position that Rome occupies in the Church** – 'holy courage' requires that prudence be combined with 'audacity': 'The kingdom of God suffers violence.'"[23]

> The above is an astounding and explicit denial of the dogma of the Papacy and the infallible canon below! Benedict XVI announces the position of the schismatic patriarch, which acknowledges no primacy of supreme jurisdiction of the popes, and he not only tells us that the position of the schismatic is acceptable (as we saw already), but that <u>the schismatic position may in fact be the true position</u> on the Bishop of Rome! In other words, the Papacy (the supreme jurisdiction of the popes over the universal Church by the institution of Christ as successors of St. Peter) may not exist at all! This is an astounding, incredible and huge heresy!

The fact that this man now claims *to be* the pope when he doesn't even believe in the Papacy is surely one of the greatest frauds in human history. Those who obstinately hold that this non-Catholic is the pope assist in perpetuating that monumental fraud.

Pope Pius IX, *Vatican Council I*, Sess. 4, Chap. 3, Canon, *ex cathedra*: "If anyone thus speaks, that the Roman Pontiff has only the office of inspection or direction, but not the full and supreme power of jurisdiction over the universal Church, not only in things which pertain to faith and morals, but also in those which pertain to the discipline and government of the Church spread over the whole world; or, that he possesses only the more important parts, but not the whole plenitude of this supreme power… let him be anathema."[24]

Benedict XVI also denies that the Papacy was even held in the first millennium and tells us that this is why we cannot bind the schismatics to believe in it!

Benedict XVI with schismatic Patriarch Mesrob II, rejecter of the Papacy and head of the Turkish Armenian schismatic Orthodox sect[25]

Benedict XVI, *Principles of Catholic Theology* (1982), pp. 198-199: "… **In other words, Rome must not require more from the East with respect to the doctrine of the primacy than had been formulated and was lived in the first millennium**. When the Patriarch Athenagoras [the non-Catholic, schismatic Patriarch], on July 25, 1967, on the occasion of the Pope's visit to Phanar, **designated him as the successor of St. Peter, as the most esteemed among us, as one who presides in charity, this great Church leader was expressing the ecclesial content of the doctrine of the primacy as it was known in the first millennium. Rome need not ask for more**."[26]

This is another astounding major heresy against the Papacy and Vatican I. Benedict XVI again says that the schismatic position of the non-Catholic Patriarch Athenagoras, which rejects the Papacy and merely acknowledges the Bishop of Rome as the successor of St. Peter with a primacy of honor BUT NOT OF SUPREME JURISDICTION, is sufficient. Further, Benedict XVI says that the reason we cannot expect the "Orthodox" to believe in the Papacy (the primacy of supreme jurisdiction of the popes, not just a primacy of honor) **is because it wasn't even held in the first millennium (according to him)!** Therefore, Benedict XVI holds that the primacy of supreme jurisdiction conferred by Jesus Christ upon St. Peter and his successors is just a fiction, an invention of later ages, not held in the early Church. **He says that the schismatic position of Athenagoras – holding that the successor of St. Peter possesses a mere primacy of honor – is "the doctrine of the primacy as it was known in the first millennium"** and that "Rome need not ask for more"! Notice how directly Benedict XVI denies Vatican I, which defined that *in all ages* the primacy of jurisdiction was recognized:

> Pope Pius IX, *Vatican Council I*, Sess. 4, Chap. 2, *ex cathedra*: "**Surely no one has doubt, rather all ages have known** that the holy and most blessed Peter, chief and head of the apostles and pillar of faith and foundation of the Catholic Church, **received the keys of the kingdom from our Lord Jesus Christ**, the Savior and Redeemer of the human race; **and he up to this time and always lives and presides and exercises judgment in his successors**, the bishops of the holy See of Rome, which was founded by him and consecrated by his blood. **Therefore, whoever succeeds Peter in this chair, he according to the institution of Christ Himself, holds the primacy of Peter over the whole Church.**"[27]

Ratzinger (now Benedict XVI) totally rejects this dogma and the entire Catholic Faith.

Moving back to Benedict XVI's heretical teaching that non-Catholics are not *bound* to believe in the Papacy, this has also been taught by Benedict XVI's Prefect for Promoting Christian Unity, "Cardinal" Walter Kasper.

> "Cardinal" Walter Kasper: "… **today we no longer understand ecumenism in the sense of a return, by which the others would 'be converted' and return to being Catholics. This was expressly abandoned by Vatican II.**"[28]

Kasper's statement is so heretical that even many of the defenders of Benedict XVI have labeled Kasper a heretic. But as we've seen, Benedict XVI believes the exact same thing. In the following quote, we see that Benedict XVI uses basically the exact same words as Kasper in rejecting Catholic dogma!

> Benedict XVI, *Address to Protestants at World Youth Day*, August 19, 2005: "And we now ask: What does it mean to restore the unity of all Christians?... **this unity does not mean what could be called ecumenism of the return: that is, to deny and to reject one's own faith history. Absolutely not!**"[29]

CARDINAL KASPER AND BENEDICT XVI BOTH REJECT THE ECUMENISM OF THE RETURN – CONVERTING PROTESTANTS

Cardinal Walter Kasper: "… today <u>we no longer understand ecumenism in the sense of a return, by which the others would 'be converted'</u> and return to being Catholics. **This was expressly abandoned by Vatican II.**"[30]	Benedict XVI, *Address <u>to</u> <u>Protestants</u> at World Youth Day*, August 19, 2005: "And we now ask: What does it mean to restore the unity of all Christians?... **this unity does not mean what could be called ecumenism of the return: that is, <u>to deny and to reject one's own faith history</u>. Absolutely not!**"[31]

The Heresies of Benedict XVI

As this comparison shows clearly, just like the notorious heretic "Cardinal" Kasper, Benedict XVI blatantly rejects the "ecumenism of the return," that is, that non-Catholics need to return to the Catholic Church by conversion and reject their heretical sects. They both reject the teaching of Pope Pius XI word for word.

> Pope Pius XI, *Mortalium Animos* (# 10), Jan. 6, 1928:
> "… the union of Christians can only be promoted by promoting the <u>return</u> to the one true Church of Christ of those who are separated from it…"[32]

Benedict XVI is formally heretical. He holds that Protestants and Eastern Schismatics don't need to be converted and accept Vatican I. He is a blatant rejecter of the necessity of the Catholic Faith for salvation, and the dogmatic teaching of Vatican I.

That is why Benedict XVI joins Paul VI and John Paul II in praising the overturning of the excommunications against the "Orthodox" – and therefore in denying Vatican I

> Benedict XVI, *Ecumenical Message to Schismatic Patriarch of Constantinople*, Nov. 26, 2005:
> "This year we commemorate the 40th Anniversary of 7 December 1965, that day on which Pope Paul VI and Patriarch Athenagoras, **dissatisfied with what had occurred in 1054, decided together at Rome and Constantinople 'to cancel from the Church's memory the sentence of excommunication which had been pronounced.'"**[33]

In the year 1054, the Patriarch of Constantinople, Michael Cerularius, broke communion with the Catholic Church and the pope of Rome. Cerularius rejected the supreme authority of the pope and closed Roman Rite churches in Constantinople. Cerularius was excommunicated by Pope St. Leo IX, and the Great Schism of the East was formalized.[34]

Thus, what "occurred in 1054," mentioned by Benedict XVI above, refers to the excommunications leveled by the Catholic Church against those who followed Michael Cerularius into schism and into a rejection of the Papacy. Paul VI "lifted" these excommunications at the end of Vatican II, and John Paul II praised and commemorated the lifting of them many times. Now we see that Benedict XVI follows John Paul II's example and also commemorates the event.

All of this simply means that Paul VI, John Paul II and now Benedict XVI have attempted to overturn <u>the Papacy as a dogma</u> which must be believed <u>under pain of heresy and excommunication</u>. But as we saw already, Vatican I declared many times and in many ways that those who reject the dogma of the Papacy are anathematized, cut off from the Faith. Hence, to attempt to overturn the excommunications against those who still reject the Papacy is simply to boldly reject the teaching of Vatican I. It's formal heresy and schism signified in word and deed.

Benedict XVI with Lutheran "minister"

Benedict XVI prays ecumenical Vespers with schismatics and Protestants and says he loves the schismatic Orthodox Church

Benedict XVI praying ecumenical Vespers on Sept. 12, 2006.[35] This is active participation in non-Catholic worship. It is a manifestation of heresy by deed.

Benedict XVI, *Address during ecumenical Vespers service*, Sept. 12, 2006: "Dear Brothers and Sisters in Christ! We are gathered, <u>Orthodox Christians, Catholics and Protestants – and together with us there are also some Jewish friends</u> – to sing together the evening praise of God… This is an hour of gratitude for the fact that **we can pray together in this way** and, by turning to the Lord, at the same time grow in unity among ourselves… Among those gathered for this evening's Vespers, I would like first to greet warmly the representatives of the Orthodox Church. I have always considered it a special gift of

God's Providence that, as a professor at Bonn, **I was able to come to know and to love the Orthodox Church**, personally as it were, through two young Archimandrites, Stylianos Harkianakis and Damaskinos Papandreou, both of whom later became Metropolitans… **Our koinonia [communion] is above all communion with the Father** and with his Son Jesus Christ in the Holy Spirit; it is communion with the triune God, made possible by the Lord through his incarnation and the outpouring of the Spirit. This communion with God creates in turn koinonia among people, as a participation in the faith of the Apostles…"[36]

This is another major heresy of Benedict XVI. First, he takes active part in the prayer and worship of non-Catholics, which is condemned in Catholic teaching.

Pope Pius XI, *Mortalium Animos* (# 10): "So, Venerable Brethren, it is clear why **this Apostolic See has never allowed its subjects to take part in the assemblies of non-Catholics**…"[37]

Second, **he says that he loves the Orthodox Church** – a schismatic and heretical non-Catholic sect. What can be more heretical than saying: "I love the schismatic Church"? He then indicates that he, the schismatics, and the Protestants have a communion with God, communion with each other, and communion with the Faith of the Apostles. This is all totally heretical. Benedict XVI is a public heretic in communion with non-Catholics.

Benedict XVI's worst heresy? He prays with the leader of the world's "Orthodox" schismatics and signs a Joint Declaration with him telling him he's in the Church of Christ

Benedict XVI embracing the leader of the world's Eastern "Orthodox" schismatics, Bartholomew I, in his Nov. 2006 visit to Turkey

BBC News, Nov. 29, 2006 –"Benedict XVI has met Ecumenical Patriarch Bartholomew I in Turkey, on the second day of a landmark visit to the largely Muslim country. The Istanbul talks with the spiritual leader of the world's Orthodox Christians aimed to heal an old rift. **The two leaders began their meeting by holding a joint prayer service at the St George [Orthodox] Church in Istanbul**."[38]

During his 2006 trip to Turkey, Benedict XVI went into two schismatic cathedrals and met with three schismatic patriarchs, including the leader of the world's schismatics: Eastern Orthodox Patriarch of Constantinople, Bartholomew I. Benedict XVI not only committed a forbidden act of communication in sacred things with the schismatic, but he may have committed his worst heresy in his joint declaration with him.

> Benedict XVI, *Joint Declaration with Schismatic Patriarch Bartholomew*, Nov. 30, 2006: "This fraternal encounter which brings us together, Pope Benedict XVI of Rome and Ecumenical Patriarch Bartholomew I, is God's work, and in a certain sense his gift. We give thanks to the Author of all that is good, who allows us once again, in prayer and in dialogue, to express the joy we feel as brothers and to renew our commitment to move towards full communion. This commitment comes from the Lord's will and **from our responsibility as Pastors in the Church of Christ**… As far as relations between the Church of Rome and the Church of Constantinople are concerned, we cannot fail to recall the solemn ecclesial act effacing the memory of the ancient anathemas which for centuries had a negative effect on our Churches."[39]

Did you get that? He says: "… *our responsibility as pastors IN THE CHURCH OF CHRIST*"! What could be more heretical than: declaring **in a joint declaration with the leader of the world's schismatics that the schismatic leader, who rejects the Papacy and Papal Infallibility, is "in the Church of Christ"?**

Benedict XVI made this formally heretical declaration *in a schismatic cathedral* as part of a joint declaration *during a divine liturgy with a notorious schismatic*! Thus, it's official: Benedict XVI has declared in a public joint declaration that one can reject the Papacy, Papal Infallibility, Vatican I, etc. and be **in the Church of Christ**. He is without any doubt a public heretic. Anyone who denies this, in light of these facts, is also a heretic. Even the most dishonest and hardened defender of Antipope Benedict XVI will find it impossible to explain this one away.

> Pope Leo XIII, *Satis Cognitum* (#15), June 29, 1896 – **Bishops Separated from Peter and his Successors Lose All Jurisdiction**: "From this it must be clearly understood that **Bishops are deprived of the right and power of ruling, if they deliberately secede from Peter and his successors**; because, by this secession, they are separated from the foundation on which the whole edifice must rest. **They are therefore outside the edifice itself; and for this very reason they are separated from the fold**, whose leader is the Chief Pastor; they are exiled from that Kingdom, the keys of which were given by Christ to Peter alone… **No one, therefore, unless in communion with Peter can share in his authority, since it is absurd to imagine that he who is outside can command in the Church.**"[40]

All of this heresy from Benedict XVI is also a total mockery of the saints and martyrs who suffered because they refused to become Eastern "Orthodox," as was covered earlier in the section entitled: **Catholics who were tortured and martyred because they refused to become Eastern Schismatics.**

That is why Benedict XVI even encourages the Schismatic Patriarch to Resume His Ministry

> Benedict XVI, *Address*, Nov. 12, 2005: "In this regard, **I ask you, venerable Brothers, to convey my cordial greeting to Patriarch Maxim, First Hierarch of the Orthodox Church of Bulgaria. Please express to him my best wishes for his health and for the happy resumption of his ministry**."[41]

Benedict XVI encourages the non-Catholic, schismatic patriarch to resume his non-Catholic and schismatic ministry. Further, on his trip to Turkey, Benedict XVI recalled John Paul II's gesture of giving relics to the schismatics. Benedict XVI said that such an action is a sign of communion.

> Benedict XVI, *Speech to schismatic patriarch Bartholomew,* Nov. 29, 2006: "… St. Gregory of Nazianzus and St. John Chrysostom… **Their relics rest in basilica of St. Peter in the Vatican, and a part of them were given to your Holiness as a sign of communion** by the late Pope John Paul II for veneration in this very cathedral."[42]

This proves again that the "gestures of ecumenism" signify a rejection of the dogma that schismatics must accept the Papal Primacy to be in communion with the Church.

Benedict XVI's incredible heresy on the schismatic "Archbishop" of Athens

> Benedict XVI, *Address,* Oct. 30, 2006: "**I am also pleased to address my thoughts and good wishes to His Beatitude Christodoulos, Archbishop of Athens and All Greece**: I ask the Lord to sustain his farsightedness and prudence in carrying **the demanding service that the Lord has entrusted to his care**. Through him I wish to greet with deep affection the holy synod of the Orthodox Church of Greece and the faithful whom it serves lovingly and with apostolic dedication."[43]

Benedict XVI says that Christodoulos, the schismatic, non-Catholic "Orthodox" bishop in Greece, has authority over all of Greece! He also indicates that the schismatics are the "faithful" and that the Lord entrusted the schismatic bishop with a "demanding service." Further, notice the amazing headline which appeared in the official Vatican newspaper when this non-Catholic bishop came to visit Benedict XVI. The official Vatican newspaper (quoting Benedict XVI) referred to this non-Catholic schismatic "archbishop" in Greece as the "Archbishop of Athens and All Greece" in huge headlines which were repeated throughout its newspaper. All of this is an utter rejection of Catholic dogmatic teaching on the unity of the Church.

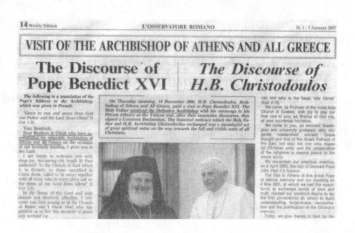

MORE HERESIES WITH THE PROTESTANTS FROM BENEDICT XVI

Benedict XVI with Protestant Evangelical "Bishop" Wolfgang Huber in 2005[44]

Benedict XVI explicitly rejects converting Protestants again in his book *Principles of Catholic Theology*.

> Benedict XVI, *Principles of Catholic Theology* (1982), p. 202: "**It means that the Catholic does not insist on the dissolution of the Protestant confessions** and the demolishing of their churches **but hopes, rather, that they will be strengthened in their confessions and in their ecclesial reality.**"[45]

Notice that Benedict XVI doesn't want the Protestant religions dissolved and converted to Catholicism, but hopes, rather, that they will be strengthened in their confession of Protestantism.

Benedict XVI's ecumenical prayer meeting in the Lutheran church: he powers ahead with major ecumenical heresy

Benedict XVI in common prayer during an Ecumenical Meeting at a Lutheran temple in Warsaw on May 25, 2006 – don't be confused by the crucifix; many Lutheran churches use crucifixes

The Heresies of Benedict XVI

> Benedict XVI, *Address at Ecumenical Meeting in Lutheran church in Warsaw*, May 25, 2006: "Together with you I give thanks **for the gift of this encounter of <u>common prayer</u>**… our ecumenical aspirations must be steeped in prayer, in **mutual forgiveness**… The words of the Apocalypse remind us that we are all on a journey towards the definitive encounter with Christ, when he will reveal before our eyes the meaning of human history… **<u>As a community of disciples</u>**, we are directed towards that encounter, **<u>filled with hope and trust that it will be for us the day of salvation</u>**, the day when our longings will be fulfilled, thanks to our readiness to let ourselves be guided by the mutual charity which his Spirit calls forth within us… Allow me to recall once more the ecumenical encounter that took place in this church with the participation of your great compatriot John Paul II…
>
> "Since that encounter [with John Paul II in the Lutheran church], much has changed. God has granted us to take many steps towards mutual understanding and rapprochement. Allow me to recall to your attention some ecumenical events which have taken place in the world during that time: the publication of **the Encyclical Letter *Ut Unum Sint*… the signing at Augsburg of the 'Joint Declaration on the Doctrine of Justification'**; the meeting on the occasion of the Great Jubilee of the Year 2000 and **the ecumenical memorial of 20th-century witnesses of the faith** [Protestant martyrs]; the resumption of Catholic-Orthodox dialogue on the world level… **the publication of the ecumenical translation of the New Testament** and the Book of Psalms… We note much progress in the field of ecumenism and yet we always await something more."[46]

There's quite a bit of heresy in this speech that Benedict XVI gave *in* the Lutheran church. Allow us to quickly summarize the main points. First, Benedict XVI goes to the Lutheran temple and takes active part in a "common prayer" service (his words) with Lutherans, other Protestants and "Orthodox" schismatics. This is a manifestation of heresy by deed – attendance at a non-Catholic Lutheran temple.

Second, he mentions the Second Coming of Christ, and says: "*we [i.e., he and the Lutherans and "Orthodox"] are directed towards that encounter, filled with hope and trust <u>that it will be for us the day of salvation</u>*"; in other words, the Protestants and schismatics to whom he was speaking will have salvation. This is complete heresy.

Third, he describes himself and the Lutherans and "Orthodox" as a single community of disciples: "**<u>As a community of disciples</u>**…" This shows that Benedict XVI is part of the same Church as the Lutherans and the schismatics; that is, he is part of a non-Catholic sect.

Fourth, Benedict XVI recalls many false ecumenical achievements, including the totally heretical, Council-of-Trent-trashing *Joint Declaration with the Lutherans on Justification*. He also recalled the **"ecumenical memorial of 20th-century witnesses of the faith,"** which was the commemoration of non-Catholics as martyrs for the Faith. He also recalled *Ut Unum Sint*, which is filled with heresies, including the idea that there are non-Catholic saints. He also **promotes a new ecumenical translation of the Bible.** Benedict XVI is a manifestly heretical non-Catholic antipope.

Benedict XVI encourages the invalid head of the Anglican Church in his "ministry" and says the Anglican Sect is grounded in Apostolic Tradition

Benedict XVI, *Address to Anglican "Archbishop of Canterbury,"* Nov. 23, 2006: "**It is our fervent hope that the Anglican Communion will remain grounded in the Gospels and the Apostolic Tradition** which form our common patrimony… The world needs our witness… May the Lord continue to bless you and your family, and **may he strengthen you in your ministry to the Anglican Communion!**"[47]

The Anglican Sect is grounded, not in Apostolic Tradition, but in the "tradition" of Henry VIII's adultery and schismatic break from the Catholic Church. Benedict XVI encourages the schismatic and heretical head of the Anglican Sect in his "ministry," and mocks all the saints and martyrs who suffered and died as martyrs because they wouldn't become Anglicans.

AT VATICAN II, BENEDICT XVI ALSO DENIED THAT NON-CATHOLICS SHOULD BE CONVERTED

Benedict XVI, *Theological Highlights of Vatican II*, 1966, pages 61, 68: "… **Meantime the Catholic Church has no right to absorb other Churches**. … **A basic unity – of Churches that remain Churches, yet become one Church – must replace the idea of conversion**…"[48]

Benedict XVI is not even remotely Catholic.

BENEDICT XVI PRAISES THE "GREATNESS" OF LUTHER'S "SPIRITUAL FERVOR"

Martin Luther was one of the worst heretics in Church history. Luther attacked the Catholic Church and its dogmas with ferocity. While never denouncing Luther as a heretic, Benedict XVI often speaks positively of Luther's views and even praises him.

At Vatican II, Benedict XVI even complained *that the document Gaudium et Spes relied too much on Teilhard de Chardin and not enough on Martin Luther.*[49] Benedict XVI is also credited with saving the 1999 *Joint Declaration with the Lutherans on Justification*, which declared that Luther's heresy of Justification by faith alone (and many others) are somehow no longer condemned by the Council of Trent.

Benedict XVI, *Principles of Catholic Theology* (1982), p. 263: "**That which in Luther makes all else bearable because of the greatness of his spiritual fervor**…"[50]

BENEDICT XVI ENCOURAGES METHODISTS TO ENTER INTO THE TOTALLY HERETICAL JOINT DECLARATION WITH THE LUTHERANS ON JUSTIFICATION, WHICH REJECTS THE COUNCIL OF TRENT

Benedict XVI, *Address to Methodists*, Dec. 9, 2005: "**I have been encouraged by the initiative** which would bring the member churches of the World Methodist Council into association with the **Joint Declaration on the Doctrine of Justification, signed by the Catholic Church** and the Lutheran World Federation in 1999."[51]

The Heresies of Benedict XVI

As covered already, the *Joint Declaration with the Lutherans on Justification* totally rejects the Council of Trent by teaching that its infallible canons no longer apply to the Lutherans. Benedict XVI adheres to this Protestant agreement and asserts that it was signed by "the Catholic Church."

BENEDICT XVI PRAISES THE NON-CATHOLIC ECUMENICAL MONASTERY OF TAIZE AND SAYS MORE SHOULD BE FORMED

The ecumenical Monastery of Taize is located in France. It is a **monastery made up of over a hundred brothers from various non-Catholic denominations, including Protestants**.[52]

> Benedict XVI, *Principles of Catholic Theology* (1982), p. 304: "…**Taize has been, without a doubt, the leading example of an ecumenical inspiration**… <u>**Similar communities of faith and of shared living should be formed elsewhere**</u>…"[53]

So, more non-Catholic ecumenical monasteries should be formed, according to Benedict XVI.

BENEDICT XVI GAVE COMMUNION TO THE PROTESTANT FOUNDER OF TAIZE

Benedict XVI giving Communion to public heretic, Bro. Roger Schutz, the Protestant founder of Taize[54]

Benedict XVI gave Communion to Bro. Roger, the Protestant founder of the Taize community, on April 8, 2005. And when Bro. Roger died in August, 2005, Benedict XVI said that this Protestant heretic went immediately to heaven.

> Benedict XVI, Aug. 17, 2005, on Bro. Roger: "**Bro. Roger Schutz [founder of a non-Catholic sect]** is in the hands of eternal goodness, of eternal love; **he has arrived at eternal joy**…"[55]

The Heresies of Benedict XVI

So much for the fact that Bro. Roger left the Catholic Church, rejected its dogmas for decades and became the founder of his own non-Catholic sect. He still went to Heaven, according to Benedict XVI. This is manifest heresy. Benedict XVI even said that the heretic Bro. Roger is guiding us from on high.

> Benedict XVI, *Address to Protestants at World Youth Day*, August 19, 2005: "**Bro. Roger Schutz… He is now visiting us and speaking to us from on high.**"[56]

Benedict XVI also praised Bro. Roger's "witness of faith."[57] If you believe that Benedict XVI is a Catholic pope, you might as well attend the Protestant church.

> Pope St. Gregory the Great: "The holy universal Church teaches that it is not possible to worship God truly except in her **and asserts that all who are outside of her will not be saved.**"[58]

BENEDICT XVI TEACHES THAT THE PROTESTANT "EUCHARIST" IS A SAVING EUCHARIST!

> Benedict XVI, *Pilgrim Fellowship of Faith*, 2002, p. 248: "**Even a theology along the lines of the concept of [apostolic] succession, as is in force in the Catholic and in the Orthodox Church, should in no way deny the saving presence of the Lord in the Evangelical Lord's Supper.**"[59]

Protestants don't have a valid Eucharist. They don't have valid bishops and priests, since they lack apostolic succession. But Benedict XVI says above that even if one accepts the Catholic dogma of apostolic succession, one should in NO WAY DENY THE SAVING PRESENCE OF THE LORD IN THE EVANGELICAL PROTESTANT "LORD'S SUPPER." According to Benedict XVI, the Protestants are not deprived of the saving Eucharistic Presence. **This means that you can get the saving Eucharistic presence at the local Protestant church. This is astounding heresy.**

> John 6:54- "Amen, amen I say to you: except you eat the flesh of the Son of man, and drink his blood, you shall not have life in you."

BENEDICT XVI TEACHES THAT PROTESTANTISM (EVANGELICAL CHRISTIANITY) SAVES

> Benedict XVI, *Pilgrim Fellowship of Faith*, 2002, p. 251: "… the burdensome question of [apostolic] succession **does not detract from the spiritual dignity of Evangelical Christianity, or from the saving power of the Lord at work within it**…"[60]

This is a bold rejection of the dogma Outside the Church There is No Salvation. If it were true, there would be absolutely no reason to be Catholic.

> Pope Gregory XVI, *Summo Iugiter Studio* (# 2), May 27, 1832:
> "Finally some of these misguided people attempt to persuade themselves and others that men are not saved only in the Catholic religion, but that even heretics may attain eternal life."[61]

BENEDICT XVI SAYS THAT PROTESTANTISM IS NOT HERESY

Benedict XVI, *The Meaning of Christian Brotherhood*, pp. 87-88: "The difficulty in the way of giving an answer is a profound one. Ultimately it is due to the fact that **there is no appropriate category in Catholic thought for the phenomenon of Protestantism today** (one could say the same of the relationship to the separated churches of the East). **It is obvious that the old category of 'heresy' is no longer of any value. Heresy, for Scripture and the early Church, includes the idea of a personal decision against the unity of the Church, and heresy's characteristic is** *pertinacia*, **the obstinacy of him who persists in his own private way. This, however, cannot be regarded as an appropriate description of the spiritual situation of the Protestant Christian.** In the course of a now centuries-old history, **Protestantism has made an important contribution to the realization of Christian faith, fulfilling a positive function** in the development of the Christian message and, above all, often giving rise to a sincere and profound faith in **the individual non-Catholic Christian, whose separation from the Catholic affirmation has nothing to do with the** *pertinacia* **characteristic of heresy.** Perhaps we may here invert a saying of St. Augustine's: that an old schism becomes a heresy. The very passage of time alters the character of a division, so that an old division is something essentially different from a new one. Something that was once rightly condemned as heresy cannot later simply become true, but it can gradually develop its own positive ecclesial nature, with which the individual is presented as his church and in which he lives as a believer, not as a heretic. This organization of one group, however, ultimately has an effect on the whole. **The conclusion is inescapable, then: Protestantism today is something different from heresy in the traditional sense, a phenomenon whose true theological place has not yet been determined.**"[62]

Protestantism is the rejection of *many* dogmas of the Catholic Faith. Protestantism is not only heresy, but the most notorious collection of heresies with which the Church ever had to contend.

Pope Pius XI, *Rerum omnium perturbationem* (# 4), Jan. 26, 1923: "… **the heresies begotten by the [Protestant] Reformation. It is in these heresies that we discover the beginnings of that apostasy of mankind from the Church**, the sad and disastrous effects of which are deplored, even to the present hour, by every fair mind."[63]

But Benedict XVI tells us that Protestants are not heretics, and that Protestantism itself is not heresy. This is undeniable proof that Benedict XVI is not a Catholic, but a complete heretic. This is one of Benedict XVI's worst heresies.

BENEDICT XVI INDICATES AGAIN THAT UNITY WITH THE PROTESTANTS RESPECTS, NOT CONVERTS, THE MULTIPLICITY OF VOICES

Benedict XVI, *Interview with Vatican Radio*, Aug. 5, 2006: "… **the Evangelical [Protestant] Church. If I am not mistaken, in Germany we have three important communities: Lutherans, Reformed, and Prussian Union.** There are also several free Churches and within there are movements like the 'Confessing Church,' and so on. **It is therefore a collection of many voices with which we have to enter into dialogue, searching for unity while respecting the multiplicity of the voices with which we want to collaborate.**"[64]

He says he searches for unity with them while respecting multiplicity of voices. This enunciates, once again, his position that they don't need to abandon their heresies and that unity with them is not "ecumenism of the return."

BENEDICT XVI SPEAKS OF THE "RICHNESS" OF HERETICAL AND SCHISMATIC DENOMINATIONS

Benedict XVI, *Address to Conference of Secretaries of Christian World Communions*, Oct. 27, 2006: "For decades the Conference of Secretaries of Christian World Communions has provided a forum for <u>fruitful contacts between the various Ecclesial Communities</u>. This has enabled their representatives to build that reciprocal trust needed to engage seriously **in bringing the richness of different Christian traditions** to serve the common call of discipleship."[65]

BENEDICT XVI'S HERESIES AGAINST THE SACRAMENTS

In 2001, the Vatican approved a document with the Assyrian Schismatic Church of the East. The document says that members of the Vatican II Church can go to the schismatic church and receive Communion and vice versa. The document was approved by Benedict XVI. The problem with this document, besides the fact that the Assyrian schismatics are not Catholics, is that this schismatic liturgy has <u>no words of consecration</u>, no "institution narrative." Benedict XVI mentioned the problem in his book *Pilgrim Fellowship of Faith*:

> Benedict XVI, *Pilgrim Fellowship of Faith*, 2002, p. 232: "…**This case needed special studies to be made, because the Anaphora of Addai and Mari most commonly in use by the Assyrians does not include an institution narrative. But these difficulties were able to be overcome**…"[66]

Benedict XVI admits that this schismatic liturgy has no "institution narrative," which is the words of consecration. But he still approved receiving Communion at this schismatic liturgy which has <u>no words of consecration</u>.

Benedict XVI came to this incredible decision because he denies that words are necessary for a valid consecration!

> Benedict XVI, *Principles of Catholic Theology* (1982), p. 377: "…we are witnesses today of **a new integralism** [read: traditionalism] that may seem to support what is strictly Catholic **but in reality corrupts it to the core**. It produces a passion of suspicions, the animosity of which is far from the spirit of the gospel. **There is an obsession with the letter that regards the liturgy of the Church as invalid and thus puts itself outside the Church. It is forgotten here that <u>the validity of the liturgy depends primarily, not on specific words, but on the community</u>** of the Church…"[67]

This is a total rejection of Catholic sacramental teaching.

> Pope Eugene IV, Council of Florence, 1439: "**<u>All these sacraments are made up of three elements</u>**: namely, things as the matter, **words as the form**, and the person of the minister who confers the sacrament with the intention of doing what the Church does. **If any of these is lacking, the sacrament is not effected.**"[68]

The fact that Benedict XVI holds that Masses without any words of consecration are valid proves that he doesn't even have a whiff of the Catholic Faith. He is a manifest heretic against the Church's sacramental teaching. And this heresy is repeated in a number of his books.

BENEDICT XVI SAYS THAT INFANT BAPTISM HAS NO REASON TO EXIST

> Benedict XVI, *Principles of Catholic Theology*, 1982, p. 43: "**The conflict over infant baptism shows the extent to which we have lost sight of the true nature of faith**, baptism and membership in the Church… It is obvious also that the meaning of baptism is destroyed wherever it is no longer understood as an anticipatory gift but only as a self-contained rite. **<u>Wherever it is severed from the catechumenate, baptism loses its *raison d'etre*</u>** [its reason to be]."[69]

This is an incredible, astounding and gigantic heresy! Benedict XVI says that wherever baptism is severed from the catechumenate – for example, in infant baptism – it loses its reason to be. Infant baptism has no meaning or purpose, according to Benedict XVI. That is why in his book *God and the World,* Benedict XVI **REJECTS THE NECESSITY OF INFANT BAPTISM AS "UNENLIGHTENED."**

> Benedict XVI, *God and the World*, 2000, p. 401: "Q. …*what happens to the millions of children who are killed in their mothers' wombs?* A. …**the question about children who could not be baptized because they were aborted then presses upon us that much more urgently. Earlier ages had <u>devised</u> a teaching <u>that seems to me rather unenlightened</u>**. They said that baptism endows us, by means of sanctifying grace, with the capacity to gaze upon God. Now, certainly, the state of original sin, from which we are freed by baptism, consists in a lack of sanctifying grace. Children who die in this way are indeed without any personal sin, so they cannot be sent to Hell, but, on the other hand, they lack sanctifying grace and thus the potential for beholding God that this bestows. They will simply enjoy a state of natural blessedness, in which they will be happy. This state people called limbo. In the course of our century, **that has gradually come to seem problematic to us. <u>This was one way in which people sought to justify the necessity of baptizing infants as early as possible, but the solution is itself questionable.</u>**"[70]

He says that earlier ages "had devised" (not received from Christ) the teaching about the necessity of baptizing infants for them to attain sanctifying grace. He says that this teaching is "unenlightened"! This is gross heresy. It was infallibly defined by the Councils of Florence and Trent that the Sacrament of Baptism is necessary for salvation, and that infants who die without the Sacrament of Baptism cannot be saved.

Some may wonder why, then, Ratzinger practices infant baptism? It's because he sees no problem practicing and going through the motions with something that, to him, has no meaning or purpose. In the same way, he poses as "the pope" even though he doesn't even believe in the primacy of supreme jurisdiction of the popes, as proven already. In the same way, he poses as the head of the Church of Jesus Christ when he doesn't even believe that Jesus Christ is necessarily the Messiah, as proven already.

BENEDICT XVI'S HERESIES AGAINST SACRED SCRIPTURE

The Catholic Church teaches that Sacred Scripture is the infallible and inerrant word of God. Vatican I also declared that all those things in the written word of God must be believed with divine and Catholic Faith.

> Pope Pius IX, *Vatican I*, Sess. III, Chap. 3, *ex cathedra*: "Further, by divine and Catholic faith, **all those things must be believed which are contained in the written word of God** and in tradition, and those which are proposed by the Church, either in a solemn pronouncement or in her ordinary and universal teaching power, to be believed as divinely revealed."[71]

BUT BENEDICT XVI SAYS THAT SACRED SCRIPTURE'S CREATION ACCOUNT IS BASED ON PAGAN CREATION ACCOUNTS

> Benedict XVI, *A New Song for the Lord*, 1995, p. 86: "**The pagan creation accounts on which the biblical story is in part based** end without exception in the establishment of a cult, but the cult in this case is situated in the cycle of the *do ut des*."[72]

If the biblical creation account in the book of Genesis is based in part on pagan creation accounts, this means that the biblical account is neither original nor inspired directly by God. This statement from Benedict XVI is heresy and shows again that he is a faithless apostate.

Pope Leo XIII, *Providentissimus Deus* (# 20), Nov. 18, 1893: "**For all the books which the Church receives as sacred and canonical, are written wholly and entirely, with all their parts, at the dictation of the Holy Ghost**; and so far is it from being possible that any error can co-exist with inspiration, that inspiration not only is essentially incompatible with error, but excludes and rejects it as absolutely and necessarily as it is impossible that God Himself, the supreme Truth, can utter that which is not true. **This is the ancient and unchanging faith of the Church, solemnly defined in the Councils of Florence and of Trent**, and finally confirmed and more expressly formulated by the Council of the Vatican."[73]

BENEDICT XVI CALLS INTO DOUBT THE STONE TABLETS OF THE EXODUS ACCOUNT

In Exodus 31, we read that God gave Moses two stone tablets written with the finger of God.

Exodus 31:18- "And the Lord, when He had ended these words in mount Sinai, gave to Moses two stone tables of testimony, written with the finger of God."

Benedict XVI, *God and the World*, 2000, pp. 165-166, 168: "*Q. …Were these laws really handed over to Moses by God when he appeared on Mount Sinai? As stone tablets, on which, as it says, 'the finger of God had written?'… to what extent are these Commandments really supposed to come from God?* A. [p. 166] …This [Moses] is the man who has been touched by God, and on the basis of this friendly contact he is able to formulate the will of God, of which hitherto only fragments had been expressed in other traditions, in such a manner that we truly hear the word of God. **Whether there really were any stone tablets is another question**… [p. 168] How far we should take this story literally is another question."[74]

BENEDICT XVI TEACHES THAT SENTENCES IN THE BIBLE ARE NOT TRUE

Benedict XVI, *God and the World*, 2000, p. 153: "It is another thing to see the Bible as a whole as the Word of God, in which everything relates to everything else, and everything is disclosed as you go on. It follows straightaway that neither the criterion of inspiration nor that of infallibility can be applied mechanically. **It is quite impossible to pick out one single sentence and say, right, you find this sentence in God's great book, so it must simply be true in itself**…"[75]

BENEDICT XVI ON EVOLUTION

Benedict XVI, *God and the World*, 2000, p. 76: "*Q. In the beginning the earth was bare and empty; God had not yet made it rain, is what it says in Genesis. **Then God fashioned man**, and for this purpose he took 'dust from the field and blew into his nostrils the breath of life; thus man became a living creature.' The breath of life – is that the answer to the question of where we come from?* A. I think we have here a most important image, which presents a significant understanding of what man is. It suggests that man is one who springs from the earth and its possibilities. **We can even read into this representation something like evolution**."[76]

Benedict XVI, *God and the World*, 2000, p. 139: "**The Christian picture of the world is this, that the world in its details is the product of a long process of evolution** but that at the most profound level it comes from the Logos."[77]

BENEDICT XVI'S HERESIES AND APOSTASY WITH ISLAM

Islam is a false religion which rejects the Trinity and the Divinity of Our Lord. The Catholic Church officially teaches that Islam is an abomination – a false religion from which people need to be converted and saved.

> Pope Eugene IV, *Council of Basel*, 1434:
> "… there is hope that very many from **the abominable sect of Mahomet** will be converted to the Catholic faith."[78]

> Pope Callixtus III: "I vow to… exalt the true Faith, and to extirpate **the diabolical sect of the reprobate and faithless Mahomet** [Islam] in the East."[79]

BENEDICT XVI HAS "DEEP RESPECT" FOR THE FALSE RELIGION OF ISLAM

> Benedict XVI, *General Audience*, Sept. 20, 2006: "**I hope that in the various circumstances during my Visit** – for example, when in Munich I emphasized how important it is to respect what is sacred to others – **that my deep respect for the great religions, and especially the Muslims, who 'worship God…' appeared quite clear!**"[80]

Notice that he has "deep respect" for not only the false religion of Islam, but other false religions. This is apostasy. Also notice that he considers respect for the false religion itself as the same thing as respecting Muslim "believers." He speaks of the two interchangeably, as we see. This is important to keep in mind because Benedict XVI frequently says that he respects Muslim believers or *Muslims as believers*. In so doing he is respecting their false religion, as we see proven clearly in the next quote.

> Benedict XVI, *Address*, Dec. 22, 2006: "My visit to Turkey afforded me the opportunity to show also publicly **my respect for the Islamic Religion, a respect, moreover, which the Second Vatican Council (declaration *Nostra Aetate* #3) pointed out** to us as an attitude that is only right."[81]

Notice that Benedict XVI admits here that Vatican II itself teaches respect for the false religion of Islam.

BENEDICT XVI SAYS THERE IS A NOBLE ISLAM

> Benedict XVI, *Salt of the Earth*, 1996, p. 244: "And, to prescind from the schism between Sunnites and Shiites, it [Islam] also exists in many varieties. **There is a noble Islam**, embodied, for example, by the King of Morocco, and there is also the extremist, terrorist Islam, which, again, one must not identify with Islam as a whole, which would do it an injustice."[82]

He is saying that a false religion is good. This is apostasy.

BENEDICT XVI SAYS THAT ISLAM REPRESENTS GREATNESS

> Benedict XVI, *Truth and Tolerance*, 2004, p. 204: "**In Hinduism (which is actually a collective name for a whole multitude of religions) there are some marvelous elements** – but there are also negative aspects: involvement with the caste system; suttee [self immolation] for widows, which developed from beginnings that were merely symbolic; offshoots of the cult of the goddess Sakti – all these might be mentioned to give just a little idea. **Yet even Islam, with all the greatness it represents**, is always in danger of losing balance, letting violence have a place and letting religion slide away into mere outward observance and ritualism."[83]

He says that Islam, a false religion which rejects the Divinity of Jesus Christ and the entire Catholic Faith, represents "greatness." This is apostasy. **Islam represents infidelity, the rejection of the Trinity and darkness**. It's also interesting to note that while speaking of the "marvelous elements" in Hinduism, Benedict XVI mentions negative aspects such as the caste system, etc. He doesn't mention the fact that Hinduism worships false gods among the negative aspects.

> Benedict XVI, *Address to Representatives of Islam*, August 20, 2005: "**The believer – and all of us, as Christians and Muslims, are believers** – … You guide Muslim believers and train them in the Islamic faith… You, therefore, have a great responsibility for the formation of the younger generation."[84]

> Benedict XVI, *Catechesis*, August 24, 2005: "This year is also the 40th anniversary of the conciliar Declaration *Nostra Aetate*, which has ushered in a new season of dialogue and spiritual solidarity between Jews and Christians, as well as **esteem for the other great religious traditions. Islam occupies a special place among them.**"[85]

Notice that Benedict XVI doesn't merely esteem the members of false religions, but the false religions themselves. This is apostasy.

> Benedict XVI, *Address*, Sept. 25, 2006: "**I would like to reiterate today all the esteem and the profound respect that I have for Muslim believers**, calling to mind the words of the Second Vatican Council which for the Catholic Church are the magna Carta of Muslim-Catholic dialogue: 'The Church looks upon Muslims with respect. They worship the one God living and subsistent… At this time **when for Muslims the spiritual journey of the month of Ramadan is beginning, I address to all of them my cordial good wishes**, praying that the Almighty may grant them serene and peaceful lives. May the God of peace fill you with the abundance of his Blessings, together with the communities you represent!"[86]

Benedict XVI respects the believers of this diabolical sect; he says they worship God; he wishes them God's blessings during their "spiritual journey" of Ramadan. This is simply apostasy.

> Benedict XVI, *Angelus Address*, Oct. 22, 2006: "I am happy to send **a cordial greeting to the Muslims of the entire world who are celebrating** in these days the conclusion of the month of the **Ramadan** fast."[87]

BENEDICT XVI ESTEEMS ISLAMIC CIVILIZATIONS

Benedict XVI, *General Audience*, Dec. 6, 2006: "**I thus had the favorable opportunity to renew my sentiments of <u>esteem for the Muslims and for the Islamic civilizations</u>**."[88]

Islamic civilizations are among the most evil and anti-Christian things in history. This statement by Benedict XVI, therefore, is complete apostasy.

Benedict XVI, *Address in Turkey to Muslim figures*, Nov. 28, 2006: "… I was pleased to express my profound esteem for all the People of this great Country and to pay my respects at the tomb of the founder of modern Turkey, Mustafa Kemal Ataturk… **I extend my greetings to all the religious leaders of Turkey, especially the Grand Muftis** of Ankara and Istanbul. In your person, Mr. President, **I greet all the Muslims in Turkey with particular esteem** and affectionate regard… <u>**This noble Land has also seen a remarkable flowering of Islamic civilization**</u> in the most diverse fields… **There are so many Christian and Muslim monuments that bear witness to Turkey's glorious past. You rightly take pride in these**, preserving them for the admiration of the ever-increasing number of visitors who flock here… **As believers, we draw from our prayer the strength that is needed** to overcome all traces of prejudice and to bear joint witness to our firm faith in God."[89]

He first mentions that he paid respects at the tomb of the nonbeliever Ataturk. He then says that he esteems *all the Muslims in Turkey*. To esteem someone is to admire him. This means that he admires all the Muslims in Turkey. That means that he not only admires millions who reject Christ, but even the criminals among the Muslims in Turkey; for certainly there are some. He then praises the "remarkable flowering of Islamic civilization," which keeps millions in darkness and infidelity. He then praises *the Muslim monuments* of the past, and says that Muslims "rightly take pride in these." Finally, he says that as "believers" Muslims can draw strength from their prayer – indicating that the practice of Islam is true and authentic. Benedict XVI is a complete and utter apostate.

BENEDICT XVI TEACHES THAT ISLAM AND CHRISTIANITY HAVE THE SAME GOD

Benedict XVI, *Pilgrim Fellowship of Faith*, 2002, p. 273: "… **Islam, too, … has inherited from Israel and the Christians the same God**…"[90]

Islam and Christianity don't have the same God. The followers of Islam reject the Trinity. Christians worship the Trinity.

BENEDICT XVI SAYS HE RESPECTS THE KORAN AS THE HOLY BOOK OF A GREAT RELIGION

Benedict XVI, *speech apologizing for his comments on Islam*, Sept. 2006: "In the Muslim world, this quotation has unfortunately been taken as an expression of my personal position, thus arousing understandable indignation. I hope that the reader of my text can see immediately that this sentence does not express **my personal view of <u>the Qur'an, for which I have the respect due to the holy book of a great religion</u>**."[91]

The Heresies of Benedict XVI   275

Benedict XVI respects the Koran as a holy book of a great religion. The Koran blasphemes the Trinity, denies the Divinity of Christ, and says those who believe in it are as excrement. It also says that all Christians are damned. This statement by Benedict XVI is total apostasy. We already covered how John Paul II kissed the Koran; this is to kiss the Koran in words.

BENEDICT XVI GOES INTO A MOSQUE AND PRAYS TOWARD MECCA LIKE THE MUSLIMS

On Nov. 30, 2006, during his trip to Turkey, Benedict XVI took off his shoes and entered the Blue Mosque. He followed the Muslim's command to turn toward "the Kiblah" – the direction of Mecca. Then the prayer began. Benedict XVI prayed like the Muslims toward Mecca in the mosque. He even crossed his arms in the Muslim prayer gesture called "the gesture of tranquility." This incredible act of <u>apostasy</u> was reported and shown all over the mainstream media. It's no exaggeration to say that Benedict XVI was initiated into Islam.

> Benedict XVI "Hailed for Praying like Muslims Toward Mecca," Dec 1, 2006 — ISTANBUL **(Reuters)** – "<u>**Pope Benedict ended a sensitive, fence-mending visit to Turkey on Friday amid praise for visiting Istanbul's famed Blue Mosque and praying there facing toward Mecca 'like Muslims.'**</u>'... 'The Pope's dreaded visit was concluded with a wonderful surprise,' wrote daily Aksam on its front page. '<u>**In Sultan Ahmet Mosque, he turned toward Mecca and prayed like Muslims**</u>,' the popular daily Hurriyet

> said, using the building's official name… 'I would compare the Pope's visit to the mosque to Pope John Paul's gestures at the Western Wall,' said veteran Vatican mediator Cardinal Roger Etchegaray, referring to Pope John Paul II's prayers at Jerusalem's Western Wall in 2000. 'Yesterday, Benedict did with the Muslims what John Paul did with the Jews.'"[92]

This absolutely proves that Benedict XVI is an apostate. This is one of the most scandalous actions in human history.

> St. Thomas Aquinas, *Summa Theologica*, Pt. I-II, Q. 103., A. 4: "All ceremonies are professions of faith, in which the interior worship of God consists. <u>Now man can make profession of his inward faith, by deeds as well as by words</u>: and in either profession, if he make a false declaration, he sins mortally."

> St. Thomas Aquinas, *Summa Theologica*, Pt. II, Q. 12, A. 1, Obj. 2: **"… if anyone were to… worship at the tomb of Mahomet, he would be deemed an apostate."**

St. Thomas says that one who worships at the tomb of Mahomet is to be deemed an apostate; **praying in a mosque, and toward Mecca like the Muslims, is much worse.** That's why no pope in history *ever even went into a mosque*; they all knew that to even go there would be to signify the acceptance of the false religion. With this action, **the debate about whether Benedict XVI is the pope is utterly and completely over** for anyone familiar with these facts and in possession of a modicum of good will. Tell your friends and relatives: Benedict XVI is a heretic, an apostate and therefore an antipope.

> Benedict XVI, *General Audience*, Dec. 6, 2006: **"In the area of interreligious dialogue,** divine Providence granted me, almost at the end of my Journey, **an unscheduled Visit which proved rather important: my Visit to Istanbul's famous Blue Mosque. Pausing for a few minutes of recollection in that place of prayer**, I addressed the one Lord of Heaven and Earth, the Merciful Father of all humanity."[93]

BENEDICT XVI'S HERESIES WITH PAGANISM

BENEDICT XVI FULLY FAVORS ECUMENISM AND THE DEVIL-WORSHIPPING ECUMENICAL CEREMONIES AT ASSISI

We've already covered John Paul II's notorious ecumenical gatherings at Assisi in 1986 where he prayed with over 130 different religious leaders of all kinds of false and demonic religions, putting the true religion on a par with idol worship. This activity is totally condemned by Catholic Tradition. It was denounced as apostasy by Pope Pius XI.

Well, the train that took the false religious leaders from the Vatican to the 2002 Assisi event (the repeat performance) was described by Benedict XVI as **"a symbol of our pilgrimage in history**… the **reconciliation <u>of peoples and religions</u>, a great inspiration…"**[94]

In 2006, Benedict XVI also praised the 1986 interreligious prayer meeting at Assisi.

> Benedict XVI, Message, Sept. 2, 2006: "**This year is the 20th anniversary of the** *Interreligious Meeting of Prayer for Peace*, desired by my venerable Predecessor John Paul II on 27 October 1986 in Assisi. It is well known that he did not only invite Christians of various denominations to this Meeting but also **the exponents of different religions**. **It constituted a vibrant message** furthering peace and an event that left its mark on the history of our time… attestations of the close bond that exists between the relationship with God and the ethics of love are recorded in **all great religious traditions**.
>
> "Among the features of the 1986 Meeting, it should be stressed that **this value of prayer in building peace was testified to by the representatives of different religious traditions**, and this did not happen at a distance but in the context of a meeting… We are in greater need of this dialogue than ever… **I am glad, therefore, that the initiatives planned in Assisi this year are along these lines** and, in particular, that the Pontifical Council for Interreligious Dialogue has had the idea of applying them in a special way for young people… I gladly take this opportunity to greet the representatives of **<u>other</u>**

religions who are taking part in one or other of the Assisi commemorations. Like us Christians, **they know that in prayer it is possible to have a special experience of God** and to draw from it effective incentives for dedication to the cause of peace."[95]

Benedict XVI is in favor of the apostate ecumenical gatherings at Assisi where John Paul II prayed with leaders of all kinds of demonic and idolatrous religions – where John Paul II had the crucifixes removed from Catholic rooms so that pagans could worship false gods. Notice that Benedict XVI says that other religions know that prayer gives them an experience of God. This means that their religious experiences, such as worshipping false gods in prayer, are true.

BENEDICT XVI CRITICIZES AS "HOTHEADS" THOSE WHO DESTROYED PAGAN TEMPLES

Benedict XVI, *God and the World*, 2000, p. 373: "**There were in fact Christian hotheads and fanatics who destroyed temples, who were unable to see paganism as anything more than idolatry** that had to be radically eliminated."[96]

Those "hotheads" whom he criticizes would include St. Francis Xavier and St. Benedict.

St. Francis Xavier [regarding the heathen children he had converted to the Catholic faith, +1543): "**These children... show an ardent love for the Divine law, and an extraordinary zeal for our holy religion and imparting it to others. Their hatred for idolatry is marvelous. They get into feuds with the heathens about it... The children run at the idols, upset them, dash them down, break them to pieces, spit on them, trample on them, kick them about, and in short heap on them every possible outrage.**"[97]

St. Benedict overthrew a pagan altar and burned the groves dedicated to Apollo when he first arrived at Mount Cassino:

Pope Pius XII, *Fulgens Radiatur* (# 11), March 21, 1947: "… he [St. Benedict] went south and arrived at a fort 'called Cassino situated on the side of a high mountain; **on this stood an old temple where Apollo was worshipped by the foolish country people, according to the custom of the ancient heathens**. Around it likewise grew groves, in which even till that time **the mad multitude of infidels used to offer their idolatrous sacrifices.** The man of God coming to that place broke the idol, overthrew the altar, burned the groves, and of the temple of Apollo made a chapel of St. Martin. Where the profane altar had stood he built a chapel of St. John; and by continual preaching he converted many of the people thereabout.'"[98]

BENEDICT XVI TELLS US THAT PAGAN AND IDOLATROUS RELIGIONS ARE HIGH AND PURE

Benedict XVI, *Salt of the Earth*, 1996, p. 23: "And so we can also see that **in the Indian religious cosmos ('Hinduism' is a rather misleading designation for a multiplicity of religions) there are very different forms: very high and pure ones** that are marked by the idea of love, but also wholly gruesome ones that include ritual murder."[99]

He says that idolatrous religions are high and pure. This is heresy and apostasy.

The Heresies of Benedict XVI

1 Cor. 10:20- "… the things which the heathens sacrifice, they sacrifice to devils, and not to God."

Pope Leo XIII, *Ad Extremas* (#1), June 24, 1893: "… the blessed Apostle Thomas who is rightly called the founder of preaching the Gospel to the Hindus. Then, there is Francis Xavier… Through his extraordinary perseverance, **he converted <u>hundreds of thousands of Hindus from the myths and vile superstitions of the Brahmans to the true religion</u>**."[100]

BENEDICT XVI HAS A PROFOUND RESPECT FOR FALSE FAITHS

Benedict XVI, *Homily*, Sept. 10, 2006: "We do not fail to show respect for other religions and cultures, **<u>we do not fail to show profound respect for their faith</u>**…"[101]

Notice that Benedict XVI doesn't merely respect the members of false faiths, but he shows PROFOUND RESPECT for the <u>false faiths</u> themselves! This is apostasy. This means that he respects the denial of Christ, the rejection of the Papacy, the endorsement of contraception and abortion, etc. (which are all part of the teaching of other "faiths").

Pope Leo XIII, *Custodi di Quella fede* (# 15), Dec. 8, 1892:
"Everyone should avoid familiarity or friendship with anyone suspected of belonging to masonry or to affiliated groups. Know them by their fruits and avoid them. **Every familiarity should be avoided, not only with those impious libertines who openly promote the character of the sect, but also with those who hide under the mask of universal tolerance, <u>respect for all religions</u>**…"[102]

BENEDICT XVI SAYS THE PRESENCE OF FALSE RELIGIONS IS A SOURCE OF ENRICHMENT FOR ALL

Benedict XVI, *Speech*, Nov. 28, 2006: "… I am certain that religious liberty is a fundamental expression of human liberty and that **the active presence of religions in society is a source of progress and enrichment for all**."[103]

This means that the various false religions are a source of progress and enrichment for all! This is apostasy.

BENEDICT XVI SAYS THEOLOGY MUST LEARN FROM THE EXPERIENCES OF FALSE RELIGIONS

Benedict XVI, *Special Address*, Sept. 12, 2006: **"For philosophy and, albeit in a different way, for theology, listening to the great experiences and insights of the religious traditions of humanity, and those of the Christian faith in particular, is a source of knowledge, and to ignore it would be an unacceptable restriction of our listening and responding."**[104]

Benedict XVI says that Catholic theology should listen to the "great experiences" and "insights" of false religions, and that to ignore them would be irresponsible. People should think about the significance of such a statement. It clearly indicates that he doesn't regard these religions (including pagan and idolatrous ones) as false and of the Devil. His statement is simply another expression of the Modernist apostasy that all religions are basically true because one becomes a believer through one's religious "experiences."

> Pope St. Pius X, *Pascendi* (# 14), Sept. 8, 1907: "**[According to the Modernists] It is this *experience* which, when a person acquires it, makes him properly and truly a believer**. How far off we are here from Catholic teaching we have already seen in the decree of the Vatican Council. We shall see later how, with such theories, added to the other errors already mentioned, the way is opened wide for atheism. Here it is well to note at once that, **given this doctrine of *experience* united with the other doctrine of *symbolism*, every religion, even that of paganism, must be held to be true. What is to prevent such experiences from being met within every religion? In fact that they are to be found is asserted by not a few. And with what right will Modernists deny the truth of an experience affirmed by a follower of Islam? With what right can they claim true experiences for Catholics alone?** Indeed Modernists do not deny but actually admit, some confusedly, others in the most open manner, that all religions are true. That they cannot feel otherwise is clear."[105]

BENEDICT XVI DENYING OUTSIDE THE CHURCH THERE IS NO SALVATION

What we have seen thus far proves many times over that Benedict XVI rejects the defined dogma Outside the Catholic Church There is No Salvation. Benedict XVI holds that we shouldn't even convert heretics and schismatics. But here are some more examples of heresy where Benedict XVI specifically addresses and denies this crucial dogma.

BENEDICT XVI ADDRESSES OUTSIDE THE CHURCH THERE IS NO SALVATION AND COMPLETELY REJECTS IT

> Benedict XVI, *Salt of the Earth*, 1996, p. 24: "Q. *But could we not also accept that someone can be saved through a faith other than the Catholic?* A. That's a different question altogether. **It is definitely possible for someone to receive from his religion directives that help him become a pure person, which also, if we want to use the word, help him please God and reach salvation. This is not at all excluded by what I said; on the contrary, <u>this undoubtedly happens on a large scale</u>**."[106]

The Church teaches that there is <u>no</u> salvation outside of the Church. Benedict XVI teaches that there is undoubtedly salvation outside the Church on a large scale. This is a bold rejection of the dogma Outside the Church There is No Salvation.

BENEDICT XVI SAYS THAT THERE ARE PAGAN SAINTS

> Benedict XVI, *Truth and Tolerance*, 2004, p. 207: "**The fact that in every age there have been, and still are, 'pagan saints'** is because everywhere and in every age – albeit often with difficulty and in fragmentary fashion – the speech of the 'heart' can be heard, because God's Torah may be heard within ourselves…"[107]

This is bold heresy. Remember, Pope Eugene IV infallibly defined that all who die as "pagans" are not saved.

Pope Eugene IV, *Council of Florence*, ex cathedra:
"…all those who are outside the Catholic Church, not only **pagans** but also Jews or heretics and schismatics, cannot share in eternal life…"[108]

BENEDICT XVI TEACHES THAT THERE ARE MANY WAYS THAT LEAD TO HEAVEN BESIDES THE CHRISTIAN FAITH

Benedict XVI, *Co-Workers of the Truth*, 1990, p. 217: "**The question that really concerns us, the question that really oppresses us, is why it is necessary for us in particular to practice the Christian Faith in its totality; why, when there are so many other ways that lead to heaven and salvation**, it should be required of us to bear day after day the whole burden of ecclesial dogmas and of the ecclesial ethos. And so we come again to the question: What exactly is Christian reality? What is the specific element in Christianity that not merely justifies it, but makes it compulsorily necessary for us? **When we raise the question about the foundation and meaning of our Christian existence, there slips in a certain false hankering for the apparently more comfortable life of other people who are also going to heaven**. We are too much like the laborers of the first hour in the parable of the workers in the vineyard (Mt. 20:1-16). Once they discovered that they could have earned their day's pay of one denarius in a much easier way, they could not understand why they had had to labor the whole day. **But what a strange attitude it is to find the duties of our Christian life unrewarding just because the denarius of salvation can be gained without them!** It would seem that we – like the workers of the first hour – want to be paid not only with our own salvation, but more particularly with others' lack of salvation. That is at once very human and profoundly un-Christian."[109]

Benedict XVI asks that all-important question: Why is it necessary to practice the Christian Faith if there are other ways to salvation? Benedict XVI answers the question by admitting that there are many other ways besides the Christian Faith that lead to salvation. He even criticizes people for asking such a question.

Benedict XVI has bluntly rejected a revealed truth of the Catholic Faith: Jesus Christ is the only way to salvation, and the Catholic Faith is necessary for salvation.

Pope Leo XII, *Ubi Primum* (# 14), May 5, 1824:
"… by divine faith we hold one Lord, one faith, one baptism, and that no other name under Heaven is given to men except the name of Jesus Christ in which we must be saved. This is why we profess that there is no salvation outside the Church."[110]

BENEDICT XVI TEACHES THAT ALL RELIGIONS CAN LEAD TO GOD

Benedict XVI, *Salt of the Earth*, 1996, p. 29: "… **in all religions there are men of interior purity who through their myths somehow touch the great mystery and find the right way of being human**."[111]

This is <u>totally</u> heretical.

BENEDICT XVI INSULTING CATHOLIC DOGMA

BENEDICT XVI INSULTS THE COUNCIL OF TRENT'S DECREE ON THE EUCHARIST

Benedict XVI, *Feast of Faith*, 1981, p. 130: "**The Council of Trent concludes its remarks on Corpus Christi with something which offends our ecumenical ears and has doubtless contributed not a little toward discrediting this feast in the opinion of our Protestant brethren. But <u>if we purge its formulation</u>** of the passionate tone of the sixteenth century, we shall be surprised by something great and positive."[112]

Benedict XVI says the Council of Trent's infallible declaration "offends" his ecumenical ears and that its "formulation" needs to be "purged," which means to *make clean* or *rid of objectionable elements*! This is totally heretical.

BENEDICT XVI SAYS THAT TRENT'S DOCTRINE ON THE PRIESTHOOD WAS WEAK AND DISASTROUS IN ITS EFFECT

Benedict XVI, *Principles of Catholic Theology* (1982), pp. 247-248: "… [Talking about the Protestant versus Catholic views of the Priesthood] **The Council of Trent did not attempt here a comprehensive treatment of <u>the problem</u> as a whole. <u>Therein lies the weakness of the text it promulgated, the effect of which was all the more disastrous…</u>**"[113]

BENEDICT XVI TOTALLY BLASPHEMES CHURCH TRADITION

Benedict XVI, *Principles of Catholic Theology* (1982), p. 100: "… the problem of tradition as it exists in the Church…The Church is tradition… into which – let us admit – much human pseudotradition has found its way; so much so, in fact, that even, and even precisely, **the Church has contributed to the general crisis of tradition that afflicts mankind.**"[114]

This is a repudiation of one of the two sources of Revelation, Sacred Tradition.

Pope Pius IX, *Vatican I*, ex cathedra: "…all those things must be believed which are contained in the written word of God and in **tradition**…"[115]

> Benedict XVI, *Principles of Catholic Theology*, 1982, p. 378: "**Not every valid Council in the history of the Church has been a fruitful one; in the last analysis, many of them have been just a waste of time.**"[116]

BENEDICT XVI TEACHES THAT THE TERM "ORIGINAL SIN" IS FALSE

> Benedict XVI, *In the Beginning*, 1986, p. 72: "…**Theology refers to this state of affairs by the certainly misleading and imprecise term 'original sin.'**"[117]

The Council of Trent promulgated an infallible "Decree on Original Sin" in which it used the term "original sin" no fewer than four times.[118]

BENEDICT XVI CRITICIZES THE APOSTLES' CREED

> Benedict XVI, *Introduction to Christianity*, 2004, p. 326: "… **Perhaps it will have to be admitted that the tendency to such a false development**, which only sees the dangers of responsibility and no longer the freedom of love, **is already present in the [Apostles'] Creed** …'"[119]

BENEDICT XVI ADMITTING THAT VATICAN II HAS CHANGED OR REJECTED CATHOLIC DOGMA

BENEDICT XVI BLUNTLY ADMITS THAT VATICAN II CONTRADICTS THE INFALLIBLE TEACHING OF POPE PIUS IX ON RELIGIOUS LIBERTY AND FALSE RELIGIONS

> Benedict XVI, *Principles of Catholic Theology*, 1982, p. 381: "**If it is desirable to offer a diagnosis of the text [of the Vatican II document, *Gaudium et Spes*] as a whole, we might say that (in conjunction with the texts on religious liberty and world religions) it is a revision of the Syllabus of Pius IX, a kind of counter syllabus**… As a result, **the one-sidedness of the position adopted by the Church under Pius IX** and Pius X in response to the situation created by the new phase of history inaugurated by the French Revolution, **was, to a large extent, corrected**..."[120]

Benedict XVI could not be more formally heretical. He is admitting that Vatican II's teaching (which he adheres to) is directly contrary to the teaching of the Magisterium in the Syllabus of Errors condemned by Pope Pius IX. We have shown that Vatican II's teaching on religious liberty contradicts traditional Catholic teaching. Benedict XVI just admitted it. One could hardly ask for more of a confirmation that the teaching of Vatican II is heretical. In his book, Benedict XVI repeats this again and again, calling the teaching of Vatican II "the countersyllabus," and saying that there can be no return to the Syllabus of Errors.

> Benedict XVI, *Principles of Catholic Theology*, 1982, p. 385: "By a kind of inner necessity, therefore, the optimism of **the countersyllabus gave way** to a new cry that was far more intense and more dramatic than the former one."[121]

> Benedict XVI, *Principles of Catholic Theology*, 1982, p. 391: "The task is not, therefore, to suppress the Council but to discover the real Council and to deepen its true intention in the light of present experience. **That means that there can be no return to the *Syllabus*,**

BENEDICT XVI ACKNOWLEDGES THAT THE VATICAN II SECT HAS ABANDONED THE CATHOLIC CHURCH'S TRADITIONAL PROHIBITION OF CREMATION

Benedict XVI, *God and the World*, 2000, p. 436: "Q. *Is it permissible to have dead bodies cremated, or is that just a heathen ritual?* A. … **Right up to the Second Vatican Council, cremation was subject to penalties. In view of all the circumstances of the modern world, the Church has abandoned this**."[123]

The Church's traditional law condemns cremation, and forbids ecclesiastical burial to those who requested it.

BENEDICT XVI'S HERESIES AGAINST THE CHURCH

BENEDICT XVI SAYS THAT CHURCH TEACHING DOESN'T EXCLUDE THOSE WHO HOLD OPPOSING VIEWS

Benedict XVI, *Principles of Catholic Theology* (1982), p. 229: "The statement of the Congregation… **proposes to meet the crisis by a positive presentation especially of those points of Church doctrine that are under dispute and to establish the identity of Catholicism, not by excluding those who hold opposing views**…"[124]

This is blatantly heretical.

Pope Eugene IV, *Council of Florence*, 1441: "Therefore the Holy Roman Church condemns, reproves, anathematizes and **declares to be outside the Body of Christ**, which is the Church, **whoever holds opposing or contrary views**."[125]

BENEDICT XVI TEACHES THAT THE "CHURCH" EXISTS OUTSIDE THE CHURCH

Benedict XVI, *Co-Workers of the Truth*, 1990, p. 29: "… there neither can nor should be any disavowal of the presence of Christ and of Christian values among separated Christians… **Catholic theology must state more clearly than ever before that, along with the actual presence of the word outside her boundaries, 'Church' is also present there in one form or another**…"[126]

Benedict XVI **states that the Church itself exists outside of the Church**. This is heretical nonsense which denies that there is only one Church.

The Nicene-Constantinople Creed, 381, *ex cathedra*: "**We believe in… one holy Catholic and apostolic Church**."[127]

BENEDICT XVI TOTALLY REJECTS THE UNITY OF THE CATHOLIC CHURCH

The unity or oneness of the Catholic Church is a very important dogma. It's one of the four marks of the Church, as in *one, holy, Catholic and apostolic*. When heretics form sects, they don't break the unity of the Catholic Church, since the unity of the Church cannot be broken. They simply leave the Catholic Church.

> Pope Leo XIII, *Satis Cognitum* (# 4), June 29, 1896:
> "**The Church in respect of its unity belongs to the category of things indivisible by nature...**"[128]

> Pope Leo XIII, *Satis Cognitum* (# 5):
> " ... **This unity cannot be broken, nor the one body divided by the separation of its constituent parts.**"[129]

BUT BENEDICT XVI TOTALLY REJECTS THE DOGMA OF THE UNITY OF THE CATHOLIC CHURCH

> Benedict XVI, *Principles of Catholic Theology* (1982), p. 121: "...it is also ultimately through these factors that it becomes clear that **the unity of the Church is not to be brought about by human effort** but can be effected only by the Holy Spirit."[130]

> Benedict XVI, *Principles of Catholic Theology* (1982), p. 148: "**The canon of Holy Scripture can be traced back to them, or, at least, to the undivided Church of the first centuries** of which they were the representatives."[131]

Benedict XVI teaches that the Church was united in the First Millennium, but divided after that time by the schismatic revolt and the Protestant revolt. This is a total repudiation of one of the four marks of the Catholic Church; it alone would prove that he is not a Catholic.

Benedict XVI, *Principles of Catholic Theology* (1982), p. 147: "**The Fathers, we can now say, were the theological teachers of the undivided Church...**"

Benedict XVI, *Principles of Catholic Theology* (1982), p. 127: "For our purposes, this fourth type of symbolum need not be further discussed **since it forms no part of the history of the symbolum of the undivided Church.**"

Benedict XVI, *Principles of Catholic Theology* (1982), pp. 145-146: "**The Fathers are the teachers of the yet undivided Church.**"

Benedict XVI, *Co-Workers of the Truth*, 1990, p. 29: "...**This means that even in Catholic belief the unity of the Church is still in the process of formation; that it will be totally achieved only in the eschaton...**"

Benedict XVI says that the unity of the Church (the oneness of the Church), one of the four marks of the true Church, does not exist and will not exist until "the eschaton" (the end of the world)!

> Pope Pius XI, *Mortalium Animos* (# 7), Jan. 6, 1928:
> "… here it seems opportune to expound and to refute a certain false opinion… For they are of the opinion that the unity of faith and government, which is a note of the one true Church of Christ, has hardly up to the present time existed, and does not today exist."[132]

OTHER HERESIES OF BENEDICT XVI

BENEDICT XVI SAYS JUDAS MIGHT NOT BE IN HELL

Benedict XVI, Oct. 18, 2006: "This poses two questions when it comes to explaining what happened [with Judas]. The first consists in asking ourselves how it was possible that Jesus chose this man and trusted him. In fact, though Judas is the group's administrator (cf. John 12:6b; 13:29a), in reality he is also called "thief" (John 12:6a). The mystery of the choice is even greater, as Jesus utters a very severe judgment on him: "Woe to that man by whom the son of man is betrayed!" (Matthew 26:24). **This mystery is even more profound if one thinks of his eternal fate, knowing that Judas "repented and brought back the 30 pieces of silver to the chief priests and the elders, saying 'I have sinned in betraying innocent blood'" (Matthew 27:3-4). Though he departed afterward to hang himself (cf. Matthew 27:5),** <u>it is not for us to judge his gesture, putting ourselves in God's place, who is infinitely merciful and just</u>."[133]

These words of Benedict XVI indicate that he holds that Judas might not be in Hell. This is a denial of the Gospel. If Judas is not in Hell (as Benedict XVI indicates is possible), then Our Lord's words in Matthew 26:24 (quoted below) would be false.

> "Woe to that man by whom the Son of man shall be betrayed: <u>**it were better for him, if that man had not been born**</u>" (Matthew 26:24).

If Judas didn't go to Hell, then he went to Purgatory or Heaven. In that case, Our Lord (the all knowing God) could not have said that it is better for Judas not to have been born. That's very clear and very simple; but these simple truths of the Catholic Faith are all thrown out the window by the non-Catholic Vatican II sect.

It's quite interesting that, in this speech, Benedict XVI quotes the first part of Matthew 26:24 ("Woe to that man by whom the son of man is betrayed!"), but not the last part ("<u>**it were better for him, if that man had not been born**</u>"). You can see his omission of that critical part of the passage in the citation above. That's a striking example of a heretic cutting out the part of the Gospel that he doesn't like or is about to deny!

Further refuting Antipope Benedict XVI is the fact that Our Lord also says that Judas is "lost" and calls him the "son of perdition," which means "the son of damnation." Judas also ended his life with the mortal sin of suicide.

> John 17:12- "**None of them is lost, but the son of perdition**, that the scripture may be fulfilled."

The Catholic Church has always held that Judas went to Hell, based on the clear words of Our Lord.

> St. Alphonsus, *Preparation For Death*, p. 127: "**Poor Judas! Above seventeen hundred years have elapsed since he has been in Hell**, and his Hell is still only beginning."[134]

But just like the other defined dogmas on salvation, even the clearest words and messages of the Gospel are denied by the non-Catholic, manifestly heretical Vatican II sect and its antipopes.

> Pope St. Pius X, *Pascendi* (# 3), Sept. 8, 1907: "**Moreover, they [the Modernists] lay the ax not to the branches and shoots, but to the very root, that is, to the faith and its deepest fibers**. And once having struck at this root of immortality, they proceed to diffuse poison through the whole tree, so that **there is no part of Catholic truth which they leave untouched, none that they do not strive to corrupt**."[135]

BENEDICT XVI RESPECTS HANS KUNG'S PATH OF DENIAL OF JESUS CHRIST!

For those who don't know, Hans Kung denies Papal Infallibility and the Divinity of Our Lord Jesus Christ, among other things.

Hans Kung

Hans Kung can correctly be described as an Arian, since he denies that Our Lord is of the same substance as the Father.

> Benedict XVI, *Salt of the Earth*, 1996, pp. 95-96: "Q. And about Hans Kung's path? I mean, he now hopes for a rehabilitation. A. ... **he [Hans Kung] has taken back nothing of his contestation of the papal office; indeed, he has further radicalized his positions. In Christology and in trinitarian theology he has further distanced himself from the faith of the Church. I respect his path, which he takes in accord with his conscience**, but he should not then demand the Church's seal of approval but should admit that in essential questions he has come to different, very personal decisions of his own."[136]

Benedict XVI doesn't merely say that he respects Hans Kung, which would be bad enough; he says that he respects his path – that is, the denial of Jesus Christ! This is total apostasy.

BENEDICT XVI SAYS IT'S IMPORTANT THAT EVERY PERSON CAN BELONG TO THE RELIGION OF HIS CHOICE

Benedict XVI, *Address*, May 18, 2006: "Likewise, peace is rooted in respect for religious freedom, which is a fundamental and primordial aspect of the freedom of conscience of individuals and the freedom of peoples. **It is important that everywhere in the world every person can belong to the religion of his choice and practice it freely without fear, for no one can base his life on the quest of material being alone.**"[137]

According to Benedict XVI, it's important that every person can belong to the religion of his choice. This is more religious indifferentism. Benedict XVI then explains his reason for saying this: *"for no one can base his life on the quest of material being alone."* In other words, life is more than material being; there is a spiritual reality, so it's important to embrace a religion – any religion of your choice! What an apostate.

BENEDICT XVI UTTERS MORE HERESY ON RELIGIOUS LIBERTY, DIRECTLY CONTRADICTING THE DOGMATIC TEACHING OF POPE PIUS IX

Benedict XVI, *Address to ambassador of Spain*, May 20, 2006: "**The Church also insists on the inalienable right of individuals to profess their own religious faith without hindrance, both publicly and privately**, as well as the right of parents to have their children receive an education that complies with their values and beliefs without explicit or implicit discrimination."[138]

This is precisely the opposite of the infallible teaching of the Catholic Church. The Church condemns the very thing he said the Church insists! See for yourself how clearly opposed Benedict XVI's teaching is to the dogmatic teaching of Pope Pius IX. Notice especially the underlined portion, and compare it to the teaching of Benedict XVI:

Pope Pius IX, *Quanta Cura* (#'s 3-6), Dec. 8, 1864, *ex cathedra*: "From which totally false idea of social government they do not fear to foster that erroneous opinion, most fatal in its effects on the Catholic Church and the salvation of souls, called by Our predecessor, Gregory XVI, an insanity, **NAMELY, THAT 'LIBERTY OF CONSCIENCE AND WORSHIP IS EACH MAN'S PERSONAL RIGHT, WHICH OUGHT TO BE LEGALLY PROCLAIMED AND ASSERTED IN EVERY RIGHTLY CONSTITUTED SOCIETY**; and that a right resides in the citizens to an absolute liberty, which should be restrained by no authority whether ecclesiastical or civil, **WHEREBY THEY MAY BE ABLE OPENLY AND PUBLICLY TO MANIFEST AND DECLARE ANY OF THEIR IDEAS WHATEVER, EITHER BY WORD OF MOUTH, BY THE PRESS, OR IN ANY OTHER WAY**. But while they rashly affirm this, they do not understand and note that they are preaching liberty of perdition... Therefore, **BY OUR APOSTOLIC AUTHORITY, WE REPROBATE, PROSCRIBE, AND CONDEMN ALL THE SINGULAR AND EVIL OPINIONS AND DOCTRINES SPECIALLY MENTIONED IN THIS LETTER,** AND WILL AND COMMAND THAT THEY BE THOROUGHLY HELD BY ALL THE CHILDREN OF THE CATHOLIC CHURCH AS REPROBATED, PROSCRIBED AND CONDEMNED."[139]

Benedict XVI	vs. *ex cathedra* Catholic teaching
The Church also insists on the inalienable right of individuals <u>to profess their own religious faith without hindrance, both publicly and privately</u>	...that a right resides in the citizens <u>...**WHEREBY THEY MAY BE ABLE OPENLY AND PUBLICLY TO MANIFEST AND DECLARE ANY OF THEIR IDEAS WHATEVER...**, **BY OUR APOSTOLIC AUTHORITY, WE REPROBATE, PROSCRIBE, AND CONDEMN [such an evil opinion]**</u>

BENEDICT XVI DENIES THE RESURRECTION OF THE BODY

The Resurrection of the Body is a very important dogma. Besides being part of the Apostles' Creed, <u>this dogma has been defined more than almost any other dogma</u> of the Faith.

> Pope Gregory X, *Second Council of Lyons*, 1274, *ex cathedra*: "The same most holy Roman Church firmly believes and firmly declares that nevertheless on the day of judgment **all men will be brought together <u>with their bodies</u>** before the tribunal of Christ to render an account of their own deeds."[140]

> Pope Innocent III, 1215, *ex cathedra*: "...all of whom will rise with **their bodies which they now bear**..."[141]

> Pope Benedict XII, 1336, *ex cathedra*: "... <u>**all men with their bodies**</u> will make themselves ready to render an account of their own deeds ..."[142]

Benedict XVI blatantly denies this dogma and proves again that he is a manifest heretic.

> Benedict XVI, *Introduction to Christianity*, 2004, p. 349: "<u>**It now becomes clear that the real heart of faith in the resurrection does not consist at all in the idea of the restoration of bodies**</u>, to which we have reduced it in our thinking; such is the case even though this is the pictorial image used throughout the Bible."[143]

> Benedict XVI, *Introduction to Christianity*, p. 353: "The foregoing reflections may have clarified to some extent what is involved in **the biblical pronouncements about the resurrection: their essential content is <u>not the conception of a restoration of bodies to souls</u>** after a long interval..."[144]

> Benedict XVI, *Introduction to Christianity*, 2004, pp. 357-358: "To recapitulate, <u>**Paul teaches, not the resurrection of physical bodies**</u>, but the resurrection of persons..."[145]

We can see that Benedict XVI denies this dogma in his book *Introduction to Christianity* (as quoted above) by teaching that St. Paul <u>doesn't</u> teach the resurrection of physical bodies, and that the resurrection does <u>not</u> consist in the restoration of bodies. This is astounding heresy.

Benedict XVI giving *El Diablo* satanic sign

Below we see Benedict XVI giving *El Diablo* (the Devil) sign. This satanic gesture is popular among Satanists and satanic rock groups. **Many give this satanic hand gesture without knowing it because they're taken over by the evil spirit.** Some point out that the Devil sign is similar to the hand gesture for "I love you" in sign language. That's true, but that's probably because **the inventor of the deaf signing system, Helen Keller, was herself an occultist and a Theosophist.** She wrote a book called *My Religion* in which she explained her occult views.[146] Some believe that she designed the "I love you" sign to correspond with the Devil sign so that one making it would be saying that he or she loves Satan.

Regardless, we believe that above Benedict XVI is giving the Devil sign – the double Devil sign, in fact – and that he knows what he's doing. We say this because, having read many of his books, we can say that he is clearly one of the most intelligent men in the world, in addition to having an encyclopedic knowledge of matters Catholic. Thus, when he repeatedly says in his books that one is free <u>not</u> to see Jesus as the Messiah (as we've documented), **Benedict XVI (being an extremely knowledgeable man) knows very well that he is preaching a new anti-Christian Gospel from inside the physical structures of the Catholic Church,** all the while posing as the pope who is supposedly dedicated to the Gospel. Thus, he is fully aware of the evil deception which he is pulling off. **Only a person who knowingly worships Satan or is very controlled or possessed by Satan could do such a thing.**

CONCLUSION ABOUT BENEDICT XVI

Benedict XVI is a manifest heretic. We have proven this without any doubt. He teaches that Our Lord may not be the Messiah; that the Old Covenant is valid; that Jews and others can be saved without believing in Christ; that schismatics and Protestants don't need conversion; that non-Catholics are not bound to accept Vatican I; that Protestant Monasteries should be formed; that Protestantism is not even heresy; that Mass is valid without words of consecration; that infant baptism has no purpose; that Scripture is filled with myths; that the false religion of Islam is noble; that pagan religions are high; that salvation can be had outside the Church; that Catholic dogmas need to be purged; that Vatican II rejected Catholic teaching on religious liberty; that the unity of the Church does not exist; and that the Resurrection of the Body will not occur, *just to name a few.*

Since he is a heretic, he could not have been a validly elected pope. As quoted already, Pope Paul IV solemnly taught in his Feb. 15, 1559 Bull, *Cum ex Apostolatus officio*, that it is impossible for a heretic to be validly elected pope.

Therefore, <u>**according to the teaching of the Catholic Church, Benedict XVI is not a pope, but a non-Catholic antipope whom Catholics must completely reject**</u>. He presides over the new religion of Vatican II, a counterfeit Catholicism that has abandoned the Catholic Church's traditions and dogmas.

One of Benedict XVI's main characteristics is that he is a deceiver. While he teaches undeniable, astounding and manifest heresies, one of the ways by which he has convinced so many that he is conservative is that, among these astounding heresies in his writings, there are many conservative passages. But this is nothing new. Pope Pius VI pointed out that heretics, inspired by the Devil, have always used such tactics to inculcate heresies and deceive people.

> Pope Pius VI, Bull "Auctorem fidei," August 28, 1794: **"[The Ancient Doctors] knew the capacity of innovators in the art of deception.** In order not to shock the ears of Catholics, **they sought to hide the subtleties… by the use of seemingly innocuous words such as would allow them to insinuate error into souls in the most gentle manner**. Once the truth had been compromised, they could, **by means of slight changes or additions in phraseology, distort the confession of the faith** which is necessary for our salvation, and lead the faithful by subtle errors to their eternal damnation."

Pope Pius VI points out that camouflaging the heresies in statements that are ambiguous or seemingly conservative or contradictory was the tactic of the heretic Nestorius, and that Catholics cannot allow heretics to get away with this or deceive them by it. They must hold such heretics to their heresies regardless:

> Pope Pius VI, "Auctorem fidei": "… it cannot be excused in the way that one sees it being done, **under the erroneous pretext that the seemingly shocking affirmations in one place are further developed along orthodox lines in other places, and even in yet other places corrected; as if allowing for the possibility of either affirming or denying the statement… such has always been the fraudulent and daring method used by innovators to establish error. It allows for both the possibility of promoting error and of excusing it.**

> "…It is a most reprehensible technique for the insinuation of doctrinal errors and one condemned long ago by our predecessor Saint Celestine who found it used in the writings of Nestorius, Bishop of Constantinople, and which he exposed in order to condemn it with the greatest possible severity. Once these texts were examined carefully, the impostor was exposed and confounded, for he expressed himself in a plethora of words, <u>mixing true things with others that were obscure; mixing at times one with the other in such a way that he was also able to confess those things which were denied while at the same time possessing a basis for denying those very sentences which he confessed.</u>"

Heretics have always used ambiguity and deception to insinuate their heresies and make them seem not quite as bad. In fact, the more deceptive the heretic is usually equates to how successful he is for the Devil. The heretic Arius effectively spread his denial of the Divinity of Christ because he impressed people with his appearance of asceticism and devotion.

> Pope Pius XI, *Rite expiatis* (# 6), April 30, 1926: "…**heresies gradually arose and grew in the vineyard of the Lord, propagated either by open heretics or by sly deceivers** who, because they professed a certain austerity of life and gave a false appearance of virtue and piety, easily led weak and simple souls astray."[147]

Pope Pius VI concludes his point by giving Catholics instructions on how to deal with such deception or ambiguity among the writings of heretics:

> "In order to expose such snares, something which becomes necessary with a certain frequency in every century, no other method is required than the following: **WHENEVER IT BECOMES NECESSARY TO EXPOSE STATEMENTS WHICH DISGUISE SOME SUSPECTED ERROR OR DANGER UNDER THE VEIL OF AMBIGUITY, ONE MUST DENOUNCE THE PERVERSE MEANING UNDER WHICH THE ERROR OPPOSED TO CATHOLIC TRUTH IS CAMOUFLAGED.**"

Pope Pius VI teaches us that if someone veils a heresy in ambiguity, a Catholic must hold him to the heretical meaning and denounce the heretical meaning which is camouflaged in ambiguity. But this is only common sense: if a man says that he is against abortion, but repeatedly votes in favor of it, he is a supporter of abortion and a heretic. The fact that he sometimes claims to hold Church teaching against abortion means nothing.

Likewise, the fact that Benedict XVI says some conservative, ambiguous or contradictory things doesn't change the fact that he teaches astounding heresies and is not a Catholic.

BENEDICT XVI'S RETRACTION OF HIS STATEMENT ON ISLAM REVEALS HIS TRUE NATURE AS A DECEIVER

Almost all of those who are reading this book probably heard about Benedict XVI's controversial remarks about Muhammad in a speech in Bavaria on Sept. 12, 2006. In this now-famous speech, Benedict XVI quoted a medieval emperor who denounced Muhammad's policy (and therefore Islam) as evil and inhuman.

> Benedict XVI, *Speech in Bavaria*, Sept. 12, 2006: "In the seventh conversation… the emperor touches on the theme of the holy war… saying: '**Show me just what Muhammad brought that was new, and there you will find things only evil and inhuman, such as his command to spread by the sword the faith he preached**.' The emperor, after having expressed himself so forcefully, goes on to explain in detail the reasons why spreading the faith through violence is something unreasonable. **Violence is incompatible with the nature of God and the nature of the soul**. 'God,' he says, 'is not pleased by blood - and not acting reasonably is contrary to God's nature.'"[148]

In context, we can clearly see that Benedict XVI doesn't merely quote the statement from the emperor against Muhammad's policy, but he endorses the statement of the emperor.

So, why would Benedict XVI make a statement against Islam? Is it because he believes that Islam is evil? Of course not. Benedict XVI has said that Islam represents "greatness" (*Truth and*

Tolerance, p. 204). Benedict XVI fully endorses Vatican II's teaching in favor of Islam, as we saw already. Benedict XVI thinks that John Paul II – who loved the false religion of Islam and committed countless acts of apostasy praising it – was a great pope worthy of canonization. The reason that Benedict XVI made this one statement is simply because his mission is, as we've pointed out, *to occasionally make some conservative statements and do some conservative things in order to deceive traditionalist-minded folks* back into the clutches of the false Church – all the while preaching the Vatican II apostasy. And this one conservative statement had its intended effect, *until God allowed it to backfire on him*.

Immediately after Benedict XVI's Sept. 12 speech got around, we were contacted by individuals who had, in the past, struggled with issues pertaining to whether or not the antipopes are true popes. One of the individuals wrote to us and made reference to Benedict XVI's speech on Islam; his faith against the Counter Church was clearly weakening. It's truly pathetic and actually *disgusting* that one conservative statement or action here or there from the antipope – even though the antipope denies Christ, worships at the synagogue, says we shouldn't convert Protestants, etc., etc., etc. – is all this person's weak faith needed to see to be obliterated.

But that's the way it is with many. They don't have a true faith in Christ, they don't hate evil, or their faith is as fragile as a reed. Many of them can be swept away by a single conservative statement here or there, *even from a well-documented public heretic and apostate who doesn't even believe that Jesus is the Messiah*, as we've proven. That's why Benedict XVI, who is thoroughly under the power of the Devil, does this type of thing.

THE TRUTH COMES OUT: BENEDICT XVI APOLOGIZES FOR HIS SPEECH ON ISLAM AND SAYS THAT THE STATEMENT AGAINST MUHAMMAD'S TEACHING DOESN'T "IN ANY WAY EXPRESS" HIS PERSONAL THOUGHT!

> Benedict XVI, *Apology for his Sept. 12, 2006 speech*: "At this time, I wish also to add that I am deeply sorry for the reactions in some countries to a few passages of my address at the University of Regensburg, which were considered offensive to the sensibility of Muslims. **These in fact were a quotation from a medieval text, which do not in any way express my personal thought**."[149]

This is very, very interesting on a number of levels.

First, this is ABSOLUTE PROOF THAT BENEDICT XVI IS A LIAR AND A DECEIVER. It proves that he is a liar because we already saw that Benedict XVI clearly endorsed the quote from the emperor in the speech on Sept. 12. That is undeniable. **But now he is saying that the statement from the emperor doesn't in any way express his personal thought**, which totally contradicts the Sept. 12 speech. Thus, no matter which way you look at it, **Benedict XVI is caught in a huge lie**.

Second, in addition to PROVING that Benedict XVI is a public liar and a deceiver, his statement that the quote from the emperor doesn't in any way express his personal thought proves that he is an apostate. For in the face of the reaction to his speech, he had every chance to stand by his ostensible position that Islam is evil. He was presented with a great opportunity during the swirling controversy to persuade people that the position of his speech was proven true by the Muslims' evil reaction and desire to kill; but no… he repudiated the statement against Islam instead. He followed it up by being initiated into Islam by prayer toward Mecca in a mosque with a mufti on Nov. 30, 2006.

Thus, what was originally surely intended as a neat plan by the Devil, through his Antipope Benedict XVI, to make a conservative statement which would deceive certain "traditionalists" was foiled when God allowed the plan to backfire after the Muslim reaction became so volatile that Benedict XVI had to apologize and reveal his true feelings – **thus obliterating his credibility with anyone who has eyes to see what a liar he therefore has proven himself to be**.

So don't be fooled if the manifest heretic and raging liar, Antipope Benedict XVI, says or does something else that is conservative with the intention of deceiving traditionalists. **Don't be fooled if Benedict XVI grants a universal indult to say the Latin Mass at a time when most of the priests are invalid and would have to accept the Vatican II apostasy to take advantage of it. The Devil will concede all of this as long as one accepts Benedict XVI's new religion, or accepts Benedict XVI and his apostate Bishops as Catholics while they teach that Jesus Christ and the Catholic Faith are meaningless. Don't be fooled if he reaches out in other ways to traditionally-minded groups to keep them under, or bring them back to, the Vatican II sect.** It won't change the fact that he is a manifest heretic who presides over a non-Catholic sect.

This is all part of the deception of the last days which is predicted in Catholic prophecy.

> Our Lady of La Salette, France, Sept. 19, 1846: **"Rome will lose the Faith and become the seat of the Anti-Christ... the Church will be in eclipse."**

This prophecy of La Salette coincides with the prophecies in Sacred Scripture (Apocalypse 17 and 18) that the city of seven hills (Rome) will become a harlot (a counterfeit Church), as we will cover later. The great harlot prophesied in the Bible is not the Catholic Church; it is the counterfeit Catholic Church (the Vatican II sect), the apostate, phony bride which arises in the last days to deceive Catholics and eclipse the true Church which has been reduced to a remnant.

We have shown that Our Lady's message at La Salette has been fulfilled before our very eyes: Benedict XVI and the Vatican II sect teach that Jews are perfectly free not to believe in Jesus Christ. This is published in Benedict XVI's and the Vatican's own books; it proves that Rome has become the seat of antichrist. A series of antipopes reigning from Rome has made Rome the seat of the Antichrist.

Our Lord also indicates that in the last days there will be "the abomination of desolation" "<u>in the holy place</u>" (Mt. 24:15). He tells us that there will be a deception so profound that, if it were possible, even the elect would be deceived (Mt. 24:24). He even asks if there would be any Faith left on the earth:

> Luke 18:8 "But yet the Son of man, when He cometh, shall He find, think you, faith on earth?"

This deception will happen in the very heart of the Church's physical structures – in "the Temple of God" (2 Thess. 2:4) and "the holy place" (Mt. 24:15) – and will arise because people receive not the love of the truth. God allows this as the supreme punishment for the world's sins. We are currently living through this apostasy and deception. People need to completely reject Antipope Benedict XVI, the other Vatican II antipopes, and the new Vatican II religion.

Benedict XVI is one of the most wicked men in human history, for he alleges to wield the authority of the Church of Christ while teaching that one is free to deny Jesus Christ. He alleges to be the pope while he teaches that people are free to reject the Papacy. He alleges to be the leader of the Christian Faith, while teaching that Our Lord Jesus Christ doesn't even have to be seen as the Messiah.

Endnotes for Section 20:

1 Reuters.com, Fri, Dec. 1, 2006.
2 *30 Days Magazine*, July, 1990.
3 *Decrees of the Ecumenical Councils*, Sheed & Ward and Georgetown University Press, 1990, Vol. 1, pp. 550-553; Denzinger, *The Sources of Catholic Dogma*, B. Herder Book. Co., Thirtieth Edition, 1957, no. 39-40.
4 Denzinger 712.
5 http://www.vatican.va/roman_curia/congregations/cfaith/pcb_documents/rc_con_cfaith_doc_20020212_popolo-ebraico_en.html
6 http://www.vatican.va/roman_curia/congregations/cfaith/pcb_documents/rc_con_cfaith_doc_20020212_popolo-ebraico_en.html
7 Benedict XVI, *God and the World*, San Francisco, CA: Ignatius Press, 2000, p. 209.
8 Benedict XVI, *Milestones*, Ignatius Press, 1998, pp. 53-54.
9 Zenit.org, news story for Sept. 5, 2000.
10 Benedict XVI, *God and the World*, p. 209.
11 *The Sunday Sermons of the Great Fathers*, Regnery, Co: Chicago, IL, 1963, Vol. III, p. 223.
12 Synagogue photos: *European Jewish Press*, http://www.ejpress.org
13 *Decrees of the Ecumenical Councils*, Vol. 1, p. 578; Denzinger 714.
14 *America*, October 3, 2005.
15 *L'Osservatore Romano* (the Vatican's Newspaper), Jan. 25, 2006, p. 2.
16 *L'Osservatore Romano*, Jan. 24, 2007, p. 11.
17 http://syriacchristianity.org/PZakka/PhotoGallery.htm
18 Benedict XVI, *Principles of Catholic Theology*, Ignatius Press, 1982, pp. 197-198.
19 Benedict XVI, *Principles of Catholic Theology*, p. 198.
20 Denzinger 1826-1827.
21 Denzinger 469.
22 *The Papal Encyclicals*, by Claudia Carlen, Raleigh: The Pierian Press, 1990, Vol. 3 (1903-1939), p. 315.
23 Benedict XVI, *Principles of Catholic Theology*, pp. 216-217.
24 Denzinger 1831.
25 http://www.Iraper.org
26 Benedict XVI, *Principles of Catholic Theology*, pp. 198-199.
27 Denzinger 1824.
28 *Adista*, Feb. 26, 2001.
29 *L'Osservatore Romano*, August 24, 2005, p. 8.
30 *Adista*, Feb. 26, 2001.
31 *L'Osservatore Romano*, August 24, 2005, p. 8.
32 *The Papal Encyclicals*, Vol. 3 (1903-1939), p. 317.
33 *L'Osservatore Romano*, Dec. 7, 2005, p. 4.
34 Fr. John Laux, *Church History*, Rockford, IL: Tan Books, 1989, pp. 295-296.
35 *L'Osservatore Romano*, Sept. 20, 2006, p. 10.
36 *L'Osservatore Romano*, Sept. 20, 2006, p. 10.
37 *The Papal Encyclicals*, Vol. 3 (1903-1939), p. 317.
38 http://news.bbc.co.uk/2/hi/europe/6194224.stm
39 www.zenit.org, *Zenit news report*, Nov. 30, 2006.
40 *The Papal Encyclicals*, Vol. 2 (1878-1903), pp. 400-401.
41 *L'Osservatore Romano*, Nov. 23, 2005, p. 9.
42 *L'Osservatore Romano*, Dec. 6, 2006, p. 6.
43 *L'Osservatore Romano*, Nov. 15, 2006, p. 5.
44 *EKD Bulletin*.
45 Benedict XVI, *Principles of Catholic Theology*, p. 202.
46 *L'Osservatore Romano*, May 31, 2006, p. 3.
47 *L'Osservatore Romano*, Nov. 29, 2006, p. 6.
48 Quoted in *Catholic Family News*, "Father Ratzinger's Denial of Extra Ecclesia [sic] Nulla Salus," July 2005, Editor's Postscript, p. 11.
49 http://www.nationalcatholicreporter.org/word/word081205.htm#protestant
50 Benedict XVI, *Principles of Catholic Theology*, p. 263.

[51] *L'Osservatore Romano*, Dec. 21/28, p. 5.
[52] http://www.taize.fr/en
[53] Benedict XVI, *Principles of Catholic Theology*, p. 304.
[54] *Catholic News Service*, 2005
[55] *L'Osservatore Romano*, August 24, 2005, p. 19; *Zenit News Report*, Aug. 17, 2005.
[56] *L'Osservatore Romano*, August 24, 2005, p. 9.
[57] Benedict XVI, *General Audience*, Aug. 16, 2006; *L'Osservatore Romano*, August 23, 2006, p. 11.
[58] Quoted by Pope Gregory XVI in *Summo Iugiter Studio* #5, May 27, 1832: *The Papal Encyclicals*, Vol. 1 (1740-1878), p. 230.
[59] Benedict XVI, *Pilgrim Fellowship of Faith*, Ignatius Press, 2002, p. 248.
[60] Benedict XVI, *Pilgrim Fellowship of Faith*, p. 251.
[61] *The Papal Encyclicals*, Vol. 1 (1740-1878), p. 229.
[62] Benedict XVI, *The Meaning of Christian Brotherhood*, Ignatius Press, pp. 87-88.
[63] *The Papal Encyclicals*, Vol. 3 (1903-1939), p. 242.
[64] *L'Osservatore Romano*, August 30, 2006, pp. 6-7.
[65] *L'Osservatore Romano*, Nov. 29, 2006, p. 2.
[66] Benedict XVI, *Pilgrim Fellowship of Faith*, p. 232.
[67] Benedict XVI, *Principles of Catholic Theology*, p. 377.
[68] Denzinger 695.
[69] Benedict XVI, *Principles of Catholic Theology*, p. 43.
[70] Benedict XVI, *Principles of Catholic Theology*, p. 401.
[71] Denzinger 1792.
[72] Benedict XVI, *A New Song for the Lord*, New York, NY: Crossroad Publishing, 1995, p. 86.
[73] *The Papal Encyclicals*, Vol. 2 (1878-1903), p. 335.
[74] Benedict XVI, *God and the World*, pp. 165-166, 168.
[75] Benedict XVI, *God and the World*, p. 153.
[76] Benedict XVI, *God and the World*, p. 76.
[77] Benedict XVI, *God and the World*, p. 139.
[78] *Decrees of the Ecumenical Councils*, Vol. 1, p. 479.
[79] Warren H. Carroll, *A History of Christendom*, Front Royal, VA: Christendom Press, 1993, Vol. 3 (*The Glory of Christendom*), p. 571.
[80] *L'Osservatore Romano*, Sept. 27, 2006, p. 11.
[81] *L'Osservatore Romano*, Jan. 3, 2007, p. 7.
[82] Benedict XVI, *Salt of the Earth*, Ignatius Press, 1996, p. 244
[83] Benedict XVI, *Truth and Tolerance (Christian Belief and World Religions)*, Ignatius Press, 2004, p. 204
[84] *L'Osservatore Romano*, August 24, 2005, p. 9.
[85] *L'Osservatore Romano*, August 31, 2005, p. 11.
[86] *L'Osservatore Romano*, Sept. 27, 2006, p. 2.
[87] *L'Osservatore Romano*, Oct. 25, 2006, p. 1.
[88] *L'Osservatore Romano*, Dec. 13, 2006, p. 11.
[89] *L'Osservatore Romano*, Dec. 6, 2006, p. 2.
[90] Benedict XVI, *Pilgrim Fellowship of Faith*, p. 273.
[91] http://www.vatican.va/holy_father/benedict_xvi/speeches/2006/september/documents/hf_ben-xvi_spe_20060912_university-regensburg_en.html#_ftn3
[92] Reuters.com, Fri, Dec. 1, 2006.
[93] *L'Osservatore Romano*, Dec. 13, 2006, p. 11.
[94] Zenit.org, *Zenit news report*, Feb. 21, 2002.
[95] *L'Osservatore Romano*, Sept. 13, 2006, p. 3.
[96] Benedict XVI, *God and the World*, 2000, p. 373
[97] *The Life and Letters of St. Francis Xavier* by Henry James Coleridge, S.J. (Originally published: London: Burns and Oates, 1874) Second Reprint, New Delhi: Asian Educational Services, 2004, Vol. 1, p. 154.
[98] *The Papal Encyclicals*, Vol. 4 (1939-1958), p. 113.
[99] Benedict XVI, *Salt of the Earth*, p. 23.
[100] *The Papal Encyclicals*, Vol. 2 (1878-1903), p. 307.
[101] *L'Osservatore Romano*, Sept. 13, 2006, p. 7.
[102] *The Papal Encyclicals*, Vol. 2 (1878-1903), p. 304.

103 *L'Osservatore Romano*, Dec. 6, 2006, p. 4.
104 *L'Osservatore Romano*, Sept. 20, 2006, p. 11.
105 *The Papal Encyclicals*, Vol. 3 (1903-1939), p. 76.
106 Benedict XVI, *Salt of the Earth*, p. 24.
107 Benedict XVI, *Truth and Tolerance*, 2004, p. 207.
108 Denzinger 714.
109 Benedict XVI, *Co-Workers of the Truth*, Ignatius Press, 1990, p. 217.
110 *The Papal Encyclicals*, Vol. 1 (1740-1878), p. 201.
111 Benedict XVI, *Salt of the Earth*, p. 29.
112 Benedict XVI, *Feast of Faith*, Ignatius Press, 1981, p. 130.
113 Benedict XVI, *Principles of Catholic Theology*, pp. 247-248.
114 Benedict XVI, *Principles of Catholic Theology*, p. 100.
115 Denzinger 1792.
116 Benedict XVI, *Principles of Catholic Theology*, p. 378.
117 Benedict XVI, *In the Beginning (A Catholic Understanding of the Story of Creation and the Fall)*, Grand Rapids, MI: William B. Eerdmans Publishing Co., 1986, p. 72.
118 See Session V of the *Council of Trent* (June 17, 1546), Denzinger 787.
119 Benedict XVI, *Introduction to Christianity*, Ignatius Press, 2004, p. 326.
120 Benedict XVI, *Principles of Catholic Theology*, p. 381.
121 Benedict XVI, *Principles of Catholic Theology*, p. 385.
122 Benedict XVI, *Principles of Catholic Theology*, p. 391.
123 Benedict XVI, *God and the World*, p. 436.
124 Benedict XVI, *Principles of Catholic Theology*, p. 229.
125 Denzinger 705.
126 Benedict XVI, *Co-Workers of the Truth*, p. 29.
127 Denzinger 86.
128 *The Papal Encyclicals*, Vol. 2 (1878-1903), p. 389.
129 *The Papal Encyclicals*, Vol. 2 (1878-1903), p. 390.
130 Benedict XVI, *Principles of Catholic Theology*, p. 121.
131 Benedict XVI, *Principles of Catholic Theology*, p. 148.
132 *The Papal Encyclicals*, Vol. 3 (1903-1939), p. 315.
133 *L'Osservatore Romano*, Oct. 25, 2006, p. 11.
134 St. Alphonsus Liguori, *Preparation for Death*, Tan Books, Abridged Version, p. 127.
135 *The Papal Encyclicals*, Vol. 3 (1903-1939), p. 72.
136 Benedict XVI, *Salt of the Earth*, pp. 95-96.
137 *L'Osservatore Romano*, May 24, 2006, p. 5.
138 *L'Osservatore Romano*, June 7, 2006, p. 4.
139 Denzinger 1690, 1699.
140 Denzinger 464.
141 Denzinger 429.
142 Denzinger 531.
143 Benedict XVI, *Introduction to Christianity*, p. 349.
144 Benedict XVI, *Introduction to Christianity*, p. 353.
145 Benedict XVI, *Introduction to Christianity*, pp. 357-358.
146 Texe Marrs, *Codex Magica*, Austin, TX: Rivercrest Publishing, 2005, pp. 120, 134.
147 *The Papal Encyclicals*, Vol. 3 (1903-1939), p. 294.
148 http://news.bbc.co.uk/2/hi/europe/5348456.stm
149 http://news.bbc.co.uk/2/hi/europe/5353774.stm

21. Answers to the Most Common Objections Against Sedevacantism

END NOTES - PAGE 345

Pope Vigilius, *Second Council of Constantinople*, 553:
"… we bear in mind what was promised about the holy Church and Him who said *the gates of Hell will not prevail against it* **(by these we understand the death-dealing tongues of heretics)**…"[1]

There are many objections launched against the sedevacantist position – that is, the position expounded in this book according to which the Chair of St. Peter is vacant because the post-Vatican II "popes" are not true popes, but non-Catholic antipopes. We will now address all of the major objections that are launched against this position.

> Objection 1): The Gates of Hell cannot prevail against the Church, as Christ said (Matthew 16). He said He would be with His Church all days until the end of the world (Matthew 28). What you are saying is contrary to the promises of Christ.

Answer: No, indefectibility (the promise of Christ to always be with His Church, and that the gates of Hell will not prevail against it) means that the Church will, until the end of time, remain essentially what she is. The indefectibility of the Church requires that *at least a remnant* of the Church will exist until the end of the world, and that a true pope will never authoritatively teach error to the entire Church. It <u>does not</u> exclude antipopes posing as popes (as we've had numerous times in the past, even in Rome) or a counterfeit sect that reduces the adherents of the true Catholic Church to a remnant in the last days. This is precisely *what is predicted* to occur in the last days and what happened during the Arian crisis.

St. Athanasius: "**Even if Catholics faithful to tradition are reduced to a handful, they are the ones who are the true Church of Jesus Christ.**"[2]

Further, it should be noted that the Church has defined that heretics are the gates of Hell which Our Lord mentioned in Matthew 16!

Pope Vigilius, *Second Council of Constantinople*, 553:
"… we bear in mind what was promised about the holy Church and Him who said *the gates of Hell will not prevail against it* **(by these we understand the death-dealing tongues of heretics)**…"[3]

Pope St. Leo IX, Sept. 2, 1053: "The holy Church built upon a rock, that is Christ, and upon *Peter*… because by **the gates of Hell, that is, by the disputations of heretics** which lead the vain to destruction, it would never be overcome."[4]

St. Thomas Aquinas (+1262): "Wisdom may fill the hearts of the faithful, **and put to silence the dread folly of heretics, fittingly referred to as the gates of Hell.**"[5] (*Intro. To Catena Aurea*.)

Notice that heretics are the gates of Hell. Heretics are not members of the Church. That's why a heretic could never be a pope. The gates of Hell (heretics) could never have authority over the Church of Christ. It's not those who expose the heretical Vatican II antipopes who are asserting that the gates of Hell have prevailed against the Church; it's those who obstinately defend them as popes, even though they can clearly be proven to be manifest heretics.

> Pope Innocent III, *Eius exemplo*, Dec. 18, 1208:
> "By the heart we believe and by the mouth we confess **the one Church, not of heretics**, but the Holy Roman, Catholic, and Apostolic Church outside of which we believe that no one is saved."[6]

> St. Francis De Sales (17th century), Doctor of the Church, *The Catholic Controversy*, pp. 305-306: "**Now when he [the Pope] is explicitly a heretic, he falls *ipso facto* from his dignity and out of the Church**..."

There is not one teaching of the Catholic Church that can be quoted which is contrary to the fact that there is presently a counterfeit sect which has reduced the true Catholic Church to a remnant in the days of the Great Apostasy, which is presided over by antipopes who have falsely posed as popes. Those who assert that the Vatican II sect is the Catholic Church assert that the Catholic Church officially endorses false religions and false doctrines. This is impossible and would mean that the gates of Hell have prevailed against the Catholic Church.

Objection 2): What's your authority for making these judgments? Your use of dogmatic statements is private interpretation.

Answer: The authority a Catholic has to determine that heretics are not members of the Church is Catholic *dogma*, which teaches us that those who depart from the Faith are considered alien to the Church.

> Pope Leo XIII, *Satis Cognitum* (# 9), June 29, 1896:
> "The practice of the Church has always been the same, as is shown by the unanimous teaching of the Fathers, who were wont to hold as outside Catholic communion, AND ALIEN TO THE CHURCH, WHOEVER WOULD RECEDE IN THE LEAST DEGREE FROM ANY POINT OF DOCTRINE PROPOSED BY HER AUTHORITATIVE MAGISTERIUM."[7]

Moreover, to assert that adhering to this Catholic dogma is to engage in private interpretation, as this objection does, is to assert precisely what Pope St. Pius X condemned in his Syllabus of Errors against the Modernists.

> Pope St. Pius X, *Lamentabile*, The Errors of the Modernists, July 3, 1907, #22:
> "**The dogmas** which the Church professes as revealed are not truths fallen from heaven, **but they are a kind of interpretation** of religious facts, which the human mind by a laborious effort prepared for itself."- **Condemned**[8]

> Pope Pius X, *Lamentabile*, The Errors of the Modernists, July 3, 1907, #54:
> "**The dogmas**, the sacraments, the hierarchy, **as far as pertains both to the notion and to the reality, are nothing but interpretations** and the evolution of Christian intelligence, which have increased and perfected the little germ latent in the Gospel."- **Condemned**[9]

Notice, the idea that dogmas are interpretations is condemned. But that's exactly what this objection is asserting, whether those who make it will admit it or not. They are saying that to apply the truth of a dogma is "private interpretation." Further refuting this objection is the fact that, in its *Decree on the Sacrament of Order*, the Council of Trent solemnly declared that the dogmatic canons are for the use of <u>all</u> the faithful.

> Pope Pius IV, *Council of Trent*, Sess. 13, Chap. 4: "These are the matters which in general it seemed well to the sacred Council to teach to the faithful of Christ regarding the sacrament of order. **It has, however, resolved to condemn the contrary <u>in definite and appropriate canons in the following manner, so that all, making use of the rule of faith</u>, with the assistance of Christ, <u>may be able to recognize more easily the Catholic truth in the midst of the darkness of so many errors</u>**."[10]

The word "canon" (in Greek: *kanon*) means a reed; a straight rod or bar; a measuring stick; something serving to determine, rule, or measure. The Council of Trent is infallibly declaring that its canons are measuring rods for **"<u>all</u>"** so that they, <u>making use</u> of these <u>rules of Faith</u>, may be able to recognize and defend the truth in the midst of darkness! This very important statement <u>blows away</u> the claim of those who say that using dogmas to prove points is "private interpretation." Catholic dogma is the authority of all who come to these correct conclusions.

> Pope Gregory XVI, *Mirari Vos* (# 7), Aug. 15, 1832: "… nothing of the things appointed ought to be diminished; nothing changed; nothing added; **but they must be preserved both as regards expression and meaning**."[11]

Objection 3): You cannot know if someone is a heretic or denounce him as such without a trial and declaratory sentence.

Answer: Not so. The declaratory sentence which follows an automatic excommunication is merely a legal recognition of something which already exists. If this were not true, the automatic excommunication would be meaningless.

> Canon 2314, 1917 Code of Canon Law: "All apostates from the Christian faith and each and every heretic or schismatic: 1) Incur *ipso facto* [by that very fact] excommunication…"[12]

The excommunicated person is already severed from the Church. Most heretics are known to be heretics without a trial or declaratory sentence, and must be denounced as such.

> Pope Pius VI, *Auctorem fidei*, Aug. 28, 1794:
> "47. Likewise, **the proposition which teaches that it is necessary, according to the natural and divine laws, <u>for either excommunication or for suspension, that a personal examination should precede</u>**, and that, therefore, **sentences called 'ipso facto' have no other force than that of a serious threat without any actual effect**" – **<u>false</u>, rash, pernicious, injurious to the power of the Church, erroneous**.[13] DENZ 1547

As we see here, the Catholic Church teaches that formal processes and judgments are <u>not</u> necessary for *ipso facto* (by that very fact) excommunications to take effect. They are very often, as in the case of the heretic Martin Luther, formal recognitions of the *ipso facto* excommunication that has already occurred. This should be obvious to a Catholic; but to illustrate this point, here is what Martin Luther said before he was formally condemned as a heretic by the pope.

> Martin Luther, <u>speaking before the Bull of Pope Leo X giving him the final sixty days</u> to retract before a declaration of excommunication was published: "As for me, the die is cast: I despise alike the favor and fury of **Rome; I do not wish to be reconciled with her, or ever to hold any communion with her. Let her condemn and burn my books; I, in turn, unless I can find no fire, will condemn and publicly burn the whole pontifical law, that swamp of heresies.'"**[14]

Are we to believe that the man who uttered this quotation (well before he was formally condemned as a heretic by a declaratory sentence) was a Catholic or could have been considered one? If such an idea isn't patently absurd, then nothing is. Obviously, Martin Luther was a manifest heretic prior to the formal declaration, and any Catholic aware of his beliefs could have and *should have* denounced him as a manifest heretic once that Catholic encountered his outrageously heretical views.

That's why, prior to the trial of Luther, Cardinal Cajetan "contacted Elector Frederick, Luther's sovereign and protector, urging him not to 'disgrace the good name of his ancestors' by supporting a heretic."[15]

The same principle applies to a heretic such as John Kerry, the notorious supporter of abortion. Almost all conservative-minded professing Catholics would immediately agree that John Kerry is a heretic and not a Catholic, since he obstinately rejects Catholic teaching against abortion. **But they are making this "judgment" on their own, since no declaratory sentence has ever been issued against him**. They are thus proving the point that a declaration is not necessary to condemn a heretic. Most heretics in Church history, and almost all heretics in the world today, have been and must be considered heretics without any declaration by virtue of their heresy being manifest.

When the heresy is manifest and clearly obstinate, as in the case of Luther or Benedict XVI (who says we shouldn't convert non-Catholics and takes active part in Synagogue worship), Catholics not only can denounce him as a non-Catholic without a trial, but must do so. That is precisely why St. Robert Bellarmine, Doctor of the Church, <u>in addressing this precise question</u>, states unequivocally that the manifest heretic is deposed and must be avoided as a non-Catholic with no authority **before any "excommunication** or judicial sentence." In this context, St. Robert uses the word "excommunication" to refer to the *ferendae sententiae* penalty (the formal declaration by the pope or judge).

> St. Robert Bellarmine, *De Romano Pontifice*, II, 30, speaking of a claimant to the Papal Office: "For, in the first place, **it is proven with arguments from authority and from reason that the manifest heretic is 'ipso facto' deposed**. The argument from authority is based on St. Paul (Titus 3:10), who orders that the heretic be avoided after two warnings, that is, after showing himself to be manifestly obstinate - **which means before any excommunication or judicial sentence**. And this is what St. Jerome writes, adding that the other sinners are excluded from the Church by sentence of excommunication, but the heretics exile themselves and separate themselves by their own act from the body of Christ."

Let us repeat that: WHICH MEANS BEFORE ANY EXCOMMUNICATION OR JUDICIAL SENTENCE! So, we can see that non-sedevacantists, in arguing that Catholics cannot denounce manifest heretics such as Benedict XVI since there hasn't been a formal trial, have gotten it all wrong. Their conclusion makes a complete mockery out of the unity of Faith in the Church. In case we have forgotten, there is a unity of Faith in the Catholic Church (as in **one**, holy, Catholic and apostolic.)

> Pope Pius XII, *Mystici Corporis Christi* (# 22):
> "As therefore **in the true Christian community** there is only one Body, one Spirit, one Lord, and one Baptism, so **there can be only one faith**. And therefore if a man refuse to hear the Church let him be considered – so the Lord commands – as a heathen and a publican. It follows that **those who are divided in faith or government cannot be living in the unity of such a Body**, nor can they be living the life of its one Divine Spirit."[16]

According to the non-sedevacantists' conclusion, Catholics would have to affirm communion with a man who publicly avowed that he wanted no communion with the Catholic Church, and held that the whole Pontifical law is a swamp of heresies; or a man who is obstinately pro-abortion, just because no formal declaration was made against him. To state that Catholics should hold communion with such a manifest heretic because no process against him had been completed, is contrary to Catholic teaching, Catholic Tradition and Catholic sense.

> St. Robert Bellarmine, *De Romano Pontifice*, II, 30:
> "… for men are not bound, or able to read hearts; BUT WHEN THEY SEE THAT SOMEONE IS A HERETIC BY HIS EXTERNAL WORKS, THEY JUDGE HIM TO BE A HERETIC PURE AND SIMPLE, AND CONDEMN HIM AS A HERETIC."

Objection 4): What about material heresy? Can't the Vatican II Popes only be material heretics?

Answer: A "material" heretic is a Catholic erring in good faith about a dogmatic issue. The Vatican II antipopes are without doubt real heretics. They cannot be material heretics (Catholics erring in good faith) for many reasons, most important among those reasons being: 1) they don't hold the essential mysteries of Faith; 2) they reject obvious dogmas of which they are fully aware.

"Material heretic" is a term used by theologians to describe a Catholic erring in good faith regarding some Church teaching, who has not denied it deliberately. The only way that one can be a "material heretic" is by being unaware that the position that he holds is contrary to the teaching of the Church. Such a person would change his position immediately upon being informed of the Church's teaching on the matter. Thus, a so-called "material heretic" is not a heretic, but rather a confused Catholic who denies nothing of that which he knows the Church to have taught. The fact that a so-called "material heretic" is not a heretic is proven by the fact that a so-called "material heretic" does not cease to be part of the Church; and we have already shown by many quotations that <u>all</u> heretics cease to be members of the Church.

> Pope Eugene IV, *Council of Florence*, "Cantate Domino," 1441:
> "The Holy Roman Church firmly believes, professes and preaches that **all those <u>who are outside the Catholic Church</u>**, not only pagans **but also** Jews or <u>heretics</u> and schismatics…"[17]

Furthermore, a so-called "material heretic" (an erring Catholic) does not bring down on his head eternal punishment for denying the faith; and <u>all</u> heretics bring down on their heads eternal punishment for denying the faith.

> Pope St. Celestine I, *Council of Ephesus*, 431:
> "… <u>ALL</u> HERETICS corrupt the true expressions of the Holy Spirit with their own evil minds and they draw down on their own heads an inextinguishable flame."[18]

A material heretic, therefore, is <u>not a heretic</u>, but a Catholic who is innocently mistaken about some Church teaching. Hence, **those who claim that Benedict XVI is unaware of all of the dogmas that he denies, and is therefore only a "material heretic" (in other words, a mistaken Catholic) are not only arguing that which is absurd, but that which is IMPOSSIBLE.** It is impossible that Benedict XVI is only a so-called "material heretic" for three reasons:

> **Number 1):** It is a fact that Benedict XVI knows of the many dogmas of the Church which he denies. He knows more about Catholic teaching than almost anyone in the world. He discourses on the Church's dogmatic pronouncements – the very same ones he contradicts and rejects, such as Vatican I – all the time.

> Benedict XVI, *Principles of Catholic Theology* (1982), p. 239: "Anyone who inquires about the Church's teaching with regard to holy orders finds at his disposal a relatively rich supply of source materials; **three councils have spoken extensively on the subject: Florence, Trent, and Vatican II.** Mention should also be made of the important apostolic constitution of Pius XII (*Sacramentum ordinis*) of the year 1947."[19]

> Benedict XVI, *Principles of Catholic Theology* (1982), pp. 197-198: "**On the part of the West, <u>the maximum demand would be that the East recognize the primacy of the bishop of Rome in the full scope of the definition of 1870</u> [Vatican I] and in so doing submit in** practice, to a primacy such as has been accepted by the Uniate churches… <u>none of the maximum solutions offers any real hope of unity</u>."[20]

In these quotations we see just a glimpse of Benedict XVI's familiarity with Catholic teaching, including the very councils he denies. The same applies to John Paul II and his "predecessors." For example, in the 1999 agreement with the Lutheran Church on Justification, approved by John Paul II, John Paul II agreed that the Council of Trent no longer applies.

> Vatican-Lutheran Agreement on the Doctrine of Justification, approved by Benedict XVI: "# 13. **IN LIGHT OF THIS CONSENSUS, THE CORRESPONDING DOCTRINAL CONDEMNATIONS OF THE 16TH CENTURY** [i.e., the canons of the Council of Trent] **DO NOT APPLY TO TODAY'S PARTNER.**"[21]

It goes without saying that he cannot be unaware of the Council of Trent if he agrees that it no longer applies. Further, **Benedict XVI holds several doctorates in theology and has written many books dealing with the intricacies of Catholic dogma. One of us has read 24 of his books, and can say that Benedict XVI is more familiar with what the Catholic Church teaches than almost anyone in the world.** To assert that Benedict XVI or John Paul II or Paul VI or John XXIII remained unaware of the simplest Church teachings which they denied on Our Lord, against Protestantism, on salvation, against false religions, on religious liberty, etc. is false and

Answers to Objections

ridiculous in the highest degree. To assert, for instance, that Benedict XVI is unaware of the dogma that Protestants are bound under pain of heresy to accept the Papacy – remember that he teaches just the opposite – is <u>pure insanity</u>. It's equivalent to asserting that one can be the head chef at a five star restaurant and not know what lettuce is. But that's exactly what those who advance the "material heretic" argument would have us believe.

> Number 2): It's impossible for Benedict XVI to be only a "material heretic" or a mistaken Catholic because – supposing for a moment that he were unaware of the many dogmas which he denies (which, as we have stated, is definitely not true) – being a man who claims to be a bishop and the pope, he is bound to have learned them. Therefore, there is no excuse for him on the grounds that he is unaware of the fundamental Church dogmas which he denies.

A canon law manual: "**If the delinquent making this claim be a cleric, his plea for mitigation must be dismissed,** either as untrue, or else as indicating ignorance which is affected, or at least crass and supine… His ecclesiastical training in the seminary, with its moral and dogmatic theology, its ecclesiastical history, not to mention its canon law, all insure that the Church's attitude towards heresy was imparted to him."[22]

> Number 3): It is impossible that Benedict XVI is merely a "material heretic" because there are certain things that every adult must hold by a necessity of means in order to be a Catholic, and Benedict XVI doesn't hold those things. Every adult Catholic must believe in the Trinity, the Incarnation, that Jesus Christ and His Church are true, and that other religions outside of Jesus Christ are false. These essential mysteries must be known by *a necessity of means*.

Pope Benedict XIV, *Cum Religiosi* (# 1), June 26, 1754:
"We could not rejoice, however, when it was subsequently reported to Us that in the course of religious instruction preparatory to Confession and Holy Communion, it was very often found that these people were ignorant of the mysteries of the faith, **even those matters which must be known by** *necessity of means*; consequently they were ineligible to partake of the Sacraments."[23]

In other words, every Catholic above the age of reason must have a positive knowledge of certain mysteries of faith to be saved. There are no excuses, even for ignorance. Thus, if one holds a belief which destroys faith in those mysteries, even if he has been taught incorrectly, he is not a Catholic.

Pope Benedict XIV, *Cum Religiosi* (# 4):
"… confessors should perform this part of their duty whenever anyone stands at their tribunal who does not know **what he must by** *necessity of means* **know to be saved…**"[24]

Pope St. Pius X, *Acerbo Nimis* (# 2), April 15, 1905:
"And so Our Predecessor, Benedict XIV, had just cause to write: 'We declare that a great number of those who are condemned to eternal punishment suffer that everlasting calamity **because of ignorance of those mysteries of faith which must be known and believed in order to be numbered among the elect.'**"[25]

For instance, if one really believes in three different gods and not *one God in three divine persons*, then he is not a Catholic – period. This is true even if he was never taught the true doctrine on the Trinity. He is not a Catholic, since his belief contradicts an *essential mystery* he must possess to hold the true Faith.

Likewise, if one believes that other religions, such as Islam, Judaism, etc. are also good, then one doesn't believe that Christ (and, by extension, His Church) is the only truth. If one doesn't believe that Christ (and, by extension, His Church) is the only truth, then one doesn't have the Catholic Faith – period. This is true even if he was never taught the true doctrine on this matter, which is why Pope Pius XI says that all who hold the opinion that all religions "are more or less good and praiseworthy" have abandoned the true religion – period.

> Pope Pius XI, *Mortalium Animos* (# 2):
> "… Certainly such attempts can nowise be approved by Catholics, founded as they are on **that false opinion which considers all religions to be more or less good and praiseworthy**, since they all in different ways manifest and signify that sense which is inborn in us all, and by which we are led to God and to the obedient acknowledgment of His rule. **Not only are those who hold this opinion in error and deceived, but also in distorting the idea of true religion they reject it**, and little by little, turn aside to naturalism and atheism, as it is called; **from which it clearly follows that one who supports those who hold these theories and attempt to realize them, is altogether abandoning the divinely revealed religion.**"[26]

Well, we have shown that Benedict XVI and his "predecessors" believe that Judaism, Islam, etc. are good. Benedict XVI was even initiated into Islam in a mosque on Nov. 30, 2006. He and his "predecessors" praise these religions. Benedict XVI specifically called Islam "noble" and said that it represents "greatness." It's not possible for him to believe this and be a Catholic "material heretic," since he doesn't believe in an *essential mystery* he must possess to hold the true Faith: that Christ is the only truth. Therefore, Benedict XVI is not a Catholic – period.

This is also proven from another angle. Since it's an essential mystery of Catholic Faith that Christ (and, by extension, his Church) is the only truth, it follows that those who believe this mystery also hold that *Christ's Church must be believed*. This is the teaching of Pope Leo XIII.

> Pope Leo XIII, *Satis Cognitum* (# 13), June 29, 1896:
> "**You are not to be looked upon as holding the true Catholic faith if you do not teach that the faith of Rome is to be held.**"[27]

If one holds that the Catholic religion doesn't have to be accepted by non-Catholics, then one is not a Catholic. As we've shown, the Vatican II antipopes teach that the Catholic religion doesn't have to be accepted by non-Catholics; they specifically teach that the Eastern Schismatics don't need to convert to the Catholic Faith.

> Paul VI, Joint Declaration with the Schismatic "Pope" Shenouda III, May 10, 1973: "Paul VI, Bishop of Rome and Pope of the Catholic Church, and **Shenouda III, Pope of Alexandria and Patriarch of the See of St. Mark**… In the name of this charity, **we reject all forms of proselytism… Let it cease, where it may exist**…"[28]

> John Paul II, *Homily*, Jan. 25, 1993: "'**The way to achieve Christian unity, in fact,' says the document of the Pontifical Commission for Russia, 'is not proselytism but fraternal dialogue**…"[29]

> Benedict XVI, *Address to Protestants at World Youth Day*, August 19, 2005: "And we now ask: What does it mean to restore the unity of all Christians?... <u>this unity does not mean what could be called ecumenism of the return</u>: that is, <u>to deny and to reject one's own faith history. Absolutely not!</u>"[30]

Furthermore…

The law of the Church presumes pertinacity in heresy unless the contrary is proven.

In addition to the above facts which demonstrate that the Vatican II antipopes are definitely formal heretics, the presumption of the law is against them:

> Canon 2200.2, 1917 Code of Canon Law: "<u>**When an external violation of the law has been committed**</u>, **malice is presumed** in the external forum until the contrary is proven."

A commentary on this canon by Rev. Eric F. Mackenzie, A.M., S.T.L., J.C.L, states:

> "**The very commission of any act which signifies heresy, e.g., the statement of some doctrine contrary or contradictory to a revealed and defined dogma, gives sufficient ground for juridical presumption of heretical depravity…** [E]xcusing circumstances have to be proved in the external forum, and **the burden of proof is on the person whose action has given rise to the imputation of heresy. In the absence of such proof, all such excuses are presumed not to exist.**"[31]

Not only have the Vatican II antipopes made literally hundreds of statements contrary to revealed and defined dogma, but they have also explicitly declared themselves to be in communion with – in the same Church as – schismatics and heretics. They have, furthermore, confirmed these statements with acts which further manifest their adherence to heresy, such as *communicatio in sacris* (communication in sacred things) with various false religions. It is not, therefore, the law or the spirit of the Church to exonerate someone publicly spewing heresy, but rather to presume him guilty.

> Pope Innocent IV, *First Council of Lyons*, 1245:
> "The civil law declares that **those are to be regarded as heretics, and ought to be subject to the sentences issued against them, who even on slight evidence are found to have strayed from the judgment and path of the Catholic religion.**"[32]

St. Robert Bellarmine explains why this must be.

> St. Robert Bellarmine, *De Romano Pontifice*, II, 30:
> "… for men are not bound, or able to read hearts; but **when they see that someone is a heretic by his external works, they judge him to be a heretic pure and simple, and condemn him as a heretic.**"

A simple illustration will also demonstrate why this must be.

> Suppose you had some sheep and you appointed a shepherd to watch over them. Suppose one day the shepherd <u>became a wolf and began eating the sheep and tearing them to pieces</u>. Would you, looking after the welfare of these sheep, **maintain the wolf**

as head of the sheep? Would you demand that <u>the other sheep not yet eaten subject themselves to the wolf</u>, and thus place themselves in proximate danger of being eaten? Of course you wouldn't, and neither would God.

God could never allow one who is promulgating manifest heresy in the external forum to maintain authority in the Church or be able to demand the submission of Catholics, regardless of what his intentions are. Remember, heresy kills souls. Suppose the wolf in our story is just hungry, or having a bad day. Does this change the fact that the sheep are being eliminated? No.

Furthermore, what wolf who was trying to deceive people would openly declare himself to be a non-Catholic or an enemy of the Church?

> Matthew 7:15-
> "Beware of false prophets, *who come to you in clothing of sheep*, but inwardly they are ravening wolves."

There is no more effective way to assist a false prophet than to insist that he, despite his public profession of heresy, maintains authority in the Church. **Pope St. Celestine authoritatively confirms the principle that we cannot regard a public heretic as a person with authority when dealing with the case of the heretic Nestorius.** Nestorius, Patriarch of Constantinople, began to preach the heresy that Mary was not the Mother of God. The faithful reacted by breaking communion with him, having realized that since Nestorius was preaching public and notorious heresy he could not have authority in the Catholic Church. The following quote from Pope St. Celestine is found in *De Romano Pontifice*, the work of St. Robert Bellarmine.

> Pope St. Celestine:
> "**The authority of Our Apostolic See has determined** that the bishop, cleric, or simple Christian who had been deposed or excommunicated by Nestorius or his followers, **after the latter began to preach heresy *shall not be considered deposed or excommunicated*. <u>For he who had defected from the faith with such preachings, cannot depose or remove anyone whatsoever</u>**."[33]

Pope Pius IX confirms this principle by teaching that one is considered a heretic or a schismatic even if one has not yet been declared as such by the Holy See.

> Pope Pius IX, *Quartus Supra* (# 12), Jan. 6, 1873:
> "Since the faction of Armenia is like this, **they are schismatics even if they had not yet been condemned as such by Apostolic authority.**"[34]

This is why the saints, theologians, doctors, canonists and popes who speak to the issue of a "heretical pope" avoid the terms "material" and "formal" heresy, for these are terms that imply a judgment of the internal forum. Rather, they use the words public, manifest, notorious, etc. – terms corresponding to the external forum.

> F.X. Wernz, P. Vidal (1943):
> "Through <u>notorious</u> and openly revealed heresy, **the Roman Pontiff, should he fall into heresy, by that very fact is deemed to be deprived of the power of jurisdiction even before any declaratory judgment of the Church…**"[35]

> Canon 192, *1917 Code of Canon Law:*
> "A person may be **unwillingly deprived** of, **or removed from, an office**, either by **operation of law** or an act of the lawful superior."

> Canon 188.4, *1917 Code of Canon Law*:
> "There are certain causes which effect the tacit (silent) resignation of an office, **which resignation is accepted in advance by operation of the law, and hence is effective without any declaration.** These causes are… (4) <u>if he has publicly fallen away from the faith.</u>"

What is a public defection from the faith?

> Canon 2197.1, *1917 Code of Canon Law*:
> "A Crime is *public*: (1) if it is already commonly known or the circumstances are such as to lead to the conclusion that it can and will easily become so…"

Thus, we have shown in great detail why it's utterly false to assert that the Vatican II antipopes are merely "material heretics." They cannot be material heretics because 1) they know very well of the dogmas which they deny; 2) they are bound to know the Catholic Faith as "bishops," especially the dogmas which they deny; and 3) they lack and contradict the essential mysteries of Faith which one must hold to be a Catholic.

Objection 5): The Church cannot exist without a pope, or at least it cannot exist for 40 years without a pope, as sedevacantists say…

Answer: The Church has existed for years without a pope, and does so every time a pope dies. The Church has experienced a papal interregnum (i.e. period without a pope) over 200 different times in Church history. The longest papal interregnum (before the Vatican II apostasy) was between Pope St. Marcellinus (296-304) and Pope St. Marcellus (308-309). It lasted for more than three and a half years.[36] Further, theologians teach that the Church can exist *for even decades without a pope*.

FR. EDMUND JAMES O'REILLY CRUSHES THE NON-SEDEVACANTISTS' MAIN ARGUMENT ON THE LENGTH OF A PAPAL INTERREGNUM (PERIOD WITHOUT A POPE) BY TEACHING THAT THE CHURCH CAN EXIST FOR DECADES WITHOUT A POPE

Fr. Edmund James O'Reilly was an eminent theologian who lived at the time of Vatican I. Writing *after* Vatican I and its definitions on the perpetuity of the Papal Office, he taught that God could leave the Church without a pope for over 39 years – e.g., during the entire span of the Great Western Schism (1378-1417). Here is a quote from Father O'Reilly's discussion of the Great Western Schism:

> "We may here stop to inquire what is to be said of the position, at that time, of the three claimants, and their rights with regard to the Papacy. In the first place, there was all through, from the death of Gregory XI in 1378, a pope – with the exception, of course, of the intervals between deaths and elections to fill up the vacancies thereby created. There was, I say, at every given time a pope, really invested with the dignity of the Vicar of Christ and Head of the Church, whatever opinions might exist among many as to his genuineness; **not that an interregnum covering the whole period would have been**

Answers to Objections

> **impossible or inconsistent with the promises of Christ, for this is by no means manifest**, but that, as a matter of fact, there was not such an interregnum."[37]

Fr. O'Reilly says that an interregnum (a period without a pope) covering the entire period of the Great Western Schism is by no means incompatible with the promises of Christ about His Church. The period Fr. O'Reilly is speaking about began in 1378 with the death of Pope Gregory XI and ended essentially in 1417 when Pope Martin V was elected. **That would be a 39-year interregnum (period without a pope).** And Fr. O'Reilly was one of the most eminent theologians of the 19th Century.

It's obvious that Fr. O'Reilly is on the side of those who, in rejecting the Vatican II antipopes, hold the possibility of a long-term vacancy of the Holy See. In fact, on page 287 of his book, Fr. O'Reilly gives this prophetic warning:

> "The great schism of the West suggests to me a reflection which I take the liberty of expressing here. **If this schism had not occurred, the hypothesis of such a thing happening would appear to many chimerical [absurd]. They would say it could not be; God would not permit the Church to come into so unhappy a situation.** Heresies might spring up and spread and last painfully long, through the fault and to the perdition of their authors and abettors, to the great distress too of the faithful, increased by actual persecution in many places where the heretics were dominant. **But that the true Church should remain between thirty and forty years without a thoroughly ascertained Head, and representative of Christ on earth, this would not be. Yet it has been; and we have no guarantee that it will not be again**, though we may fervently hope otherwise. What I would infer is, that **we must not be too ready to pronounce on what God may permit. We know with absolute certainty that He will fulfill His promises**… We may also trust that He will do a great deal more than what He has bound Himself by His promises. We may look forward with cheering probability to exemption for the future from some of the trouble and misfortunes that have befallen in the past. **But we, or our successors in the future generations of Christians, shall perhaps see stranger evils than have yet been experienced**, even before the immediate approach of that great winding up of all things on earth that will precede the day of judgment. I am not setting up for a prophet, nor pretending to see unhappy wonders, of which I have no knowledge whatever. **All I mean to convey is that contingencies regarding the Church, not excluded by the Divine promises, cannot be regarded as practically impossible, just because they would be terrible and distressing in a very high degree.**"[38]

This is an excellent point. Fr. O'Reilly explains that if the Great Western Schism had never occurred, Catholics would say that such a situation (three competing claimants to the Papacy with no thoroughly ascertained head for decades) is impossible – just like those today who say the sedevacantist "thesis" is impossible, even though the facts prove that it is true.

The Great Western Schism did happen, Fr. O'Reilly says, and we have no guarantee that worse things, that are not excluded by divine promises, won't happen. There is nothing contrary to indefectibility in saying that we haven't had a pope since the death of Pope Pius XII in 1958. **There is everything contrary to the indefectibility of the Catholic Church in asserting that true popes could promulgate Vatican II, officially endorse false and pagan religions, promulgate the Protestant New Mass, and hold that non-Catholics don't need to convert for salvation.** Leaving the Church without a pope for an extended period of the Great Apostasy is the punishment inflicted by God on our generation for the wickedness of the world.

> Prophecy of St. Nicholas of Fluh (1417-1487): "The Church will be punished because the majority of her members, high and low, will become so perverted. **The Church will sink**

Answers to Objections

deeper and deeper until she will at last seem to be extinguished, and the succession of Peter and the other Apostles to have expired. But, after this, she will be victoriously exalted in the sight of all doubters." [39]

> **Objection 6): Vatican I's definitions on the perpetuity of the Papal Office contradict the claims of the sedevacantists.**

Answer: Vatican I's dogmas <u>don't</u> contradict a vacancy of the Papal See; in fact, it's only those who reject the Vatican II antipopes who can consistently accept these papal dogmas, since Benedict XVI utterly rejects them.

ANSWERS TO SPECIFIC PASSAGES FROM VATICAN I CITED BY NONSEDEVACANTISTS – AND THE ABSURDITY OF A "POPE" WHO DOESN'T BELIEVE IN VATICAN I

People attempting to refute sedevacantism often cite three passages from Vatican I. We will specifically address all three of those passages. Before we do that, we must emphasize the fact we just discussed: there have been long periods of time when the Church has had no pope. We've already mentioned the three and a half year interregnum between Pope St. Marcellinus and Pope St. Marcellus.

Although Pope St. Gregory VII died on May 25, 1085, it was not until almost two years later - May 9, 1087 - that his successor, Pope Victor III, was elected. On June 25, 1243, Pope Innocent IV became the 179th successor to St. Peter; his immediate predecessor, Pope Celestine IV, however, had died over a year and a half before - November 10, 1241. Later in the same century, Catholics would be forced to wait nearly three years as the Church, upon the death of Pope Clement IV on November 29, 1268, delayed naming a new Pope until St. Gregory X was picked on September 1, 1271. Other examples of a year or more space between popes can be cited, the point here being that while the quick transfer of papal power has been common, exceptions are to be found. **Today's crisis, then, certainly is not the first time in which the Church has suffered for a significant period of time without a pope**.

We've already discussed antipopes who reigned from Rome while posing as the pope, something we saw in the case of Anacletus II and the Great Western Schism. There is also a theological axiom, "plus or minus does not mutate the species, a change in degree does not affect the principle." If the Church did not defect or lose perpetual papal succession during a 3 year and 7 month vacancy, then the Church will not defect or lose perpetual papal succession during a 40 year vacancy. The principle is the same, unless one can cite a specific teaching of the Church which declares a limit to a papal interregnum.

Since there is <u>no teaching which puts a limit on such a papal interregnum</u> (a period without a pope), <u>and since the definitions of Vatican I on the perpetuity of Papal Office make absolutely no mention of papal vacancies</u> or how long they can last, if the definitions of Vatican I disprove the sedevacantist position (as some claim), then they also disprove the indefectibility of the Catholic Church – every single time the Church finds itself without a pope. But this is impossible and ridiculous, of course.

Thus, in order to be consistent, non-sedevacantists who quote Vatican I against the sedevacantist "thesis" must argue that the Church can never be without a pope, not even for a moment (a patent absurdity). But this is exactly what one of them argued in a very interesting slip-up in an article. This serves to reveal his profound bias and the errors at the heart of his position:

> Chris Ferrara, "Opposing the Sedevacantist Enterprise," Catholic Family News, August 2005, p. 19: "**Never in Her history has the Church, even for a moment, been without a successor to Peter**, validly elected upon the death of his validly elected predecessor."[40]

This is obviously absurd and completely false. The writer knows that this is false because, in the next sentence, he declares:

> Ferrara: "Indeed, **the longest interregnum between two popes in Church history was only two years and five months**, between the death of Pope Nicholas IV (1292) and the election of Pope Celestine V (1294)."[41]

First, the interregnum he mentions was not the longest in Church history (as we saw above). Second, he admits that the Church existed without a pope for years. So there have been quite a few "moments" in Church history that the Church has been without a pope. Why would he say that the Church cannot be without a pope "even for a moment" when he knows that this is not true?

Now that the fact that the Church can be without a pope for a long period of time has been established, let's look at the passages of Vatican I:

1. Vatican I declares that the Papacy is the Perpetual Principle and Visible Foundation of Unity

   > Vatican I, Dogmatic Constitution on the Church of Christ, Sess. 4, July 18, 1870: "But, that the episcopacy itself might be one and undivided, and that the entire multitude of the faithful through priests closely connected with one another might be preserved in the unity of faith and communion, **placing Peter over the other apostles He established in him the perpetual principle and visible foundation of both unities**, upon whose strength the eternal temple might be erected, and the sublimity of the Church might rise in the firmness of this faith."[42]

That what Christ instituted in St. Peter (THE OFFICE OF PETER) remains the perpetual principle and visible foundation of unity <u>EVEN TODAY, AND WHEN THERE IS NO POPE</u>, is proven every time a Catholic who is a sedevacantist converts an Eastern "Orthodox" Schismatic to the Catholic Faith.

The Catholic (who is a sedevacantist) charitably informs the Eastern Schismatic that <u>he (the Eastern Schismatic) is not in the unity of the Church</u> because he doesn't accept what Christ instituted in St. Peter (the office of the Papacy), in addition to not accepting what the successors of St. Peter have bindingly taught in history (the Council of Trent, etc.). **This is a clear example of how the Office of the Papacy still serves – and will always serve – as the perpetual principle of visible unity, distinguishing the true faithful from the false (and the true Church from the false)**. This is true when there is no pope, and for the sedevacantist today. This dogmatic teaching of Vatican I doesn't exclude periods without a pope and it is not contrary to the sedevacantist thesis in any way.

Answers to Objections 312

In fact, while this definition remains true for the sedevacantist, it must be stated clearly that **THIS DEFINITION OF VATICAN I ONLY REMAINS TRUE FOR THE SEDEVACANTIST.** THIS DEFINITION OF VATICAN I ON THE PAPACY BEING THE PERPETUAL PRINCIPLE AND VISIBLE FOUNDATION OF UNITY IS MOST CERTAINLY NOT TRUE FOR THOSE UNDER BENEDICT XVI. This teaching of Vatican I only remains true for the sedevacantist (not those under Benedict XVI) because Vatican II teaches just the opposite:

> Vatican II document, *Lumen Gentium* (# 15):
> "For several reasons the Church recognizes that it is joined to those who, though baptized and so honoured with the Christian name, do not profess the faith in its entirety or do not preserve communion under the successor of St. Peter."[43]

We see that Vatican II teaches that the Papacy is not the visible foundation of the unities of faith and communion. It teaches that those who reject the Papacy are in communion with the Church. Since this is the official teaching of the Vatican II sect and its antipopes, those who adhere to them contradict the above teaching of Vatican I.

Second, the teaching of Vatican I on the perpetuity of the Papal Office only remains true for the sedevacantist because **Benedict XVI explicitly teaches that accepting the Papacy is not essential for unity**!

> Benedict XVI, *Principles of Catholic Theology*, 1982, pp. 197-198: "**On the part of the West, the maximum demand would be that the East recognize the primacy of the bishop of Rome in the full scope of the definition of 1870 [Vatican I]** and in so doing submit in practice, to a primacy such as has been accepted by the Uniate churches… **As regards Protestantism, the maximum demand of the Catholic Church would be that the Protestant ecclesiological ministers be regarded as totally invalid and that Protestants be converted to Catholicism;… none of the maximum solutions offers any real hope of unity.**"[44]

We've already shown – but it was necessary to quote it again here – that Benedict XVI specifically mentions, and then bluntly rejects, the traditional teaching of the Catholic Church that the Protestants and Eastern Schismatics must be converted to the Catholic Faith and accept Vatican I ("the full scope of the definition of 1870") for unity and salvation. He specifically rejects that the dogmatic definition of Vatican I (accepting the Papacy, etc.) is binding for Church unity. Besides the fact that this is another clear example of manifest heresy from the Vatican II antipopes, **this proves that BENEDICT XVI (THE MAN THEY ACTUALLY CLAIM IS THE "POPE") DENIES THE VERY DOGMA FROM VATICAN I THAT THIS OBJECTION BRINGS FORWARD!**

2. The Papacy will endure forever

> Vatican I, Dogmatic Constitution on the Church of Christ, Sess. 4, Chap. 2: "Moreover, **what the Chief of pastors and the Great Pastor of sheep, the Lord Jesus, established in the blessed Apostle Peter** for the perpetual salvation and perennial good of the Church, this by the same Author **must endure always in the Church which was founded upon a rock and will endure firm until the end of ages.**"[45]

Yes, what Christ instituted in St. Peter (i.e., THE OFFICE OF THE PAPACY) must endure always until the end of ages. What is the Office of the Papacy? The Office of the Papacy is the office of St. Peter which is occupied by every true and lawful Bishop of Rome. This means and guarantees that every time there is a true and valid occupant of the office he is endowed by Christ with infallibility (in his authoritative and binding teaching capacity), he is endowed with supreme

Answers to Objections 313

jurisdiction over the universal Church, and he is the visible head of the Church. **That remains true for every true and lawful occupant of the Papal Office until the end of time. This doesn't mean that the Church will always have such an occupant, as Church history and more than 200 papal vacancies prove**, nor does it mean that antipopes reigning from Rome are an impossibility (such as Antipope Anacletus II, who reigned in Rome from 1130-1138). This definition proves nothing for the non-sedevacantist, so let's move on.

3. Peter will have perpetual successors in the Primacy over the Universal Church

> Pope Pius IX, *First Vatican Council*, Sess. 4, Chap. 2, [Canon]. "<u>If anyone then says that it is not</u> from the institution of Christ the Lord Himself, or <u>by divine right that the blessed Peter has perpetual successors in the primacy over the universal Church, or that the Roman Pontiff is not the successor of blessed Peter in the same primacy</u>, let him be anathema."[46]

This is the favorite canon of those who argue against the sedevacantist "thesis"; but, as we will see, it also proves nothing for their position. Words and distinctions are very important. Understanding distinctions and words can often be the very difference between Protestantism and Catholicism.

The canon from Vatican I condemns those who deny "*that Peter has <u>perpetual successors in the primacy</u> over the universal Church.*" Notice the phrase "perpetual successors **IN THE PRIMACY**." This, as we have seen, does not mean and cannot mean that we will always have a pope. That is why it doesn't say that "we will always have a pope." It's a fact that there have been periods without a pope. So what does the canon mean?

In understanding this canon, we must remember that there are schismatics who hold that St. Peter himself was given the primacy over the universal Church by Jesus Christ, <u>but that the primacy over the universal Church stopped with St. Peter</u>. **They hold that the Bishops of Rome aren't successors to the same primacy that St. Peter had**. They hold that the full-blown force of the primacy doesn't descend to the popes, even though they succeed St. Peter as Bishop of Rome. **Again: the "Orthodox" schismatics <u>would admit that the Bishops of Rome are successors of St. Peter in a certain way</u> because they succeed him as Bishops of Rome, <u>but not successors with the same jurisdictional primacy</u>** over the universal Church which St. Peter held in his life. This is the heresy that is the subject of the canon above.

This heresy – which denies that a pope is the successor of St. Peter <u>in the same primacy perpetually</u> (that is, *every time there is a pope until the end of time, he is a successor in the same primacy, with the same authority St. Peter possessed*) – is precisely what this canon condemns.

> Pope Pius IX, *First Vatican Council*, Sess. 4, Chap. 2, [Canon]. "<u>If anyone then says that it is not</u> from the institution of Christ the Lord Himself, or <u>by divine right that the blessed Peter has perpetual successors in the primacy over the universal Church</u>, or that the Roman Pontiff is not the successor of blessed Peter <u>in the same primacy</u>, let him be anathema."[47]

When we understand this we clearly see the meaning of this canon. This is emphasized at the end by the words "or that the Roman Pontiff is not the successor of blessed Peter **in the same primacy**" let him be anathema. The canon is <u>not</u> declaring that we will have a pope at all times or that there won't be gaps, as <u>we clearly have had</u>. The meaning of the canon is clear from what it says. It condemns those who deny that Peter has perpetual successors in the primacy – that is, those who deny that every time there is a true and lawful pope until the end of time he is a successor in the same primacy, with the same authority that St. Peter possessed.

This canon proves nothing for the non-sedevacantist, but it does prove something for us. Remember, Benedict XVI also rejects this dogma on the primacy of the popes!

BENEDICT XVI COMPLETELY REJECTS THIS CANON AND VATICAN I

> Benedict XVI, *Principles of Catholic Theology* (1982), p. 198: "**Nor is it possible, on the other hand, for him to regard as the only possible form and, consequently, as binding on all Christians the form this primacy has taken in the nineteenth and twentieth centuries** *[ed.- This means the schismatics don't have to accept Vatican I]*. **The symbolic gestures of Pope Paul VI and, in particular, his kneeling before the representative of the Ecumenical Patriarch [the schismatic Patriarch Athenagoras] were an attempt to express precisely this** and, by such signs, to point the way out of the historical impasse… **In other words, Rome must not require more from the East with respect to the doctrine of the primacy than had been formulated and was lived in the first millennium**. When the Patriarch Athenagoras [the non-Catholic, schismatic Patriarch], on July 25, 1967, on the occasion of the Pope's visit to Phanar, **designated him as the successor of St. Peter, as the most esteemed among us, as one who presides in charity, this great Church leader was expressing the ecclesial content of the doctrine of the primacy as it was known in the first millennium. Rome need not ask for more.**"48

This means, once again, that **according to Benedict XVI all Christians are not bound to believe in the Papacy as defined by Vatican I in 1870. This means that the "Orthodox" schismatics are free to reject the Papacy.** This is a blatant denial of Vatican Council I and the necessity of accepting the primacy by the man who claims to be "the pope." Who will cry out against this abominable madness?

> Pope Pius IX, *Vatican Council I*, 1870, Sess. 4, Chap. 3, ex cathedra: "… **all the faithful of Christ must believe that the Apostolic See and the Roman Pontiff hold primacy over the whole world**, and the Pontiff of Rome himself is the successor of the blessed Peter, the chief of the apostles, and is the true vicar of Christ and head of the whole Church… Furthermore We teach and declare that the Roman Church, by the disposition of the Lord, holds the sovereignty of ordinary power over all others… **This is the doctrine of Catholic truth from which no one can deviate** and keep his *faith* and salvation."49

Moreover, notice that Benedict XVI admits that Paul VI's symbolic gestures with the schismatic Patriarch "were an attempt to express precisely this" – that is to say, his gestures (such as kneeling before the representative of the non-Catholic, schismatic Patriarch Athenagoras) expressed that the schismatics don't have to believe in the Papacy and Vatican I! Consider this a smashing vindication of all that we have said with regard to John Paul II's incessant gestures toward the schismatics: giving them relics; giving them donations; praising their "Churches"; sitting on equal chairs with them; signing common declarations with them; lifting the excommunications against them.

We pointed out again and again that these actions alone (not even considering his other statements) constituted a teaching that the schismatics don't have to accept the dogma of the Papacy. Countless false traditionalists and members of the Vatican II Church denied this and tried to explain these gestures away as either merely scandalous or something else, but not heretical. Well, here we have Ratzinger – now Benedict XVI, the new "head" of the Vatican II Church – admitting precisely what we said.

In the section on Benedict XVI's heresies, we covered in even more detail his other denials of Vatican I. We will not repeat all of that here; please consult that section for more.

So, please tell me, dear reader: who denies Vatican I? Who denies the dogmas on the perpetuity, authority, and prerogatives of the Papal Office? Who denies what Christ instituted in St. Peter? Is it the sedevacantists, who correctly point out that a man who denies Vatican I is outside the Church, outside of the unity – since he rejects, among other things, the perpetual principle of unity (the Papacy) – and therefore cannot occupy an office or head a Church which he doesn't even believe in?

> St. Robert Bellarmine (1610), Doctor of the Church: "**A pope who is a manifest heretic automatically (*per se*) ceases to be pope and head,** just as he ceases automatically to be a Christian and a member of the Church. Wherefore, he can be judged and punished by the Church. This is the teaching of all the ancient Fathers who teach that manifest heretics immediately lose all jurisdiction."

> St. Francis De Sales, Doctor of the Church:
> "It would indeed be <u>one of the strangest monsters that could be seen</u> – <u>if the head of the Church *were not of the Church*</u>."[50]

Or are the real deniers of the Papacy and Vatican I those who profess union with a man who clearly doesn't even believe in Vatican I; a man who doesn't even believe that the Papacy and Vatican I are binding on all Christians; a man who doesn't even believe that the Papacy was held in the first millennium?

The answer is obvious to any sincere and honest person who considers these facts. It is Antipope Benedict XVI, and all who obstinately insist on union with him, who deny the Papacy; it is the sedevacantists who are faithful to the Papacy.

Objection 7): No one can judge the Holy See… thus the Vatican II popes are true popes.

Answer: <u>First</u>, people need to understand what the teaching "No one can judge the Holy See" means. It comes from the early Church. In the early Church, when a bishop was accused of a crime, there would sometimes be a trial presided over by other bishops or by a patriarch of greater authority. These bishops would sit in judgment on the accused bishop. The Bishop of Rome, however, since he is the supreme bishop in the Church, cannot be subjected to any trial by other bishops or by other people.

> Pope St. Nicholas, epistle (8), *Proposueramus quidem*, 865:
> "… Neither by Augustus, nor by all the clergy, nor by religious, nor by the people will the judge be judged… '**The first seat will not be judged by anyone.**'"[51]

Answers to Objections   316

This is what "No one can judge the Holy See" means. It does not refer to recognizing a manifest heretic who claims to be the pope as one who is not a true pope. And this brings us to the second point, which is the most important in this regard.

Second, the Holy See has told us that no heretic can be accepted as the valid occupant of the Holy See (the Pope)! With the fullness of his authority, Pope Paul IV defined that anyone who has been promoted to the Papacy as a heretic is not a true and valid pope, and that he can be rejected as a warlock, heathen, publican and heresiarch.

> Pope Paul IV, Bull *Cum ex Apostolatus Officio*, Feb. 15, 1559: "6. In addition, [by this Our Constitution, which is to remain valid in perpetuity, We enact, determine, decree and define:] that if ever at any time it shall appear that any Bishop, even if he be acting as an Archbishop, Patriarch or Primate; or any Cardinal of the aforesaid Roman Church, or, as has already been mentioned, any legate, **or even the Roman Pontiff, prior to his promotion or his elevation as Cardinal or Roman Pontiff, has deviated from the Catholic Faith or fallen into some heresy:**
>
> (i) the promotion or elevation, even if it shall have been uncontested and by the unanimous assent of all the Cardinals, shall be null, void and worthless;
> (ii) it shall not be possible for it to acquire validity (nor for it to be said that it has thus acquired validity) through the acceptance of the office, of consecration, of subsequent authority, nor through possession of administration, nor through the putative enthronement of a Roman Pontiff, or Veneration, or obedience accorded to such by all, nor through the lapse of any period of time in the foregoing situation;
> (iii) it shall not be held as partially legitimate in any way...
> (vi) those thus promoted or elevated shall be deprived automatically, and without need for any further declaration, of all dignity, position, honour, title, authority, office and power...
>
> 7. Finally, [by this Our Constitution, which is to remain valid in perpetuity, We] also [enact, determine, define and decree]: that any and all persons who would have been subject to those thus promoted or elevated if they had not previously deviated from the Faith, become heretics, incurred schism or provoked or committed any or all of these, be they members of anysoever of the following categories:
> (i) the clergy, secular and religious; (ii) the laity; (iii) the Cardinals [etc.]... shall be permitted at any time to withdraw with impunity from obedience and devotion to those thus promoted or elevated and to avoid them as warlocks, heathens, publicans, and heresiarchs (the same subject persons, nevertheless, remaining bound by the duty of fidelity and obedience to any future Bishops, Archbishops, Patriarchs, Primates, Cardinals and Roman Pontiff canonically entering).
>
> 10. No one at all, therefore, may infringe this document of our approbation, re-introduction, sanction, statute and derogation of wills and decrees, or by rash presumption contradict it. If anyone, however, should presume to attempt this, let him know that he is destined to incur the wrath of Almighty God and of the blessed Apostles, Peter and Paul.
>
> Given in Rome at Saint Peter's in the year of the Incarnation of the Lord 1559, 15th February, in the fourth year of our Pontificate.
>
> + I, Paul, Bishop of the Catholic Church..."

Thus, one is obeying and adhering to the teaching of the Holy See in rejecting as invalid the heretical post-Vatican II claimants. They are not true popes, according to the teaching of the Holy See.

Third, it was near the beginning of this Bull, prior to the declaration that the faithful can reject as totally invalid the "election" of a heretic, that Pope Paul IV repeated the teaching that no one can judge the pope.

> Pope Paul IV, Bull *Cum ex Apostolatus Officio*, Feb. 15, 1559: "1. In assessing Our duty and the situation now prevailing, We have been weighed upon by the thought that a matter of this kind [i.e. error in respect of the Faith] is so grave and so dangerous that **the Roman Pontiff, who is the representative upon earth of God and our God and Lord Jesus Christ, who holds the fullness of power over peoples and kingdoms, <u>who may judge all and be judged by none in this world</u>**, may nonetheless be contradicted if he be found to have deviated from the Faith."

> Could there be a more stunning confirmation that the sedevacantist position doesn't contradict the teaching that "No one can judge the pope or the Holy See" than the fact that Pope Paul IV's Bull repeats this teaching about no one judging the pope **immediately prior to declaring that the faithful must recognize as invalid the election of a heretic**!

Pope Paul IV, unlike non-sedevacantists who use the "no one can judge the Holy See" argument, correctly distinguishes between a true Catholic pope whom none can judge, and a manifest heretic (e.g. Benedict XVI) who has shown himself to be a non-Catholic <u>who is not the pope,</u> since he is outside of the true Faith. This is striking proof that sedevacantists who hold as invalid the "election" of the manifest heretic Joseph Ratzinger <u>are not judging a pope</u>.

Fourth, many of the people who attempt to defend the Vatican II "popes" by saying "no one can judge the Holy See" are themselves guilty of judging the most authoritative actions of the men they think occupy the Holy See. Most of the traditionalists reject Vatican II, the "canonizations" of the Vatican II "popes," etc. This is a schismatic position, which rejects the authoritative actions of that which they deem to be the Holy See. It proves that these "popes" are not popes at all and do not, in fact, occupy the Holy See.

> Objection 8): St. Robert Bellarmine said that one cannot depose a pope, but that one can licitly resist him. Sedevacantists judge, punish and depose the pope…

> St. Robert Bellarmine, *De Romano Pontifice*, Book II, Chap. 29: "Just as it is licit to resist the Pontiff who attacks the body, so also is it licit to resist him who attacks souls or destroys the civil order or above all, tries to destroy the Church. I say that it is licit to resist him by not doing what he orders and by impeding the execution of his will. **It is not licit, however, to judge him, to punish him, or to depose him.**"

Answer: Many of those who believe Benedict XVI is the pope, yet reject the official actions of his "Church," such as Vatican II, attempt to see a justification for their false position in this passage from St. Robert Bellarmine. In fact, this passage is one of the most commonly used pieces of evidence that people attempt to throw against the sedevacantist position. Unfortunately, **the passage has been completely misapplied and distorted**.

First, in the chapter immediately following the above quote from Bellarmine, he teaches this:

> "**A pope who is a manifest heretic automatically (*per se*) ceases to be pope and head**, just as he ceases automatically to be a Christian and a member of the Church. **Wherefore, he can be judged and punished** by the Church. *This is the teaching of all the ancient Fathers* who teach that manifest heretics immediately lose all jurisdiction."[52]

Now, hold on a second. In chapter 29 (the quote cited in objection 2), St. Robert says that you cannot "judge, punish or depose" the pope. In chapter 30, he says that a manifest heretic ceases to be pope (i.e., he is deposed) and he can be "judged and punished" by the Church.

My question to the objector is this: *Is St. Robert Bellarmine an idiot?*

St. Robert Bellarmine, *De Romano Pontifice*, chapter 29	One cannot "judge, punish or depose" a pope
St. Robert Bellarmine, *De Romano Pontifice*, chapter 30	A pope who is a manifest heretic is deposed, "judged and punished"

St. Robert Bellarmine is neither an idiot nor contradicting himself. He is a doctor of the Church, and knows exactly what he is trying to say. It is blatantly obvious, therefore, that **he is not speaking about a manifestly heretical pope in chapter 29**, but rather a true pope who gives bad example, who is not a manifest heretic. The context of the chapter confirms this beyond any doubt.

Chapter 29 involves St. Robert's lengthy refutation of nine arguments favoring the position that the pope is subject to secular power (emperor, king, etc.) and to an ecumenical council (the heresy of conciliarism). During the Middle Ages, the heresy of conciliarism (subjecting a pope to an ecumenical council) became a major problem. In contradiction to this heresy, St. Robert Bellarmine says that while a Catholic can resist a bad pope, he cannot depose him, even if the pope gives bad example, disturbs the state or kills souls by his action. He is speaking of a bad pope who is not a manifest heretic; for he deals with the proper reaction to manifest heresy in the next chapter! It's quite simple. He says that a manifest heretic is considered not to be the pope in the next chapter!

With this in mind, the objection raised from Bellarmine against sedevacantism is refuted. He is not talking about a manifest heretic in chapter 29, but a true pope who acts inappropriately; for he explains that a manifestly heretical pope *is* deposed, judged and punished in chapter 30. It is a mortal sin of omission for "Catholic" writers to quote over and over again the passage of chapter 29, without ever giving St. Robert's statement on manifestly heretical popes in chapter 30. Among such people we include those who write for some of the more popular "traditional" publications. These writers suppress St. Robert's teaching in chapter 30, along with all the other saints, popes and canonists who teach that manifestly heretical popes lose their office, because they want to deceive their readers into thinking that St. Robert condemns sedevacantism, when in reality he and *all the early Church Fathers* support the fact that a manifest heretic is not a pope.

> St. Robert Bellarmine, *De Romano Pontifice*, II, 30:
> "For, in the first place, **it is proven with arguments from authority and from reason that the manifest heretic is 'ipso facto' deposed**. The argument from authority is based on St. Paul (Titus 3:10), who orders that the heretic be avoided after two warnings, that is, after showing himself to be manifestly obstinate – **which means before any**

Answers to Objections

> **excommunication or judicial sentence**. And this is what St. Jerome writes, adding that the other sinners are excluded from the Church by sentence of excommunication, but the heretics exile themselves and separate themselves by their own act from the body of Christ."

And again St. Robert Bellarmine teaches:

> **"This principle is most certain. The non-Christian cannot in any way be Pope**, as Cajetan himself admits (ib. c. 26). The reason for this is that he cannot be head of what he is not a member; now he who is not a Christian is not a member of the Church, **and a manifest heretic is not a Christian**, as is clearly taught by St. Cyprian (lib. 4, epist. 2), St. Athanasius (Scr. 2 cont. Arian.), St. Augustine (lib. De great. Christ. Cap. 20), St. Jerome (contra Lucifer.) and others; **therefore the manifest heretic cannot be Pope**."[53]

Objection 9): Pope Liberius gave in to the Arian heretics and excommunicated St. Athanasius, yet he remained the pope…

Answer: It is **not true** that Pope Liberius gave in to the Arians, signed any Arian formula, **or even excommunicated St. Athanasius**. Pope Liberius was a staunch defender of the truth during the Arian crisis, but his return from exile gave some the idea that he had compromised, when, in fact, he had not. We quote Pope Pius IX.

> Pope Pius IX, *Quartus Supra* (# 16), January 6, 1873, On False Accusations:
> "And previously **the Arians falsely accused Liberius**, also Our predecessor, to the Emperor Constantine, because ***Liberius refused to condemn St. Athanasius, Bishop of Alexandria, and refused to support their heresy.***"[54]

> Pope Benedict XV, *Principi Apostolorum Petro* (# 3), Oct. 5, 1920:
> "Indeed, lest they should prove faithless from their duty, **some went fearlessly into exile, as did Liberius** and Silverius and Martinus."[55]

According to Pope Pius IX and Pope Benedict XV, Pope Liberius didn't falter in any way during the Arian crisis, and was **falsely accused** by the Church's enemies for standing firm. Pope St. Anastasius I bears witness to this as well.

> Pope St. Anastasius I, epistle *Dat mihi plurimum*, about 400 AD:
> "For at this time when Constantius of holy memory held the world as victor, the heretical African faction was not able by any deception to introduce its baseness because, as we believe, our God provided that the holy and untarnished faith be not contaminated through any vicious blasphemy of slanderous men… ***For this faith those who were then esteemed as holy bishops gladly endured exile, that is*** *Dionysius, thus a servant of God, prepared by divine instruction, or those following his example of holy recollection,* **LIBERIUS bishop of the Roman Church**, Eusebius also of Vercelli, Hilary of the Gauls, to say nothing of many, on whose decision the choice could rest to be fastened to the cross rather than blaspheme God Christ, which the Arian heresy compelled, or call the Son of God, God Christ, a creature of the Lord."[56]

It was not Pope Liberius, but the pseudo-bishop Ischyras, who, before he usurped the See of Alexandria, ejected St. Athanasius from his See.

> Pope Pius VI, *Charitas* (# 14), April 13, 1791:
> "Perhaps in appreciation of these actions, the bishop of Lidda, Jean Joseph Gobel, was elected Archbishop of Paris, while the archbishop was still living. **He is following the example of Ischyras, who was proclaimed bishop of Alexandria at the Council of Tyre as payment for his sinful service in accusing St. Athanasius and ejecting him from his See.**"[57]

Objection 10): Pope Pius XII declared in *Vacantis Apostolicae Sedis* that a cardinal, no matter what excommunication he's under, can be elected pope.

> Pope Pius XII, *Vacantis Apostolicae Sedis*, Dec. 8, 1945: "34. None of the cardinals may in any way, or by pretext of any excommunication, suspension, or interdict whatsoever, *or of any other ecclesiastical impediment*, be excluded in the active and passive election of the Supreme Pontiff. We hereby suspend such censures solely for the purposes of the said election; at other times they are to remain in vigor (AAS 38 [1946], p. 76)."

ANSWER: As we've already shown, it's a dogma that 1) heretics are not members of the Church; and 2) that a pope is the head of the Church. It is a dogmatic fact, therefore, that a heretic cannot be the head of the Church, since he is not a member of it.

What, then, does Pope Pius XII mean in *Vacantis Apostolicae Sedis*? First off, one needs to understand that excommunication can be incurred for many things. **Historically, excommunications were distinguished by the terms *major* and *minor*.** Major excommunications were incurred for heresy and schism (sins against the faith) and certain other major sins. Those who received major excommunication for heresy were not members of the Church (as we have just proven at length). Minor excommunication, however, *did not remove one from the Church*, but forbade one to participate in the Church's sacramental life. Pope Benedict XIV made note of the distinction.

> Pope Benedict XIV, *Ex Quo Primum* (# 23), March 1, 1756:
> "*Moreover heretics and schismatics are subject to the censure of <u>major</u> excommunication by the law of Can. de Ligu. 23, quest. 5, and Can. Nulli, 5, dist. 19.*"[58]

Minor excommunication, on the other hand, was incurred for things such as violating a secret of the Holy Office, falsifying relics (c. 2326), violating a cloister (c. 2342), etc. These are all ecclesiastical or Church penalties. Such actions, though gravely sinful, *did not separate a person from the Church*. And though the terms major and minor excommunication are no longer used, it remains a fact that **a person could incur an excommunication (for something other than heresy) which would <u>not</u> separate him from the Church**, and he could incur an excommunication for heresy which would separate him from the Church.

Therefore, a cardinal who receives an excommunication <u>for heresy</u> is no longer a cardinal because heretics are outside the Catholic Church (*de fide*, Pope Eugene IV). But a cardinal who receives an excommunication for something else is still a cardinal, though in a state of grave sin.

Answers to Objections

So when Pope Pius XII says that all cardinals, whatever *ecclesiastical impediment* they are under, can vote and be elected in a Papal conclave, **this presupposes cardinals who have received an excommunication for something other than heresy, since a cardinal who has received an excommunication for heresy is not a cardinal at all**. The key point to understand is that heresy is not merely an *ecclesiastical impediment* – thus it is not what Pius XII is talking about – but an impediment by divine law.

> The canonist Maroto explains: "**Heretics and schismatics are barred from the Supreme Pontificate by the divine law itself**, because, although by divine law they are not considered incapable of participating in certain types of ecclesiastical jurisdiction, nevertheless, they must certainly be regarded as excluded from occupying the throne of the Apostolic See..."[59]

Notice, heretics are not excluded from the Papacy by merely ecclesiastical impediments, but impediments flowing from the divine law. Pius XII's legislation doesn't apply to heresy because he was speaking about ecclesiastical impediments: "...or any other *ecclesiastical* impediment...". Thus, his legislation does not show that heretics can be elected and remain popes, which is why he didn't mention heretics. Pope Pius XII was referring to Catholic cardinals who may have been under excommunication.

To further prove the point, let's assume *for the sake of argument* that Pope Pius XII's legislation did mean that a heretical cardinal could be elected pope. Notice what Pius XII says:

> "We hereby suspend such censures solely for the purposes of the said election; **at other times they are to remain in vigor**."

Pius XII says that the excommunication is suspended *only for the time of the election*; at other times it remains in vigor. This would mean that the excommunication for heresy would fall back into force immediately after the election and then the heretic who had been elected pope would lose his office! Thus, no matter what way you look at it, a heretic could not be validly elected and remain pope.

> St. Antoninus (1459): "**In the case in which the pope would become a heretic, he would find himself, by that fact alone and without any other sentence, separated from the Church.** A head separated from a body cannot, as long as it remains separated, be head of the same body from which it was cut off. A pope who would be separated from the Church by heresy, therefore, would by that very fact itself cease to be head of the Church. **He could not be a heretic and remain pope, because, since he is outside of the Church, he cannot possess the keys of the Church.**" (*Summa Theologica*, cited in *Actes de Vatican I*. V. Frond pub.)

If a heretic (one who denies the faith) could be the head inside the Church, then the dogma that the Church is **one in faith** (as in *one, holy, Catholic and apostolic*) would be false.

> **Objection 11): What does it matter whether or not Benedict XVI is a pope? The issue does not concern me.**

Answer: If whether or not Benedict XVI is a pope does not matter, then the non-Catholicism of the Vatican II sect does not matter, the New Mass doesn't matter, etc. One cannot separate one from the other. You cannot separate pope and Church. Furthermore, to maintain that Benedict XVI is the head of the Catholic Church is to assert that the gates of Hell have prevailed against Her.

Further, to obstinately recognize Benedict XVI as the pope is to commit a sin against the Faith; for it is to assert that one has the true Faith who, in fact, is a manifest heretic and apostate against it. Moreover, to recognize Benedict XVI and the other Vatican II antipopes as true popes is to scandalize non-Catholics; it is to be unable to consistently present the Faith to a non-Catholic. On this point, we must now see *The Devastating Dilemma* to demonstrate just how much this issue matters.

The Devastating Dilemma: Why Catholics cannot even present the Faith to a Protestant if they accept the Vatican II antipopes as true popes

Suppose that tomorrow you encounter a well-informed Protestant who is interested in becoming a Catholic. While this man claims to be interested in becoming "Catholic," he has major problems with the teaching of the Catholic Church on justification: he rejects the canons and decrees of the 16th century Council of Trent. As he explains his position you think to yourself: "How does this man expect to become Catholic when he doesn't believe in the teaching of the Council of Trent on justification?"

So you, being a charitable Catholic, inform him that if he wants to become Catholic he <u>***must***</u> accept and believe the Council of Trent's teaching on justification and repudiate Luther's view of justification by faith alone (*sola fide*), since the Catholic Church (not to mention scripture – James 2:24) condemns the idea of justification by faith alone.

> Pope Paul III, *Council of Trent*, Session 6, Chap. 10, *ex cathedra*:
> "'You see, that by works a man is justified **AND NOT BY FAITH ALONE' (James 2:24)."**[60]

But the Protestant responds by saying:

> "Excuse me sir, I do not have to accept and believe the Council of Trent's teaching on justification to become Catholic. Nor do I have to believe that justification by faith alone is a heresy, as you say. Your pope, Benedict XVI, and his predecessor, John Paul II, who are both Catholics agree with and have approved of a document that says that faith alone is not a heresy, and that Trent's canons on justification do not apply to the Lutheran explanation of justification." And he proceeds to make three points in succession to prove this.

Answers to Objections 323

#1) The Protestant first cites the *Joint Declaration with the Lutherans on the Doctrine of Justification*, approved by the Vatican on Oct. 31, 1999. He quotes two selections from the *Joint Declaration with the Lutherans on the Doctrine of Justification*, which he happens to have in his briefcase.

> **Joint Declaration With Lutherans:** "# 5. THE PRESENT JOINT DECLARATION has this intention: namely, to show that on the basis of their dialogue the subscribing Lutheran churches and the Roman Catholic Church are now able to articulate a common understanding of our justification by God's grace through faith in Christ. It does not cover all that either church teaches about justification; it does encompass a consensus on basic truths of the doctrine of justification and **SHOWS THAT THE REMAINING DIFFERENCES ARE NO LONGER THE OCCASION FOR DOCTRINAL CONDEMNATIONS.**"[61]

After citing this, the Protestant correctly explains that this rules out any condemnation of the Lutheran view of justification (*faith alone*, etc.). He then cites # 13.

> **Joint Declaration With Lutherans:** "# 13. IN LIGHT OF THIS CONSENSUS, THE CORRESPONDING DOCTRINAL CONDEMNATIONS OF THE 16TH CENTURY DO NOT APPLY TO TODAY'S PARTNER."[62]

After citing this, the Protestant rightly explains that this also means that Trent's condemnations (in the 16th century) of the Lutheran view of justification no longer apply.

#2) To further substantiate his point, the Protestant proceeds to cite two more selections from the same Joint Declaration With the Lutherans.

> **Joint Declaration With Lutherans:** "# 41. Thus the doctrinal condemnations of the 16th century, in so far as they are related to the doctrine of justification, appear in a new light: THE TEACHING OF THE LUTHERAN CHURCHES PRESENTED IN THIS DECLARATION DOES NOT FALL UNDER THE CONDEMNATIONS FROM THE COUNCIL OF TRENT."[63]

The Protestant points out the obvious fact that this means that none of the Lutheran teaching contained in the Joint Declaration is condemned by the Council of Trent. He then proves that justification by *faith alone* is among the teaching of the Lutheran churches in the Joint Declaration.

> **Joint Declaration With Lutherans:** "# 26. ACCORDING TO THE LUTHERAN UNDERSTANDING, GOD JUSTIFIES SINNERS IN FAITH ALONE** (*sola fide*). In faith they place their trust wholly in their Creator and Redeemer and thus live in communion with him."[64]

He concludes, with perfect logic, that according to the Vatican's own agreement with the Lutherans on justification, faith alone is most assuredly not condemned by the Council of Trent. Thus, he says to you:

> "**You see, sir, the Catholics who adhere to and believe in the *Joint Declaration with the Lutherans on the Doctrine of Justification* do not hold that faith alone is a heresy that is anathematized** infallibly by decree of the Council of Trent, as you claim a Catholic must believe in order to be Catholic."

Answers to Objections

#3) Finally, this smart Protestant knows that you will try to say that John Paul II and Benedict XVI didn't sign the *Joint Declaration with the Lutherans on the Doctrine of Justification*. So he points out that the Joint Declaration was signed under John Paul II's auspices and repeatedly approved by Benedict XVI.

> John Paul II, Jan. 19, 2004, *At a Meeting with Lutherans From Finland*: "… I wish to express my gratitude for the ecumenical progress made between Catholics and Lutherans in the five years **since the signing of the *Joint Declaration on the Doctrine of Justification*.**"[65]

> Benedict XVI, *Address to Methodists*, Dec. 9, 2005: "**I have been encouraged by the initiative which would bring the member churches of the World Methodist Council into association with the Joint Declaration on the Doctrine of Justification, signed by the Catholic Church and the Lutheran World Federation in 1999.**"[66]

The Protestant concludes his presentation by saying:

> "Benedict XVI (and, before him, John Paul II) is a Catholic and adheres to the Joint Declaration with the Lutherans on the doctrine of justification, **which declaration explicitly teaches that faith alone is not anathematized by Trent, and that the remaining differences between Lutherans and Catholics on justification are not the occasion for any doctrinal condemnations. Therefore, when I become a Catholic, I will hold the same position as Benedict XVI and as the Joint Declaration with the Lutherans sets forth. I will hold that faith alone justifies, and I will not hold that it is an anathematized heresy!** And I will not embrace the canons and decrees of the Council of Trent, because John Paul II and Benedict XVI have accepted, endorsed and agreed with the Joint Declaration, which explains that Trent's canons are no longer in force."

You know that as a Catholic, you have a strict obligation to tell him that belief in faith alone and belief in the Catholic religion are incompatible. So what do you say in response?

If you hold that Benedict XVI and John Paul II are/were valid popes, you spit back the following response, which is the only thing that you can think of:

> "*John Paul II and Benedict XVI are wrong. They aren't infallible in everything they say or do. The Joint Declaration is not infallible. The Council of Trent is infallible.*"

And the smart Protestant, quickly detecting the flaws in this illogical and poor response, replies:

> "*Sir, I never said that the Joint Declaration is infallible. Infallibility has nothing to do with our discussion.* **The bottom-line is that you admit that Benedict XVI is a Catholic with whom you are in communion**, *and with whom every Catholic must be in communion.* **You admit that he is not a heretic who is outside the communion of the Catholic Church for embracing the Joint Declaration with the Lutherans on the Doctrine of Justification, so you must admit that I will also be a Catholic in communion with the Church (not a heretic) when I take the same position.**"

If you hold that Benedict XVI is a valid pope, you would then have nothing to say in response to this Protestant. The debate is over, and you have lost. You cannot on the one hand say that acceptance of *faith alone and the Joint Declaration With the Lutherans on the Doctrine of Justification* is incompatible with this Protestant's entrance into the Catholic Church (which you must as a Catholic, since this was defined infallibly at Trent), while you simultaneously give obedience to Benedict XVI as head of the Catholic Church, who has demonstrated his acceptance of the *Joint*

Declaration with the Lutherans on the Doctrine of Justification quite publicly. The Protestant has cornered you and you are forced to admit that he can indeed become Catholic and hold to what is taught in the Joint Declaration. This proves that those who accept Benedict XVI as the pope cannot even consistently present the Catholic Faith to a Protestant. **THEY MUST ADMIT THAT ONE CAN BE A "CATHOLIC" AND HOLD THAT FAITH ALONE IS NOT AN ANATHEMATIZED HERESY, AND THAT TRENT'S CANONS DO NOT APPLY TO THE LUTHERAN VIEW OF JUSTIFICATION.**

As long as one acknowledges Benedict XVI as the Catholic pope, he is defending a Church that has repudiated the Council of Trent, a "Church" that is, by definition, a non-Catholic Church – a Church of heretics.

> Pope Innocent III, *Eius exemplo*, profession of faith, Dec. 18, 1208: "By the heart we believe and by the mouth we confess **THE ONE CHURCH, NOT OF HERETICS**, but the Holy Roman, Catholic, and Apostolic Church outside of which we believe that no one is saved."[67]

The same judgment and authority by which you determined that this non-denominational Protestant was a heretic and outside the Catholic Church – a judgment you made upon meeting him and finding out what he believed and how he repudiated the Council of Trent – is the same exact judgment that you absolutely are forced to make about Benedict XVI. It should hit you in a striking and illuminating way that you are not guilty of judging the Holy See or a pope when you correctly judge that Benedict XVI is a non-Catholic; rather, you are identifying a non-Catholic for what he is, just as you correctly identified the non-denominational Protestant you met as a non-Catholic, as well as any Calvinist, Methodist or Episcopalian.

Objection 12): How could the entire Church and all the cardinals recognize an antipope, such as in the case of John XXIII (1958-1963)?

Answer: Pope Paul IV declared that Catholics could not accept such a heretical claimant, **even if obedience were given to him by "all" – indicating by such a statement that all giving obedience to such an antipope is a possibility.**

> Pope Paul IV, Bull *Cum ex Apostolatus Officio*, Feb. 15, 1559: "6. **In addition, [by this Our Constitution, which is to remain valid in perpetuity We enact, determine, decree and define:]** that if ever at any time it shall appear that… the Roman Pontiff, prior to his promotion or his elevation as Cardinal or Roman Pontiff, has deviated from the Catholic Faith or fallen into some heresy… (ii) **it shall not be possible for it to acquire validity (nor for it to be said that it has thus acquired validity) through the acceptance of the office, of consecration, of subsequent authority, nor through possession of administration, nor through the putative enthronement of a Roman Pontiff, or Veneration, or obedience accorded to such by all**, nor through the lapse of any period of time in the foregoing situation;…"

But we've already had a situation where all of the cardinals recognized an antipope! As covered earlier in the book, during the Great Western Schism **15 of the 16 cardinals who had elected Pope Urban VI withdrew from his obedience on the grounds that the unruly Roman mob had made the election uncanonical**. The one cardinal who did not repudiate Pope Urban VI was Cardinal Tebaldeschi, but he died shortly thereafter, on Sept. 7 – **leaving a situation where not**

<u>one of the cardinals of the Catholic Church recognized the true pope, Urban VI. All of the living cardinals then regarded his election as invalid.</u>[68]

In the 12th century, Antipope Anacletus II – who reigned eight years in Rome while rivaling the true Pope, Innocent II – gained the majority of the cardinals, the Bishop of Porto, the Dean of the Sacred College, and the entire populace of Rome as his supporters.[69]

> **Objection 13): John XXII was a heretic, who was even denounced by Cardinal Orsini as a heretic, yet he remained the pope.**

> Chris Ferrara, "Opposing the Sedevacantist Enterprise," Catholic Family News, August 2005, p. 21: "**Compare the [Sedevacantist] Enterprise's lack of success in finding 'manifest' heresy in the pronouncements of the conciliar popes with the historical example of Pope John XXII. In 1331, certain French theologians and Cardinal Orsini denounced John XXII as a heretic when, in a series of sermons, he taught that the souls of the blessed departed, after finishing their appointed time in Purgatory, do not see God until after the last judgment. Cardinal Orsini called for a general council to pronounce the Pope a heretic…** Confronted in this public manner, John XXII replied that he had not intended to bind the whole Church to his sermons, and he impaneled a commission of theologians to consider the question. The commission informed the Pope that he was in error, and he did retract the error several years later, the day before his death. <u>**Yet despite being denounced as a heretic and threatened with a general council to declare his heresy**</u>, John XXII never ceased to be regarded by the Church as Pope, and Church history duly records him as such."[70]

Answer: John XXII was not a heretic, and his reign is no proof that heretics can be popes.

First, we want the reader to notice something very interesting: when Ferrara (the person launching this objection) is discussing John XXII, notice that the affair is exaggerated. He doesn't hesitate to label it as an example of actual heresy. But when he is addressing the clear heresies of the Vatican II "popes," they are all diminished so much that he denies that any of them even constitute heresy. For instance:

> Chris Ferrara, "Opposing the Sedevacantist Enterprise," Catholic Family News, August 2005, p. 21: "But **the [Sedevacantist] Enterprise does not even get to first base since**, as we shall see, despite its indefatigable efforts <u>**it has failed to identify any 'manifest' heresy among the many ambiguous pronouncements and disturbing (even scandalous) actions of John Paul II or Paul VI**</u>…"[71]

Okay, so none of the clear heresies from John Paul II and Paul VI (e.g., teaching that there are saints in other religions; stating that we shouldn't convert non-Catholics; etc.) even constitute heresy, according to Ferrara; but the case of John XXII *certainly* rose to the level of heresy. What complete nonsense! Does anyone not see the profound hypocrisy and utter dishonesty here? When Ferrara and other non-sedevacantists feel that it is an advantage to belittle the heresy, they raise the bar for heresy, so that basically nothing rises to the level of actual heresy. But when they deem it useful to exaggerate a heresy (as in the case of John XXII), because they think it will successfully oppose sedevacantism, they overstate it and make it seem much worse than it was.

The fact of the matter is that John XXII was not a heretic. John XXII's position that the souls of the blessed departed don't see the Beatific Vision until after the General Judgment was not a matter that had yet been specifically defined as a dogma. This definition occurred two years after Pope John XXII's death by Pope Benedict XII in *Benedictus Deus*,[72] but apparently Ferrara didn't feel that it was important to mention that fact.

The fact that Cardinal Orsini denounced John XXII as a heretic doesn't prove anything, especially when we consider the context of the events. To provide a brief background: **John XXII had condemned as heretical the teaching of "the Spirituals."** This group held that Christ and the apostles had no possessions individually or in common. John XXII condemned this view as contrary to Sacred Scripture, and declared that all who persistently adhere to it are heretical.[73] "The Spirituals" and others like them, including King Louis of Bavaria, were condemned as heretics.

When the controversy about John XXII's statements on the Beatific Vision occurred, the Spirituals and King Louis of Bavaria profited by it and accused the pope of heresy. **These enemies of the Church were supported by Cardinal Orsini, the man Ferrara mentions in his article.**

> *The Catholic Encyclopedia*, "John XXII," Vol. 8, 1910, p. 433: "**The Spirituals, always in close alliance with Louis of Bavaria, profited by these events to accuse the pope of heresy, being supported by Cardinal Napoleon Orsini. In union with the latter, King Louis wrote to the cardinals, urging them to call a general council and condemn the pope.**"[74]

With this background, we can see that Ferrara's statement that "Cardinal Orsini called for a general council to pronounce the pope a heretic…" takes on a different light: Yes, Cardinal Orsini and his good friends, the excommunicated heretics. In fact, even Ferrara's own "pope," in his book *Dogmatic Theology*, notes that the scandal was exploited by the enemies of the Church for political ends:

> "Cardinal" Joseph Ratzinger (Benedict XVI), *Dogmatic Theology*, 1977, p. 137: "**The scandal [of John XXII] was exploited for political ends in the accusation of heresy brought by the pope's Franciscan opponents** [the Spirituals] in the circle of William of Ockham at the court of the emperor Louis of Bavaria."[75]

Ferrara places himself right in the company of the enemies of the Church with his exaggeration of the case of John XXII. John XXII was not a heretic. **In addition to the fact that the matter had not yet been specifically defined as a dogma, John XXII also made it clear that he bound no one to his (false) opinion and was not arriving at a definitive conclusion on the matter:**

> *The Catholic Encyclopedia*, on Pope John XXII:
> "**Pope John wrote to King Phillip IV on the matter (November, 1333), and emphasized the fact that, as long as the Holy See had not given a decision, the theologians enjoyed perfect freedom in this matter**. In December, 1333, the theologians at Paris, after a consultation on the question, decided in favor of the doctrine that the souls of the blessed departed saw God immediately after death or after their complete purification; **at the same time they pointed out that the pope had given no decision on this question but only advanced his personal opinion,** and now petitioned the pope to confirm their decision. John appointed a commission at Avignon to study the writings of the Fathers, and to discuss further the disputed question. **In a consistory held on 3 January, 1334, the pope explicitly declared that he had never meant to teach anything contrary to**

> **Holy Scripture or the rule of faith and in fact had not intended to give any decision whatever**. Before his death he withdrew his former opinion, and declared his belief that souls separated from their bodies enjoyed in heaven the Beatific Vision."[76]

All of this serves to show that John XXII was not a heretic. He held a personal opinion that was dead wrong, one which he explicitly declared was nothing more than opinion. In fact, despite his significant error, John XXII was quite vigorous against heresy. His condemnation of the Spirituals and King Louis of Bavaria is proof that he did condemn heresy. To compare him to the Vatican II antipopes who don't even believe that heresy exists is utterly ridiculous. As established already, Benedict XVI doesn't even believe that Protestantism is heresy! What a satanic joke that anyone would *obstinately* (in the face of these facts) assert that this man is a Catholic! The fact is wherever non-sedevacantists want to turn (to the dogma of the Papacy, or the actions of Luther, etc.), they are refuted. For instance, since we're on the topic of John XXII and the General Judgment, it should remembered that Benedict XVI denies perhaps the most central Catholic dogma regarding the General Judgment: the Resurrection of the Body, as we demonstrated in the previous section on his heresies.

> Benedict XVI, *Introduction to Christianity*, 2004, p. 349: "**It now becomes clear that the real heart of faith in the resurrection does not consist at all in the idea of the restoration of bodies**, to which we have reduced it in our thinking; such is the case even though this is the pictorial image used throughout the Bible."[77]

> Benedict XVI, *Introduction to Christianity*, 2004, pp. 357-358: "To recapitulate, **Paul teaches, not the resurrection of physical bodies**, but the resurrection of persons…"[78]

So, when non-sedevacantists bring up the issue of John XXII and the Last Judgment, they do nothing except remind us of another dogma which Benedict XVI denies and another proof why he is not the pope.

Objection 14): Pope Honorius was condemned for heresy by a general council after his death, yet the Church does not consider him to have ceased to be pope, even though he was accused of heresy during his reign.

Answer: As we have already seen, it's a dogmatic fact that a heretic cannot be the pope, since it's an infallibly defined dogma that a heretic is not a member of the Catholic Church.

> Pope Eugene IV, *Council of Florence, ex cathedra*: "The Holy Roman Church firmly believes, professes and preaches that **all those who are outside the Catholic Church**, not only pagans **but also** Jews or **heretics** and schismatics …"[79]

The case of Pope Honorius doesn't prove that a heretic can be the pope. In condemning Pope Honorius as a heretic after his death, **the *III Council of Constantinople* made no statement – nor has the Church ever made a statement – that he remained pope until his death.**

> *Third Council of Constantinople*, Exposition of Faith, 680-681:
> "… the contriver of evil did not rest, finding an accomplice in the serpent and through him bringing upon human nature the poised dart of death, so now too he has found instruments suited to his own purpose – namely, Theodore… Sergius, Pyrrhus, Paul and

Peter... and further Honorius, who was pope of elder Rome, Cyrus... and Macarius... - and has not been idle in raising through them obstacles of error against the full body of the Church, sowing with novel speech among the orthodox people the heresy of a single will and a single principle of action..."[80]

The Church didn't address the issue of whether Honorius lost the Papal Office after falling into heresy; it simply condemned him. (Honorius was also condemned by the *Fourth Council of Constantinople* and the *Second Council of Nicea*.) Since Honorius was a validly elected pope (which is why he is listed in the list of true popes), if he became a true heretic during his reign then he did lose the Papal Office; for, as even non-sedevacantists who make this argument admit, **"heretics are not Catholics, and non-Catholics cannot be popes."**

Pope Honorius had been dead for more than 40 years when he was condemned by the *III Council of Constantinople*. Honorius had issued no dogmatic decrees, and only "reigned" for three and ½ years after the incident of heresy occurred. Hence, the question of whether he remained the pope and ruled the universal Church for the last three and ½ years of his thirteen-year pontificate wasn't especially relevant to the faithful at the time.

Therefore, it is perfectly understandable that the Church didn't issue any proclamation that Honorius lost his office because nothing was riding on the issue at the time, and it would have involved a major theological discussion and an entire can of worms that didn't need to be opened.

Further, there still remains some confusion among people (including among Honorius's successors) as to whether Pope Honorius had been a heretic or merely guilty of failing to stamp out heresy or whether he had been completely misunderstood, as *The Catholic Encyclopedia* of 1907 states. Certain scholars who have even studied the question in great detail remain unconvinced that Honorius was condemned as a true heretic by the *III Council of Constantinople*. Their argument rests in the fact that **Pope St. Agatho, who was alive during the council, died before it was over.** Since a council's decrees only possess the authority which are given to them in the confirmation by the pope, they argue that Pope St. Leo II, the pope who actually confirmed the council, *only confirmed the condemnation of Honorius in the sense that he failed to stamp out heresy*, and therefore allowed the faith to be polluted. This confusion is surely why we see that St. Francis De Sales says what he says (see below) about Honorius.

In order to further differentiate the case of Honorius from the Vatican II antipopes, it's important to point out that **the lapse of Pope Honorius was almost completely unknown during his reign and for years after his reign.** Honorius's two letters which favored the monothelite heresy (written in 634) were letters to Sergius, the Patriarch of Constantinople. These letters were not only almost completely unknown at the time, but were also misunderstood by a pope who reigned just after Honorius.

For instance, **Pope John IV (640-643), who was the second pope to reign after Pope Honorius, defended Honorius from any charge of heresy**. Pope John IV was convinced that Honorius had not taught the monothelite heresy (that Christ has only one will), but that Honorius merely emphasized that Our Lord doesn't have two contrary wills.

> Pope John IV, "Dominus qui dixit" to Constantius the Emperor, Regarding Pope Honorius, 641: "...So, **my aforementioned predecessor [Honorius] said** concerning the mystery of the incarnation of Christ, that there were not in Him, as in us sinners, contrary wills of mind and flesh; **and certain ones converting this to their own meaning,**

<u>suspected that he taught one will of His divinity and humanity which is altogether contrary to the truth."</u>[81]

With these facts in mind, one can see: 1) the case of Pope Honorius doesn't prove that heretics can be popes, since the Church has never declared that he remained the pope after his lapse; and 2) **the facts of the case of Pope Honorius are drastically different from the case of the Vatican II antipopes, since Honorius's two letters containing heresy were almost completely unknown at the time, and were even misunderstood by popes who succeeded him.** To compare Pope Honorius's two letters to the acts and statements of the manifest heretics Paul VI, John Paul II and Benedict XVI is like comparing a grain of sand to the seashore.

Finally, if you want further confirmation that heretics *ipso facto* cease to be popes, **and that the case of Pope Honorius provides no evidence to the contrary**, you don't have to take our word for it.

> St. Francis De Sales (17th century), Doctor of the Church, *The Catholic Controversy*, pp. 305-306: "**Thus we do not say that the Pope cannot err in his private opinions, as did John XXII; or be altogether a heretic, <u>as perhaps Honorius was</u>. <u>Now when he [the Pope] is explicitly a heretic, he falls *ipso facto* from his dignity and out of the Church</u>**..."[82]

<u>In the same paragraph in which St. Francis De Sales (Doctor of the Church) mentions Pope Honorius</u>, **he states unequivocally that a pope who would become a heretic would cease to be pope**. St. Francis De Sales wasn't sure if Pope Honorius was a heretic or merely failed to stamp out heresy; but, whatever it was, St. Francis knew the case of Honorius didn't affect the truth that heretics cannot be popes.

St. Robert Bellarmine and St. Alphonsus were also familiar with the case of Pope Honorius. His case didn't cause them to hesitate in declaring:

> St. Robert Bellarmine (1610), Doctor of the Church: "**A pope who is a manifest heretic automatically (*per se*) ceases to be Pope and head, just as he ceases automatically to be a Christian and a member of the Church**. Wherefore, he can be judged and punished by the Church. <u>This is the teaching of all the ancient Fathers</u> who teach that manifest heretics immediately lose all jurisdiction."

> St. Alphonsus Liguori (1787), Doctor of the Church: "**If ever a pope, as a private person, should fall into heresy, he would at once fall from the Pontificate.**"[83]

With these facts in mind, we can see that the argument from Honorius doesn't prove anything for the non-sedevacantist; but rather it reminds us of the Doctors of the Church who, while recalling his case, simultaneously declared that heretics cannot be popes.

> **Objection 15):** The Church and the hierarchy will always be visible. If the Vatican II Church is not the true Catholic Church, then the Church and hierarchy are no longer visible.

Answer: 1) People misunderstand in what the visibility of the Church consists; 2) the Vatican II sect cannot be the visible Church of Christ; and 3) the Vatican II sect denies this very teaching on the visibility of the Church.

No one denies that the Catholic Church could cease to exist in all the countries of the world except one. The visibility of the Church does not require that the faithful or the hierarchy be seen in every single geographical location around the globe. This has never been the case. Simply, the visibility of the Church signifies real Catholic faithful who externally profess the one true religion, even if they are reduced to a very small number. These faithful who externally profess the one true religion will always remain the visible Church of Christ, even if their ranks are reduced to just a handful.

And that is <u>precisely what is predicted to happen</u> at the end of the world.

> St. Athanasius: "Even if Catholics faithful to tradition are reduced to a handful, they are the ones who are the true Church of Jesus Christ."[84]

Our Lord Himself indicates that the size of the Church will become frighteningly small in the last days.

> Luke 18:18: **"But yet, when the Son of man cometh, shall He find, think you, faith on earth?"**

The Apocalypse of St. John seems to indicate the same.

> Apocalypse 11:1-2:
> "And there was given me a reed like unto a rod, and it was said to me: Arise, and measure the temple of God, and *the altar*, and them that adore in it. But the court, which is without the temple, cast out, and measure it not, because it is given to the Gentiles..."

The *Haydock version of the Douay-Rheims Bible*, a popular compilation of Catholic commentary on the Scriptures by Rev. Fr. Geo. Leo Haydock, contains the following comment on Apoc. 11:1-2.

> Catholic Commentary on Apoc. 11:1-2, *Haydock version of the Douay-Rheims Bible*:
> **"The churches consecrated to the true God, are so much diminished in number, that they are represented by St. John as one church; its ministers officiate at *one altar*; and all the true faithful are so few, with respect to the bulk of mankind, that the evangelist sees them assembled in one temple, to pay their adorations to the Most High. - Pastorini."**[85]

The Magisterium of the Catholic Church has never taught that there must always be a certain number of bishops or faithful for the Church to exist. As long as there is at least one priest or bishop and at least a few faithful, the Church and the hierarchy are alive and visible. Today there is much more than a handful of faithful left who maintain the unchanging Catholic Faith. Thus,

Answers to Objections

the argument of our opponents from the standpoint of visibility lacks any merit and is contrary to the prophecies of Sacred Scripture.

Further, during the Arian crisis the true Faith was eliminated from entire regions, so much so that there were hardly any Catholic bishops to be found anywhere.

> Fr. William Jurgens: "At one point in the Church's history, only a few years before Gregory's [Nazianz] present preaching (+380 A.D.), <u>perhaps the number of Catholic bishops in possession of sees, as opposed to Arian bishops in possession of sees, was no greater than something between 1% and 3% of the total</u>. **Had doctrine been determined by popularity, today we should all be deniers of Christ and opponents of the Spirit.**"[86]

> Fr. William Jurgens: "In the time of the Emperor Valens (4th century), Basil was virtually the only orthodox Bishop in all the East who succeeded in retaining charge of his see… If it has no other importance for modern man, **a knowledge of the history of Arianism should demonstrate at least that the Catholic Church takes no account of popularity and numbers in shaping and maintaining doctrine**: else, we should long since have had to abandon Basil and Hilary and Athanasius and Liberius and Ossius and call ourselves after Arius."[87]

The Arian heresy became so widespread in the 4th century that the Arians (who denied the Divinity of Christ) came to occupy almost all the Catholic churches and appeared to be the legitimate hierarchy basically everywhere.

> St. Ambrose (+382): **"There are not enough hours in the day for me to recite even the names of all the various sects of heretics."**[88]

Things were so bad that St. Gregory Nazianz felt compelled to say what the Catholic remnant today could very well say.

> St. Gregory Nazianz, "Against the Arians" (+380): "Where are they who revile us for our poverty and pride themselves in their riches? **They who define the Church by numbers and scorn the little flock?**"[89]

This period of Church history, therefore, proves an important point for our time: If the Church's indefectible mission of teaching, *governing* and sanctifying <u>required</u> a governing (i.e., jurisdictional) bishop for the Church of Christ to be present and operative in a particular see or diocese, then one would have to say that the Church of Christ <u>defected</u> in all those territories where there was no governing Catholic bishop during the Arian heresy. However, it is a fact that in the 4th century, <u>where the faithful retained the true Catholic faith, even in those sees where the bishop defected to Arianism</u>, the faithful Catholic remnant constituted the true Church of Christ. In that remnant, the Catholic Church existed and endured in her mission to teach, govern and sanctify without a governing bishop, thus proving that **the Church of Christ's indefectibility and mission to teach, govern and sanctify does not require the presence of a jurisdictional bishop.**

It should also be noted that the hierarchy can be defined in two ways: the jurisdictional hierarchy and the ecclesiastical hierarchy.[90]

> Pope Pius XII, *Ad Sinarum gentum* (# 13), Oct. 7, 1954: "Besides – as has also been divinely established – **the power of orders (through which the ecclesiastical hierarchy is**

> **composed of bishops, priests, and ministers) comes from receiving the Sacrament of Holy Orders."**[91]

Only those who have ordinary jurisdiction (i.e., jurisdiction which is attached to an office) constitute the jurisdictional hierarchy. All valid Catholic priests, on the other hand, constitute parts of the ecclesiastical hierarchy. It is possible that as long as the ecclesiastical hierarchy remains the hierarchy exists.

Non-sedevacantists who raise this objection cannot point to one real Catholic bishop with ordinary jurisdiction. To whom are they going to point? Are they going to point to "Bishop" Bruskewitz, who conducted an interfaith Seder Supper with a group of rabbis in his own cathedral during Holy Week?[92] Are they going to point to "Cardinal" Mahony or "Cardinal" Keeler?

If it's true that there must be one bishop with ordinary jurisdiction somewhere (which is something that has not been proven), then he is somewhere. But it doesn't change the fact that Benedict XVI and his apostate bishops are not Catholic and therefore not part of the hierarchy. Against a fact there is no argument; against this fact there is no argument.

Finally, and perhaps most importantly, the Vatican II sect rejects the visibility of the Catholic Church, thus proving again that it's not the visible Catholic Church!

> Vatican II document, *Unitatis Redintegratio* (# 1):
> "Yet almost all, though in different ways, <u>long for</u> the one visible Church of God, <u>that truly universal Church</u> whose mission is to convert the whole world to the gospel, so that the world may be saved, to the glory of God."[93]

Remember this one? At the very beginning of its Decree on Ecumenism, Vatican II teaches that almost everyone longs for a truly universal and visible Church whose mission is to convert the world to the Gospel. Again, for those who doubt that Vatican II was here denying that the Catholic Church exists, we will quote Antipope John Paul II's own interpretation of this passage.

> John Paul II, *Homily*, Dec. 5, 1996, <u>speaking of prayer with non-Catholics</u>: **"When we pray together, we do so with the longing 'that there may be one visible Church of God, <u>a Church truly universal</u> and sent forth to the whole world that the world may be converted to the Gospel and so be saved, to the glory of God'** (*Unitatis Redintegratio*, 1)."

> John Paul II, *Ut Unum Sint* (# 7), May 25, 1995: **"And yet almost everyone, though in different ways,** *longs that there may be one visible Church of God*, **a Church truly universal** and sent forth to the whole world that the world may be converted to the Gospel and so be saved, to the glory of God (Vatican II document *Unitatis Redintegratio*, 1.)."[94]

So, if you accept the Church's teaching on its visibility, that's just one more reason to reject the Vatican II sect and its antipopes.

By the way, the idea of an invisible Church – taught by the Vatican II sect – has been condemned at least three times: Pope Leo XIII, *Satis Cognitum* (# 3), June 29, 1896;[95] Pope Pius XI, *Mortalium Animos* (# 10), Jan. 6, 1928;[96] Pope Pius XII, *Mystici Corporis Christi* (# 64), June 29, 1943.[97]

> Pope Leo XIII, *Satis Cognitum* (# 3), June 29, 1896:

> "'Now you are the Body of Christ' (1 Cor. 12:27) – and precisely because it is a body is the Church **visible... From this it follows that those who arbitrarily conjure up and picture to themselves a hidden and invisible Church are in grievous and pernicious error."**[98]

Moreover, here is an interesting quote from the Lay Investiture crisis (1075-1122). During this crisis the evil King of Germany, Henry IV, instituted an antipope (who was supported by many German bishops). Henry also appointed his own bishops who were also subject to the antipope. The result was **two bishops in most dioceses and massive confusion**.

> The Catholic Encyclopedia, Vol. 8, 1910, "Investitures," p. 86: "There was now much confusion on all sides... **Many dioceses had two occupants**. Both parties called their rivals perjurers and traitors..."[99]

The point is: while we are currently dealing with an unprecedented apostasy, the Church has seen confusing times before, including those in which the true hierarchy was not easily ascertainable.

Objection 16): The Vatican II popes haven't taught manifest heresy, because their statements are ambiguous and require commentary.

> Chris Ferrara, *Catholic Family News*, "Opposing the Sedevacantist Enterprise, Part II," Oct. 2005, p. 8: "**Now that which is manifest – i.e., plain, evident, obvious, unmistakable and undoubted – <u>requires no explanation</u>**. The very quality of not needing to be explained is what makes a thing manifest. Thus, before the Enterprise can even get to first base, it must show us not merely papal statements made openly, but statements whose alleged heresy requires no explanation to demonstrate. **The papal words themselves – not sedevacantist *interpretations* of those words – must denote heresy.**
>
> "**If a Pope were to proclaim to the whole Church in some document or public pronouncement 'There is no Holy Trinity. There is only God the Creator, just as the Muslims believe!' his heresy would be manifest in the full and correct sense of the word.**"[100]

Answer: The one making this objection, Chris Ferrara, is completely wrong, as usual. First, there are many examples of manifest heresies from the post-conciliar antipopes which require no explanation or commentary, as we have seen. Second, papal authority teaches us that some heresies do require explanation, deep study and analysis to uncover and condemn, as we will also see.

Before we expand on those two points, it is necessary for the reader to examine the example of heresy that Ferrara gives. Ferrara gives the example of heresy: "There is no Holy Trinity." According to Ferrara, this is an undeniable example of manifest heresy. He is correct that this statement is heretical, but notice that **even in this example we are not dealing with an exact *word-for-word* denial of a dogmatic definition**. As far as we're aware, there is no dogmatic definition on the Holy Trinity which states "There is a Holy Trinity." There are definitions, such as the following:

> Pope Gregory X, *Council of Lyons II*, 1274, ex cathedra: "**We believe that the Holy Trinity, the Father, and the Son, and the Holy Spirit, is one God omnipotent...**"[101]

Of course, Catholics immediately recognize that the statement "There is no Holy Trinity" *equates* to a direct denial of this dogmatic definition, even though it doesn't deny the dogmatic definition *verbatim*. So, **in giving his single example of heresy** – a single example Ferrara probably concocted because he feels confident that that the sedevacantists can produce no equivalent heresy on the Trinity from Benedict XVI – **Ferrara proves our point: statements that equate to a direct denial of dogma, even though they are not <u>exact word-for-word</u> denials of a dogmatic definition, are examples of manifest heresy.**

So, just as Catholics immediately recognize that the statement "There is no Holy Trinity" is a manifest heresy, even though there is no dogma declaring *exactly the opposite word-for-word*, they likewise immediately recognize that Benedict XVI's declaration that **Protestantism is not heresy** is, of course, a direct denial of the Catholic dogmas which condemn Protestant teachings as heresies. Thank you for proving our point again, Mr. Ferrara.

We will now quote more than 10 statements from Benedict XVI (and just one from John Paul II) and give no commentary whatsoever. Everyone who is sincere and honest will see that they equate to direct rejections of Catholic dogma without any analysis being required.

> "Cardinal" Joseph Ratzinger, *The Meaning of Christian Brotherhood*, pp. 87-88: "The difficulty in the way of giving an answer is a profound one. Ultimately it is due to the fact that <u>there is no appropriate category in Catholic thought for the phenomenon of Protestantism today (one could say the same of the relationship to the separated churches of the East). It is obvious that the old category of 'heresy' is no longer of any value</u>... Protestantism has made an important contribution to the realization of Christian faith, fulfilling a positive function in the development of the Christian message... <u>The conclusion is inescapable, then: Protestantism today is something different from heresy in the traditional sense, a phenomenon whose true theological place has not yet been determined</u>."[102]

No comment necessary.

> Joseph Ratzinger, *Theological Highlights of Vatican II*, pp. 61, 68: "... **Meantime <u>the Catholic Church has no right to absorb other Churches</u>**. The Church has not yet prepared for them a place of their own, but this they are legitimately entitled to... <u>**A basic unity – of Churches that remain Churches, yet become one Church – must replace the idea of conversion**</u>, even though conversion retains its meaningfulness for those in conscience motivated to seek it."[103]

No comment necessary.

> "Cardinal" Ratzinger, *Principles of Catholic Theology*, pp. 197-198: "Against this background we can now weigh the possibilities that are open to Christian ecumenism. The maximum demands on which the search for unity must certainly founder are immediately clear. **On the part of the West, <u>the maximum demand would be that the East recognize the primacy of the bishop of Rome in the full scope of the definition of 1870</u>** and in so doing submit in practice, to a primacy such as has been accepted by the Uniate churches. On the part of the East, the maximum demand would be that the West declare the 1870 doctrine of primacy erroneous and in so doing submit, in practice, to a primacy such as has been accepted with the removal of the Filioque from the Creed and including the Marian dogmas of the nineteenth and twentieth centuries. **As regards Protestantism, <u>the maximum demand of the Catholic Church would be that the Protestant ecclesiological ministers be regarded as totally invalid and that Protestants</u>**

be converted to Catholicism… **none of the maximum solutions offers any real hope of unity**."[104]

No comment necessary.

"Cardinal" Joseph Ratzinger, *God and the World*, 2000, p. 209: "**It is of course possible to read the Old Testament so that it is not directed toward Christ; it does not point quite unequivocally to Christ**. And if Jews cannot see the promises as being fulfilled in him, this is not just ill will on their part, but genuinely because of the obscurity of the texts and the tension in the relationship between these texts and the figure of Jesus. Jesus brings a new meaning to these texts – yet it is he who first gives them their proper coherence and relevance and significance. **There are perfectly good reasons, then, for denying that the Old Testament refers to Christ and for saying, No, that is not what he said**. And there are also good reasons for referring it to him – that is what the dispute between Jews and Christians is about."[105]

No comment necessary.

"Cardinal" Ratzinger, *Principles of Catholic Theology* (1982), p. 377: "…**There is an obsession with the letter that regards the liturgy of the Church as invalid and thus puts itself outside the Church. It is forgotten here that the validity of the liturgy depends primarily, not on specific words, but on the community** of the Church…"[106]

No comment necessary.

"Cardinal" Ratzinger, *Principles of Catholic Theology* (1982), p. 202: "**It means that the Catholic does not insist on the dissolution of the Protestant confessions** and the demolishing of their churches **but hopes, rather, that they will be strengthened in their confessions and in their ecclesial reality**."[107]

No comment necessary.

John Paul II, *Ut Unum Sint* (# 84), May 25, 1995:
"…[Speaking of non-Catholic "Churches"] **These *saints* come from all the Churches and Ecclesial Communities WHICH GAVE THEM ENTRANCE INTO THE COMMUNION OF SALVATION**."[108]

No comment necessary.

"Cardinal" Joseph Ratzinger, *Principles of Catholic Theology*, 1982, p. 381: "If it is desirable to offer a diagnosis of the text [of the Vatican II document, Gaudium et Spes] as a whole, **we might say that (in conjunction with the texts on religious liberty and world religions) it is a revision of the Syllabus of Pius IX, a kind of counter syllabus**… As a result, the one-sidedness of the position adopted by the Church under Pius IX and Pius X in response to the situation created by the new phase of history inaugurated by the French Revolution **was, to a large extent, corrected** *via facti*, especially in Central Europe, but there was still no basic statement of the relationship that should exist between the Church and the world that had come into existence after 1789."[109]

No comment necessary.

Answers to Objections 337

> "Cardinal" Joseph Ratzinger, *Co-Workers of the Truth,* 1990, p. 217: "**The question that really concerns us, the question that really oppresses us, is why it is necessary for us in particular to practice the Christian Faith in its totality; why, when there are so many other ways that lead to heaven and salvation**, it should be required of us to bear day after day the whole burden of ecclesial dogmas and of the ecclesial ethos. And so we come again to the question: What exactly is Christian reality? What is the specific element in Christianity that not merely justifies it, but makes it compulsorily necessary for us? **When we raise the question about the foundation and meaning of our Christian existence, there slips in a certain false hankering for the apparently more comfortable life of other people who are also going to heaven**. We are too much like the laborers of the first hour in the parable of the workers in the vineyard (Mt. 20:1-16). Once they discovered that they could have earned their day's pay of one denarius in a much easier way, they could not understand why they had had to labor the whole day. **But what a strange attitude it is to find the duties of our Christian life unrewarding just because the denarius of salvation can be gained without them!** It would seem that we – like the workers of the first hour – want to be paid not only with our own salvation, but more particularly with others' lack of salvation. That is at once very human and profoundly un-Christian."[110]

No comment necessary.

> "Cardinal" Joseph Ratzinger, *Co-Workers of the Truth,* 1990, p. 29: "To borrow Congar's cogent phrase, **it would be both foolish and perverse to identify the efficacy of the Holy Spirit with the work of the ecclesial apparatus. This means that even in Catholic belief the unity of the Church is still in the process of formation; that it will be totally achieved only in the eschaton** [the end of the world], just as grace will not be perfected until its effects are visible – although the community of God has already begun to be visible."[111]

No comment necessary.

> "Cardinal" Joseph Ratzinger, *Introduction to Christianity,* 2004, p. 349: "**It now becomes clear that the real heart of faith in the resurrection does not consist at all in the idea of the restoration of bodies**, to which we have reduced it in our thinking; such is the case even though this is the pictorial image used throughout the Bible."[112]

No comment necessary.

> *The Jewish People and the Holy Scriptures in the Christian Bible*, Section II, A, Prefaced by Benedict XVI: "**Jewish messianic expectation is not in vain**... to read the Bible as Judaism does necessarily involves an implicit acceptance of all its presuppositions... **which exclude faith in Jesus as Messiah and Son of God... Christians can and ought to admit that the Jewish reading of the Bible is a possible one...**"[113]

There are <u>many</u> others, but these constitute more than ten examples of manifest heresies which equate to a direct denial of Catholic dogma without any commentary being necessary.

CHRIS FERRARA VS. POPE PIUS VI ON AMBIGUITY IN HERESY = A KNOCKOUT FOR POPE PIUS VI

In addition to the fact that there are manifest heresies which require no commentary from the Vatican II antipopes, as we saw above, **WHAT UTTERLY DESTROYS FERRARA'S POINT is the fact that Pope Pius VI teaches exactly the opposite of Ferrara on heresy and ambiguity. Pope Pius VI declares that heretics, such as Nestorius, have always camouflaged their heresies and doctrinal errors in self-contradiction and ambiguity!**

Pope Pius VI, condemning the Synod of Pistoia, Bull "Auctorem fidei," August 28, 1794: **"[The Ancient Doctors] knew the capacity of innovators in the art of deception.** In order not to shock the ears of Catholics, they sought to hide the subtleties of their tortuous maneuvers by the use of seemingly innocuous words such as would allow them to insinuate error into souls in the most gentle manner. Once the truth had been compromised, they could, by means of slight changes or additions in phraseology, distort the confession of the faith which is necessary for our salvation, and lead the faithful by subtle errors to their eternal damnation. This manner of dissimulating and lying is vicious, regardless of the circumstances under which it is used. For very good reasons it can never be tolerated in a synod of which the principal glory consists above all in teaching the truth with clarity and excluding all danger of error.

"Moreover, if all this is sinful, <u>it cannot be excused</u> in the way that one sees it being done, <u>under the erroneous pretext that the seemingly shocking affirmations in one place are further developed along orthodox lines in other places, and even in yet other places corrected; as if allowing for the possibility of either affirming or denying the statement</u>, or of leaving it up to the personal inclinations of the individual – <u>such has always been the fraudulent and daring method used by innovators to establish error. It allows for both the possibility of promoting error and of excusing it.</u>

"It is as if the innovators pretended that they always intended to present the alternative passages, especially to those of simple faith who eventually come to know only some part of the conclusions of such discussions which are published in the common language for everyone's use. Or again, as if the same faithful had the ability on examining such documents to judge such matters for themselves without getting confused and avoiding all risk of error. **It is a most reprehensible technique for the insinuation of doctrinal errors and one condemned long ago by our predecessor Saint Celestine who found it used in the writings of Nestorius, Bishop of Constantinople, and which he exposed in order to condemn it with the greatest possible severity.** Once these texts were examined carefully, the impostor was exposed and confounded, for he expressed himself in a plethora of words, <u>mixing true things with others that were obscure; mixing at times one with the other in such a way that he was also able to confess those things which were denied while at the same time possessing a basis for denying those very sentences which he confessed</u>.

"In order to expose such snares, something which becomes necessary with a certain frequency in every century, no other method is required than the following: <u>WHENEVER IT BECOMES NECESSARY TO EXPOSE STATEMENTS WHICH DISGUISE SOME SUSPECTED ERROR OR DANGER UNDER THE VEIL OF AMBIGUITY, ONE MUST DENOUNCE THE PERVERSE MEANING UNDER WHICH THE ERROR OPPOSED TO CATHOLIC TRUTH IS CAMOUFLAGED."</u>

Pope Pius VI teaches us that if someone veils a heresy in ambiguity, as heretics have done throughout the ages, a Catholic must hold him to the heretical meaning and denounce the heretical meaning which is camouflaged in ambiguity! **This alone blows Chris Ferrara's entire series of articles and objections against sedevacantism out of the water.** (And please note an important distinction: we are not asserting that documents or statements that are merely ambiguous, but which teach no clear doctrinal contradiction of Catholic Faith, are heretical; no, we are asserting with Pope Pius VI that documents which contain heretical statements or assertions which <u>clearly</u> contradict Catholic dogma ("shocking affirmations," according to Pius VI) but which *also* contain self-contradiction and ambiguity along with those heretical statements, are still just as heretical despite the ambiguity and self-contradiction that accompanies the heresy. An example would be an alleged "Catholic" who consistently supports abortion, but sometimes says that he accepts Church teaching on abortion. This person is a manifest heretic, despite the self-contradiction and ambiguity that his position implies. Another example would be a man who states that we shouldn't convert Protestants (a manifest heresy), but who also states that the Catholic Church alone is the fullness of the Christian Faith which all should embrace. He is a manifest heretic, despite the fact that the latter statement seems to some to contradict the former statement. Heretics are dishonest and liars, so they often attempt to contradict or mitigate the offensiveness of their heresies through subtle tactics of self-contradiction and accompanying ambiguity; that is the point of Pope Pius VI.)

Notice how directly Chris Ferrara contradicts the teaching of Pope Pius VI.

| Chris Ferrara, *Catholic Family News*, "Opposing the Sedevacantist Enterprise, Part II," Oct. 2005, p. 25: "**Thus, we are dealing with a document [*Dignitatis Humanae* of Vatican II] that contains apparent self-contradictions**, which seem to have resulted from the Council's attempt to appease both conservative and liberal factions among the Council Fathers. **A document that contradicts itself by appearing to uphold and negate the traditional teaching at one and the same time can hardly be said to constitute a manifest contradiction of the traditional teaching**… For what is at issue are **ambiguities, internal inconsistencies**, and novelties…" | Pope Pius VI: "Moreover, if all this is sinful, <u>it cannot be excused in the way that one sees it being done, under the erroneous pretext that the seemingly shocking affirmations in one place are further developed along orthodox lines in other places, and even in yet other places corrected; as if allowing for the possibility of either affirming or denying the statement, or of leaving it up to the personal inclinations of the individual – such has always been the fraudulent and daring method used by innovators to establish error. It allows for both the possibility of promoting error and of excusing it.</u>

" It is a most reprehensible technique for the insinuation of doctrinal errors and one condemned long ago by <u>our predecessor Saint Celestine who found it used in the writings of Nestorius, Bishop of Constantinople, and which he exposed in order to condemn it with the greatest possible severity</u>…" |

Obviously, Pope Pius VI is correct and Chris Ferrara is completely wrong. Notice that Pius VI also says that some of these doctrinal errors (**which are also <u>heresies</u> in this case, since he is referring to the *heresies* of the *arch-heretic* Nestorius**) were <u>only uncovered through careful study and analysis</u>!

> Pius VI: "It is a most reprehensible technique for the insinuation of doctrinal errors and one condemned long ago by our predecessor Saint Celestine who found it used in the writings of Nestorius, Bishop of Constantinople, and which he exposed in order to condemn it with the greatest possible severity. **<u>Once these texts were examined carefully</u>, the impostor was exposed and confounded**, for he expressed himself in a plethora of words, <u>mixing true things with others that were obscure; mixing at times one with the other in such a way that he was also able to confess those things which were denied while at the same time possessing a basis for denying those very sentences which he confessed.</u>"

But we thought that such analysis and study wouldn't be needed for manifest contradictions of Catholic teaching? That's what Chris Ferrara said.

> Chris Ferrara, *The Remnant*, Sept. 30, 2005, p. 18: "…where are the objectively heretical statements? If they exist, it should be a simple matter to quote the heretical propositions uttered… **The 'heresies' should speak for themselves without any helpful 'commentary' by sedevacantist accusers**."[114]

Chris Ferrara couldn't be more wrong. Heretics deceive through contradictions and ambiguity because heresy itself is a lie and a contradiction.

> Pope Pius XI, *Rite expiatis* (# 6), April 30, 1926: "…**<u>heresies gradually arose and grew in the vineyard of the Lord, propagated either by open heretics or by sly deceivers</u>** who, because they professed a certain austerity of life and gave a false appearance of virtue and piety, easily led weak and simple souls astray."[115]

Notice, <u>heresies</u> arise both through open and undeceiving heretics as well as by <u>sly deceivers, such as Benedict XVI,</u> who mixes in conservative statements and actions among his astounding and undeniable heresies. Illustrating this point again is the fact that the arch-heretic Arius got himself approved by Constantine by giving him an <u>ambiguous</u> profession of faith. St. Athanasius was not fooled, however, and refused to consider him a Catholic.

> "**Arius presented himself** with Euzoios, his ally in doctrine and exile. **He left with the Emperor [Constantine] a wary profession of Faith which could be interpreted either in the Arian or the orthodox sense but which did not contain the word 'consubstantial.'** Constantine was content, revoked his sentence of exile, and ordered that Arius should be readmitted to his rank in the clergy. Arius' ecclesiastical superior, <u>Athanasius, however, refused to accept him</u>."[116]

According to Chris Ferrara, Catholics should have accepted the Christ-denier Arius as a Catholic, as Constantine did, since his profession was ambiguous. **Chris Ferrara is the perfect dupe of Satan; all the Devil needs to have the heretic do after teaching his heresy is spice in a little ambiguity, and pepper in a little contradiction, and he will be telling the world to follow the**

heretic and remain under his aegis. And that is exactly how the Devil has been so successful in keeping people in the apostate, manifestly heretical Vatican II sect. People see a few conservative statements or actions from the heretics, and they convince themselves that they couldn't be malicious heretics, even though they are denying and destroying the Faith all around them, as we've shown. In this way, the Devil wins.

To further illustrate the "patent absurdity" of Chris Ferrara's "theology" John Doe could write a document which denies that Our Lady is immaculate over and over again, and then state at the end that he upholds Church teaching on the Immaculate Conception, and the document wouldn't be manifestly heretical because it contains "self-contradiction." Could anything be more stupid? Ferrara applies this false theology, which is directly contrary to the teaching of Pope Pius VI (as we saw above), to his analysis of Vatican II's Declaration on Religious Liberty.

> Chris Ferrara, *Catholic Family News*, "Opposing the Sedevacantist Enterprise, Part II," Oct. 2005, p. 25: "**The [Sedevacantist] Enterprise's claim of manifest heresy** in DH [*Dignitatis Humanae*, Vatican II's Declaration on Religious Liberty] **becomes even weaker when one considers that Article 1 of DH states that the Council 'leaves untouched traditional Catholic doctrine on the moral duty of men and societies toward the true religion and toward the one Church of Christ.'"[117]

Vatican II's Declaration on Religious Liberty contains clear heresy against the Church's dogma that the State has the right to repress the public expression of false religions. The fact that Vatican II's Declaration on Religious Liberty claims to "leave untouched traditional Catholic doctrine" means absolutely nothing. The "Old Catholics" said exactly the same, as did heretics throughout history.

> Pope Pius IX, *Graves ac diuturnae* (# 2), March 23, 1875: "**They [the 'Old Catholics'] repeatedly state openly that they do not in the least reject the Catholic Church** and its visible head **but rather that they are zealous for the purity of Catholic doctrine**… But in fact they refuse to acknowledge all the divine prerogatives of the vicar of Christ on earth and do not submit to His supreme Magisterium."[118]

According to Ferrara, then, the case that the "Old Catholics" are heretics is invalid, for they repeatedly state that they are zealous for the purity of Catholic doctrine, and they openly declare that they don't reject Catholic teaching. But no, the Catholic Church teaches that they are manifest heretics, and all who adhere to their teachings and sect are considered heretics.

> Pope Pius IX, *Graves ac diuturnae* (#'s 1-4), March 23, 1875: "… the new heretics who call themselves 'Old Catholics'… these schismatics and heretics… their wicked sect… these sons of darkness… their wicked faction… this deplorable sect… This sect overthrows the foundations of the Catholic religion, shamelessly rejects the dogmatic definitions of the Ecumenical Vatican Council, and devotes itself to the ruin of souls in so many ways. **We have decreed and declared in Our letter of 21 November 1873 that those unfortunate men who belong to, adhere to, and support that sect should be considered as schismatics and separated from communion with the Church.**"[119]

> Pope Pius IX, *Quartus Supra* (# 6), Jan. 6, 1873: "It has always been the custom of heretics and schismatics to call themselves Catholics and to proclaim their many excellences in order to lead people and princes into error."[120]

We can see that Chris Ferrara's "theology" is directly at variance with not only the teaching of the popes, but common sense. In fact, the satanic idiocy of Ferrara's (and many others') position – that the Vatican II apostates and antipopes are not manifest heretics because they sometimes contradict themselves and employ ambiguity along with their astounding heresies – is perhaps best exemplified by looking at the case of the apostate John Kerry.

We would doubt that almost anyone reading this article believes that John Kerry is a Catholic. Even the people at Franciscan University admit that: **"You cannot be a Catholic and be pro-abortion,"** as their signs declared in protest when he spoke in Ohio. **But John Kerry states that he accepts Catholic teaching**, even though he consistently votes in favor of abortion.

During the 2004 Presidential Debate with George W. Bush, John Kerry stated: **"I cannot impose my article of faith on someone else."** Did you get that? John Kerry has stated publicly that the Church's teaching against abortion is his article of faith, but that he simply cannot apply that or impose that in the public sphere. His argument is absurd, a lie, a contradiction, of course – as all heresies are. But according to Chris Ferrara, John Kerry must be considered a Catholic, for something that:

> "… contradicts itself by appearing to uphold and negate the traditional teaching at one and the same time can hardly be said to constitute a manifest contradiction of the traditional teaching…"[121]

We can see that this statement is pure nonsense. If it were true, then John Kerry can hardly be said to be a manifest heretic when he publicly affirms that Church teaching against abortion is his article of faith, but contradicts that by adamantly supporting abortion. John Kerry must be considered a Catholic, according to the despicable perversion of Catholic teaching, inspired by Satan, that the heretic Chris Ferrara is peddling in "traditional" publications. This conclusion would also put Ferrara at variance with another of his colleagues and good friends, Michael Matt, who declared unequivocally (on his own authority, since this has not been declared by his "pope") that John Kerry is an apostate.

> Michael Matt, *The Remnant*, April 15, 2004, p. 5: **"Take Senator John F. Kerry, for example, the first Catholic nominated for the presidency by either major party since 1960.** Kerry, whose paternal grandparents were Jewish, by the way, is doing a remarkably good Kennedy impersonation these days: 'We have a separation of Church and state in this country,' Kerry recently told *Time* magazine. 'As John Kennedy said very clearly, I will be a President who happens to be Catholic, not a Catholic president.' On that, at least, we can agree with the gentleman from Massachusetts! **In fact, we would take it one step further by noting that presidential candidate Kerry isn't Catholic at all.**
> **"Oh, yes, the former altar boy says he's Catholic; he allegedly complains when his staff doesn't leave adequate time on his schedule for Sunday Mass; his official web site announces that 'John Kerry was raised in the Catholic faith and continues to be an active member of the Catholic church.' But he's not Catholic, and neither is his wife** – another anti-Catholic who claims to be a practicing one. John Kerry's description of himself and his wife is simply untrue: '[I'm a] believing and practicing Catholic, married to another believing and practicing Catholic.' Sounds nice. Trouble is, **John Kerry is an apostate.**"[122]

It seems that Ferrara and Matt have some talking to do. And really, the case of John Kerry proves the point, for if you cannot say that Benedict XVI, who takes active part in Jewish worship, doesn't believe that Jesus is necessarily the Messiah and Son of God, teaches that we shouldn't convert Protestants, was initiated into Islam, etc. can't be considered a heretic – then you have no justification whatsoever to label John Kerry one. In fact, the dogmas that Benedict XVI denies have been defined far more times than the dogma that Kerry denies.

> ## Objection 17): Both the 1917 and 1983 Codes of Canon Law teach that a declaration is needed for one to lose his office due to heresy.

Chris Ferrara, "A Challenge to the Sedevacantist Enterprise, Part II," *The Remnant*, Sept. 30, 2005, p. 18: "Indeed, **both the 1917 and 1983 codes** of canon law provide that no one may insist that an ecclesiastical office has been lost due to heresy unless this has been established by a declaration of the competent authority."[123]

Answer: This is simply not true. Antipope John Paul II's heretical and invalid 1983 Code states that such a declaration is necessary in Canon 194 § 3. But the 1917 Code doesn't. The 1917 Code's parallel canon to canon 194 is canon 188. **Canon 188 of the 1917 Code does not contain this provision**, but simply declares that a cleric who "Publicly defects from the Catholic faith" (188 § 4) loses his office by that very fact "without any declaration."

Canon 188.4, *1917 Code of Canon Law*:
"There are certain causes which effect the tacit (silent) resignation of an office, **which resignation is accepted in advance by operation of the law, and hence is effective without any declaration**. These causes are… (4) if he has publicly fallen away from the faith."[124]

Notice that the 1917 Code doesn't say anything about a declaration being necessary; it says just the opposite – "without any declaration"! When one compares the two canons, one sees the glaring difference.

Canon 194.1-3, *1983 Code of Canon Law*: "One is removed from an ecclesiastical office by the law itself: … 2- who has publicly defected from the Catholic faith or from the communion of the Church… The removal from office referred to in nn. 2 and 3 can be enforced only if it is established by the declaration of a competent authority."[125]

This is probably why Ferrara provides no citation to the 1917 Code in his footnote; he only provides a reference to the 1983 code. Thus, we are dealing with another blatant falsehood from Ferrara.

> ## Objection 18): The Council of Constance condemned the idea that a heretic would cease to be the pope.

Errors of John Hus, Condemned by the Council of Constance: "#20. **If the Pope is wicked** and especially if he is foreknown (as a reprobate), then as Judas, the Apostle, he is of the devil, a thief, and a son of perdition, **and he is not the head of the holy militant Church, since he is not a member of it.**"[126] – Condemned

Answer: No, the Council of Constance didn't condemn the idea that a heretic would cease to be the pope at all. This is a serious misunderstanding of this proposition. As we see clearly above, the Council condemned something significantly different. It condemned the proposition that **a wicked man** would cease to be the head of the Church, since he is not a member of it. The proposition from the heretic Hus rightly asserts that one who is not a member of the Church cannot be the head of the Church, but it falls into trouble by stating that the pope ceases to be a member if he is "wicked."

> Pope Pius XII, *Mystici Corporis Christi* (# 23), June 29, 1943:
> "For <u>not every sin, however grave it may be</u>, is such as of its own nature **to sever a man from the Body of the Church, as does schism or heresy or apostasy.**"[127]

A merely wicked pope doesn't cease to be pope, but <u>a heretic or schismatic does</u>. This is because heresy and schism and apostasy separate one from the Church, while other sins (no matter how grave or wicked they are) do not. Thus, we can see clearly that the proposition is condemning the idea that wickedness separates one from the Church. It is not condemning the truth that a heretic ceases to be the pope. In fact, many of the other propositions from John Hus which were condemned by the Council of Constance repeat the false idea expressed above in different ways: that the wicked are not part of the Church.[128]

> St. Robert Bellarmine, *De Romano Pontifice*, Book II, Chap. 30:
> "This principle is most certain. **The non-Christian cannot in any way be pope, as Cajetan himself admits (ib. c. 26). The reason for this is that he cannot be head of what he is not a member;** now he who is not a Christian is not a member of the Church, **and a manifest heretic is not a Christian, as is clearly taught by St. Cyprian (lib. 4, epist. 2), St. Athanasius (Scr. 2 cont. Arian.), St. Augustine (lib. De great. Christ. Cap. 20), St. Jerome (contra Lucifer.) and others;** <u>therefore the manifest heretic cannot be pope.</u>"

> Objection 19): The Joint Declaration with the Lutherans is not manifest heresy because John Paul II and Benedict XVI didn't sign it.

Answer: The Joint Declaration with the Lutherans by itself proves that the Vatican II "popes" are non-Catholic antipopes. The fact that John Paul II and Benedict XVI neither wrote the document nor signed it is completely irrelevant. **<u>They both approved of it publicly numerous times</u>**, and agreed with it.

> John Paul II, Jan. 19, 2004, *At a Meeting with Lutherans From Finland*: "… I wish to express my gratitude for the ecumenical progress made between Catholics and Lutherans in the five years <u>**since the signing of the *Joint Declaration on the Doctrine of Justification***</u>."[129]

> Benedict XVI, *Address to Protestants at World Youth Day*, August 19, 2005: "… **the important Joint Declaration on the Doctrine of Justification (1999)** …"[130]

James Smith could draw up a document denying the Immaculate Conception, and if you were to go around giving speeches about how great Smith's document is, that would make you a manifest heretic. The fact that you didn't write Smith's document or sign it means nothing; you publicly approved of it. John Paul II and Benedict XVI publicly approved of the *Joint Declaration with the Lutherans on Justification*, which teaches that the worst Lutheran heresies are not condemned by the Council of Trent. They are manifest heretics.

There is No Reason not to accept the Sedevacantist Position

We have addressed in much detail the major objections launched against the sedevacantist position. We can see that there is nothing in the teaching of the Catholic Church which should cause one not to accept the undeniable fact that the Vatican II sect is not the Catholic Church, and that the men who have headed this sect (the post-Vatican II "popes") are not popes at all, but non-Catholic antipopes. On the contrary, there is undeniable proof for this position and every reason to accept it.

Endnotes for Section 21:

[1] *Decrees of the Ecumenical Councils*, Sheed & Ward and Georgetown University Press, 1990, Vol. 1, p. 113.
[2] *Coll. Selecta SS. Eccl. Patrum*. Caillu and Guillou, Vol. 32, pp 411-412
[3] *Decrees of the Ecumenical Councils*, Vol. 1, p. 113.
[4] Denzinger, *The Sources of Catholic Dogma*, B. Herder Book. Co., Thirtieth Edition, 1957, no. 351.
[5] *The Sunday Sermons of the Great Fathers*, Regnery, Co: Chicago, IL, 1963, Vol. 1, pp. xxiv.
[6] Denzinger 423.
[7] *The Papal Encyclicals*, by Claudia Carlen, Raleigh: The Pierian Press, 1990, Vol. 2 (1878-1903), p. 393.
[8] Denzinger 2022.
[9] Denzinger 2054.
[10] Denzinger 960.
[11] *The Papal Encyclicals*, Vol. 1 (1740-1878), p. 236.
[12] *The 1917 Pio-Benedictine Code of Canon Law*, translated by Dr. Edward Von Peters, San Francisco, CA: Ignatius Press, 2001, canon 2314, p. 735.
[13] Denzinger 1547.
[14] *The Catholic Encyclopedia*, "Luther," Robert Appleton Company, 1910, pp. 445-446.
[15] Warren H. Carroll, *A History of Christendom*, Front Royal, VA: Christendom Press, 2000, Vol. 4 (*The Cleaving of Christendom*), p. 10.
[16] *The Papal Encyclicals*, Vol. 4 (1939-1958), p. 41.
[17] *Decrees of the Ecumenical Councils*, Vol. 1, p. 578.
[18] *Decrees of the Ecumenical Councils*, Vol. 1, p. 74.
[19] Benedict XVI, *Principles of Catholic Theology*, Ignatius Press, 1982, p. 239.
[20] Benedict XVI, *Principles of Catholic Theology*, pp. 197-198.
[21] *L'Osservatore Romano*, Special Insert, Joint Declaration of the Doctrine of Justification, November 24, 1999, #13.
[22] G. McDevitt, *The Delict of Heresy*, 48, CU, Canon Law Studies 77. Washington: 1932.
[23] *The Papal Encyclicals*, Vol. 1 (1740-1878), p. 45.
[24] *The Papal Encyclicals*, Vol. 1 (1740-1878), p. 46.
[25] *The Papal Encyclicals*, Vol. 3 (1903-1939), p. 30.
[26] *The Papal Encyclicals*, Vol. 3 (1903-1939), pp. 313-314.
[27] *The Papal Encyclicals*, Vol. 2 (1878-1903), p. 399.
[28] *L'Osservatore Romano* (the Vatican's Newspaper), May 24, 1973, p. 6.
[29] *L'Osservatore Romano*, Jan. 27, 1993, p. 2.
[30] *L'Osservatore Romano*, August 24, 2005, p. 8.
[31] Eric F. Mackenzie, A.M., S.T.L., J.C.L. Rev., *The Delict of Heresy*, Washington, D.C.: The Catholic Univ. of America, 1932, p. 35. (Cf. Canon 2200.2).
[32] *Decrees of the Ecumenical Councils*, Vol. 1, p. 283.
[33] St. Robert Bellarmine, *De Romano Pontifice*, II, 30.
[34] *The Papal Encyclicals*, Vol. 1 (1740-1878), p. 416.
[35] *Ius Canonicum*. Rome: Gregorian 1943. 2:453.

[36] Denzinger 51-52e; Warren H. Carroll, *A History of Christendom*, Vol. 1 (*The Founding of Christendom*), p. 494; J.N.D. Kelly, *Oxford Dictionary of Popes*, Oxford University Press, 2005, p. 25.
[37] Fr. Edmund James O'Reilly, *The Relations of the Church to Society – Theological Essays*, 1882.
[38] Fr. O'Reilly, *The Relations of the Church to Society – Theological Essays*, p. 287.
[39] Yves Dupont, *Catholic Prophecy*, Rockford, IL: Tan Books, 1973, p. 30.
[40] Chris Ferrara, "Opposing the Sedevacantist Enterprise," *Catholic Family News*, Niagra Falls, NY, August 2005, p. 19
[41] Chris Ferrara, "Opposing the Sedevacantist Enterprise," *Catholic Family News*, August 2005, p. 19
[42] Denzinger 1821.
[43] *Decrees of the Ecumenical Councils*, Vol. 2, p. 860.
[44] Benedict XVI, *Principles of Catholic Theology*, pp. 197-198.
[45] Denzinger 1824.
[46] Denzinger 1825.
[47] Denzinger 1825.
[48] Benedict XVI, *Principles of Catholic Theology*, p. 198.
[49] Denzinger 1826-1827.
[50] St. Francis De Sales, *The Catholic Controversy*, Tan Books, 1989, p. 45.
[51] Denzinger 330.
[52] St. Robert Bellarmine, *De Romano Pontifice*, II, 30.
[53] St. Robert Bellarmine, *De Romano Pontifice*, II, 30.
[54] *The Papal Encyclicals*, Vol. 1 (1740-1878), p. 417.
[55] *The Papal Encyclicals*, Vol. 3 (1903-1939), p. 195.
[56] Denzinger 93.
[57] *The Papal Encyclicals*, Vol. 1 (1740-1878), p. 180.
[58] *The Papal Encyclicals*, Vol. 1 (1740-1878), p. 84.
[59] *Institutiones Iuris Canonici*, 1921.
[60] *Decrees of the Ecumenical Councils*, Vol. 2, p. 675.
[61] *L'Osservatore Romano*, Special Insert, Joint Declaration of the Doctrine of Justification, November 24, 1999, #5.
[62] *L'Osservatore Romano*, Special Insert, Joint Declaration of the Doctrine of Justification, November 24, 1999, #13.
[63] *L'Osservatore Romano*, Special Insert, Joint Declaration of the Doctrine of Justification, November 24, 1999, #41.
[64] *L'Osservatore Romano*, Special Insert, Joint Declaration of the Doctrine of Justification, November 24, 1999, #26.
[65] *L'Osservatore Romano*, Jan. 28, 2004, p. 4.
[66] *L'Osservatore Romano*, Dec. 21/28, p. 5.
[67] Denzinger 423.
[68] Warren H. Carroll, *A History of Christendom*, Vol. 3 (*The Glory of Christendom*), pp. 432-434.
[69] *The Catholic Encyclopedia*, Vol. 1, p. 447.
[70] Chris Ferrara, "Opposing the Sedevacantist Enterprise," *Catholic Family News*, August 2005, p. 21.
[71] Chris Ferrara, "Opposing the Sedevacantist Enterprise," *Catholic Family News*, August 2005, p. 21
[72] Denzinger 530.
[73] Denzinger 494.
[74] *The Catholic Encyclopedia*, "John XXII," Vol. 8, 1910, p. 433.
[75] Benedict XVI, *Dogmatic Theology*, The Catholic University of America Press, 1977, p. 137.
[76] *The Catholic Encyclopedia*, Vol. 8, p. 433.
[77] Benedict XVI, *Introduction to Christianity*, p. 349.
[78] Benedict XVI, *Introduction to Christianity*, pp. 357-358.
[79] *Decrees of the Ecumenical Councils*, Vol. 1, p. 578; Denzinger 714.
[80] *Decrees of the Ecumenical Councils*, Vol. 1, pp. 125-126.
[81] Denzinger 253.
[82] St. Francis De Sales, *The Catholic Controversy*, pp. 305-306.
[83] *Oeuvres Complètes*, 9:232.
[84] *Coll. Selecta SS. Eccl. Patrum*, Caillu and Guillou, Vol. 32, pp 411-412.

Answers to Objections

85 *The Douay-Rheims New Testament with a Catholic Commentary*, by Rev. Leo Haydock, Monrovia, CA: Catholic Treasures, 1991, p. 1640.
86 Jurgens, *The Faith of the Early Fathers*, Collegeville, MN: The Liturgical Press, 1970, Vol. 2, p. 39.
87 Jurgens, *The Faith of the Early Fathers*, Vol. 2, p. 3.
88 Jurgens, *The Faith of the Early Fathers*, Vol. 2, p. 158.
89 Jurgens, *The Faith of the Early Fathers*, Vol. 2, p. 33.
90 Donald Attwater, *A Catholic Dictionary*, "Hierarchy," Tan Books, p. 229.
91 *The Papal Encyclicals*, Vol. 4 (1939-1958), p. 267.
92 *Catholic Family News*, January, 1999.
93 *Decrees of the Ecumenical Councils*, Vol. 2, p. 908.
94 *The Encyclicals of John Paul II*, Huntington, IN: Our Sunday Visitor Publishing Division, 1996, p. 918.
95 *The Papal Encyclicals*, Vol. 2 (1878-1903), p. 388.
96 *The Papal Encyclicals*, Vol. 3 (1903-1939), p. 317.
97 *The Papal Encyclicals*, Vol. 4 (1939-1958), p. 50.
98 *The Papal Encyclicals*, Vol. 2 (1878-1903), p. 388.
99 *The Catholic Encyclopedia*, Vol. 8, 1910, "Investitures," p. 86
100 Chris Ferrara, *Catholic Family News*, "Opposing the Sedevacantist Enterprise, Part II," Oct. 2005, p. 8.
101 Denzinger 461.
102 Benedict XVI, *The Meaning of Christian Brotherhood*, pp. 87-88.
103 Benedict XVI, *Theological Highlights of Vatican II*, New York: Paulist Press, 1966, pp. 61, 68.
104 Benedict XVI, *Principles of Catholic Theology* (1982), pp. 197-198.
105 "Cardinal" Joseph Ratzinger, *God and the World*, Ignatius Press, 2000, p. 209.
106 "Cardinal" Ratzinger, *Principles of Catholic Theology*, p. 377.
107 "Cardinal" Ratzinger, *Principles of Catholic Theology*, p. 202.
108 *The Encyclicals of John Paul II*, p. 965.
109 "Cardinal" Joseph Ratzinger, *Principles of Catholic Theology*, p. 381.
110 "Cardinal" Joseph Ratzinger, *Co-Workers of the Truth*, Ignatius Press, 1990, p. 217.
111 "Cardinal" Joseph Ratzinger, *Co-Workers of the Truth*, p. 29.
112 "Cardinal" Joseph Ratzinger, *Introduction to Christianity*, Ignatius Press, 2004, p. 349.
113 *The Jewish People and the Holy Scriptures in the Christian Bible*, Section II, A, Prefaced by Benedict XVI, www.vatican.va.
114 Chris Ferrara, *The Remnant*, Forest Lake, MN, Sept. 30, 2005, p. 18.
115 *The Papal Encyclicals*, Vol. 3 (1903-1939), p. 294.
116 Abbot Ricciotti, *The Age of Martyrs*, Tan Books, p. 275; see also Fr. Laux, *Church History*, Tan Books, 1989, p. 113; Warren H. Carroll, *A History of Christendom*, Vol. 2 (*The Building of Christendom*), p. 18.
117 Chris Ferrara, *Catholic Family News*, "Opposing the Sedevacantist Enterprise, Part II," Oct. 2005, p. 25.
118 *The Papal Encyclicals*, Vol. 1 (1740-1878), p. 451.
119 *The Papal Encyclicals*, Vol. 1 (1740-1878), pp. 451-452.
120 *The Papal Encyclicals*, Vol. 1 (1740-1878), p. 414.
121 Chris Ferrara, *Catholic Family News*, Oct. 2005, p. 25.
122 Michael Matt, *The Remnant*, April 15, 2004, p. 5.
123 Chris Ferrara, "A Challenge to the Sedevacantist Enterprise, Part II," *The Remnant*, Sept. 30, 2005, p. 18.
124 *The 1917 Pio-Benedictine Code of Canon Law*, translated by Dr. Edward Von Peters, p. 83.
125 *The Code of Canon Law (1983), A Text and Commentary*, Commissioned by the Canon Law Society of America, Edited by James A. Coriden, Thomas J. Green, Donald E. Heintschel, Mahwah, NJ: Paulist Press, 1985, p. 111.
126 Denzinger 646.
127 *The Papal Encyclicals*, Vol. 4 (1939-1958), p. 41.
128 Denzinger 627 ff.
129 *L'Osservatore Romano*, Jan. 28, 2004, p. 4.
130 *L'Osservatore Romano*, August 24, 2005, p. 8.

START OF PART II:

BY THEIR FRUITS YOU SHALL KNOW THEM – THE ROTTEN FRUITS AND INEXHAUSTIBLE SCANDAL OF THE VATICAN II SECT PROVE THAT IT'S NOT THE CATHOLIC CHURCH AND THAT WE ARE IN THE GREAT APOSTASY

A teen in leotards, in an inappropriate position, performs for an applauding John Paul II – just one of a myriad of examples of the scandal, immorality and bad fruits universally exemplified by the Vatican II sect

JESUS CHRIST, Matthew 7:16-19- "**By their fruits you shall know them.** Do men gather grapes of thorns, or figs of thistles? Even so **every good tree bringeth forth good fruit, and the evil tree bringeth forth evil fruit. A good tree cannot bring forth evil fruit, neither can an evil tree bring forth good fruit.** Every tree that bringeth not forth good fruit, shall be cut down, and shall be cast into the fire."

The Catholic Church is the one, *holy*, Catholic and apostolic. In considering these four marks of the true Church, we sometimes forget to consider the Church's holiness. Vatican I summed it up well.

> Pope Pius IX, *Vatican Council I*, Sess. 3, Chap. 3, on Faith: "…**the Church itself by itself, because of its marvelous propagation, <u>its exceptional holiness, and inexhaustible fruitfulness</u>** in all good works; because of its Catholic unity and invincible stability, <u>**is a very great and perpetual motive of credibility**</u>, and <u>an incontestable witness of its own divine mission</u>." (Denzinger 1794)

Vatican I defined that the Catholic Church is recognized by its *exceptional holiness* and inexhaustible fruitfulness in good works. Its holiness is a "great and perpetual motive of [its] credibility." Now, in discussing this point, we must make a distinction. We are <u>not</u> suggesting that all the members of the true Catholic Church are holy or that scandals cannot arise within the ranks of the true faithful. Such an idea has been condemned by the Church. Since faith is distinct from charity, one might possess the true Faith while disregarding charity or morality. The true Church has always contained some good people and some bad people. However, we are pointing out in accordance with Vatican I, that *generally speaking* where the true Faith is found holiness is also found. To put it another way: where the dictates of the true Church are lived up to and put into practice a holy life necessarily follows.

On the other hand, **where massive and almost universal sin, immorality and scandal are present, the dictates, precepts and teachings of the true Church are almost necessarily rejected and/or denied**. Hence, if one is confronted by a "Church" which purports to be the Catholic Church, but is characterized, not by inexhaustible holiness, <u>but by inexhaustible and almost universal scandal among its representatives</u>, this in itself is almost sufficient to prove that such a "Church" is not the Catholic Church, but a non-Catholic sect which has also departed from the faith of the true Church. **Their departure from the true Faith explains why holy lives are not found within their ranks.** This couldn't be more true than in the case of the Vatican II sect, the counterfeit "Catholic Church" of the last days.

22. The Massive Sexual Scandal among the Vatican II/Novus Ordo "priests"

"Cardinal" Bernard Law, formerly of Boston, who presided over the Vatican II sect's massive sexual scandal there

CBS News – "Clergy members and others in the Boston Archdiocese likely sexually abused more than 1,000 people over a period of six decades, Massachusetts' attorney general said Wednesday, calling the scandal so massive **it 'borders on the unbelievable.'**"[1]

Almost everyone reading this book is probably familiar with the massive sexual scandal among Novus Ordo/Vatican II "priests" that was unceasingly exposed by the mainstream media from approximately 2002-2004. The sexual perversion of the Novus Ordo/Vatican II "priests" is so pervasive that whole dioceses of the Vatican II sect have gone into bankruptcy to pay out legal settlements to abused victims. The Diocese of Davenport provides the most recent example.

Traditional Catholics need to seriously consider how severely this scandal has damaged the Catholic Church in the eyes of the world. Even though we can prove that the Vatican II sect is not the Catholic Church and that the men intimately involved in this scandal adhere to the new religion, not the real Catholic religion – as we will continue to do in this book – for those outside the scandal is seen as coming from "Catholic priests." Non-Catholic after non-Catholic uses this priestly sex scandal as a cheap way to attack the true Church and dissuade potential converts. It is truly one of the worst scandals in human history when we consider the truth of the holy priesthood and the Catholic Faith.

We've spoken to so many non-Catholics who, when approached about embracing the truth of the Catholic Faith, have immediately answered back with facts about the Vatican II sect's pervert priests. "Why would I want to join a Church whose priests molest children?," they say (or words to this effect). In trying to convert people, we've been rejected for this reason dozens of times. People need to realize that *the fact that God allowed this massive scandal to occur, which has undoubtedly discouraged millions and will continue to discourage millions from investigating or seeing the Catholic Faith as true,* shows us that we are in the time of the Great Apostasy and Great Spiritual deception. It's only Catholics who are fully aware of the truth who can take heart in the realization that these priests are not adherents of the true Catholic Faith at all, but adherents of the non-Catholic counterfeit sect. **This manifestation of perversion is simply the underlying reality of the post-Vatican II apostasy coming out for what it really is.**

During "Cardinal" Law's tenure in Boston, Paul Shanley and John Geoghan were moved from parish to parish within the diocese, despite repeated allegations of molestation of children against them. Later, it was discovered that Father Shanley advocated the North American Man-Boy Love Association.

BOSTON CONSIDERS BANKRUPTCY – The Archdiocese of Boston is reportedly considering filing a claim in U.S. Bankruptcy Court unless prospects for a mediated settlement improve, the Boston Globe reported Dec. 1… A spokeswoman said the archdiocese has to consider all its options but said there is no timetable for deciding whether to file for bankruptcy. (National Catholic Register, Dec. 8-14, 2002, p. 1.)

BOSTON ARCHDIOCESE SELLS OR MORTGAGES ONCE UNTOUCHABLE PROPERTY TO PAY SEX SCANDAL SETTLEMENT

The Associated Press-

BOSTON (AP) – THE SEX SCANDAL IN THE BOSTON ARCHDIOCESE HAS SHAKEN THE CHURCH ALMOST LITERALLY TO ITS FOUNDATIONS. To help pay the $85 million settlement reached with more than 500 victims of child-molesting priests, the archdiocese has mortgaged its very seat of power -- the Cathedral of the Holy Cross -- and is putting up for sale the archbishop's residence, an Italian Renaissance-style mansion that was a symbol of the church's grandeur and authority. Dozens of churches are also expected to be closed in a move at least accelerated by the scandal. (Dec. 18, 2003)

"And I will accomplish in my fury, and will cause my indignation to rest upon them, and I will be comforted: and they shall know that I the Lord have spoken it in my zeal, when I shall have accomplished my indignation in them.

"And I will make thee desolate, and a reproach amongst the nations that are round about thee, in the sight of every one that passeth by. And thou shalt be a reproach, and a scoff, an example, and an astonishment amongst the nations that are round about thee, when I shall have executed judgments in thee in anger, and in indignation, and in wrathful rebukes. I the Lord have spoken it…" (Ezechiel 5:13-16)

> **CBS News** - Clergy members and others in the Boston Archdiocese likely sexually abused more than 1,000 people over a period of six decades, Massachusetts' attorney general said Wednesday, calling the scandal so massive **it "borders on the unbelievable."** ... The sheer number of abuse allegations documented by investigators **in Boston appears unprecedented, even amid a scandal that has touched dioceses in virtually every state** and has prompted about 1,000 people to come forward with new allegations nationwide in the last year. (CBSNews.com, July 23, 2003)
>
> **ABC NEWS, Sept. 9**— The Boston Archdiocese and lawyers for victims of sex abuse by priests announced today that they reached a settlement of $85 million, **the largest known payout in the child molestation scandal that has rocked the Roman Catholic Church**. (ABCNews.com, Sept. 9, 2003)

But this scandal was by no means limited to Boston.

> On May 3, 2003, Phoenix Bishop Thomas J. O'Brien acknowledged that he hid allegations of sex abuse by priests. He then surrendered some of his authority. [2]
>
> June 28, 2003 – "In one of the largest out-of-court settlements to abuse victims in the Catholic sex scandal, **the Louisville Archdiocese in Kentucky announced that it will pay nearly $25.7 million** to people who said they were sexually molested by priests and other employees of the church... William McMurry, who represented many of the plaintiffs, said that **the archdiocese is using more than half of its liquid assets to pay the settlement**."[3]
>
> On July 6, 2004, "Facing dozens of pending lawsuits accusing clergy of sexual abuse, the Archdiocese of Portland, Ore., files for bankruptcy. **The Portland church has already paid more than $53 million** to settle more than 130 abuse claims, and the archbishop says, 'The pot of gold is pretty much empty right now.'"[4]
>
> On Sept. 20, 2004, "The Roman Catholic **Diocese of Tucson,** Ariz., becomes the second in the nation to seek bankruptcy protection, in the wake of extensive and continuing legal action stemming from sexual abuse of children by parish priests."[5]
>
> On Sept. 24, 2004, "Bishop Thomas Dupre is indicted on child rape charges, becoming the first bishop to face charges in the church sex abuse scandal. Dupre was the head of the **Springfield, Mass.** diocese, but resigned in February after the allegations came to light."[6]
>
> On Dec. 2, 2004, "**The Orange County** diocese reaches a settlement with 87 victims of clergy abuse. Terms of the agreement are not disclosed, but a source tells the Associated Press the payout will be bigger than the record $85 million agreement with the Boston Archdiocese. The lawsuits allege sexual misconduct by 30 priests, 11 lay personnel and two nuns."[7]
>
> **The Diocese of Spokane, WA** "filed for Chapter 11 bankruptcy protection in December 2004, listing more than $81 million in claims. The diocese sought bankruptcy protection in advance of court trials over claims of clergy sexual abuse."[8] In 2006, the Diocese of Spokane auctioned off its chancery to pay off sex abuse claims.[9]

"The child sex abuse scandal in the Roman Catholic **diocese on Long Island** has resulted in the defrocking of eight priests and the permanent suspension of nine [for alleged sex abuse], while three await canonical trials, the bishop of the diocese said."[10]

On Oct. 12, 2005, "Newly released records of sex abuse **claims against 126 priests** that are at the core of hundreds of lawsuits against the **Archdiocese of Los Angeles** show that church officials for decades moved accused priests between counseling and new assignments." [11]

Recently in 2006, "the Roman Catholic **Diocese of Davenport** filed for Chapter 11 bankruptcy protection today, less than two weeks before it defends itself at a trial involving a former priest accused of sexually abusing a high school student. Bishop William Franklin says he regrets the decision, but the financial pressure and demands for settling as many as 25 outstanding claims of sexual abuse by its priests is too great."[12] (IOWA CITY, Iowa)

Examples of this corruption among the Vatican II clergy <u>could be multiplied for pages</u>, but the reader should get the idea: this unspeakable scandal is present among the Vatican sect simply because it's not the *holy* Catholic Church. Who would dare say it is? The scandal we're talking about is so outrageous – indeed one of the very worst scandals in history – that **it could only be a sign of the end times and of the apocalyptic counterfeit church which will characterize the last days**. You know things are bad when **the most prominent thing at the top of the website for the Diocese of Pittsburgh is a toll-free number for sex abuse response.**[13]

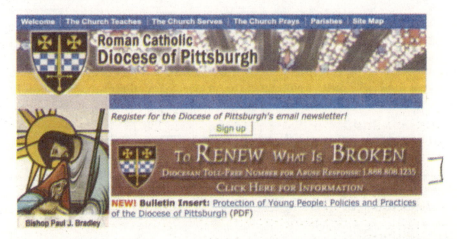

The website for the Archdiocese of Philadelphia has as its fifth option a section on "Children and Youth Protection" [14] – protection, that is, from its pervert "priests." It's such a problem that **every diocesan website we checked has a prominent place for the abuse problem**. What follows are just a few more examples from the diocesan websites of Miami[15] and Milwaukee.[16] Notice that the sexual abuse issue is one of the most prominent things mentioned on the websites (underlining and bracketing are our own).

The massive Sex Scandal among priests 354

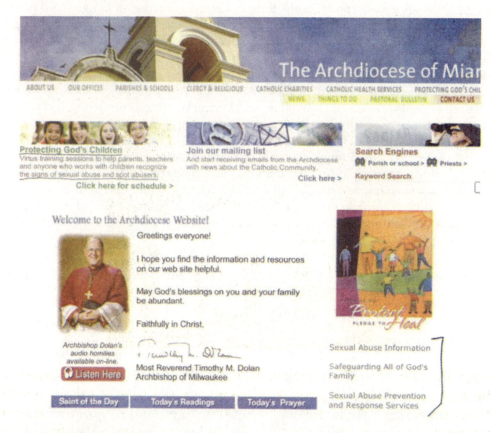

Nor is the Vatican II sect's sexual scandal limited to the U.S. The sexual scandal that has engulfed the Vatican II sect has indeed spread all over the world. On July 8, 2002, "The Catholic Bishops Conference of **the Philippines** apologized for 'grave sexual misconduct' by Filipino priests, and promises a protocol to address future cases of abuse."[17]

In the Archdiocese of Vienna in 2004, for instance, 10,000 people left the Novus Ordo church in a few months over two high profile sex scandals involving clergy, child pornography and alleged molestation.[18]

Endnotes for Section 22:

[1] CBSNews.com, July 23, 2003.
[2] http://www.nytimes.com – Jan. 25, 2005.
[3] The Christian Century Foundation: http://www.findarticles.com/p/articles/mi_m1058/is_13_120/ai_104681885
[4] http://www.nytimes.com – Jan. 25, 2005.
[5] http://www.nytimes.com – Jan. 25, 2005.
[6] http://www.nytimes.com – Jan. 25, 2005.
[7] http://www.nytimes.com – Jan. 25, 2005.
[8] http://www.spokesmanreview.com/sections/diocese/?ID=132420
[9] www.kxly.com, Oct. 3, 2006.
[10] http://www.nytimes.com – Jan. 25, 2005.
[11] http://www.nytimes.com – Jan. 25, 2005.
[12] http://www.whotv.com/Global/story.asp?S=5522807&nav=2HAB
[13] http://www.diopitt.org/
[14] http://www.archdiocese-phl.org/links.htm
[15] http://www.miamiarch.org
[16] http://www.archmil.org
[17] http://www.cbsnews.com/htdocs/catholic_crisis/timeline.html
[18] http://news.scotsman.com/international.cfm?id=1122942004

23. The Seminaries of the Vatican II sect are unspeakable cesspools of homosexuality and heresy

Pope Pius XI, *Ad catholici sacerdotii* (# 66), Dec. 20, 1935: **"Give the best of your clergy to your seminaries;** do not fear to take them from other positions. These [other] positions may seem of greater moment, but in reality their importance is not to be compared with that of the seminaries, which is capital and indispensable. Seek also from elsewhere, wherever you can find them, men really fitted for this noble task. Let them be such as teach priestly virtues, rather by example than by words, <u>men who are capable of imparting, together with learning, a solid, manly and apostolic spirit</u>."[1]

In 2002, the book *Goodbye, Good Men* by Michael Rose was published. This book documented the almost unbelievable perversion and debauchery of the seminaries of the Vatican II/Novus Ordo "Church." The corrupt seminaries produced the "priests" who, in turn, produced the notorious sexual scandal. The author (Rose) is a defender of the Vatican II sect, so his exposé (coming from one who is inclined to defend the Vatican II clergy) reveals how horrible the situation really is.

Some of the anecdotes about life at the seminary are so horrifying that only one conclusion follows from them: the "Church" which presents these places as "seminaries for the formation of Catholic priests" could only be the apocalyptic Whore of Babylon which Scripture predicts will arise in the last days to deceive Catholics. A few excerpts from *Goodbye, Good Men* are necessary to establish the point:

> Michael Rose, *Goodbye, Good Men*, pp. 56-57: "According to former seminarians and recently ordained priests, **this 'gay subculture' is so prominent at certain seminaries that these institutions have earned nicknames such as Notre Flame (for Notre Dame Seminary in New Orleans) and Theological Closet** (for Theological College at the Catholic University of America in Washington, D.C.). **St. Mary's Seminary in Baltimore has earned the nickname the 'Pink Palace.'**"[2]

The antipopes and "bishops" of the Vatican II sect do nothing about these seminaries or the massive homosexual problem, of course! But when someone under their authority opposes the New Religion they act with lightning-fast speed. **For instance: when the head of the Fraternity of St. Peter Seminary, Fr. Bisig, showed that he was not inclined to accept in his fraternity men who wanted to say the New Mass, the Vatican promptly removed him and appointed Father Arnaud Devillers in his place.** How quickly the Vatican acts when the New Religion is opposed! Also remember that, in 1988, a bishop was excommunicated immediately after acting to spread the Traditional Latin Mass. Yet the post-Vatican II Vatican does nothing about perverted seminaries all over the world. This is because it is the Counter Church of the Devil.

Prior to Vatican II, it was the policy that those with the perverse tendency to homosexuality (which is a result of demonic takeover as a result of some form of idolatry, as is taught in Romans 1) <u>were forbidden to become priests</u>.

> "Father Andrew Walter, ordained for the Diocese of Bridgeport, Connecticut, in 2000, spent several semesters at the Baltimore school as a seminarian for the Diocese of Paterson, New Jersey. **The [homosexual] problem was so bad when he was there, he explained, that 'some of the students and faculty used to get dressed up in leather to go to 'the block,'** Baltimore's equivalent to 42nd Street in Manhattan.'"[3]

> Michael Rose, *Goodbye, Good Men*, p. 57: "Father John Trigilio of the Harrisburg, Pennsylvania, diocese remembers visiting St. Mary's in Baltimore when he was a seminarian in Pennsylvania. 'There was no discretion at all,' he said of the gay subculture there. 'The few times I was there, **some of the seminarians would literally dress like gays from the Village. They would even go so far as to wear pink silk;** it was like going to see *La Cage aux Folles.*'
>
> 'In my day at St. Mary's,' said Father John Despard, now a religious order priest from the Southeast, **'down the hall there would be two guys together in the shower and everybody knew it.'**
>
> "Ada Mason, a philosophy professor at a prominent Catholic university, once served on the board of a seminary in the upper Midwest. In that position she was shocked to discover a gay subculture extremely active there. 'Open homosexual behavior was more than tolerated,' she admitted. 'I was even told by one of the seminary faculty that **every Friday a van took priesthood students to a nearby city to cruise the gay bars.'"**[4]

As awful as it sounds, this is actually just the tip of the iceberg of the perversion and rampant homosexuality of the Vatican II sect. *Goodbye, Good Men* also documents that the seminaries of the Novus Ordo sect endorse and accept a rejection of the most basic teachings of the Catholic Faith.

> "'Many seminarians lost their faith there [at the seminary],' he lamented. 'One guy I remember in particular,' he recounted. **'He lost his faith because of a Christology course we were all required to take.'** In that course, Perrone explained, the seminarians were taught the German Protestant biblical exegesis popularized by German Lutheran Rudolph Bultmann, and **the first book they read was Albert Schweitzer's *Quest for the Historical Jesus*, which Perrone called 'a very damaging book' that dismissed all of the Church's teachings as unreliable myths**. 'And we had similar books in the same vein.'"[5]

The first book they read at the seminary attacked Our Lord's historicity and dismissed all the Church's teachings as myths. Again, this is just a tiny sampling of what goes on and is taught at the "seminaries" of the Vatican II sect. Rose's book also documents that men who are opposed to the ordination of women are discouraged from pursuing a vocation. It documents how the Papal Primacy, the inerrancy of Scripture, etc. are commonly denied at these seminaries. It documents how a witch attended one seminary (p. 108), and how candidates for the seminary were interviewed and screened by a Mason:

> "The next step **in the admissions process [to the seminary]** was the psychological evaluation. Carrigee was sent to an independent psychological clinic, where **he spent two days taking tests and 'being interviewed by a stone-faced stoic who wore a Masonic ring.'"**[6]

Things are so bad at these "seminaries" that one prominent "priest" of the Vatican II sect, "Fr." John Trigilio, had this to say about his seminary days:

> "Trigilio lamented, hinting at the campy subculture that permeated the seminary atmosphere. **'We used to say, if you wore a cassock you were a reactionary 'daughter of Trent.' If you wore women's underwear, they'd make you seminarian of the year. We had a few guys who sometimes wore women's clothing, lingerie, makeup, etc., and some who were as effeminate as could be... The campy ones at MIS [Mary Immaculate Seminary, Northampton, P.A.] would call each other by female names...'"**[7]

> "'I can say this,' he explained, 'but it's not an absolute: If a guy through his seminary career at **MIS had never had any opposition from the faculty, there was something wrong with him**. If you were anything near orthodox, you had to fight tooth and nail to keep your sanity and your faith... The formation team would tell my bishop that 'He's having trouble adjusting to contemporary theology; he remains very rigid.' **But for those who were openly homosexual, their bishops were not informed.'"**[8]

These are the words of a Novus Ordo "priest" who is currently featured on EWTN. This "priest" is a promoter of false ecumenism, salvation outside the Church, and many other post-Vatican II heresies. The point is that he's by no means a traditional Catholic. He's very far away from the traditional Catholic Faith, yet he was considered a reactionary at his seminary simply because he wasn't open to things such as homosexuality and women's ordination. This shows us how wicked the Vatican II sect is, and how far it is from Catholic.

AN INCREDIBLE ACCOUNT OF THE STATE OF THE SEMINARIES FROM ONE WHO SPENT TIME AT A PROMINENT NOVUS ORDO SEMINARY

In the 1995 issue of *The Homiletic and Pastoral Review* (which was subsequently published on the internet), an article appeared by an individual who had attended one of the nation's most prominent Novus Ordo seminaries. He was appalled by what he saw. Some of the things he said include:

> "After spending four years in a Neo-Modernist Roman Catholic seminary, I have come to the firm belief that the source of the current crisis in the Church in the United States can be traced directly to the seminaries. The seminary is literally the seedbed of the faith... **A man would inevitably find trouble [at the seminary], however, if he used language like "the Holy Sacrifice of the Mass."** He would have two strikes against him if he in turn stood in opposition to the concept of "priestesses" in the Roman Catholic Church.

> **"The Rosary was looked upon as being suitable for those without the capacity to approach God intellectually, and it was beneath one of theological sophistication**...

To begin with, we were instructed upon entry to the seminary that we could not kneel at the consecration during Mass, nor could we kneel after receiving communion. This would 'break community.'...

"At Mass, the priest was often simply referred to as the "presider." He was the one leading us in prayer, "animating" the community. Many "presiders" improvised upon the Mass, adding their own touch to the eucharistic prayers. Making sure the readings were inclusivized was the responsibility of the reader for the day...

"**We, as Roman Catholic seminarians, were not allowed to wear clerical clothing**. This was because the collar was a sign of "clericalism." Though the rector had been known to tell bishops he did not want to 'confuse ministry with the wearing of the collar,' the reality behind abolishing the collar in our seminary was that it was a cause of great anxiety for the feminists...

"We were told from the beginning that seminarians were not to refer to any of the faculty as "Father" or "Sister." We were not to be caught up with "titles," as this was another form of clericalism. These things would also offend against the "ecumenical" mission that the seminary was committed to. In terms of a "confusion of ministries," one might question the very practice inculcated in the seminary...

"**During a class conference, the question that was raised was the unchecked effeminate, scandalous behavior of some seminarians, the negative reputation of the seminary gained by this recurring image, and the kinds of role models the seminary was tacitly approving in recommending these men for orders. The Vice Rector replied by saying the seminary admitted men of both orientations**, but the policy was that all had to be celibate...

"**For our entire first academic year, we had to study Richard P. McBrien's** *Catholicism*. This book set the most fertile foundations for doubt and intellectual departure from the true Catholic Faith. It was through subtle and clever deception by veiled, ambiguous language, that McBrien's book was so effective. It became the basis for the reasonableness and goodness of dissent. **Some of his more exemplary ideas, implied and cleverly suggested throughout the book, are that we don't have to believe in the virginity of the Blessed Mother**; that we don't have to believe or assent to follow Church teaching unless it explicitly states it has dogmatic status; and that we must admit to Jesus having been ignorant and in error. McBrien expertly employed his language so that he remained within a "legal" framework, and made outrageous suggestions which to some appear compelling. I recall seeing the firsthand results of this book's use in a discussion I had with another seminarian - he was firmly convinced that 'It's totally naive to think that Mary didn't have sex.'

"**We often studied Protestant theologies right alongside Rahner, Schillebeeckx, Kung, Boff (even on occasion Matthew Fox)** and so forth. Since there was no reliance upon the Magisterium for guidance or point of reference in most theological discussions, we seminarians would be adrift in a sea of opinion and interpretations, both Protestant and Catholic.

"In the area of spirituality, we had workshops on "women's spirituality," or something about "collaborative ministry" and "social justice," because this was perceived as "where the Spirit was" in today's world. Devotion to Mary as "Blessed Mother" was allowed, but generally not encouraged... **The Rosary, prayed in the main chapel by a group of seminarians, was tolerated for a time. But eventually the tension created in the seminary over this group brought it to an end**. However, to please bishops, and as a kind of token gesture to the conservative element in the seminary, the Rosary was suddenly allowed again - with official seminary approval - but then only in a small hall chapel where there was no Blessed Sacrament, one day a week, between breakfast and classes. The reason behind not allowing the Rosary in the main chapel was that 'the chapel is for liturgical celebrations - not devotions.' And yet the chapel was used for a number of functions outside Catholic worship, including on occasion the rehearsals of a local symphony orchestra.

"The greatest of spiritual tests came in my fourth year, in a course of so-called "Pastoral Counseling." A laywoman with a very vocal agenda taught the course. Not only did she proudly inform us one day that she'd be taking off a class to attend the Call to Action seminars in Chicago (where everyone joined in the Eucharistic prayers as a woman in stole "presided" - and with a Catholic Bishop in the congregation), but she openly canvassed for gay and lesbian rights, radical feminism, and even abortion. Because I openly questioned this woman's arguments, I was penalized...

"Through a discouraging dilemma, I knew that what was being taught directly contradicted what the Church taught, and I knew that the bishop in my home diocese supported me... **After four years in the seminary of standing up for what was right, I was finally punished with dismissal**. I was asked to leave at the end of the academic year and to not return. Even though I was pointing out direct cases where the seminary stood contrary to Catholicism in its spiritual climate, members of the faculty protected themselves and the institution by making it appear I was the one who opposed the Church, her authority, and seminary formation... Because of the ramifications of the rector's rage, and to my surprise, the bishop in turn also "released" me, as the matter had become quite political for him.

"I wondered if, in seminaries like the one I attended, men are in a sense still being placed before the images of various gods and told to make a choice."[9]

Notice that this conservative-minded seminarian thought that his Novus Ordo "bishop" would support him. After his dismissal, he discovered that the "bishop" stood with the apostates at the seminary and against him.

Endnotes for Section 23:

[1] *The Papal Encyclicals*, by Claudia Carlen, Raleigh: The Pierian Press, 1990, Vol. 3 (1903-1939), p. 509.
[2] **Michael Rose, *Goodbye, Good Men*, Washington, D.C.: Regnery Publishing, Inc., 2002, p. 56.**
[3] **Michael Rose, *Goodbye, Good Men*, p. 56.**
[4] **Michael Rose, *Goodbye, Good Men*, p. 56.**
[5] **Michael Rose, *Goodbye, Good Men*, p. 97.**
[6] **Michael Rose, *Goodbye, Good Men*, p. 44.**
[7] **Michael Rose, *Goodbye, Good Men*, p. 171.**
[8] **Michael Rose, *Goodbye, Good Men*, p. 172.**
[9] http://mafg.home.isp-direct.com/priest01.htm

24. The idolatry of the Vatican II sect, and the formation of "priests" for its idolatry in the Vatican II seminaries, is connected with its rampant homosexuality

Scripture teaches that homosexuality is a result of idolatry.

> **Romans 1- "Because that, when they knew God, they have not glorified him as God, or given thanks; but became vain in their thoughts, and their foolish heart was darkened... who changed the truth of God into a lie; and worshipped and served the creature rather than the Creator, who is blessed for ever. Amen. For this cause God delivered them up to shameful affections. For their women have changed the natural use into that use which is against nature. And, in like manner, the men also, leaving the natural use of the women, have burned in their lusts one towards another, men with men working that which is filthy, and receiving in themselves the recompense which was due to their error... they who do such things, are worthy of death; and not only they that do them, but they also that consent to them that do them."**

The Vatican II Sect contradicts this teaching of Scripture by asserting that the cause of homosexuality is unknown, and that the homosexual orientation is not wrong.

> John Paul II, New Catechism, #2357: "Homosexuality... Its psychological genesis remains largely unexplained."[1]

rampant homosexuality is connected with the V-2 Sect's idolatry

But Romans 1 clearly teaches that homosexuality is *"against nature,"* which means that **this orientation is foreign to man's nature**; that is, it is NOT INSTILLED BY GOD. As a result of idolatry, God sometimes allows a demon to take people over, possess them, and change their sexual orientation, as St. Paul describes.

Men and women are given over to homosexuality for inundating themselves with sins of impurity – thereby worshipping the flesh rather than God. For this sin they can get possessed by the demon of lust, which takes them over and corrupts their entire orientation. (And they can be cured of this.) People also become homosexuals by engaging in idolatry by either harboring a perverse fascination with human beings over God – thereby worshipping the creature rather than the Creator – or by simply worshipping something that is a creature or the works of one's hands. The fact that all homosexuals are possessed by a demon is corroborated by the fact that most homosexual males can be identified by their effeminate external mannerisms. What explains this? It's obviously the demon's presence in the person making itself manifest externally – *the external, unnatural mannerisms revealing the internal corruption of the soul.*

> Isaias 3:9 – "***The shew of their countenance doth witness against them; and they declare their sin as Sodom***, they hide it not. Woe unto their soul! For they have rewarded evil unto themselves."

Notice that the prophet Isaias, referring to homosexuals, says that *"they have **rewarded** evil unto themselves."* This is strikingly similar to Romans 1 above, where St. Paul says that homosexuals have *received "in themselves the **recompense** [reward] which was due to their error."*

An examination of the most demonic cultures in history corroborates Scripture's teaching on the connection between idolatry (whether of the flesh or of the work of one's hands or of oneself) with homosexuality. **All of this is relevant because homosexuality is rampant among the Vatican II clergy.**

The Aztec culture in Mexico in the 15th and 16th centuries, which the Catholic conquistadors physically overthrew – and which the appearance of Our Lady of Guadalupe (1531) spiritually crushed – was arguably the wickedest culture in human history.

> Warren H. Carroll, *Our Lady of Guadalupe and the Conquest of Darkness*, pp. 8-11:
> "**Many primitive peoples have practiced occasional human sacrifice and some have practiced cannibalism. None has ever done so on a scale remotely approaching that of the Aztecs**. No one will ever know how many they sacrificed; but the law of the empire required a thousand sacrifices to the Aztec tribal god Huitzilopochtli in every town with a temple, every year; and there were 371 subject towns in the Aztec empire…
>
> "**Every Aztec city and large town had a central square, from which a high pyramidal temple rose,** and four gates opening upon four roads approaching the town in straight lines extending at least five miles, each ending at one side of the pyramid temple… **Month after month, year after year, in temple after temple, the sacrificial victims came down the roads to the steps**, climbed up the steps to the platform at the top, **and there were bent backwards over large convex slabs of polished stone** by a hook around the neck wielded by a priest with head and arms stained black, never-cut black hair all caked and matted with dried blood, and once-white garments soaked and stained with innumerable gouts of crimson. **An immense knife with a blade of midnight black volcanic glass rose and fell, cutting the victim open. His heart was torn out while still beating** and held up for all to see, while his ravaged body was kicked over the edge of

the temple platform where it bounced and slithered in obscene contortions down the steps to the bottom a hundred feet below. Later, the limbs of the body were eaten…

"The early Mexican historian Ixtlilxochitl estimated that one out of every five children in Mexico was sacrificed… **An almost universal symbol in Mexican religion was the serpent.** Sacrifices were heralded by the prolonged beating of an immense drum made of skins of huge snakes, which could be heard two miles away. **Nowhere else in human history has Satan so formalized and institutionalized his worship with so many of his own actual titles and symbols.**"[2]

Here is a description of the 1487 Aztec dedication of a new pyramid temple to their false god, Huitzilopochtli:

"**Tlacaellell decided that this central temple should be dedicated with the greatest mass sacrifice of his fifty-eight years of dominance** in the Aztec empire. As always, he had his way. In R.C. Padden's memorable description: '<u>**Well before daybreak of the opening day, legionnaires prepared victims, who were put in close single file down the steps of the great pyramid**</u>, through the city, out over the causeways, and as far as the eye could see. **For the average person viewing the spectacle from roof top, it would appear that the victims stretched in lines to the end of the earth**. The bulk of unfortunates were from hostile provinces and the swollen ranks of slavery. <u>**On the pyramid's summit, four slabs had been set up, one at the head of each staircase**</u>, for Tlacaellel and the three kings of the Triple Alliance, all of whom were to begin the affair as sacrificial priests. All were in readiness; the lines of victims were strung out for miles, with great reservoirs at their ends, **thousands of trapped humans milling about like cattle, awaiting their turn in the line that was about to move**. Suddenly, the brilliantly arrayed kings approached Huitzilopochtli's [the false god's] chapel and made reverent obeisance. As they turned to join their aides at the four slabs, <u>**great snakeskin drums began to throb, announcing that the lines could now begin to move**</u>.

"**Relays of priests dispatched the victims. As each group tired [of killing], others of the thousands who were to live below in the new temple stepped forward to relieve them and keep up the pace**. Years of practice had given them a skill and speed almost incredible. Reliable evidence indicates that it took only fifteen seconds to kill each victim. <u>**Blood and bodies cascaded in an endless stream down the temple steps. Hearts were assembled in piles and skulls in endless racks**</u>.

"It went on four days and four nights. More than eighty thousand men were killed. Tlacaellel had commanded all the high nobility of Mexico to be present, watching from scented, rose-covered boxes; but eventually the bonds of custom and even of fear were burst by overwhelming horror, and most of the spectators fled, along with many people of the city. Even those who could hide from the sight of what was happening were unable any longer to endure the stench. **But Tlacaellel [the leader of the Empire] at eighty-nine remained to the very end, watching the victims killed at fifteen seconds per man, <u>until the last of the eighty thousand had their hearts torn out before his devouring eyes</u>.**"[3]

Perhaps this bit of history, more than any other, illustrates the truth of the scriptural teaching that the gods of the heathen are actually devils.

Psalms 95:5- "For all the gods of the Gentiles are devils…"

> 1 Cor. 10:20- "But the things which the heathens sacrifice, they sacrifice to devils, and not to God. And I would not that you should be made partakers with devils."

It also demonstrates the connection of idolatry with homosexuality, for the Catholic conquistadors, "After repelling the attack [of the Aztecs], saw their first small temples. '**There were clay idols made of pottery,**' Bernal Diaz tells us, '**with the faces of demons or women and other evil figures <u>that showed Indians committing acts of sodomy with each other</u>.**'"[4]

It was such a problem that Cortes told the Aztecs: "I would have you know that we have come from afar… **<u>Give up your sodomy</u>** and all your other evil practices, for so commands Our Lord God, Whom we believe and Whom we adore…"[5]

St. Francis Xavier (16th century) witnessed the same thing when preaching the faith in pagan Japan. "Fucarandono then went on with the general subject, and afterwards asked Francis Xavier why he forbade **<u>the unnatural lusts so common in Japan</u>**."[6] These unnatural lusts were so common because they worshipped some 33,000 idols at the temple at Kioto.[7] As Romans 1 teaches, unnatural lusts are connected with idolatry.

That's why unnatural lusts are so common among the clergy of the Vatican II sect: they are steeped in idolatry.

Endnotes for Section 24:

---

[1] *The Catechism of the Catholic Church*, by John Paul II, St. Paul Books & Media, 1994, # 2357.
[2] Warren H. Carroll, *Our Lady of Guadalupe and the Conquest of Darkness*, Front Royal, VA: Christendom Press, 1983, pp. 8-11.
[3] Warren H. Carroll, *Our Lady of Guadalupe and the Conquest of Darkness*, pp. 8-11.
[4] Warren H. Carroll, *Our Lady of Guadalupe and the Conquest of Darkness*, p. 17.
[5] Warren H. Carroll, *Our Lady of Guadalupe and the Conquest of Darkness*, p. 33.
[6] *The Life and Letters of St. Francis Xavier* by Henry James Coleridge, S.J. (Originally published: London: Burns and Oates, 1874) Second Reprint, New Delhi: Asian Educational Services, 2004, Vol. 2, p. 320.
[7] *The Life and Letters of St. Francis Xavier* by Henry James Coleridge, S.J., Vol. 2, p. 350.

25. The Vatican II sect promotes idolatry by its general worship of man, by its particular worship of man in the New Mass, and by its acceptance of idolatrous religions

"Those who undertake the tedious task of wading through **even a fraction of the propaganda which has accompanied the New Mass in any Western country would certainly concur that almost invariably it sees the meaning of the Mass in the assembly**, not the sacrifice for which, in theory at least, the assembly comes together... Professor Salleron noted at once [in 1970] that **the New Mass represented the liturgical expression of the Cult of Man...**"[1]

We've already covered in great detail the Vatican II sect's acceptance of idolatrous religions. We must now look at how man has replaced God in the New Mass, and how this is reflected in the seminaries.

Lex Orandi, lex credendi – The Novus Ordo Law of Prayer corresponds to the Novus Ordo Law of Belief: that Man is God

Lex Orandi, lex credendi is a principle in Catholic teaching. It simply means that the manner in which the Church prays or worships reflects what the Church believes. This is so true that when the Protestant heretics split from the Church they most effectively indoctrinated people with the Protestant heresies (denying the Real Presence of Christ in the Eucharist, denying the Mass as sacrifice, etc.) by changing the Mass in ways which reflected their new beliefs (e.g., treating the Eucharist like an ordinary piece of bread, removing references to sacrifice, etc.)

We see the same thing in the Novus Ordo Missae (the New Mass). Let's focus briefly on how the Novus Ordo law of prayer reflects the post-Vatican II teaching (enunciated by John Paul II) that man is God. Even Michael Davies, the late defender of the validity of the New Mass, clearly recognized that the worship of the New Mass is the Cult of Man.

> Michael Davies, *Pope Paul's New Mass*, p. 149: "**Perhaps the most dramatic symbol of the man-centered nature of the new liturgy is the turning round of the altar, or rather, its replacement by a table… Man has turned away from God to face his fellow men**. Not all liturgical experts would state formally that they are **replacing the Cult of God by the Cult of Man**. For some it is a subconscious process. But it is all part of a trend which, if not stated formally, **is nonetheless clear**."[2]

The turning around of the altar, and its replacement by a table *which faces man*, replaces the cult of God with the cult of man.

> Michael Davies, *Pope Paul's New Mass*, p. 141: "The late T.S. Gregory… was very disturbed by the post-conciliar liturgical reforms… he warned: '… But though we can no more change the Catholic Mass than we can change the nature of God… We can even think that **the heart of the matter is not the sacrificed Son of God but the assembled faithful**.' This was a prophetic warning of the nature of the New Mass as defined by its compilers in the notorious Article 7, i.e. the essence of the Mass consists in the coming together of the faithful. **Those who undertake the tedious task of wading through even a fraction of the propaganda which has accompanied the New Mass in any Western country would certainly concur that almost invariably it sees the meaning of the Mass in the assembly**, not the sacrifice for which, in theory at least, the assembly comes together… Professor Salleron noted at once [in 1970] that the New Mass represented the liturgical expression of the Cult of Man…"[3]

Notice this important point: the meaning of the New Mass is in the assembly, according to the Vatican II sect, because its creed is that the assembly – man – is now Christ.

> Antipope John Paul II, Very First Homily, Forever Marking the Beginning of his Pastoral Ministry, Sunday, Oct. 22, 1978: "All of you who are still seeking God, all of you who already have the inestimable good fortune to believe, and also you who are tormented by doubt: please listen once again, today, in this sacred place, to the words uttered by Simon

Peter [Mt. 16:16]. In those words is the faith of the Church. In those same words is the new truth, indeed, **the ultimate and definitive truth about man: the Son of the living God – 'You are the Christ, the Son of the living God.'"**⁴

This replacement of God with man in the (New) Mass is also inculcated in the official Vatican II document on the liturgy (*Sacrosanctum Concilium*).

> Vatican II Constitution on the Sacred Liturgy, *Sacrosanctum Concilium* # 14: "In the restoration and promotion of the sacred liturgy, this **full and active participation by all the people [in the liturgy] is the aim to be considered *before all else*;** for it is the primary and indispensable source from which the faithful are to derive the true Christian spirit."⁵

Regarding this teaching, Michael Davies commented:

> Michael Davies, *Pope Paul's New Mass*, pp. 142-143: "What matters in the Tridentine Mass is the reverence due to God, that the sacrifice should be celebrated in a manner appropriate to the majesty of God to Whom it is offered. **Article 14 of the Constitution on the Sacred Liturgy is unambiguous, attention must be focused upon the congregation rather than God**."⁶

Thus, Vatican II officially teaches that attention in the Mass must be on man rather than on God.

That's why we hear about every kind of abomination at the New Mass, including Clown Masses, Kiddie Masses, Polka Masses, etc., etc., etc., etc., *which are all directed toward making the worship conform to the assembly* – conforming to man, who is really the object of its worship.

Body Surfing at the New Mass

Michael Davies, *Pope Paul's New Mass*, p. 170: "…**the most evident characteristic of the new liturgy is that it is the Cult of Man rather than the Cult of God**. The last thing it intends to convey is that we are in but not of the world; the last thing it intends is that we should be drawn out of our ordinary lives. **The leit-motiv of contemporary writing on the [new] liturgy is that the congregation must be made to feel at home** during Mass and this is best done by insuring that that the liturgy reflects its particular milieu… This is particularly true in the case of children… the Directory on Children's Masses…"[7]

This worship of man in the New Mass was strikingly captured in an April 3, 1978 exposé by *The Boston Globe*.

A Clown Mass that took place in Boston on April 2, 1978

Here is the Eucharistic prayer from this Novus Ordo Clown "Mass," which was celebrated by Fr. Joachim Lally:

> "Send Your Spirit over these gifts of bread and wine and over each of us **so that together we might be the living and breathing and moving Body and Blood of Jesus Christ** Your Son and our Brother."[8]

In this Eucharistic prayer from the Novus Ordo Clown Mass, we see the blatant teaching that **man is Christ**. The prayer stated that "*we* might be the living and breathing and moving Body and Blood of Jesus Christ…"! This is the doctrine of Antichrist, the dissolving of Jesus into everyone (1 John 4:2-3). This religion of man as Christ is also inculcated in a ruling laid down on how Novus Ordo "Communion" must <u>not</u> be distributed.

> Michael Davies, *Pope Paul's New Mass*, p. 340: "Many readers will be shocked to learn that the American hierarchy is actually preparing the way for Catholic acceptance of the concept **that the sacrifice in the Mass is that of Christ being offered in virtue of His presence in <u>the congregation who offer themselves</u>**. In the official Newsletter of the Bishops' Committee on the Liturgy, <u>a ruling was laid down that when distributing Holy Communion a priest must not say: 'Receive the Body of Christ' or 'This is the Body of Christ.' The reason given is that the congregation itself is the Body of Christ</u>.

> "[Bishops' statement]: 'The use of the phrase *The Body of Christ. Amen*, in the Communion rite asserts in a very forceful way the presence and role of the community… **The change to the use of the phrase *The Body of Christ* rather than the long formula which was previously said by the priest has several repercussions in the liturgical renewal. First, <u>it seeks to highlight the important concept of the community as the body of Christ</u>…'"[9]

Notice: the official statement of the Novus Ordo bishops says that a priest must <u>not</u> say "Receive the Body of Christ" or "This is the Body of Christ" when distributing Communion, but rather "the Body of Christ" in order to emphasize that the "Body of Christ" is present in the community! This is the worship of man!

This idolatry is reflected in the Novus Ordo seminaries. At many of these seminaries, **devotion to what they think is the Blessed Sacrament** [remember, the Real Presence of Christ is not present in the New Mass, as we've covered] **is actually discouraged because it fails to recognize the presence of Christ** *in everyone*!

> Michael Rose, *Goodbye, Good Men*, p. 121, an exposé of Novus Ordo Seminaries: "**The [Novus Ordo] seminarian who kneels and receives Communion on the tongue is guilty of** three things: respect, reverence, and piety, which are indicators that the seminarian has **'outdated' understanding of the Real Presence of Christ** in the Eucharist."[10]

Some of those who even kneel for what they deem to be the Blessed Sacrament are rebuked for their "outdated" understanding of the Real Presence of Christ, i.e., "failing" to "understand" that Christ is present in *everyone!* This is the doctrine of Antichrist, fully imbibed by the Vatican II sect. And we know this from first-hand experience. Many years ago one of us visited a Novus Ordo seminary in the Philadelphia area. The New "Mass" was ridiculously irreverent and featured seminarians strumming their guitars at what was more like a folk concert than a Mass. When one of us complained to a seminary authority that the antics at "Mass" were not reverent to Christ who is present in the Blessed Sacrament (which one of us mistakenly thought at the time, not knowing about the invalidity of the New Mass), the seminary authority actually replied, **"But what about Christ who is present in each person?"**

> Michael Rose, *Goodbye, Good Men*, p. 121: "Sister Katarina Schuth of St. Paul's Seminary in Minnesota explains that '**students may accuse faculty of not** supporting their devotions or **loving the Blessed Sacrament, to which faculty respond that they are simply asking students also to see Christ in others**…'"[11]

Notice how the Devil subtly insinuates the worship of man under the false pretext of a concern for others. Hiding evil under the cloak of a false charity or a phony "love" has always been one of the Devil's most effective means of spreading heresy and lies.

These people fail to realize that Pope Pius XII expressly condemned confusing the Mystical Body of Christ (the members of the Church) with the actual Body and Person of Jesus Christ.

> Pope Pius XII, *Mystici Corporis Christi* (# 86), June 29, 1943: "For there are some who neglect the fact that the Apostle Paul has used *metaphorical* language of speaking of this doctrine [of the Mystical Body], and failing to distinguish as they should the precise and proper meaning of the terms the physical body, the social body, and the mystical Body, arrive at a distorted idea of unity. **They make the Divine Redeemer and the members of the Church coalesce in one physical person**, and while they bestow divine attributes on man, they make Christ our Lord subject to error and to human inclination to evil. **But Catholic faith and the writings of the holy Fathers reject such false teaching as impious and sacrilegious; and to the mind of the Apostle of the Gentiles it is equally abhorrent**, for although he brings Christ and His Mystical Body into a wonderfully intimate union, **he nevertheless distinguishes one from the other, as Bridegroom and Bride**."[12]

We will conclude this section with the following mind-boggling story of what occurred in St. Mark's Novus Ordo Minor Seminary. This story takes this doctrine of man as Christ to its full conclusion. It shows us how this doctrine of the assembly as Christ rules in the New Church. It illustrates how the Vatican II sect, the New Mass and the Novus Ordo seminaries are unspeakably demonic.

Michael Rose, *Goodbye, Good Men*, p. 166: "One of the most memorable moments for Trigilio **came during a rare benediction of the Blessed Sacrament prayer service [at St. Mark's] in the chapel. 'The priest took the monstrance,'** Trigilio recounted, **'and held it at waist level, <u>walked over to the tabernacle, and replaced the Blessed Sacrament. Then he took a clay pot that looked like a Grecian urn, holding it much higher than he had held the monstrance, carried it over to the altar, and placed it in the spot where the Blessed Sacrament had been; he then incensed the pot and knelt before it, saying, 'Abba, you are the potter, we are the clay</u>.'** There was nothing in the pot, but the priest was incensing it, and praying to it…' This, said Trigilio, was the attitude of many of the formation team at St. Mark's: in short, idolatrous."[13]

The worship of man (the assembly) as Christ in the New Mass had so fully consumed this apostate Novus Ordo "priest" that he worshipped the clay pot, just as he worships the assembly of people in the New Mass. And this is precisely what the Novus Ordo/Vatican II religion of John Paul II is all about. It's why the Assisi interreligious apostasy has been fully embraced by the Vatican II clergy, whereby all religious leaders, including Christ-deniers, are accepted. They are invited and accepted because (according to the false Vatican II religion) <u>their dignity as men is more important than the fact that they reject Christ</u>.

So, idolatry exists on three fronts in the Vatican II religion: 1) the worship of an invalidly consecrated piece of bread in the New Mass, since the form of consecration in the New Mass doesn't suffice for validity (as we've shown); 2) the worship of man by conforming the service to the assembly, rather than to God, by the turning around of the altar and many other things; and 3) the elevation of man's dignity above the teaching of Christ by accepting men's false religions, despite the fact that they contradict the teaching of Christ.

This worship of man is a main reason why the Novus Ordo "priesthood" is a cesspool of abominations, homosexuality and unspeakable perversion. As we've seen, a study of the missionaries reveals that where idolatry is common (such as in mission territories fully under Satan's yoke), homosexuality is common. The idolatry of the New Mass is a major factor in the *massive* perversion of the Novus Ordo "priests."

Obviously, these facts should show us once again why the Novus Ordo Mass can never be attended for any reason under pain of grave sin.

> Pope St. Pius X, *E Supremi Apostolatus*, Oct. 4, 1903: "While, on the other hand, and this according to the same apostle is **the distinguishing mark of Antichrist, man has with infinite temerity put himself in the place of God**."[14]

Endnotes for Section 25:

[1] Michael Davies, *Pope Paul's New Mass*, Kansas City, MO: Angelus Press, p. 141.
[2] Michael Davies, *Pope Paul's New Mass*, p. 149.
[3] Michael Davies, *Pope Paul's New Mass*, p. 141.
[4] *L'Osservatore Romano* (the Vatican's Newspaper), Nov. 2, 1978, p. 1.
[5] Walter M. Abbott, *The Documents of Vatican II*, The America Press, 1966, p. 144.
[6] Michael Davies, *Pope Paul's New Mass*, pp. 142-143.
[7] Michael Davies, *Pope Paul's New Mass*, p. 170.
[8] Michael Davies, *Pope Paul's New Mass*, pp. 197-198.
[9] Michael Davies, *Pope Paul's New Mass*, p. 340.
[10] Michael Rose, *Goodbye, Good Men*, Washington, D.C.: Regnery Publishing, Inc., 2002, p. 121.
[11] Michael Rose, *Goodbye, Good Men*, p. 121.
[12] *The Papal Encyclicals*, by Claudia Carlen, Raleigh: The Pierian Press, 1990, Vol. 4 (1939-1958), p. 54.
[13] Michael Rose, *Goodbye, Good Men*, p. 166.
[14] *The Papal Encyclicals*, Vol. 3 (1903-1939), p. 6.

26. The Deplorable State of "Catholic" Parochial and High Schools

"I believed in the beginning it would be easy to stop <u>the filthy material from being taught in schools</u>. I was confident that if any decent person would just look at the material, they would be repulsed and stop it immediately. <u>I was naive to think the Archbishop or his "department heads" cared anything for souls</u>."[1]

Since the Vatican II revolution, the once-Catholic school system has been laid waste. Even many supporters of the Vatican II/Novus Ordo "Church," who have made themselves vigorous defenders of the antipopes we've exposed in the preceding sections, have been forced to abandon the Novus Ordo "Catholic" school system in droves. The heresy and immorality of the "Catholic" school system allows one to say that it's no longer Catholic except in name only. Chief among its many problems is sex education.

Pope Pius XI condemned sex education. In doing so, he pointed out that it's not ignorance of such things which lead to sins in this regard, but rather exposure to such enticements.

> Pope Pius XI, *Divini illius magistri*, Dec. 31, 1931: "But much more pernicious are those opinions and teachings regarding the following of nature absolutely as a guide. These enter upon a certain phase of human education which is full of difficulties, namely, that which has to do with moral integrity and chastity. **For here and there a great many foolishly and dangerously hold and advance the method of education, which is disgustingly called 'sexual,' since they foolishly feel** that they can, by merely natural means, after discarding every religious and pious aid, warn youth against sensuality and excess, by initiating and instructing all of them, without distinction of sex, even publicly, in hazardous doctrines; and what is worse, **by exposing them prematurely to the occasions, in order that their minds having become accustomed**, as they say, may grow hardened to the dangers of puberty.
>
> "But in this such persons gravely err, because they do not take into account the inborn weakness of human nature, and that law planted within our members, which, to use the words of the Apostle Paul, 'fights against the law of my mind' (Rom. 7:23); and besides, they rashly deny what we have learned from daily experience, that <u>**young people certainly more than others fall into disgraceful acts, not so much because of an imperfect knowledge of the intellect as because of a will exposed to enticements**</u> and unsupported by divine assistance."[2]

In blatant disregard of this teaching, sex education programs, including graphic ones, are implemented in all "Catholic schools," thus corrupting the innocence of Catholic children from their earliest years. In fact, it would be a gross understatement to merely call these programs "sex education." They are more correctly labeled "sex initiation" or indoctrination in filth. As partially quoted at the beginning of this section, one mother, whose child was receiving this "sex education" in the "Catholic" school, expressed her outrage to the "bishop"; but to no avail:

> "The last two months have been a nightmare. **I believed in the beginning it would be easy to stop <u>the filthy material from being taught in schools</u>. I was confident that if any decent person would just look at the material, they would be repulsed and stop it immediately. <u>I was naive to think the Archbishop or his "department heads" cared anything for souls</u>.** Instead, what I found was a Chancery full of people with **deadened consciences and deformed judgments----- "white washed sepulchers with**

dead men's bones." Every parent in this diocese should be alarmed that such people have been put in charge of caring for and teaching innocent and vulnerable children. It is scandalous!"[3]

To illustrate the perversion of this "sex education," it's necessary to expose some specifics. If specifics are never given, most never realize how bad the situation really is. In the Diocese of San Antonio, for instance, the book *Growing in Love* is used for sex education grades K-8. This book is also used in dioceses all over the country. A complaining mother noted about this book:

> "The sexology begins <u>in kindergarten</u> where children learn correct body terms such as: penis, testes, breasts, vagina, buttocks, anus, urinate, and defecate. **They are introduced to the idea of self-touch (masturbation) "For comfort or pleasurable sensation."** Each year the program explores sexual activity a little more in depth rehashing body parts and progressing to <u>how-to instructions</u> regarding French kissing, foreplay, orgasms, **oral and anal sex**. If that isn't bad enough, *Growing In Love* teaches about sex toys (dildos and vibrators), and sadism and masochism."[4]

Another man noted:

> "<u>*Growing in Love*, is so utterly disgusting and depraved in its explicit description of perverted sex acts including oral sex techniques for male and female heterosexuals and homosexuals</u>, and so in-your-face with 'gay and lesbian agit-prop,' that it just might spark enough public outrage to force the American hierarchy and the Vatican to bring this fifty-year anti-life, anti-child, anti-family and anti-God experiment to a merciful end."[5]

This book is used to educate children in "Catholic" schools! We've covered in great detail how evil and heretical the Vatican II sect is, but it's still somewhat difficult to believe that this is being taught. We're talking about a full demonic takeover here: the very education given in "Catholic" schools encourages the youngest children to commit mortal sins (such as masturbation) which will send them to Hell forever!

> Matthew 18:6- "But he that shall scandalize one of these little ones that believe in me, it were better for him that a millstone should be hanged about his neck, and that he should be drowned in the depth of the sea."

And while this abominable and satanic *sex initiation* is taught in "Catholic" schools, it's actually illegal to present such sexually graphic material, as is found in *Growing in Love,* in public schools in the state of Louisiana.[6] The book *Growing in Love* bears the Nihil obstat of Rev. Richard L. Schaefer, Censor DePutatus and the imprimatur of Archbishop Jerome Hanus of the Archdiocese of Dubuque (IA).

In light of the above situation, it's not surprising that basic Catholic dogma and morality are rejected or almost universally ignored by "Catholics" who have come from these schools. Immorality, immodesty and indifferentism are rampant, and in many ways the Novus Ordo "Catholics" are as bad or worse than the pagans. For instance, **almost all "Catholic" high schools host proms and balls which feature Rap, Rock, and Heavy Metal music** – as well as lascivious dress and dancing. There's no aversion to the modern culture and the worldly celebrations, which Scripture and traditional Catholic Faith teach are at variance with the ways of God. **Rather, there is a union of pagan culture and the Novus Ordo school system.** Since this is the opposite of what a real Catholic education imparts, this shows again that the Novus Ordo school system is devoid of the true Catholic Faith.

> Pope Leo XIII, *Exeunte iam anno* (# 10), Dec. 25, 1888: "Now the whole essence of a Christian life is to reject the corruption of the world and to oppose constantly any indulgence in it…"[7]

People go through four years of "Catholic" high school without having been taught the concept of mortal sin.[8] As the aforementioned mother noted, "It is a real tragedy that in today's Catholic schools, children today can recite the litany of sexual body parts, but cannot recite the Lord's Ten Commandments."[9] A study written by a professor of sociology at Notre Dame concluded that American "Catholic" teens are "largely indifferent to faith and practice matters."[10] That revealing assessment is also probably an understatement if we consider that it comes from a professor who teaches at one of the post-Vatican II sect's universities.

Both in America and abroad, the post-Vatican II "Catholic" school system is fraught with religious indifferentism and a celebration of false religions. For instance, Holy Rood Roman Catholic Primary School in South Yorkshire, England – approved by the Diocese of Hallam – held a Sikh and a Jewish Day in order to celebrate these false religions.[11]

Jewish Day at Holy Rood "Catholic" Primary School

This is so evil and so sad; they're turning these little children into apostates.

The post-Vatican II "Catholic" school system is a complete joke, and perhaps the only reason it still has even a semblance of respect or recognition as "Catholic" from the modern world is because of its athletic programs. The "Catholic Leagues" are now identified with competitive high school athletics, which boast some of the top sports programs in the country, especially in football and basketball. The "Catholic Leagues" are certainly not outstanding for their formation of people in the Catholic Faith, which is non-existent.

Since the Catholic Faith is no longer held to be necessary for salvation, Novus Ordo priests no longer tell families they are obliged to send their children to "Catholic" schools. "The number of Catholic schoolchildren in the Archdiocese of Boston has plunged from 152,869 in 1965 to 50,742 today, and the archdiocese has closed multiple schools during each of the last several years."[12]

The statistics of decline for the U.S. as a whole are even more striking.

> "-- Catholic schools. **Almost half of all Catholic high schools in the United States have closed since 1965**. The student population has fallen from 700,000 to 386,000. Parochial schools suffered an even greater decline. Some 4,000 have disappeared, **and the number of pupils attending has fallen below 2 million – from 4.5 million. Though the number of U.S. Catholics has risen by 20 million** since 1965, Jones' statistics show that the power of Catholic belief and devotion to the Faith are not nearly what they were."[13]

In considering these figures, one must remember that the population of professing Catholics increased by 20 million since 1965.[14] Thus, if the number of Catholic schoolchildren had remained the same since 1965, that would represent, in itself, a tremendous failure. But when we consider that not only has the number not remained the same, but almost half of all Catholic high schools have closed, and parochial school attendance had decreased by 2.5 million, this represents a catastrophic crisis and a deep-seated spiritual rot. It's all tied up with what we've been covering and exposing in the first part of this book: the Vatican II antipopes, the New Mass and the Vatican II apostasy.

Endnotes for Section 26:

[1] Quoted in a discussion on the topic: http://www.dotm.org/sexed-notes.htm
[2] Denzinger, *The Sources of Catholic Dogma*, B. Herder Book. Co., Thirtieth Edition, 1957, no. 2214.
[3] http://www.dotm.org/sexed-notes.htm
[4] http://www.dotm.org/gil-flores.htm
[5] http://www.diocesereport.com/diocese_report/pr/homo_kinder_pr.shtml
[6] http://www.dotm.org/gil-new.htm
[7] *The Papal Encyclicals*, by Claudia Carlen, Raleigh: The Pierian Press, 1990, Vol. 2 (1878-1903), p. 199.
[8] Personal testimony given to MHFM.
[9] http://www.dotm.org/gil-flores.htm
[10] Christian Smith, *Soul Searching: The Religious and Spiritual Lives of American Teenagers* (Oxford, 2005); quoted by *Inside Fordham Online*, Jan. 19, 2007.
[11] http://holyroodschool.catholicweb.com/index.cfm/NewsItem?SlideID=51536&ID=159375&From=Home#headline
[12] Michael Paulson, "Church Turns to Critic to Aid Catholic Schools," *The Boston Globe*, Oct. 23, 2005, http://www.boston.com.
[13] http://www.townhall.com/opinion/columns/patbuchanan/2002/12/11/165161.html
[14] http://www.townhall.com/opinion/columns/patbuchanan/2002/12/11/165161.html

27. The Deplorable State of "Catholic" Colleges and Universities

Every "Catholic" college or university in communion with Benedict XVI is rife with heresy and indifferentism and/or the promotion of the gay agenda and/or attacks on Sacred Scripture and/or attacks on the historicity of Our Lord or all of the above. Honorary degrees are frequently given to pro-abortionists. Pro-abortionists are often commencement speakers at these "Catholic" colleges, where the most outrageous scandals abound. Now we will look at just a few snapshots of the heresy, apostasy and immorality that characterize "Catholic" colleges and universities. One could write an entire book filled with examples of what we're about to cover.

In 2004, 29 so-called "Catholic Colleges" actually showed the abominable play, *The Vagina Monologues*.[1] In February of 2005, 27 showed the play.[2] People need to consider the level of apostasy that such a fact reveals; this outrage was actually performed on these "Catholic" campuses, where they have members of the clergy in positions of authority! In the same year, at least 16 "Catholic" colleges had pro-abortion commencement speakers. In May 2005, "Catholic" Marymount Manhattan College had Hillary Clinton as commencement speaker.[3] Clinton has spoken at other "Catholic" colleges, including Canisius in Buffalo, NY.[4] Non-Catholic and pro-abortion commencement speakers are so common at "Catholic" universities that it would be a major project to keep track of them all.

Loyola University Chicago, "Chicago's Jesuit University," actually welcomed Kyan Douglas, the homosexual actor from "Queer Eye for the Straight Guy," with a prominent link and picture on its website.[5] The same university openly promotes lesbianism and homosexuality.[6]

A "study conducted by the University of California-Los Angeles showed that Catholic students' moral views were weaker, rather than stronger, after four years on a 'Catholic' college campus. At thirty-eight of the Catholic colleges surveyed, 37.9 percent of Catholic freshmen said in 1997 that abortion should be legal. Four years later, as seniors, 51.7 percent supported legalized abortion."[7]

The U.S. school named after Mary – the University of Notre Dame – has twice <u>hosted a Queer Film Festival</u>. Its head of theology, "Fr." Richard McBrien, denies the most basic Catholic dogmas.

Jesuit University of San Francisco offers benefits to homosexual couples.[8]

Santa Clara University, a "Jesuit" institution in California, featured two speakers from the National Center for Lesbian Rights in Feb. 2004 to promote legal issues facing homosexual partners.[9]

DePaul University, the largest "Catholic" university in America, offers a minor in "Queer Studies."[10]

The "Catholic University of America," like all the major "Catholic" colleges and universities, is rife with heresy and apostasy. On April 26, 2006, CUA hosted an interfaith luncheon. "**Approximately 100 guests, representing Roman Catholic, Eastern Orthodox/Oriental Christian, Protestant, Jewish, Muslim and Eastern faith groups**, participated in a 1 p.m. luncheon hosted by Rev. David M. O'Connell, C.M., President of Catholic University. In his welcoming remarks to those assembled, Father O'Connell reflected that religion has always played a significant role in the development of world cultures,"[11] *as if their false religions of the Devil were a positive and God-willed aspect of the establishment of cultures.*

"Fr." O'Connell **also encouraged them in their own prayers**, commemorated the spirit of Assisi, and "joined together in prayer" with the infidels, pagans and heretics. Someone we know who attended CUA called it the most wicked place he's ever been: the spirit of apostasy from the true Faith in a place claiming to represent it was such a unique and deep form of evil that one could feel it.

"Catholic" Seton Hall University is a home for people of all religions. Its official website declares: "**Whether you are looking for a nearby synagogue, a Muslim group to join for Friday prayers** or an interfaith Bible study, Campus Ministry [at Seton Hall] will connect you with students who share in your beliefs."[12] This is total apostasy, of course – encouraging people to practice Judaism, Islam, etc.

Seton Hall also gave the "Sandra Day O'Connor Award" to pro-abortion judge Maryanne Trump Barry. Sandra Day O'Connor, who is herself pro-abortion and was the key vote in striking down the anti-abortion laws in almost 30 states, presented the award named after herself to the pro-abortion judge who struck down New Jersey's partial-birth abortion ban.[13] There are only two words for this: insanity and apostasy.

"Catholic" Marquette University promotes interfaith apostasy. As one of many examples, its website states: "University Ministry will hold an interfaith prayer for peace… Please join us to hear the call from **religious leaders from diverse faith traditions** and denominations **as they join their voices in prayer** for a peaceful resolution to the potential for war in Iraq."[14]

"Catholic" Duquesne University is particularly open about its apostasy. Its website also goes so far as to compile a list with the addresses of the local non-Catholic churches and temples so that its students can go worship at them. **This list includes Protestant and schismatic churches, synagogues, mosques and the Hindu Jain Temple!** So much for it being a "Catholic" University dedicated to the one true Faith!

> "The Office of Spiritan Campus Ministry has compiled this list for all students to use so that they may practice their faith while away at school. If no listing of a time is given, a phone number is listed to call and inquire. The starred locations (*) are within walking distance. Duquesne is an urban campus with many churches and other places of worship nearby. **We will be happy to help you find one that suits your needs**."[15]

"Catholic" **Xavier University** in Ohio openly encourages people to practice non-Catholic religions. It "**provides opportunities for worship** and spiritual development **for those of all faith traditions**. Information about Protestant, Jewish and other local faith communities is available at the office of campus ministry."[16] This is total apostasy.

"Jesuit" **Georgetown University** features a course called "Problem of God." The goal of the course is to bring about an acceptance of all religions.

> "The [non-Catholic] students admit they were skeptical when first learning the course was part of their curriculum. When Kholoud told her family she would be taking a class called Problem of God taught by a Catholic priest, they wondered if she would be converted.

> "'**He's not here to do that,' Kholoud says of Maher**. 'He's here to talk about faith. My idea is different from his, but **he helps us develop acceptance of other faiths**.' Maher also helped lay such fears [that he wanted to convert anyone] to rest during the first week of class when he said matter-of-factly: 'I'm sure that people will be asking, '**Does Father Maher want to convert us?' ... Of course, the answer is yes. I want to convert all of us from a childhood understanding and grasp on our faith to an adult understanding and grasp on our faith**.'"[17]

So, the "priest" teaching at "Catholic" Georgetown University admits that he doesn't want to convert people to the Catholic Faith, but rather to "convert" them to a deeper understanding of their own faiths, whatever they may be. And the purpose of his course "Problem of God" is to bring about an acceptance of all religions. This is <u>total</u> apostasy.

2006 Interfaith Apostasy at Georgetown in commemoration of Assisi[18]

On the 20th anniversary of John Paul II's interreligious prayer meeting at Assisi, many "Catholic" colleges and universities held small gatherings of the same type to commemorate the event. "Catholic" Georgetown held *International Prayer for Peace 2006: A Meeting of Peoples and Religions in the Spirit of Assisi*.[19] Georgetown also offers Ministry programs for the promotion of Judaism, Islam, Protestantism and Eastern "Orthodoxy."

> "In addition to extensive worship services offered by specific religious traditions, **the Office of Campus Ministry provides opportunities for interfaith prayer** and dialogue throughout the school year. Events include interfaith dialogues, **interfaith meditation**, Hallelujah Shabbat, **Interfaith Seder** and an interfaith art exhibit." [20]

This means Georgetown promotes the practice of Judaism directly on its website.

> "**Protestant, Jewish and Muslim worship takes place on campus [at Georgetown] in services organized by the Office of Campus Ministry** and student groups. Bible studies, daily retreats and three Sunday worship services in the Protestant tradition take place on campus. **The Jewish Chaplains and the Jewish Student Association hold a Shabbat dinner each Friday. A Muslim prayer room in Copley Hall is used for Islamic prayer** and worship daily and there is a large Muslim community worship service each Friday. On Tuesday evenings there is an Orthodox prayer service in Copley Crypt."[21]

"Jesuit" **Boston College** is likewise fraught with apostasy. On Feb. 9, 2005, it hosted a panel discussion on the American "bishops" August 2002 document *Reflections on Covenant and Mission*. This notorious document stated that "… campaigns that target Jews for conversion to Christianity are no longer theologically acceptable in the Catholic Church." **Three Boston College "theologians" addressed the issue: "Should Catholics Seek to Convert Jews (If Jews are in a true covenant with God)?"** All three indicated – in their modernist way of saying a lot while saying almost nothing – that there is no necessity whatsoever for Jews to be converted. The clearest answer came from Boston College "theologian" Philip Cunningham, who stated:

> "If, as Christians would certainly posit, the birth of the Church was part of the divine plan, **then Christians must contemplate the possibility that the Jewish "no" to the Gospel and the development of the post-Temple rabbinic heritage were also parts of the divine plan."**[22]

"No" to the Gospel may be part of the divine plan, according to "Catholic" Boston College.

Arguably the most "prestigious" "Catholic" university in the world is **the Angelicum** in Rome. It promotes the same apostasy exemplified by all the other "Catholic" colleges and universities. It offers a course on ecumenism which promotes ecumenism in line with *The Directory for the Application of the Principles and Norms on Ecumenism*, which was promulgated by John Paul II.[23] This incredible Directory discourages converting non-Catholics, promotes interfaith worship services, sharing of churches with false religions and sects, etc., as covered earlier in this book.

The Gregorian in Rome is another famous "Catholic" institution. Well, the former Anglican "Archbishop" of Canterbury, George Carey, teaches ecumenism there.[24] This means that a non-Catholic heretic – a layman who posed as a valid bishop – is teaching heretical ecumenism to Novus Ordo seminarians and clergy. We suspect that they won't be covering the invalidity of Anglican orders.

We could continue for many pages documenting the apostasy, immorality and scandal at the so-called "Catholic" colleges and universities, but one should see very clearly that the apostasy of the educational institutions of the Vatican II sect is universal. It goes from the local college of the Vatican II sect here in America, all the way to the most prestigious ones in Rome. This is simply because they're all following the new religion of the Vatican II sect. They are, like the Vatican II sect that endorses them, Catholic in name only.

Endnotes for Section 27:

[1] http://www.tfp.org/student_action/activities/protests/monologues_protest.htm
[2] Tim Drake, "No Longer Catholic," *This Rock*, Nov. 2005 issue, El Cajon, CA: Catholic Answers.
[3] Tim Drake, "No Longer Catholic," *This Rock*, Nov. 2005 issue, El Cajon, CA: Catholic Answers.
[4] http://transcripts.cnn.com/TRANSCRIPTS/0502/01/ltm.06.html
[5] http://www.catholiccitizens.org/press/contentview.asp?c=12556; http://www.luc.edu/info/kyan.shtml
[6] http://www.luc.edu/orgs/rainbow/
[7] Tim Drake, "No Longer Catholic," *This Rock*, Nov. 2005 issue, El Cajon, CA: Catholic Answers.
[8] http://www.sffaith.com/ed/articles/2004/0405jh.htm
[9] http://seattletimes.nwsource.com/html/localnews/2001869154_seattleusex02m.html
[10] http://www.npr.org/templates/story/story.php?storyId=5173232
[11] http://publicaffairs.cua.edu/news/06PeaceLuncheonFinal.htm
[12] http://www.shu.edu/catholic_mission/index.html
[13] http://www.lifenews.com/state512.html
[14] http://www.marquette.edu/pages/home/resourcecommons/campus/archives/2003/02_10_2003/
[15] http://www.campusministry.duq.edu/worshipsites.html

16 http://www.xavier.edu/campus_ministry/
17 http://explore.georgetown.edu/news/?ID=14756
18 www.georgetown.edu
19 http://prayerforpeace.georgetown.edu/
20 http://explore.georgetown.edu/documents/?DocumentID=12052
21 http://explore.georgetown.edu/documents/?DocumentID=12052
22 http://www.bc.edu/research/cjl/meta-elements/texts/center/events/cunningham_9Feb05.htm
23 http://www.angelicum.org/facolta/paginephp/dxcorsiteo.php?xt=t3e&xa=2005
24 http://www.ianpaisley.org/article.asp?ArtKey=ecumenism

Developing Leaders in Mind, Heart and Spirit

Our Catholic tradition is evident in other ways, too. More than 40 priests reside on campus (including student residence halls) and many serve as faculty or staff. Mass is offered three times a day, including Sunday evenings (for those of you who aren't morning people). Campus Ministry also provides opportunities for spiritual counseling and exploration.

A Home for People of All Faiths

We strive to meet the spiritual needs of all students, regardless of faith. Although the majority of our students are Catholic (about 70 percent, according to information voluntarily submitted on admissions applications), there also are significant groups of Jewish, Muslim, Protestant and Buddhist students, among others. <u>Whether you are looking for a nearby synagogue, a Muslim group to join for Friday prayers or an interfaith Bible study, Campus Ministry will connect you with students who share in</u> your beliefs.

No matter what your faith, the Catholic ideals and values that we will share with you while you are at Seton Hall will make you feel good about who you are and your ability to make a real difference in the community.

Seton Hall University •

A striking image of the Vatican II apostasy promoted on the website of "Catholic" Seton Hall University, which we covered in this section (underlining added by us)

28. The Annulment Fiasco – The Vatican II Sect's *De Facto* acceptance of Divorce and Remarriage

> Pope Leo XIII, *Dum Multa* (# 2), Dec. 24, 1902: "It follows then that **the marriage of Christians when fully accomplished… cannot be dissolved for any reason other than the death of either spouse**, according to the holy words: 'What God has joined, let no man put asunder.'"[1]

According to Catholic dogma, the essential properties of marriage are unity and indissolubility. A marriage validly contracted and consummated is binding until death separates the spouses. *"There is no such thing as the annulment of a consummated sacramental marriage. The expression is sometimes used inaccurately for the declaration of nullity of a union reputed to be a marriage but which upon examination is proved not to have been such."*[2] It's important for us to understand that there is no such thing as "an annulment" of a consummated marriage, but only a declaration of nullity that a certain union never was a marriage to begin with <u>if there is clear-cut evidence proving that a particular union was not validly contracted.</u>

With this in mind, it's easy to see why "annulments" (that is, declarations that certain unions *were not actually marriages to begin with*) <u>were traditionally given very rarely</u>. Such cases are extremely difficult to prove, and if there's a doubt about whether a particular union was a validly contracted marriage, the Church presumes the validity of the marriage.

> Canon 1014, 1917 Code of Canon Law: "Marriage enjoys the favor of law; therefore <u>in doubt the validity of marriage is to be upheld</u> until the contrary is proven, with due regard for the prescription of Canon 1127."[3]

A good example of "an annulment" that could be given on solid grounds would be if a woman were to "marry" (through no fault of her own) a man whom she later discovered to be a validly ordained priest. Since priests cannot enter into matrimony (canon 1972),[4] the union between this priest and the woman was not a valid marriage. She would be given a decree of nullity that she was never married. She would be free to marry another person.

Another obvious example for an "annulment" would be if the person you "married" turned out to have been married before, but he hid this information from you. An example from the past would be if a woman married a slave whom she actually thought was a free man, but was not. A declaration of nullity would be given, since that particular error about the person one is marrying is so grave that it renders the marriage invalid (canon 1083.2).[5]

In all of these cases, the reason must be grave and the evidence that there never was a valid marriage must be <u>clear</u>. That's why **<u>only 338 annulments were granted in 1968 in the U.S., when the pre-Vatican II teaching on marriage was still held by most</u>**.

However, with the explosion of the post-Vatican II apostasy, the teaching of the indissolubility of marriage has been thrown out the window along with the other dogmas. **<u>From 1984 to 1994, the Vatican II Church in the U.S. granted just under 59,000 annually</u>**, even though the number of Catholic marriages has fallen one third since 1965![6]

In 2002 alone, the Vatican II sect granted 50,000 annulments in the United States![7] **An astounding 97% of all annulments requested are granted in the United States!** This means that almost everyone who wants an "annulment" of his or her marriage gets one!

> Fr. Leonard Kennedy: "From 1984 to 1994 **it was 97% for First Instance trials**. All cases however have to have a second trial. **The percentage of decisions overturned in the United States is 4/10 of 1%.**"[8]

This means that almost 100 percent of requested annulments are granted in the first trial, with the chances of such an annulment being overturned in a second trial being <u>less than 1/2 of 1%</u>! This is a total rejection of the indissolubility of marriage <u>in fact and in deed</u>. This annulment fiasco was the subject of Sheila Rauch Kennedy's famous book, *Shattered Faith: A Woman's Struggle to Stop the Catholic Church from Annulling Her Marriage*. This allowance of divorce and remarriage under the pretext of phony marriage annulments has destroyed countless families and mocked the Catholic Church before the world.

Things are so bad that, "**<u>There is advertising in church bulletins, Catholic newspapers, and even the secular press, that annulments are available</u>**, sometimes with a suggested guarantee that they will be granted. '**Some invitations practically promise an annulment to all who apply**. The promotional efforts . . . may evoke responses from . . . spouses who dream of greener marital pastures but would not seriously consider separation and divorce were annulment not presented as a convenient and acceptable alternative.'"[9]

Basically anyone who wants a declaration that they aren't married can get one. They issue them for all kinds of ridiculous reasons, such as alcoholism, personality incompatibility, etc., etc., etc., none of which are valid grounds. **11.68% of annulments today are granted because of "defective consent," which involves at least one of the parties not having sufficient knowledge or maturity to know what was involved in marriage!**[10] In other words, if after a few years of marriage a person discovers that he doesn't like his spouse anymore, he wasn't properly "mature" or didn't know what he was getting into when he decided to exchange the perpetual vows with this person. This is obviously absurd, completely bogus and outrageous.

The people that think they are free to marry based on such false and dishonest grounds are deceiving themselves; they are placing themselves on the road to damnation. And the Vatican II sect confirms them on their false path. When people take the marriage vows, it's until they are parted by death. They wanted the benefits of marriage; they're the ones that chose to contract it. The obligations accompanying marriage didn't seem to bother them when they took advantage of their marriage rights. It's their own fault if, after some time, they don't like their choice or weren't prepared for it. **The capitulation of the Vatican II sect on this issue is another proof of its worship of man,** appeasing man at all costs, **relieving him of all his responsibilities and contracts before God because they're inconvenient for him or not to his liking.** This abominable annulment fiasco is one of the most despicable aspects of the Vatican II sect.

Robert H. Vasoli, author of the book *What God Has Joined Together*, was part of a totally valid marriage for 15 years when he suddenly found himself as a respondent for the annulment of his own marriage. He writes that the scandal generated by an annulment which people who know the spouses can't possibly approve of "is infinitesimal compared to the scandal generated by the tribunal system. The system as a whole is scandalous."[11]

The antipopes of the Vatican II sect do nothing to curb this outrage or enforce the sanctity of the marriage bond. This mockery of marriage by the issuance of phony annulments continues inexorably under their watch like lava spilling out of an erupting volcano.

Based on these amazing facts, one can truly say that the Vatican II sect allows divorce and remarriage, proving once again that it's not the Catholic Church, but a counterfeit sect of the final days. Notice how differently the true popes of the Catholic Church acted when confronted with these problems.

While the Vatican II sect denies the indissolubility of marriage, the Catholic Church and the true popes have defended it at all costs

In the year 995, King Robert of France put away his wife Suzanne and "married" Bertha of Chartres. Despite the problems which might have arisen from opposing the powerful king, **Pope Gregory V condemned Robert's union with Bertha as bigamous and ordered him to put Bertha away or face excommunication**. Robert then sent an ambassador to Rome in the hope that the pope would compromise; but to no avail:

> "…**Pope Gregory V could only say with his Lord: 'What God has joined together, let no man put asunder.'** Almost a thousand years before, Jesus Christ had given to His disciples this, which seemed to them one of the hardest of his teachings. Still it re-echoed down the corridors of time, the terror of the mighty, the shield of the innocent, as the one hundred and thirty-eighth of His Vicars on earth spoke His mind once more on the sacred, unbreakable bond of marriage, on behalf of Princess Suzanne. **When King Robert still did not send Bertha away, he was excommunicated, about the end of the year 988**. Three years later he finally submitted, and sent her away."[12]

In 1141, the sister of Queen Eleanor of France, Peronelle, desired marriage to one of the richest nobles and most powerful officials at court, the Seneschal Raoul of Vermandois. The problem was that the Seneschal Raoul of Vermandois was already married to another Eleanor. A three-man commission of bishops, certainly influenced by King Louis VI, pronounced Raoul's marriage to Eleanor invalid on the specious grounds of consanguinity. He promptly married Peronelle. **St. Bernard denounced the decision of the bishops in words that apply strikingly to the post-Vatican II situation, with one crucial difference**:

> "**St. Bernard denounced the three bishops as 'shameless men… who, despite the law of God, have not scrupled to separate what God has joined together**. Nor is this all. They have gone further and added one sin to another by uniting what should not be united. The sacred rites of the Church have been violated and the robes of Christ have been torn, and to make matters worse <u>this has been done by those very persons whose business it ought to be to mend them</u>.' He did not hesitate to point out that Louis' own marriage to Eleanor was within the prohibited degrees of consanguinity, yet had received no Papal dispensation. **<u>Pope Innocent III responded in 1142 by excommunicating Raoul of Vermandois and imposing an interdict on his lands</u>, and suspending the three bishops.**"[13]

In this episode we see a striking analogy to the present situation. St. Bernard denounces the bishops for granting a phony annulment when there weren't grounds to do so, and condemns them for tearing the union of matrimony when it is their business to see that it remains. But the difference is that St. Bernard was living when there was a true pope, unlike those living today. The true pope, Innocent III, promptly backed up St. Bernard by excommunicating the culprit and suspending the bishops. Nothing like this is done by the antipopes of the Vatican II sect, of course, because they are not Catholic and their sect endorses divorce and re-marriage under the cover of easy and fraudulent annulments.

In 1193, the powerful King Philip II of France announced that he would seek an annulment one day after marrying Princess Ingeborg. The French bishops obediently granted Philip an annulment without even giving Ingeborg a hearing. **But in 1195 Pope Celestine III overruled the annulment** given by the French bishops and demanded that Philip take Ingeborg back; he further warned him that no future marriage of his would be recognized by the Church while Ingeborg lived.

> "The king resisted furiously, and in 1196 bigamously married Agnes of Meran; but Pope Celestine III and his successor… continued to insist on Ingeborg's rights. **In January 1200 Pope Innocent placed the whole kingdom of France under an interdict to enforce them**. Philip made a pretense of yielding, but his heart remained hardened; only thirteen years later did he finally take Ingeborg back and reign with her at his side. Once again, **the Vicars of Christ had defended a royal marriage bond regardless of the political cost.**"[14]

Perhaps the most obvious case that should be mentioned in this regard is the Anglican Schism. The Anglican Schism (16th century) resulted from the Catholic Church's just refusal to grant King Henry VIII of England an annulment of his valid marriage to Catherine of Aragon. King Henry VIII wanted it to be considered invalid because he desired to marry Anne Boleyn (whom some scholars suggest was actually his illegitimate daughter),[15] so Henry put away Catherine and invalidly married Anne Boleyn. On July 11, 1533, Pope Clement VII excommunicated King Henry VIII and commanded all the faithful to avoid him for putting away Catherine and sacrilegiously and invalidly "marrying" Anne. The next year (1534), King Henry VIII declared himself head of the Church in England. He denied that the pope had supreme jurisdiction over the universal Church by denying the pope's authority over the Church in England. He declared his own marriage to Catherine invalid, and his marriage to Anne valid.

If the popes had simply granted Henry VIII the annulment he wanted based on "defective consent" or psychological incompatibility or some other bogus reason, *as the Vatican II sect is wont to do*, the entire Anglican Schism would have been avoided. But no, **the truth and the sanctity of the marriage bond had to be defended at all costs, even if it meant that a king would take an entire country into schism**. That's the difference between the Catholic Church and the Vatican II sect; one is Catholic and the other is not.

Endnotes for Section 28:

[1] *The Papal Encyclicals*, by Claudia Carlen, Raleigh: The Pierian Press, 1990, Vol. 2 (1878-1903), pp. 517-518.
[2] Donald Attwater, *A Catholic Dictionary*, Tan Books, 1997, p. 23.
[3] *The 1917 Pio-Benedictine Code of Canon Law*, translated by Dr. Edward Von Peters, San Francisco, CA: Ignatius Press, 2001, p. 352.
[4] *The 1917 Pio-Benedictine Code of Canon* Law, translated by Dr. Edward Von Peters, p. 369.
[5] *The 1917 Pio-Benedictine Code of Canon* Law, translated by Dr. Edward Von Peters, p. 373.
[6] Fr. Leonard Kennedy, *Catholic Insight*, "The Annulment Crisis in the Church," March 1999 Issue, http://catholicinsight.com/online/church/divorce/c_annul.shtml
[7] http://www.townhall.com/opinion/columns/patbuchanan/2002/12/11/165161.html
[8] Fr. Leonard Kennedy, *Catholic Insight*, "The Annulment Crisis in the Church," March 1999 Issue, http://catholicinsight.com/online/church/divorce/c_annul.shtml
[9] Fr. Leonard Kennedy, *Catholic Insight*, "The Annulment Crisis in the Church," March 1999 Issue, http://catholicinsight.com/online/church/divorce/c_annul.shtml
[10] Fr. Leonard Kennedy, *Catholic Insight*, "The Annulment Crisis in the Church," March 1999 Issue, http://catholicinsight.com/online/church/divorce/c_annul.shtml

[11] Quoted by Fr. Leonard Kennedy, *Catholic Insight*, "The Annulment Crisis in the Church," March 1999 Issue, http://catholicinsight.com/online/church/divorce/c_annul.shtml
[12] Warren H. Carroll, *A History of Christendom*, Vol. 2 *(The Building of Christendom)*, Front Royal, VA: Christendom Press, 1987, pp. 437-438.
[13] Warren H. Carroll, *A History of Christendom*, Vol. 3 *(The Glory of Christendom)*, p. 55.
[14] Warren H. Carroll, *A History of Christendom*, Vol. 3 *(The Glory of Christendom)*, pp. 141-142.
[15] Rev. Dr. Nicholas Sander, *The Rise and Growth of the Anglican Schism*, Tan Books, 1988, pp. 96-100.

29. The Figures on the post-Vatican II decline

The figures on the post-Vatican II decline were summarized by Pat Buchanan in a Dec. 11, 2002 article called "An index of Catholicism's decline" on townhall.com. Pat Buchanan was drawing on the research of Kenneth Jones' work, *Index of Leading Catholic Indicators: The Church Since Vatican II*.

"While the number of priests in the United States more than doubled to 58,000, between 1930 and 1965, since then that number has fallen to 45,000. By 2020, there will be only 31,000 priests left, and more than half of these priests will be over 70.

"-- Ordinations. In 1965, 1,575 new priests were ordained in the United States. In 2002, the number was 450. In 1965, only 1 percent of U.S. parishes were without a priest. Today, there are 3,000 priestless parishes, 15 percent of all U.S. parishes. -- Seminarians. Between 1965 and 2002, the number of seminarians dropped from 49,000 to 4,700, a decline of over 90 percent. Two-thirds of the 600 seminaries that were operating in 1965 have now closed.

"-- Sisters. In 1965, there were 180,000 Catholic nuns. By 2002, that had fallen to 75,000 and the average age of a Catholic nun is today 68. In 1965, there were 104,000 teaching nuns. Today, there are 8,200, a decline of 94 percent since the end of Vatican II.

"-- Religious Orders. **For religious orders in America, the end is in sight**. In 1965, 3,559 young men were studying to become Jesuit priests. In 2000, the figure was 389. With the Christian Brothers, the situation is even more dire. Their number has shrunk by two-thirds, with the number of seminarians falling 99 percent. In 1965, there were 912 seminarians in the Christian Brothers. In 2000, there were only seven. **The number of young men studying to become Franciscan and Redemptorist priests fell from 3,379 in 1965 to 84 in 2000.**

"-- Catholic schools. **Almost half of all Catholic high schools in the United States have closed since 1965**. The student population has fallen from 700,000 to 386,000. Parochial schools suffered an even greater decline. Some 4,000 have disappeared, and the number of pupils attending has fallen below 2 million -- from 4.5 million. <u>**Though the number of U.S. Catholics has risen by 20 million**</u> since 1965, Jones' statistics show that the power of Catholic belief and devotion to the Faith are not nearly what they were.

"--Catholic Marriage. **Catholic marriages have fallen in number by one-third since 1965**, while the annual number of annulments has soared from 338 in 1968 to 50,000 in 2002.

" -- Attendance at Mass. A 1958 Gallup Poll reported that three in four Catholics attended church on Sundays. A recent study by the University of Notre Dame found that **only one in four now attend**. Only 10 percent of lay religious teachers now accept church teaching on contraception. Fifty-three percent believe a Catholic can have an abortion and remain a good Catholic. Sixty-five percent believe that Catholics may divorce and remarry. Seventy-seven percent believe one can be a good Catholic without going to mass on Sundays. By one *New York Times* poll, 70 percent of all Catholics in the age group 18 to 44 believe the Eucharist is merely a "symbolic reminder" of Jesus.

At the opening of Vatican II, reformers were all the rage. They were going to lead us out of our Catholic ghettos by altering the liturgy, rewriting the Bible and missals, abandoning the old traditions, making us more ecumenical, and engaging the world. And their legacy? Four decades of devastation wrought upon the church, and the final disgrace of a hierarchy that lacked the moral courage of the Boy Scouts to keep the perverts out of the seminaries, and throw them out of the rectories and schools of Holy Mother Church. Through the papacy of Pius XII, the church resisted the clamor to accommodate itself to the world and remained a moral beacon to mankind. Since Vatican II, the church has sought to meet the world halfway. Jones' statistics tell us the price of appeasement."[1]

Endnotes for Section 29:

[1] http://www.townhall.com/opinion/columns/patbuchanan/2002/12/11/165161.html

30. One can be pro-abortion and part of the Vatican II sect at the same time

"...no pro-abortion politician, no matter how prominent the figure nor how boldly he supports abortion, has been excommunicated (i.e. expelled from the "Church") by the Vatican II antipopes."

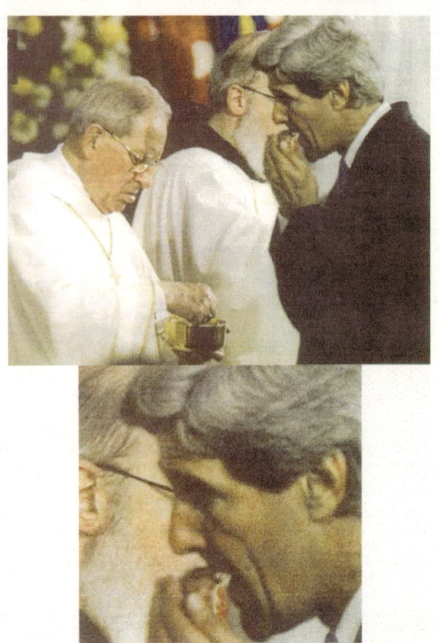

John Kerry receiving "Communion" in a Vatican II church in Boston.[1] Notice the miraculous image of a baby which appears as if Kerry is eating!

We've catalogued in great detail that the Vatican II sect is fraught with religious indifferentism and a denial of basic Catholic dogmas. The only issues which it pretends to hold are issues pertaining to morality and human dignity, not the issues of the Faith. For instance, while the Vatican II sect is certainly in favor of false religions, such as Islam and Judaism, it pretends to be against abortion and artificial contraception.

However, no pro-abortion politician, no matter how prominent the figure nor how boldly he supports abortion, has been excommunicated (i.e. expelled from the "Church") by the Vatican II antipopes. When we consider this fact, remember that it took John Paul II fewer than 72 hours to "excommunicate" Archbishop Marcel Lefebvre for consecrating bishops without a Papal mandate! Lefebvre consecrated these bishops for the spread of the Traditional Latin Mass. John Paul II was very concerned that more Traditional Latin Masses would be available, which he desperately wanted to stop, **so he wasted no time bringing down the hammer**. If he or Benedict XVI were really against abortion, they would have acted swiftly against obstinate pro-abortion politicians with the penalty of excommunication, just like John Paul II did with Lefebvre.

The most notorious case was Democratic Presidential Candidate, John Kerry. Kerry "boasted" a 100% pro-abortion voting record, and flaunted his pro-abortion position before the whole world when he became one of the world's most well known figures in the 2004 Presidential Campaign. He consistently received "Communion" in the Novus Ordo Church, to the protest of millions of professing Catholics. John Paul II did absolutely nothing about it, and Benedict XVI does nothing.

If anyone would have been excommunicated by the Vatican II sect for a pro-abortion stance, it would have been John Kerry. Not only was he not excommunicated, but almost every single Novus Ordo bishop who addressed the issue refused to say that Kerry should *even be refused Communion*. At the end of this section, we will consider the theological implications of this fact for the hierarchy of the Vatican II/Novus Ordo Church.

Bishop Robert Vasa of Baker (Oregon) described the bishops' discussion and decision on the matter of pro-abortion Catholic politicians:

> "Very specifically the question was asked whether the denial of Holy Communion is 'necessary because of their public support for abortion on demand.'
>
> **"The view ultimately accepted by the body of bishops was that such a denial was not necessarily 'necessary'** but such a denial was certainly possible and permissible, if, in the judgment of the local ordinary, it was deemed 'the most prudent course of pastoral action.'"[2]

This means that the official policy adopted by the U.S. "bishops" about this grave matter was that pro-abortion politicians need not even be refused Communion, and that every "bishop" can decide for himself. **This proves that one can officially receive "Communion" and be a "Catholic" in good standing *in the Vatican II sect* while being pro-abortion.**

After reviewing the policy whereby the "bishops" decide for themselves whether those who advocate murder in the womb should be given Communion or not, **"Cardinal" Ratzinger said that it was "very much in harmony"** with the principles of the Congregation of the Doctrine of the Faith.[3]

We must remember the context in which these conclusions were reached. In 2004, the scandal of pro-abortion "Catholic" politicians receiving "Communion" and not being declared excommunicated was put front and center by the "Catholic" media and many mainstream media outlets. Everyone knew about it, but the question was: would the Vatican II sect do anything to stop it? Would the Vatican II sect accept as "Catholic" pro-abortionists or would it not? Would it declare that their very membership in the "Church" was dependent upon their rejection of abortion? Or would it, by its silence, indicate that one can hold anything in the Vatican II sect and not be excommunicated? The answer was that nothing was done. The inaction in this context was definitely tantamount to an official statement by the Vatican II sect that one can be a Catholic and pro-abortion at the same time.

To summarize: the Vatican II sect not only refuses to excommunicate pro-abortion politicians, such as John Kerry, **but the very head of the Congregation for the Doctrine of the Faith, "Cardinal" Ratzinger (the now Benedict XVI), agreed that pro-abortion politicians need not be refused Communion**, thus proving that the Vatican II sect doesn't hold that it's a binding dogma that one must be against abortion.

The Vatican's Secretary of State, "Cardinal" Angelo Sodano, awarded the Knighthood to Julian Hunte, a pro-abortion politician in the West Indies.[4]

The "very conservative" "Archbishop" of Denver, Charles Chaput, doesn't hold that pro-abortion politicians must be denied Communion; but he doesn't "rule it out." Wow… he's really a "hammer of heretics."

> **"The archbishop [of Denver, Chaput] refused to rule out denying communion saying,** 'Denying anyone Communion is a very grave matter. It should be reserved for extraordinary cases of public scandal.'"[5]

He's quite a "Catholic" – **not**; and Chaput is radically conservative by Novus Ordo standards! "Bishop" Mengeling of Lansing, Michigan – another complete apostate – flatly refuses to punish pro-abortion Governor Granholm. *"Bishop Mengeling now has officially told the media that he will DO NOTHING to discipline Granholm or any other pro-abortion Catholic politician."*[6] The heretic who wrote this article says that "Bishop" Mengeling has broken with Rome (the Vatican II "popes"). Not so, for the Vatican II antipopes have done nothing to excommunicate or to stop pro-abortion politicians from receiving Communion. They could have very easily and immediately excommunicated John Kerry and all pro-abortion politicians, but they deliberately chose not to, because they are apostates who aren't really opposed to abortion.

The "Cardinal" of Baltimore, William Keeler, also said that John Kerry should not be denied Communion. He said that it's not the business of bishops to do such a thing: "We don't need bishops to get into the act."[7] We wonder what he thinks a "bishop" should do: act as figureheads and shuffle around pedophiles, and then hire lawyers to negotiate sex scandal settlements?

Keeler is the apostate who also said that we shouldn't convert Jews, but then again, that's basically every Novus Ordo "bishop"!

The former Pittsburgh apostate, "Bishop" Donald Wuerl, also won't deny pro-aborts Communion. *"Pittsburgh's Catholic bishop said yesterday that Catholic politicians should not support legalized abortion but that he does not advocate denying them Holy Communion."*[8]

Cincinnati "Archbishop" Daniel Pilarczyk says that pro-abortion politicians shouldn't be refused Communion, because then you would have to refuse Communion to everybody who denied any teaching of the Church! That's exactly right, you apostate!

"Archbishop" Daniel Pilarczyk: "… it seems to me **we need to be very cautious about denying people the sacraments on the basis of what they say they believe,** especially when those are political beliefs. So Kerry believes abortion is a good thing for our society, let's say. Do you refuse him communion on the basis of his opinions? What about people who don't like *Humanae Vitae*? **What about people who don't like the church's teaching on the death penalty, or on homosexual marriages? Are we going to refuse them?**

Mr. Allen: "There's a swath of Catholic opinion that would say yes to that question.

Abp. Pilarczyk: "I know there is. **But there's also a justice issue here. It seems to me that the last thing any church, or any representative or agent of the church wants to do, is to deny the sacraments to anybody unjustly.** It seems to me at this point that <u>**it makes a lot more sense to presume people's good will, presume erroneous conscience or perplexed conscience and give them Communion**</u>, rather than say, 'I think you think such-and-such.' …"[9]

"Bishop" John **Steinbock** of **Fresno**, California also doesn't advocate denying pro-aborts Communion: "*I pointed out to the priests and deacons that this document did not say, as was falsely reported by the secular media, that Catholic politicians who vote for abortion may not receive Communion. It did not refer to Catholic politicians at all.*"[10]

"Archbishop" Alexander **Brunett of Seattle** has said that pro-abortion politicians should **not be** denied Holy Communion: "*Ministers of the Eucharist should not take it upon themselves to deny Holy Communion to anyone who presents themselves* [sic]."[11]

"Bishop" Joseph A. **Fiorenza of Galveston**-Houston took issue with the tiny handful of Novus Ordo "bishops" who **advocated denying Communion:**

"As you know, **a few bishops have made public statements in which they favor the denial of Holy Communion to Catholic politicians** who are consistently in opposition to the teaching of the Church on the most fundamental human rights issue, the right to be born. I really wish these bishops had waited for the report of the task force. They didn't, and now many people are asking their own diocesan bishop to speak on the issue.

"Without going into detail on the pastoral and canonical issues involved in this issue, **I believe that the tradition of the Church does not favor denying the Eucharist as a sanction for Catholic pro-abortion politicians**. In fact, I believe that such a sanction would be counter-productive and at the end of the day, would harm the pro-life movement."[12]

"Bishop" Fiorenza obviously doesn't know anything about the tradition of the Church. Popes throughout the ages have proclaimed the dogma that non-Catholics who receive the Lamb outside the Church receive it to their own condemnation.

Pope Pius VIII, *Traditi Humilitati* (# 4), May 24, 1829:
"Jerome used to say it this way: **he who eats the Lamb outside this house will perish as did those during the flood who were not with Noah in the ark.**"[13]

> Pope Gregory XVI, *Commissum divinitus* (# 11), May 17, 1835:
> "… whoever dares to depart from the unity of Peter might understand that he no longer shares in the divine mystery.' St. Jerome adds: '**Whoever eats the Lamb outside of this house is unholy**. Those who were not in the ark of Noah perished in the flood.'"[14]

> Pope Pius IX, *Amantissimus* (# 3), April 8, 1862: "He who deserts the Church will vainly believe that he is in the Church; **whoever eats of the Lamb and is not a member of the Church, has profaned.**"[15]

And Pope Benedict XIV (not Antipope Benedict XVI) makes it clear that not only must avowed non-Catholics be refused the sacraments, but anyone who is known to oppose even one official teaching of the Church.

> Pope Benedict XIV, *Ex Omnibus* (# 3), Oct. 16, 1756:
> "The authority of the apostolic constitution which begins *Unigenitus* is certainly so great and lays claim everywhere to such sincere veneration and obedience that no one can withdraw the submission due it or oppose it without risking the loss of eternal salvation. Now, a controversy has risen concerning whether viaticum must be denied to those who oppose the constitution. **The answer must be given without hesitation that as long as they are opposed publicly and notoriously, viaticum must be denied them; this follows for** <u>the universal law</u> **which prohibits a known public sinner to be admitted to Eucharistic communion, whether he asks for it in public or in private.**"[16]

The Arizona bishops won't deny John Kerry Communion: "…two Arizona bishops say they won't deny communion to Roman Catholic politicians who support abortion rights. **Bishop Thomas J. Olmsted of Phoenix said that instead of refusing to offer communion,** <u>he will attempt to use persuasion</u> to educate politicians about church teachings."[17]

We could continue quoting Novus Ordo "bishop" after "bishop" saying the same thing, but the point should be clear. <u>In the Vatican II sect, opposition to **abortion is an optional thing which the** "hierarchy" of the Vatican II sect will "persuade" you to hold</u>. In other words, it's just a matter of opinion, not a dogma binding under pain of Hell, excommunication and anathema.

We must now consider the theological implications of this position, or rather, non-position of the Vatican II sect. Heresy is manifested not only by word and deed, <u>but also by omission</u>. If a man says he's in favor of Catholic dogma, but refuses to condemn a heresy which is opposed to that dogma when asked to, he is not a Catholic. This truth was shown during the Arian crisis. The famous Bishop Eusebius of Nicomedia signed the Council of Nicaea's profession of Trinitarian dogma, but he refused to condemn the Arians who denied this dogma.

> "There were no more whispers, winks and nods from the Arians. **The Church had taken her first great step to define revealed doctrine more precisely in response to a challenge from heretical theology.** A creed was drawn up, embodying this new formulation, to convey a better awareness – though **never full understanding** – of the supernal mystery. It was presented for signature June 19, 325. All the bishops signed it but two from Libya who had been closely associated with Arians from the beginning. They and Arius were exiled to Illyricum. **Even Eusebius of Nicomedia signed, <u>though refusing to join in the condemnation of Arius</u>**."[18]

Since Eusebius of Nicomedia <u>refused to condemn the Arians</u> and "gave hospitality" to them, even though he signed the profession of the true dogma, **he was rightly banished with the**

heretics. [19] Likewise, the Novus Ordo/Vatican II "bishops" may *claim* to oppose abortion – which, as we've seen, is about the only heresy or evil which they sometimes speak against – and may sign statements saying it's wrong, but since they don't excommunicate or condemn obstinate advocates of abortion, they really aren't opposed to it. We've seen that, **as a body – and with the agreement of Rome – they refuse to excommunicate or even hold as unworthy of Communion obstinate advocates of murder in the womb who are put right in their face, such as John Kerry.**

On May 10, 2004, 48 House Democrats – including "Catholics" in favor of abortion – sent a letter to Cardinal Theodore McCarrick of Washington, D.C., boldly stating that denying Communion as a way of getting Catholic politicians in line on abortion rights would be counterproductive and would possibly prompt anti-Catholic bigotry.[20] In other words, they were basically putting their rejection of Catholic teaching boldly in the bishops' faces – a veritable challenge to them to do something about it. Of course, nothing was done by the phony "bishops" of the Vatican II sect to condemn these heretics who were putting their heresy right in their faces.

Thus, it's a fact that one can be a member of the Vatican II sect without being opposed to abortion. In fact, on June 22, 2006, at the installation "Mass" for Archbishop Donald W. Wuerl, John Kerry was given "Communion" by Benedict XVI's nuncio to the American bishops:

> "During the Mass, **Kerry, who supports keeping abortion legal, received Communion in the hand from Archbishop Pietro Sambi, apostolic nuncio to the United States and Pope Benedict XVI's representative** to the U.S. bishops. Archbishop Wuerl distributed Communion alongside the nuncio."[21]

These facts prove abundantly that being against abortion is not something that must be held to be a part of the Vatican II sect. But you cannot consecrate bishops for the spread of the Traditional Latin Mass without being excommunicated within 72 hours (e.g. Lefebvre). This demonstrates once again that the Vatican II sect, which is currently headed by Benedict XVI, is not the Catholic Church, but the Counter Church.

Endnotes for Section 30:

[1] *Time Magazine*, June 21, 2004, p. 4.
[2] http://www.wf-f.org/Bishops_Catholics_Politics.html#anchor36189926
[3] http://www.usccb.org/comm/archives/2004/04-133.htm
[4] http://www.lifesite.net/ldn/2004/sep/04092702.html
[5] http://www.lifesite.net/ldn/2004/may/04052603.html
[6] http://www.catholiccitizens.org/press/contentview.asp?c=14536
[7] *The Baltimore Sun*, May 28, 2004; http://www.wf-f.org/Bishops_Catholics_Politics.html#anchor69086
[8] http://www.pittsburgpostgazette.com/pg/04147/322065.stm
[9] http://www.wf-f.org/Bishops_Catholics_Politics.html#anchor932576
[10] http://www.dioceseoffresno.org/letters/20040701knxtcommunion.html
[11] http://www.wf-f.org/Bishops_Catholics_Politics.html#anchor3484970
[12] http://www.wf-f.org/Bishops_Catholics_Politics.html#anchor114660
[13] *The Papal Encyclicals*, by Claudia Carlen, Raleigh: The Pierian Press, 1990, Vol. 1 (1740-1878), p. 222.
[14] *The Papal Encyclicals*, Vol. 1 (1740-1878), p. 256.
[15] *The Papal Encyclicals*, Vol. 1 (1740-1878), p. 364.
[16] *The Papal Encyclicals*, Vol. 1 (1740-1878), pp. 105-106.
[17] http://www.tucsoncitizen.com/news/local/052204b1_abortion

[18] Warren H. Carroll, *A History of Christendom*, Vol. 2 (*The Building of Christendom*), Front Royal, VA: Christendom Press, 1987, p. 11.
[19] Fr. John Laux, *Church History*, Rockford, IL: Tan Books, 1989, p. 112.
[20] http://www.msnbc.msn.com/id/5017313/
[21] http://www.catholic.org/international/international_story.php?id=20313

31. The Vatican II sect literally turns away converts at the door

We've already documented that Paul VI, John Paul II and Benedict XVI explicitly taught/teach that non-Catholics, such as the Protestants and Eastern Orthodox, don't need to be converted to the Catholic Faith for unity and salvation. In keeping with this heretical theology, Vatican officials have actively turned away non-Catholics who have presented themselves for conversion to the Catholic Faith!

> "There are reported cases of Vatican Cardinals actively discouraging non-Catholics who desire to convert to Catholicism… **Father Linus Dragu Popian, who had been raised in the Romanian Orthodox religion. In 1975 he risked his life to escape Communist Romania and presented himself as a seminarian to the Vatican, expressing his wish to convert to Catholicism.** The then-Secretary of State, Cardinal Villot, and other Vatican Cardinals were horrified. **They told young Popian that he must not flee Communism and must not become Catholic**, because this would damage the Vatican's relations with Communist Romania and the Romanian Orthodox Church." (*The Devil's Final Battle*, p. 68.)

The Vatican officials told him that he must not become Catholic! They were just following the evil policy taught by the Vatican II antipopes, Paul VI, John Paul II and Benedict XVI.

In 2005, we were contacted by an Eastern Orthodox bishop who was interested in converting to Catholicism. He informed us via e-mail (which provided his full name and address, but which he asked us not to publish) that he was discouraged by the Archdiocese of Boston from converting to the Catholic Faith.

> "Greetings in Christ! I have been watching your site for sometime now and wanted to know more about your organization. I was at one time very active in the Ecumenical Movement but left sometime ago due to what I had seen as being problematic. I do have many questions though and hope you can provide me with some answers please.
>
> "But let me tell you a little bit about myself: I am a Coptic Orthodox Bishop and retired at present. I am also fairly new to the internet as well. I know of several priests and another bishop in Cairo that are thinking of converting to the Catholic faith.
>
> **For myself, I was told by the Diocese of Boston that: 'There is no need to Convert, there is salvation for non-Catholics.'** I was very disheartened and confused as I am sure you can understand. I do have many concerns and questions concerning Catholic doctrine though."

Of course, this is perfectly in line with the Vatican II sect's teaching, enunciated by John Paul II and Benedict XVI, that conversion of the "Orthodox" is not the way for unity. It is perfectly in line with the Vatican II sect's handbook on ecumenism, the outrageous *Directory for the Application of the Principles and Norms of Ecumenism*.

Once again, this is absolute and total proof that the Vatican II sect is not the Catholic Church.

32. The Religious Orders in the Vatican II Sect: Totally Apostate

"We devoted two full days to sharing our personal spiritual journeys… attending the Buddhist community's chanting services, meditating together and enjoying superb Chinese vegetarian cuisine."[1]

Novus Ordo "Benedictines" at the "Monks in the West" Conference with Buddhists[2]

"- Religious Orders. **For religious orders in America, the end is in sight**. In 1965, 3,559 young men were studying to become Jesuit priests. In 2000, the figure was 389. With the Christian Brothers, the situation is even more dire. Their number has shrunk by two-thirds, with the number of seminarians falling 99 percent. In 1965, there were 912 seminarians in the Christian Brothers. In 2000, there were only seven. **The number of young men studying to become Franciscan and Redemptorist priests fell from 3,379 in 1965 to 84 in 2000.**"[3]

It's not a surprise that the religious orders in the Vatican II sect are almost dead. Why would a Catholic young man or woman want to join when basically the only thing they stand for is the promotion of false religions and "human dignity"?

"Franciscans" in Massachusetts welcome gay "Catholics," with no denunciation of the abominable homosexual lifestyle, thus encouraging them in their activity.[4]

Novus Ordo nuns worship with Buddhists in front of a Buddhist statue.[5]

The official website of the Irish "Jesuits" prominently states that there can be: "No service of faith without… *openness to other religious experiences.*"[6] This is from the General Congregation of Irish Jesuits – total apostasy.

The official website for the Novus Ordo "Order of St. Benedict" links to the Anglican and "Orthodox" Benedictines![7]

The practice of Yoga is also rampant in Novus Ordo religious orders. Since the wicked practice of Yoga is rampant in not only Novus Ordo religious orders but also secular institutions, such as the YMCA, we feel that it is important to quickly discuss what's wrong with it. Isn't Yoga just stretching? No. We will quote a Novus Ordo "priest," "Fr." James Manjackal, who is very knowledgeable about the subject:

> "What is Yoga? **The word Yoga means "union", the goal of Yoga is to unite one's transitory (temporary) self, "JIVA" with the infinite "BRAHMAN", the Hindu concept of God. <u>This God is not a personal God, but it is an impersonal spiritual substance which is one with nature and cosmos</u>. Brahman is an impersonal divine substance that 'pervades, envelopes and underlies everything.'** Yoga has its roots in the Hindu Upanishads, which is as old as 1.000 BC, and it tells about Yoga thus, 'unite the light within you with the light of Brahman.' 'The absolute is within one self' says the Chandogya Upanishads, 'TAT TUAM ASI' or 'THOU ART THAT.' The Divine dwells within each one of us through His microcosmic representative, the individual self called Jiva. In the Bhagavad Gita, the lord Krishna describes the Jiva as 'my own eternal portion,' and 'the joy of Yoga comes to yogi who is one with Brahman.' In A.D. 150, the yogi Patanjali explained the eight ways that lead the Yoga practices from ignorance to enlightenment – the eight ways are like a staircase – They are self-control (yama), religious observance (niyama), postures (asana), breathing exercises (pranayama), sense control (pratyahara), concentration (dharana), deep contemplation (dhyana), enlightenment (samadhi). **It is interesting to note, here, that postures and breathing-exercises, often considered to be the whole of Yoga in the West, are steps 3 and 4 towards union with Brahman! Yoga is not only an elaborate system of physical exercises, it is a spiritual discipline, purporting to lead the soul to samadhi, total union with the divine being**. Samadhi is the state in which the natural and the divine become one, man and God become one without any difference (Brad Scott: Exercise or religious practice? Yoga: What the teacher never taught you in that Hatha Yoga class" in *The Watchman Expositor*, Vol. 18, No. 2, 2001)."[8]

To summarize, <u>**Yoga is a spiritual discipline**</u> which attempts to unite one with <u>**the divine within oneself and united with all of creation**</u> through breathing, physical exercises, concentration, etc. The idea that the divine is to be found within oneself is, of course, occultic. The idea that the divine permeates all of creation – the idea upon which the practice of Yoga is based and toward which it is geared – is Pantheism and condemned by Vatican I.

> Pope Pius IX, *First Vatican Council*, Session 3, Chap. 1, On God the Creator of all things:
> "**The holy, Catholic, Apostolic, Roman Church believes and confesses that there is one, true, living God**, Creator and Lord of heaven and earth... **who**, although He is one, singular, altogether simple and unchangeable spiritual substance, **must be proclaimed distinct in reality and essence from the world**..."[9]

> Pope Pius XI, *Mit Brennender Sorge* (# 7), March 14, 1937:
> "**Whoever identifies, by pantheistic confusion, God and the universe**, by either lowering God to the dimensions of the world, or raising the world to the dimensions of God, **is not a believer in God**."[10]

As an aside, John Paul II himself taught this condemned pantheistic notion in his encyclical *Dominum et Vivificantem* (50.3), May 18, 1986. He stated:

> "'The Word became flesh.' **The Incarnation of God the Son signifies the taking up into unity not only of human nature, but in this human nature, in a sense, of everything that is 'flesh': the whole of humanity, the entire visible and material world**. The Incarnation, then, also has a cosmic significance, a cosmic dimension."[11]

Notice that as he was expounding (as usual) on his heretical belief that Christ is united to each and every man, in this case John Paul II decided to take it one step further: not only has Christ united Himself with every man (he says), but with the "entire visible and material world." According to Antipope John Paul II, the grass, trees, rivers, lakes, oceans, etc. were all united with Christ by virtue of the Incarnation. He develops the thought in the next sentence of this encyclical.

> John Paul II, *Dominum et Vivificantem* (50.3), May 18, 1986:
> The 'first-born of all creation,' becoming incarnate in the individual humanity of **Christ, <u>unites himself</u> in some way with the entire reality of man, which is also 'flesh' - and in this reality with all 'flesh,' <u>with the whole of creation</u>.**"[12]

What we had in Antipope John Paul II was a Pantheist. In Pantheism, the world and God make a single thing.

> A Catholic Dictionary, by Attwater: "**Pantheism** - A false philosophy which consists in confounding God with the world. *According to some the world is absorbed by God* (Indian pantheists, Spinoza); others teach that God is absorbed by the world of which he is the force and the life… **But all [Pantheists] seek to establish an identity of substance between God and the world**."[13]

> The Catholic Encyclopedia:
> "Pantheism, the view according to which God and the world are one."[14]

Since, as we saw above, the practice of Yoga is based on the idea of union with the divine within oneself and within all of creation, <u>the practice of Yoga is therefore an expression of belief in the condemned pantheistic heresy that God and His creation are a single thing.</u> Practicing Yoga, therefore, is practicing a false religion and expressing belief in a false god. The conservative Novus Ordo priest we quoted above, who is outraged by the rampant practice of Yoga in "Christian" and "Catholic" circles, summed the situation up quite well:

> "**<u>The practice of Yoga is pagan at best, and occult at worst. This is the religion of antichrist and for the first time in history it is being widely practiced throughout the Western world and America</u>**. It is ridiculous that even yogi masters wearing a Cross or a Christian symbol deceive people saying that Yoga has nothing to do with Hinduism and say that it is only accepting the other cultures. Some have masked Yoga with Christian gestures and call it "Christian Yoga." **Here it is not a question of accepting the culture of other people, it is a question of accepting another religion**…"[15]

The Monastery of the Holy Spirit offers a special "Fundamentals of Yoga and Christianity" Retreat.[16] **The Carmelite Spiritual Center** in Darien, Illinois offered a "Living Your Light" Yoga Retreat.[17] **The "Catholic" Ecclesia Center** in Girard, Pennsylvania – which is approved by the Diocese in which it resides[18] – includes on its staff <u>a Yoga instructor!</u>

> "Michael Plasha is a credentialed Yoga Therapist and a Yoga Alliance registered teacher… He has also trained in Zen and Vipassana meditation. Since 1980 Michael has

taught over 3,000 classes in yoga and meditation… Yoga … is a non-dogmatic approach to union with the Divine presence within everyone."[19]

Notice that **the Ecclesia Center** admits that Yoga is an approach to the Divine presence "within everyone," thus proving that it's rooted in, and directed toward, Pantheism and the occult. The website also states that Ecclesia Center "provides spiritual renewal to persons of <u>all faiths</u>."[20] This is total apostasy, fully approved by the diocese.

Other examples could be given, but the evil practice of Yoga is so rampant at "Catholic" monasteries that Budget Travel Online actually advertises for it!

"More than 2,000 monasteries, abbeys, and spiritual retreat centers are scattered throughout the United States and Canada. About 80 percent are linked to a religious order. **But most take a more ecumenical, interfaith approach to accommodate this increased interest**. 'In the old days if you were a Catholic retreat center, you advertised yourself that way. Now most of them want everybody to come,' Stone says. **<u>Many places offer yoga</u>**, Buddhist thought, prayers of all sorts."[21]

Novus Ordo "Trappists" and "Jesuits" are officially installed in Novus Ordo Monasteries as teachers of Zen Buddhism!

Trappist "priest," Fr. Kevin Hunt, on his knees as he is installed as Zen Teacher by "Jesuit" Fr. Robert Kennedy.[22] Notice the statue of Buddha in the background.

Monastic Interreligious Dialogue (Newsletter)- Sponsored by North American Benedictine and Cistercian monasteries of men and women

> "**Fr. Kevin Hunt Installed as Zen Teacher-** On April 17, 2004, **Fr. Kevin Hunt, OCSO, a Trappist monk of St. Joseph's Abbey in Spencer, Massachusetts, and a former member of the MID board, <u>was installed as a Zen teacher (Sensei) in a ceremony held at the abbey</u>**. The installation was led by Fr. Robert Kennedy, S.J., who is the only North American Jesuit who is also a Zen Master (Roshi) and who served as Fr. Kevin's teacher. **The installation was witnessed by the abbot of St. Joseph's and the rest of the monastic community as well as by over seventy guests, <u>including Zen teachers and members of Catholic religious orders from around the country</u>.**
>
> "Fr. Kevin thereby became the first Trappist monk who is also a Zen teacher. **In recognition of this unique event, letters of commendation were written by His Holiness the Dalai Lama and <u>by Fr. Peter-Hans Kolvenbach, the superior general of the Society of Jesus</u>**. Fr. Kolvenbach wrote, 'Many Christians have found Zen to be a valuable instrument for progressing in the spiritual life. By coming to focus on the present moment through the practice of the techniques of Zen meditation, the Christian can become aware of God's immediate loving presence.'
>
> "Fr. Kolvenbach's remarks reflect the commitment made by the Jesuits at their 34th General Congregation to foster dialogue with other religions… **Noting that Pope John Paul II has wished to make interreligious dialogue an apostolic priority for the third millennium, Fr. Kennedy said that his work with Fr. Kevin was one way in which this priority could be carried out…**"
>
> **Seventh Annual Vaishnava-Christian Dialogue**
> "On April 16-17, 2004, three persons directly connected with the North American MID were among the sixteen who participated in **the seventh annual Vaishnava-Christian Dialogue**, held at Rockwood Manor Park in Potomac, Maryland, **under the co-sponsorship of the Office of Ecumenical and Interreligious Affairs of the United States Conference of Catholic Bishops** and the International Society of Krishna Consciousness (ISKCON)…
>
> "As in most past years, the first day of the program included addresses by a Christian and a Vaishnava participant, each commenting on texts from the two traditions… [The] opening talks elicited lively dialogue among the other participants for the rest of the day and **on into the next day, which began with the singing of hymns and chanting of prayers from the two traditions**."[23]

So now we have ceremonies going on in the Novus Ordo Monasteries to induct men as teachers of the occultic practice of Zen Buddhism. But once again, all of this happens because they're just following Vatican II and the lead of the New Church in Rome.

Please note that "Fr." Peter-Hans Kolvenbach, **the alleged Superior General of the Society of Jesus,** wrote a letter of commendation for this event. This is the leader of the entire "Jesuit" Order in the Vatican II sect.

Note that the newsletter (quoted above), which is sponsored by "North American Benedictine and Cistercian" monasteries, referred to the satanic Dalai Lama (who claims to be a god) as "His Holiness." Note that **John Paul II's program of interreligious dialogue is used as the justification for this event.**

Finally, please note that the United States "Conference of Catholic Bishops" sponsored the **seventh annual Vaishnava-Christian Dialogue in which took place the chanting of Hindu prayers!** Behold the members, the religious, and the leaders of your Church, if you believe that the Vatican II sect is the Catholic Church.

Cloistered Nuns on Mt. Carmel pray for Jews to remain Jews

An article was posted online about cloistered Novus Ordo nuns who spend most of their day in silence and want Jews to remain Jews:

> "While Pope John Paul II pleads for religious harmony in the Holy Land, 17 **cloistered nuns on Mount Carmel quietly pray for their Jewish neighbors. Not to win souls for Christendom. These nuns want Jews to be Jewish**…
>
> "'**How can you be a servant in Israel if you speak about conversion?**' says Sister Angela del Bono, mother superior of the Monastery of Our Lady of Mount Carmel, in a rare interview from behind a metal grille in the parlor of a sprawling granite convent. She pounds her hand on her forehead beneath a veil. 'Imagine someone coming in here and telling me to become an Adventist or a Muslim,' she says, smiling at her own fervor…
>
> "'**We pray that Jews remain true to their covenant**,' says Sister Angela del Bono, 68, holding a thick wool sweater tightly around her floor-length brown habit in the unheated convent.
>
> "We pray that people come to the full revelation of God… If they are good Jews and we are good Christians this is already glory to God without forcing anyone to change,' the native Italian nun says, speaking in English. 'We pray for all to be happy and be righteous in front of God. **Each man can go to Heaven--Jews, Catholics, Muslims, Zulus--if they are… of goodwill**. If they feel godly, **if they follow their own conscience, they will go to Heaven**."[24]

People really need to consider how bad this is. This shows us again that the Vatican II sect is the sect of Antichrist. The belief that one can freely reject Jesus Christ – the doctrine of Antichrist – has been imbibed by the religious orders which are supposedly dedicated to Jesus Christ.

> 1 John 2:22 – "Who is a liar, but **he who denieth that Jesus is the Christ? He is antichrist**, who denieth the Father, and the Son."

This also reminds us that people can spend much time in supposedly religious acts for God, and it will profit them nothing if they don't have the true Faith. These nuns spend much of their day in silence and their convent is unheated; yet they are complete apostates, rejecters of God and headed for Hell. This shows us that without the true faith it is impossible to please God, no matter how many other religious and devotional acts one thinks he performs. Notice that the nun also expressed precisely the heresy condemned by Pope Gregory XVI, that Heaven is open to the naturally "good" members of any religion.

> Pope Gregory XVI, *Mirari Vos* (# 13), Aug. 15, 1832: "With the admonition of the apostle, that 'there is one God, one faith, one baptism' (Eph. 4:5), **may those fear who contrive the notion that the safe harbor of salvation is open to persons of any religion whatever.** They should consider the testimony of Christ Himself that 'those who are not with Christ are against Him,' (Lk. 11:23) and that they disperse unhappily who do not gather with Him. **Therefore, 'without a doubt, they will perish forever, unless they hold the Catholic faith whole and inviolate' (Athanasian Creed)."**[25]

The Apostasy of the Novus Ordo "Benedictine" Nuns; need one say more?

We've already cited the fact that the Novus Ordo "Benedictines" actually link to the Anglicans and Eastern "Orthodox." Mary Lou Kownacki, "OSB," is executive director of Alliance of International Monasticism, <u>which links 200 Novus Ordo "Benedictine" and "Cistercian" communities</u> in the developing world with those in the United States. She is also director of development and communications for the Novus Ordo "Benedictine" sisters of Erie, PA. In line with the Vatican II religion, she exemplifies total interreligious apostasy. In her poem quoted below, she invokes the "Cosmic Christ," whom she says spoke through the apostate Teilhard de Chardin. She also says he spoke through the idolater Mahatma Gandhi, the heretic Martin Luther King, Jr., and the Jews Anne Frank and Rabbi Heschel.

> "O Cosmic Christ… Through Teilhard de Chardin, scientist of the cosmos, you imagined a new heaven and a new earth. Through Mahatma Gandhi, great soul, you became nonviolent in the struggle for justice… Through Anne Frank… you preserved goodness in the midst of a great evil… Through Martin Luther King, Jr.,… Through Rabbi Abraham Heschel, Hasidic sage, you answered our search for meaning."[26]

What more does one really have to say? This <u>apostate directs</u> an **alliance which links 200 Novus Ordo "Benedictine" and "Cistercian" communities**. And to think that people ask us why we are not in communion with the Novus Ordo "Benedictines." Those who accept people such as this as Catholics are not in communion with the Catholic Church.

Saint John's Abbey: a typical example of outrageous apostasy in the Vatican II sect's religious orders

Saint John's Abbey, located in Collegeville, Minnesota, is one of the major and historic monasteries of the Vatican II sect in America. The "Benedictines" at St. John's Abbey, like the Vatican II sect to which they belong, are unfortunately not even remotely Catholic. As we introduced at the beginning of this section, in 2004 St. John's Abbey held a "Monks in the West" meeting with Buddhist "monks."

> Their magazine states: "**We devoted two full days to sharing our personal spiritual journeys… <u>attending the Buddhist community's chanting services</u>**, meditating together and enjoying superb Chinese vegetarian cuisine."[27]

This is complete and utter apostasy.

Novus Ordo "Benedictines" attended Buddhist prayer services at "Monks in the West" Conference.[28] Notice that their "cross" is neither a crucifix nor a cross, but a plus sign.

> The same magazine states: "… **Christianity can also learn from wisdom of the Buddhist tradition, especially in the area of thought and fantasy**. For example, in one session a monk from Shasta Buddhist Abbey… **described the Buddhist method of accepting sexual feelings without either acting on them or repressing them**, but just letting them pass through... We explored the possibility of publishing a book on what we learned about the meaning and practice of celibacy in our two traditions."[29]

So, the members of St. John's Abbey not only meditated with pagans and idolaters and also attended their idolatrous services, but allowed them to promote their evil philosophy of not rejecting impure thoughts. The Catholic Church, based on the teaching of Jesus Christ (Matthew 5:28), has always taught that impure thoughts and desires must be rejected. What we've covered here is a profound example of apostasy in the Vatican II sect, but it's quite typical.

A member of our religious community, prior to becoming a traditional Catholic, spent time at a Novus Ordo Monastery in South Carolina. During his stay at the monastery, he attended a talk by a Novus Ordo "priest" who appeared to be a theologian. The "priest" told the brothers that all religions lead to Heaven, and that there is no necessity to be Catholic to be saved. The Novus Ordo monks who were present appeared to have no reaction, outrage or even surprise at these blatantly heretical teachings of the "priest." The young man, however, was so bewildered and stunned that he stayed up much of the night writing down scripture verses on the necessity of accepting Jesus Christ for salvation in order to refute the apostasy of the "priest." The next day he presented the information to the Novus Ordo monks in order to refute what had been said; they didn't seem to care at all.

An article by a "Benedictine" Nun, Sr. Mary Margaret Funk, further confirms the utter apostasy of the Vatican II sect's religious orders

Many argue that the teachings of Vatican II don't contradict Catholic dogma in any way. They strenuously assert that the Vatican II religion is in perfect continuity with the unchanging Catholic religion. Some people call these individuals (who defend everything in Vatican II and the post-conciliar apostasy) neo-Catholics; we call them neo-apostates, since they attempt to explain away everything from kissing the Koran to allowing idol-worshippers to take over and pray to false gods at Assisi. **But one of the most interesting and clear ways of proving that the**

Vatican II sect is not the Catholic Church is simply by looking at what its members believe at the local level. We've done a great deal of this already, but the amount of stories from individuals who have actually been discouraged from becoming Catholic by members of the Novus Ordo Church, including bishops, Vatican officials and RCIA teachers, seem almost endless. So, if you ever want to be stirred to a holy indignation against the Vatican II apostasy, or if you ever want proof of what an abominable outrage the Vatican II sect is, or if you ever want to be convinced that it is a matter of Heaven or Hell to completely reject this false, non-Catholic sect falsely posing as the Catholic Church, then just call some Novus Ordo churches and ask them: *"Do you accept the dogma Outside the Church There is No Salvation? Is Islam a false religion? Is Judaism a false religion?"*

The responses that you will get will astound you, if you know and possess the true Catholic Faith. The responses you will get will confirm for you, if you are sincere, that the religion of these individuals (the Vatican II religion) is not the Catholic religion. **It will confirm for you, if you are sincere, that the entire Vatican II sect is apostate, since these individuals are simply putting into practice what is taught and exemplified by Vatican II concerning non-Christian religions**.

In that vein, one of us was paging through the *St. Anthony Messenger* and came across an article entitled ***Islam: What Every Catholic Should Know* by Mary Margaret Funk, "O.S.B."** (*St. Anthony Messenger* is one of the most prominent publications of the Vatican II sect.) So here was an article by a supposed Benedictine Nun on Islam. What did she say?

> Mary Margaret Funk, "O.S.B.," *Islam: What Catholics Should Know*, p. 36, St. Anthony Messenger, August, 2005: "Unlike Christians, who believe that Jesus was the Son of God and an indivisible part of God, **Muslims believe that the Holy Prophet Mohammed (570-632)** was a man and that he followed Adam, Abraham, Moses, David, Solomon, and Jesus as the last of the great prophets to receive divine revelation."[30]

While referring to Mohammed as "the Holy Prophet," Mary Margaret didn't think it necessary to mention to her "Catholic" readership that Mohammed was a false prophet and the originator of a false religion. She continues:

> Mary Margaret Funk, "O.S.B.," *Islam: What Catholics Should Know*, St. Anthony Messenger, August, 2005, p. 36: "**Mohammed tested the authenticity of his revelations with prayer and fasting**. It was two years before he went public with **his profound religious experience**."[31]

The impression that any reasonable reader of this article gets is that Mary Margaret holds that Mohammed's false revelations were authentic or could be authentic (which is apostasy).

> Mary Margaret Funk, "O.S.B.," *Islam: What Catholics Should Know*, St. Anthony Messenger, August, 2005, p. 38: "I am struck by the absolute grasp of and reverence for the Quran communicated by the Muslims. The name *Allah*, after all, is simply the Arabic word for God, **the one God of Judaism, Christianity and Islam**."[32]

Here we see that Mary Margaret bases her effusive praise for the false religion of Islam on the false teaching of Vatican II that Jews, Christians and Muslims supposedly worship the same God. We see this very clearly illustrated in the next quote:

> Mary Margaret Funk, "O.S.B.," *Islam: What Catholics Should Know*, St. Anthony Messenger, August, 2005, p. 39: "**When I was present for the Muslim *salat*, I felt as**

though I was at home with my nuns in Beech Grove, Indiana. It was the same God, the same praise and the same bended knee."³³

This is pure religious indifferentism. But it is all based precisely on the teaching of Vatican II on Muslims:

> *Vatican II document, Nostra aetate* (# 3): "The Church also looks upon <u>Muslims</u> with respect. They worship the one God living and subsistent, merciful and mighty, creator of heaven and earth, who has spoken to humanity and to whose decrees, even the hidden ones, they<u> seek to submit themselves whole-heartedly</u>, just as Abraham, to whom the Islamic faith readily relates itself, submitted <u>to God</u>… <u>Hence they have regard for the moral life and worship God in prayer, almsgiving and fasting.</u>"³⁴

Mary Margaret Funk continues:

> Mary Margaret Funk, "O.S.B.," *Islam: What Catholics Should Know*, St. Anthony Messenger, August, 2005, p. 39: **"My community of 82 nuns carries me when my devotion is tepid and my inclination is capricious. I see that same zeal among my Muslim friends. The stopping for prayer is the norm allowing us to be God-conscious during the in-between times and to help God-consciousness become pervasive. What then happens is that we return to ritual prayer thankful for this felt presence of God."**³⁵

Obviously, Mary Margaret Funk considers the false religion of Islam – which is considered to be an abomination by the Catholic Church – as a perfectly valid way of worshipping and "pleasing" God. Mary Margaret Funk is a member of Our Lady of Grace Monastery in Beech Grove, Indiana. She is not a member of the Catholic Church. She is a Christ-rejecter and an apostate who believes in salvation outside the Church and that false religions are not false. She is the former prioress of her large religious community, and **she is the executive director of Monastic Interreligious Dialogue**. She is simply following the teaching of Vatican II and post-conciliar ecumenism; she is typical of the hierarchy and the religious of the Vatican II sect.

How many stories such as this could be duplicated? **They could be duplicated without end, in every diocese under Benedict XVI, and in every single religious community in communion with him**. Have Mary Margaret Funk and millions of others misunderstood the teaching of Vatican II? No, she has understood perfectly that Vatican II teaches that Muslims worship God truly in prayer, almsgiving and fasting. Have Mary Margaret Funk and millions of others misunderstood the meaning of John Paul II's attending of the mosque, the Assisi event, the Buddhist temple, the Lutheran church and the synagogue? No, they have understood quite well that such actions are a validation of those false religions. It is because they have followed the official teaching of Vatican II that they have come to apostasy as a result.

The Apostasy of Mother Teresa and her Religious Order, The Missionaries of Charity

Mother Teresa of Calcutta was the founder of the Missionaries of Charity, one of the largest and most famous religious orders in the Vatican II sect. **Mother Teresa is considered to be one of the shining lights of the post-Vatican II religion.** The sad truth is that she wasn't even Catholic. Her religious indifferentism and apostasy from the Catholic Faith was illustrated in a 1989 interview with *Time* Magazine.

Mother Teresa's 1989 Interview with *Time Magazine* – She loved all religions!

"**Time:** What do you think of Hinduism?

Mother Teresa: I love all religions, but I am in love with my own. No discussion. That's what we have to prove to them. Seeing what I do, **they realize that I am in love with Jesus.**"[36]

As quoted here, Mother Teresa loved all religions. Mother Teresa loved religions of Satan! She loved religions of idolatry, religions that reject Christ, etc. This is apostasy. And she will soon be a "saint" in the Vatican II sect, thus proving again that the Vatican II sect is not the Catholic Church.

1 Corinthians 13:3- "**And if I should distribute all my goods to feed the poor**, and if I should deliver my body to be burned, and have not charity, it profiteth me nothing."

Mother Teresa's charity was false, because it was not founded on the true Faith. It profited her nothing.

Pope Pius XI, *Mortalium Animos* (# 9), Jan. 6, 1928: "For which reason, since charity is based on a complete and sincere faith, the disciples of Christ must be united principally by the bond of one faith."[37]

Hebrews 11:6: "But without faith it is impossible to please God…"

Mother Teresa venerating the Hindu Gandhi

The Apostasy of the Religious Orders 408

Here is a picture of Mother Teresa worshipping Buddha in 1975.

In the picture on the left, we see Mother Teresa worshipping Buddha in a ceremony of thanksgiving for the 25th anniversary of the Missionaries of Charity. She is kneeling in prayer in the bottom-left corner of the picture. The picture on the right is a close-up of the same ceremony, which took place on October 7, 1975. When we consider this act, together with Mother Teresa's many other statements of apostasy below, there is no doubt that she was among the worst apostates and biggest false prophets in all of Catholic history.

After John Paul II held his idolatrous inter-religious prayer meeting in Assisi in 1986 where, among other abominations, the Dalai Lama placed a Buddhist statue on top of the Tabernacle, Mother Teresa referred to the day as "the most beautiful gift of God."[38]

A recently released book, *Everything Starts From Prayer, Mother Teresa's Meditations on Spiritual Life for People of all Faiths*, also shows Mother Teresa's thorough rejection of the Catholic Faith and the necessity of Christ for salvation. The foreword quotes one of her most famous statements, which reveals the demonic spirit of Mother Teresa's work:

> Mother Teresa: "I've always said **we should help a Hindu become a better Hindu, a Muslim become a better Muslim**, a Catholic become a better Catholic."[39]

This is apostasy from Jesus Christ and the Catholic Faith. Mother Teresa also stated:

> "**Some call Him Ishwar, some call Him Allah, some simply God**, but we have to acknowledge that it is He who made us for greater things: to love and be loved. What matters is that we love. We cannot love without prayer, and so **whatever religion we are, we must pray together.**"[40]

So, in short, Mother Teresa believed that God (the Most Holy Trinity) and demons (the false gods of the heathens) are one and the same. The fact that she is considered "saintly" by the Vatican II sect constitutes one of the biggest spiritual frauds in Christian history. Mother Teresa expressed a general attitude of indifference to what religion a man professed, and manifested her approval of false religions of the Devil (non-Christian religions) consistently.

"Once, **when Mother Teresa was ministering to a dying Buddhist man, a visitor overheard her whisper, 'You say a prayer in your religion,** and I will say a prayer as I know it. Together we will say this prayer and it will be something beautiful for God.'"[41]

In *Mother Teresa, A Pictorial Biography* by Joanna Hurley, we read the following on page 68 about Mother Teresa's Order, *The Missionaries of Charity*:

> "A Catholic Order, *The Missionaries of Charity* is nonetheless ecumenical in its work. **The nuns bury the dying they have nursed according to the rites of each individual's religion**, and they observe local holidays [of the other religions] along with those of the Church. **Here a group of young nuns help children light sparklers for Diwali, India's Festival of Lights.**"[42]

This means that the nuns of Mother Teresa's order not only approved of, but actually participated in, the pagan rites of non-Christian religions. **This is because they are following the religious indifferentism of their founder, Mother Teresa.** On page 68 of this book, there is a picture of **the nuns of Mother Teresa's order lighting the sparklers for the Hindu festival of Diwali** with gigantic smiles on their faces. This is sin against the Faith of the worst kind; nay, it is religion of Antichrist – where man, and his personal preference for false religions, supersedes and replaces Jesus Christ.

A friend of ours from Canada recently called the superior of one of Mother Teresa's convents. Our friend said, "How come Mother Teresa never tried to convert anyone?" "Mother Superior" from Canada responded: "*It is the ultimate respect for the human person to respect his religion.*" "Mother Superior" told our friend that these non-Catholics are going to Heaven even if they reject Christ, as long as they are "good people," for that's what matters, according to her. In other words, man and his choice of religion are greater and more important than Jesus Christ. This is the Gospel of Antichrist, and Mother Teresa was its main false prophet and exemplar outside of the Vatican II antipopes. She cloaked her apostasy in purely natural works which gave her the appearance of true charity when, in fact, she had none.

> Pope St. Pius X, *Editae Saepe* (# 28), May 26, 1910: "As a matter of fact, however, **merely naturally good works are only a counterfeit of virtue** since they are neither permanent nor sufficient for salvation."[43]

Mother Teresa fed and clothed the bodies of many people, but she left their souls starving for what they needed most, Our Lord Jesus Christ. She deprived these souls of the only thing that really mattered, and therefore was not their true friend, but their enemy.

> Luke 12:4-5: "[Jesus saith] And I say to you, my friends: **Be not afraid of them who kill the body**, and after that have no more that they can do. But I will shew you whom you

shall fear: fear ye him, who after he hath killed, hath power to cast into hell. Yea, I say to you, fear him."

John 17:3- "Now **this is life everlasting, that they may know thee, the only true God, and Jesus Christ**, whom thou hast sent."

1 John 5:11-12: "And this is the testimony, that God hath given to us eternal life. **And this life is in his Son. He that hath the Son, hath life. He that hath not the Son, hath not life.**"

We have spent some extended time on this issue because it's likely that the Vatican II sect will soon "canonize" the apostate Mother Teresa, who exemplified some of the worst religious indifferentism of any of the members of the Vatican II sect. Since canonizations are infallible, this will be further proof that the Vatican II antipopes are not true popes.

We could continue with page after page of examples of the apostasy of the religious orders, but the point should be clear. The religious orders of the Vatican II sect are apostate since they are following the teaching of Vatican II.

Endnotes for Section 32:

[1] *The Abbey Banner – Magazine of St. John's Abbey*, Collegeville, MN, Winter, 2006, p. 24.
[2] *The Abbey Banner – Magazine of St. John's Abbey*, Winter, 2006, p. 24.
[3] http://www.townhall.com/opinion/columns/patbuchanan/2002/12/11/165161.html; also Kenneth Jones, *Index of Leading Catholic Indicators: The Church Since Vatican II*.
[4] http://www.faithfulvoice.com/convertino.htm
[5] http://www.urbandharma.org/images/NunsoftheWest/31_JPG.html
[6] http://www.jesuit.ie/main/
[7] http://www.osb.org/
[8] http://www.jmanjackal.net/eng/engyoga.htm
[9] Denzinger, *The Sources of Catholic Dogma*, B. Herder Book. Co., Thirtieth Edition, 1957, no. 1782.
[10] *The Papal Encyclicals*, by Claudia Carlen, Raleigh: The Pierian Press, 1990, Vol. 3 (1903-1939), p. 526.
[11] *The Encyclicals of John Paul II*, Huntington, IN: Our Sunday Visitor Publishing Division, 1996, p. 316.
[12] *The Encyclicals of John Paul II*, p. 316.
[13] Donald Attwater, *A Catholic Dictionary*, Tan Books, 1997, p. 366.
[14] *The Catholic Encyclopedia*, Vol. 11, New York: Robert Appleton Co., 1911, p. 447.
[15] http://www.jmanjackal.net/eng/engyoga.htm
[16] http://www.trappist.net/newweb/enews_03_18_05.html
[17] http://www.carmelitespiritualcenter.org/living-light.asp?a=retreats
[18] Confirmed in a personal telephone communication with Ecclesia Center.
[19] http://www.ecclesiacenter.org/staff.htm
[20] http://www.ecclesiacenter.org/index.htm
[21] http://www.budgettravelonline.com/bt-dyn/content/article/2005/06/04/AR2005060400391.html
[22] *National Catholic Reporter*, July 16, 2004.
[23] http://www.monasticdialog.com/bulletins/73/boardnews.htm
[24] http://www.beliefnet.com/story/16/story_1675_1.html
[25] *The Papal Encyclicals*, Vol. 1 (1740-1878), pp. 237-238.
[26] http://www.spiritualityandpractice.com/days/features.php?id=10953
[27] *The Abbey Banner – Magazine of St. John's Abbey*, Winter, 2006, p. 24.
[28] *The Abbey Banner – Magazine of St. John's Abbey*, Winter, 2006, p. 24.
[29] *The Abbey Banner – Magazine of St. John's Abbey*, Winter, 2006, p. 25.
[30] Mary Margaret Funk, *Islam: What Catholics Should Know*, St. Anthony Messenger, August, 2005, p. 36.
[31] Mary Margaret Funk, *Islam: What Catholics Should Know*, St. Anthony Messenger, August, 2005, p. 36.
[32] Mary Margaret Funk, *Islam: What Catholics Should Know*, St. Anthony Messenger, August, 2005, p. 38.
[33] Mary Margaret Funk, *Islam: What Catholics Should Know*, St. Anthony Messenger, August, 2005, p. 39.

[34] *Decrees of the Ecumenical Councils*, Sheed & Ward and Georgetown University Press, 1990, Vol. 2, p. 969.
[35] Mary Margaret Funk, *Islam: What Catholics Should Know*, St. Anthony Messenger, August, 2005, p. 39.
[36] http://www.servelec.net/mothertheresa.htm
[37] *The Papal Encyclicals*, Vol. 3 (1903-1939), p. 316.
[38] *Time Magazine*, Nov. 10, 1986.
[39] Anthony Stern, *Everything Starts From Prayer, Mother Teresa's Meditations on Spiritual Life for People of all Faiths*.
[40] Anthony Stern, *Everything Starts From Prayer, Mother Teresa's Meditations on Spiritual Life for People of all Faiths*.
[41] Anthony Stern, *Everything Starts From Prayer, Mother Teresa's Meditations on Spiritual Life for People of all Faiths*.
[42] Joanna Hurley, *Mother Teresa: A Pictorial Biography*, Courage Books, 1997, p. 68.
[43] *The Papal Encyclicals*, Vol. 3 (1903-1939), p. 121.

33. Shocking News items provide a summary of the Apostasy of the Vatican II Sect's dioceses, faithful, clergy, religious orders, etc.

The seemingly <u>bottomless pit of scandal</u> produced by the Vatican II sect in the areas of outrageous New Masses (many of which we have already catalogued), "Catholic" colleges and universities, and the actions of its apostate hierarchy and members, is documented on the internet basically on a daily basis.

Here are just some of the headlines which we have posted in the "News and Commentary" section of our website about the scandal of the Vatican II sect in the past year or so. Obviously, we cannot reproduce the full articles which corroborated these headlines. We have endnotes for almost all of the headlines listed here; those without a reference are from real articles that we linked to, but which have been moved to a different place or are no longer stored on the host website. All of these headlines are <u>real reflections of true occurrences</u> in the Vatican II sect. **More of the same come out every day**.

-Novus Ordo "Cardinal" Cheong of Seoul sends greetings for Buddha's Birth and says: "We need Buddha's teaching more and more"[1]

Wow, that's some apostasy... but the "cardinal" is just following the lead of the Vatican II antipopes. Remember this one:

> John Paul II, May 6, 1984: "... the Korean people throughout history have sought, in the great ethical and religious visions of Buddhism and Confucianism, the path to renewal of self... **May I address a particular greeting to the members of the Buddhist tradition as they prepare to celebrate the festivity of** <u>the Coming of the Lord Buddha</u>? May your rejoicing be complete and your joy fulfilled."[2]

-Buddhist Ritual in Novus Ordo Cathedral

"Pyeonghwa Broadcasting Corporation (PBC), the cable TV station run by Seoul Archdiocese, invited Buddhists to perform the Yeongsanjae ritual at Coste Hall in the Myongdong Cathedral compound on April 19. The performance was part of a mostly musical program for an audience of about 200 Buddhists and Catholics.

"It marked the first time that Myongdong Cathedral has held such a Buddhist ritual in its compound, according to the cathedral office."[3]

-So-called "Catholic priest" denies that Jesus even founded a Church on *Larry King Live's* (CNN's) promotional for "God or the Girl"

> "KING: And Father Manning, did Christ in fact form a church?
>
> "MANNING: **Not necessarily**.
>
> "KING: Did he die a Jew?
>
> "MANNING: As the church -- he was very much that. We started to move later on in

that -- certainly there were the apostles, there were the group. But, yes, no I agree, yes.

"KING: You can chime in, too. You're more than a student.

"DEMATTE: Christ -- the Catholic Church does not believe that Christ did not start a church. The Catholic Church teaches -- we proclaim every day in the creed, we believe in one holy Catholic apostolic church. We believe in one church, founded by Christ, and that church was founded in Matthew Chapter 16, where Jesus gave Peter the keys to the kingdom of God.

"And with that, it goes back to the Old Testament where the Old Testament kings would hand over the keys to the kingdom to the prime minister when that king was going to leave.

"And so while Jesus was leaving our kingdom here on earth, he was going to the kingdom of God and he gave his keys over to Peter, the prime -- with primary lead in our church and that's where our papal primacy comes from. That's where our authority comes from. And that's where Jesus establishes the church."[4]

On April 13, 2006, *Larry King Live* hosted a program called "God or the Girl" about young men torn between choosing the Novus Ordo "priesthood" or marriage. It was a promotional for a program by the same title that appeared on another network. As part of the panel, Larry King had so-called "Catholic priest" Fr. Michael Manning, the host of "The Word in the World." Fr. Manning is frequently shown on *Larry King Live* supposedly to give the official "Roman Catholic" perspective. Well, as we can see above, when asked whether Jesus even founded a Church, Fr. Manning said "not necessarily," and that this was formed much later on! This is such an outrage that one is at a loss for words to comment on it.

One of the young men on the show named Dematte – who is considering the Novus Ordo "priesthood" – actually chimed in, to his credit, and refuted the heresy, as we see in the transcript above. But this tells us where we are in history, and how far from Catholic the Vatican II sect is: a supposed Catholic priest, featured by CNN to give the official "Catholic" line **to millions of viewers**, denies that Jesus even founded a Church.

-New Novus Ordo "Archbishop" of San Francisco finds Gay Cowboy movie "Very Powerful"[5]

-Circus and Clown "Mass" in Florida

"**Priests in multicolored vestments depicting lions, tigers, clowns and other circus performers** concelebrated the circus Sunday Mass **for a more-than-capacity congregation Jan. 15 [2006]**. The annual Mass at St. Martha Parish in Sarasota was celebrated by Father Fausto Stampiglia, SAC, pastor, and Bishop John Kinney of the Diocese of St. Cloud, Minn."[6]

Shocking News items summarize the Apostasy

"Dressed in multicolored vestments, from left, Father Fausto Stampiglia, pastor of St. Martha Parish; Father Gavin Griffith of Monterrey, Calif., seated; Bishop John Kinney of St. Cloud, Minn.; Father Charles Watkins of Chicago; and Father Jim Challancin of Crystal Falls, Mich., concelebrated the circus Mass Jan. 15." [7]

This is a complete mockery of God and the Catholic Faith, but it's just another day in the Vatican II sect. Notice that a Novus Ordo "bishop" was fully involved with this outrage. It was also performed before a more-than-capacity congregation.

-Vatican newspaper agrees that Intelligent Design should not be taught in schools[8]

What more proof could one possibly need that we are in the Great Apostasy, and that Rome is occupied by a counterfeit non-Catholic sect, than the fact that the official Vatican newspaper agrees that Intelligent Design should not be taught in schools? Wow!

-With the "Bishop's" permission, Novus Ordo "priest" announces he's gay during the Novus Ordo "Mass," and declares that he will be leaving to pursue a gay relationship[9]

Thunder Bay (Ontario) Diocesan Bishop Fred Colli also said that he "admires" the priest's decision.

-Archdiocese of Los Angeles officially invites all to ecumenical Taize prayer services

-Muslims are going to Heaven, says EWTN priest[10]

- Rabbi Made a "Papal" Knight by the Vatican II sect

"Rabbi David Rosen, the American Jewish Committee's international director of interreligious affairs on Thursday became the first Israeli citizen, the first Orthodox rabbi and the fifth living

Jew to be invested with a papal knighthood... The investiture was conducted by Cardinal Walter Kasper, President of the Holy See's Commission for Religious Relations with Jewry."[11]

-Novus Ordo "Priests" seek to adopt Hindu rituals

"A gathering <u>of leading Catholic clergymen</u> from all over India have asked the Vatican to endorse their proposal to include Hindu rituals in the church. The Pune Papal seminary said **priests from all over India were unanimous that the Catholic clergy must incorporate Hindu practices** like performing *aarti* during mass, studying Sanskrit and the Vedas, and experiencing ashram life."[12]

-Novus Ordo Diocesan Agency helps Gays Adopt Children

-The official website of the Novus Ordo "Bishops" officially pays homage to pro-abortion and pro-homosexual Rabbi Balfour[13]

The website also declared that this Jewish Rabbi may rest in peace with the Lord, and asks that his name may forever be a blessing. If this isn't apostasy then nothing has ever been apostasy.

-Lutheran funeral service for non-Catholic Rehnquist to be held in Novus Ordo Cathedral[14]

-Canadian Novus Ordo Diocese of St. George to sell all of its churches to pay Sex Abuse Claims[15]

-Diocese Settles Lawsuit over accused molestation by "traditional" Society of St. John priests[16]

-45% of "Catholic" Hospitals in US Dispense Abortion Drugs[17]

-Benedict XVI Invites Rabbi of Rome to Installation

-Novus Ordo "Bishop" of San Diego Apologizes for Not having Catholic Funeral for Gay Nightclub Owner! The "bishop" now agrees to have "Mass" in memory of the sodomy promoter.[18]

-St. Petersburg's "Bishop" Lynch Favors Starving Terri Schiavo[19]

-Novus Ordo "Mass" with firecrackers, drums, gongs and a costumed dragon dance

-England's "Bishops" Adopt Gay Equality Agenda[20]

-Another Pro-Gay/ "Sodomy Mass" in the Novus Ordo[21]

-EWTN Priest says that it's okay to attend Protestant services[22]

The EWTN "priest," Rev. Mark J. Gantley, JCL, even agrees that it's okay to attend a JW or LDS service, which means a Jehovah's Witness or Mormon service! Jehovah's Witnesses reject the Most Holy Trinity. Mormons allow polygamy and believe that men can become gods. But, if you believe that the Vatican II "popes" are legitimate, don't complain about this advice. This apostate "priest" is just following what is officially taught by John Paul II in #118 of the incredible *Directory for the Application of the Principles and Norms of Ecumenism,* as we covered earlier.

In # 118, the Directory says that <u>Catholics who attend non-Catholic churches are "encouraged to take part in the psalms, responses, hymns and common actions of the Church in which they are guests</u>."

> On March 25, 1993, John Paul II "approved this Directory, confirmed it by his authority and ordered that it be published. Anything to the contrary notwithstanding."[23]

This is why a manifest heretic could never be a true pope. These people are following the official teachings of the Vatican II religion and they are following it right to Hell! The authoritative teachings of a true pope don't lead one to Hell!

-Jews, Buddhists and Unitarians worship together with "Catholics" at a Novus Ordo church

-Kickapoo Tribe member preaches at another interfaith service at a Novus Ordo church

-"Catholic" University of Notre Dame has Gay Lifestyle Celebration[24]

-Hundreds of Baptisms declared invalid at Novus Ordo church in Australia[25]

-Novus Ordo "Archbishop" of Dublin favors Homosexual Spousal Rights[26]

-Novus Ordo Chaplains will be combined with Protestant Chaplains

-Novus Ordo "Catholic Bishops" Celebrate Anniversary of Protestant Revolution with the Lutherans!

The question must be asked: Is this your hierarchy? If you are a Catholic the answer must be a resounding *no*. The apostate "Catholic Bishop" of Bismarck also made sure to quote the incredible *Joint Declaration with the Lutherans on Justification* in this celebration.

-"Cardinal" of Mexico unveils plate commemorating Dalai Lama's visit[27]

-Buddhists Defile Mexico City Cathedral with "cardinal's" permission[28]

Shocking News items summarize the Apostasy   417

Please notice the striking contrast in the picture on the left with Mexico's "Cardinal" Norberto Rivera and the Dalai Lama. Above, we see the large crucifix of Our Lord Jesus, while below – like the serpent slithering on the ground – we see his enemy, the Dalai Lama, invading His space and corrupting the children, with the Novus Ordo "cardinal" looking on, encouraging and enabling him. This picture captures in one shot the striking reality of what has occurred: a phony, antichrist, non-Catholic sect has arisen with Vatican II, and it attempts to eclipse the true Church of Christ (the true Catholic Church), which has been reduced to a remnant of faithful Catholics.

> Our Lady of La Salette, Sept. 19, 1846: "Rome will lose the faith and become the Seat of the Antichrist… the Church will be in eclipse."

-Novus Ordo Nun Obsessed with Elvis

-Two Novus Ordo hospitals Commit Live-Birth Abortions, condoned by bishops[29]

-"Catholic" Loyola University Chicago Invites totally pro-abortion Howard Dean to speak[30]

-Kid dressed as Harry Potter helps priest at New Mass[31]

-Occult-like practices rampant in the Novus Ordo[32]

Shocking News items summarize the Apostasy

-St. Joan of Arc church promotes Gay/Lesbian/Bisexual/Transgender Agenda[33]

-Only 8 Novus Ordo "priests" to be ordained in all of Ireland[34]

There is only one seminary left in the entire country; all the rest have been closed.

-Only 18 Novus Ordo "priests" to be ordained in all of England and Wales[35]

-Bishop Bernard Harrington of Winona Diocese says *yes* and appoints gay predator "priest"[36]

-"Cardinal" Law's prestigious new role in Rome, given by John Paul II

Thanks to John Paul II, one of the most abominable men in the Novus Ordo sect, "Cardinal" Law of Boston – the man who shuffled pedophile "priests" from parish to parish in Boston, including the founder of the unspeakable man-boy love association – is now on commissions overseeing the appointment of bishops and the oversight of priests. Law "is the titular head of two significant churches there: the Basilica of St. Mary Major, one of the four patriarchal basilicas of the Catholic Church, and Santa Susanna, an ancient parish now dedicated to serving Americans in Rome. He is seen about town with some frequency, patronizing some of the same restaurants he preferred when Rome was just a place he visited, and sitting in the front row at important Vatican events."[37]

-Novus Ordo Molesters Were Moved From Country to Country[38]

-"Cardinal" Maida of Detroit OK's Tridentine Mass only to keep people away from independent Traditional Masses[39]

This is an interesting article. It demonstrates that the Novus Ordo bishops are quite evil. Maida is concerned that too many people in Detroit are going to the Traditional Mass because they see the Novus Ordo for the bad joke it is. This he must stop, while he allows all kinds of other sacrileges and abominations and every heresy under the sun.

-Scranton Seminary closes

"Citing a shortage of priests and the lack of those interested in becoming priests, Diocese of Scranton Bishop Joseph F. Martino announced Thursday the shutting down of St. Pius X Seminary… Priest shortages have crippled dioceses throughout the country. The Diocese of Scranton, with 355,000 Catholics in 11 counties, is served by 224 priests -- fewer than half the number serving in 1966."[40]

Why would this seminary remain open? According to the Vatican II sect, Islam should be protected, Protestant religions are a means of salvation, Eastern schismatics should not be converted, and Christ is united with everyone because of the Incarnation.

-"Cardinal" Mahony, the apostate phony, says Rainbow Sash Protesters OK to receive Communion

This article also mentions that "Cardinal" George, the apostate Archbishop of Chicago, has instructed the Novus Ordo "priests" to deny the Rainbow Sash protesters (active homosexuals) Communion. The Novus Ordo "conservatives" are really emphasizing this fact. George is considered to be an "ultra-conservative" among the pack of heretics that makes up the Vatican II sect. Yet George recently celebrated the Muslim holyday of Ramadan in a Mosque together with a group of priests and nuns from his diocese. The Chicago Tribune noted that George "was the first Chicago archbishop to attend such an event," and that "as the last verses of the Imam Senad Agic's melodious prayer resonated under the white and gold dome... clerics and laypeople of both faiths bowed their heads."[41] This is utter apostasy, of course.

"Cardinal" George in his diocesan newspaper also wrote that "The Church has also sinned against the Jewish people, first of all, in teaching that God's covenant with Israel is no longer valid..."[42] This means that George holds that the Jews have a valid covenant with God and don't need to convert to the Catholic Faith or Jesus Christ for salvation. Remember, he's a "conservative" among the Vatican II sect's bishops!

-Pictures of the Novus Ordo "bishop" who threw his election party at a Masonic Temple![43]

-John Paul II Applauds the Charismatic Renewal[44]

-Boston "Archdiocese" will close 65 parishes and 60 churches

"The Boston Archdiocese will lose 65 of its 357 parishes in a massive restructuring brought on partly by the sex abuse scandal that aggravated already shrinking Mass attendance and weekly collections."[45]

-Novus Ordo Priest Denies "Holy Communion" to Pro-life Politician because he was kneeling

"On September 22, the Cathedral Rector, Fr. Dominic Irace, refused to give Communion to Delegate Black since Black was kneeling to receive. Fr. Irace told him he must stand to receive, but Black chose rather to genuflect and withdraw."[46]

-Gymnastics practiced inside this French Novus Ordo parish!

-John Paul II's Envoy Favors Recognition of Sodomite Unions

"Departing from his prepared speech, the 'papal nuncio' added that although the law in Spain, and many other countries, defined marriage as the union of a man and a woman, 'there are other forms of cohabitation and it is good that they be recognized.'"[47]

-Britain's vocation crisis deepens

"As Catholics around the world prayed for vocations yesterday, congregations in Britain were asking for nothing short of a miracle. Only 38 men entered the country's seminaries this year meaning that, with the deaths and retirements of their predecessors, the number of priests in Britain could be halved in less than ten years."[48]

-Toronto "Catholic" University Alumni Magazine Boasts of Homosexual "Marriage"[49]

-Ontario "Catholic" Teachers' Union Website Promotes Transvestites and Drag Queens!

"The conference keynote address, titled Loving the Difference: Drag Queens, Transvestites and Me, will be given by professed transvestite Sky Gilbert. The occasion also features such offerings as: Enhancing sexual empowerment: Therapeutic use of sex toys; Tantra: Ancient sex for modern times; and Outside of the boxes: Youth perspectives on gender and sexual identities."[50]

-Inter-religious service at Arcadia Parish

The Blessed Sacrament (or, rather, what they wrongly deem to be the Blessed Sacrament) was removed from the parish so that "pastors" of various heretical denominations could partake in an ecumenical prayer service and intone prayers in the "Catholic" church.[51]

-"Cardinal" Martini says "Catholic Church" should abandon the Papal Monarchy and become a democracy[52]

Martini, now retired, was actually one of the most prominent "cardinals" in the world as "Archbishop" of Milan. The article indicates that he favors women deacons, laymen selecting bishops, and a governing council to rule his "Church" along with the "pope."

-John Kerry Receives "Communion" and is applauded at the New "Mass"!

-Novus Ordo Priest's New Way of Praying the Rosary: Focus on Yourself, Not Christ[53]

-What a Surprise: Pro-Abort Politician Durbin Receives "Communion" in the Novus Ordo[54]

-More Paganism in the Novus Ordo: Kansas City members celebrate "Year of the Monkey"[55]

-The "Cardinal Archbishop" of Paris, Jean-Marie Lustiger, Condemns *The Passion*[56]

"Cardinal" Lustiger, who was raised a Jew, stated in a 1981 interview: "*I am a Jew. For me the two religions are one.*"[57] So the Vatican II sect has two openly Jewish bishops, Gourion in Jerusalem (see next section) and Lustiger in Paris. What an absolute joke that this man was the head of the Vatican II sect in Paris, an archdiocese which is one of the largest and most prominent in the world. The Vatican II sect is a sick joke.

-The Vatican II sect is the "Church" of Sodom[58]

Here is a partial list of "Gay Friendly" parishes in the Vatican II sect. The promotion of homosexuality and lesbianism is rampant in the dioceses of the Vatican II sect.

-Novus Ordo "Priests" dying of AIDS all over the place

The death rate of priests from AIDS is at least four times that of the general population, the newspaper said.[59]

-Novus Ordo "Franciscans" welcome homosexuality[60]

St. Anthony's will hold a gay and lesbian Sunday brunch Dec. 8, which it calls an "Afternoon of Reflection: Body, Mind & Spirit."

- John Paul II "canonized" and "beatified" more people than all the popes combined since the formal process was created

Antipope John Paul II did this in order to demean the significance of sainthood and in order to make the road to Heaven seem very wide, so that not only are all men saved (as he repeatedly taught), but basically everyone is a saint. Fortunately for Catholics, Antipope John Paul II had no authority to canonize or beatify anyone, since he was a non-Catholic antipope.

-Novus Ordo "Franciscan" Friars in Boston angrily oppose the distribution of flyers against homosexual "marriage"[61]

Hmmm, we wonder why…

-The Novus Ordo "Archbishop" of Johannesburg, South Africa, supports the offering of the blood of sacrificed animals during the Novus Ordo "Mass"[62]

-Here is another article reporting the same[63]

"Archbishop" Buti Tlhagale of Bloemfontein, South Africa proposes that the blood of the slain animal – be it goat, chicken, sheep or cow – can be presented during the Mass as 'a gift to the ancestors…' He also asserts that "Animal sacrifice has a special place in the scheme of things and is celebrated in almost all African families. We have kept it out of God's Church for too long."

This is satanic. But again, this wicked "archbishop" is just following John Paul II's lead. Remember that it was John Paul II who was a good buddy of the voodooists and allowed them to preach from "Catholic" pulpits and practice their satanic rites in "Catholic" churches, such as on the World Day of Prayer for Peace, Jan. 24, 2002.

-A Witch gets Novus Ordo Burial[64]

-L.A. Cathedral features a liturgy with 50-foot dragons representing the god of rainfall!

The "Cardinal Archbishop" of Los Angeles, Roger Mahony, was in attendance, **while "the program handed out before the Mass dedicated the first page to justifying the presence of the dragon and lion dances**. The dragon, according to the program, is a legendary animal in Chinese mythology, signifying power, prosperity, fertility, majesty, and regal dignity. **Believed to be the governing god of rainfall**, and China being traditionally an agricultural country, the 'veneration to the dragon,' read the program, 'slowly evolved as a cult.'"[65]

Those who consider Benedict XVI as the pope must recognize Roger Mahony as the leader of the "Catholic Church" in Los Angeles. Such an idea is obviously insane.

-Novus Ordo priest commemorated by liturgical dancers with face paint during Sunday "Mass"

-Bishop of San Jose Denies Historical Accuracy of the Gospels

> "The Roman Catholic bishop of San Jose, California **has written an editorial for the local paper in which he denies the historical truth of the Gospels**. In response to the accusations of anti-semitism which have been made against the film, "The Passion of the Christ," Bishop Patrick J. McGrath wrote in *The Mercury News* on February 18, that the charge of anti-Semitism cannot be leveled against Catholicism since Catholics do not adhere to the literal, historical truth of Scripture."[66]

Pope St. Pius X condemned anyone who would deny the historical accuracy of the Gospels in "Lamentabili Sane," #'s 11, 14 and 16.[67] Besides all of the other heresies, when we consider the fact that this Novus Ordo bishop publicly denies one of the foundations of divine revelation (Sacred Scripture), and nothing was done to him since many others feel the same, it is further proof that the Novus Ordo/Vatican II sect is not the Catholic Church.

-Crowd erupts into wild frenzy as six Novus Ordo "Priests" sing love songs

"The crowd erupted into a wild frenzy near the end of the show, with the priests dancing and singing "Mr. Suave" and "Otso-otso," which was performed twice and had the people dancing to the ubiquitous tune."[68]

-The Vatican II sect has basically eliminated the Catholic Faith from Ireland

"The Catholic Church in Ireland faces the worst crisis in its history. The scandal of clerical sexual abuse has compounded the catastrophic decline in vocations to the priesthood. All but one of the diocesan seminaries have closed and a generation of religious illiterates is being produced by the current catechetical program. **The pews are emptying more rapidly than ever before**. In some Dublin parishes, Sunday Mass attendance has fallen to well below 10 per cent."[69]

-Novus Ordo "Church" in Australia openly promotes Occultism and Witchcraft

This article shows how the Australian Vatican II "church" is rife with occultism, witchcraft and goddess worship. "That the Australian church today has been seriously compromised by Goddess worshippers can be seen on a number of fronts: For example, **many churches, as a matter of custom, contain "pagan blessing trees"** — dead tree limbs festooned with red, large yellow, green, and blue ribbons. Also, prayers — even official prayers such as that used for the success of the Brisbane Archdiocese's Synod 2003 — omit any reference to "God" or the traditional formulary "through Jesus Christ our Lord," but rather refer to the "Holy Spirit of Fire . . . [to] help us recognize wisdom even from unlikely sources."[70]

-Michigan Basilica Featured Buddhist Prayer Chants[71]

Buddhist monks had a chanting prayer service in a Michigan basilica. Certain traditionalist-minded folks, who were not part of the Novus Ordo church where this was occurring, protested this outrage. They actually made moves to force the Buddhist chanting to stop. The traditionalist-minded protesters were opposed by angry members of the Novus Ordo, who said: "maybe you should take it up with John Paul II – he's a good friend of the Dalai Lama." The members of the Novus Ordo also complained to the protesters: we came to see the monks – referring to the Buddhist monks!

-Diocese of the Vatican II sect in Cleveland is Worried about "The Passion of the Christ"

"The Diocese of Cleveland <u>sent a February memo to all its parishes</u> asking Catholics to be aware of the potential for anti-Semitism [from the film]."[72]

Let's get this straight: the Novus Ordo "bishops" allow every kind of heresy and abomination to occur and do nothing to stop it, but get worried and take immediate action against anything that might be good and Catholic. **Would they ever send a letter to all of their parishes warning about the rise of modernism, liturgical abuse, the acceptance of contraception and permissive lifestyles, and the gay agenda in "Catholic" circles?** No. But when something good is out there, especially something that the Christ-rejecting Jews don't like, they move immediately and contact every single parish. It's just amazing. It's truly the Counter Church.

-Toronto Novus Ordo "Catholic" Priest Files Supreme Court Affidavit Supporting Gay Marriage[73]

This priest is "highly credentialed" and in good standing in the Vatican II sect in Toronto.

-Novus Ordo "Priest" has Puppet "Masses"

"The idea to use ventriloquism in his children's liturgies came to Father Sweet during his time as a seminarian when he had first met Father Charles… He started out with hand puppets as a way to boost the children's interest and it has evolved into a wonderful talent… There was so much laughter at church by the young and young at heart. The children that I teach say he is awesome, hilarious and so cute. **They hope to see the puppet again at Mass**… We all love Fr. Doug, he is so full of joy. **His puppet Masses are a true delight for everyone.** <u>The children get so excited they can hardly stay seated in the pews</u>. The first time Fr. Doug did a Mass with his grandfather puppet was at our grandparent liturgy. You could feel the joy in our church that day."[74]

"The children get so excited [at "Mass" about a puppet!] that they can hardly stay seated in the pews"! Whew! This is truly a new religion! This article about "Fr." Doug and the puppet "Masses" is featured on the official website of the Diocese of Shreveport, Louisiana.

-Novus Ordo priest uses Muppets Fr. Kermit and Sr. Piggy at Sunday Mass in Alaska[75]

A woman from Anchorage informed us that every Sunday at her parish (for many months during the year), the Novus Ordo "priest" Fr. Patrick Fletcher uses muppets. "Fr. Kermit" and "Sr. Piggy" emerge from a box on the altar and carry on a dialogue in their distinctive voices in order to instruct the people. This is truly a new religion and a false religion.

-Break-Dancers perform for Antipope John Paul II and Get His Blessing

VATICAN CITY – "In an unusual spectacle at the Vatican, Pope [sic] John Paul II presided Sunday over a performance of break-dancers who leaped, flipped and spun their bodies to beats from a tiny boom box. The 83-year-old pontiff seemed to approve, waving his hand after each dancer completed a move, then applauding for the entire group. He watched the performance from a raised throne. '**For this creative hard work I bless you from my heart,'** he said."[76]

-"Fr." Stan Fortuna is the Rapping "Priest"

The "Rapping Priest," "Fr." Stan Fortuna, is promoted even by "conservative" sectors of the Vatican II "Church," such as EWTN and "Franciscan" University. **Stan has stated publicly that he was "inspired" to his current activity by John Paul II's promotion of Rock Music**. One of his songs is called, "Say Yes to Sex (Theology of the Body)."[77] Notice that in the photo[78] "Fr." Stan seems to be giving the *El Diablo* (the horned Devil sign), which is popular among Satanists and satanic rock groups. Many give this satanic hand gesture without knowing it because they're taken over by the evil spirit, as the "Rapping Priest" probably was at this time. As stated earlier, some point out that the *El Diablo* (Devil's horns) sign is similar to the hand gesture for "I love you" in sign language. That's true, but that's probably because the inventor of the deaf signing system, Helen Keller, was herself an occultist and a Theosophist. She wrote a book called *My Religion*, in which she explained her occult views.[79] Some believe that she designed the "I love you sign" to correspond with the horned Devil sign so that the one making it is literally saying that he or she loves Satan.

-German Diocese Offers Zen Meditation[80]

The bulletin is in German, but you can see the promotion of satanic Zen Meditation at the top.

-Novus Ordo Priest says, "I hate the Rosary."

This was an article about **a Novus Ordo priest who carries off statues to the trash and dresses up as superman or the grinch for "Mass,"** and much more. What is perhaps almost as bad as this satanic (obviously possessed) priest is that he operates in good standing in his diocese. His wicked bishop and the Vatican do nothing, but this shouldn't be a surprise. He presides over a large Novus Ordo congregation and the numbers of his "church" are growing.

Here are a few quotes from the priest: On life after death, in a 1981 interview:``*There's just God and me and you. No Devil. No angels. But there is a Heaven, and Jesus is in it. And I can't wait to get there.*" On the Rosary: ``*I hate the Rosary.*" On himself: "*I hope I haven't scandalized you. I wouldn't mind if I did.*" On the design of his last church: ``*I hired a Jewish architect. I told him, "If you make it look like a church, I'll kill you.*"

This article not only reminds us how wicked the apostate religion of the Novus Ordo is (something one can tend to forget if one has been removed from this for a long time), but the article shows how (sadly) most of the people at the church are almost as bad as the priest; for they accept and even embrace his antics. The fact that these people consider themselves "Catholics" and still attend this man's "church" is mind-boggling. In fact, the article points out how this priest's parishioners are the most dedicated donors in the diocese!

-St. Louise Novus Ordo church Conducts Interfaith Service at a Synagogue With Jews

Temple B'nai Torah was host facility this year for the annual Joint Community Prayer Service with St. Louise, Cross of Christ and Church of the Resurrection.[81] This is heresy, apostasy and a rejection of Our Lord Jesus Christ. But once again, the "priests" of this church are just following the lead of the Vatican II antipopes.

-Novus Ordo Nun who is responsible for education for a parish of 3000 says that she is happy that she has homosexuals at her Parish

"This parish of 3,000 is diverse, friendly and welcoming," says Holy Names Sister Dolores Barling, responsible for RCIA, adult education, liturgy and Bible study. "It's a wonderful parish," she adds, praising the parish's outreach to the poor. "We have elderly, lesbians, gays and a variety of ethnic backgrounds --- lots of diversity." "I love the people. I think sometimes that I am surrounded by saints."

-The Official Website of the Novus Ordo Bishops Endorses Teilhardian Pagan Spirituality[82]
(Look at "Cosmic Artist": Sister Blanche Marie Gallagher)

Conclusion on these sections concerning the scandals and unholiness of the Vatican II Counter-Church

The headlines and sections that we've covered are just the tip of the iceberg. Examples like the ones covered above could be continued for many pages. The Vatican II/Novus Ordo sect is characterized by its **inexhaustible scandal**. *More scandals and acts of unholiness come out almost daily. Since holiness is one of the marks of the true Church, if scandal and immorality are basically universal* in a Body which purports to be the true Church, that serves to prove it's not the true Church and that the true Catholic Faith is also not present. **And we've already proven that the Vatican II sect rejects the true Faith**, and thus cannot be the Catholic Church based on doctrinal grounds. To sum it up simply: the scandals and unholiness we've exposed are **the fruits** of the heresies and false doctrines embraced by **the Counter Church**. And by their fruits you shall know them (Matthew 7:16). What we have just covered about its inexhaustible scandal **serves to confirm this fact by showing that it's not the Holy Catholic Church.**

> Pope Pius IX, *Vatican Council I*, Sess. 3, Chap. 3, on Faith: "…**the Church itself by itself, because of its marvelous propagation, its exceptional holiness, and inexhaustible fruitfulness** in all good works; because of its Catholic unity and invincible stability, **is a**

very great and perpetual motive of credibility, and an incontestable witness of its own divine mission."[83]

We must now continue with this theme. We will now take a closer look at the beliefs of the hierarchy, and some of the prominent members, who are underneath the Vatican II antipopes.

Endnotes for Section 33:

[1] http://www.catholic.org/international/international_story.php?id=19634
[2] *L'Osservatore Romano* (the Vatican's Newspaper), May 14, 1984, p. 7.
[3] http://www.catholic.org/international/international_story.php?id=19563
[4] http://transcripts.cnn.com/TRANSCRIPTS/lkl.html
[5] http://www.lifesite.net/ldn/2006/feb/06021306.html
[6] Story and photo by Lois Kindle: http://www.thefloridacatholic.org/articles/2006/060203/060203-venice-circusmass.htm
[7] Story and photo by Lois Kindle: http://www.thefloridacatholic.org/articles/2006/060203/060203-venice-circusmass.htm
[8] http://www.catholicnews.com/data/stories/cns/0600273.htm
[9] http://www.lifesite.net/ldn/2006/jan/06010607.html
[10] http://www.ewtn.com/vexperts/showresult.asp?RecNum=453781&Forums=0&Experts=0&Days=14&Author=&Keyword=&pgnu=1&groupnum=0&record_bookmark=20&ORDER_BY_TXT=ORDER+BY+ID+DESC&start_at
[11] http://www.jpost.com/servlet/Satellite?cid=1131035504811&pagename=JPost/JPArticle/ShowFull
[12] http://www.ndtv.com/morenews/showmorestory.asp?category=National&slug=Catholic+priests+seek+Hindu+rituals&id=80561
[13] Text of the press release issued by the Office of Media Relations of the United States Catholic Conference, Sept. 2, 2005.
[14] http://www.beliefnet.com/story/174/story_17441_1.html
[15] http://www.theglobeandmail.com/servlet/Page/document/v4/sub/MarketingPage?user_URL=http://www.theglobeandmail.com%2Fservlet%2FArticleNews%2FTPStory%2FLAC%2F20050510%2FABUSE10%2FTPNational%2FCanada&ord=1158701757405&brand=theglobeandmail&force_login=true
[16] http://www.bishop-accountability.org/news2005_01_06/2005_05_10_Birk_DioceseOf.htm
[17] http://www.tldm.org/news8/AbortionCatholicHospitals.htm
[18] http://www.signonsandiego.com/news/metro/20050321-2013-bromapology.html
[19] http://www.worldnetdaily.com/news/article.asp?ARTICLE_ID=43624
[20] http://www.lifesite.net/ldn/2005/feb/05020803.html
[21] http://www.freerepublic.com/focus/f-religion/1317047/posts
[22] http://www.ewtn.com/vexperts/showmessage.asp?Pgnu=1&Pg=Forum9&recnu=6&number=421395
[23] *Directory for the Application of the Principles and Norms of Ecumenism*, by the Pontifical Council for Promoting Christian Unity, Boston, MA: St. Paul Books & Media, p. 124.
[24] http://www.lifesite.net/ldn/2005/feb/05021406.html
[25] http://www.findarticles.com/p/articles/mi_m0MKY/is_1_29/ai_n8709004
[26] http://www.lifesite.net/ldn/2004/nov/04111603.html
[27] http://www.phayul.com/news/article.aspx?t=3&c=1&id=7876
[28] http://www.phayul.com/news/article.aspx?t=3&c=1&id=7868
[29] http://www.worldnetdaily.com/news/article.asp?ARTICLE_ID=40465
[30] http://www.luc.edu/info/howarddean.shtml
[31] http://www.kath-kirche-kaernten.at/pages/aktuell.asp?menuopt=1000
[32] http://www.edith-stein-exerzitienhaus.de/rundgang/rund7.html
[33] http://www.stjoan.com/er1fr.htm
[34] http://www.montgomerycountynews.net/travel08-18-04.htm
[35] http://www.telegraph.co.uk/news/main.jhtml?xml=/news/2004/07/08/nrc08.xml&sSheet=/news/2004/07/08/ixhome.html
[36] http://www.cruxnews.com/rose/rose-09july04.html
[37] http://www.boston.com/news/local/massachusetts/articles/2004/07/04/in_romes_shadow/
[38] http://www.cwnews.com/news/viewstory.cfm?recnum=30298
[39] http://www.cruxnews.com/articles/crux-03june04.html
[40] http://thetimestribune.com/site/news.cfm?newsid=11815432&BRD=2185&PAG=461&dept_id=415898&rfi=6

41 *Chicago Tribune*, "George Breaks Fast with Muslims, Jan. 21, 1998, Section 2, p. 3.
42 Cardinal Francis George, "The Sins of the Church: God's Forgiveness and Human Memories, Catholic New World," March 19, 2000.
43 http://www.rcf.org
44 http://www.dici.org/actualite_read.php?id=358&loc=US
45 http://www.boston.com/news/local/massachusetts/articles/2004/05/25/archdiocese_announces_60_churches_will_close/
46 http://www.lifesite.net/ldn/2002/oct/02101001.html
47 http://www.theage.com.au/articles/2004/05/05/1083635202645.html
48 http://www.cwnews.com/news/viewstory.cfm?recnum=29304
49 http://www.lifesite.net/ldn/2004/apr/04042306.html
50 http://www.lifesite.net/ldn/2004/apr/04041309.html
51 http://www.losangelesmission.com/ed/roamincatholic/0103roam.htm
52 http://www.cathnews.com/news/404/43.php
53 http://home.catholicweb.com/sthomasapostle/index.cfm/NewsItem?id=102904&From=Home
54 http://www.renewamerica.us/columns/abbott
55 http://catholickey.org/index.php3?gif=news.gif&mode=view&issue=20040130&article_id=2741
56 http://www.cathnews.com/news/402/126.php
57 Romano Amerio, *Iota Unum*, Kansas City, MO: Angelus Press, 1998, p. 578.
58 http://catholiclesbians.org/pastoral/pastoral_orgs.html
59 http://www.sdnewsnotes.com/ed/articles/2000/1200ps.htm
60 http://www.faithfulvoice.com/convertino.htm
61 http://www.catholiccitizens.org/press/contentview.asp?c=13192
62 http://www.all-creatures.org/hr/hrasacrificeinchurch.htm
63 http://www.christianitytoday.com/ct/2000/115/46.0.html
64 http://www.cruxnews.com/ftm/ftm-12march04.html
65 http://www.losangelesmission.com/ed/articles/2004/0403ff.htm
66 http://www.lifesite.net/ldn/2004/feb/04022304.html
67 Denzinger *The Sources of Catholic Dogma*, B. Herder Book. Co., Thirtieth Edition, 1957, nos. 2011, 2014, 2016.
68 http://www.inq7.net/reg/2004/feb/19/reg_7-1.htm
69 http://archives.tcm.ie/businesspost/2004/02/15/story730395567.asp
70 http://www.cruxnews.com/articles/likoudis-11feb04.html
71 http://mycalendar.net/webcal1/asp1/editEvent.asp?ID=2977116&
72 http://www.freerepublic.com/focus/f-religion/1073389/posts
73 http://www.lifesite.net/ldn/2004/feb/04020308.html
74 http://www.dioshpt.org/connection/frdoug.htm
75 Personal communication to MHFM.
76 http://media.www.houstonianonline.com/media/storage/paper229/news/2004/01/27/Entertainment/BreakDancers.Perform.For.Pope.Atican-588703.shtml?sourcedomain=www.houstonianonline.com&MIIHost=media.collegepublisher.com
77 http://www.francescoproductions.com/lyrics/lyrics.html
78 http://www.dioceseofcheyenne.org/cyjoe/frstan2/images/pic32.jpg
79 Texe Marrs, *Codex Magica*, pp. 120, 134.
80 http://www.kirche-im-bistum-aachen.de/kiba/opencms/traeger/3/jesuitenkirche-st-alfons-aachen/zen/aktuell.html
81 http://www.stlouise.org/eic/eic_events/eic_event_011121ThanksEve.html
82 http://www.usccb.org/consecratedlife/az.htm
83 Denzinger 1794.

34. The Apostasy of the Hierarchy and prominent members of the Vatican II sect – is this your hierarchy?

The Bishop of Buffalo getting vested by the Dalai Lama in a massive interreligious service of apostasy[1] (more on this below)

St. Robert Bellarmine, *De Romano Pontifice*, lib. II, cap. 30: "Finally, the Holy Fathers teach unanimously not only that heretics are outside of the Church, but also that they are 'ipso facto' deprived of all ecclesiastical jurisdiction and dignity."

It's important to emphasize once again the teaching of the Catholic Church that bishops who become heretics immediately lose all authority and any offices they might possess. This is clearly illustrated by the case of the 5th century heresiarch, Nestorius, who was Patriarch of Constantinople. On Christmas Day in the year 428, Nestorius denied that Mary was the Mother of God from his pulpit. A simple layman named Eusebius stood up and protested the public heresy. This resulted in the Catholics of Constantinople breaking communion with their bishop, Nestorius; for they recognized that since he was a public heretic, he had no authority in the Church: he lost his office automatically. They even chanted: "An emperor we have, but no bishop." This reaction was praised by councils and popes, as we see described below. Notice that Pope St. Celestine says that Nestorius had no power to excommunicate after he began to preach heresy. This confirms that heretical bishops lose their offices ipso facto (by that very fact) when they become heretics. And this teaching on the loss of Episcopal office due to heresy applies precisely to the manifestly heretical "bishops" of the Vatican II sect: they have no authority and are outside the Catholic Church, even though they hold the buildings and possess the putative authority of a diocese.

> Dom Prosper Guéranger, *The Liturgical Year*, Vol. 4 (St. Cyril of Alexandria), p. 379: "It was then that Satan produced **Nestorius… enthroned in the Chair of Constantinople**… In the very year of his exaltation, on Christmas Day 428, Nestorius, taking advantage of the immense concourse which had assembled in honor of the Virgin Mother and her Child, **pronounced from the Episcopal pulpit the blasphemous words**: 'Mary did not bring forth God; her Son was only a man, the instrument of the Divinity.' The multitude shuddered with horror. <u>**Eusebius, a simple layman, rose to give expression to the**</u>

general indignation, and protested against this impiety. Soon a more explicit protest was drawn up and disseminated in the name of the members of this grief-stricken Church, **launching an anathema against anyone who should dare to say**: 'The Only-begotten Son of the Father and the Son of Mary are different persons.' **This generous attitude was the safeguard of Byzantium, and won the praise of popes and councils**. When the shepherd becomes a wolf, the first duty of the flock is to defend itself.'"[2]

Pope St. Celestine, quoted by St. Robert Bellarmine:
"**The authority of Our Apostolic See** has determined that the bishop, cleric, or simple Christian who had been deposed or excommunicated by Nestorius or his followers, **after the latter began to preach heresy** shall not be considered deposed or excommunicated. **For he who had defected from the faith with such preachings, cannot depose or remove anyone whatsoever**."[3]

The "Bishop" of Buffalo gets vested by the Dalai Lama in a massive ecumenical service with Jews, Muslims and heretics which expresses his complete apostasy from the Catholic Faith

"The remarkable service brought the red-and-gold robed Dalai Lama on a dais with a Muslim imam, Catholic bishop, Baptist preacher and Jewish rabbi, as well as 10 other clergy and area religious leaders… There were readings, prayers and chants from sacred texts, as well as a ritual gonging and three minutes of meditative silence."[4]

People ask us all the time, "what diocese are you under?" "Are you under the bishop?" If we were part of the Vatican II sect, we would be in communion with "Bishop" Edward U. Kmiec, the putative "Bishop" of Buffalo. In the picture above, you can see "Bishop" Kmiec of the Vatican II sect – the putative head of the diocese where our monastery resides – taking part in an interreligious prayer service with the Dalai Lama. Also present were a Muslim imam, a Protestant heretic, and a rabbi. This is exactly the type of interreligious prayer service which Pope Pius XI condemned in *Mortalium Animos,* and which Pius XI said represents apostasy from the Catholic Faith.

By the way, the Dalai Lama – in addition to being the spiritual leader of a pagan religion which leads souls to idolatry and to Hell – actually claims to be an incarnation of God; he literally represents antichrist. So, who is in communion with the Catholic Church? "Bishop" Kmiec? Or is it those who reject him and hold fast to the fullness of the Faith? Of course, it's not "Bishop" Kmiec and his false-religion-loving sect. He is outside the Catholic Faith and part of a religion of apostasy. Hence, we can truly say with Catholics of the past, who cried out similarly during the Nestorian heresy (see above): We don't have a bishop. The teaching of St. Robert Bellarmine cited above, which explains that heretics possess no authority in the Church, applies precisely to this situation.

Also notice that "Bishop" Kmiec is clothed ROUND ABOUT (i.e. around his waist) in purple.

> Apocalypse 17:4 – "And **the woman was clothed round about with purple and scarlet**, and gilt with gold, and precious stones and pearls, having a golden cup in her hand, full of the abomination and filthiness of her fornication."

We will explain more about this later in the book.

The Head of Russian Bishops tells us that the Vatican II sect has no intention of converting Russian "Orthodox" Schismatics

"There is no proselytism <u>as a directive on the part of the Holy See</u>, nor is there any intention to convert Russia to Roman Catholicism."[5] --Igor Kovalevsky, Secretary General of the *Novus Ordo* "Conference of Roman Catholic Bishops" of Russia

Comment: This is easily one of the worst heresies of Vatican II sect, and quite devastating to its claim to be the Catholic Church.

U.S. Novus Ordo Bishops Officially Join "Christian Churches Together in the U.S.A." – a Protestant Communion

WASHINGTON (AP) – 11/17/04: "The nation's Roman Catholic bishops voted Wednesday to join a new alliance that would be the broadest Christian group ever formed in the United States, linking American evangelicals and Catholics in an ecumenical organization for the first time. The alliance, called Christian Churches Together in the U.S.A., is set to kick off next year. It would include mainline Protestants, Orthodox Christians, and black and other minority churches. With about 67 million U.S. members, **the Catholic Church would be the largest denomination."**[6]

Comment: All over the internet you can find articles about this amazing act of heresy by the U.S. bishops. The Novus Ordo bishops have officially joined "Christian Churches Together in the U.S.A.," a Protestant communion which is part of the National Council of Churches. This act is definitely on a level with the incredible *Joint Declaration with the Lutherans on Justification,* and the Vatican II "popes" repeated acts of repudiating proselytizing the Eastern schismatics.

With this agreement, **the Novus Ordo Church in the U.S.A. has officially repudiated any claim to be the one true Church of Jesus Christ, and has admitted that it is just one of many heretical denominations**. It also has officially recognized that the Protestant and schismatic sects which belong to **"Christian Churches Together in the U.S.A." are part of the true Church of Jesus Christ.** If the Novus Ordo bishops didn't officially recognize these (non-Catholic) heretical sects and denominations as part of the Christian Church, they would never have joined this heretical group.

Here is the Profession of Faith of the National Council of Churches, of which "Christian Churches Together in the U.S.A." is a part:

Statement of Faith: "The National Council of Churches is a community of Christian communions, which, in response to the gospel as revealed in the Scriptures, confess Jesus Christ, the incarnate Word of God, as Savior and Lord. <u>These communions covenant with one another to manifest ever more fully the unity of the Church.</u>

> **Relying upon the transforming power of the Holy Spirit, the communions come together as the Council in common mission, serving in all creation to the glory of God."** *--from the Preamble to the NCC Constitution.*

This means that the members of the National Council of Churches share a communion covenant with all of the other denominations and recognize all the other denominations as manifesting the unity of the Church. This is totally heretical.

John Paul II's appointment as New Bishop in Jerusalem says that the Catholic Church has no intention of converting Jews to Christianity!

(FROM *ISRAEL TODAY*, JAN. 22, 2004) "**NEW BISHOP IN JERUSALEM IS JEWISH** – For the first time since the Apostle James served as bishop of Jerusalem, **the Holy City has a *Jewish* bishop**! Benedictine Abbot **Jean-Baptiste Gourion** was ordained as the new bishop at the Catholic church in Kiryat Ye'arim, above the Israeli Arab village of Abu Ghosh near Jerusalem. Bishop Gourion will be responsible for the Hebrew-speaking Catholic community in Israel, many of whom are of Jewish origin… Explaining how he (Bishop Gourion), as a Jew, became a Catholic, he told us: '<u>For me, Christianity and Judaism are the same. I didn't have to leave Judaism to come to Christianity. The Jew and the Christian form the same body</u>." As such, he makes it clear that he will not engage in 'missionary' activities…

After his ordination, **Israel today** editor Aviel Schneider interviewed the new bishop.

Israel today: Congratulations, Bishop Gourion… How did your family react to your new title of bishop?

Bishop Gourion: I have a very close relationship with my three siblings, who attended my ordination in Jerusalem and gave me God's blessing. All in all, I think my appointment by the Catholic Church points to a new era between Jews and Catholic Christians. We have to learn to understand each other better. <u>The Catholic Church has no intention of converting Jews to Christianity</u>. Therefore, the Pope advocated a Jewish bishop in Israel…

Israel today: …the Vatican was reluctant to recognize the Jewish state, establishing diplomatic ties with Israel just 10 years ago. One of the reasons is that the Catholic Church thinks of itself as God's chosen people.

Bishop Gourion: Well, 40 years ago in the Second Vatican Council, the Church adopted a new theological position toward Israel as God's chosen people. <u>The Catholic Church does not replace the Jewish people with whom God made an eternal covenant</u>…

Israel today: Do you still think of yourself as part of the Jewish people?

Bishop Gourion: Sure. **I see myself as a Jew**."

Comment: In 2004, "Bishop" Gourion was appointed by John Paul II as the new auxiliary Bishop of Jerusalem. In the interview, Gourion says that <u>John Paul II specifically appointed Gourion to</u>

Jerusalem because of who he is and what he believes. Well, the "new Bishop" Gourion says that he is "a Jew"; that his "Church" (the Vatican sect) "*has no intention of converting Jews to Christianity*"; that the Jewish covenant with God is still valid and not replaced by the Catholic Church; that the Body of Christ (the Catholic Church) and Judaism are one Body.

Are those under Benedict XVI going to tell us that "Bishop" Gourion is a Catholic? Is "Bishop" Gourion a bishop in their "Church" with whom Catholics must share faith and communion – yes or no?

> Pope Pius XII, *Mystici Corporis Christi* (# 22), June 29, 1943:
> "As therefore **in the true Christian community** there is only one Body, one Spirit, one Lord, and one Baptism, so **there can be only one faith**. And therefore if a man refuse to hear the Church let him be considered – so the Lord commands – as a heathen and a publican. It follows that **those who are divided in faith or government cannot be living in the unity of such a Body**, nor can they be living the life of its one Divine Spirit."[7]

To assert that Gourion is a Catholic in the face of this information (i.e., that he is in your Church) is a mortal sin against the Faith and a denial of Jesus Christ. **But those who believe that Benedict XVI is the pope must say that Bishop Gourion is their fellow Catholic who has the same Faith** and is in the same Church (Body), as we can see above, because all in the Church have the same Faith (*de fide*). But if they correctly assert that Gourion is an apostate who is outside the Catholic Church and has no authority, then they must also say the same of Benedict XVI who, as we already saw, believes in the same apostasy on the Jews.

John Paul II's "Cardinal Archbishop" of Washington, D.C. confirms John Paul II's rejection of proselytism (converting others)

> "Cardinal Archbishop" Theodore McCarrick, Interview with *National Catholic Register* about his trip to Moscow to give the Icon of Our Lady of Kazan back to the Schismatics, Sept. 2004:
>
> Q. What did you observe about the relations between Orthodox and Roman Catholics?
>
> A. Cardinal McCarrick: "I think our Orthodox brothers and sisters still may feel threatened by the Roman Catholic Church... There are always going to be some people in communities who feel troubled by other religious communities, **possibly fearing that they're going to proselytize [try to convert them]. I THINK THE HOLY FATHER HAS REALLY BEEN SO CLEAR THAT HIS ROLE IS NEVER TO PROSELYTIZE**; his role is to find the key to unity."[8]

Comment: Here we see the "head" of the Novus Ordo sect in Washington D.C., a supposed "cardinal," bluntly admitting that John Paul II "has really been so clear that his role is never to proselytize"! To proselytize is to convert people. If you live in Washington, D.C. and believe that John Paul II is the pope, you would have to admit that this arch-apostate Theodore McCarrick is actually the leader of the Catholic Church in your area.

The "Archbishop" of Strasbourg admits that the Vatican II sect has abandoned Catholic teaching on the Jews!

Archbishop Joseph Dore of Strasbourg, France, Speech to B'nai B'rith (Jewish Freemasons), August, 2003: "Whatever the depiction [of the Jews in traditional Catholic art]… **the theological message is the same – God's election has now passed to the Christian people; and the Church, the true Israel, may triumph, She who confesses the saving truth brought by Christ**.

"**At Vatican II, the Catholic Church finally revised this teaching** and understood to what extent it contradicts the Bible itself… In 1973, the French episcopacy, particularly under the influence of Msgr. Elchinger, [past] Bishop of Strasbourg, published a document of unparalleled moral force on Judeo-Christian relations, while **Pope John Paul II recalled on numerous occasions the permanence of the First Covenant** [*Ed.* the Old Covenant], 'which was never revoked' by God [John Paul II, Mainz, Germany, 1980]. Today, we desire to work together with our elder brothers toward reconciliation and fraternal dialogue. Yet **we must have the humility to recognize that the doctrine of contempt and the 'theology of substitution' – making the Church to be the new and only Israel of God – still penetrate the minds of a large number**. Only by a great labor of education will we ever manage to extirpate all seed of anti-Judaism. Only by a continual purification of memory, making them conscious of their own temptations, will Christians be moved to vigilance and responsibility.

"Today the Church calls Christians to take the first steps on the path to conversion, inviting them to construct a future with their Jewish brothers in which, together, they might be a 'blessing for one another' [John Paul II, 1983]."[9]

Comment: This is apostasy. It is utter contempt for – and rejection of – the dogma we've quoted throughout this book, which declares that the Old Covenant ceased with the coming of Christ and was replaced with the New and Eternal Covenant of Jesus Christ.

Notice how the execrable apostate, "Archbishop" Dore, references John Paul II's speech in 1980 (and other statements from John Paul II) to attempt to justify his apostasy. Notice how he refers to the Old Covenant as the "First Covenant," not the "Old" Covenant, because "Old" implies that it is no longer in force. Notice how he says that *"we must have the humility"* to abandon the Catholic dogma that the Old Covenant has ceased. Notice how he says that it will require "a great labor" to extirpate (root out) this dogmatic truth from Catholic minds. This is **the "archbishop" of the Vatican II sect in Strasbourg, France**, following the teaching of the Vatican II antipopes. Again, this is nothing other than the counterfeit "Catholic sect" of the Antichrist.

> 1 John 2:22 – "**Who is a liar, but he who denieth that Jesus is the Christ? He is antichrist,** who denieth the Father, and the Son."

The Novus Ordo Bishops Bluntly Repudiate the Dogmatic Second Council of Lyons and the Council of Florence!

"*An Agreed Statement of the North American Orthodox-Catholic Theological Consultation Saint Paul's College, Washington, DC, October 25, 2003* * (*U.S. Catholic Bishops – Secretariat for Interreligious Affairs:*)*

"**IV. Recommendations** -"We are aware that <u>the problem of the theology of the *Filioque*</u>… Although dialogue among a number of these Churches and the Orthodox communion has already touched on the issue, any future resolution of the disagreement between East and West on the origin of the Spirit must involve all those communities that profess the Creed of 381 as a standard of faith. Aware of its limitations, <u>our Consultation nonetheless makes the following theological and practical recommendations</u> to the members and the bishops of our own Churches…

- that in the future, because of the progress in mutual understanding that has come about in recent decades, Orthodox and Catholics refrain from labeling as heretical the traditions of the other side on the subject of the procession of the Holy Spirit…
- that the Catholic Church, as a consequence of the normative and irrevocable dogmatic value of the Creed of 381, <u>use the original Greek text alone</u> in making translations of that Creed for catechetical and liturgical use.
- that the Catholic Church, following a growing theological consensus, and in particular the statements made by Pope Paul VI, **<u>declare that the condemnation made at the Second Council of Lyons (1274) of those "who presume to deny that the Holy Spirit proceeds eternally from the Father and the Son" is no longer applicable.</u>**

"We offer these recommendations to our Churches in the conviction, based on our own intense study and discussion, that our traditions' different ways of understanding the procession of the Holy Spirit need no longer divide us."[10]

Comment: This is an incredible heresy, but first a little background. It's a defined dogma of the Catholic Church that God the Holy Ghost proceeds eternally from the Father and the Son.

Pope Gregory X, *Second Council of Lyons*, 1274, ex cathedra: "**We profess faithfully and devotedly that the Holy Ghost proceeds eternally from the Father and the Son**, not as from two principles, but as from one principle… **This the holy Roman Church, mother and mistress of all the faithful, has till now professed, preached and taught; this she firmly holds, preaches, professes and teaches**… But because some, on account of ignorance of the said indisputable truth, have fallen into various errors, <u>**we, wishing to close the way to such errors, with the approval of the sacred council, condemn and reprove all who presume to deny that the Holy Ghost proceeds eternally from the Father and the Son**</u>, or rashly to assert that the Holy Ghost proceeds from the Father and the Son as from two principles and not as from one."[11]

The Eastern schismatics (i.e., the so-called "Orthodox") reject this dogma. They only believe that the Holy Ghost proceeds from the Father; they don't believe that the Holy Ghost proceeds from the Father <u>and the Son</u> (*Filioque*). So, what do the bishops of the Vatican II sect do in their dialogue with these "Orthodox" schismatics? In their dialogue with these schismatics and heretics, they have issued the above statement which is carried <u>on the official website of the U.S. bishops</u> in union with Benedict XVI. This statement, as can be seen above, **bluntly asserts that the dogmatic definition of the Second Council of Lyons – which declared that the Holy Ghost proceeds from the Father <u>and the Son</u> (*Filioque*) – is no longer applicable!** Nothing could be more formally heretical! **The U.S. bishops in union with John Paul II (and now Benedict XVI)** declared that a solemn, *ex cathedra* pronouncement of a pope at an ecumenical council of the Catholic Church no longer applies!

The U.S. bishops of the Vatican II sect also recommended that the current version of the Nicene-Constantinople Creed (which is recited every Sunday at Mass), which declares that the Holy Ghost proceeds from the Father *and the Son* (*Filioque*), <u>be dropped from all catechetical and liturgical use</u> (see above) – and that only the original creed of 381, which only declared that the Holy Ghost proceeds from the Father, be used. For those who don't know, the Catholic Church lawfully added the phrase "*and the Son*" to the Nicene-Constantinople Creed.

> Pope Eugene IV, *Council of Florence*, "Laetentur coeli," July 6, 1439, ex cathedra: "In the name of the Holy Trinity, of the Father, and of the Son, and of the Holy Spirit, with the approbation of this holy general Council of Florence **we define that this truth of faith be believed and accepted by all Christians, and that all likewise profess that the Holy Ghost is eternally from the Father and the Son… <u>We define in addition that the explanation of the words 'Filioque' for the sake of declaring the truth and also because of imminent necessity has been lawfully and reasonably added to the Creed</u>.**"[12]

By declaring that the "Filioque" ("*and the Son*") dogma is not binding and no longer applicable, the Novus Ordo bishops repudiate two dogmatic councils of the Catholic Church (Lyons II and Florence) at the same time.

Vatican Commission under John Paul II again rejects trying to convert Jews!

> Joint Jewish-"Catholic" Meeting- "**Delegations of the Chief Rabbinate of Israel and of the Holy See's Commission for Religious Relations with the Jews met for the fourth time** from 17-19 October [2004] in Grottaferrata, Italy. This Joint Committee was established in June 2002. The following is the Committee's Report of the meeting… 3. **<u>The bilateral Committee [of Jews and "Catholics"] reiterated its commitment to the principal declarations of the previous meetings, which included a call for mutual respect of our different religious identities, and affirmed a common rejection of any attempts to persuade people to reject their own heritage</u>**… As believers in the One God whose name is Peace, prayer was offered up to him to bring an end to war…"[13]

Comment: This joint declaration with rabbis appeared in the official Vatican newspaper because it was an act of an official Vatican commission. The joint declaration was signed by five different chief rabbis, two "cardinals," two bishops, two monsignors, one "archbishop" and a priest, including "Cardinal" Jorge Mejia, Chairman of the "Catholic" delegation of the Vatican. Allow us to put it bluntly: this is antichrist. "**The bilateral Committee [of Jews and Catholics]… affirmed a common rejection of any attempts to persuade people to reject their own heritage**." This means that the Vatican commission rejects any attempts to persuade the Jews to convert to Jesus Christ and the Catholic Faith. People wonder when the following prophecy of Our Lady of La Salette will come to fruition:

> Our Lady of La Salette, Sept. 19, 1846: "*Rome will lose the faith and become the Seat of the Antichrist… the Church will be in eclipse.*"

It has come to fruition. The statement of this Vatican commission is perfectly in line with the teaching of John Paul II and Benedict XVI on the Jews, as we saw already.

Hindus Worship the Devil at the Shrine of Our Lady of Fatima

Frontpage Online, Portugal's Weekend Newspaper in English, May 22, 2004: "…we can report that the first steps in developing Fátima as a multi-faith centre could have been taken. **On May 5th… Notícias carried a report on a Hindu religious service held in the Chapel of the Apparitions [of Our Lady of Fatima] at the shrine… Sixty Hindus led by a high priest had traveled from Lisbon to pay homage to the Goddess Devi, the divinity of nature**. SIC's reporter described how before leaving Lisbon the Hindus had gathered at their temple in the city to pray to and worship various statues of Hindu gods.

"**Arriving in Fátima the pilgrims made their way to the Chapel of the Apparitions, where from the altar a Hindu priest led prayer sessions**. A commentary on the service was given by the TV reporter who explained: 'This is an unprecedented unique moment in the history of the shrine. **The Hindu priest, or Sha Tri, prays on the altar the Shaniti Pa**, the prayer for peace.' The Hindus can be seen removing their shoes before approaching the altar rail of the chapel as the priest chants prayers from the altar's sanctuary… **After worshipping their gods and praying in the chapel the Hindus are shown being escorted to an exhibition hall** where a model of the controversial new basilica currently being constructed is on display. In a setting described as ambassadorial by the commentator, **each Hindu is personally greeted by the Bishop of Leiria - Fátima, who bows to the Hindu priest repeating his gesture of greeting. The Hindu priest is then seen clothing the Rector of the Fátima Shrine and the bishop with a Hindu priestly shawl**. 'On the shoulders of the highest representatives of the Church in Fátima, the Hindu priest places a shawl with the inscriptions of the Bhagavad Gita, one of the sacred books of Hinduism,' the reporter tells his viewers.

"**The newscast finishes with scenes of the Hindu priest lighting a candle at the shrine while his followers dance outside the Chapel of the Apparitions chanting praises to their gods**."

Comment: There you have it. Pagan, idolatrous, demonic worship was conducted at the very chapel built over the spot where Our Lady of Fatima appeared. It happened with the full approval of the Shrine Rector, Msgr. Guerra, and with the full approval of the Bishop of Leiria-Fatima, and with the full approval of the head of the Pontifical Council for Interreligious Dialogue, "Archbishop" Michael Fitzgerald. But how can they do this? **They can do it because they learned it from Benedict XVI, John Paul II**, Paul VI and Vatican II, as we have documented.

This latest abomination also shows how misled and deceived are the useful heretics who try to explain away everything. On an April 25 EWTN broadcast, Fr. Mitch Pacwa and Fr. Robert Fox discussed the rumors that Fatima was being turned over to non-Catholic religions. Fr. Robert Fox assured the audience that the whole idea is a "fabrication," that nothing like this was going on or would go on! Yeah, it is a fabrication all right… and now we see the Hindu idolaters in Fatima conducting their satanic rites in the Chapel of the Apparitions. How long will people listen to these heretics who lead souls to Hell?

Pope Leo XIII, *Ad Extremas* (#1), June 24, 1893: "Our thoughts turn first of all to the **blessed Apostle Thomas who is rightly called the founder of preaching the Gospel to the Hindus**. Then, there is Francis Xavier… Through his extraordinary perseverance, **he** converted **hundreds of thousands of Hindus from the myths and vile superstitions of the Brahmans to the true religion**. In the footsteps of this holy man followed numerous priests… they are continuing these noble efforts; nevertheless, in the vast reaches of the Earth, **many are still deprived of the truth, miserably imprisoned in the darkness of superstition**."[14]

St. Francis Xavier, Sept. 18, +1542: "**I told him that God, most Faithful and True, held the misbelievers and their prayers in abomination, and so willed that their worship, which He rejected altogether, should come to naught.**"[15]

St. Francis Xavier, Spring +1543: "One day I turned out of my road into a village of heathens… There was a woman with child, who had been three days in labor with so much difficulty, that many despaired of her life. **Their prayers for her were not heard, for the prayer of the wicked is an abomination in the eyes of God, because the gods of the heathens are all devils** [Psalm 95:5; 1 Cor. 10:20]."[16]

Apocalypse 18:2-5- "**Babylon the great is fallen, is fallen: and is become the habitation of devils, and the hold of every unclean and hateful bird:** Because all nations have drunk of the wine of the wrath of her fornication… And I heard another voice from heaven, saying: **Go out from her, my people; that you be not partakers of her sins, and that you receive not of her plagues. For her sins have reached unto heaven, and the Lord hath remembered her iniquities.**"

The Vatican II Sect commemorates Mennonite "martyrdom"

Mons. John A. Rodano, Vatican Council for Promoting Christian Unity, March, 2004: "An international dialogue between the Catholic Church and the Mennonite World Conference took place 1998-2003… Part III, 'Toward a Healing of Memories,' was written in light of bitter memories of the past and especially, from **the Mennonite perspective, their memory of persecution and martyrdom in the 16th century**, and in light of our isolation from one another since that time. **It outlines four steps that could be taken toward a healing of memories**…

"In a common statement, **Catholics and Mennonites together regret that they and other Christians 'were unable to resolve the problems of the Church of that time in such a way as to prevent divisions in the Body of Christ that have lasted to the present day.**'"[17]

Comment: In early March of 2004, the Vatican II sect was following John Paul II's lead by commemorating the Lutheran pastor, Paul Schneider. Late in March of the same year, the Vatican II sect commemorated Mennonite "martyrdom." This is formal heresy coming out basically on a weekly basis. Could the Vatican II sect deny the dogma Outside the Church There is No Salvation any more clearly or consistently? What kind of "Catholic" could affirm communion with such a "hierarchy" while aware of these facts?

The common statement above presents the divisions between Catholics and Mennonites (in other words, the heresies of the Mennonites) as *"problems of the Church at that time,"* for which seemingly both sides were to blame. In other words, the Mennonites aren't the ones guilty of heresy for leaving the Body of Christ and following their man-made religion!

Non-Catholic "Saints" and "Martyrs" Commemorated by the Vatican II sect, following John Paul II's teaching

Fr. Matthias Turk, Vatican Council for Promoting Christian Unity, March, 2004: "Among the more significant events was **the touching ecumenical celebration organized by the Community of Sant'Egidio on 1 February 2003 in Rome's Basilica of St. Bartholomew in order to commemorate the Lutheran Pastor Paul Schneider**, who was killed in the Buchenwald concentration camp. Those attending on this occasion included Cardinal Walter Kasper... and other ecumenical representatives of Roman Parishes.

"This testimony, as the Holy Father has said, 'speaks louder than the things which divide us.'"[18]

Comment: Here we see the Vatican Council for Promoting Christian Unity commemorating a Lutheran heretic as a martyr for the faith. This is formal heresy against the Council of Florence. Consult the earlier sections of this book which deal with proving that John Paul II repeatedly taught that there are saints outside the Church.

Pope Eugene IV, Council of Florence, *Cantate Domino*, Session 11, Feb. 4, 1442, *ex cathedra*: "... no one, whatever almsgiving he has practiced, even if he has shed blood for the name of Christ, can be saved, unless he has remained within the bosom and unity of the Catholic Church."[19]

Pope Pelagius II, epistle (2) *Dilectionis vestrae*, 585: "Those who were not willing to be at agreement in the Church of God, cannot remain with God; although given over to flames and fires, they burn, or thrown to wild beasts, they lay down their lives, there will not be for them that crown of faith, but the punishment of faithlessness, not a glorious result (of religious virtue), but the ruin of despair. Such a one can be slain; he cannot be crowned."[20]

The Vatican II sect praises and celebrates John Wesley, the founder of the Methodist sect

Fr. Donald Bolen, Vatican Council for Promoting Christian Unity, Feb. 2004: "2003 was an eventful year in relations between the Catholic Church and the World Methodist Council... **In June 2003, Methodists worldwide celebrated the 300th anniversary of the birth of John Wesley**, and in small but significant ways, invited the Catholic Church to join in these celebrations... **Cardinal Walter Kasper, President of the Pontifical Council for Promoting Christian Unity, preached at the Methodist Church in Rome on the occasion of the 300th anniversary of the birth of John Wesley. Later in the year, he sent a message to a celebration marking both the anniversary of Wesley's birth and that of the Chapel Wesley opened in London 225 years ago.**

"Cardinal Kasper made use of the opportunity provided by these occasions to contribute to a Catholic reassessment of John Wesley, particularly attentive to 'his wholehearted commitment to spreading the good news of salvation, his fostering of Scriptural holiness and structuring of communities of Christians for witness and mission.'

"Cardinal Kasper noted that 'We must also seek a wider view, to see what dynamized Wesley's ministry, to see the evangelical passion which gave direction to his life and the movement he started.'

> "Kasper stressed that <u>this reassessment of Wesley, which was 'rich with possibilities</u>,' was possible because Catholics could now look to Wesley through eyes educated by our international dialogue and by the emergence of friendship and shared mission in various local contexts throughout the world, wherein '<u>we have come to recognize each other as brothers and sisters in Christ</u>.'
>
> "Addressing the congregation of Methodists Cardinal Kasper noted that just as Methodists '**continue to turn to the ministry of John Wesley for inspiration and guidance, <u>we can look to see and find in him the evangelical zeal, the pursuit of holiness</u>**, the concern for the poor, <u>the virtues and goodness which we have come to know and respect in you</u>. Cardinal Kasper's homily and message were warmly received and much appreciated."[21]

Comment: John Wesley was a non-Catholic heretic, and the founder of his own religion. He started out as an Anglican, and then formed Methodism. Wesley denied the Papacy; he denied many of the dogmatic councils of the Catholic Church; he denied apostolic succession; he denied all but two of the seven sacraments, admitting only Baptism and the Eucharist, but he rejected that Baptism confers sanctifying grace and he denied that Our Lord is truly present in the Eucharist. He denied Purgatory, and he held that man is justified by faith alone and thereby assured of his salvation. How is that for "*wholehearted commitment to spreading the good news of salvation*"? How is that for "*fostering of Scriptural holiness and structuring of communities of Christians*"? How is that for "*evangelical zeal, the pursuit of holiness… the virtues and goodness which we have come to know and respect in you*"? Yes, heresy, schism and the spreading of false doctrines of the worst kind – including the evil doctrine of faith alone – are "virtues" that the Vatican II sect wants to come to know and respect in everyone.

The article also calls for the Methodists to affirm the *Joint Declaration with the Lutherans on Justification*, which totally repudiates the Council of Trent.

No Words of Consecration, No Problem. The Vatican, with the approval of John Paul II and Benedict XVI, approves a "Mass" as valid which has no words of Consecration!

Preliminary Comment: The following is an excerpt from a document issued by the Vatican, and approved by "Cardinal" Ratzinger and John Paul II, on whether Chaldean Eastern Rite Catholics are permitted to have inter-Communion with the Assyrian schismatics of the East, who are non-Catholics who reject the Catholic Church.

The document says *yes*; therefore, the Assyrian schismatic non-Catholics are allowed to receive Holy Communion from Catholic ministers, while the Chaldean "Catholics" are also allowed to receive Communion at the Assyrian Schismatic churches.

Besides the obvious sin of heretical inter-Communion with non-Catholics, there is an additional problem. **These Assyrian Schismatics – unlike most Eastern Schismatics – don't have any words of Consecration in their liturgy!** Their liturgy doesn't even have "This is My Body" or "This is My Blood, etc."; it doesn't have *the words of Institution*, as the words of consecration are frequently called! Thus, the Assyrian Schismatic Liturgy isn't even valid. But the following document of the Vatican essentially tells us: *no words of consecration, no problem!*

"**PONTIFICAL COUNCIL FOR PROMOTING CHRISTIAN UNITY-** *GUIDELINES FOR ADMISSION TO THE EUCHARIST BETWEEN THE CHALDEAN CHURCH AND THE ASSYRIAN CHURCH OF THE EAST, July 20, 2001:*

"The present guidelines subsequently have been elaborated by the *Pontifical Council for Promoting Christian Unity,* in agreement with the *Congregation for the Doctrine of the Faith and the Congregation for the Oriental Churches*… 3. … **The principal issue for the Catholic Church in agreeing to this request**, related to the question of the validity of the Eucharist celebrated with the Anaphora of Addai and Mari, one of the three Anaphoras traditionally used by the Assyrian Church of the East. The Anaphora of Addai and Mari is notable because, from time immemorial, it has been used without a recitation of the Institution Narrative. **As the Catholic Church considers the words of the Eucharistic Institution a constitutive and therefore indispensable part of the Anaphora or Eucharistic Prayer,** a long and careful study was undertaken of the Anaphora of Addai and Mari, from a historical, liturgical and theological perspective, at the end of which the Congregation for the Doctrine of the Faith on January 17th, 2001 concluded that this Anaphora can be considered valid. H.H. **Pope John Paul II has approved this decision** … the words of Eucharistic Institution are indeed present in the Anaphora of Addai and Mari, **not in a coherent narrative way and** *ad litteram*, but rather in a dispersed euchological way, that is, integrated in successive prayers of thanksgiving, praise and intercession."

Comment: Here the official Vatican document, approved by John Paul II, is admitting that the words of "Eucharistic Institution" (the words of Consecration which Christ Himself instituted as necessary for the confection of the Eucharist) are not present in this Assyrian liturgy. After admitting this fact, it tries to explain it away by asserting that the words of consecration are present in a "dispersed euchological way," which is a neat way of saying that they're not actually present, but they are somehow accounted for in other "prayers *of thanksgiving, praise and intercession*" which mention nothing of them! How convenient!

According to this outrageous document, the words of consecration are accounted for in other prayers of thanksgiving, praise and intercession which don't mention them. This heresy devastates all Catholic sacramental teaching.

> Pope Eugene IV, *Council of Florence,* Session 8, Nov. 22, 1439, "Exultate Deo": "All these sacraments are made up of three elements: namely, things as the matter, words as the form, and the person of the minister who confers the sacrament with the intention of doing what the Church does. **If any of these is lacking, the sacrament is not effected."**[22]

> Pope St. Pius V, *De Defectibus*, chapter 5, Part 1:
> "The words of Consecration, which are the FORM of this Sacrament, are these: *FOR THIS IS MY BODY. And: FOR THIS IS THE CHALICE OF MY BLOOD, OF THE NEW AND ETERNAL TESTAMENT: THE MYSTERY OF FAITH, WHICH SHALL BE SHED FOR YOU AND FOR MANY UNTO THE REMISSION OF SINS.* Now if one were to remove, or change anything in the FORM of the consecration of the Body and Blood, and in that very change of words the [new] wording would fail to mean the same thing, he would not consecrate the sacrament."

In light of these facts, one can see that this heresy of the Vatican II sect, John Paul II and Benedict XVI is equivalent to saying that one can validly baptize without water. It's a rejection of the *substance of the sacraments*, those things specifically instituted by the Lord Himself as necessary for the confection of the Sacraments, which no man – not even a *true* Pope – has any power to change or alter.

> Pope Pius XII, *Sacramentum Ordinis* (# 1), Nov. 30, 1947:
> "... **the Church has no power over the 'substance of the sacraments**,' that is, over those things which, with the sources of divine revelation as witnesses, Christ the Lord Himself decreed to be preserved in a sacramental sign..."[23]

> Pope St. Pius X, *Ex quo*, Dec. 26, 1910: "... **it is well known that to the Church there belongs no right whatsoever to innovate anything touching on the substance of the sacraments.**"[24]

We continue with another short excerpt from this document:

> "**4. Guidelines for admission to the Eucharist-** ...1. When necessity requires, Assyrian faithful are permitted to participate and to receive Holy Communion in a Chaldean celebration of the Holy Eucharist; in the same way, **Chaldean faithful** for whom it is physically or morally impossible to approach a Catholic minister, **are permitted to participate and to receive Holy Communion in an Assyrian celebration of the Holy Eucharist**. 2. In both cases, Assyrian and Chaldean ministers celebrate the Holy Eucharist according to the liturgical prescriptions and customs **of their own tradition**. 3. When Chaldean faithful are participating in an Assyrian celebration of the Holy Eucharist, the Assyrian minister **is warmly invited to insert the words of the Institution** in the Anaphora of Addai and Mari, as allowed by the Holy Synod of the Assyrian Church of the East." (*Rome, July 20th, 2001*)

Notice how the Vatican document "warmly invites" the Assyrian schismatics to use the words of Institution. But if the schismatics aren't "warmed up" to this idea, no problem – it's somehow valid anyway according to the Vatican II sect. In light of these facts, how is affirming communion with these men any different from affirming communion with Protestant ministers?

The Novus Ordo Bishop of Kansas City denies the Perpetual Virginity of Our Lady

FROM AN ARTICLE IN *THE ANGELUS*, publication of the Society of St. Pius X (SSPX), Dec. 2003, pp. 32-37: "... I pointed out to you [Bishop Boland of Kansas City] that George Noonan, on the radio program [an allegedly 'Catholic' program in Bishop Boland's diocese], had denied the necessity of sanctifying grace for the salvation of one's soul. **You [Bishop Boland] immediately defended Mr. Noonan by stating that it is not necessary for [to have] sanctifying grace to save one's soul**... When I informed you [Bishop Boland] that George Noonan (on the radio program) was silent as to whether or not he believed in the principle of logic of non-contradiction, **you stated that the law of non-contradiction – where two contradictory statements could not both be true – was in fact, false**... During our conversation, we also got off on a tangent as regards the lack of respect shown by Rabbi Michael Zedik concerning the Blessed Mother and how George Noonan, as the Catholic co-host, did not defend Our Lady's dignity as being a perpetual virgin. **You indicated that it has yet to be proven that Our Lady did not have any children other than Our Lord**... This quickly led into our last discussion in which

<u>you stated that the Church's doctrine can change and has changed</u>. My father and I wholeheartedly disagreed with you on this point…"[25]

Comment: Would you believe that "Bishop" Boland is the "head" of the Novus Ordo/Vatican II sect in Kansas City?

> Pope Pius IX, *First Vatican Council*, Session 4, Chap. 3, *ex cathedra*:
> "This power of the Supreme Pontiff is so far from interfering with that power of ordinary and immediate Episcopal jurisdiction by which the **bishops**… have succeeded to the places of the apostles, as true shepherds individually feed **and rule the individual flocks entrusted to them.**"

"Bishop" Boland denies that sanctifying grace is necessary for salvation; he denies the law of non-contradiction; he denies the perpetual virginity of Our Lady; and he holds that Catholic doctrine can change. Bishop Boland is a manifest heretic.

> Pope Paul IV, Cum quorundam, *Council of Trent*, 1555: "… the most blessed and **ever Virgin Mary**…"[26]

> Pope Martin I, *First Lateran Council*, 649, Can. 3: "**If anyone does not properly and truly confess** in accord with the holy Fathers, that the holy Mother of God and ever Virgin and immaculate Mary… **her virginity remaining indestructible even after His birth, let him be condemned.**"[27]

"Bishop" Boland is obviously not the visible head and authority of the Catholic Church in Kansas City, but the ruler of a non-Catholic sect which poses as the Catholic Church in Kansas City (the Vatican II/Novus Ordo sect). And as incredibly heretical as he is, **"Bishop" Boland is probably average among the Novus Ordo bishops**. But groups like the SSPX still recognize Boland as a Catholic and the head of the diocese; their priests in Kansas City pray for him as their legitimate bishop each Sunday at Mass, and they continue to call him "Your Excellency"! Since they are obstinate in this position, this is very offensive to God and to Our Lady.

> FROM THE SAME ARTICLE IN *THE ANGELUS*, publication of the SSPX, Dec. 2003, pp. 33-37: "Your Excellency… Your Excellency… Your Excellency… Your Excellency… Most of all, Your Excellency… Your Excellency… **May God bless you [Bishop Boland] in your work as Bishop of our diocese** so that the Traditional Catholic Faith is nourished and spreads **such that your crown in Heaven is ornamented by the many souls entrusted to your spiritual care.**"[28]

At the 2003 Fatima Conference hosted by the Novus Ordo clergy, the dogmatic definition of the Council of Florence was called "horrible"!

> *Catholic Family News*, Dec. 2003, pp. 20-21: "… I have covered a number of these post-conciliar conferences including New Evangelization Seminars, Rock'n'-Roll World Youth Days, screaming charismatic meetings, and evenings of Jewish-Catholic dialogue. **Yet the most explicit heresy I have ever heard at any of these events came from the mouth of the Belgian Jesuit Father Jacques Dupuis, only a few hundred yards from where Our Lady of Fatima appeared… On the point of 'outside the Church there is no**

salvation,' Fr. Dupuis said in disgust, 'There is no need to invoke here that horrible text from the Council of Florence in 1442.'"[29]

Comment: We've already documented that the shrine of Our Lady of Fatima was invaded by the Hindus with the full permission of the Vatican II sect. It's also said that it's going to be turned into an interfaith shrine open to all religions. At the Fatima conference where this diabolical idea was put forward, Fr. Jacques Dupuis called the following dogmatic definition of the Council of Florence on outside the Church there is no salvation "horrible."

> Pope Eugene IV, Council of Florence, "Cantate Domino," 1441-1442, ex cathedra: "The Holy Roman Church firmly believes, professes and preaches that all those who are outside the Catholic Church, not only pagans but also Jews or heretics and schismatics, cannot share in eternal life and will go into the everlasting fire which was prepared for the devil and his angels, unless they are joined to the Church before the end of their lives; that the unity of this ecclesiastical body is of such importance that only for those who abide in it do the Church's sacraments contribute to salvation and do fasts, almsgiving and other works of piety and practices of the Christian militia produce eternal rewards; and that nobody can be saved, no matter how much he has given away in alms and even if he has shed blood in the name of Christ, unless he has persevered in the bosom and unity of the Catholic Church."[30]

Msgr. Guerra (the Fatima Shrine Rector), as well as John Paul II's own Apostolic Delegate to Portugal and the Bishop of Leiria-Fatima, were also present and applauded Fr. Dupuis' heresy. This means that the man put in charge of the shrine by the Vatican II sect, as well as the bishop over the territory, applauded the aforementioned speech which called the Council of Florence's solemn teaching "horrible"! The crowd in attendance also applauded the speech, which was filled with heresy and apostasy throughout.

To maintain the Faith, it is not enough to oppose these incredible abominations and heresies, if one still affirms communion and faith with these men. **To affirm communion and faith with such men is to deny the Faith by mixing Fatima with apostasy, by saying that one can be an apostate and hold the authority of the Church of Christ in Fatima.**

Even "conservative" Novus Ordo "bishops," such as "Bishop" Fabian Bruskewitz and "Cardinal" George, are complete apostates

Even if one looks at the most conservative members of the "hierarchy" under Benedict XVI, such as "Bishop" Fabian Bruskewitz of Lincoln, Nebraska, one sees that they are complete apostates. **"Bishop" Bruskewitz "presided over an ecumenical prayer service and breakfast together with an Anglican 'bishop' and assorted Lutheran 'ministers.'"**[31]

"Bishop" Bruskewitz "also respectfully attended the [invalid] 'consecration' of Methodist 'bishop' Joel Martinez, who has publicly recalled (in a sermon on May 21, 2000) the joyous day his mother left the Catholic Church..."[32] One of Bruskewitz's own parishes "conducts what it calls a 'Sermon a la Carte' program, in which parishioners are urged to attend sermons by the ministers of these very sects [i.e. various Protestant sects], as well as the local Methodist and Lutheran 'churches.'"[33] This is heretical.

Pope Pius IX, *Graves ac diuturnae* (# 4), March 23, 1875: "**They [the faithful] should totally shun their religious celebrations, their buildings,** and their chairs of pestilence which they have with impunity established to transmit the sacred teachings. They should shun their writings and all contact with them. They should not have any dealings or meetings with usurping priests and apostates from the faith who dare to exercise the duties of an ecclesiastical minister without possessing a legitimate mission or any jurisdiction."[34]

Worst of all, **"Bishop" Bruskewitz actually conducted an interfaith Seder Supper with a group of rabbis in his own cathedral** during Holy Week, thus committing a horrible act of apostasy, heresy and mortal sin.[35] All of this proves that "Bishop" Bruskewitz, perhaps the most conservative "bishop" of the Vatican II hierarchy, is also a manifest heretic and an apostate.

Regarding "Cardinal" George, we already pointed out that in his diocesan newspaper he wrote that "The Church has also sinned against the Jewish people, first of all, in teaching that God's covenant with Israel is no longer valid…"[36] This means that George holds that the Jews have a valid covenant with God and don't need to convert to the Catholic Faith or Jesus Christ for salvation. All of these "bishops" also accept the heresies of Vatican II, the incredible *Joint Declaration with the Lutherans on Justification*, and the ecumenism of the Vatican II antipopes.

Every year the Vatican sends a message commemorating Buddhist feast of Vesakh

Vatican Message to Buddhists on feast of Vesakh, Archbishop Michael Fitzgerald, **president of the Pontifical Council for Interreligious Dialogue, 4/30/04**:

"**Dear Buddhist Friends**: 1. I am writing to you again this year **to express my heartfelt greetings on the occasion of your festival of Vesakh. I pray that each and every one of you may have a joyful and peaceful feast**. Vesakh offers an opportunity for us Christians to visit our Buddhist friends and neighbors to exchange greetings, and this helps to strengthen the bonds of friendship already established and to create new ones. It is my wish that such cordial links may continue to grow generation after generation, sharing with each other our joys and hopes, our sorrows and preoccupations…"[37]

Every year the Vatican Congratulates Muslims for the end of Ramadan

"Archbishop" Michael Fitzgerald, Head of Vatican Pontifical Council for Interreligious Dialogue:

Dear Muslim Friends,

1. **It is a pleasure for me to address you on the occasion of 'Id al-Fitr, which concludes the month of Ramadan,** in order to offer you friendly greetings on behalf of the Pontifical Council for Interreligious Dialogue and indeed on behalf of the whole Catholic Church… 4. **As believers in the One God** we see it as our duty to strive to bring about peace. Christians and Muslims, we believe that peace is above all a gift from God. This

The Apostasy of the "Hierarchy" of the V-2 Sect 445

is why our two communities pray for peace; it is something they are always called to do. **As you know, Pope John Paul II invited representatives of different religions to come to Assisi, the city of St Francis, on 24 January 2002,** in order to pray and to commit themselves to peace in the world…

5. In bringing about peace, and maintaining it, **religions have an important role to play**… 6. It is at what is a very special time for you, the month of Ramadan **in which fasting, prayer and solidarity bring you interior peace,** that I am sharing with you these reflections on the ways to peace. I express to you, therefore, good wishes of peace, peace in your hearts, in your families and in your respective countries, and I invoke upon you the Blessing of the God of Peace."[38] –**Archbishop Michael L. Fitzgerald,** *President*

Comment: This is total apostasy. And this is why Pope Pius XI says (as quoted already) that those who favor interreligious prayer gatherings, such as the Vatican II antipopes and its apostate bishops, <u>are not only in error and deceived</u>, but have completely rejected the true religion.

Pope St. Leo the Great (+ c. 450): "For whoever is led away from the path of the true faith, and changed to another, **his whole journey is an apostasy; and the further he travels from the Catholic light, the nearer he comes to the darkness of death."**[39]

Every year the Vatican Sends a Message to Hindus on the Feast of Diwali!

"Dear Hindu Friends,

"1. This year again, I am pleased to greet you and share with you a short message on the occasion of Diwali, the feast **which you celebrate according to your venerable religious tradition.** I know that among many Hindu festivals which are celebrated by you throughout the year this one, in particular, has a special place and deep relevance for you and your families. **Diwali is a time for families to get together, and celebrate in a meaningful way the rites prescribed by the ancient dharma**… **Do not your various Hindu traditions (sampradaya) eloquently speak not only of God's love** for us and our love for God but also of the love that human beings must have for one another?… <u>**The occasion of the festival of Diwali provides us with ample food for thought when the Hindu tradition informs us of how light overcomes darkness, how the victory of good is achieved over evil**</u> and how hatred gives way to love through forgiveness. Dear Hindu friends, may you, your families, friends and even the strangers in your midst experience joy, peace, serenity, and light on the feast of Diwali, as symbolized by the innumerable flames, the Deepavali."[40] - Sent by Archbishop Michael L. Fitzgerald (10-14-2003), President of the Vatican Council for Interreligious Dialogue

Comment: **Fitzgerald even tells the Hindus that their false religion of the Devil "informs us of how light overcomes darkness."** If Fitzgerald were not a complete apostate himself who unfortunately lies in spiritual darkness, he would discover that those outside the kingdom of Christ lie in the kingdom of darkness (Colossians 1:13).

Colossians 1:13: "Who hath delivered us from the power of darkness, and hath translated us into the kingdom of the Son of His love."

Pope Leo XIII, *Ad Extremas* (#1), June 24, 1893: "Our thoughts turn first of all to the **blessed Apostle Thomas who is rightly called the founder of preaching the Gospel to the Hindus.** Then, there is Francis Xavier… Through his extraordinary perseverance, **he converted** hundreds of thousands of Hindus from the myths and vile superstitions of the Brahmans to the true religion. In the footsteps of this holy man followed numerous priests… they are continuing these noble efforts; nevertheless, in the vast reaches of the Earth, **many are still deprived of the truth, miserably imprisoned in the darkness of superstition.**"[41]

> So, to summarize, every year on the Buddhist day of Vesakh, and during the Muslim month of Ramadan, and on the Hindu feast of Diwali, the Vatican II sect officially sends out greetings in praise and esteem for these false religions. This proves that the New Church of the Vatican II sect is just one among these false religions.

The Vatican II sect teaches that Jews and Muslims are the spiritual seed of Abraham, which is a denial of Jesus Christ

A common heresy of the Vatican II sect is the idea that Jews and Muslims are the spiritual seed of Abraham; or, to put it another way, the idea that Christianity, Islam and Judaism are all heirs to the faith of Abraham. This heresy is taught by many in the Vatican II sect, but was most prominently inculcated by John Paul II. This heresy rejects the divinely revealed truth that Christ is the seed of Abraham, and that *only those who accept Christ are the spiritual seed of Abraham*.

When God promised Abraham that, *"In your descendants all nations of the earth will be blessed, because you have obeyed my voice"* (Gen. 22:18), He was referring to Our Lord Jesus Christ, as St. Paul makes quite clear.

> Galatians 3:14- *"That the blessing of Abraham might come on the Gentiles through Christ Jesus*: **that we may receive the promise of the spirit by faith."**

> Galatians 3:29- **"And if you be Christ's; then you are the seed of Abraham."**

The following *truly great* popes make this clear as well.

> Pope St. Gregory the Great (+ c. 590): "… *if you be Christ's then you are the seed of Abraham* (Gal. 3:29). **If we because of our faith in Christ are deemed children of Abraham, the Jews therefore because of their perfidy have ceased to be His seed**."[42]

> Pope St. Leo the Great, Dogmatic Letter to Flavian (449), read at Council of Chalcedon (451), *ex cathedra*: "The promises were spoken to Abraham and his seed. He does not say "to his seeds" – as if referring to multiplicity – but to a single one, **'and to thy seed,' which is Christ** (Gal. 3:16)."[43]

Yet, the leaders of the Vatican II sect frequently deny this infallible truth of Scripture and Catholic dogma by asserting that the Jews and Muslims are the spiritual descendants or "children" of Abraham.

John Paul II, *Homily*, March 7, 1982: "**Abraham's descendants in faith** are, in a certain sense, the followers of the three great monotheistic religions of the world: Judaism, Christianity, Islam.** '*In your descendants all nations of the earth will be blessed, because you have obeyed my voice*' (Gen. 22:18)."

John Paul II, *Address to Roman Citizens*, Jan. 15, 1998: "**I cordially greet you**, Roman citizens, who belong to other religious traditions: **you, Jews, heirs to the faith of Abraham**, who for centuries have shared in the spiritual and civil life in Rome; you, brothers and sisters of the Christian confessions; **you, believers of the Muslim religion. May common adoration of the Most High** foster mutual respect and make you all active builders of an open and united society."

John Paul II, *Homily*, Jan. 1, 2002: "This appeal is first and foremost for those who believe in God, **in particular for the great 'Abrahamic religions': Judaism, Christianity and Islam**, called to declare their firm and decisive rejection of violence."

Comment: This is a major denial of Jesus Christ. Notice above how John Paul II even quoted the promise made to Abraham in Gen. 22:18 and attributed this blessing to Judaism and Islam!

Galatians 3:29- "**And if you be Christ's**; then you are the seed of Abraham."

Summary of the Apostasy of the Hierarchy and Members of the Vatican II Sect

We have exhaustively documented the blatant heresies and apostasy of the hierarchy and prominent members of the Vatican II sect. We could continue for many pages, but this suffices to establish that we are definitely in the Great Apostasy, and that the religion to which they adhere (the post-Vatican II "Catholicism") is a counterfeit sect which Catholics must completely reject.

Endnotes for Section 34:

[1] http://www.buffalonews.com/editorial/20060919/1039091.asp
[2] Dom Prosper Gueranger, *The Liturgical Year*, Fitzwilliam, NH: Loreto Publications, 2000, Vol. 4, p. 379.
[3] Quoted by St. Robert Bellarmine, *De Romano Pontifice*, II, 30.
[4] http://www.buffalonews.com/editorial/20060919/1039091.asp
[5] *Itar-Tass News Agency*, May 7, 2004
[6] http://www.usatoday.com/news/religion/2004-11-17-catholic-bishops_x.htm?csp=34
[7] *The Papal Encyclicals*, by Claudia Carlen, Raleigh: The Pierian Press, 1990, Vol. 4 (1939-1958), p. 41.
[8] *National Catholic Register*, Sept. 19-25, 2004, p. 10.
[9] Bulletin *du prieure Marie-Reine* [195 rue de Bale, 68100 Mulhouse]; also *The Angelus*, Feb-March 2004, p. 70.
[10] http://www.usccb.org/seia/filioque.shtml
[11] *Decrees of the Ecumenical Councils*, Sheed & Ward and Georgetown University Press, 1990, Vol. 1, p. 314; Denzinger, *The Sources of Catholic Dogma*, B. Herder Book. Co., Thirtieth Edition, 1957,460.
[12] Denzinger 691.
[13] *L'Osservatore Romano* (the Vatican's Newspaper), Nov. 17, 2004, p. 8.
[14] *The Papal Encyclicals*, Vol. 2 (1878-1903), p. 307.
[15] *The Life and Letters of St. Francis Xavier* by Henry James Coleridge, S.J. (Originally published: London: Burns and Oates, 1874) Second Reprint, New Delhi: Asian Educational Services, 2004, Vol. 1, p. 116.
[16] *The Life and Letters of St. Francis Xavier* by Henry James Coleridge, Vol. 1, p. 147.
[17] *L'Osservatore Romano*, March 24, 2004, p. 10.

[18] *L'Osservatore Romano*, March 10, 2004, p. 11.
[19] Denzinger 714.
[20] Denzinger 247.
[21] *L'Osservatore Romano*, Feb. 18, 2004.
[22] Denzinger 695.
[23] Denzinger 2301.
[24] Denzinger 2147a.
[25] *The Angelus*, Kansas City, MO, Dec. 2003, pp. 32-37.
[26] Denzinger 993.
[27] Denzinger 256.
[28] *The Angelus*, Kansas City, MO, Dec. 2003, pp. 32-37.
[29] *Catholic Family News*, Niagra Falls, NY, Dec. 2003, pp. 20-21.
[30] Denzinger 714.
[31] Thomas Woods and Chris Ferrara, *The Great Façade*, Wyoming, MN: The Remnant Publishing Co., 2002, pp. 147-148.
[32] Thomas Woods and Chris Ferrara, *The Great Façade*, p. 148.
[33] Thomas Woods and Chris Ferrara, *The Great Façade*, p. 148.
[34] *The Papal Encyclicals*, Vol. 1 (1740-1878), p. 452
[35] *Catholic Family News*, January, 1999.
[36] Cardinal Francis George, "The Sins of the Church: God's Forgiveness and Human Memories, Catholic New World," March 19, 2000.
[37] Archbishop Michael Fitzgerald, *Vatican Message to Buddhists on feast of Vesakh*, April 30, 2004.
[38] *L'Osservatore Romano*, Nov. 26, 2003, p. 3.
[39] *The Sunday Sermons of the Great Fathers*, Regnery, Co: Chicago, IL, 1963, Vol. 2, p. 148.
[40] http://www.zenit.org/english/visualizza.phtml?sid=42717
[41] *The Papal Encyclicals*, Vol. 2 (1878-1903), p. 307.
[42] *The Sunday Sermons of the Great Fathers*, Vol. 1, p. 92.
[43] *Decrees of the Ecumenical Councils*, Vol. 1, p. 78.

35. EWTN: The Global "Catholic" Network and the Charismatic Movement

"In the chapel, [the Charismatic] **Schlemon and the [Charismatic] priest laid hands on Mother**, invoking the baptism of the Holy Spirit."[1] About a week later "**a foreign tongue spilled from Mother Angelica's mouth inexplicably.** When Sister Regina came to deliver a glass of orange juice, Mother tried to say thank you, but '**something else came out.**'"[2]

Mother Angelica, the foundress of the Eternal Word Television Network (EWTN)[3]

One of the "conservative" organizations affiliated with the Vatican II sect is EWTN, the global "Catholic" television network. Some misguided people have persuaded themselves and others that EWTN is a strong defender of Catholic truth spreading light to millions in a dark world. However, despite what many think, EWTN is actually a vehicle for some of the worst of the post-Vatican II apostasy. EWTN promoted John Paul II's interreligious apostasy at Assisi, and covered with approval Benedict XVI's apostasy at the synagogue in Germany, as well as his initiation into Islam in a mosque in Turkey. EWTN promotes the heresy of salvation outside the Church; its show, *The Journey Home*, treats conversion to the Catholic Faith from Protestant sects as a preference, but not a necessity. This heretical and evil idea, that adhering to Protestant sects which reject the teaching of the true Church doesn't bar one from salvation, is articulated by almost all of the "converts" from Protestantism featured on *The Journey Home*.

EWTN's foundress Mother Angelica, who has been one of the most significant figures in the post-Vatican II sect, especially for its more "conservative" members, is someone for us to consider. Speaking about other religions during one show, EWTN foundress Mother Angelica asserted with pure religious indifferentism that we all have the same God. She specifically said: "You call

EWTN and the Charismatic Movement

him Allah, and we call him Jesus." For the Jubilee Year in 2000, Mother Angelica was repeatedly featured citing a Jubilee prayer. In the prayer, Mother Angelica mentioned the "great religions" of the world – a quotation of John Paul II's and Paul VI's frequent expression of religious indifferentism.

On another show with Mother Angelica, Alice Von Hildebrand (a frequent guest on EWTN) bluntly asserted that one can get to Heaven as a Buddhist. The way it was stated not only indicated that Buddhists can be saved (which is heresy, of course), but that there is no obligation *whatsoever* for a Buddhist to be a Catholic. In the face of this tremendous heresy and religious indifferentism, which was asserted right in front of her face, Mother Angelica posed no objection, and even commented with approval. Mother Angelica and EWTN have always been defenders of the heretical teachings of Vatican II.

Mother Angelica was also an outspoken defender of the worst kind of false ecumenism, including with Jews. In one show, Mother Angelica and Fr. Benedict Groeschel were discussing the recent death of "Cardinal" John O'Connor. Fr. Groeschel mentioned that the Jews held a Jewish service <u>in St. Patrick's Cathedral</u> after the death of "Cardinal" John O'Connor. Groeschel, an incredible apostate, thought that the Jewish service in the Cathedral was a great thing. **Mother Angelica also wasted no time in blurting out: "That's awesome!"**

Thus, Mother Angelica held that the worst kind of false ecumenism – a Jewish service in St. Patrick's Cathedral itself – is "awesome." These facts, by the way, refute the ridiculous assertion which was made in a book which is cited below: that EWTN supposedly went Modernist only after the departure of Mother Angelica from the reins of power. There is an article on our website giving more detail about this issue. But even Raymond Arroyo, who wrote the biography for Mother Angelica and is one of her biggest supporters, bluntly admitted that *she was a promoter of ecumenism whose work could therefore be supported by members of non-Catholic religions.* "The monastery [under Mother Angelica] had become **an ecumenical touchstone** in Birmingham, an inspired project **that Protestants, Jews,** and Catholics could **support**. The personality of Mother Angelica made it so."[4]

In short, EWTN is a mechanism by which the Devil made post-Vatican II conservative-minded professing Catholics comfortable with the post-Vatican II apostasy.

In 1980, Mother Angelica went to North Carolina and appeared on the Protestant television network called PTL, which was founded by Assembly of God minister Jim Bakker and his wife, Tammy Faye. "Mother Angelica had appeared on PTL several times throughout 1979, to great acclaim, and was ranked in the polls as an audience favorite… **Bakker was so taken with the nun, he dispatched a team of scenic designers to Birmingham to build her first studio set**."[5] The fact that a Protestant minister was so impressed with her that he actually sent a team to design her studio demonstrates, once again, that her message was not Catholic, but ecumenical.

Mother Angelica was also actively involved in **the Charismatic movement**, a movement which is quite widespread in the Vatican II sect. The Charismatic movement is a false movement heavily infected with heretical and Protestant tendencies and ideas. On February 11, 1971, "Barbara Schlemon, a charismatic reputed to have the gift of healing, passed through Birmingham and asked Fr. De Grandis [a Charismatic priest] to take her to meet Mother Angelica… In the chapel, **Schlemon and the priest laid hands on Mother**, invoking the baptism of the Holy Spirit."[6] **About a week later "a foreign tongue spilled from Mother Angelica's mouth inexplicably.** When Sister Regina came to deliver a glass of orange juice, Mother tried to say thank you, **but 'something else came out**.'"[7] We must emphasize that this very significant fact is admitted in a biography about Mother Angelica which was written by one of her biggest supporters: the anchor of her network, Raymond Arroyo.

"**On Holy Saturday in 1971, Father De Grandis and Mother prayed over each member of the community**. All but one nun experienced the baptism of the Holy Spirit, and everyone received something. Following this experience, Sister Joseph and other nuns believed the Lord began speaking to them. **By Easter Sunday, the whole community was 'speaking in tongues.'**"[8]

Speaking in languages not known by the individual who is speaking them, speaking in gibberish, etc. is very often a sign of diabolical possession. This is especially true when it comes as a result of a Charismatic experience in which one has had hands laid on him or her in order to receive "the spirit." Readers are, of course, perfectly free to take this or leave it: but an individual we know from Massachusetts, who was heavily involved in the Charismatic movement years ago, actually told one of us that he felt a demon enter him after a Charismatic had laid his hand on him at a service. He also told us that, at one Charismatic conference, God allowed him to see a small demon enter a room. Amazed, he followed the demon and waited to see if it would come back out of the room; but the only thing which emerged from the room was the Charismatic priest who was about to perform his "healing" service by praying over people. This experience caused this individual to abandon the Charismatic movement.

We believe that God allows the Devil to take people over in these Charismatic services because *by partaking in them people are essentially saying that the sacraments of the Catholic Church, the seven instituted by Jesus Christ, are not sufficient.* They are professing, therefore, that they need a new set of man-made rites – rites which are outside the sacramental system – **in order to really receive "the spirit."** By participation in such "rites," they are essentially participating in a new religion in order to gain access to "the spirit" outside the means specifically set up by Christ. As a consequence, these Charismatic "rites" become new "sacraments" of a false religion which give access to the evil, not the Holy, spirit.

It should be emphasized that the laying on of hands is present throughout the New Testament as the matter for the Sacrament of Confirmation (e.g. Acts 8:17; Acts 19:6) – a sacrament instituted by Jesus Christ. It's ironic that in the new "Confirmation" in the Vatican II sect the laying on of hands has been abolished, but Charismatics continue to use the laying on of hands in their own services in order to transmit "the spirit." **Since we know that** *their laying on of hands in an attempt to transmit the "spirit" is <u>not</u> the Sacrament of Confirmation* **(for even women and laymen do it), it is actually the Counter Confirmation – a false sacrament which therefore gives access, once again, not to the Holy, but to the evil spirit.**

So, as a worthy recipient of the Sacrament of Confirmation receives a deeper endowment of the Holy Ghost, the active participation in such new "rites" or "sacraments" of the false Charismatic religion – by partaking in things such as the laying on of hands – gives these unfortunate individuals a deep endowment of the evil spirit. **That's why at many of these Charismatic meetings the "Catholics" actually find themselves oinking like pigs, barking like dogs, and breaking out into outrageously uncontrollable laughter.** These things, especially oinking like pigs and barking like dogs, are clear signs of demonic possession.

We make reference to this individual's experience because Mother Angelica herself not only spoke repeatedly of her own mystical "experiences," but she also admitted something striking about her reaction to having hands laid on her by Charismatics. Her reaction dovetails with this gentleman's experience. Mother Angelica said that her experience, *in which words she hadn't intended to speak spilled out of her mouth after having had hands laid on her by Charismatics*, scared her. She recalled: **"Words came out, but I didn't know what they were. It scared me."**[9]

Mother Angelica didn't realize that it was an evil spirit which she had picked up after involvement with the Charismatics. She continued to promote this movement.

On Dec. 2, 1977, Mother Angelica led a Charismatic retreat in Birmingham with 28 leaders in her work, who were called "Guardians." Standing in the chapel, "**Mother laid her hands on each guardian, praying in tongues for their fidelity. Some sang out in** holy **gibberish**, others were 'slain in the Spirit.'"[10] One of the participants said afterwards that it was "**charismania at its height.**"[11] After the death of Paul VI, "**Mother Angelica laid hands on Matt Scalici, Jr.** in her chapel."[12]

Mother Angelica's biography claims that after this time she "gradually" pulled out of the Charismatic movement. This is an empty claim, for her network continued to promote the biggest charismatics in the country, such as the figures at Franciscan University and those of their ilk.

We find Mother Angelica's early involvement in the diabolical Charismatic movement very significant. It's significant because EWTN has been a vehicle by which the Devil has kept many "conservatives" inside the Vatican II sect by its mixture of conservatism (i.e. some things which are true to Catholic Tradition) with the apostasy of the Vatican II religion. Personalities such as Mother Angelica have acted as magnets to keep "conservatives" deceived and devoted to the Counter Church. Many are persuaded that figures such as Mother Angelica in the post-Vatican II "Church" are proof that true spiritual vitality is still to be found there when, in truth, it is a false "Church" and adherence to its apostasy leads to damnation. It makes sense that the leader of this deceptive apostolate at EWTN, Mother Angelica, got her start by receiving a diabolical spirit at a Charismatic event.

In fact, Mother Angelica has claimed that numerous mystical experiences guided her course at EWTN.

> "During a bright spot in her convalescence, **Mother claims to have seen the child Jesus dashing down the halls of the monastery**. This was by no means an isolated event."[13]

Does it sound like the Child Jesus to be "dashing down the halls"? Or does it sound more like what a demon would be doing as he goes about his work for the destruction of souls? Based on what we've covered already about Mother Angelica's endorsement of heresy, false religions and the diabolical Charismatic movement, a true Catholic would have to conclude that Mother Angelica actually saw the latter, not the former.

> Matthew 24:24-25- "For there shall arise false Christs and **false prophets, and shall show great signs and wonders, insomuch as to deceive (if possible) even the elect**. Behold I have told it to you, beforehand."

Mother Angelica also claimed that the Child Jesus appeared to her and told her, "**Build me a temple** and I will help those who help you."[14] While churches can be described as "temples" – as we covered earlier in the section on 2 Thess. 2:4 – a "temple" can also describe a Jewish house of worship and a Masonic lodge. Since Mother Angelica has promoted the heretical and false idea that Jews don't need Jesus Christ for salvation – proven by, among other things, her adherence to the antipopes who teach this – it's certain that it was not Our Lord Jesus telling her to build a Catholic temple. Rather, it was another evil spirit (one similar to that which she received at the Charismatic event) cryptically telling her to build a "temple" for the New Church religion of the Vatican II sect. It's very interesting that the top of the Cross on the outside of this "temple" (a temple that Mother Angelica spent about 50 million dollars to build!) was incredibly blown off cleanly by a bolt of lightning during a powerful storm, leaving only a "T," not the regular Cross. It remains that way to this day.

Moving back to the apostasy promoted by EWTN, Fr. Benedict Groeschel is a huge figure at EWTN. Groeschel has turned away converts, declared that he never "bought" that non-Catholics can't be saved (a defined dogma), preached in "200 Protestant churches and a hundred synagogues," and said that the sacraments are not necessary for salvation, and <u>even denied that Our Lord even said</u> "Unless you eat the flesh of the Son of Man and drink his blood you shall not have life in you" (John 6:54)![15]

EWTN's "experts" totally reject the necessity of the Catholic Church for salvation. EWTN's "experts" inform non-Catholic inquirers – including a Jew who rejects Christ and the wife of an "Orthodox" schismatic wondering about her husband's obligation to convert – that they are fine for Heaven right where they are.[16]

EWTN also promotes an organization called the Association of Hebrew Catholics (AHC). The Association of Hebrew Catholics is composed of supposed "converts" from Judaism. They are attempting to create, in effect, a Jewish sect inside the "Catholic Church." This organization is headed by David Moss, who has been featured on EWTN numerous times. David Moss is the brother of Rosalind Moss, who also has hosted shows on EWTN and is employed by "Catholic Answers." This AHC – composed of supposed converts from Judaism – promotes that Catholics converted from Judaism may continue to practice the Old Law (an idea solemnly condemned by the Council of Florence).

> "Ignoring the Church's teaching that the rituals and observances of the Mosaic law have been abolished with the New Covenant and that it is mortally sinful to observe them, **Moss recommended that the Catholic inquirer <u>'go to a local synagogue and watch what they do and listen to it. You can take part in a Seder,'</u>** he added... <u>**Moss then recommended that Catholics follow suit [that is, follow the practice of 'Messianic Jews'] by celebrating Passover and Rosh haShanah**</u>... This conclusion is supported by an item on AHC's website entitled: 'Through the Hebrew Catholic Year: A Collection of Traditions and Prayers for the Jewish Holidays for Catholics.' **Here AHC advocates a 'Catholic' celebration of Rosh haShanah, Yom Kippur, Succoth, Purim, Passover, Shavuoth, and Hanukkah, using prayers 'adapted from traditional Jewish prayer books.'**"[17]

This is a promotion of mortal sin, heresy and apostasy.

EWTN is unfortunately a very heretical, modernist, false ecumenical network, which mixes apostasy, a promotion of Vatican II, the New Mass and the New Religion with some interesting programming. Here's an interesting e-mail we received on this issue:

> "Good morning, **Turned on EWTN this morning**. I find myself occasionally viewing the Novus Ordo service during this my decision process, i.e., what to do (relative to my Catholic Faith). I heard the "main celebrant" Fr. Francis state: '...**the Church never said other Christians will not receive salvation...those that say this are liars or misinformed...the Catholic Church is like a five course meal, if you want the whole meal, come to the Church.**.'

> "The day's homily is available online (I think next day). Perhaps you can use this statement, after you verify, as your "Heresy of the Week." This "doctrine" has gone, real

time, to untold numbers. If not included as a "Heresy" installment - send the poor fellow a copy of your "No Salvation" book.

Pray for me,
G. M."

We wonder if any of the EWTN supporters who heard or watched the sermon ever deeply considered its implications: what it means about their presence at church, their entire effort to attend "Mass," etc. We wonder if it hit any of them that this means that being a Catholic, praying the Rosary, going to confession, etc. is pointless.

We certainly hope for the conversion of "Fr." Francis, but we must say that he is too blinded by his apostasy to realize his foolishness. He is too blinded to realize that he holds that his own "priesthood" – the entire EWTN Network – is a complete waste of time. If you believe what EWTN and "Fr." Francis do, you would have to be a **complete idiot** to be Catholic. You could just head down to the local Lutheran church, confess your faith in Jesus as Lord, and head on your way.

So don't be fooled by externals. Heretics have always had externals to one degree or another. Don't be fooled by those who claim to have some attachment to the Catholic Faith or Our Lord or Our Lady or the Saints, but reject a dogma. Unless they accept the entire truth, they are phonies. "Fr." Francis sometimes speaks of bringing the young to Christ on his show "Life on the Rock." Sounds great and devoted, doesn't it? But then he publicly commented on and praised Benedict XVI's Christ-denying visit to the synagogue and endorsement of the Jewish religion. He speaks of bringing the young to Christ when he believes that Christ is meaningless.

This e-mail shows us again that phonies mix an attachment to some things Catholic with a rejection of its truth. They act as if they are devoted to God, and surely say some good and conservative things, but they are abominations in God's sight.

Since we're speaking of phonies, mention must be made of "Fr." John Corapi of EWTN. Those who have seen him know that Corapi gives talks as if he is devoted to Our Lord and the Catholic Faith – "thundering" against sin and defending the Eucharist in his melodramatic fashion. He is an utter phony, for he holds that it is all meaningless. He holds that you can be a Protestant who completely rejects Our Lady, the Papacy and the Eucharist, or even a Jew who completely rejects Christ.

> **They are like "whitewashed tombs, which outwardly appear beautiful, but within are full of dead men's bones and all uncleanness. [They] outwardly appear righteous to men, but within are full of hypocrisy and iniquity."** (Matthew 23:28)

One of us called "Fr." Corapi's secretary once, and asked her: "Is it necessary to be a Catholic to be saved?" She responded with the blunt answer: "No." One of us then said, "then why be a Catholic?" She said: "Because it is the fullness of truth." **One of us responded: "But it's not necessary according to you." She agreed.** Behold the emptiness, the stupidity and the evil of the Vatican II religion.

Endnotes for Section 35:

---

[1] Raymond Arroyo, *Mother Angelica*, Random House, Inc., 2005, p. 120.
[2] Raymond Arroyo, *Mother Angelica*, p. 121.
[3] Shown in Raymond Arroyo, *Mother Angelica*; from OLAM.

[4] Raymond Arroyo, *Mother Angelica*, p. 98.
[5] Raymond Arroyo, *Mother Angelica*, pp. 148-149.
[6] Raymond Arroyo, *Mother Angelica*, p. 120.
[7] Raymond Arroyo, *Mother Angelica*, p. 121.
[8] Raymond Arroyo, *Mother Angelica*, p. 123.
[9] Raymond Arroyo, *Mother Angelica*, p. 121.
[10] Raymond Arroyo, *Mother Angelica*, p. 135.
[11] Raymond Arroyo, *Mother Angelica*, p. 135.
[12] Raymond Arroyo, *Mother Angelica*, p. 142.
[13] Raymond Arroyo, *Mother Angelica*, p. 314.
[14] Raymond Arroyo, *Mother Angelica*, p. 255.
[15] Chris Ferrara, *EWTN: A Network Gone Wrong*, Pound Ridge, NY: Good Counsel Publications, 2006, p. 79; pp. 86-90.
[16] EWTN Q & A Forum, advice by Richard Geraghty of Feb. 19, 2005 on "Non-Catholic Salvation."
[17] EWTN broadcast of March 7, 2005; quoted by Chris Ferrara, *EWTN: A Network Gone Wrong*, p. 146.

START OF PART III –

THE TRADITIONALIST RESISTANCE – SOME ISSUES PERTAINING TO THOSE WHO HAVE FIGURED OUT, TO ONE DEGREE OR ANOTHER, THAT THE POST-VATICAN II CHURCH MUST BE RESISTED OR REJECTED

As we've shown in this book, the Vatican II sect is not the Catholic Church and the Vatican II "popes" aren't true popes at all, but non-Catholic antipopes. All over the world there are groups of individuals who have, to one degree or another, recognized the truth that we have been covering in this volume. They have resisted Vatican II and the New Mass and attempted to cling to the traditional Catholic Faith – recognizing them both to be departures from the traditional Catholic Faith. While resisting Vatican II and the New Mass, however, many of these groups and individuals maintain certain untenable positions.

Concerning those who reject the Vatican II religion but accept the Vatican II "popes"

There are those who have rightly acknowledged that the Vatican II sect is clearly not the Catholic Church, but they still maintain that Benedict XVI, John Paul II, John Paul I, Paul VI and John XXIII are/were valid popes. They admit that the post-Vatican II "popes" *are bad and that they have departed from Tradition*; some of them recognize them as heretics, but they hold that one cannot say they are antipopes. They hold that they can be valid popes, despite the fact that they have headed a new, non-Catholic religion. Such a position **asserts that a true pope heads a false Church.** Thus, such a position separates a true pope from the true Church, which is impossible.

Pope Leo XIII, Jan. 22, 1899 : "Where Peter is, there is the Church."[1]

A true pope heads the true Church, and a false antipope heads a false Church. Therefore, to acknowledge the Vatican II Church as a false Church **requires that one acknowledge its head (currently Benedict XVI) as a false Peter**. On the other hand, to acknowledge Benedict XVI as a true Peter requires that one acknowledge his false Vatican II Church as a true Church – which is contrary to the Faith.

Pope Leo XIII, *Satis Cognitum* (# 15) June 29, 1896: "When the divine founder decreed that the Church should be *one in faith, in government, and in communion,* **He chose Peter and his successors as <u>the principle and center</u>, as it were, of this unity.**"[2]

Moreover, to obstinately acknowledge that Benedict XVI is a true pope requires that you have the same faith as he does, and are in communion with his Vatican II Church.

Pope Leo XIII, *Satis Cognitum* (# 10), June 29, 1896:
"For this reason, **as the unity of the faith is of necessity required for the unity of the Church,** inasmuch as it is the *body of the faithful,* so also for this same unity, inasmuch as the Church is a divinely constituted society, unity of government, which effects and involves ***unity of communion,* is necessary *jure divino* (by divine law).**"[3]

Start of Part III – Issues pertaining to the Traditionalist Resistance 457

And this is precisely why this issue is so important. Because to affirm that a particular person is your pope, the head of your Church, means, by divine law, that you share communion and faith with that person and with his Church.

> Pope Gregory XVI, *Commissum divinitus* (# 10), May 17, 1835:
> "… Christ established this ecclesiastical power for the benefit of unity. **And what is this unity unless one person is placed in charge of the whole Church who protects it and joins all its members in the one profession of faith…**"[4]
>
> Pope Pius XI, *Mortalium Animos* (# 9), on the unity of the Church: "… that unity can only arise from one teaching authority, one law of belief and **one faith of Christians.**"[5]
>
> Pope Pius X, *Editae saepe* (# 8), May 26, 1910: "… the Church remains immutable and constant, 'as the pillar and foundation of truth,' **in professing one identical doctrine**…"[6]
>
> St. Francis De Sales, Doctor of the Church: **"The Church is a holy university or general company of men united and collected together in the profession of one same Christian faith…"**[7]

But to affirm that you profess the same faith as Benedict XVI, John Paul II, etc., after seeing the facts that we have presented, is literally to deny the faith and to break communion with the Catholic Church. So, in order to profess the Catholic Faith whole and undefiled, and in order to declare that one is not part of a false Church, one must denounce Benedict XVI and his predecessors after Vatican II as non-Catholic antipopes.

Many of these traditionalists also hold that while the traditional Mass is superior to the New Mass, the New Mass can still be attended, since it is still valid. Some of them cite alleged apparitions from Heaven to attempt to prove it. Others hold that even though Vatican II was an erroneous or heretical council, it doesn't matter because Paul VI never made it binding on anyone, and therefore he can still be held to have been a valid pope.

The articles which follow deal with different angles of these controversies and disputes among "traditionalists." The facts will show that there is only one position which a Catholic can and must take. The only true position is a complete rejection of the Vatican II sect as a counterfeit Church, which means that one must completely reject Vatican II, the New Mass and the antipopes who imposed them. One must also reject the non-Catholic, manifestly heretical Novus Ordo "bishops."

Endnotes for Introduction to Part III:

[1] Denzinger, *The Sources of Catholic Dogma*, B. Herder Book. Co., Thirtieth Edition, 1957, 1976.
[2] *The Papal Encyclicals*, by Claudia Carlen, Raleigh: The Pierian Press, 1990, Vol. 2 (1878-1903), p. 401.
[3] *The Papal Encyclicals*, Vol. 2 (1878-1903), p. 396.
[4] *The Papal Encyclicals*, Vol. 1 (1740-1878), p. 255.
[5] *The Papal Encyclicals*, Vol. 3 (1903-1939), p. 317.
[6] *The Papal Encyclicals*, Vol. 3 (1903-1939), p. 117.
[7] St. Francis De Sales, *The Catholic Controversy*, Rockford, IL: Tan Books, 1989, p. 161.

36. The False Apparitions at Bayside, New York

(This section exposes the lengths to which the Devil has been allowed to go to deceive people about the Vatican II apostasy, the Vatican II antipopes and the New Mass)

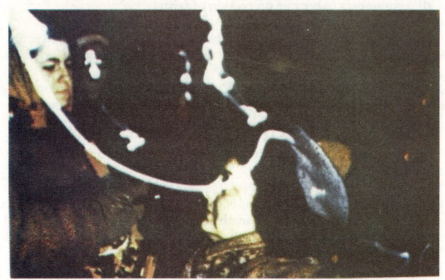

A sign at Bayside - but, as we will see, not a sign from Heaven

We're often contacted by those who follow the alleged apparitions of Our Lady and Our Lord that have occurred in various parts of the world over the past few decades. Among these, the apparitions at Bayside, New York are prominent. Veronica Lueken allegedly received messages from Our Lord and Our Lady starting in the 1970's and lasting into the 1990's. Veronica's messages were known as the Message of Bayside. These messages were – and still are – extremely influential in how many view the post-conciliar crisis.

The False Apparitions at Bayside, NY 459

Veronica Lueken in "ecstasy" at Bayside, NY - As we will see, she was seeing something, but not Our Lady or Our Lord

The messages allegedly received by Veronica were accompanied by prodigies and signs that were witnessed by many at the Bayside apparition site. At the top of this section is a picture from the grounds at Bayside, in which there appears to be a miraculous sign of grace in the area of Veronica Lueken's head. Apparently, there are thousands of such pictures from the grounds at Bayside. These indeed appear to be "signs"; but, as we will see, these signs are not from Heaven.

Speaking of the last days, Our Lord warns the world that there will be false signs and wonders to deceive (if it were possible) even the elect.

> Matthew 24:24-25: "*Then if any man shall say to you: Lo here is Christ, or there, do not believe him. For there shall arise false Christs and **false prophets, and shall show great signs and wonders, insomuch as to deceive (if possible) even the elect**. <u>Behold I have told it to you, before hand</u>*. If therefore they shall say to you: Behold He is in the desert, go ye not out: Behold He is in the closets, believe it not."

In this warning, Our Lord makes the very specific statement that **if people say they see Him here or there in those days, do not believe it**. He even uses the very interesting phrase, "in the closet." In other words, if they say Our Lord is appearing to them in their closets or in their rooms, do not believe it. This admonition would obviously apply also to those who say that His Mother is here or there in those days. St. Paul warns us of the same thing in 2 Thessalonians, when speaking about the time of the Great Apostasy and the coming of Antichrist:

> 2 Thessalonians 2:9-12: "Whose coming is according to the working of Satan, <u>**in all power, and signs, and lying wonders**</u>, And in all seduction of iniquity to them that perish; <u>because they receive not the love of the truth</u>, that they might be saved. Therefore God shall send them the operation of error, to believe lying. That all may be judged who have not believed the truth, but have consented to iniquity."

> Prophecy of Marie Julie Jahenny, *Briton Stigmatist* (1891): "**During the time of the approach of the punishments announced at La Salette, an unlimited amount of false revelations will arise from Hell like a swarm of flies**; a last attempt of Satan to choke and destroy the belief in the true revelations by false ones."[1]

Faced with this situation, <u>**the way that a Catholic judges everything is by the teaching of the Catholic Church**</u>. **If an apparition apparently from Heaven gives a message that contains one clear heresy, or anything contrary to the teaching of the Catholic Church, that is sufficient to prove that it cannot be from God, but that it is from the Devil**. God does not contradict Himself.

> Galatians 1:8-9- "But though we, or an angel from Heaven, preach a gospel to you besides that which we have preached to you, let him be anathema. As we said before, so now I say again: If anyone preach to you a gospel, besides that which you have received, let him be anathema."

What follows are some of the heresies and clearly false messages in Bayside. These serve to prove that the apparitions of Bayside were not authentic messages from Our Lady or Our Lord. We will cover just a few of the false messages in Bayside. There are many others which we will not include in order to avoid making this section too long. These facts are sufficient to prove that Our Lord and Our Lady did not appear or speak to Veronica Lueken. **It was actually the Devil posing as Our Lady and Our Lord who gave Veronica Lueken false messages in order to lead people astray.**

The False Apparitions at Bayside, NY   461

BAYSIDE TEACHES THAT THERE ARE OTHER FAITHS IN HEAVEN

"Our Lady" of Bayside, August 14, 1979: "Do not judge your brothers and sisters who have not been converted. For My Father's House, **My Son has repeated over and over, remember always – that in My Father's House, there are many rooms in the Mansion, signifying faiths and creeds**."[2]

The statement above allegedly from "Our Lady of Bayside," that in the Father's House *there are many mansions representing many faiths and creeds,* is blatantly heretical. It is an infallibly defined dogma that only those who die with the Catholic Faith go to Heaven, as we've covered throughout this book.

Pope Eugene IV, The Athanasian Creed, *Council of Florence,* Sess. 8, Nov. 22, 1439, *ex cathedra*: "**Whoever wishes to be saved, needs above all to hold the Catholic faith;** unless each one preserves this whole and inviolate, he will without a doubt perish in eternity."[3]

This heresy in Bayside gives it away as a false apparition of the Devil, for Our Lady does not contradict infallible dogma and the Chair of St. Peter. To say otherwise is blasphemous heresy.

Pope Leo XII, *Ubi Primum* (# 14), May 5, 1824:
"**It is impossible for the most true God**, who is Truth itself, the best, the wisest Provider, and the Rewarder of good men, **to approve all sects who profess false teachings** which are often inconsistent with one another and contradictory, **and to confer eternal rewards on their members**… **by divine faith we hold one Lord, one faith**, one baptism… **This is why we profess that there is no salvation outside the Church.**"[4]

The Bayside Message contradicts what Catholics must hold by divine faith, that there is only one faith that leads to Heaven, the Catholic Faith, outside of which there is no salvation. The *many mansions* in the Father's house that Our Lord refers to in the Gospel represent different rewards for Catholics who die in the state of grace.

BAYSIDE'S FALSE PROPHECY ON THE MARKET CRASH

"Our Lady" of Bayside, June 18, 1988: "Within two years or less, there will be a great crash of the market. The whole world's monetary systems will be paralyzed. That, My child, is why you had to come this evening to the grounds."[5]

This never happened.

BAYSIDE'S FALSE PROPHECY ON THE BALL OF REDEMPTION

"Our Lady" of Bayside, June 18, 1988: "Do not be affrighted, My child; you must see this, for it is important. Within this century this Ball will be sent upon mankind… It is almost too late… a Ball that is fast hurtling towards earth! It will be here within this century, if not sooner."[6]

A common characteristic of many of the recent false apparitions is the claim that a ball of redemption will come to crush the Earth or much of it. Personally, we believe that the Devil's purpose in promoting this idea is to get people to focus on a physical chastisement, rather than on the spiritual deception occurring with the Vatican II sect. Bayside clearly prophesied that this comet/ball of redemption would arrive "within" the 20th century. **This never happened,** thus proving that the Message of Bayside is false. Further, look at the wording of the message allegedly from "Our Lady." She supposedly says that this ball would arrive "within this century, if not sooner," AS IF SHE DOESN'T KNOW. It is not the statement of Our Lady, but the lie of the Devil.

When Our Lady communicates, she usually says very little. She expresses herself precisely, and she certainly doesn't make false prophecies. She is the Queen of Prophets.

BAYSIDE TEACHES HERESY ON GOD'S POWERS, AND THAT JOHN PAUL II WAS GOOD

"Our Lord" of Bayside, August 21, 1985: "My children – three figures with great power, who are planning the fate of your Vicar [John Paul II]. You must warn him to be clear of those about him. When he reads their writings he will understand. However, **We also ask that he spend less time in going to and fro across the nations, <u>for he makes it doubly difficult for Us to protect him</u>**. Pray a constant vigilance of prayer. You have a <u>good and holy Father</u> now in Rome, but should he be removed there will come disaster."[7]

According to this, Our Lord said it's doubly hard for Him to protect someone who travels. This is clearly false.

Pope Pius IX, *Vatican Council I*, Sess. 3, Chap. 1, On God the creator of all things: "EVERYTHING THAT GOD HAS BROUGHT INTO BEING HE PROTECTS AND GOVERNS BY HIS PROVIDENCE, *which reaches from one end of the earth to the other and orders all things well. All things are open and laid bare before His eyes*, even those which will be brought about by the free activity of creatures."[8]

God's providence and power extend from one end of the earth to the other. It's not hard for Him to do anything. The statement of Bayside not only contradicts Vatican I, but also the Gospel. Our Lord tells His Apostles that He could instantly have more than 12 legions of angels (Mt. 26:53) from His Father, if He asked for them. But Bayside would have us believe that it makes it difficult for God if you travel! This is just one example of many which proves that there is outrageous heresy and error in the Bayside Message.

While God allows the Devil to work false signs at these apparition sites, at the same time He allows (or even forces) the Devil to make major mistakes, so that those who really want the truth can see that the message is a deception of the Devil.

The above message also tells us that John Paul II was "good." This is arguably the worst part of the Bayside Message. John Paul II praised all the different false religions and taught that we shouldn't convert non-Catholics, as we've documented in this book. John Paul II was an evil, Christ-rejecting heretic. Through Veronica Lueken, the Devil wanted to convince people that a man who preached a new Gospel, promoted idolatry and religious indifferentism, was actually "good."

The False Apparitions at Bayside, NY 463

John Paul II at Assisi, 1986, at an ecumenical gathering, which Pope Pius XI condemned as apostasy in *Mortalium Animos*

BAYSIDE TEACHES A CLEAR FALSEHOOD ON THE TELEVISION

> "Our Lady" of Bayside, Sept. 27, 1975: "I have, many times, cautioned you, and all my children, against the use of the diabolical machine, your television. **There will be no excuses for having these in your presence.**"[9]

According to the Message of Bayside, "Our Lady" says that there are no excuses for having a television in your presence. This is clearly ridiculous. That means that one could never watch a Catholic video or the news or some other perfectly acceptable program. Our Lady would certainly condemn the misuse of the television, and most things on television; but this statement of Bayside is clearly false, and it contradicts the teaching of Pope Pius XI in *Vigilanti Cura*, June 29, 1936.

Speaking of motion pictures (movies) – and therefore what he says obviously applies to the television as well – Pius XI points out the "**potentialities for good as well as for harm**." Movies and the television are <u>not</u> intrinsically evil; they can be used for good or for evil.

> Pope Pius XI, *Vigilanti cura* (#'s 18-19), June 29, 1936: "The power of the cinema is due to the fact that it speaks through the medium of living images, which are assimilated with delight and without difficulty, even by those who are untrained and uneducated, and who would be incapable or unwilling to make the efforts of induction or deduction necessary in reasoning. For to read, or to listen to another reading aloud demands a certain concentration and mental effort; an effort which in the cinema is replaced by the delight of a continuous stream of living images presented to the eyes… These theatres, being like the school of life itself, have a greater influence in <u>inciting men to virtue or vice</u> than abstract reasoning."[10]

It's interesting that Pius XI points out that watching a movie requires less mental effort than reading a book, which is why movies and the television are so popular. Most people are unwilling to make the mental effort it requires to read. Since this continuous stream of living images is presented directly to the eyes by a motion picture, Pius XI points out that <u>it possesses great power to incite men</u> "**to virtue or vice…**" Thus, movies and television *can* lead men to virtue, if the program is wholesome and Catholic. Movies and television are not intrinsically evil. The Message of Bayside is proven again to be false.

BAYSIDE'S FALSE PROPHECY ON THE ONE FOLLOWING JOHN PAUL II

"Our Lady" of Bayside, June 18, 1988: "Please, my children, pray for your Holy Father, the pope. You must not lose him, for the one who comes after him will destroy if he can – he will attempt to destroy Pope John Paul II."[11]

This is another false prophecy. The one after John Paul II, who is Benedict XVI, doesn't try to destroy him, but wants to "canonize" him! Further, the prophecy is inherently contradictory, for how could the one after John Paul II attempt to destroy him when John Paul II will already be dead?

THE REAL PURPOSE OF THE FALSE BAYSIDE MESSAGES: STAY IN YOUR PARISH AT THE INVALID NEW MASS AND WITH THE ANTIPOPE

"Our Lady" of Bayside, Aug. 14, 1981, STAY IN YOUR PARISH: "My heart, My Son's heart has been grieved, as we go about the world… We can see a division bordering on schism… it is promoted by Satan… Do not judge My Son's House, His Church, by the man, though he is a representative – legal, a legal representative of My Son… at the time that My Son comes in the Consecration, He shall not turn aside from you, My Son. Therefore, <u>you cannot say that the Mass is invalid</u>. **This has brought great sorrow to Our Hearts, for many left the fold on this matter.**"[12]

"Our Lady" of Bayside, May 3, 1978, Stay in your parish: "**<u>You will all remain in your Parish churches</u>**."[13]

Notice the insistence with which the Message tells people to remain at the New Mass!

"Our Lady" of Bayside, Aug. 14, 1981, Stay in your parish: "I have asked you in the past, and I ask and continue to beg you, my children, **not to abandon your Vicar in Rome**, and **not to abandon your parish church**."[14]

"Our Lord" of Bayside, Sept. 14, 1986, Traditionalists are being led astray: "We hear all names coming forward to Our ears of churches being born anew, called the Traditional

Roman Catholic Church. My child and My children, **We need no more Traditionalists running around** and creating new churches."[15]

The Devil wants people to stay with the counterfeit Church of the Vatican II sect. He wants people to stay with the invalid New Mass. This is the whole purpose of the Bayside Messages, and many similar false messages. The Devil wants to keep conservative-minded "Catholics" inside the Vatican II parishes, in communion with the new Vatican II religion, and under the manifestly heretical and non-Catholic Vatican II antipopes. In order to accomplish this, the Devil uses false seers such as Veronica Lueken. And in order to be ultra-effective, in the false messages which he gives them he includes conservative statements. These conservative statements – such as encouraging the people to pray the Rosary, wear the scapular, denounce modernism, reject liturgical abuses, etc. – are meant to deceive. All of these things were part of the Bayside messages. Since people receive not the love of the truth (2 Thess. 2), God allows them to be deceived by the false signs that have occurred at these apparition sites.

Sadly, the Devil's plan has been incredibly effective. We've been in contact with many who continue to attend the New Mass – while deploring its abuses, of course, as the Bayside Message instructs them – simply because they believe in Bayside. They won't hear the Magisterial arguments (arguments from the traditional teaching authority of the Church) which show that the New Mass is no Mass; rather, they just stick with Bayside. They dismiss all the proof that Paul VI, John Paul II and Benedict XVI weren't/aren't even Catholic; they just stick with Bayside. We know entire families who have been raised in the Conciliar religion – for instance, attending both the indult Mass and the New Mass, rather than strictly the Traditional Mass at an independent chapel – <u>simply because they follow Bayside</u>.

Unfortunately, if they remain on their present path it will cost them their salvation, since they have chosen to follow strange voices rather than the truth communicated through the teaching of the Catholic Church. At their judgments, Our Lord will repeat to them what He warned all of us in the Gospel:

> Matthew 24:24-25: "Then if any man shall say to you: Lo here is Christ, or there, do not believe him. For there shall arise false Christs and false prophets, and shall show great signs and wonders, insomuch as to deceive (if possible) even the elect. <u>Behold I have told it to you, before hand</u>. If therefore they shall say to you: Behold He is in the desert, go ye not out: Behold He is in the closets, <u>believe it not</u>."

Below is just one of countless examples that could be given of a "conservative" message that the Devil spiced in among the Bayside messages. The Devil tells them to <u>remain at the Vatican II parish</u> and under the antipope, while also...

> "Our Lady" of Bayside, Aug. 14, 1974 – Vatican II: "**Satan was present – He listened with careful ears at the Great Council [Vatican II].** He awaited every move, and he placed his agents among you! Recognize and reconstruct your path! You have been deluded."[16]

This tickles the ears of those who know that Vatican II caused the spiritual crisis. So the Devil tells them that there were problems with Vatican II, while keeping them in the very sect that Vatican II created. It's brilliant. Veronica also said that it was revealed to her that if the Latin Mass were returned the coming chastisement would be averted. Hence, the people are told that the Latin Mass is preferable, but the New Mass is also valid and should not be abandoned.

VERONICA LUEKEN WAS A VOICE-BOX FOR THE DEVIL

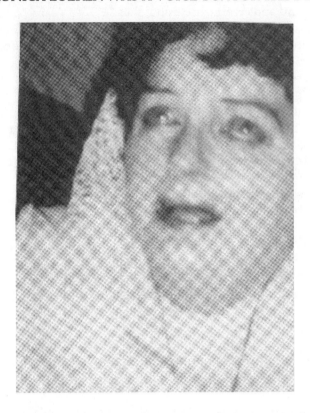

"Our Lady" of Bayside, July 25, 1985: "…By the time We had reached you in Bayside, in your home, My Child, We had looked with Theresa a long time for a Veronica… the highest of Heaven approach many souls to be messengers, **voice-boxes**, for the Eternal Father, through My Son…"[17]

Veronica Lueken was chosen and used as a voice-box for the Devil. Her false messages, which contradict Catholic teaching, have had disastrous effects on innumerable souls. For the most part, what is said in this article also applies to the many other false apparitions of the past few decades. It applies to the false apparitions at Medjugorje, which contain clear heresy; it applies to the false apparitions/locutions to **Don Gobbi, John Leary**, etc., etc., etc. Some of these other apparitions are slightly more conservative, while some of them are slightly more liberal. The Devil has various flavors to appeal to different kinds of people, but they all deliver a false message on the post-Vatican II apostasy. Almost all of them say similar things about John Paul II.

In conclusion, these facts should show us the lengths to which Satan has gone (with God's permission) to deceive people and keep them with the New Mass and the Vatican II antipopes, etc. **This should be a wake up call to us all about the gravity of the spiritual deception we are dealing with now.**

Endnotes for Section 36:

[1] Rev. R. Gerald Culleton, *The Reign of Antichrist*, Rockford, IL: Tan Books, 1974, p. 177.
[2] *Our Lady of the Roses (Blue Book)*, the "messages" of Bayside, published by Apostles of Our Lady, Inc. Lansing, MI, 1993, p. 81.

[3] *Decrees of the Ecumenical Councils*, Sheed & Ward and Georgetown University Press, 1990, Vol. 1, pp. 550-553; Denzinger, *The Sources of Catholic Dogma*, B. Herder Book. Co., Thirtieth Edition, 1957, 39-40.
[4] *The Papal Encyclicals*, Vol. 1 (1740-1878), p. 201.
[5] *Our Lady of the Roses (Blue Book)*, the "messages" of Bayside, p. 108.
[6] *Our Lady of the Roses* (Blue Book), the "messages" of Bayside, p. 108.
[7] *Our Lady of the Roses (Blue Book)*, the "messages" of Bayside, p. 103.
[8] Denzinger 1784.
[9] *Our Lady of the Roses (Blue Book)*, the "messages" of Bayside, p. 86.
[10] *The Papal Encyclicals*, Vol. 3 (1903-1939), p. 519.
[11] *Our Lady of the Roses (Blue Book)*, the "messages" of Bayside, p. 108.
[12] *Our Lady of the Roses (Blue Book)*, the "messages" of Bayside, p. 83.
[13] *Our Lady of the Roses (Blue Book)*, the "messages" of Bayside, p. 83.
[14] *Our Lady of the Roses (Blue Book)*, the "messages" of Bayside, p. 83.
[15] *Our Lady of the Roses (Blue Book)*, the "messages" of Bayside, p. 104.
[16] *Our Lady of the Roses (Blue Book)*, the "messages" of Bayside, p. 87.
[17] *Our Lady of the Roses (Blue Book)*, the "messages" of Bayside, p. 102.

37. What Does Medjugorje Say? Its message proves that it is also a false apparition

"The Madonna always stresses that there is but one God and that people have enforced unnatural separation. **One cannot truly believe, be a true Christian, if he does not respect other religions as well.**"[1] – "Seer" Ivanka Ivankovic

"The Madonna said that religions are separated in the earth, **but the people of all religions are accepted by her Son.**"[2] – "Seer" Ivanka Ivankovic

Question: "Is the Blessed Mother calling all people to be Catholic?" Answer: "No. The Blessed Mother says all religions are dear to her and her Son."[3] – "Seer" Vicka Ivankovic

This is total apostasy in the Message of Medjugorje. It is a rejection of Catholic dogma; it is a rejection of the dogma Outside the Catholic Church There is No Salvation; and it is a total rejection of the clear teaching of the Gospel on the necessity of believing in Jesus Christ, the Son of God, for salvation. This proves that Medjugorje, like the rest of the false modern apparitions, is a deception of the Devil. Those who are aware of these facts and refuse to reject it as a false apparition are rejecting the Catholic Faith.

Endnotes for Section 37:

[1] *The Apparitions of Our Lady of Medjugorje*, Franciscan Herald Press, 1984.
[2] *The Apparitions of Our Lady of Medjugorje*, Franciscan Herald Press, 1984.
[3] Janice T. Connell, *The Visions of the Children, The Apparitions of the Blessed Mother at Medjugorje*, St. Martin's Press, August, 1992.

38. Was Vatican II infallible? If you believe that Paul VI was a true pope, *yes*.

"**Each and every one of the things set forth in this Decree** has won the consent of the fathers. **We, too, by the Apostolic Authority conferred on us by Christ, join with the venerable fathers in approving, decreeing, and establishing these things** in the Holy Spirit, and we direct that what has thus been enacted in synod [council] be published to God's glory… **I, Paul, Bishop of the Catholic Church.**" [1] (Paul VI, solemnly closing every document of Vatican II)

We have exposed in detail the heresies of Vatican II. We have also shown that the men who implemented this non-Catholic Council were **not true popes of the Catholic Church, but antipopes**. Despite all of the evidence, some people remain unconvinced. They hold that there are indeed doctrinal problems with Vatican II; but, according to them, this is no problem for Paul VI because he did not infallibly promulgate any of the Vatican II heresies. "The heresies of Vatican II don't matter," they say, "because Vatican II was not infallible!" We will now show that if Paul VI had been a true pope, the documents of Vatican II would have been promulgated infallibly. This will prove, again, that Paul VI (the heretic who promulgated the apostate documents of Vatican II, changed the rites to all seven sacraments, changed the Mass into a Protestant service, oversaw the systematic and world-wide dismantling of Catholicism, ruined the world-wide Catholic school system, and initiated the greatest apostasy from Catholicism in history) was not and could not have been a true pope. He was an antipope.

There are three conditions that need to be met for a pope to teach infallibly: **[1] the pope must carry out his duty as pastor and teacher of all Christians; [2] he must teach in accord with his supreme apostolic authority**; and **[3] he must explain a doctrine of faith or morals to be believed by the universal Church**. If a pope fulfills these conditions, he, through the divine assistance promised him as successor of Peter, operates infallibly, as the following definition of Vatican Council I teaches.

> Pope Pius IX, *Vatican Council I*, Session 4, Chap. 4:
> "… the Roman Pontiff, when he speaks *ex cathedra*, that is, **[1] WHEN CARRYING OUT THE DUTY OF THE PASTOR AND TEACHER OF ALL CHRISTIANS [2] IN ACCORD WITH HIS SUPREME APOSTOLIC AUTHORITY [3] HE EXPLAINS A DOCTRINE OF FAITH OR MORALS TO BE HELD BY THE UNIVERSAL CHURCH**, through the divine assistance promised him in blessed Peter, <u>operates with that infallibility</u> with which the divine Redeemer wished that His Church be instructed in defining doctrine on faith and morals; and so such definitions of the Roman Pontiff from himself, but not from the consensus of the Church, are unalterable. But if anyone presumes to contradict this definition of Ours, which may God forbid: let him be anathema."[2]

We will now prove, point by point, that Paul VI's promulgation of the documents of Vatican II fulfilled all three of these requirements, which would make the documents of Vatican II infallible if he had been a true pope.

1) A Pope must act as Pastor and teacher of all Christians

The first requirement for a pope to teach infallibly is that he must act as pastor and teacher of all Christians. If he was the true pope, Paul VI fulfilled this requirement.

EACH ONE OF THE 16 DOCUMENTS OF VATICAN II BEGINS WITH THESE WORDS:

> "PAUL, BISHOP, SERVANT OF THE SERVANTS OF GOD, TOGETHER WITH THE FATHERS OF THE SACRED COUNCIL FOR EVERLASTING MEMORY."[3]

Pope Eugene IV began the 9th session of the dogmatic Council of Florence with these words: "**Eugene, bishop, servant of the servants of God, for an everlasting record.**"[4] Pope Julius II began the 3rd session of the dogmatic 5th Lateran Council with these words: "**Julius, bishop, servant of the servants of God, with the approval of the sacred council, for an everlasting record.**"[5] And Pope Pius IX began the 1st session of the dogmatic First Vatican Council with these words: "**Pius, bishop, servant of the servants of God, with the approval of the sacred council, for an everlasting record.**"[6] This is the customary way in which the decrees of general/dogmatic/ecumenical councils are solemnly begun by popes. **Paul VI began every document of Vatican II in the very same way, with the very same words!**

By beginning each document of Vatican II in this way, Paul VI (if he was a true pope) clearly fulfilled the first requirement to teach infallibly.

2) A Pope must teach in accord with his supreme apostolic authority

The second requirement for a pope to teach infallibly is that he must teach in accord with his supreme apostolic authority. If he was the pope, Paul VI fulfilled this requirement.

EACH ONE OF THE 16 DOCUMENTS OF VATICAN II ENDS WITH THESE WORDS (OR WORDS BASICALLY IDENTICAL TO THESE):

> "EACH AND EVERY ONE OF THE THINGS SET FORTH IN THIS DECREE HAS WON THE CONSENT OF THE FATHERS. WE, TOO, <u>BY THE APOSTOLIC AUTHORITY CONFERRED ON US BY CHRIST, JOIN WITH THE VENERABLE FATHERS IN APPROVING, DECREEING, AND ESTABLISHING THESE THINGS IN THE HOLY SPIRIT,</u> AND WE DIRECT THAT WHAT HAS THUS BEEN ENACTED IN SYNOD BE PUBLISHED TO GOD'S GLORY... I, PAUL, BISHOP OF THE CATHOLIC CHURCH."[7]

Wow! This little known fact is utterly devastating to any claim that Paul VI could have been a true pope. Paul VI ended each Vatican II document by invoking his "apostolic authority," followed by his signature! He clearly fulfilled the second requirement for infallibility. In fact, this paragraph in itself fulfills not just the second requirement for Papal Infallibility, but all three; for in it we see Paul VI is "approving, decreeing and establishing" in "the holy Spirit" and "by his apostolic authority" all the things contained in each document! This is infallible language. Anyone who would deny this simply doesn't know what he is talking about.

The approval given to Vatican II by Paul VI (quoted above) is even more solemn than the approval given to the infallible *Council of Nicaea* (325) by Pope St. Sylvester. It's more solemn than the approval given to the infallible *Council of Ephesus* (431) by Pope St. Celestine. In other words, in approving the true councils of the Catholic Church, these true popes approved the documents of these councils in ways that were even less extraordinary than the way in which Paul VI approved Vatican II; and yet their approval of these true councils was sufficient to qualify as infallible and binding – a fact which no Catholic questions.

It is, therefore, a fact that each Vatican II document is a solemn act of Paul VI. Each document is signed by him; each one is begun with him speaking as "pastor and teacher of all Christians"; and each one finished with him "approving, decreeing and establishing" all of the document's contents in virtue of his "apostolic authority."

This proves that if Paul VI was the pope the documents of Vatican II are infallible! But the documents of Vatican II are not infallible; they are evil and heretical. **Consequently, this DESTROYS ANY POSSIBILITY that Paul VI was ever a true pope**; for a true pope could never promulgate the evil documents of Vatican II in this authoritative manner.

3) A Pope must explain a doctrine of faith or morals to be held by the universal Church

We've already proven that Paul VI fulfilled all three requirements to teach infallibly at Vatican II if he were the pope. For the sake of completeness, however, we will finish the point-by-point proof by noting that the Vatican II documents are filled with teachings on faith and morals (part of the third requirement). And they must be held by the universal Church, if Paul VI was the pope, because Paul VI solemnly approved, decreed and established them, in virtue of his "apostolic authority," ordering that they be published.

Therefore, the third requirement for infallibility was also fulfilled by Paul VI in his promulgation of Vatican II. But there's still more!

In his brief declaring the council closed, Paul VI again invoked his "apostolic authority" and acknowledged that all the constitutions, decrees and declarations of Vatican II have been approved and promulgated by him. He further stated that all of it must be "religiously observed by all the faithful"! He further declared all efforts contrary to these declarations null and void.

Paul VI says Vatican II is to be Religiously Observed

Paul VI, "*Papal*" *Brief declaring Council Closed*, Dec. 8, 1965:
"At last all which regards the holy Ecumenical Council has, with the help of God, been accomplished and **ALL THE CONSTITUTIONS, DECREES, DECLARATIONS, AND VOTES HAVE BEEN APPROVED BY THE DELIBERATION OF THE SYNOD AND PROMULGATED BY US.** Therefore, we decided to close for all intents and purposes, **WITH OUR APOSTOLIC AUTHORITY**, this same Ecumenical Council called by our predecessor, Pope John XXIII, which opened October 11, 1962, and which was continued by us after his death. **WE DECIDE MOREOVER THAT ALL THAT HAS BEEN ESTABLISHED SYNODALLY IS TO BE RELIGIOUSLY OBSERVED BY ALL THE FAITHFUL**, for the glory of God and the dignity of the Church… **WE HAVE APPROVED AND ESTABLISHED THESE THINGS, DECREEING THAT THE PRESENT LETTERS ARE AND REMAIN STABLE AND VALID, AND ARE TO HAVE LEGAL EFFECTIVENESS**, so that they be disseminated and obtain full and complete effect, and so that they may be fully convalidated by those whom they concern or may concern now and in the future; and so that, as it be judged and described, **ALL EFFORTS CONTRARY TO THESE THINGS BY WHOEVER OR WHATEVER AUTHORITY, KNOWINGLY OR IN IGNORANCE, BE INVALID AND WORTHLESS FROM NOW ON**. Given at Rome, at St. Peter's, under the [seal of the] ring of the fisherman, December 8… the year 1965, the third year of our Pontificate."[8]

Was Vatican II infallible?

There you have it. The apostate Second Vatican Council is to be "<u>**religiously observed**</u>," if you accept Paul VI. There can be no doubt that if Paul VI was a true pope the gates of Hell prevailed against the Catholic Church on Dec. 8, 1965. If Paul VI was the pope, Jesus Christ's promises to His Church failed. If Paul VI was the pope, all of Vatican II's teaching on faith or morals was promulgated infallibly (*ex cathedra*). **But this is impossible** – and anyone who would say that it is possible doesn't believe in Catholic teaching on the indefectibility of the Catholic Church. **Thus we know that Giovanni Montini (Paul VI) was not a true successor of Peter, but an invalid antipope – which <u>we already proved so clearly in exposing his incredible heresies</u> which showed that his "election" – since he was a manifest heretic – was invalid.**

And if you are not convinced of this, ask yourself this question: Is it possible for a true Catholic pope to "*approve, decree and establish*" all of the heresies of Vatican II "*in the Holy Spirit*" and by his "*apostolic authority*"? Your Catholic sense tells you the answer. No way. Therefore, those who recognize the heresies of Vatican II and the facts that we are presenting here, and yet still maintain that it was possible that Antipope Paul VI was a true pope, are unfortunately in heresy for denying Papal Infallibility and for holding a position which means that the gates of Hell have prevailed against the Catholic Church.

Some people will erroneously argue that for a pope to speak *ex cathedra* he must condemn the opposing view or set forth penalties for non-observance. This is not true. Nowhere in the definition of Pope Pius IX on papal infallibility does he say that the pope must condemn in order to operate infallibly. There are a number of infallible definitions where popes don't condemn or set forth any penalties.

> **Objections-** We will now refute the common objections made by those who argue that Vatican II wasn't infallibly promulgated by Paul VI even if he was the pope.

<u>**Objection #1)**</u> At his speech to open Vatican II, John XXIII said that Vatican II was to be a "pastoral council." This proves that Vatican II was not infallible!

<u>**Response:**</u> This is not true. John XXIII <u>did not say</u> in his opening speech at the council that Vatican II was to be a pastoral council. Here is what John XXIII actually said:

> John XXIII, *Opening Speech at Vatican II*, Oct. 11, 1962: "The substance of the ancient deposit of faith is one thing, and the way in which it is presented is another. And it is the latter that must be taken into great consideration with patience if necessary, everything being measured in the forms and proportions **OF A MAGISTERIUM WHICH IS PREDOMINANTLY PASTORAL IN CHARACTER.**"[9]

Here we see that John XXIII did not say that Vatican II would be a pastoral council. He said that it would reflect the Church's Magisterium, which is predominantly pastoral in character. So, despite the incredibly widespread myth, the truth is that John XXIII never even called Vatican II a pastoral council in his opening speech. By the way, even if John XXIII had called Vatican II a pastoral council in his opening speech, this wouldn't mean that it is not infallible. To describe something as pastoral does not mean *ipso facto* (by that very fact) that it's not infallible. This is proven by John XXIII himself in the above speech when he described the Magisterium as "pastoral," and yet it's *de fide* (of the faith) that the Magisterium is infallible. Therefore, even if John XXIII did describe Vatican II as a pastoral council (which he did not) this would not prove that it is not infallible.

Most importantly, however, the fact that John XXIII did not actually call Vatican II a pastoral council in his opening speech at Vatican II doesn't actually matter. **This is because, as we saw already, it was Paul VI who solemnly confirmed the heresies of Vatican II**; and it is Paul VI's confirmation (not John XXIII's) which proves that Vatican II is binding upon those who accept him.

Objection #2) Paul VI said in his *General Audience* on Jan. 12, 1966, that Vatican II "had avoided proclaiming in an extraordinary manner dogmas affected by the mark of infallibility."

Response: It is true that Paul VI stated in 1966 (after Vatican II had already been solemnly promulgated) that Vatican II "*had avoided proclaiming in an extraordinary manner dogmas affected by the mark of infallibility.*" However, Antipope Paul VI's statement in 1966 is **irrelevant.** It does not and cannot change the fact that he solemnly promulgated (in a way that would be infallible if he were the pope) all of the documents of Vatican II on Dec. 8, 1965. **Paul VI had already signed and sealed Vatican II long before Jan. 12, 1966. Vatican II was solemnly closed on Dec. 8, 1965.** This means that *if Paul VI was the pope* (which he wasn't), the gates of Hell prevailed against the Church on Dec. 8, 1965 because of his solemn and final promulgation of all the heretical Vatican II documents on that day.

The Magisterium is a teaching authority whose teachings are "irreformable" (*de fide definita*, Vatican I, Denz. 1839). Since they are irreformable, they are unalterable from the date on which they are declared. If Antipope Paul VI had been a true Pope, Vatican II was irreformable and infallible on Dec. 8, 1965. Nothing said or done after Dec. 8, 1965 could undo (if Paul VI were a true pope) that which was done already, for then the Magisterium's teaching *would become reformable*. Hence, the speech of Antipope Paul VI in 1966 (after the council was closed) has no relevance to whether or not Vatican II was infallible.

But why, then, would Antipope Paul VI make such a statement? The answer is simple. The diabolical (satanic) intelligence guiding Antipope Paul VI knew that, eventually, everyone with a traditionally Catholic mindset would not accept these decrees of Vatican II as infallible, since they are filled with errors and heresies. Consequently, if he hadn't made this statement in 1966 that Vatican II had avoided extraordinary definitions with infallibility, a *vast body* of people would have come to the immediate conclusion that he (Giovanni Montini - Antipope Paul VI) **was not a real pope**. So the Devil had quite a bit riding on this statement.

The Devil had to propagate among "traditionalists" the idea that Paul VI did not "infallibly" promulgate Vatican II. It was essential to the Devil's entire post-Vatican II apostasy; he was scared to death that millions would have become sedevacantists denouncing Antipope Paul VI, his false Church and his false mass (the *Novus Ordo)*. Hence, the Devil inspired Antipope Paul VI to say (well after Vatican II had been solemnly promulgated by him) that Vatican II didn't issue dogmatic statements. This assurance, the Devil hoped, would give Paul VI the appearance of legitimacy among those who maintained some attachment to the traditional Faith. But this diabolical ploy collapses when one considers the fact that Vatican II had already been closed in 1965.

Furthermore, and perhaps most importantly, it must be pointed out that in the same Jan. 12, 1966 *General Audience*, Paul VI said:

> Paul VI, *General Audience*, Jan. 12, 1966: "**The Council is a great act of the magisterium of the Church, and anyone who adheres to the Council is,**

by that very fact, recognizing and honoring the magisterium of the Church…"

If people are going to quote Paul VI's Jan. 12, 1966 *General Audience* to attempt to prove that Vatican II wouldn't have been infallible even if Paul VI was the pope, then logically <u>they must accept other statements about Vatican II which Paul VI made in that *General Audience*</u>, such as the one quoted above and the one quoted below. In this quotation above, we clearly see that Paul VI says (in the very same *General Audience*) that Vatican II is an act of the Magisterium and that anyone who adheres to Vatican II is "honoring the magisterium of the Church"! [The Magisterium is the infallible teaching authority of the Church.]

> Pope Pius XI, *Rappresentanti in Terra* (# 16), Dec. 31, 1929: **"Upon this magisterial office Christ conferred infallibility**, together with the command to teach His doctrine to all."[10]

Therefore, Paul VI's speech means that, according to him, Vatican II is infallible – since he says that it is the teaching of the Magisterium, which is infallible. **His speech further says that anyone who accepts Vatican II's teaching (i.e., its heresies) – such as that non-Catholics may receive Holy Communion or the heresies on religious liberty or that Muslims and Catholics worship the same God, etc. – is honoring Catholic teaching. Anyone who wants to "go by" this speech, therefore, must admit that those who accept these heresies honor Catholic teaching!** This is clearly absurd and false; it proves that, **no matter which way one wants to look at this issue in conjunction with this *General Audience* of Paul VI, Vatican II is binding upon all who hold that Paul VI was a valid pope** – which proves that Paul VI definitely was not a true pope. You cannot quote this *General Audience* to say one is not bound to accept Vatican II, when the same *General Audience* says that anyone who follows it is honoring the Magisterium! Paul VI goes on to say in the same speech:

> **"…it [the Council] still provided its teaching with the authority of the supreme ordinary magisterium. This ordinary magisterium, which is so obviously official, <u>has to be accepted with docility, and sincerity by all the faithful</u>, in accordance with the mind of the Council on the nature and aims of the individual documents."**

This part of the speech is almost never quoted by the defenders of Paul VI, probably because they know that the teaching of the Supreme Ordinary Magisterium is infallible, which means that even this *General Audience* of Antipope Paul VI affirms the infallibility of Vatican II. In the same *General Audience*, Paul VI also said this:

> "It is the duty and the good fortune of men in the post-Conciliar period to get to know these documents, to study them and to apply them."

Furthermore, Paul VI stated in his encyclical *Ecclesiam Suam* (addressed to the entire Church) that Vatican II had the task of defining doctrine.

> Paul VI, *Ecclesiam Suam* (# 30), Aug. 6, 1964:
> "It is precisely because **the Second Vatican Council has the task of dealing once more with the doctrine *de Ecclesia* (of the Church) <u>and of defining it</u>**, that it has been called the continuation and complement of the First Vatican Council."[11]

This means that Vatican II had the task of teaching infallibly. And in the next section we will quote from Paul VI's 1976 speech where he addresses the very subject of whether Vatican II and the New Mass are binding and specifically rejects the claims of false traditionalists who want to be able to hang on to Paul VI's legitimacy while rejecting his Mass and council.

Was Vatican II infallible?

Objection #3) Vatican II was not infallible because there was a note attached to the document *Lumen Gentium* that said it was not infallible.

Response: [Note: the response to this objection is in-depth and involved, and some might not find it interesting. If you are not looking for the answer to this objection, you might want to skip this one.]

Some defenders of Paul VI make reference to a theological note that was attached to the document *Lumen Gentium*. They think this clarification proves that Paul VI didn't promulgate Vatican II infallibly or authoritatively. But this argument doesn't hold up under scrutiny. Here is the crucial portion of the theological note that was attached to the document *Lumen Gentium*:

> "Taking into account conciliar custom and the pastoral aim of the present council, this holy synod defines as binding on the Church only those matters of faith and morals which it openly declares to be such. **THE OTHER MATTERS WHICH THE SYNOD PUTS FORWARD AS THE TEACHING OF THE SUPREME MAGISTERIUM OF THE CHURCH, <u>EACH AND EVERY MEMBER OF THE FAITHFUL SHOULD ACCEPT AND EMBRACE ACCORDING TO THE MIND OF THE SYNOD ITSELF, WHICH IS CLEAR EITHER FROM THE SUBJECT MATTER OR THE WAY IT IS SAID</u>**, IN ACCORDANCE WITH THE RULES OF THEOLOGICAL INTERPRETATION."[12]

<u>First</u>, this note is not even part of the actual text of the document *Lumen Gentium*; it's an appendix to the text of *Lumen Gentium*.[13]

<u>Second</u>, this note is attached only to *Lumen Gentium,* not the rest of the documents. In other words, even if this theological note did "save" Paul VI's promulgation of the heresies in *Lumen Gentium* (which it didn't), it still did not "save" his promulgation of the rest of the Vatican II heresies.

<u>Third</u>, if one reads the above note one can see that it declares that the subject matter, or the way something is said within Vatican II, identifies that Vatican II is enacting the supreme Magisterium of the Church, in accordance with the rules of theological interpretation – that is to say, as the Church in the past has enacted the supreme Magisterium. **Paul VI's declaration at the beginning and end of every Vatican II document (quoted already) definitely indicates, by "the way it is said," "in accordance with the rules of theological interpretation" (that is, paralleling past dogmatic decrees), that he is enacting the supreme Magisterium (if he had been a pope).** Therefore, this theological clarification attached to the document *Lumen Gentium* does not diminish or negate the solemn language of Paul VI found at the end of every Vatican II document. Rather, his language at the end of every Vatican II document fulfills the requirements of the theological note.

<u>Fourth</u>, those who attempt to use this note in order to "save" all of the documents of Vatican II from compromising Papal Infallibility <u>don't pay much attention to what it actually said</u>. The note clearly stated that **"the other matters which the synod (Vatican II) puts forward as the teaching of the supreme Magisterium of the Church, <u>each and every member of the faithful should accept and embrace according to the mind of the synod itself, which is clear either from the subject matter or the way it is said</u>, in accordance with the rules of theological interpretation."**

This is a very important point! There are numerous instances in Vatican II where Vatican II is setting forth what it believes to be the teaching of the supreme Magisterium, which *"each and every member of the faithful <u>should accept and embrace according to the mind of the synod itself</u>,* *which is clear either from the subject matter or the way it is said…"* For instance, in its heretical Declaration on Religious Liberty (*Dignitatis Humanae*), Vatican II says this:

> Vatican II document, *Dignitatis Humanae* (# 9): "The statements made by this Vatican synod on the right to religious freedom have their basis in the dignity of the person, the demands of which have come to be more fully known to human reason from the experience of centuries. **But this teaching on freedom also has its roots in divine revelation, and is for that reason to be held all the more sacred by Christians.**"[14]

Here Vatican II explicitly indicates that its heretical teaching on religious liberty is rooted in divine revelation and is to be held sacred by Christians. This clearly fulfills the requirements of the theological note for a teaching that "each and every member of the faithful should accept and embrace according to the mind of the (Vatican II) synod itself, **which is clear either from the subject matter or the way it is said**…" And there is more:

> Vatican II document, *Dignitatis Humanae* (# 12): "**Hence the Church is being faithful to the truth of the Gospel and is following the way of Christ and the apostles, when it sees the principle of religious freedom as in accord with human dignity and the revelation of God**, and when it promotes it. Throughout the centuries it has guarded and handed on the teaching received from the master and the apostles."[15]

Here Vatican II explicitly indicates that its heretical teaching on religious liberty is: 1) faithful to the truth of the Gospel; 2) follows the way of Christ and the apostles; and 3) is in accord with the revelation of God! We remind the reader again of the wording of the theological note, which stated that *"the other matters which the (Vatican II) synod puts forward as the teaching of the supreme Magisterium of the Church, each and every member of the faithful should accept and embrace according to the mind of the synod itself, **which is clear either from the subject matter or the way it is said**, in accordance with the rules of theological interpretation."*

Therefore, according to the theological note itself, those who accept Paul VI as a pope are bound to accept Vatican II's heretical teaching on religious liberty as the teaching of the supreme Magisterium of the Church! The theological note binds them to accept Vatican II's heretical teaching on religious liberty as: 1) faithful to the truth of the Gospel; 2) following the way of Christ and the apostles; and 3) in accord with the revelation of God **because this is** *"the mind of the synod itself (Vatican II), which is clear from the subject matter or the way it is said…"* It's very simple: those who believe that Antipope Paul VI was the pope are bound to the heretical document on religious liberty.

To summarize all of the points made so far: 1) the theological note attached to *Lumen Gentium* does not apply to every document; 2) the theological note attached to *Lumen Gentium* does not diminish or negate the language of Paul VI at the end of every Vatican II document, but rather proves that his language at the end of every document fulfills the requirements for infallible teaching of the Magisterium; 3) even if the theological note did apply to every document – and somehow did make Paul VI's solemn language at the end of each document non-binding (which it most certainly doesn't) – **the theological note itself still proves that various documents in Vatican II are infallible and binding by the way Vatican II presents its teaching on these matters**. No matter which way one tries to escape the reality that Antipope Paul VI could not have been a true pope and at the same time promulgate Vatican II, he fails.

St. Peter vs. Anti-Peter

In his dogmatic encyclical *Quanta Cura*, Pope Pius IX infallibly condemned the heretical doctrine of religious liberty (which had also been condemned by numerous other popes). Pope Pius IX explicitly anathematized the heretical idea that religious liberty should be a civil right in every rightly constituted society. The Catholic Church teaches that a government which recognizes the right to religious liberty - like the U.S.A. – is, of course, preferable to one which suppresses Catholicism. Nevertheless, this situation is only the lesser of two evils. The ideal is a government which recognizes the Catholic religion as the only religion of the state and does not give every person the "freedom" to practice and propagate his/her false religion in the public domain. Therefore, the idea that religious liberty should be a universal civil right is heretical, as Pope Pius IX infallibly defined in *Quanta Cura*.

> Pope Pius IX, *Quanta Cura* (#'s 3-6), Dec. 8, 1864, *ex cathedra*:
> "From which totally false idea of social government they do not fear to foster that erroneous opinion, most fatal in its effects on the Catholic Church and the salvation of souls, called by Our predecessor, Gregory XVI, an insanity, NAMELY, THAT 'LIBERTY OF CONSCIENCE AND WORSHIP IS EACH MAN'S PERSONAL RIGHT, WHICH OUGHT TO BE LEGALLY PROCLAIMED AND ASSERTED IN EVERY RIGHTLY CONSTITUTED SOCIETY... But while they rashly affirm this, they do not understand and note that they are preaching liberty of perdition... Therefore, BY OUR APOSTOLIC AUTHORITY, WE REPROBATE, PROSCRIBE, AND CONDEMN ALL THE SINGULAR AND EVIL OPINIONS AND DOCTRINES SPECIALLY MENTIONED IN THIS LETTER, AND WILL AND COMMAND THAT THEY BE THOROUGHLY HELD BY ALL THE CHILDREN OF THE CATHOLIC CHURCH AS REPROBATED, PROSCRIBED AND CONDEMNED."[16]

Pope Pius IX condemned, reprobated and proscribed (outlawed) by his apostolic authority the heretical idea that every state should grant the civil right to religious liberty. But watch this! Whereas Pope Pius IX condemned, reprobated and proscribed (outlawed) this doctrine by his apostolic authority, Antipope Paul VI approves, decrees and establishes this condemned teaching by his "apostolic authority." In other words, **that which Pope Pius IX solemnly condemns by his apostolic authority is exactly what Antipope Paul VI solemnly teaches by his "apostolic authority"**!

> Antipope Paul VI, *Vatican II Declaration on Religious Liberty*: "PAUL, BISHOP, SERVANT OF THE SERVANTS OF GOD, TOGETHER WITH THE FATHERS OF THE SACRED COUNCIL FOR EVERLASTING MEMORY... This Vatican synod declares that the human person has the right to religious freedom ... **THIS RIGHT OF THE HUMAN PERSON TO RELIGIOUS FREEDOM SHOULD HAVE SUCH RECOGNITION IN THE REGULATION OF SOCIETY BY LAW AS TO BECOME A CIVIL RIGHT**... Each and every one of the things set forth in this decree has won the consent of the Fathers. WE, TOO, **BY THE APOSTOLIC AUTHORITY CONFERRED ON US BY CHRIST, JOIN WITH THE VENERABLE FATHERS IN APPROVING, DECREEING, AND ESTABLISHING THESE THINGS** IN THE HOLY SPIRIT, and we direct that what has thus been enacted in synod be published to God's glory... I, Paul, Bishop of the Catholic Church."[17]

The Authority of St. Peter	vs.	The Authority of Anti-Peter
Pope Pius IX, *Quanta Cura* (#'s 3-6), Dec. 8, 1864, *ex cathedra*: "From which totally false idea of social government they do not fear to foster that erroneous opinion, most fatal in its effects on the Catholic Church and the salvation of souls, called by Our predecessor, Gregory XVI, **an insanity, NAMELY, THAT 'LIBERTY OF CONSCIENCE AND WORSHIP IS EACH MAN'S PERSONAL RIGHT, WHICH OUGHT TO BE LEGALLY PROCLAIMED AND ASSERTED IN EVERY RIGHTLY CONSTITUTED SOCIETY**… But while they rashly affirm this, they do not understand and note that they are preaching liberty of perdition… Therefore, **BY OUR APOSTOLIC AUTHORITY, WE REPROBATE, PROSCRIBE, AND CONDEMN ALL THE SINGULAR AND EVIL OPINIONS AND DOCTRINES SPECIALLY MENTIONED IN THIS LETTER,** AND WILL AND COMMAND THAT THEY BE THOROUGHLY HELD BY ALL THE CHILDREN OF THE CATHOLIC CHURCH AS REPROBATED, PROSCRIBED AND CONDEMNED."[18]		Antipope Paul VI, *Vatican II Declaration on Religious Liberty*: "PAUL, BISHOP, SERVANT OF THE SERVANTS OF GOD, TOGETHER WITH THE FATHERS OF THE SACRED COUNCIL FOR EVERLASTING MEMORY… This Vatican synod declares that the human person has the right to religious freedom … **THIS RIGHT OF THE HUMAN PERSON TO RELIGIOUS FREEDOM SHOULD HAVE SUCH RECOGNITION IN THE REGULATION OF SOCIETY BY LAW AS TO BECOME A CIVIL RIGHT**… Each and every one of the things set forth in this decree has won the consent of the Fathers. WE, TOO, **BY THE APOSTOLIC AUTHORITY CONFERRED ON US BY CHRIST, JOIN WITH THE VENERABLE FATHERS IN APPROVING, DECREEING, AND ESTABLISHING THESE THINGS** IN THE HOLY SPIRIT, and we direct that what has thus been enacted in synod be published to God's glory… I, Paul, Bishop of the Catholic Church."[19]

Is it possible for Paul VI to possess the same "apostolic authority" as Pope Pius IX? Does the apostolic authority of St. Peter contradict itself? No way! It is heresy to say so! (Lk. 22:32; *Vatican I*, Sess. 4, Chap. 4.)

Pope Leo XIII, *Satis Cognitum* (# 9), June 29, 1896:
"… Christ instituted a living, authoritative and permanent Magisterium, which by His own power He strengthened, by the Spirit of truth He taught, and by miracles confirmed… As often, therefore, as it is declared on the authority of this teaching that this or that is contained in the deposit of divine revelation, it must be believed by every one as true. If it could in any way be false, an evident contradiction follows; for then God Himself would be the author of error in man."[20]

Pope Pius IX, *Vatican Council I*, Session 4, Chap. 4, ex cathedra:
"So, this gift of truth and **a never failing faith was divinely conferred upon Peter and his successors in this chair**… that with the occasion of schism removed the whole Church might be saved as one, and relying on her foundation might stay firm against the gates of Hell."[21]

With these facts in mind, one can see why those who obstinately maintain that Paul VI was a true pope deny Papal Infallibility. They deny the indefectibility of the Church; they assert that the apostolic authority conferred by Christ upon the successor of Peter contradicts itself; and they assert that the gates of Hell have prevailed against the Catholic Church.

The truth is that Antipope Paul VI was never the validly elected pope of the Catholic Church; and therefore his solemn promulgation of the heresies of Vatican II did not infringe upon Papal Infallibility. As we saw already, the Catholic Church teaches that it's impossible for a heretic to be elected pope, since a heretic is not a member of the Catholic Church. This was defined in Pope Paul IV's Apostolic Constitution *Cum ex Apostolatus Officio*.

Endnotes for Section 38:

[1] Walter M. Abbott, *The Documents of Vatican II*, The America Press, 1966, p. 366, etc.
[2] Denzinger, *The Sources of Catholic Dogma*, B. Herder Book. Co., Thirtieth Edition, 1957, no. 1839.
[3] Walter M. Abbott, *The Documents of Vatican II*, pp. 137, 199, etc.
[4] *Decrees of the Ecumenical Councils*, Sheed & Ward and Georgetown University Press, 1990, Vol. 1, p. 559.
[5] *Decrees of the Ecumenical Councils*, Vol. 1, p. 597.
[6] *Decrees of the Ecumenical Councils*, Vol. 2, p. 802.
[7] Walter M. Abbott, *The Documents of Vatican II*, p. 366, etc.
[8] Walter M. Abbott, *The Documents of Vatican II*, pp. 738-739.
[9] Walter M. Abbott, *The Documents of Vatican II*, p. 715.
[10] *The Papal Encyclicals*, by Claudia Carlen, Raleigh: The Pierian Press, 1990, Vol. 3 (1903-1939), p. 355.
[11] *The Papal Encyclicals*, Vol. 5, p. 140.
[12] *Decrees of the Ecumenical Councils*, Vol. 2, p. 898.
[13] Walter M. Abbott, *The Documents of Vatican II*, p. 97.
[14] *Decrees of the Ecumenical Councils*, Vol. 2, p. 1006.
[15] *Decrees of the Ecumenical Councils*, Vol. 2, pp. 1008-1009.
[16] Denzinger 1690, 1699.
[17] Walter M. Abbott, *The Documents of Vatican II*, pp. 675, 679, 696.
[18] Denzinger 1690, 1699.
[19] Walter M. Abbott, *The Documents of Vatican II*, pp. 675, 679, 696.
[20] *The Papal Encyclicals*, Vol. 2 (1878-1903), p. 394.
[21] Denzinger 1837.

39. Paul VI ends a very popular and significant false traditionalist myth by declaring that Vatican II and the New Mass are binding

"It is even affirmed that the Second Vatican Council is not binding… The adoption of the new Ordo Missae is certainly not left to the free choice of priests or faithful."[1] (Paul VI, *Address*, May 24, 1976)

(Following up on the points just made, this section further refutes one of the biggest false traditionalist myths, that Antipope Paul VI never made Vatican II and the New Mass binding. Since Vatican II is heretical, and the New Mass is a false "Mass," this is powerful proof that Paul VI was not the pope)

As we've been discussing, among those who recognize problems with the post-Vatican II apostasy, there are many "traditionalists" who reject the New Mass and Vatican II, but maintain that Paul VI, the man who promulgated them, never bound anyone to either the New Mass or Vatican II.

Chris Ferrara, *The Remnant*, "A Challenge to the Sedevacantist Enterprise," Nov. 15, 2005, p. 11: "As already mentioned, **even Vatican officials, including the 1984 cardinalate commission, have conceded that the traditional Mass was never actually abolished** *de jure* by the promulgation of the New Mass, and that priests have always been free to continue using the preconciliar Missal… In essence, Paul VI merely created a new rite alongside the old rite, leaving the old intact and never actually forbidding its continued use."[2]

Well, let's quote Paul VI himself to explode and destroy this falsehood. You will probably never see it quoted in *false traditionalist publications* who want to hang on to the myth that Paul VI could have been a true pope, since it is devastating to their FALSE TRADITIONALIST ENTERPRISE. Here it is (brace yourselves false traditionalists):

Paul VI, *Address*, May 24, 1976: "And the fact is all the more serious in that the opposition of which we are speaking is not only encouraged by some priests, but is lead by a prelate, **Archbishop Marcel Lefebvre,** who nevertheless still has our respect.
" It is so painful to take note of this: but how can we not see in such an attitude – whatever may be these people's intentions – **the placing of themselves outside obedience and communion with the Successor of Peter and therefore outside the Church? For this, unfortunately, is the logical consequence,** when, that is, it is held as preferable to disobey with the pretext of preserving one's faith intact, and of working in one's way for the preservation of the Catholic Church, while at the same time refusing to give her effective obedience. And this is said openly. **It is even affirmed that the Second Vatican Council is not binding**: that the faith would also be in danger because of the reforms and post-conciliar directives, that one has the duty to disobey in order to preserve certain traditions. What traditions? It is for this group, not the Pope, not the College of Bishops, not the Ecumenical Council, to decide which among the innumerable traditions must be considered as the norm of faith! As you see, Venerable Brothers, **such an attitude sets itself up as a judge of that**

divine will which placed Peter and his lawful successors at the head of the Church to confirm the brethren in the faith, and to feed the universal flock, and which established him as the guarantor and custodian of the deposit of faith…

"**The adoption of the new Ordo Missae is certainly not left to the free choice of priests or faithful.** The instruction of 14 June 1971 has provided for, with authorization of the Ordinary, the celebration of the Mass in the old form <u>only</u> by aged and infirm priests, who offer the divine Sacrifice *sine populo* [without people]. **The new Ordo was promulgated to take the place of the old, after mature deliberation, following upon the requests of the Second Vatican Council. In no different way** did our holy predecessor Pius V make **obligatory** the Missal reformed under his authority, following the Council of Trent…

"We have called the attention of Archbishop Lefebvre to the seriousness of his behavior, the irregularity of his principal present initiatives, the inconsistency and often falsity of the doctrinal positions on which he bases this behavior and these initiatives, and the damage that accrues to the entire Church because of them."[3]

There you have it. Paul VI himself <u>directly refutes</u> the false traditionalists on their two main contentions. Paul VI declares that it is **"<u>certainly not</u>"** the "free choice" of priests or faithful to <u>not</u> adopt the New Ordo Missae (the New Mass). He also denounces their assertion that the Second Vatican Council is not binding, and he indicates that the logical consequence of the position of Lefebvre, which rejects the New Mass and Vatican II, and operates independently of the hierarchy it recognizes, is to place him outside the Church.

It's time for everyone to wake up and realize that the Vatican II sect is a counterfeit sect from head to toe, and there is no way to salvage it or its antipopes. That's why all the "bishops" with "ordinary jurisdiction" in the Vatican II sect hold that Vatican II is the official teaching of the Church. It's why all of the "traditional" groups which receive "official approval" from the Vatican II sect must accept Vatican II. It's why Benedict XVI recently told the leader of the SSPX that they cannot be accepted fully in the Vatican II sect unless they accept Vatican II.

Endnotes for Section 39:

[1] *L'Osservatore Romano* (the Vatican's Newspaper), June 3, 1976, p. 2.
[2] Chris Ferrara, *The Remnant*, "A Challenge to the Sedevacantist Enterprise," Nov. 15, 2005, p. 11
[3] *L'Osservatore Romano*, June 3, 1976, p. 2.

40. The File on the positions of the Society of St. Pius X (SSPX)

Archbishop Lefebvre (founder of the SSPX) and the four bishops he consecrated[1] on June 30, 1988

"We are faced with a serious dilemma which, I believe, has never existed in the Church: the one seated on the chair of Peter takes part in the worship of false gods. What conclusions will we have to draw, perhaps in a few months' time, faced with these repeated acts of taking part in the worship of false religions, I do not know. But I do wonder. **It is possible that we might be forced to believe that the pope is not the pope.**"[2] (Archbishop Lefebvre, Sermon, Easter, 1986)

[**Note:** What is said in this section applies not only to the Society of St. Pius X, but to many other similarly-minded, independent "traditionalist" groups which resist the Vatican II apostasy and the New Mass by holding positions similar to the SSPX.]

The SSPX is a "traditionalist" order of priests founded by the late Archbishop Marcel Lefebvre. Lefebvre was an archbishop in France who resisted many things about the post-Vatican II religion, recognizing them to be departures from traditional Catholicism. He recognized the New Mass to be Protestant and opposed to Tradition. He also opposed the heresies of "ecumenism" and religious liberty, which were taught at Vatican II. He began seminaries for the formation of priests who would be offering exclusively the traditional Mass, and he ordained them in the traditional rite of ordination. In order to do this, he had to remain independent of the Vatican II antipopes, even though he continued to take the position that they were legitimate popes who held the office of the Papacy. He was also independent of the working communion of the "bishops" who had gone along with the new religion. On June 30, 1988, Lefebvre decided (independently of the Vatican II antipopes) to consecrate four bishops in the traditional rite of Episcopal Consecration, so that these bishops could continue to ordain priests for the traditional rites. He was "excommunicated" by John Paul II within 72 hours, even though (as we've discussed already) no prominent pro-abortion politician has yet been excommunicated by any of the Vatican II antipopes.

The positions of the Society of St. Pius X 483

The SSPX has many traditional Mass locations around the world, and is a major force influencing and providing sacraments for those who profess to be traditionalist-minded Catholics. We want to emphasize that the SSPX does many good things; it has been an avenue by which many have been introduced, and come back, to the traditional Catholic Faith. However, in various areas the SSPX's positions are unfortunately heretical and contrary to the Catholic Faith. First, the SSPX holds and teaches that souls can be saved in non-Catholic religions, which is heretical.

> Fr. Schmidberger, *Time Bombs of the Second Vatican Council*, Angelus Press [SSPX], p. 10: "Ladies and gentlemen, **it is clear that the followers of other religions can be saved under certain conditions**, that is to say, if they are in invincible error."

> Archbishop Marcel Lefebvre, Against the Heresies, Angelus Press [SSPX], p. 216: "Evidently, certain distinctions must be made. **Souls can be saved in a religion other than the Catholic religion (Protestantism, Islam, Buddhism, etc.),** but not by this religion."

These statements constitute blatant heresy against the dogma Outside the Church There is No Salvation; yet they are printed in the very best-selling materials of the SSPX. In fact, almost all priests who even celebrate the traditional Mass hold this same heresy.

> Pope Gregory XVI, *Summo Iugiter Studio* (# 2), May 27, 1832:
> **"Finally some of these misguided people attempt to persuade themselves and others that men are not saved only in the Catholic religion, but that even heretics may attain eternal life."**[3]

Also, while resisting the Vatican II apostasy, the SSPX *obstinately* maintains an allegiance to the manifestly heretical "bishops" of the Novus Ordo/Vatican II Church, as mentioned above. At the same time, however, the SSPX doesn't operate in communion with what it calls "the New Church" – the Novus Ordo Church – the Church of the Vatican II "bishops" and "popes" (who are actually antipopes). Their position is a contradiction. It's an affront to Catholic teaching on three counts: 1) They recognize manifest heretics (the Novus Ordo bishops and the Vatican II antipopes) as Catholics who possess authority in the Church, which is heretical They need to recognize that these heretical bishops are outside the Church and have no authority at all.

> St. Robert Bellarmine, *De Romano Pontifice*, lib. II, cap. 30: "Finally, the Holy Fathers teach unanimously not only that heretics are outside of the Church, but also that they are "ipso facto" deprived of all ecclesiastical jurisdiction and dignity."

> St. Robert Bellarmine, *De Romano Pontifice*, II, 30:
> "A pope who is a manifest heretic automatically (*per se*) ceases to be pope and head, just as he ceases automatically to be a Christian and a member of the Church. Wherefore, he can be judged and punished by the Church. *This is the teaching of all the ancient Fathers* who teach that manifest heretics immediately lose all jurisdiction."

2) The SSPX *obstinately* operates outside of communion with the Novus Ordo hierarchy, even though it recognizes it as the Catholic hierarchy. This is actually schismatic. In fact, the SSPX boldly refuses communion with the Novus Ordo Church (see below), even though it recognizes the Novus Ordo hierarchy as the true Catholic hierarchy!

> Archbishop Marcel Lefebvre, *Declaration* of August, 1976:
> "**All those enter into schism who cooperate in this realization of this upheaval and adhere to this new Conciliar Church**, as His excellency Bishop Benelli designated it in the letter he addressed to me in the Holy Father's name last June 25th." (Quoted in *Sacerdotium*)

> Fr. Franz Schmidberger, former Superior General of the Society of St. Pius X:
> "**We have never wished to belong to this system which calls itself the Conciliar Church**, and identifies itself with the Novus Ordo Missae… **The faithful indeed have a strict right to know that priests who serve them are not in communion with a counterfeit church.**" (Quoted in *Sacerdotium*)

> *The Angelus*, Official publication of the Society of St. Pius X (SSPX), May, 2000:
> "This current of renewal **has given birth to a new church within the bosom of the Catholic Church**, to that which Msgr. Benelli himself called '*the conciliar church,*' whose limits and paths are very difficult to define… **It is against this conciliar church that our resistance stands. We do not refuse our adherence to the Pope as such, but to this conciliar church**, for its ideas are foreign to those of the Catholic Church."4

To refuse communion with the Novus Ordo Church and not the head of the Novus Ordo Church is like saying that one refuses communion with the Communist Party but not the head of the Communist Party! It's a contradiction.

Moreover, by its recognition of the Vatican II "popes" and "bishops" as the Catholic hierarchy, the SSPX is in communion with this "counterfeit Church." At the same time, the SSPX is in schism with this "counterfeit Church" because it blatantly refuses communion with the members of this Church, as we see above. (If it sounds contradictory, that's because it is.) The position is schismatic.

> Canon 1325.2, *1917 Code of Canon Law*: "One who after baptism… rejects the authority of the Supreme Pontiff **or refuses communion with the members of the Church who are subject to him, he is a schismatic.**"

> St. Ignatius of Antioch, *Letter to the Trallians*, (A.D. 110): "He that is within the sanctuary is pure; but he that is outside the sanctuary is not pure. In other words, **anyone who acts without the bishop and the presbytery and the deacons does not have a clean conscience.**"5

For decades now, the SSPX has been obstinately working outside of communion with the "bishops" and "pope" it deems to constitute the Catholic hierarchy. This is schismatic.

> St. Jerome, *Commentaries on the Epistle to Titus*, (A.D. 386): "Between heresy and schism there is a distinction made, that heresy involves perverse doctrine, **while schism separates one from the Church on account of disagreement with the Bishop.**"6

3) The SSPX holds that the Catholic Church has become a "New Church," a modernist sect – a non-Catholic sect which is rife with heresy and apostasy – which is impossible. The Church is the immaculate Bride of Christ, which cannot officially teach error.

> Pope Pius XI, *Mortalium Animos* (# 10), Jan. 6, 1928: "During the lapse of centuries, the mystical Spouse of Christ has never been contaminated, nor can she ever in the future be contaminated, as Cyprian bears witness: '**The Bride of Christ cannot be made false to**

her Spouse: she is incorrupt and modest. She knows but one dwelling, she guards the sanctity of the nuptial chamber chastely and modestly.'"[7]

Pope Pius XI, *Quas Primas* (# 22), Dec. 11, 1925:
"Not least among the blessings which have resulted from the public and legitimate honor paid to the Blessed Virgin and the saints is **the perfect and perpetual immunity of the Church from error and heresy.**"[8]

Pope Pius IX, *Vatican Council I*, Session 4, Chap. 4, ex cathedra: "… **knowing full well that the See of St. Peter always remains unimpaired by any error**, according to the divine promise of our Lord the Savior made to the chief of His disciples: 'I have prayed for thee [Peter], that thy faith fail not: and thou, being once converted, confirm thy brethren' (Lk. 22:32)."[9]

For instance, the SSPX even rejects the solemn canonizations of the Vatican II "popes" it recognizes. This position is terribly schismatic, for it asserts that a true pope and the Catholic Church have officially erred in canonizing saints.

St. Alphonsus Liguori, *The Great Means of Salvation and Perfection*, 1759, p. 23: "**To suppose that the Church can err in canonizing, is a sin, or is heresy, according to St. Bonaventure, Bellarmine, and others;** or at least next door to heresy, according to Suarez, Azorius, Gotti, etc.; because the Sovereign Pontiff, according to St. Thomas, is guided by the infallible influence of the Holy Ghost in an especial way when canonizing saints."[10]

Pope Benedict XIV: "**If anyone dared to assert that the Pontiff had erred in this or that canonization, we shall say that he is, if not a heretic, at least temerarious, a giver of scandal to the whole Church, an insulter of the saints, a favorer of those heretics who deny the Church's authority in canonizing saints**, savoring of heresy by giving unbelievers an occasion to mock the faithful, the assertor of an erroneous opinion and liable to very grave penalties."[11]

Since so many have a high regard for the SSPX, they have been led into the same schismatic position. **All of these false positions on the post-Vatican II situation are a result of the SSPX's unwillingness to see the truth that the Vatican II sect is a counterfeit Church from top to bottom, and that the post-Vatican II "popes" are actually invalid antipopes.**

Some very interesting statements by Archbishop Lefebvre expressing his view that the Vatican II "popes" might not be valid popes

No matter how untenable their present position is – nor how clear the evidence in favor of the sedevacantist position – the SSPX continues (even at this late stage in the Vatican II apostasy) to publish books and tracts which attack the sedevacantist position. They fail to realize that the founder of their Society, Archbishop Lefebvre, made numerous statements which demonstrated that he was on the verge of the sedevacantist position back in the 1970's and 1980's. These quotations should be known by members of the Society of St. Pius X.

Archbishop Lefebvre, Aug. 4, 1976: "The Council [Vatican II] turned its back on Tradition and broke with the Church of the past. It is a schismatic council… **If we are certain that** the Faith taught by the Church for twenty centuries can contain no error, <u>we are much less certain that the pope is truly pope</u>. **Heresy, schism, excommunication *ipso facto*, or invalid election are all causes that can possibly mean the pope was never pope, or is no longer pope**... Because ultimately, since the beginning of Paul VI's pontificate, the conscience and faith of all Catholics have been faced with a serious problem. How is it that the pope, the true successor of Peter, who is assured of the help of the Holy Ghost, can officiate at the destruction of the Church – the most radical, rapid, and widespread in her history – something that no heresiarch has ever managed to achieve?"[12]

Archbishop Lefebvre, Sermon, Aug. 29, 1976: "**The new rite of Mass is an illegitimate rite**, the sacraments are illegitimate sacraments, the priests who come from the seminaries are illegitimate priests..."[13]

Archbishop Lefebvre, Meeting with Paul VI, Sept. 11, 1976: "**[The document of Vatican II on religious liberty] contains passages that are word for word contrary to what was taught by Gregory XVI, and Pius IX.**"[14]

Archbishop Lefebvre, Sermon, Feb. 22, 1979: "Insofar as it is opposed to Tradition, **we reject the Council [Vatican II].**"[15]

Archbishop Lefebvre, Sermon, Easter, 1986: "This is the situation in which we find ourselves. I have not created it. I would die to make it go away! **We are faced with a serious dilemma which, I believe, has never existed in the Church: the one seated on the chair of Peter takes part in the worship of false gods**. What conclusions will we have to draw, perhaps in a few months' time, faced with these repeated acts of taking part in the worship of false religions, I do not know. But I do wonder. <u>**It is possible that we might be forced to believe that the pope is not the pope**</u>. Because it seems to me initially – I do not yet want to say it solemnly and publicly – that it is impossible for a pope to be publicly and formally heretical."[16]

Archbishop Lefebvre, Sermon, Aug. 27, 1986: "**He who now sits upon the Throne of Peter mocks publicly the first article of the Creed and the first Commandment of the Decalogue [The Ten Commandments]**. The scandal given to Catholics cannot be measured. The Church is shaken to its very foundations."[17]

Archbishop Lefebvre, Sermon, Oct. 28, 1986: "**John Paul II has encouraged false religions to pray to their false gods**: it is an unprecedented and intolerable humiliation to those who remain Catholic..."[18]

Archbishop Lefebvre, Meeting with "Cardinal" Ratzinger, July 14, 1987: "If there is a schism, it is because of what the Vatican did at Assisi... **being excommunicated by a liberal, ecumenical, and revolutionary Church is a matter of indifference to us.**"[19]

Archbishop Lefebvre, Meeting with "Cardinal" Ratzinger, July 14, 1987: "**Rome has lost the Faith. Rome is in apostasy.**"[20]

Archbishop Lefebvre, Aug. 29, 1987: "**The See of Peter and the posts of authority in Rome being occupied by anti-Christs,** the destruction of the Kingdom of our Lord is being rapidly carried out... This is what has brought down upon our heads persecution by the **Rome of the anti-Christs**."[21]

Archbishop Lefebvre, Declaration given to the Press before 1988 Episcopal Consecrations: "**The Church holds all communion with false religions and heresy... in** horror... **To safeguard the Catholic priesthood which perpetuates the Church and not an adulterous Church**, there must be Catholic bishops."[22]

Archbishop Lefebvre, Speaking of the leaders of the Vatican II sect: "**We cannot work together with these enemies of our Lord's reign.**"[23]

Archbishop Lefebvre, Speaking of the leaders of the Vatican II sect: "**We cannot follow these people. They're in apostasy,** they do not believe in the divinity of our Lord Jesus Christ who must reign. What is the use in waiting? Let's do the consecration!"[24]

-Some more important points pertaining to the positions of the SSPX are found on our website under the following titles; they are summarized briefly here-

Bishop Fellay of the SSPX rejects Catholic dogma by teaching that Hindus can be saved

Bishop Bernard Fellay, *Conference in Denver, Co.*, Feb. 18, 2006: "… **And the Church has always taught that you have people who will be in Heaven, who are in the state of grace, who have been saved without knowing the Catholic Church. We know this. And yet, how is it possible if you cannot be saved outside the Church? It is absolutely true that they will be saved through** the Catholic Church because they will be united to Christ, to the Mystical Body of Christ, which is the Catholic Church. It will, however, remain invisible, because this visible link is impossible for them. <u>Consider a Hindu in Tibet who has no knowledge of the Catholic Church. He lives according to his conscience and to the laws which God has put into his heart. He can be in the state of grace</u>, and if he dies in this state of grace, **he will go to Heaven.**" (*The Angelus*, "A Talk Heard Round the World," April, 2006, p. 5.)

The SSPX rejects John Paul II's "canonization" of Josemaria Escriva, thus revealing its Schism

Fr. Peter Scott, Nov. 1, 2002, from SSPX's Holy Cross Seminary in Australia: "<u>A typical example of this was the shameful and highly questionable canonization</u> of Msgr. Josemaria Escriva de Balaguer last October 6… After having pointed out that the process was uncanonical and dishonest, they had this to say: '**It (the canonization) will offend God. It will stain the Church forever. It will take away from the saints their special holiness**. It will call into question the credibility of all the canonizations made during your Papacy. It will undermine the future authority of the Papacy'… <u>Their letter will certainly turn out to be prophetic</u>, for in time they will be proven to be right in their assessment concerning Escriva … For all the reasons that they give, **<u>we cannot possibly consider this 'canonization' as a valid, infallible Papal pronouncement</u>**. We trust that he is in heaven, but we cannot possibly regard as a Saint this herald of Vatican II…" (SOUTHERN SENTINEL - No. 3 - November 2002)

Since they recognize that John Paul II was a true pope, to reject his solemn "canonization" is clearly schismatic.

Bishop Richard Williamson of the SSPX says John Paul II was a "good man" and says the SSPX's religion is not the same as that of the Vatican II "popes" it recognizes!

"A. Bishop Williamson: I was a little surprised, at first, because some people had said he wasn't really in the running. After that, to tell you the honest truth, **I don't expect a great deal from Rome as it stands. They are too far gone in the "New Religion," and the "New Religion" is too radically different and distant from the True Religion**. Rome is Rome, though, and I do believe there the popes are, and there are the cardinals, and that is where the official structure of the Church is to be found. But, I'm afraid, for the defense of the Faith, you've got to wait for some grave event to shake Rome and/or to drive the true cardinals out of Rome to start again somewhere else. I'm afraid that Rome is too deeply in the grips of the enemies of God."[25]

Bishop Williamson of the SSPX boldly states that he doesn't have the same religion as the "pope" and "bishops" he recognizes as the Catholic hierarchy! This, ladies and gentlemen, sums up the completely ridiculous – and schismatic – position of the SSPX, which is (for lack of a better description) so obstinately inconsistent that it is correctly labeled **THEOLOGICAL PUKE**.

Pope Pius XII, *Mystici Corporis Christi* (# 22):
"As therefore **in the true Christian community** there is only one Body, one Spirit, one Lord, and one Baptism, so **there can be only one faith**. And therefore if a man refuse to hear the Church let him be considered – so the Lord commands – as a heathen and a publican. It follows that **those who are divided in faith or government cannot be living in the unity of such a Body**, nor can they be living the life of its one Divine Spirit."[26]

Bishop Tissier De Mallerais of the SSPX rejects the concept of Church communion and says Benedict XVI has taught heresies

"A. Bishop Tissier De Mallerais: "Firstly, I am not familiar with this text. I do not know it. It is not interesting to me as I do not follow such news. That is not the problem here. **The problem is not "communion." That is the stupid idea of these bishops since Vatican II – there is not a problem of communion**, there is a problem of the profession of faith. "Communion" is nothing, it is an invention of the Second Vatican Council. **The essential thing is that these people (the bishops) do not have the Catholic Faith.** "Communion" does not mean anything to me – it is a slogan of the new Church. **The definition of the new Church is "communion" but it was never the definition of the Catholic Church**. I can only give you the definition of the Church as it has been understood traditionally."

"A. Bishop Tissier De Mallerais: It was when he was a priest. When he was a theologian, he professed heresies, **he published a book full of heresies**… Yes, sure. **He has a book called *Introduction to Christianity*, it was in 1968. It is a book full of heresies. Especially the negation of the dogma of the Redemption**."[27]

Pope Leo XIII, *Satis Cognitum* (# 10), June 29, 1896: "For this reason, as the unity of faith is of necessity for the unity of the Church, inasmuch as it is the body of the faithful, so also for this same unity, inasmuch as the Church is a divinely constituted society, unity of government, which effects and involves **unity of communion, is necessary *jure divino*** (by divine law)."[28]

It makes sense that the SSPX (or, at least Bishop Tissier De Mallerais) would not believe in the concept of *being in communion with all in the Church*. "Communion means nothing to me," Bishop Tissier De Mallerais says. Yes, we can all see that very well. Since he doesn't believe in it, refusing communion with the hierarchy and members of what he deems to be the Catholic Church is obviously not a conscience-problem.

The Society of St. Pius X's book *Most Asked Questions about the Society of St. Pius X* says the Vatican II "popes" CANNOT teach infallibly

> *Most Asked Questions about the Society of St. Pius X*, Question 7: But shouldn't we be following John Paul II?, pp. 38-40: "**The Pope is infallible** primarily in matters of faith and morals, and secondarily in matters of discipline (legislation for the Universal Church, canonizations, etc.) to the extent that these involve faith and morals (cf. Principle 4), and then **only when imposing for all time a definitive teaching**.
>
> "**Now 'infallible' means immutable and irreformable (Principle 6), but, the hallmark of the conciliar Popes, like the Modernists, is a spirit of evolution. To what extent can such minds want irreformably to define or absolutely to impose? They do not and, in fact, 'they cannot**...' (Archbishop Lefebvre, Econe, June 12, 1984.) Cf. Question 15, n. 3." (Angelus Press, 1997)

The Society of St. Pius X is not merely stating here that John Paul II did not fulfill the requirements to speak infallibly; the SSPX (writing during the reign of John Paul II) stated that he (the man they considered to be the true pope) *cannot* speak infallibly.

For those who are for some reason not grasping the impact of this statement by the SSPX, allow us to summarize it: the SSPX correctly points out that an infallible teaching by a pope on faith or morals is irreformable, as Vatican I declared (Denz. 1839). But according to the SSPX, the Vatican II "popes" are such Modernists that they believe in the evolution of doctrine; they don't believe that anything is irreformable. So, according to the SSPX, even though they are valid popes, the post-conciliar "popes" **CANNOT** teach infallibly! This is a rejection of the dogma of Papal Infallibility.

> Pope Pius IX, *Vatican Council I*, 1870, Session 4, Chap. 4:
> "...**the Roman Pontiff, when he speaks ex cathedra** [from the Chair of Peter], that is, when carrying out the duty of the pastor and teacher of all Christians in accord with his supreme apostolic authority he explains a doctrine of faith or morals to be held by the universal Church... **operates with that infallibility** with which the divine Redeemer wished that His Church be instructed in defining doctrine on faith and morals... **But if anyone presumes to contradict this definition of Ours, which may God forbid: let him be anathema**."[29]

By definition, a pope is the Bishop of Rome who possesses supreme jurisdiction in the Church and who CAN teach infallibly, if he fulfills the requisite conditions. If he is incapable of speaking infallibly, he is therefore not a valid pope!

All of these schismatic positions (e.g, the SSPX's rejection of "canonizations" proclaimed by their "pope") and perversions of the Papal Office are a result of the SSPX's failure to see the truth of the sedevacantist position (i.e., that the Vatican II "popes" are not popes at all, but antipopes).

Benedict XVI personally tells SSPX that it must accept Vatican II

In his *Conference in Denver* in 2006 (carried in an article in *The Angelus*), Bishop Fellay of the SSPX mentioned a very important point. He admitted that, in his personal meeting with Antipope Benedict XVI, the antipope made it very clear to him that the SSPX must accept Vatican II.

> Bishop Bernard Fellay, *Conference in Denver*, Feb. 18, 2006: "Then he [Benedict XVI] went to the second level. And he said that the second level is the acceptance of the Council… **The Pope clearly indicated in the words he used during the audience, that for him, it is impossible to accept someone in the Church, at least in his, let's say, modern way of looking at the Church, who would not accept the Council**. He was very clear. When I heard these words there, and especially one word afterwards, for me, the big fight we will have under this pontificate will be the fight about the Council."[30]

How many times does this have to be proven? The false traditionalists need to give up their impossible position, according to which it's acceptable to reject Vatican II and accept the Vatican II "popes" as legitimate. They must reject Vatican II *and* the non-Catholic antipopes who enforced it.

Important points regarding the claim of SSPX supporters – and those who hold similar positions – that they just live a Catholic life, attend the SSPX (or some other independent chapel) and don't get involved with these issues, such as sedevacantism

We frequently hear from people, especially supporters of the SSPX, that they are just laypeople who cannot get involved in these theological issues, such as the sedevacantist issue. They just go to Mass at the SSPX, support them and try to be good, spiritual people who live the Faith. This is the response of many SSPX supporters when confronted by sedevacantist arguments.

Okay, if that's the case – if you don't have the authority to get involved with these issues and you are just a "simple layman who goes to Mass" and tries to live the Catholic Faith – THEN YOU HAVE NO RIGHT TO ATTEND THE SSPX OR ANOTHER INDEPENDENT CHAPEL.

IF YOU ARE TOO SIMPLE TO "FIGURE THIS STUFF OUT" AND YOU CANNOT GET INVOLVED WITH THESE ISSUES – IF THAT IS YOUR POSITION (WHICH GOD FORBID) – THEN LOGICALLY YOU WOULD HAVE TO SIMPLY ACCEPT YOUR LOCAL NOVUS ORDO CHURCH, GO TO THE NEW MASS, AND ACCEPT VATICAN II, WHICH IS THE RELIGION APPROVED BY THE LOCAL NOVUS ORDO "BISHOP." But "no," the would-be "simple" layman who "*just goes to the SSPX and tries to live a good life*" and doesn't get involved in "these issues" **all of a sudden gets involved in the issues and becomes a "theologian." He "knows" that he cannot accept the New Mass and his local Novus Ordo religion**. He thus condemns himself out of his own mouth, refutes his own argument and shows his hypocrisy *by only "getting involved" where he wants to get involved.*

For the bottom-line is that if one can accept the New Mass and Vatican II religion and save his soul then there is no justification whatsoever for going to an independent chapel or the SSPX. It's all a matter of preference, in that case. **But if one holds that Faith obliges him to reject the New Mass and the Vatican II religion as something which will cause the loss of his salvation (which is the truth), then the local church and the New Mass (and the authorities who**

imposed it) cannot represent the Catholic Church. That leads one inescapably to the sedevacantist position, for the Holy Catholic Church does not lead us to Hell.

All of this hopefully shows us again that the only Catholic position is, of course, the sedevacantist position, and that all the other false positions are inconsistent with Catholic teaching. Since the SSPX promotes heretical positions which are inconsistent with Catholic teaching, no Catholic can financially support them under pain of mortal sin.

> Pope Innocent III, *Fourth Lateran Council*, 1215: "**Moreover, we determine to subject to excommunication believers who receive, defend, or support heretics.**"[31]

Quick Thoughts on a Possible Reunion of the SSPX completely with the New Church

At the time this book is being finalized (2007), there is some talk that the SSPX will enter into full communion with the Vatican II sect, in exchange for Antipope Benedict XVI's wider permission for the Latin Mass and a possible lifting of the excommunications against their society. If this occurs, this will represent a complete selling out by the SSPX to the Counter Church. Benedict XVI, being guided by the Devil, is well aware that, at this point, the apostasy of the Vatican II sect is so firmly in place, *and almost all of the priests are invalid since they were ordained in the New Rites of Paul VI*, that he can afford to make concessions to traditionalist-minded groups in order to lure them back into the Counter Church whereby they will be completely denying Christ by full acceptance of the new religion and things such as a "canonization" of the apostate John Paul II.

If Benedict XVI does make a deal of this type with the SSPX, don't be deceived; it will be a tactical move by the Devil to attempt to deceive traditionalists at this late stage of the Great Apostasy. If this does occur, we think it would result in the fracture of the SSPX into factions pro and con the full reunion with the Counter Church.

Endnotes for Section 40:

---

[1] Bishop Tissier De Mallerais, *The Biography of Marcel Lefebvre*, Kansas City, MO: Angelus Press, 2004.
[2] Bishop Tissier De Mallerais, *The Biography of Marcel Lefebvre*, p. 536.
[3] *The Papal Encyclicals*, by Claudia Carlen, Raleigh: The Pierian Press, 1990, Vol. 1 (1740-1878), p. 229.
[4] *The Angelus*, Angelus Press, May 2000, p. 21.
[5] Jurgens, *The Faith of the Early Fathers*, Collegeville, MN: The Liturgical Press, 1970, Vol. 1:50.
[6] Jurgens, *The Faith of the Early Fathers*, Vol. 2:1371a.
[7] *The Papal Encyclicals*, Vol. 3 (1903-1939), p. 317.
[8] *The Papal Encyclicals*, Vol. 3 (1903-1939), p. 275.
[9] Denzinger, *The Sources of Catholic Dogma*, B. Herder Book. Co., Thirtieth Edition, 1957, 1836.
[10] St. Alphonsus Liguori, *The Great Means of Salvation and Perfection*, 1759, p. 23.
[11] Quoted by Tanquerey, "*Synopsis Theologiae Dogmaticae Fundamentalis*" (Paris, Tournai, Rome: Desclee, 1937), new edition ed. by J.B. Bord, Vol. I. p. 624, footnote 2.
[12] Bishop Tissier De Mallerais, *The Biography of Marcel Lefebvre*, p. 487.
[13] Bishop Tissier De Mallerais, *The Biography of Marcel Lefebvre*, p. 489.
[14] Bishop Tissier De Mallerais, *The Biography of Marcel Lefebvre*, p. 492.
[15] Bishop Tissier De Mallerais, *The Biography of Marcel Lefebvre*, p. 501.
[16] Bishop Tissier De Mallerais, *The Biography of Marcel Lefebvre*, p. 536.
[17] Bishop Tissier De Mallerais, *The Biography of Marcel Lefebvre*, pp. 537, 623.
[18] Bishop Tissier De Mallerais, *The Biography of Marcel Lefebvre*, p. 537
[19] Bishop Tissier De Mallerais, *The Biography of Marcel Lefebvre*, p. 547.
[20] Bishop Tissier De Mallerais, *The Biography of Marcel Lefebvre*, p. 548.
[21] Bishop Tissier De Mallerais, *The Biography of Marcel Lefebvre*, pp. 549, 625.

[22] Bishop Tissier De Mallerais, *The Biography of Marcel Lefebvre*, p. 561.
[23] Bishop Tissier De Mallerais, *The Biography of Marcel Lefebvre*, p. 548.
[24] Bishop Tissier De Mallerais, *The Biography of Marcel Lefebvre*, p. 549.
[25] Interview with *The Remnant*, May 15, 2005 issue.
[26] *The Papal Encyclicals*, Vol. 4 (1939-1958), p. 41.
[27] Interview printed in *The Remnant*, Forest Lake, MN.
[28] *The Papal Encyclicals*, Vol. 2 (1878-1903), p. 396.
[29] Denzinger 1839.
[30] *The Angelus*, "A Talk Heard Round the World," April, 2006, p. 15.
[31] *Decrees of the Ecumenical Councils*, Sheed & Ward and Georgetown University Press, 1990, Vol. 1, p. 234.

41. Sister Faustina's *Divine Mercy Devotion* is something to avoid

Sister Faustina Kowalski and the image of her *Divine Mercy Devotion*

Over the years we had heard different opinions about the Divine Mercy Devotion; we didn't know exactly what to think about it. **The fact is that in the 1950's the Divine Mercy Devotion was suppressed and Sr. Faustina's diary was on the index of forbidden books.** It was only rehabilitated around the world by John Paul II after Vatican II. In addition to that, something that concerned us was that it seemed to be popular among the Charismatic "Catholics," and that it seemed to be used as a substitute for the Rosary. Some time ago one of us decided to quickly flip through the more than 600-page book *Divine Mercy in my Soul Diary* by Sister Faustina Kowalski. Below are just a few strange things that were found in that investigation that are enough to convince us that this "devotion" is something to be avoided.

> On page 23 of the book *Divine Mercy in My Soul* (The Diary of Sr. Faustina), it says: "… **and the host came out of the tabernacle and came to rest in my hands** and I, with joy, placed it back in the tabernacle. This was repeated a second time, and I did the same thing. Despite this, it happened a third time…"[1]

> On page 89 of the book *Divine Mercy in My Soul,* it says: "When the priest approached me again, I raised the host for him to put back into the chalice, because when I had first received Jesus I could not speak before consuming the host, and so could not tell Him that the other host had fallen. **But while I was holding the host in my hand, I felt such a power of love** that for the rest of the day I could neither eat nor come to my senses. I heard these words from the host: **I desired to rest in your hands**, not only in your heart."[2]

> On page 168, it says: "The moment I knelt down to cross out my own will, as the Lord had bid me to do, I heard this voice in my soul: From now on, **do not fear God's judgment, for you will not be judged**."[3] (From Feb. 4, 1935)

Sr. Faustina's Divine Mercy Devotion is something to avoid

On page 176, "Jesus" says to her: "You are a sweet grape and a chosen cluster; **I want others to have a share in the juice that is flowing within you.**"[4]

On page 191, "Jesus" says to her: "For your sake I will withhold the hand which punishes; **for your sake I will bless the Earth.**"[5] (Also see page 378.)

On page 247, "Jesus" says: "**And know this, too, My daughter: All creatures, whether they know it or not, and whether they want to or not, always fulfill my will**... My daughter, if you wish, I will this instant create a new world, more beautiful than this one, and you will live there for the rest of your life."[6]

On page 260, "Jesus" says: "For many souls will turn back from the gates of Hell and **worship My mercy.**"[7]

On page 374, "Jesus" says: "**If they will not adore My mercy**, they will perish for all eternity."[8]

On page 382, "Jesus" says: "**I desire that My mercy be worshipped.**"[9]

On page 288, "Jesus" says: "That is why **I am uniting myself with you so intimately as with no other creature**."[10]

On page 400, "Jesus" says: "I see your love so pure, purer than that of the angels, and all the more so because you keep fighting. **For your sake I bless the world.**"[11]

On page 417, we read that "Jesus" supposedly gave Sr. Faustina this instruction: "**Tell the Superior General to count on you as the most faithful daughter in the Order.**"[12]

On page 583, we read that Sr. Faustina said: "When I took the Messenger of the Sacred Heart into my hand and read the account of the canonization of St. Andrew Bobola, **my soul was instantly filled with a great longing that our congregation, too, might have a saint and I wept like a child that there was no saint in our midst**. And I said to the Lord, 'I know your generosity, and yet it seems to me that you are less generous towards us.' And I began again to weep like a little child. And the Lord Jesus said to me, 'Don't cry. <u>You are that saint</u>.'"[13]

On page 602, we read that "Jesus" supposedly said: "**I cannot stand them, because they are neither good nor bad.**"[14]

On page 612, we read that "Jesus" supposedly said: "**I bear a special love for Poland**, and if she will be obedient to My will, I will exalt her in might and holiness. <u>**From her will come forth the spark that will prepare the world for My final coming**</u>."[15]

On page 643, we read that Sr. Faustina said after receiving Communion: "**Jesus transform me into another host**!... You are a great and all-powerful Lord; you can grant me this favor. And the Lord answered me, '**You are a living host**.'"[16]

On page 208 we learn that "Jesus" supposedly told Sr. Faustina about the new Divine Mercy Devotion and supposedly instructed her that it is to be said on the beads of the Rosary: "This prayer [the Divine Mercy Devotion] will serve to appease my wrath. **You will recite it for nine days, on the beads of the Rosary,** in the following manner: First of all, you will say one Our Father and Hail Mary and the I Believe in God. Then **on the**

Our Father beads you will say the following words: 'Eternal Father I offer you the Body and Blood, Soul and Divinity of your dearly beloved Son, Our Lord Jesus Christ, in atonement for our sins and those of the whole world.' **On the Hail Mary beads you will say the following words**: 'For the sake of His sorrowful Passion have mercy on us and on the whole world.' In conclusion, three times you will recite these words: 'Holy God, holy mighty one, holy immortal one, have mercy on us and on the whole world.'"[17] (Saturday, Sept. 14, 1935)

The above statements present a number of problems. The first problem is the promotion of Communion in the hand, which is supposedly endorsed by Our Lord. The Host flies into her hand numerous times; Our Lord supposedly says that He desires to rest in her hands. We believe this is a diabolical snare to get Communion in the hand accepted intellectually in advance of the Vatican II religion.

Second, we see unnecessary praise heaped upon this sister. We see things said to her supposedly by Our Lord that wouldn't foster humility, but vanity – that she is basically the greatest thing in the world. We don't believe Our Lord would ever instruct her to tell her superior that she is the most faithful daughter in the Order. Our Lord could have told the superior such a thing, if he wanted it known.

Third, we see that Sr. Faustina is told that God's spark – which will prepare the world for His Second Coming – comes out of Poland! This has been interpreted to mean that God's chosen person was John Paul II, who was from Poland! Since we know that John Paul II was an apostate, a non-Catholic antipope, a man who endorsed the false religions of the world, this shows us again that Sr. Faustina's revelations were from the Devil. In fact, it shows us how much the Devil wanted to prop up support for John Paul II.

Fourth, the Divine Mercy Devotion is centered around mercy at a time when mankind was coming closer and closer to having filled up the cup of divine justice. The problem at that time, and today, of course, was that men didn't fear God and continued to offend Him. They needed to hear about His justice. But the Divine Mercy devotion was the perfect false devotion and message to make people believe that they will receive God's mercy even if they stay in their sins; it even instructs people to "worship" His mercy.

Fifth, and perhaps most importantly, would God reveal a new devotion to be said *on the beads of the Rosary* shortly after His Mother came to Fatima to work a profound miracle to reveal, among other things, the necessity of the Rosary? The specific direction given to Sister Faustina for the Divine Mercy Devotion to be prayed *on the beads of the Rosary* is clearly, we believe, the Devil's substitute for the Rosary. And we've seen it used that way with so many souls. The Divine Mercy Devotion is a clever counterfeit which, being traditional in so many ways, serves the Devil's purpose to get this counter-devotion inserted into conservative-minded circles, which the Devil hopes will use it as a substitute for the Rosary.

All these things considered, **the Divine Mercy Devotion is something which should be avoided by Catholics**. Catholics should say an extra rosary or the Stations of the Cross instead.

Endnotes for Section 41:

[1] *Divine Mercy in My Soul, The Diary of Sr. Faustina*, Stockbridge, MA: Marian Press, 1987, p. 23.
[2] *Divine Mercy in My Soul, The Diary of Sr. Faustina*, p. 89.
[3] *Divine Mercy in My Soul, The Diary of Sr. Faustina*, p. 168.
[4] *Divine Mercy in My Soul, The Diary of Sr. Faustina*, p. 176.

[5] *Divine Mercy in My Soul, The Diary of Sr. Faustina*, p. 191.
[6] *Divine Mercy in My Soul, The Diary of Sr. Faustina*, p. 247.
[7] *Divine Mercy in My Soul, The Diary of Sr. Faustina*, p. 260.
[8] *Divine Mercy in My Soul, The Diary of Sr. Faustina*, p. 347.
[9] *Divine Mercy in My Soul, The Diary of Sr. Faustina*, p. 382.
[10] *Divine Mercy in My Soul, The Diary of Sr. Faustina*, p. 288.
[11] *Divine Mercy in My Soul, The Diary of Sr. Faustina*, p. 400.
[12] *Divine Mercy in My Soul, The Diary of Sr. Faustina*, p. 417.
[13] *Divine Mercy in My Soul, The Diary of Sr. Faustina*, p. 583.
[14] *Divine Mercy in My Soul, The Diary of Sr. Faustina*, p. 602.
[15] *Divine Mercy in My Soul, The Diary of Sr. Faustina*, p. 612.
[16] *Divine Mercy in My Soul, The Diary of Sr. Faustina*, p. 643.
[17] *Divine Mercy in My Soul, The Diary of Sr. Faustina*, p. 208.

42. Natural Family Planning is Sinful Birth Control

In this Article:
- **What is Natural Family Planning?**
- **Why is NFP wrong?**
- **The Teaching of the Catholic Papal Magisterium**
- **God's Word**
- **People Know that NFP is a Sin**
- **Planned Parenthood and NFP of the same cloth**
- **NFP has eternal and infinite consequences**
- **Objections**
- **Conclusion**

What is Natural Family Planning?

Natural Family Planning (NFP) is the practice of deliberately restricting the marital act exclusively to those times when the wife is infertile so as to avoid the conception of a child. It is also called "the rhythm method." NFP or rhythm is used for the same reasons that people use artificial contraception: to deliberately avoid the conception of a child while carrying out the marital act.

Antipope Paul VI explained correctly that NFP is birth control when he promoted it in his encyclical *Humanae Vitae*.

> Paul VI, *Humanae Vitae* (# 16), July 25, 1968:
> "…married people may then take advantage of the natural cycles immanent in the reproductive system **and engage in marital intercourse only during those times that are infertile, thus controlling birth** in a way which does not in the least offend the moral principles which We have just explained."[1]

Why is NFP wrong?

NFP is wrong because it's birth control; it's *against* conception. It's a refusal on the part of those who use it to be open to the children that God planned to send them. **It's no different in its purpose from artificial contraception,** and therefore it's a moral evil just like artificial contraception.

The Teaching of the Catholic Papal Magisterium

Pope Pius XI spoke from the Chair of Peter in his 1931 encyclical *Casti Connubii* on Christian marriage. His teaching shows that <u>all forms of birth prevention are evil</u>. We quote a long excerpt from his encyclical which sums up the issue.

> Pope Pius XI, *Casti Connubii* (#'s 53-56), Dec. 31, 1930: "And now, Venerable Brethren, we shall explain in detail the evils opposed to each of the benefits of matrimony. First consideration is due to the offspring, which many have the boldness to call the disagreeable burden of matrimony and which they say is to be carefully avoided by married people not through virtuous continence (which Christian law permits in matrimony when both parties consent) but by frustrating the marriage act. Some justify

this criminal abuse on the ground that they are weary of children and wish to gratify their desires without their consequent burden. Others say that they cannot on the one hand remain continent nor on the other can they have children because of the difficulties whether on the part of the mother or on the part of the family circumstances.

"**But no reason, however grave, may be put forward by which anything intrinsically against nature may become conformable to nature and morally good**. Since, therefore, the conjugal act is destined primarily by nature for the begetting of children, **those who in exercising it deliberately frustrate its natural powers and *purpose* sin against nature and commit a deed which is shameful and intrinsically vicious.**

"Small wonder, therefore, if Holy Writ bears witness that the Divine Majesty regards with greatest detestation this horrible crime and at times has punished it with death. As St. Augustine notes, '**Intercourse even with one's legitimate wife is unlawful and wicked where the conception of offspring is prevented.**' Onan, the son of Judah, did this and the Lord killed him for it (Gen. 38:8-10).

"Since, therefore, openly departing from the uninterrupted Christian tradition some recently have judged it possible solemnly to declare another doctrine regarding this question, **the Catholic Church**, to whom God has entrusted the defense of the integrity and purity of morals, standing erect in the midst of the moral ruin which surrounds her, in order that she may preserve the chastity of the nuptial union from being defiled by this foul stain, **raises her voice** in token of her divine ambassadorship **and through Our mouth proclaims anew: any use whatsoever of matrimony exercised in such a way that the act is deliberately frustrated in its natural power to generate life is an offence against the law of God and of nature, and those who indulge in such are branded with the guilt of a grave sin.**"[2] DENZ 2239-2240

One can see that Pope Pius XI condemns all forms of contraception as mortally sinful because they frustrate the marriage act. Does this condemn NFP? Yes it does, but the defenders of Natural Family Planning say "no." They argue that in using *the rhythm method* to avoid conception they are not deliberately frustrating the marriage *act* or designedly depriving it of its natural *power* to procreate life, as is done with artificial contraceptives. They argue that NFP is "natural."

Common sense should tell those who deeply consider this topic that these arguments are specious because NFP has as its entire purpose the avoidance of conception. However, the attempted justification for NFP – the claim that it doesn't interfere with the marriage act *itself* and is therefore permissible – must be specifically refuted. This claim is specifically refuted by a careful look at the teaching of the Catholic Church on marriage and ITS PRIMARY PURPOSE. It is the teaching of the Catholic Church on the primary purpose of marriage (and the primary purpose of the marriage act) which condemns NFP.

Catholic dogma teaches us that the primary purpose of marriage (and the conjugal act) is the procreation and education of children.

> Pope Pius XI, *Casti Connubii* (# 17), Dec. 31, 1930: "**The primary end of marriage is the procreation and the education of children**."[3]

> Pope Pius XI, *Casti Connubii* (# 54), Dec. 31, 1930:
> "Since, therefore, **the conjugal act is destined primarily by nature for the begetting of children**, those who in exercising it deliberately frustrate its natural powers and *purpose* sin against nature and commit a deed which is shameful and intrinsically vicious."[4]
>
> DENZ 2239

Besides this primary purpose, there are also secondary purposes for marriage, such as mutual aid, the quieting of concupiscence, and the cultivating of mutual love. **But these secondary purposes must always remain subordinate to the primary purpose of marriage (the procreation and education of children).** This is the key point to remember in the discussion on NFP.

> Pope Pius XI, *Casti Connubii* (# 59), Dec. 31, 1930: "For in matrimony as well as in the use of the matrimonial right there are also secondary ends, such as mutual aid, the cultivating of mutual love, and the quieting of concupiscence which husband and wife are not forbidden to consider **SO LONG AS THEY ARE SUBORDINATED TO THE PRIMARY END** and so long as the intrinsic nature of the act is preserved."[5]

Therefore, even though NFP doesn't directly interfere with the marriage *act itself*, as its defenders love to stress, it makes no difference. **NFP is wrong because practicing it subordinates the primary end (or purpose) of marriage and the marriage act (the procreation and education of children) to the secondary ends.**

NFP subordinates the primary end of marriage to other things by deliberately attempting to avoid children (i.e., to avoid the primary end) while having marital relations. NFP therefore inverts the order intended by God. It does the very thing that Pope Pius XI solemnly teaches may not lawfully be done. And this point *refutes* all of the arguments made by those who defend NFP; for all of the arguments made by those who defend NFP focus on the marriage act itself, while they ignore the fact that it makes no difference if a couple does not interfere with the act itself *if they subordinate or thwart the primary PURPOSE of marriage.*

To summarize: the only difference between artificial contraception and NFP is that artificial contraception frustrates the power of the marriage *act itself*, while NFP frustrates its primary purpose (by subordinating the procreation of children to other things).

God's Word

It's not a complicated matter to understand that using Natural Family Planning to avoid pregnancy is wrong. It's written on man's heart that such activity is wrong.

> Genesis 30:1-2- "And Rachel seeing herself without children, envied her sister, and said to her husband: Give me children, otherwise I shall die. **And Jacob being angry with her, answered: Am I as God, who hath deprived thee of the fruit of thy womb?**"

We all know that God is the One who opens the womb, the One who killeth and maketh alive.

> Genesis 30:22- "The Lord also remembering Rachel, heard her, **and opened her womb.**"

> 1 Kings 2:6- "The Lord killeth and maketh alive, he bringeth down to Hell, and bringeth back again."

So why would a woman who desires to fulfill the will of God make a systematic effort to avoid God sending her a new life? What excuse could such a person possibly make for going out of her way to calculate how to have marital relations without getting pregnant with the child God was going to send? Why would a woman (or a man) who believes that God opens the womb try to avoid His opening of the womb by a meticulous and organized effort, involving charts, cycles and thermometers? The answer is that those who engage in such behavior as NFP turn from God (which is the essence of sin) and refuse to be open to His will.

When a married couple goes out of their way to avoid children, by deliberately avoiding the fertile times and restricting the marriage act exclusively to infertile times, they are committing a sin against the natural law – they are sinning against the God whom they know sends life. NFP is, therefore, a sin against the natural law, since God is the author of life and NFP thwarts His designs.

People Know that NFP is a sin

Below are a few very interesting testimonies from people who have either used NFP or were taught NFP. Their comments have been taken from "the letters to the editor" section of a publication which carried an article on NFP.[6] (Their names were given in the original letter.) Their letters demonstrate that the women who use NFP, as well as the men who tolerate or cooperate with it, are convicted of its sinfulness by the natural law written on their hearts. Those who use NFP know that they are thwarting the will of God and practicing contraception.

"Dear Editor… I was a non-religious divorced pagan before I met my husband who was, at the time, a minimal practicing Catholic. I became Catholic in 1993 and we were married in 1994. I had no idea at that time that Catholics were allowed to do anything to prevent a child. I had never even heard of NFP until the priest we were meeting with during the six months prior to our wedding handed me a packet of papers and basically said, 'here, you'll want to learn this.' When I got home, I briefly thumbed through the papers. I saw calendars, stickers, and charts. To be honest, it was mind-boggling all the effort people would go through just so they could have intimacy without consequence. It was also shocking to me that this was being promoted before I even took the vows on my wedding day! I threw the packet away and have never looked back. I am thankful that I never learned NFP… I wonder which of my children wouldn't be here had I chosen to keep those papers and learn NFP?"

"Dear Editor… I am a mother to seven children and can share my own experiences. NFP did NOT bring my marriage closer. I struggled with reconciling myself to the fact that scripture states a husband and wife should be submissive and not separate unless for prayer. We were avoiding pregnancy… plain and simple. There can be nothing spiritual about telling your spouse that you can't participate in the marital embrace for fear of a child being conceived. Webster's dictionary defines contraception as: 'deliberate prevention of conception or impregnation.' Systematically charting and watching out for those fertile days is the deliberate prevention of conception. I know friends who use it. I've talked to them in a very personal way. They do not want any more children. They are using NFP as birth control, which it is. And one friend has been using it for 11 years and 'hasn't had any accidents.' … I can say that St. Augustine was right on target when he wrote in *The Morals of the Manichees*: 'Marriage, as the marriage tablets themselves proclaim, joins male and female for the procreation of children. Whoever says that to procreate children is a worse sin than to copulate thereby prohibits the purpose of marriage; and he makes the woman no more a wife than a harlot, who, when she has been given certain gifts, is joined to a man to satisfy his lust. If there is a wife, there is matrimony. But there is no matrimony where motherhood is prevented, for then there is no wife.'… My favorite comment recently was made by another author comparing NFP to a farmer who plants his corn in the dead of winter so as to avoid a plentiful harvest."

"Dear Editor… Let me put the NFP debate simply: if it is your intention to avoid having children it really doesn't matter what method you use. You've already committed the sin. If, however, you use contraception as your method of choice, you add to the first sin a second one. As to the oft-repeated mantra of 'grave reasons,' allow me to say this:

name one. Look deep into your heart and name one that is really, truly grave... We did the NFP bit for awhile... and have felt revulsion over it ever since. During that time we might have had at least two more children."

"To the Editor: NFP is one of the chief infiltrations of the new-age sex cult into the Church, along with sex-ed and immodest dress... As modern Catholics have been conditioned to embrace mutually contradictory ideas while defending them as consonant, they have been easily deceived by the notion that NFP, as commonly practiced, is somehow different from birth control. I have no training in moral theology, but even I know that the goal of an action determines its substance. When a couple engages in deliberately sterile relations, this is known as birth control, plain and simple."

Planned Parenthood and NFP of the Same Cloth

Have you noticed the similarities between Planned Parenthood (the world's largest abortion provider) and Natural Family Planning? Artificial contraceptives and abortifacients are found under store aisles marked "Family Planning." Like abortionists, family planners consider children as something undesirable, at least temporarily; whereas the true faithful have always considered them as an undeniable blessing from God Himself, planned by His providence from all eternity. "Behold, children are the inheritance of the Lord; the fruit of the womb is a reward... Blessed is the man whose desire is filled with them; he shall not be confounded..." (Psalm 126:3,5).

In publications promoting NFP, the fertile period of the wife is sometimes classified as "not safe" and "dangerous," as though generating new life were considered a serious breach of national security and a little infant a treacherous criminal! This is truly abominable.

Could it be more clear that those who subscribe to this type of behavior and this method shut God and children out and replace them with their own selfish agenda?

> Tobias 6:17 – "The holy youth Tobias approaches his bride Sara after three days of prayer, not for fleshly lust but only for the love of posterity. <u>Having been instructed by the Archangel Saint Raphael that to engage in the marital act he must be moved rather for love of children than for lust</u>. **For they who in such manner receive matrimony, as to shut out God from themselves, and from their mind, and to give themselves to their lust, as the horse and mule, which have not understanding, <u>over them the Devil hath power</u>.**"

The word *matrimony* means "the office of motherhood." Those who use NFP attempt to avoid matrimony (the office of motherhood) and shut out God from themselves.

> Saint Caesar of Arles: "As often as he knows his wife without a desire for children... without a doubt he commits sin."[7]

> Errors Condemned by Pope Innocent XI: "9. **The act of marriage exercised for pleasure only is entirely free of all fault** and venial defect."–Condemned[8] DENZ 1159

NFP has eternal and infinite consequences

The following facts may be the most incriminating to the practice of "Natural Family Planning."

If family planners had their way, there would have been no St. Bernadette of Lourdes, who was born from a jail flat; nor St. Therese of Lisieux, who came from a sickly mother who lost three children in a row; nor St. Ignatius Loyola, who was the thirteenth of thirteen children;[9] **and most certainly not a St. Catherine of Siena, who was the twenty-fifth child in a family of twenty-five children!**[10]

Examples of saints who were the last of many children could probably be multiplied for pages. St. Catherine of Siena and the rest of the saints who would have been phased out of existence by NFP will rise in judgment against the NFP generation. Natural Family Planners would have been sure to inform St. Catherine's mother that there was no need having five children (let alone twenty-five!), and that she was wasting her time going through all those pregnancies.

Only in eternity shall we know the immortal souls who have been denied a chance at Heaven because of this selfish behavior. The only thing that can foil the will of the all-powerful God is the will of His puny creatures; for He will not force offspring on anyone, just as He will not violate anyone's free will. NFP is a crime of incalculable proportions. (Just contemplate for a second the thought: if your mom had decided not to have you.)

If family planners had their way, the appearances of Our Lady of Fatima would not have occurred, as she appeared to Lucia (the seventh of seven children), Francisco (the eighth of nine children) and Jacinta (the ninth of nine children). Family Planners, by their selfish thwarting of the will of God, **would have erased from human history the entire message of Fatima**, as well as the incredible miracle of the sun, the extraordinary lives of these three shepherd children, and all the graces of conversion obtained by their heroic sacrifices. How many saints, conversions and miracles have been erased by this abominable birth control practice? Only God knows.

A mother of many children, who was about to be a mother once more, came to Ars (the place where St. John Vianney resided) to seek courage from him. She said to him, "Oh, I am so advanced in years, Father!" St. John Vianney responded: *"Be comforted my child; if you only knew the women who will go to Hell because they did not bring into the world the children they should have given to it!"*

> 1 Timothy 2:15- "**Yet she shall be saved through child-bearing**; if she continue in faith, and love, and sanctification, with sobriety."

Scripture teaches that a woman can be saved through child-bearing (if she is Catholic and in the state of grace). But NFP advocates would have us believe that a woman can be saved through child-avoiding. Moreover, just as a woman who fulfills the will of God and maintains the state of grace in the state of matrimony is saved by her childbearing, so too are countless women going to be damned for not bearing the children that God wanted them to have.

> "Seek first the kingdom of God and His justice and all things will be added unto you." (Mt. 6:33)

Objections

> Objection 1) Natural Family Planning is a justifiable practice of birth control because it does nothing to obstruct the natural power of procreation.

Response: We've already responded to this objection above. We won't repeat all of that here. We will simply summarize again that NFP is condemned because it subordinates the primary PURPOSE of marriage and the conjugal act to other things. This makes the fact that NFP does nothing to obstruct the marriage act itself irrelevant, since the primary <u>purpose</u> is being frustrated.

> Objection 2) Pope Pius XII taught that NFP is lawful for at least certain reasons. So you have no right to condemn it, as he was the pope.

Response: It is true that Pope Pius XII taught that Natural Family Planning is lawful for certain reasons in a series of <u>fallible</u> speeches in the 1950's. However, this does not justify NFP. Pius XII's speeches were fallible, and were therefore vulnerable to error.

In studying papal errors throughout history in preparation for its declaration of papal infallibility, the theologians at Vatican I found that over 40 popes held wrong theological views. In a notorious case of papal error, Pope John XXII held the false view that the just of the Old Testament don't receive the Beatific Vision until after the General Judgment. Pope Honorius I, a validly elected Roman Pontiff, encouraged the heresy of monotheletism (that Our Lord Jesus Christ only had one will), for which he was later condemned by the *Third Council of Constantinople*. But none of these errors were taught by popes from the Chair of St. Peter, just like Pius XII's speech to Italian midwives is not a declaration from the Chair of St. Peter.

One of the most notorious cases of papal error in Church history is the "Synod of the Corpse" of 897. This was where the dead body of Pope Formosus – who by all accounts was a holy and devoted pope – was condemned after his death by Pope Stephen VII for a number of supposed violations of canon law.[11] Pope Sergius III was also in favor of the judgment, while later Popes Theodore II and John IX opposed it. This should show us very clearly that **not every decision, speech, opinion or judgment of a pope is infallible**.

One can argue that Pius XII was one of the weakest popes in the history of the Church. (We are not including the Vatican II antipopes, as they are not popes). Pius XII allowed heresy and modernism to flourish; he modernized the holy week liturgy; he taught that theistic evolution could be held and taught by Catholic priests and theologians; and he allowed the denial of the dogma Outside the Church There is No Salvation to run rampant, just to name a few. He was a valid pope, but he was truly the bridge to the apostate Second Vatican Council and the antipopes who imposed it. Those who think that they're safe following something simply because it was endorsed by pre-Vatican II theologians or by Pope Pius XII in his <u>fallible</u> capacity are mistaken. Even though the explosion of the Great Apostasy occurred at Vatican II, its momentum by a departure from the Faith was well in motion prior to Vatican II, as is evidenced from many pre-Vatican II books which promoted condemned heresy and modernism. Most of the priests had already fallen into heresy in the 1950's, as is proven by the fact that almost all of them accepted and embraced the new religion of the Vatican II Church when it was imposed.

The bottom-line remains that it's an infallible teaching of the Catholic Church that the primary end of marriage (and the conjugal act) is the procreation and education of children. Natural Family Planning subordinates the primary end of marriage and the conjugal act to other things and is therefore gravely sinful.

> Objection 3) I know that NFP is always wrong, except for certain reasons, and in those cases it is allowable.

Response: We will quote again Pope Pius XI to respond to this objection.

> Pope Pius XI, *Casti Connubii* (# 54), Dec. 31, 1930:

> "**But no reason, however grave, may be put forward by which anything intrinsically against nature may become conformable to nature and morally good**. Since, therefore, the conjugal act is destined primarily by nature for the begetting of children, **those who in exercising it deliberately frustrate its natural powers and _purpose_ sin against nature and commit a deed which is shameful and intrinsically vicious.**"[12] DENZ 2239

No reason, however grave it may be, can bring it about that something that is intrinsically evil can become good. NFP subordinates the primary purpose of the conjugal act (the procreation and education of children) to other things and is therefore forbidden.

And this brings us to another point. If NFP is not a sin – if it is simply "natural," as they say – then why can't married couples use NFP during the whole marriage and have zero children? If NFP isn't a sin, then all women are perfectly free to use this method of birth control to phase out of existence all children so that not even one is born. However, basically all of the defenders of NFP would admit that it would be immoral and gravely sinful to use NFP to avoid all new life. But when they make this admission they are admitting that NFP is a sin; otherwise, let them confess that it can be used by all couples for any reason to avoid all children.

> Objection 4) In *Casti Connubii* itself, Pope Pius XI taught that married couples could use the periods where the wife cannot become pregnant.
>
> Pope Pius XI, *Casti Connubii* (# 59), Dec. 31, 1930: "Nor are those considered as acting against nature who in the married state use their right in the proper manner although on account of natural reasons either of time or of certain defects, new life cannot be brought forth. For in matrimony as well as in the use of the matrimonial right there are also secondary ends, such as mutual aid, the cultivating of mutual love, and the quieting of concupiscence which husband and wife are not forbidden to consider **SO LONG AS THEY ARE SUBORDINATED TO THE PRIMARY END** and so long as the intrinsic nature of the act is preserved."[13] DENZ 2241

Response: Yes, Pope Pius XI taught that married couples could use their marriage rights in the infertile periods of the wife (or when there is a defect of nature or age which prevents new life from being conceived). But he did not teach that they could designedly restrict the marriage act to the infertile periods to avoid a pregnancy, as in Natural Family Planning.

This is why, in the very passage quoted above, Pope Pius XI reiterates that all use of the marriage rights – including when new life cannot be brought forth due to time or nature – must keep the secondary ends of marriage subordinate to the primary end! This teaching is the deathblow to NFP, as NFP itself is the subordination of the primary end of marriage (the procreation and education of children) to other things. So, in summary, the passage above does not teach NFP, but merely enunciates the principle that married couples may use their marriage rights at any time. Further, in the same paragraph, the very paragraph that the defenders of NFP erroneously twist to justify their sinful birth control practice, Pope Pius XI condemns NFP by reiterating the teaching on the primary purpose of marriage, which NFP subordinates to other things.

> Objection 5) Everyone admits that "Natural Family Planning" can be used to help a woman achieve a pregnancy. Therefore, the same method can be used to avoid pregnancy.

Response: If a couple is using Natural Family Planning to achieve a pregnancy, it is lawful because in this case they are doing their utmost to fulfill the primary end of marriage (the procreation and education of children). If a couple is using Natural Family Planning to avoid pregnancy, it is unlawful because in this case they are doing their utmost <u>to avoid</u> the primary end of marriage (the procreation and education of children).

Objection 6) But my traditional priest instructed me in NFP.

Response: When the blind lead the blind, they both fall into the pit (Matthew 15:14). Couples who use NFP know that they are committing a sin. It's written on their hearts. They don't need a priest to tell them it's wrong. Yes, the priests who obstinately instruct people that NFP is okay and defend this birth control method are also guilty, but this doesn't take away the responsibility of the couples who follow their bad advice.

This is why we stress that those who are contributing money to "traditionalist" priests who promote or accept NFP must cease immediately if they don't want to share in their sin and follow them to Hell, as these priests are leading souls to Hell.

This includes the priests of the Society of St. Pius X, the Society of St. Pius V, the C.M.R.I. and almost all independent priests in this time of the Great Apostasy.

Conclusion

Couples who have used NFP, but who are resolved to change, should not despair. NFP is an evil, but God is merciful and will forgive those who are firmly resolved to change their life and confess their sin. Those who have used NFP need to be sorry for their sin and confess to a validly ordained priest that they have practiced birth control (for however long it may have been used). Both the wife and the husband who agreed with the use of NFP need to confess. They should then be open to all of the children that God wishes to bestow upon them – without concern or knowledge of charts, cycles, fertile or infertile, seeking first the kingdom of God and His justice, letting God plan their family.

Endnotes for Section 42:

[1] *The Papal Encyclicals*, by Claudia Carlen, Raleigh: The Pierian Press, Vol. 5, p. 227.
[2] *The Papal Encyclicals*, Vol. 3 (1903-1939), pp. 399-400.
[3] *The Papal Encyclicals*, Vol. 3 (1903-1939), p. 394.
[4] *The Papal Encyclicals*, Vol. 3 (1903-1939), p. 399.
[5] *The Papal Encyclicals*, Vol. 3 (1903-1939), p. 394.
[6] http://www.seattlecatholic.com
[7] Jurgens, *The Faith of the Early Fathers*, Collegeville, MN, The Liturgical Press, 1970, Vol. 3:2233.
[8] Denzinger, *The Sources of Catholic Dogma*, B. Herder Book. Co., Thirtieth Edition, 1957, no. 1159.
[9] John. J. Delaney, *Pocket Dictionary of Saints* (abridged edition), New York: Double Day, 1980, p. 251.
[10] John. J. Delaney, *Pocket Dictionary of Saints* (abridged edition), 110.
[11] Warren H. Carroll, *A History of Christendom*, Vol. 2 (*The Building of Christendom*), Front Royal, VA: Christendom Press, 1987, p. 387.
[12] *The Papal Encyclicals*, Vol. 3 (1903-1939), p. 399.
[13] *The Papal Encyclicals*, Vol. 3 (1903-1939), p. 394.

43. The Whole Truth about the Consecration and Conversion of Russia and the impostor Sr. Lucy

-The question is: Can you handle the truth on this issue?
-The truth that you won't hear from "Fr." Gruner; the stunning facts on an issue that we've all been brainwashed only to consider from one angle
-This is something that every traditional Catholic needs to read

Proverbs 16:7- "When the ways of man shall please the Lord, He will convert even his enemies to peace."	Our Lady: "If they listen to my requests, Russia will be converted and there will be peace."

Proverbs 16:7- "When the ways of man shall please the Lord, He will **convert** even His enemies **to peace**."

"…cum placuerint Domino viae hominis inimicos quoque eius **convertet ad pacem**."

IN THIS ARTICLE:

-FACT #1: POPE PIUS XII CONSECRATED RUSSIA TO THE IMMACULATE HEART OF MARY - POPE PIUS XII CONSECRATED NOT THE WORLD, BUT SPECIFICALLY RUSSIA, ON JULY 7, 1952
-FACT #2: **WHAT OUR LADY MEANS BY THE CONVERSION OF RUSSIA – THE STRIKING EVIDENCE**
-THIS POSITION IS FURTHER SUBSTANTIATED BY CONSIDERING PORTUGAL – "THE SHOWCASE OF OUR LADY"
-THIS POSITION IS FURTHER SUBSTANTIATED BY SR. LUCY'S SUMMARY OF THE TUY VISION
-"THE GOOD WILL BE MARTYRED" AND "VARIOUS NATIONS WILL BE ANNIHILATED" ARE PROPHECIES THAT HAVE ALREADY BEEN FULFILLED
-WHAT RUSSIA WAS CONVERTED FROM – SNAPSHOTS OF THE SATANIC REGIME IN COMMUNIST RUSSIA
-HE WILL DO THE CONSECRATION, BUT IT WILL BE "LATE"
-OUR LADY'S WORDS REVEAL TO US THAT HER TRIUMPH IS NOT A UNIVERSAL TRIUMPH OR REIGN OF PEACE, BUT ONLY A "CERTAIN" PERIOD OF PEACE
-THE CONVERSION OF RUSSIA =…
-THE EVIDENCE
-SOME LEFTOVER OBJECTIONS – AND SR. LUCY DIDN'T EVEN KNOW IF PIUS XII'S 1942 CONSECRATION OF THE WORLD WAS ACCEPTED IN HEAVEN
-PART II: THE EVIDENCE EXPOSING THE IMPOSTOR SR. LUCY
-THE FALSE MESSAGE OF "FR." NICHOLAS GRUNER

One of the most frequent questions that we receive concerns Our Lady's statement at Fatima on July 13, 1917:

> "*You see Hell, where the souls of poor sinners go. To save them God wishes to establish in the world the devotion to my Immaculate Heart. If they do what I will tell you, many souls will be saved, and there will be peace. The war is going to end. But if they do not stop offending God, another and worse war will begin in the reign of Pius XI. When you shall see a night illuminated by an unknown light, know that it is a great sign that God gives you that He is going to punish the world for its crimes by means of war, of hunger, and of persecution of the Church and of the Holy Father. To prevent this I come to ask the consecration of Russia to my Immaculate Heart and the Communion of reparation on the first Saturdays. If they listen to my requests, Russia will be converted and there will be peace. If not she will scatter her errors through the world, provoking wars and persecutions of the Church. The good will be martyred, the Holy Father will have much to suffer, various nations will be annihilated. In the end my Immaculate Heart will triumph. The Holy Father will consecrate Russia to me, and it will be converted and a certain period of peace will be granted to the world.*"[1]

The Vatican II "popes" must be true popes, so the objection goes, because one of them will finally consecrate Russia to the Immaculate Heart of Mary, and the entire nation will be converted to the Catholic Faith. That hasn't happened, so you cannot be right that these are antipopes.

First, in examining this issue it is important for people to clear their minds of any pre-conceived notions or prejudices in this area. **They must be prepared to take a fresh new look at the facts.** Let's jump right into this very important issue:

FACT #1: POPE PIUS XII SPECIFICALLY CONSECRATED RUSSIA TO THE IMMACULATE HEART OF MARY ON JULY 7, 1952

Many know that Pope Pius XII consecrated the world to the Immaculate Heart of Mary in 1942. Many do not know that Pope Pius XII specifically consecrated Russia to the Immaculate Heart of Mary in 1952.

We didn't know this until we began studying this issue in some depth. But this important fact is revealed even in the books promoted by "Fr." Nicholas Gruner's apostolate.

> Frere Michel de la Sainte Trinite, *The Whole Truth About Fatima*, Vol. 1, p. 498: "…**in 1952. On July 7 of the same year, a month after the article by Dhanis, Pope Pius XII in his apostolic letter *Sacro Vergente Anno*, accomplished this consecration of Russia and it alone, by name** – so much for Dhanis declaring it impossible!"[2]

This fact can also be found in the book *Fatima in Twilight*:

> Mark Fellows, *Fatima in Twilight*, p. 119: "**The letter went on to request that Pius consecrate Russia to the Immaculate Heart. He [Pius XII] did so in a letter to all Russians** (*Sacro vergente anno*), writing in pertinent part, 'today we consecrate and in a most special manner entrust all the peoples of Russia to this Immaculate Heart…'"[3]

Here are the words of Pope Pius XII:

> Pope Pius XII, *Sacro Vergente Anno* (Apostolic Letter), July 7, 1952: "**…just as a few years ago We consecrated the entire human race to the Immaculate Heart of the Virgin Mary, Mother of God, so today We consecrate and in a most special manner We entrust all the peoples of Russia to this Immaculate Heart…**"[4]

Thus, it is an undeniable fact that Pope Pius XII specifically consecrated Russia to the Immaculate Heart of Mary.

But didn't Our Lady promise that Russia would be consecrated in union with all the bishops of the world? No! This is a key point. Our Lady *requested* that Russia be consecrated in union with all the bishops of the world, but on July 13 she only promised that *"In the end my Immaculate Heart will triumph. <u>The Holy Father will consecrate Russia to me</u>, and it will be converted and a certain period of peace will be granted to the world."* Notice that Our Lady didn't promise: "The Holy Father and all the bishops will consecrate Russia to me…" Further, Heaven revealed that the actual fulfillment of the consecration of Russia would not be fully in accord with Heaven's original wishes; for instance, it would be "late" (more on this in a bit).

FACT #2: OUR LADY NEVER SAID THAT THE CONVERSION OF RUSSIA MEANS THAT RUSSIA WOULD BE CONVERTED TO THE CATHOLIC FAITH

The question that we must re-examine is: **did Our Lady ever say that Russia would be converted to "the Catholic Faith"? Is there any evidence that Our Lady ever said that Russia would be converted to the Catholic Faith?** The answer, which will probably surprise many, is *no*. One of us recently completed a careful study of Frere Michel's 3-volume work *The Whole Truth About Fatima* (more than 2000 pages on the issue). We were looking for some evidence, any evidence, that Our Lady ever said that the "conversion" of Russia means that the nation of Russia will be converted to the Catholic Faith. In the entire 3-volume set, there is no evidence whatsoever that Our Lord or Our Lady ever promised that Russia would be converted to *the Catholic Faith*. [Please note: *we're not examining the question of whether Heaven would want the conversion of Russia to the Catholic Faith, which of course it would, since outside the Catholic Church there is no salvation. Rather, we're addressing the question of whether Heaven ever <u>said or promised</u> that the nation of Russia would be converted to the Catholic Faith. There is no evidence that Heaven ever promised that Russia would be converted to the Catholic Faith.*]

"But of course it means that the entire country will be converted to the Catholic Faith," as one person told us, *"for it couldn't mean anything else!"* This person even said that it's absurd to think that Our Lady would ever use the word "conversion" to mean anything but a conversion to the true Faith. Oh really? Well, this person may be surprised to learn that in Proverbs 16:7, Almighty God Himself uses the word "conversion" not to mean a conversion to the true Faith, but the conversion of a persecuting enemy to peace (i.e. to a cessation of his persecuting ways).

Proverbs 16:7- "When the ways of man shall please the Lord, He will <u>**convert**</u> even His enemies <u>**to peace**</u>."

In fact, what is striking is that Our Lady's words of July 13 appear to be structured on Proverbs 16:7: in the context of both, *conversion is immediately linked with peace, after a man fulfills the request of the Lord.*

| Proverbs 16:7- "When the ways of man shall please the Lord, He will convert even his enemies to peace." | Our Lady: "If they listen to my requests, Russia will be converted and there will be peace." |

After studying this issue in depth, and taking a fresh new look at the facts, we are of the firm opinion that Our Lady's words are structured on the promise of Proverbs 16:7: the "conversion" of Russia does not mean the conversion of the nation to the Catholic Faith, but rather the conversion of a persecuting enemy (Russia) to a certain period of peace. We will see exactly what this means as we go along, and that the evidence from the message of Fatima bears this out.

THIS POSITION IS FURTHER SUBSTANTIATED BY CONSIDERING PORTUGAL – "THE SHOWCASE OF OUR LADY"

To attempt to substantiate their position that Russia has not been consecrated, "Fr." Gruner and his supporters often bring up the case of Portugal as the "Showcase of Our Lady." They point out that when the Portuguese bishops consecrated their nation to the Immaculate Heart of Mary on May 13, 1931, the result was an incredible Catholic renaissance and social reform. They say that Our Lady used Portugal as a "showcase" of what she would do for Russia and the rest of the world.

> John Vennari, "It Doesn't Add Up," *The Fatima Crusader*, Issue #70: "Thus it is not hard to understand why Portugal at this time has been called the "Showcase of Our Lady." **And this triple miracle of Portugal stands as a preview of how Russia and the world will look after the Collegial Consecration of Russia**."[5]

However, in bringing up the example of Portugal, they provide more evidence that Our Lady's promise of the "conversion" of Russia did not mean the conversion of the entire nation to the Catholic Faith. For they fail to note that even **after the bishops consecrated the nation of Portugal (a nation that was already almost entirely Catholic in population) the country did not become a Catholic country**!

> Frere Michel de la Sainte Trinite, *The Whole Truth About Fatima*, Vol. 2, p. 420: "**Curiously**, in this accord [of the Portuguese nation], **the Catholic religion is not recognized as the official religion of the Portuguese State**, and therefore in theory the separation of Church and State remains."[6]

If Portugal itself (a nation that was already almost entirely Catholic) wasn't even changed into a Catholic country after its consecration, this is further evidence that the conversion of Russia does not mean a conversion of the nation to the Catholic Faith. The 1959 Portuguese Constitution doesn't even mention the name of God.[7]

THIS POSITION IS FURTHER SUBSTANTIATED BY SR. LUCY'S SUMMARY OF THE TUY VISION

In order to attempt to substantiate their position that Russia will be converted to the Catholic Faith, many cite the vision of Tuy, in which Our Lady promised to "save" Russia:

Our Lady to Sr. Lucy, June 13, 1929, at Tuy: "The moment has come when God asks the Holy Father to make, in union with all the bishops of the world, the consecration of Russia to My Immaculate Heart, promising to save it by this means."[8]

What is HUGELY SIGNIFICANT is that Frere Michel admits that Sr. Lucy summarized this communication at Tuy in a slightly different manner in two letters to Fr. Goncalves:

Frere Michel de la Sainte Trinite, *The Whole Truth About Fatima*, Vol. 2, p. 465: **"[page after quoting what you just read] Let us point out right away that in 1930, in two letters to Father Goncalves, Sister Lucy was to express in a slightly different manner the requests of Heaven…** [Sister Lucy]: '**The good Lord promises to end the persecution in Russia**, if the Holy Father will himself make a solemn act of reparation and consecration of Russia to the Sacred Hearts of Jesus and Mary, as well as ordering all the bishops of the Catholic Church to do the same. The Holy Father must then promise that upon the ending of this persecution he will approve and recommend the practice of the reparatory devotion already described.'"[9]

So, according to Sr. Lucy, the message at Tuy that Our Lord will "save" Russia means that the Lord promises to "**end the persecution in Russia**," thus corroborating the point that there is no evidence that Heaven ever promised that Russia would be converted to the Catholic Faith. We find the same thing in another vision that Our Lord granted to Sr. Lucy in 1940:

Our Lord to Sr. Lucy, Oct. 22, 1940: "I will punish the nations for their crimes by means of war, famine and persecution of My Church and this will weigh especially upon My Vicar on earth. **His Holiness will obtain an abbreviation of these days of tribulation** if he takes heed of My wishes by **promulgating the Act of Consecration** of the whole world to the Immaculate Heart of Mary, with a special mention of Russia."[10]

The consecration of Russia will "obtain an abbreviation" of the tribulation that is caused by the persecutions of Russia, perfectly coinciding with our point about what Our Lady meant by the "conversion" of Russia. Most importantly, however, we can see what Our Lady meant in context by the conversion of Russia in a careful consideration of her words on July 13.

*"The **war** is going to end. But if they do not stop offending God, **another and worse war** will begin in the reign of Pius XI. When you shall see a night illuminated by an unknown light, know that it is a great sign that God gives you that **He is going to punish the world for its crimes by means of war, of hunger, and of persecution of the Church** and of the Holy Father. **To prevent this** I come to ask the consecration of Russia to my Immaculate Heart and the Communion of reparation on the first Saturdays. If they listen to my requests, Russia will be converted and there will be peace. If not she will scatter her errors through the world, provoking wars and persecutions of the Church. The good will be martyred, the Holy Father will have much to suffer, various nations will be annihilated. In the end my Immaculate Heart will triumph. The Holy Father will consecrate Russia to me, and it will be converted and a certain period of peace will be granted to the world."*

Notice, the consecration of Russia was specifically requested to prevent "war… hunger and persecution of the Church…" This shows us how firmly set within this specific context Our Lady's words were on the consecration of Russia – converting this enemy to peace from these persecutions of "war… hunger… of the Church."

This point is corroborated when one considers **the "great sign"** mentioned by Our Lady in the context of her request for the consecration of Russia. Our Lady says: *"**When you shall see a night illuminated by an unknown light**, know that it is **a great sign** that God gives you that He is going to punish the world for its crimes by means of war, of hunger, and of persecution of the Church and of the Holy Father. To prevent this…"* This "sign" was not some "small sign," but the "great sign" that Heaven gave <u>in the context of the consecration of Russia and the punishments the consecration of Russia would prevent</u>.

Well, this "great sign" (as basically every Fatima scholar admits) was the unknown light that lit up the sky on Jan. 25, 1938, just prior to the events that precipitated World War II.

> **"An aurora borealis of exceptional size furrowed the sky of Western Europe last night**; it caused an uproar in a number of departments, which at first believed it to be a gigantic fire. In the entire region of the Alps, the population was much intrigued by this strange spectacle. **The sky was ablaze like an immense moving furnace**, provoking a very strong blood-red glow."[11]

We think that most people can agree that this sign doesn't seem that significant to us from our vantage point today. Yet, **within the context of the consecration of Russia, and the "war… hunger… and persecution of the Church…" which it was requested to prevent, this was the "great sign" that Heaven gave**. This shows us again <u>how firmly within this specific context Our Lady's words for the consecration of Russia were</u> – converting this enemy to peace from its persecutions of war, persecutions of the Church, etc.

"THE GOOD WILL BE MARTYRED" AND "VARIOUS NATIONS WILL BE ANNIHILATED" ARE PROPHECIES THAT HAVE ALREADY BEEN FULFILLED

In order to further understand what Our Lady meant by the "conversion" of Russia, **it is important for us to understand what she meant by things she mentioned in the same context; for instance, "various nations will be annihilated" and "the good will be martyred."**

> *Our Lady of Fatima, July 13, 1917: "If they listen to my requests, Russia will be converted and there will be peace. If not she will scatter her errors through the world, provoking wars and persecutions of the Church. **The good will be martyred**, the Holy Father will have much to suffer, **various nations will be annihilated**…"*

Many believe that Our Lady's words "various nations will be annihilated" and "the good will be martyred" (as a result of the spread of Russia's errors) still have not been fulfilled. However, the truth is that both of these things have already been fulfilled.

VARIOUS NATIONS WERE ANNIHILATED

As we will see, even Frere Michel, an author whose work is promoted by Nicholas Gruner's apostolate, **admits that the Soviet Union's takeover of the Baltic nations and other small States during the period of World War II, which it simply annexed to itself** *making them exist no longer*, **constituted the annihilation of nations of which Our Lady spoke**.

> Frere Michel de la Sainte Trinite, *The Whole Truth About Fatima*, Vol. 3, p. 190: "In 1939 the USSR was still the only communist state in the world… **Six years later… <u>several nations were erased from the map, absorbed by the Soviet empire</u>, a dozen countries entered Moscow's orbit and retained only the appearance of liberty,** while others were agitated

by internal wars or gravely threatened by communist subversion. **The prophecy of Fatima was being fulfilled to the letter.**"[12]

Besides the nations of Poland, Hungary, Czechoslovakia, Romania, Bulgaria, etc. which entered the orbit of the Soviet Empire and were reduced to puppets of its machine, **the Baltic nations, Lithuania, Latvia and Estonia, were actually erased from the map** – completely annihilated by full absorption into the Soviet Empire.

"**The small Baltic nations – Lithuania, Latvia and Estonia – were now ready for Stalin to pluck.** He moved at once to impose 'mutual assistance treaties' on them, whose only significant clause provided for stationing large numbers of Soviet troops on their territory. These treaties were signed on September 28 (Estonia), October 5 (Latvia), and October 10 (Lithuania). **They could now be taken over at any time.**"[13] (Warren H. Carroll, *The Rise and Fall of the Communist Revolution*, Christendom Press, p. 310)

An article carried on the website of the Joint Baltic American National Committee notes that:

"On July 23, 1940, Sumner Welles, acting US Secretary of State, stated that the '**devious processes whereby the political independence and territorial integrity of the three small Baltic republics** – Estonia, Latvia and Lithuania – **were to be deliberately annihilated** by one of their more powerful neighbors, have been rapidly drawn to their conclusion.'"[14] (Joint Baltic American Committee)

Notice, the absorption of the Baltic nations by the Soviet Union "annihilated" the political independence and territorial integrity of these nations (i.e., annihilated their nationhood itself)! Another article on the website of the Joint Baltic American Committee notes that "…communism will be remembered not so much for what it left behind as for what it didn't. **The decades of totalitarian rule annihilated cultures**…"[15]

Our Lady's words about the annihilation of nations clearly refer to the Soviet Union's takeover of the Baltic nations, which literally erased them from the map by absorption. But there are some who believe that Our Lady's words refer to nuclear catastrophe that will happen in the future. To attempt to prove this point, they will quote Sr. Lucy's words to Fr. Fuentes.

Sister Lucy to Fr. Fuentes, 1957: "Tell them, Father, that many times the Most Holy Virgin told my cousins Francisco and Jacinta, as well as myself, that **many nations will disappear** from the face of the earth. She said that Russia will be the instrument of chastisement chosen by Heaven to punish the whole world if we do not beforehand obtain the conversion of that poor nation."[16]

Sr. Lucy is obviously reiterating Our Lady's words about the annihilation of nations. However, if a nation were devastated by nuclear catastrophe, it wouldn't disappear. It would still be visible, but as an empty and devastated wasteland. The only way to make a nation literally "disappear" is by erasing it from the map by incorporation into another country, as happened with the Soviet Union's takeover of the Baltic nations. **In stunning confirmation of this point**, here is what the Soviet Foreign Minister, Molotov, said to the Lithuanian Foreign Minister (concerning the Soviet Union's imminent takeover of the Baltic nations):

Soviet Foreign Minister, Molotov, to Lithuanian Foreign Minister: "You must take a good look at reality and understand

The truth about the Consecration and Conversion of Russia 513

that in the future **small nations will have to disappear. Your Lithuania along with the other Baltic nations**…"[17] (quoted by Warren H. Carroll, *The Rise and Fall of the Communist Revolution*, p. 306.)

This map (above) of Eastern Europe before World War II defines the Baltic nations (Estonia, Latvia and Lithuania) before they were annihilated and made to disappear by full absorption into the satanic Soviet Empire

This map of Eastern Europe and the Communist Bloc after WWII defines the disappearance and annihilation of the Baltic nations by full absorption into the Soviet Empire

The annihilation of nations, the making of nations "disappear," clearly refers to the Soviet Union and its takeover of the Baltic States. Frere Michel even applies the "annihilation of nations" to the other nations that the Soviet Union incorporated into its orbit as satellites, such as Poland, etc. However, it most specifically refers to the erasing of the Baltic nations, as well as other small provinces such as North Bukovina and Bessarabia. And this surely would have happened to "many" other nations if Russia had not been consecrated.

> Frere Michel de la Sainte Trinite, *The Whole Truth About Fatima*, Vol. 3, pp. 193-194: "<u>Is it necessary to enumerate these nations, which perhaps Our Lady of Fatima designated, announcing that 'various nations will be annihilated'?</u> Torn from their age-old traditions, and from their Church, their society destroyed by the great Bolshevik machine, in effect, these countries are no longer themselves… **There is Albania, where the persecution against the Church began in 1945. There is Hungary,** with its 7 million Catholics out of 10 million inhabitants, where the apostolic nuncio was expelled in April, 1945… **There is Poland (22 million Catholics**), where in September, 1945, the government decided to break the concordat. **There is Czechoslovakia**, where out of 12 million inhabitants, almost nine million were Catholics. There is Orthodox **Romania** with its valiant minority of 3 million Eastern Rite faithful, where the government awaits the favorable hour to perform the same forced integration to the schismatic Church as in Ukraine. There is Bulgaria, where the Church numbers only 57,000. **There is Tito's Yugoslavia… where a bloody persecution began in June – July, 1945.**"[18]

In every communist nation controlled by the Soviet Union, the press, the radio and education were totally controlled by the State. This became the sad and gloomy reality in country after country that fell to communism. All of these satellites also vigorously persecuted the Church. For instance:

> "**In Romania**, with the active complicity of Patriarch Alexis of Moscow and the entire Orthodox national hierarchy, **the communists decided on the liquidation, pure and simple, of the Greek-Catholic Church,** which numbered 1,600,000 Faithful at the time. 'Towards the end of October, 1948, they proceeded to arrest the Byzantine Catholic Bishops, vicar generals, canons, and the majority of priests, about 600 in all. **The government then proceeded to the confiscation of churches, and convents of monks and religious**, in spite of their resistance.' On December 1 [1948], **the communist government published the decree suppressing the Eastern Catholic Church.**"[19] (*WTAF*, Vol. 3, pp. 255-256)

And this led to the "good being martyred," which has also been fulfilled:

THE GOOD WERE MARTYRED

It is simply a fact that countless Catholics were martyred at the hands of the Soviet Union and its communist satellites. Since this is well known, we won't give many quotes to prove the point. But it is significant to note again that even Frere Michel, whose work on Fatima is promoted by "Fr." Nicholas Gruner, admits that the "good will be martyred" has already occurred.

> Frere Michel de la Sainte Trinite, *The Whole Truth About Fatima*, Vol. 2, p. 764: "When, in a letter of January 21, 1940, **Sister Lucy mentioned in connection with the war '*the blood spilled by the martyrs,*'** which in the end would appease the divine wrath, and **when Our Lady announced in her Secret that '*the good will be martyred,*' how can we forget about these millions of Ukrainian or Polish Catholics martyred by the Bolsheviks?**"[20]

A prime example comes from Russia in 1923. At that time, Moscow attempted to blackmail the Vatican into granting its regime diplomatic recognition. Moscow gave orders for the arrest of high-placed cleric Msgr. Cieplak (apostolic administrator of the diocese of Mohilev), his vicar general, Msgr. Budkiewicz, and thirteen other priests. These clerics declared that they would not observe the 1922 law of the Soviet Union forbidding teaching the Catholic Faith to children (Warren H. Carroll, *The Rise and Fall of the Communist Revolution*, p. 310). Moscow agreed to their release if the Vatican agreed to diplomatic relations with its regime. The Russian regime knew that once the Vatican established diplomatic relations with it, the rest of Europe would follow. But the Vatican could not grant it such recognition, so Moscow executed the sentence:

> "**On Holy Thursday of 1923, Msgr. Budkiewicz was martyred with frightful cruelty. Brutally pushed across a dark corridor, he fell and broke his leg...** Stripped of his clothes and no longer able to walk, the martyr was dragged by the ears all the way to the detachment of guards. One of his ears had been severed. In the gaping hole, he was given a revolver shot.** Father Walsh... heard the shot ring out among shouts, drunken singing and bursts of laughter. So that no relics would remain, the martyr's body was burned and his ashes dispersed. And **this was the signal for a series of attacks against the hierarchy, clergy and laity, many of whom were sent to the icy prisons of Solowki on the Black Sea, where a concentration camp was specially assigned for Christians**; others died in prison, some of them reduced to madness by the torments they had endured."[21]

"...during the year 1922 alone more than 800 Catholic and Orthodox priests, brothers and nuns were shot in Russia."[22]

Pope Pius XI, *Letter to Cardinal Pompili*, Feb. 2, 1930: "**This past year during the Christmas holy days, not only were hundreds of churches [in Russia] closed, great numbers of icons burned, all workers and schoolchildren compelled to work and Sundays suppressed, but <u>they even compelled factory workers, both men and women, to sign a declaration of formal apostasy and hatred against God, or else be deprived of their bread rationing cards, without which every inhabitant of this poor country is reduced to dying of hunger, misery and cold</u>**. Among other things, in all the cities and in many villages... during the Christmas holy days last year: they witnessed a procession of tanks manned by numerous ruffians clad with sacred vestments, taking the cross in derision and spitting upon it while other armored cars transported huge Christmas trees, from which marionettes representing Catholic and Orthodox bishops were hung by the neck. In the center of the city, other young hoodlums committed all sorts of sacrileges against the cross."[23]

"**In 1946 the Soviet authorities removed every Lithuanian bishop but one from his diocese**... From 1946 to 1948, 357 priests – **one-third of all the priests in Lithuania – were deported to labor camps in Russia and Siberia. One of them, who had been sentenced to 25 years (which meant death**, since virtually no one survived more than ten years in the camps) **was offered his freedom, one of the largest churches in Vilinius, and 100,000 rubles if he would head a schismatic Lithuanian Catholic church. He refused, and disappears.**"[24] (Warren H. Carroll, *The Rise and Fall of the Communist Revolution*, pp. 364-365)

(As an aside, this priest could have been spared the horrors of the labor camps if he had simply consented to becoming an Eastern Schismatic. He refused, and suffered horribly. This shows us again the evil of false ecumenism. Post-Vatican II ecumenism, which accepts and praises Eastern Orthodoxy, holds that his martyrdom was pointless.)

dead bodies of Lithuanians after the Soviet Union eliminated those it deemed threats to full takeover

In 1936, the errors of Russian communism stirred up a revolution and the Spanish Civil War. What resulted was arguably the worst persecution of the Catholic Church in history:

"**Almost all at once the holocaust of Spain began [in 1936]. The chief target of the revolutionaries was... the Catholic Church**. During the next three months, <u>**the Catholic**</u>

> **priests, religious and laity who were caught in the half of Spain where the Republic retained control, were the victims of the bloodiest persecution the Church has experienced since that of the Roman Emperor Diocletian in the fourth century. In all, 6,549 priests and 283 nuns were martyred**, many in the classic circumstances of martyrdom, offered life if they renounced their faith and death if they upheld it."[25] (Warren H. Carroll, *The Rise and Fall of the Communist Revolution*, p. 285)

Hugh Thomas, considered the premier historian of the Spanish Civil War, gives us some details on these martyrdoms:

> "In Cervera, **rosary beads were forced into monks' ears till their eardrums were perforated… Certain persons were burned, and others buried, alive** – the latter after being forced to dig their own graves. At Alcazar de San Juan **a young man, distinguished for his piety, had his eyes dug out**. In that province, Ciudad Real, the crimes were indeed atrocious. **A crucifix was forced down the mouth of the mother of two Jesuits. Eight hundred persons were thrown down a mine shaft**."[26]

That the Spanish persecution was fueled and stirred up by the errors of Russia is beyond question; even some of the "attackers carried red banners with the hammer and sickle."[27]

One could multiply examples of the good being martyred for pages. For instance, after the Soviet Union's forced "reunification" of the schismatic "Church" with the Greek Catholic Church in 1945, there were countless Ukrainian Catholics who were martyred for their Faith:

> Cardinal Slipyi: "On April 11, 1945, **I was arrested with all the other bishops**. Less than a year later, over 800 priests had followed us into captivity. From March 8-10, 1946, the illegal Synod of Lvov took place. Under atheist pressure it proclaimed the 'reunification,' and by the very fact, **the official liquidation of our Church was effected by brutal force. The bishops were deported to every corner of the Soviet Union**. Almost all of them have died since then, or were killed in captivity… over 1,400 priests and 800 religious, to **tens of thousands of the Faithful who in captivity sealed, by the sacrifice of their life, their fidelity to the Pope, the Roman Apostolic See and the Universal Church**."[28]

It is a fact that doesn't need to be proven any further: the good were martyred in the Soviet Union, in its communist satellites, and in other countries, such as Spain, where the errors of Russia stirred up bloody persecution. **Our Lady's words that the good will be martyred, and various nations will be annihilated, have already been fulfilled.**

> *Our Lady: "If they listen to my requests, Russia will be converted and there will be peace. **If not she will scatter her errors through the world, provoking wars and persecutions of the Church. The good will be martyred**, the Holy Father will have much to suffer, various nations will be annihilated. In the end my Immaculate Heart will triumph. The Holy Father will consecrate Russia to me, and it will be converted and a certain period of peace will be granted to the world."*

> Sr. Lucy to Fr. Jongen, Feb. 1946: "**I think that now Our Lady's words are being fulfilled**: 'If this is not done (she had just recalled 'the exact request' of the Blessed Virgin) **Russia will spread her errors throughout the world**.'"[29] (*WTAF*, Vol. 3, p. 123)

Some also ask: what about the persecution of the Holy Father, who will "have much to suffer"? What is the meaning of this? We find the answer in the aforementioned message of Our Lord to Sr. Lucy from 1940:

> Our Lord to Sr. Lucy, Oct. 22, 1940: "**I will punish the nations for their crimes by means of war, famine and persecution of My Church and <u>this will weigh especially upon My Vicar on earth</u>. His Holiness will obtain an abbreviation of these days of tribulation** if he takes heed of My wishes by promulgating the Act of Consecration of the whole world to the Immaculate Heart of Mary, with a special mention of Russia."[30] (*WTAF*, Vol. 2, p. 732)

The persecution of the Church during this period – the torture and martyrdom of priests and faithful, the suppression of ecclesiastical activity – weighed as an incredible burden and torment on the pope who felt responsible, yet helpless, in the face of this tragedy. With these facts in mind, we can see that all four aspects of Our Lady's message, the spread of Russia's errors, the martyrdom of the good, the annihilation of nations and the suffering of the Holy Father, had their application to this period.

What people fail to realize is that Our Lady's request for the consecration of Russia <u>was given in this very same context</u>. The consecration and conversion of Russia was intended *to prevent the punishments and torments and persecutions of Russia mentioned in this context.* In line with Proverbs 16:7, and Sr. Lucy's summary of the Tuy vision, it means converting this enemy to peace from its ways of persecution.

That is why Our Lady came to Tuy in <u>1929</u> to ask for the consecration of Russia. In fact, Sr. Lucy didn't mention a word about Russia until 1929. **1929 was a time when the horrors of Stalin's Gulag started to become known in the world. It was a time when the persecutions of Russia were about to reach their apex.** 1929 was just prior to Stalin's policy of "dekulakization," a policy imposed from 1930-1934, which resulted in the deaths of millions of peasant farmers. 1929 was also just prior to Stalin's unspeakable imposed famine of 1933, which killed millions. **<u>It makes sense that Our Lady would come back to ask for the consecration of Russia in order to prevent these horrible persecutions when they were at, or were about to reach, their most gruesome point</u>**. The most serious demographers count at least fifteen million victims at the hands of Bolshevik Russia from the years 1929-1933.[31]

At this point, it's very important for us to look at what those errors of Russia had become. We need to get a closer look at the satanic regime of Communist Russia to get a better grasp on the context of the message of Our Lady.

WHAT RUSSIA WAS CONVERTED FROM – SNAPSHOTS OF THE SATANIC REGIME IN COMMUNIST RUSSIA

Vladimir Lenin, maker of the Communist revolution, mass-murderer, and leader of Communist Russia from 1917-1924

In 1917, Lenin closed all Catholic churches in Petrograd.[32] In 1918, Lenin shut down all newspapers in Moscow except those published by the Communists. This was soon extended to all printed material, including periodicals, etc.[33]

"In 1918, one could read the following words in the official organ of the Soviet of Petrograd: **'We will render our hearts cruel, harsh, without pity. We will open the dams of this bloody sea. Without pity, without mercy, we will kill our enemies by the thousands. We will drown them in their own blood.'**"[34]

A decree of February 26, 1922 confiscated all the treasures of the Church, including consecrated objects. At the same time, and this was still the very early stage of the Bolshevik horrors, Cardinal Mercier published the first figures of the persecution: "Statistics for the victims of the persecution are frightening. Since November 1917, 260,000 simple soldier prisoners and 54,000 officers; 18,000 landed proprietors; 35,000 'intellectuals'; 192,000 workers; 815,000 peasants; 28 bishops and 1,215 priests were put to death."[35] (*WTAF*, Vol. 2, p. 451)

Things were so bad in Russia in 1922, that Pope Pius XI published the apostolic letter *Annus Fere*, ordering a general collection in favor of the starving Russian people. In it, he spoke of the horrors suffered by the Russian people. Though he didn't denounce the satanic Communist regime in Russia by name, Pius XI spoke of "the extreme misery of the Russian people, who were decimated by disease and famine, **victims of the greatest calamity in history**…"[36] (*WTAF*, Vol. 2, p. 565)

Shortly after taking over Russia, in 1919 Lenin established the Gulag. The Gulag was a network of concentration camps to which all "enemies" of the State could be sent.

> "**In April 1919**, following Dzerzhinsky's recommendation and with Lenin's approval, <u>**the Soviet government ordered the establishment of a network of concentration camps**</u>, **at least one per province, the first of its kind in history**, which served as a model and inspiration to Hitler and his Nazis <u>**and was later to become infamous as the GULAG.**</u> **By 1923 the number of these camps had reached 315.**"[37] (Warren H. Carroll, *The Rise and Fall of the Communist Revolution*, p. 142)

It's important for us to get a glimpse of the horrors of the Gulag. For this purpose, we will quote from Warren H. Carroll who, in turn, draws from Alexander Solzhenitsyn's famed work, *The Gulag Archipelago*.

Alexander Solzhenitsyn as Gulag labor camp prisoner

> "The famine dealt out death at home, or as far away from home as dying men could walk. <u>**The labor camps dealt out death afar**</u>… **It seems almost presumptuous for any man to write of the gulag, after Alexander Solzhenitsyn. He was in it; he made its theme his own; he changed the world and history by what he wrote about it**… **Here we can only select, here and there, from Solzhenitsyn, and annotate him – to give a bit of**

the sense, the flavor, the sound of the wind from hell that blew across those killing grounds in the wilderness."[38] (Warren H. Carroll, *The Rise and Fall of the Communist Revolution*, p. 243)

Carroll then proceeds to describe the labor camp at Orotukan:

"**We may begin with Orotukan.** In the middle of the second volume of *The Gulag Archipelago*, Solzhenitsyn concludes a brief description of Orotukan **(which he then locates only by a reference to the Kolyma River in far northern Siberia)**, whose horrors sound as bad but no worse than those of many other labor camps he has described, with this one stark sentence: '*All* **who survived Orotukan say they would have preferred the gas chamber.'** *All* **who were there and survived, and spoke about it, say they would have preferred death to survival?**... On the far side of the Chersky Range from Yakutsk, the Kolyma River flowed into the Arctic Ocean. It flowed, that is, during the summer. In the winter it was a ribbon of ice, top to bottom; for **the country around the Cherksy Range is the coldest spot on earth except for the center of Antarctica... On the Kolyma, the average winter temperature is sixty degrees below zero. Seventy-five below is common**...

"Until November they had only shelters made of branches to live in, and were given no clothing but what they had arrived in. Then they were given wooden barracks with walls made of single boards without insulation. There were stoves for heating, but the laborers had to cut their own wood – at thirty and forty and fifty degrees below zero – after completing their day's work. These, still at Magadan, were the lucky ones. **The less fortunate were sent to begin building the road to Kolyma – in the middle of the winter**... There were no barracks there, only tents and branch huts. **Patrolling dogs prevented escape. Some of the camps on the route to the Kolyma were wiped out to the last man and dog – not only did all the slave laborers die, but also all of the guards**...

A man who froze to death at a Gulag labor camp

"As soon as the ice melted in the Gulf of Okhotsk more ships began arriving carrying more 'kulaks,' saboteurs, wreckers, and other undesirable folk from the country... When the ice melted at the end of the spring in 1934, the *Dzhurma* finally arrived at the mouth of the Kolyma. **Every one of the 12,000 prisoners aboard had died**. Nearly all the crew survived. But on their return to Vladivostok, half of them had to be treated for 'mental disorders.' What had they seen?

"Orotukan was built as a punishment camp for those laborers on the Kolyma who survived and proved particularly intractable. Conditions at Orotukan, therefore, had to be made worse than at any of the other camps in the region. <u>**Solzhenitsyn tells us that every hut at Orotukan was surrounded on three sides by piles of frozen corpses.**</u> **The grand total death toll at the camps on the Kolyma was approximately three million. Every year, one-third of the prisoners in its camps died**; almost none survived more than four continuous years there. At least one man died for every kilogram of gold extracted from the Kolyma mines..."[39] (Warren H. Carroll, *The Rise and Fall of the Communist Revolution*, pp. 243-245)

Carroll also describes the Belomor Canal labor camps:

"The Belomor Canal labor force numbered about 300,000 at its peak, not counting the almost equally large number who died of overwork, mistreatment, undernourishment, or camp-induced disease, and were replaced as fast as they fell. **The death rate was 700 per day; but new prisoners came in to the camps in the Belomor Canal area at the rate of 1,500 per day. Average survival time was two years**... D.P. Vitkovsky, a Solovetsky prisoner himself who was a work supervisor on the canal, describes with calm and deadly precision the working conditions and their results, even for those who were not labor camp inmates:

'<u>**At the end of the workday there were corpses left on the work site**</u>. The snow powdered their faces. **One of them was hunched over beneath an overturned wheelbarrow; <u>he had hidden his hands in his sleeves and frozen to death in that position</u>**. Someone had frozen with his head bent down between his knees. <u>**Two were frozen back to back leaning against each other**</u>. They were peasant lads and the best workers one could possibly imagine. They were sent to the canal in tens of thousands at a time, and the authorities tried to work things out so no one got to the same subcamp as his father; they tried to break up families. **And right off they gave them norms of shingle and boulders that you'd be unable to fulfill even in summer**. No one was able to teach them anything, to warn them; and in their village simplicity <u>they gave all their strength to their work and weakened very swiftly and froze to death, embracing in pairs. At night the sledges went out and collected them.</u> **The drivers threw the corpses onto the sledges with a dull clonk**. And in the summer bones remained from corpses which had not been removed in time, and together with the shingle they got into the concrete mixer."[40] (Warren H. Carroll, *The Rise and Fall of the Communist Revolution*, pp. 248-249)

Besides the countless people who were sent off to the labor camps and other regions from within Russia, the Soviet Union deported massive amounts of people from other countries which it occupied, in order to pave the way for the full takeover of these States. People from Poland, the Baltic States, etc. were deported and dumped into regions where they had to fend for themselves, or they were sent to the labor camps. This resulted in atrocious suffering and the deaths of countless Catholics:

"Massive deportations had already begun in Soviet-occupied Poland. **In February 1940 more than 200,000 people, most families, had been moved to northern European Russia, where they were dumped in small villages or thinly populated countryside where they had to fend for themselves**; in April a still larger number, <u>about 320,000 of the wives and children whose husbands and fathers had already been executed or consigned to labor camps, were sent to the wastes of Kazakhstan where most of the children died</u>; in June a quarter of a million more were sent to Siberia."[41] (Warren H. Carroll, *The Rise and Fall of the Communist Revolution*, p. 318)

Joseph Stalin, arguably the greatest mass-murderer in history, leader of Communist Russia from 1924-1953

From 1930-1934, Stalin instituted the policy of "dekulakization." Farmers that were opposed, or perceived as threats, to the Communist policy of collectivization of farms were dubbed "kulaks" and liquidated. This unspeakable tragedy resulted in the deaths of 14.5 million:

> "Who were these 'kulaks'?... **In May 1929 the Council of People's Commissars formally defined a kulak as any farmer who made any money whatsoever from any source or activity other than the sale of agricultural produce grown in his own fields.** Any outside income, any processing of goods done on the farm (as by a small hand-operated mill), was sufficient to make a kulak. **When the campaign of liquidation was launched in 1930, <u>from ten to fifteen per cent of the small farmers in every region were arbitrarily dubbed kulaks and liquidated</u>.** If there were not enough of them fitting the May 1929 definition, others had to be added to fill up the quota. They could be selected by income level, actual or apparent; by leadership in local villages... by opposition to forced collectivization (a particularly frequent reason for designation as a kulak); or simply by being devout Christians... <u>**It was the first act of a farm holocaust from 1930 to 1934 that took ten million lives by Stalin's own estimate**</u> given to U.S. President Franklin Roosevelt at Yalta, **<u>and an estimated 14.5 million when all the victims, including those sent to the labor camps and dying there later, are taken into account</u>**."[42] (Warren H. Carroll, *The Rise and Fall of the Communist Revolution*, pp. 224-225)

Here is the harrowing account of Miron Dolot. Dolot witnessed the deportations of these "kulaks" from his hometown to the labor camps and other regions:

"**A cold wind blew snow on the unfortunates, who were not properly dressed**, for they had not been allowed to take warm clothing with them. <u>**We wanted to help somehow, and since we could assume that they would be banished to Siberia**</u>, we had to get them some heavy clothing… **Under careful supervision of soldiers, a score of sleighs moved into the square**. They were to take the arrested farmers out of the village. Loading of six to eight persons to a sleigh started immediately, controlled through the use of a list… **husbands were separated from their wives, and children from their parents**… <u>**As one sleigh moved to join a column, a young man sprang from it and raced toward another sleigh in which his helpless and weeping wife and children were riding**</u>. The father obviously wanted to be with his family, but he did not reach them. **Comrade Pashchenko**, the chairman of the village soviet who was supervising the whole action, **raised his revolver and calmly fired. The young father dropped dead into the snow, and the sleigh carrying his widow and orphans moved on.**"[43] (Warren H. Carroll, *The Rise and Fall of the Communist Revolution*, pp. 227-228)

"There are reports of 'kulaks' on trains to Kazakhstan or Siberia, locked in cars each carrying fifty of them, with a loaf of bread and a pail of tea or thin soup per day per ten people (on days when it was delivered), crawling with vermin, unheated in winter, suffocatingly hot in summer, throwing their dying babies out the windows to put an end to their suffering."[44] (Warren H. Carroll, *The Rise and Fall of the Communist Revolution*, p. 228)

In 1933, in order to starve millions in the Ukraine, Stalin imposed ridiculous grain quotas on the collective farms. The grain quotas imposed by Moscow were impossible to meet. But in an attempt to comply with Moscow's demands, all the available grain in the Ukraine was shipped off. The result was that millions were left without food, to starve and to die. To cover for his crime, Stalin falsely accused the Ukrainians of hoarding grain.

Children in the largely Catholic Ukraine, left to starve and to die in the famine

"**The cold hard essence of the situation was this**: the Ukrainian farmers were going to die; and the Communist operatives feared death, or purging, or the labor camps if they did not let them die. **They knew there was no grain. Everybody knew it. But no one dared say it… Meanwhile the people were eating rats, mice, sparrows, snails, ants, and earthworms, leather and shoe soles, old skins and furs, ground-up bones, acacia bark and nettles.** By March, in many areas, even most of these things were gone, and there was nothing at all left to eat. A ghastly silence fell over the countryside; there were no animals to make any sound, and the people still alive rarely spoke. Victor Kravchenko, then a Party activist sent to Ukraine, who later repudiated communism and escaped to freedom, recalled what he had seen:

'Here I saw people dying in solitude by slow degrees, dying hideously, without the excuse of sacrifice for a cause. They had been trapped and left to starve, each in his own home, by a political decision made in a far-off capital around conference and banquet tables. There was not even the consolation of inevitability to relieve the horror. The most terrifying sights were the little children with skeleton limbs dangling from balloon-like abdomens. Starvation had wiped every trace of youth from their faces, turning them into tortured gargoyles; only in their eyes still lingered the reminder of childhood. Everywhere we found men and women lying prone, their faces and bellies bloated, their eyes utterly expressionless… <u>**Some five million Ukrainians died in this genocidal, deliberate famine**</u>."[45] (Warren H. Carroll, *The Rise and Fall of the Communist Revolution*, pp. 240-241)

The truth about the Consecration and Conversion of Russia

At this point we can clearly see why, on July 13, 1917, Our Lady mentioned persecutions of *"war, of hunger, and of persecution of the Church and of the Holy Father. To prevent this I come to ask the consecration of Russia…"*

These facts should show us clearly the context in which Our Lady requested the consecration of Russia, and how the conversion of Russia means a conversion of this regime to peace from its persecutions of war, of hunger, of the Church, etc.

HE WILL DO THE CONSECRATION, BUT IT WILL BE "LATE" – FITS POPE PIUS XII

It is certain that Pope Pius XI failed to consecrate Russia to Our Lady's Immaculate Heart. Pope Pius XII also failed to do so for many years, but (as we saw) he finally did consecrate Russia in 1952.

> Our Lord to Sister Lucy, Summer, 1931: **"Like the King of France they will repent and do it, but it will be late. Russia will have already spread its errors throughout the world provoking wars and persecutions against the Church**: the Holy Father will have much to suffer."[46] (quoted in *The Whole Truth About Fatima*, Vol. 2, pp. 543-544)

> Pope Pius XII, *Sacro Vergente Anno* (Apostolic Letter), July 7, 1952: **"…just as a few years ago We consecrated the entire human race to the Immaculate Heart of the Virgin Mary, Mother of God, so today We consecrate and in a most special manner We entrust all the peoples of Russia to this Immaculate Heart**…"[47]

It's clear that, as most commentators agree, Our Lord's words *"They"* will repent and do it apply to the line of popes – just as popes in encyclicals refer to themselves as "We." (*"They" cannot refer to the pope and all the bishops, because all the bishops did not delay the request and therefore do not need to repent of delaying it.*)

That Pope Pius XII was the one who did it, but "late," makes perfect sense. First, Pope Pius XII consecrated the world to the Immaculate Heart of Mary in 1942. Ten years later, however, he "repented and did it" by specifically consecrating Russia.

Second, in 1939 Russia was still the only Communist nation on earth, but **in the next decade the Soviet Union overtook Estonia, Latvia and Lithuania (1940), Bulgaria (1944), Poland (1945), Romania (1945) and Hungary (1946).** Perhaps these developments – in addition to a specific request – caused Pius XII to "repent and do it." Thus, Our Lord's words that "Russia will have already spread its errors throughout the world provoking wars and persecutions against the Church" fit precisely to Pius XII; **for what Heaven had intended to prevent by the consecration of Russia – the spread of Communism, and the Soviet Union's annihilation of nations and martyrdom of the good – had, to a large extent, already occurred when he did it**.

Third, there may be another signal that Pope Pius XII (though he certainly did it late) would be the one who would actually consecrate Russia to the Immaculate Heart of Mary. This signal comes in the amazing coincidence that Pope Pius XII was consecrated a bishop the very day (and, according to Frere Michel, the very same hour) that Our Lady first appeared at Fatima.

> William Thomas Walsh, *Our Lady of Fatima*, 1954, p. 52 (note 1): **"It is an interesting coincidence that Monsignor Eugenio Pacelli [Pius XII] was being consecrated Bishop**

at the Sistine Chapel in Rome on May 13, 1917, the very day when the children [first] saw the Lady of Fatima."[48]

Fourth, a careful consideration of Our Lady's words reveals that the actual fulfillment of the consecration of Russia would not be in perfect conformity with Heaven's original requests, which coincides with the fact that Pius XII did it, but "late" and not with all the bishops.

OUR LADY'S WORDS REVEAL TO US THAT HER TRIUMPH IS NOT A UNIVERSAL TRIUMPH OR REIGN OF PEACE, BUT ONLY A "CERTAIN" PERIOD OF PEACE

"If they listen to my requests, Russia will be converted and *there will be peace."*	*"In the end* my Immaculate Heart will triumph. The Holy Father will consecrate Russia to me, and it will be converted and **a certain period of peace** will be granted to the world."

Please notice this extremely important point! In the Secret of July 13, Our Lady first expresses a conditional promise. "If they listen to my requests, Russia will be converted and there will be **peace**." If her requests are fulfilled precisely, she says that there will be "peace." But when speaking of **what will actually happen "In the end,"** she adds something, and declares that it will only be a "*certain*" period of peace!

Why does Our Lady add the word "certain" when telling us what will actually happen in the end, and not (on the left) when telling us what would happen if her requests were fulfilled precisely? **It's obviously because what would happen with the consecration of Russia would not be in perfect conformity with her original requests!** The consecration would be "late," and not with all the bishops! Thus, as Our Lady's words prove, the triumph of Our Lady is not a universal triumph or reign of peace, as so many have suggested and promoted, **but rather a "certain" period of peace – a mitigated, less profound period of peace than what Heaven would have granted if "they listened" to her requests and fulfilled them precisely.** This is similar to the message of Fatima on August 19th, when Our Lady told the children: "If you had not been taken away [by the Administrator on Aug. 13] to the City, the miracle [of Oct. 13th] would have been greater."[49] She told the children that their arrest on August 13th by the evil administrator of Ourem, which prevented them from being at the apparition site that day, caused the miracle on Oct. 13th to be less profound than what it would have been. Likewise, the pope doing the consecration of Russia "late" and not with all the bishops caused its conversion to peace not to be as profound as it would have been – but only to a "certain" period of peace.

THE CONVERSION OF RUSSIA = THE CONVERSION OF THE SATANIC REGIME IN RUSSIA TO A CERTAIN PERIOD OF PEACE FROM ITS PERSECUTION OF THE CHURCH, ETC.

In this article we've seen that Our Lady's words about the conversion of Russia parallel Proverbs 16:7, which speak of a conversion of an enemy, not to the true Faith, but to peace from its persecuting ways.

| Proverbs 16:7- "When the ways of man shall please the Lord, He will convert even his enemies to peace." | Our Lady: "If they listen to my requests, Russia will be converted and there will be peace." |

We've also seen that Sr. Lucy's summary of the Tuy vision confirms that this is what Our Lady meant by her words: *"In the end my Immaculate Heart will triumph. The Holy Father will consecrate Russia to me, and it will be converted and a certain period of peace will be granted to the world."*

> Sr. Lucy to Fr. Goncalves, summarizing the Tuy Vision: "**The good Lord promises to end the persecution in Russia**, if the Holy Father will himself make a solemn act of reparation and consecration of Russia to the Sacred Hearts of Jesus and Mary, as well as ordering all the bishops of the Catholic Church to do the same."[50] (*The Whole Truth About Fatima*, Vol. 2, p. 465)

We've also seen that Our Lady specifically requested the consecration of Russia to prevent Russia's stirring up of wars, persecutions of the Church, etc.

> *"The war is going to end. But if they do not stop offending God, another and worse war will begin in the reign of Pius XI. When you shall see a night illuminated by an unknown light, know that it is a great sign that God gives you that He is going to punish the world for its crimes by means of war, of hunger, and of persecution of the Church and of the Holy Father. To prevent this I come to ask the consecration of Russia to my Immaculate Heart and the Communion of reparation on the first Saturdays..."*

We've also seen that Heaven revealed that the actual fulfillment of the consecration of Russia would not be fully in accord with Heaven's original request.

> Our Lord to Sister Lucy, Summer, 1931: "**Like the King of France they will repent and do it, but it will be late. Russia will have already spread its errors throughout the world provoking wars and persecutions against the Church**: the Holy Father will have much to suffer."[51]

We've also seen that Our Lady's words about her triumph over Russia do not promise a universal or ideal reign of peace, as so many have suggested, but only a certain period of peace – one that is inferior to the peace that she would have given if her requests were fulfilled precisely.

| *"If they listen to my requests*, Russia will be converted and *there will be peace."* | *"In the end* my Immaculate Heart will triumph. The Holy Father will consecrate Russia to me, and it will be converted and **a certain** period of peace will be granted to the world." |

We've also seen that Pope Pius XII clearly consecrated Russia to the Immaculate Heart of Mary in 1952.

> Pope Pius XII, *Sacro Vergente Anno* (Apostolic Letter), July 7, 1952: "**…just as a few years ago We consecrated the entire human race to the Immaculate Heart of the Virgin Mary, Mother of God, <u>so today We consecrate and in a most special manner We entrust all the peoples of Russia to this Immaculate Heart</u>…**"[52]

We've also seen that another vision of Sr. Lucy shows that the conversion of Russia means a conversion to a certain period of peace from the era of persecution:

> Our Lord to Sr. Lucy, Oct. 22, 1940: "I will punish the nations for their crimes by means of war, famine and persecution of My Church and this will weigh especially upon My Vicar on earth. **His Holiness will obtain an abbreviation of these days of tribulation** if he takes heed of My wishes by promulgating the Act of Consecration of the whole world to the Immaculate Heart of Mary, with a special mention of Russia."[53] (*WTAF*, Vol. 2, p. 732)

In conclusion, we can answer the question about the consecration of Russia by stating that it is a fact that Russia has been consecrated to the Immaculate Heart of Mary by Pope Pius XII. **It is also a fact that Russia has been converted from its regime of persecution and the horrors which Our Lady specifically requested the consecration to prevent to a** *certain* **period of peace. The era of persecution of the Church in Russia and in all of its satellites – the era of the Gulag, the imposed famines, the martyrdom of priests, the annihilation of small nations annexed to the Soviet Union, the overt and vigorous persecution of the Church, etc. – formally came to an end with the dissolution of the Soviet Union – and the collapse of its satellites – on Christmas Day, 1991**. This astonishing transformation occurred <u>within one generation of Pope Pius XII's consecration of Russia in 1952</u>. Below are three different sources corroborating the fact that the collapse of the Soviet Union officially occurred on Christmas:

> "After <u>**the dissolution of the Soviet Union on 25 December, 1991**</u>, the Russian Federation claimed to be the legal successor to the Soviet state on the international stage despite its loss of superpower status. Russian foreign policy repudiated Marxism-Leninism as a guide to action, soliciting Western support for capitalist reforms in post-Soviet Russia." [54] (http://en.wikipedia.org/wiki/Soviet_Union#History)

> "…<u>**Gorbachev formally resigned his now vanished office of President of the Soviet Union on December 25, the day of the official transfer of all power from the Soviet Union to the Russian republic in the Kremlin**</u>**, solemnized by a flag change in the early evening**. That change took place at 7:35 p.m. It was the stuff of dreams for some, who had imagined how it might happen on some far-off glorious day, but had never expected it so soon. Floodlit against the darkness, the red flag with the hammer and sickle whipped and crackled in the Arctic wind. For seventy-four years it had flown over the Kremlin, vivid and terrible symbol of the ultimate revolution for which the Kremlin was headquarters. Now its day was done. The world watched on television. The cameras focused. The tricolor of pre-revolutionary Russia was made ready for raising. As the bloody banner of man-made apocalypse came fluttering down the Kremlin flagpole under the radiant stars of Christmas night, the Communist Revolution in the West was dead."[55] (Warren H. Carroll, *The Rise and Fall of the Communist Revolution*, p. 778)

> "**On Dec. 25 [1991],** Gorbachev resigned as president of the USSR and was not replaced; **on the same day the United States recognized the remaining republics of the USSR as independent nations**."[56] (http://www.answers.com/topic/union-of-soviet-socialist-republics)

Now, there are some who assert that the collapse of the Soviet Union and the fall of its Communist satellites was all a master-plan of the Communists to deceive the West. Communists still rule, they say, but they simply have a Western style of government, which doesn't persecute the Church, allows freedoms, abolished the Gulag, etc. in order to gain funds from the West. That's quite a conspiracy theory, but this is the position of many, including former KGB agent Anatoliy Golitsyn in *The Perestroika Deception*. Even those who hold this view (we do not, as we will explain below) are still admitting (regardless of *why* they think it has occurred in Russia and in all of its satellites) **that the era of persecution in Russia and its satellites is over**, thus proving the point. As Sr. Lucy put it: "The good Lord promises to end the persecution in Russia," and this has occurred. And this cessation of the persecution of the Church in Russia and in all of its satellites **represents a significant triumph of Our Lady's Immaculate Heart over the satanic Russian regime**, which was poised to, and probably would have (according to Sr. Lucy's statement to William Thomas Walsh), overtaken the entire earth if the Russian regime had not been converted beforehand. We believe this is why the official dissolution of the Soviet Union occurred on Christmas; it was a sign that the conversion of this enemy into something else and to a certain period of peace from its persecutions, etc. was a triumph of Heaven. (And those who don't think that the conversion of Russia to a certain period of peace from its era of persecution is somehow "good enough" or "big enough" to be what Our Lady meant, then I suggest they re-read those passages on the situation in Russia and its satellites during that period, and ask themselves how they would have liked to be in Gulag prison camp at Orotukan, or in the Ukraine during the famine, or deported from Lithuania to the wastes of Siberia.)

Even an article carried on "Fr." Gruner's own website is forced to admit that the Soviet Union has "converted"!

> Cornelia Ferreira, "Commentary on The Perestroika Deception by Anatoliy Golitsyn," *Catholic Family News*, March, 1996: "In order to increase Communist representation and influence in the UN, the European Union and international financial organizations, **the Soviet Union was deliberately converted into independent republics**."[57]

We don't know **what more one needs to prove that Russia (the Soviet Union) was "converted"** into something else, which resulted in a certain period of peace from its persecutions, etc., than seeing this fact admitted in publications such as these! These are the publications that would be the most opposed to the thesis of this article, yet *even they are compelled to admit that with the dissolution of the Soviet Union in 1991 a "conversion" of the regime has taken place*! This "conversion" that has occurred with the Soviet Union, regardless of why you think it has occurred, has brought an end to the particular era of persecution and the things which Our Lady specifically requested the consecration to prevent. This is an undeniable fact.

That's why it's irrelevant for people such as Nicholas Gruner and his followers to continually bring up the fact that Russia is presently rife with immorality, abortion, pornography, etc. That is certainly true, but it is beside the point. Our Lady never promised that Russia would be converted to a good nation or to a Catholic one, but rather, as shown again and again in this article, she spoke of its conversion in the context of a *conversion of an enemy from its persecuting ways*, along the lines of Proverbs 16:7. This has occurred. Just ask anyone who lives, for instance, in the Czech Republic today as opposed to under Communism.

Shortly we will take a look at how things changed in each of the satellites of the Soviet Union. These facts will show us that even if the liberalizing policies of glasnost (openness) and perestroika (restructuring) – which were adopted by the Soviet Union in 1980's – were *intended* as a deception by the higher-ups in the Communist Party, the fact is that the plan backfired. For once these ideas were promoted and put somewhat into action, they caught on with the people behind the Communist Bloc, and the momentum for freedom from Communist tyranny became unstoppable.

THE FALL OF THE SATELLITES

The Fall of Poland:

> "**In 1956 the régime became more liberal, freeing many people from prison and expanding some personal freedoms**. In 1970 the government was changed. It was a time when the economy was more modern, and the government had large credits. **Labor turmoil in 1980 led to the formation of the independent trade union, "Solidarity", which over time became a political force. It eroded the dominance of the Communist Party;** by 1989 it had triumphed in parliamentary elections, and Lech Wałęsa, a Solidarity candidate, eventually won the presidency in 1990. The Solidarity movement greatly contributed to the soon-following collapse of Communism all over Eastern Europe."[58] (http://en.wikipedia.org/wiki/Poland#History)

What further corroborates that Russia was converting from its satanic regime of persecutions to a certain period of peace is the fact that, as Poland began to free itself from Communist domination, **Russia did not roll in the tanks to restore order and re-assert the dominance of the Communist Party, as it had done in the past;** whereas in China, during the same period, when demonstrators for Democracy got "out of hand," the Chinese regime sent in the force to restore order by means of the Tiananmen Square Massacre.

The Fall of Hungary:

> "**Then in May [1989] the reform-minded Hungarian Communist government took a step unprecedented for a Communist country. It opened the national border with Austria**. The cement and barbed-wire barricades which held the people of Hungary inside their oppressed land… were taken down… On October 7 the conference [of the Hungarian Communist Party] voted 1,005-159 to abandon Leninist ideology and rename itself the Hungarian Socialist Party. A few days later the Hungarian parliament dropped the Communist-imposed name 'People's Republic' for their country… **The parliament changed the constitution to provide for a multi-party system**. The direct election of a president was approved… **On the 33rd anniversary of the Budapest uprising of 1956, October 23, 1989, Hungary officially proclaimed itself free of Soviet domination. Free elections to parliament were held in March and April 1990**. Despite a plethora of parties, the Communists, with just eight per cent of the vote, came in fourth. Historian Josef Antall, head of Democratic Forum, became prime minister of a non-Communist coalition government of Hungary in May 1990."[59] (Warren H. Carroll, *The Rise and Fall of the Communist Revolution*, pp. 735-736)

The Fall of East Germany:

> "**Rapidly as the momentum of change in the Communist world was building in the last four months of 1989, it seemed unlikely to most observers that there would be any fundamental alteration in the status of Communist East Germany soon**. Conventional wisdom held that the Soviet Union, even under Gorbachev, would not and could not afford to let go this large portion of the population and territory of their supreme enemy during two world wars, and certainly would never permit the reunification of Germany. **The boss of East Germany, Erich Honecker, was the toughest Communist leader west of China**… [he] had ruled his artificial country with an iron hand for the past eighteen

years. He had helped to build the Berlin Wall and had given repeated orders to 'shoot to kill' anyone trying to cross it, above or below, which took the lives of over two hundred men and women desperately fleeing his tyranny.

(top) guards on the Berlin Wall, ready to shoot anyone who crossed
(bottom) the lighted "death strip," painted white so that anyone crossing would be easy to see and shoot

"In Honecker's capital, **the Berlin Wall loomed as a constant reminder that travel to the West was prohibited to all but an officially favored few in East Germany**. But travel to 'fraternal socialist countries' was permitted. **The problem, for Honecker, was that by the end of the summer of 1989 two of those countries – Poland and Hungary – were ceasing to be fraternally socialist**. Hungary in particular was a favorite vacation spot for East Germans who could afford to travel. And Hungary now had an open border with Austria, beyond which lay West Germany.

By August the West German embassy in Budapest [Hungary] was besieged by persons requesting entry to West Germany and assistance in obtaining documents that would allow them to leave Hungary legally. On September 11, tired of grappling with this foreign problem while its own momentous changes were in process, **the Hungarian government announced that all East Germans then in Hungary, and any who wished to do so in the future, might cross the Austrian border without restraint. And the outward flood began.**"[60] (Warren H. Carroll, *The Rise and Fall of the Communist Revolution*, pp. 736-737)

Let us stop right here and summarize the point that is being made. Without special permission, **travel from behind the Iron Curtain was strictly forbidden during the reign of the Soviet Union. But travel to fellow Communist satellites was not forbidden. Thus, once Poland and (more significantly in this regard) Hungary (two Communist satellites) had fallen from Communist domination** (as we saw above), there was a problem.

(not pictured here is the USSR to the right of Poland and Czechoslovakia, and Communist Romania to the lower right of Hungary)

Hungary had opened its border with Austria, and East Germans in Hungary flooded to the West via Austria. Thus, if one wanted to escape to free West Germany, all he had to do was get to Hungary, cross the (now open) border of Austria, and go to West Germany. One can see how this situation couldn't last long, and would spell the end for the Communist Bloc's imprisonment of peoples.

> "**News of this spread fast**. Second to Hungary as a favorite travel destination for East Germans was Czechoslovakia, particularly Prague. **Czechoslovakia was still under hard-line Communist control. But its leaders could read the newspapers; they did not want foreigners stirring up trouble at such a time.** <u>After several thousand East German tourists crowded into the West German embassy in Prague and began camping around it, demanding to go to West Germany</u>, the Czech authorities told the West German Foreign Minister they would let them go if Honecker agreed. In a moment of fantasy which defies rational explanation, Honecker did agree on the absurd condition that the trains carrying the refugees should all be routed through East Germany, sealed. **This produced scenes of more and more people in East German cities frantically trying to climb aboard the sealed trains as they passed through – as many as ten thousand in Dresden alone.**"[61] (Warren H. Carroll, *The Rise and Fall of the Communist Revolution*, p. 738)

Not all the East Germans who wanted to flee to the West could reach Hungary, but some of them could get to Czechoslovakia. Seeing that others from their oppressed country had fled from Communist tyranny via Hungary, they besieged the West German embassy in Communist Czechoslovakia to let them go, and they camped out at the embassy. Not wanting to be troubled by a refugee situation, the Czechoslovakian government agreed to let them go if Honecker (the Communist leader of East Germany) agreed. Incredibly, he did agree – probably to save his Czechoslovakian comrades the trouble of having to deal with a refugee crisis. At that point, so many East Germans started to take advantage that Honecker banned all travel by East Germans to Czechoslovakia. This was futile:

> "On October 3 [1989] Honecker banned all travel by East Germans to Czechoslovakia. <u>But he had no wall on the Czech border; it was a fraternal socialist state.</u>"[62] (Warren H. Carroll, *The Rise and Fall of the Communist Revolution*, p. 738)

One can only imagine the enthusiasm at this point in the satellite States. Seeing that others in Poland and Hungary had been liberated from Communist domination, they longed that much more for freedom from its tyranny. The momentum was unstoppable. Huge crowds gathered in Leipzig to protest the Communist Government in East Germany.

"The anniversary ceremonies took place on October 8… The next day was Monday – prayer and rally time at St. Nicholas Church in Leipzig. **And this day there were no less than fifty thousand people present**, as though sprung up from the polluted East German earth. **Honecker had seen it coming. He had assembled a large force of secret police, regular police, and soldiers in Leipzig and had issued them live ammunition, with instructions to use whatever force was required to break up the demonstration. Another Tiananmen Square loomed. But the order to fire did not come**… But he [Honecker] adamantly refused to renounce the use of deadly force against the crowds. At a critical meeting of the East German Politburo October 10, only two members supported Honecker in this. Even hard old lifelong Communists argued against a 'Chinese solution.'… Honecker raged in vain. Three days later he issued a vague and uncharacteristic statement promising economic reforms, more consumer goods and expanded rights to travel… **On October 16 the number of Monday demonstrators in Leipzig tripled to 150,000. On the next day the East German Politburo met again… Most of the other Politburo members knew the game was up. There was to be no help from the Soviet Union**…"

Huge crowds in Leipzig protesting the East German Communist government

"The East German army, which had never fired a gun in anger and was not and never had been defending a real country, could not be counted on in a crisis. If the crowds in Leipzig had tripled to 150,000 in one week, how many might be there next Monday? Willi Stoph, the 75-year-old prime minister, belled the cat. **He told Honecker he must resign. The next day he did, citing reasons of health… If Erich Honecker could not maintain communism in East Germany, no one else could. The Party, for so long and until so recently almighty, fell like a sand castle in the rain.** On October 30 three hundred thousand marched after the Monday prayers in Leipzig; on November 4 half a million rallied for freedom in East Berlin, demanding effective restraints on the power of the government. On November 7 the entire East German government resigned, and Honecker was dismissed from the Politburo…

"In the dissolving chaos, some anonymous government official issued a statement that 'private trips abroad can be requested without fulfilling requirements.' No one knew what it meant, probably including the official who wrote it; **but crowds surging up to the Berlin Wall shouted it like a slogan, and the border guards did not know what it meant either. Late in the evening of November 9 the officers commanding them at the Wall decided to let the pressing people through**. By midnight hundreds of thousands were pouring through the opened gates, rejoicing and celebrating wildly, bashing chunks off the wall with improvised hammers. Government officials cut a huge hole in the wall at Potsdamer Platz. **On November 11 no less than a million East Germans flooded into West Berlin on foot and by every mode of transportation... No one any longer tried to stop them**... **On December 3 the entire Politburo resigned and Honecker was arrested. The [Communist] Party almost dissolved itself completely on the spot**... East Germany now had no future. In the course of 1990 it slipped unmourned into history as, contrary to all previous expectations and punditry, **Germany was fully reunified with no significant opposition from anyone, not even the Soviet government**."[63] (Warren H. Carroll, *The Rise and Fall of the Communist Revolution*, pp. 738-740)

The Fall of Czechoslovakia:

"**The fall of the Berlin Wall tolled the knell for Communist rule in Czechoslovakia**. On November 17 a student-led rally of 17,000 in Prague's broad Wenceslas Square demanded the elimination of the 'leading role' of the Czechoslovak Communist Party. Police beat some of the demonstrators, and public anger rapidly escalated... On November 20 two hundred thousand filled Wenceslas Square from end to end, calling for a change of government, shouting 'This is it! Now is the time!' Every day another rally was held at Wenceslas Square; every day the already enormous numbers grew. On November 22 more than a quarter of a million chanted 'resign! resign!' as the names of ministers in the Communist government were mentioned... **On November 27 virtually the whole country joined in a two-hour general strike, and the government... declared that the Czechoslovak Communist Party would abandon its 'leading role.'** But [Prime Minister] Adamec did not move fast enough; the still largely Communist government he proposed was rejected by Havel and the Civic Forum, and on December 7 he resigned as Prime Minister, followed two days later by the resignation of President Gustav Husak... **A new non-communist government was instituted, and millions of Czechs and**

Slovaks celebrated."[64] (Warren H. Carroll, *The Rise and Fall of the Communist Revolution*, pp. 740-741)

The Fall of Bulgaria:

"The day the Berlin Wall fell there was a change in the Communist leadership in Bulgaria. Todor Zhikov, who had governed this most obedient satellite of the Soviet Union for no less that 35 years, stepped down under pressure for reform which he was unable or unwilling to undertake… **A month later 50,000 people rallied in previously wholly quiescent Sofia, demanding the resignation of the 'leading role' of the Communist Party**. In an incautious outburst caught by a television reporter that destroyed him politically when it was revealed, Mladenov [now leading Communist Bulgaria] muttered 'the best thing to do is bring in the tanks.' But he brought in no tanks, nor does any such action seem to have been seriously proposed even by this hard-line government, which had furnished assassins to the KGB for many years. A gentle, modest philosopher named Zhelyu Zhelev formed a Democratic Union, and **on December 12 the Bulgarian Communist Party agreed to relinquish its monopoly of power and hold free elections. A second round of these, in 1990, made Zhelev president**."[65] (Warren H. Carroll, *The Rise and Fall of the Communist Revolution*, pp. 741-742)

The Fall of Romania (Rumania):

"**There remained, standing against the freedom tide, the long unchallenged Communist dictator of Rumania, Nicolae Ceausescu, and his coldly vicious wife, Elena**… The Ceausescus loved power with a consuming passion… He kept Rumania in poverty while building enormous showcase projects… **The secret police were everywhere, keeping constant watch on everyone even slightly suspected of dissidence. Every typewriter in Rumania was registered with the secret police**, along with a sample of its typing so that any compromising document could be traced to the machine that typed it. Assassins tracked the few prominent persons who successfully fled the country and hunted them down to their deaths. On November 20, with Poland and Hungary and East Germany liberated and Czechoslovakia on the way to liberation, Ceausescu said he would never follow these nations in 'blocking socialism.'

Once again, as in Poland and in East Germany, the liberation of a Communist country began with a church… The government had ordered Tokes to leave his parish. He refused to go. On December 15, the deadline given for his eviction, a thousand people rallied unexpectedly to his support. The next day the number swelled to five thousand. Ceausescu sent in the army. Its officers were reluctant to open fire, but Ceausescu condemned them for indecisiveness and on the 17th ordered a 'Chinese solution.' About a hundred people were killed and hundreds more wounded.

The people of the city responded with a general strike as the army began to withdraw from it, eager to put the scene of their killings behind them. Sympathy demonstrations began in other cities; Ceausescu warned that he would use similar force against any and all of them if they continued. On December 21 he went outside the presidential palace to harangue a crowd on live national television. For the first time in his 24 years of power he was met with shaken fists, hoots and jeers and shouts of 'Ceausescu dictator!' lasting a full three minutes. Startled, he began to wave his hands ineffectually; Elena hissed at him, 'Be calm! Be calm!' Then the nation's television screens went blank. The crowd grew to 15,000 in the course of the day and was finally broken up by the security police, who killed thirteen people.

> **The next day large crowds surrounded the building used by the Party Central Committee in Palace Square in Bucharest.** Still full of manic confidence, Ceausescu came out to speak to them. But someone had turned off the microphone. There was fighting in the streets; the people were entering the building. Nicolae and Elena Ceausescu boarded a waiting helicopter just ahead of the attacking crowd. The helicopter landed short of its destination, by an open road... Nicolae and Elena leaped out and tried to flag a passing truck. **A few minutes later they were arrested. Many of the rest of the government... shed its Communist structure and very soon its Communist name,** blamed Ceausescu of everything, and got away with it. The reconstituted government disposed of the Ceausescus with lightning speed. On Christmas day 1989 **they were brought before a drumhead court-martial, convicted, and executed."**[66] (Warren H. Carroll, *The Rise and Fall of the Communist Revolution*, pp. 742-743)

And while the era of persecution officially culminated with the fall of the satellites (1989-1991) and the dissolution of the Soviet Union (1991), the winds of change began much earlier than that. The death of Stalin in 1953 was a good start. Nikita Khrushchev actually denounced Stalin and allowed the publication of a book exposing the horrors of the Gulag labor camps:

> "Speaking at a Moscow rally July 19, 1963... **Khrushchev threw away his prepared text and made his most vehement recorded public assault on Stalin, calling him one of the worst tyrants in history, who had stayed in power only by 'the headman's axe.'...**"[67] (Warren H. Carroll, *The Rise and Fall of the Communist Revolution*, pp. 529-530)

> "...**[in 1962] Khrushchev authorized the publication of Alexander Solzhenitsyn's short novel,** *One Day in the Life of Ivan Denisovich*, **the first explicit account of the horrors of Stalin's labor camps to be printed in the Soviet Union... This act of Khrushchev may well have been, from the vantage point of history, second in importance only to his own denunciation of Stalin.** For Solzhenityn's was a voice no man and no system could silence, once it had been heard."[68] (Warren H. Carroll, *The Rise and Fall of the Communist Revolution*, p. 494)

> "**To many in the Party, Khrushchev's permission for the publication of Solzhenitsyn's book was a major error which rendered the follow-up writings inevitable and had potential for seriously endangering the regime.**"[69] (Warren H. Carroll, *The Rise and Fall of the Communist Revolution*, pp. 529-530)

Of course, Khrushchev was an evil Communist who threatened nuclear war with the U.S. (which never came to pass), told the world at the U.N. that "we will bury you," and wanted to profit politically by the denunciation of Stalin. But the fact the he could actually get away with denouncing Stalin and allowing the publication of a book exposing the Gulag showed how things were beginning to change inside the Soviet Union – how the era of persecution was coming to an end – which eventually led to the collapse of the regime in 1991.

Q. But China and North Korea still persecute Catholics as Russia did under Stalin, etc?

A. Our Lady never promised that China, etc. would convert; she indicated that Russia would be converted *to a certain period of peace*. The fact that Pope Pius XII did it "late" is surely why Communism was able to spread to these other countries even after his consecration, such as China, N. Korea, Cuba.

Our Lord to Sister Lucy, Summer, 1931: "**Like the King of France they will repent and do it, <u>but it will be late</u>. Russia will have already spread its errors throughout the world provoking wars and persecutions against the Church**: the Holy Father will have much to suffer."[70] (quoted in *The Whole Truth About Fatima*, Vol. 2, pp. 543-544)

As stated already, in the message of Fatima on August 19th Our Lady told the children: "If you had not been taken away [by the Administrator on Aug. 13] to the City, the miracle [of Oct. 13th] would have been greater." She told the children that their arrest on August 13th by the evil administrator of Ourem, which prevented them from being at the apparition site that day, caused the miracle on Oct. 13th to be less profound than what it would have been! Likewise, the Pope doing the consecration of Russia "late" caused its conversion to peace not to be as profound as it would have been – such as preventing the spread of Communism to these other countries. God and Our Lady promised that the persecution would end in Russia, and they obviously included the satellite nations of Russia – such as Poland, etc. – in the promise; for these were, in reality, only extensions of the Soviet Empire. And this has occurred.

Sr. Lucy to Fr. Goncalves, summarizing Tuy Vision, 1930: "<u>**The good Lord promises to end the persecution in Russia**</u>, if the Holy Father will himself make a solemn act of reparation and consecration of Russia to the Sacred Hearts of Jesus and Mary, as well as ordering all the bishops of the Catholic Church to do the same. The Holy Father must then promise that upon the ending of this persecution he will approve and recommend the practice of the reparatory devotion already described."[71] (*The Whole Truth About Fatima*, Vol. 2, p. 465)

SOME LEFTOVER OBJECTIONS

Q. What about Sr. Lucy. If Pope Pius XII's consecration of Russia in 1952 was accepted in heaven, how come she didn't say so?

A. Sr. Lucy knew what Heaven revealed to her; she did not know what Heaven did not reveal to her. It is extremely important to note that in 1947, when asked by William Thomas Walsh about Pope Pius XII's 1942 consecration of the world, Sr. Lucy didn't even know if it was sufficient!

William Thomas Walsh, *Our Lady of Fatima*, **p. 222: "After my return from Portugal I wrote several questions which His Excellency the Bishop of Leiria was good enough to send to Sister Dores [Sr. Lucy]. Her answers, written February 17, 1947, reached me just too late for the first edition of this book… Q. Is it your opinion that the Pope and the Bishops will consecrate Russia to the Immaculate Heart of Mary only after the laity have done their duty, in Rosaries, sacrifices, first Saturday Communions, etc.? A. [Sr. Lucy] <u>The Holy Father has already consecrated Russia, including it in the consecration of the world</u>, but it has not been done in the form indicated by Our Lady: <u>I do not know whether Our Lady accepts it, done in this way, as complying with her promises</u>.**

The truth about the Consecration and Conversion of Russia

Prayer and sacrifice are always the means necessary to draw down the graces and blessings of God."[72]

This was in reference to Pope Pius XII's consecration of the world on Oct. 31, 1942! Sr. Lucy didn't even know if this consecration of the world fulfilled the request of Heaven! Ten years later, Pius XII went further and specifically consecrated Russia to the Immaculate Heart of Mary. So how could a person say that Pope Pius XII's consecration of Russia definitely wasn't accepted in Heaven, when Sr. Lucy didn't even know if his consecration of the world wasn't accepted in Heaven? This serves to show us that Sr. Lucy only knew what Heaven revealed to her, and that she did not know – but was only speculating on – things that were not specifically revealed to her. For instance, she knew that various nations would be annihilated, as Our Lady told her, but she didn't necessarily know exactly how that prophecy would have its fulfillment.

Q. Didn't Fr. Alonso, the Fatima expert, also hold that Russia would be converted to the Catholic Faith?

A. Yes, in addition to "Fr." Gruner, Fr. Alonso has probably been the biggest proponent of the idea that the consecration of Russia will convert the nation to the Catholic Faith, and that a universal reign of peace will result, an idea which finds no proof in the words of Our Lady. What people need to know is that Fr. Alonso was a liberal heretic who 1) justified Paul VI's decision not to reveal the third secret; 2) condemned traditionalists; 3) was extremely soft on the number one enemy of Fatima, Fr. Dhanis; and 4) agreed with the bogus note from the Coimbra diocese which rejected Sr. Lucy's 1957 interview with Fr. Fuentes.

> Fr. Alonso: "**An inopportune revelation of the text [by Paul VI] would only have further exasperated the two tendencies which continue to tear the Church apart: a traditionalism** which would believe itself to be assisted by the Fatima prophecies, and a progressivism which would have lashed out against these apparitions…"[73]

Here we see Fr. Alonso condemning traditionalists and justifying Paul VI for not revealing the third secret! Remember, this is the man who, in addition to Gruner, is largely responsible for promoting the idea (now almost universally believed) that Russia will necessarily convert to the Catholic Faith resulting in universal triumph of Our Lady and peace over the earth.

> Fr. Alonso: "**It must be clearly noted that certain 'revelations' made by the press concerning Sister Lucy cannot be attributed to her**, for example, those spread by **Father Fuentes** and Father Lombardi."[74]

Here we see Fr. Alonso agreeing with the bogus note from the Diocese of Coimbra (more on this in a bit) which denounced Fr. Fuentes as a fabricator. Thus, the fact that Fr. Alonso held such and such a position or idea proves nothing. What is very interesting and unfortunate is that writer after writer has adopted the idea of Alonso and Gruner on the conversion of Russia and the triumph of Our Lady. This has been very significant in misleading them on the current apostasy. Notice how the following writer seems to bank everything on "In the end…"

> Mark Fellows, *Fatima in Twilight*, p. 334: "Mary has given us this promise: '**In the end, My Immaculate Heart will triumph. The Holy Father will consecrate Russia to Me, and she will be converted**, and some time of peace will be granted to the world.' Father Alonso also wrote, 'The final triumph of Mary's heart is certain and it will be definitive…'

> **On that day history will at last be pulled into conformity with the Divine Will. The chastisement of apostasy will cease.** In the new dawn all will realize that the darksome nightmare we are living through did not vitiate Christ's promise that the gates of hell would never conquer His Church. **Perfect mercy will follow perfect justice.** Russia will be devotedly consecrated to the Immaculate Heart. The conversion of that tortured nation will be dazzling, blinding, as the perfect humility of the Immaculate will put the red dragon and his beasts to flight… **New legends will be born that will seed cultures with the will to base society on the Kingship of Christ. This will inspire a renaissance of Christian poetry and art. Man will remember anew the supernatural reality of the Holy Sacrifice of the Mass. With trembling reverence, we will once more kneel before the Almighty.**"[75]

Sounds great, doesn't it? The problem is that it has no foundation in the words of Our Lady, as we have shown. The triumph of Our Lady is a triumph "in the end" (i.e., after Russia will have already spread its errors, annihilating certain nations and martyring the good) over the satanic regime in Russia by converting it to a certain period of peace, as we have shown. It is not a universal triumph or reign of peace, but only a "certain" period of peace.

> Frere Michel de la Sainte Trinite, *The Whole Truth About Fatima*, Vol. 3, pp. 837-838: "However, let us not be mistaken. **The third Secret cannot announce the end of the world, which will not come before the fulfillment of the wonderful promise which concludes the Secret.** But this promise of the imminent triumph of the Immaculate Heart of Mary, which is so comforting and generates such enthusiasm, a promise which ought to be preached unceasingly, in season and out of season, Cardinal Ratzinger ignores…"[76]

Notice that Frere Michel seems to hold the same position, banking everything on his version of the triumph of Our Lady. On page 845 of his third volume, Frere Michel goes so far as to move the words of Our Lady about "*In the end, My Immaculate Heart will triumph. The Holy Father will consecrate Russia to Me, and she will be converted, and a certain period of peace will be granted to the world*" to *after* the words "*In Portugal the dogma of Faith will always be preserved, etc.*" The last words given by Our Lady in the secret of July 13 were: "*In Portugal the dogma of Faith will always be preserved, etc.*"[77] The words "*In the end, My Immaculate Heart will triumph…*" come before these words because they pertain to the second part of the secret, the part dealing with the period of Russia's persecutions covered in this article.

> Q. What do you think is the meaning of the words: "In Portugal the dogma of Faith will always be preserved, etc." which come just before the third secret?

A. Since we don't have the complete sentence, we cannot say for sure, but it could be: "In Portugal the dogma of Faith will always be preserved *in a faithful remnant…*" Or: "In Portugal the dogma of Faith will always be preserved *among those truly devoted to me…*" Or: "In Portugal the dogma of Faith will always be preserved *until the Great Apostasy…*" The third secret undoubtedly deals with the present apostasy of the Vatican II sect.

PART II: THE IMPOSTOR SISTER LUCY

Q. What about Sr. Lucy's statements after 1960? She seems to be quoted every which way? Some quote her saying that John Paul II successfully consecrated Russia; others quote her as saying just the opposite. Some quote her as saying that the third secret was never intended to be revealed and that no one goes to Hell, while others quote her as talking about the diabolical disorientation in the Church.

A. **After 1960 we are undoubtedly dealing with a massive conspiracy and an impostor Sr. Lucy.** We will now cover the striking evidence that the enemies of the message of Fatima, starting during the reign of the Freemason, John XXIII, actually implanted an impostor Sr. Lucy who falsely acted as if she were the real Sr. Lucy. Nothing coming from Sr. Lucy after 1960 is reliable.

First of all, we know that there was a conspiracy involving Sr. Lucy starting in 1959. In 1957, Sr. Lucy gave her famous interview to Fr. Augustin Fuentes, postulator of the cause of Beatification for Jacinta and Francisco. In this interview, Sr. Lucy said that she had determined that we are in the last times, and that there are punishments in store for the world. Sr. Lucy also said not to wait for the hierarchy for the call to penance. Following the interview, in 1959 the Diocese of Coimbra issued a note. This note declared that Fr. Fuentes fabricated basically all the statements attributed to Lucy in the interview not dealing specifically with Jacinta and Francisco. Included in this note was a statement allegedly from Sr. Lucy, in which she supposedly declared that Fr. Fuentes' claims were <u>not truthful</u>. Here is a portion of the note:

> *Note from the Diocese of Coimbra*, July 2, 1959, on the Fuentes interview: "**Father Augustin Fuentes, postulator of the cause of beatification for the seers of Fatima… visited Sister Lucy at the Carmel of Coimbra and spoke to her exclusively about things concerning the process in question. But after returning to Mexico… this priest allowed himself to make sensational declarations of an apocalyptic, eschatological and prophetic character,** <u>which he declares that he heard from Sister Lucy's very lips</u>. Given the gravity of such statements, the chancery of Coimbra believed it its duty to order a rigorous investigation on the authenticity of such news… but also with regard to things reported as having been said by Sister Lucy, **the Diocese of Coimbra has decided to publish these words of Sister Lucy, given in answer to questions put by one who has the right to do so.**
> [Sr. Lucy]: 'Father Fuentes spoke to me in his capacity as Postulator for the causes of beatification of the servants of God, Jacinta and Francisco Marto. **We spoke solely on things connected with this subject; therefore, <u>whatever else he refers to is neither exact nor true.</u>** I am sorry about it, for I do not understand what good can be done for souls when it is not based on God, Who is the Truth. **I know nothing, and could therefore say nothing, about such punishments, <u>which are falsely attributed to me</u>**.'
> "The chancery of Coimbra is in a position to declare that since up to the present **Sister Lucy has said everything she believed it her duty to say about Fatima**, she has said nothing new and consequently has authorized nobody, at least since February 1955, to publish anything new that might be attributed to her on the subject of Fatima."[78] (*WTAF*, Vol. 3, pp. 550-551)

Even "Fr." Gruner's apostolate holds the Fuentes interview to be authentic, and this statement from the Diocese of Coimbra, in which Sr. Lucy supposedly disavows much of the Fuentes interview, to be a lie. Thus, <u>**we are dealing with a conspiracy surrounding Sr. Lucy as early as 1959 – the diocese attributing and publishing false statements in Sr. Lucy's name to disavow**</u>

The Impostor Sister Lucy

important warnings for the world. At the same time, it was conveniently declared that Sr. Lucy "has said everything she believed it her duty to say about Fatima"; in other words, Sr. Lucy has nothing more to say about Fatima. Frere Michel also notes that after the Fuentes interview it became increasingly difficult to get access to Sr. Lucy; she became "invisible."

> Frere Michel de la Sainte Trinite, *The Whole Truth About Fatima*, Vol. 3, pp. 748-749: "**From then on [after the Fuentes interview and diocesan note disavowing it], <u>she was bound to a much more rigorous silence on everything concerning Fatima</u>**, and especially the great themes of the Secret… As we have seen, in its note of July 2, 1959, the chancery of Coimbra declared authoritatively that 'Sister Lucy has nothing more to say on Fatima'! <u>**It also became increasingly difficult to see her, and for years no more of her writings were published**</u>. Her testimony was becoming bothersome. <u>**In 1962, Maria de Freitas remarked that 'more and more, visits to Sister Lucy are forbidden; more and more she is becoming invisible.'**</u>"[79]

Well, we believe that the following photographs (in addition to other evidence) reveal why, following the Fuentes interview, Sr. Lucy was subjected to a rigorous silence, why she became "invisible." It's because after that point it wasn't Sr. Lucy at all, but an impostor posing as Sr. Lucy. Here are pictures of the real Sr. Lucy from 1945, when she was 38 years old:

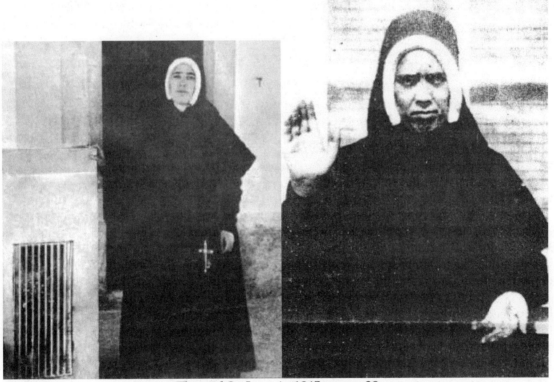

The real Sr. Lucy in 1945, at age 38

And next we see the picture of "Sr. Lucy" in 1967 at age 60!

The Impostor Sister Lucy

544

"Sr. Lucy" in 1967 at age 60

You can judge for yourself, but the woman pictured here is not the same as the woman pictured above. First, this photograph is from 1967. Thus, this is supposedly "Sr. Lucy" 22 years later, at age 60! But this woman looks as young, or even younger, than Sr. Lucy when she was 38 years old!

Second, the real Sr. Lucy (the first picture) has a different nose structure than this "Sr. Lucy." This "Sr. Lucy's" nose is much broader; it's a different woman. Of course, while a person can (and often does) noticeably age when going from middle-aged to late middle-aged, he or she is still noticeably the same person – unlike in this case.

Third, a reader of ours named Barbara Costello has pointed out that Sr. Lucy has a characteristic dimple in her chin and in her cheeks. We see this in the following photograph of Sr. Lucy in 1945, again at age 38 (as well as the first picture above, the right-hand picture from 1945):

Notice the characteristic dimple in her cheeks and the center of her chin

But this "Sr. Lucy" below does not have the characteristic dimples in her cheeks and the center of her chin. This "Sr. Lucy" has a predominant characteristic of a protruding, forward chin, which the real Sr. Lucy doesn't have (besides the different nose structure).

The Impostor Sister Lucy 546

This woman is not Sr. Lucy, but a phony Sr. Lucy that was implanted and specially picked to serve the purpose of the false Fatima line and the Vatican II religion that has been foisted on the world since the Fuentes interview. In addition to the photographic evidence, the fact that the post-Vatican II "Sr. Lucy" is not the real Lucy screams out all over the place.

> Francis Alban, *The Fatima Priest*, Intro page: "On October 11th, 1990, Carolina, <u>**the blood sister of Sister Lucy, told Father Gruner that she had visited Sister Lucy in the Carmel of Coimbra for more than 40 years and never had she been able to speak alone with her sister in the same room. They were always separated by a grille and many other sisters of the convent were in attendance at all visits**</u>."[80]

For more than 40 years, "Sr. Lucy" was unable to be seen even by her sister except through a grille and with other nuns present! This would explain why her sister would not have uncovered the fraud – she was never able to see "Sr. Lucy" <u>except behind a grille</u> and fully clothed in a habit, and never able to speak intimately with her because of the constant presence of "many" other nuns! This strange quarantining of "Sr. Lucy" was not, as "Fr." Gruner has suggested, because she would tell the world the truth about Fatima. **It was because the conspirators in the Vatican didn't want their fake "Sr. Lucy" exposed for the impostor she was, which would have occurred if she were subjected to any tough examination or scrutiny.** (And this did happen in the few cases that the Vatican allowed her to be interviewed, such as the notorious *Two Hours with Sr. Lucia* by Carlos Evaristo, as we will see.)

So Sr. Lucy was never allowed to speak with her family except from behind a grille, **but when they needed "Sr. Lucy" to publicly endorse the Vatican II sect, its antipopes, and their failure** to release the third secret, she was neatly presented to the world at Fatima in 1967, so that she could be seen hobnobbing with her fellow conspirator, Antipope Paul VI.

The phony Sr. Lucy brought out from behind the grille to be seen by the world at Fatima in 1967 with her fellow conspirator, Antipope Paul VI - to endorse the new religion, his ripping apart of Tradition, his promulgation of V-2, and his failure to release the third secret

Same thing here: the phony Sr. Lucy brought before the world to be seen hobnobbing with Antipope John Paul II

Another question that springs to mind after viewing these photographs is: when did Sr. Lucy get her teeth fixed? Here is a picture of the real Sr. Lucy; her front teeth were characteristically mangled.

"When Lucia's second teeth began to come in… **they were large, projecting and irregular**, causing the upper lip to protrude and the heavy lower one to hang…"[81] (William Thomas Walsh, *Our Lady of Fatima*, p. 11)

Another shot of the real Sr. Lucy's teeth

But in the photographs of the phony Sr. Lucy, we see that her teeth are neat and straight, not large, projecting and irregular. Sure, it's possible that Sr. Lucy had massive dental surgery or had her teeth replaced to get them looking so neat and straight as the impostor Sr. Lucy's do, but it is more likely just *another proof* of the fact that the woman pictured above is not the real Sr. Lucy pictured here.

For those who find this hard to accept, we ask them to focus on two things: 1) Our Lord said that in the last days the deception will be so profound that even the elect would be deceived if that were possible (Matthew 24), and an impostor Lucy was crucial to the Devil's plan of deceiving the world on Fatima. 2) **Every traditionalist who doesn't accept the Vatican's version of the third secret of Fatima (released in the year 2000) already believes that there was an impostor Sr. Lucy, but simply hasn't figured it out yet, or isn't honest or logical enough to admit it**. It's undeniable that the Vatican's "Sr. Lucy" fully endorsed its version of the third secret, and its accompanying interpretation that it refers to John Paul II. This fact is not known from a letter that can be forged, but from undeniable video evidence of "Sr. Lucy" at Fatima in 2000 for the "Beatifications" of Jacinta and Francisco.

At this event, "Cardinal" Sodano (in view of "Sr. Lucy") announced that the Vatican would be releasing the third secret of Fatima, and that it refers to the assassination attempt on Antipope John Paul II. Everyone who was watching the event (as we were) could see "Sr. Lucy's" reaction, so there could be no doubt about her being hidden away in order not to tell the truth on the matter (as the Grunerites might claim). **"Sr. Lucy" made clear gestures signifying that she fully endorsed and agreed with "Cardinal" Sodano, that the third secret of Fatima refers to the assassination attempt against John Paul II!** To anyone who is honest and logical, **this is absolute proof that she cannot be the real Sr. Lucy, but is an impostor and an agent of the Vatican II sect**.

In the following quote, notice that even a Grunerite acknowledges the problem. He admits how "almost disquieting" it was to see "Sr. Lucy" endorse "Cardinal" Sodano's interpretation of the third secret – yes, I would say so! – but he fails to draw the appropriate conclusion.

> Mark Fellows, *Fatima in Twilight*, p. 327: "**In fact, her [Sister Lucy's] exuberance at Fatima in 2000 was almost disquieting**. Surely the cause of her radiance, and her new graciousness towards John Paul, was her happiness over the beatification of her two cousins. **Yet she remained exuberant even in the face of Cardinal Sodano's version of the Third Secret**, going so far as to make large, awkward gestures to the crowd."[82]

There you have it: the phony "Sr. Lucy" fully endorsed the Vatican's version and interpretation of the third secret of Fatima. The only way that one could even consider her to be the real Sr. Lucy is if one fully accepts the Vatican's version of the third secret, and its interpretation that it refers to the assassination attempt against John Paul II. But almost all traditionalists agree that the Vatican's version (and interpretation) of the third secret was not authentic, but another lie – another conspiracy. The impostor "Sr. Lucy" is of the same order. And that is why the Grunerites are forced to bend over backwards to attempt to explain away statement after statement emanating from the impostor Sr. Lucy which contradicts their position.

In 1992, there was the infamous *Two Hours with Sr. Lucy* interview, conducted by "Cardinal" Padiyara of Ernaculam, India, Bishop Francis Michaelappa of Mysore, India, and "Father" Francisco V. Pacheco of Fort Ce, Brazil. Mr. Carlos Evaristo, a journalist, was also present at the interview, and he acted as the official translator. In this interview, "Sr. Lucy," among other things, said that the third secret was never intended to be revealed by 1960 and that it should <u>not</u> be revealed. This totally contradicts everything that we know the pre-Vatican II Sr. Lucy said on this matter. In the interview, this "Sr. Lucy" also said that John Paul II's consecration of Russia was accepted in Heaven. Here is a portion of the interview:

> "Cardinal Padiyara: 'And, was this[consecration] accomplished by Pope John Paul II on March 25th of 1984?'
> **Sister Lucy**: '**Yes, Yes, Yes** (In a low affirmative voice which also seemed to show that she was expecting this question)...
> Carlos Evaristo: 'So this consecration was then accepted by Our Lady?'
> **Sister Lucy**: 'Yes.'
> Carlos: 'Our Lady is content and has accepted it?'
> **Sister Lucy**: 'Yes.'...
> Cardinal Padiyara: 'Does God and Our Lady still want the Church to reveal the Third Secret?'
> **Sister Lucy**: '**The Third Secret is not intended to be revealed**. It was only intended for the Pope and the immediate Church hierarchy.'
> Carlos: 'But didn't Our Lady say that it was to be revealed to the public by 1960, at the latest?'
> **Sister Lucy**: '**Our Lady never said that**. Our Lady said that it was for the pope.'
> Father Pacheco: 'Does the Third Secret have to do with the Second Vatican Council?'
> **Sister Lucy**: 'I cannot say.'
> Carlos: 'Can the Pope reveal the Third Secret?'
> **Sister Lucy**: 'The Pope can reveal it if he chooses to, **but I advise him not to**. If he chooses to, I advise great prudence. He must be prudent.'"

The Grunerites have desperately tried to discredit this interview, since it is so devastating to their position; but one of us had a chance to speak with "Fr." Pacheco when he came to visit the monastery for a conference in the 1990's. "Fr." Pacheco told one of us that something is very wrong with this Sr. Lucy, and that she couldn't answer simple questions about her life. It's quite obvious that the interviewers were simply probing too deeply in areas with which the impostor was unfamiliar.

The Grunerites attempt to discredit this 1992 interview by pointing out that Sr. Lucy was always behind the grille, but in this interview she was supposedly out in the open, even holding hands with people. But this makes sense: the Vatican allowed one selective interview to an independent group – with Sr. Lucy out in the open and not behind the grille – *in which she would tell them (and thus the world) that John Paul II successfully consecrated Russia so that it would be on the record* with an independent group. But when "Sr. Lucy" was to meet with her sister (who could have more easily identified that she was an impostor), she was always kept behind the grille and with many other nuns.

Besides the 1992 interview, *Two Hours with Sr. Lucy*, there are numerous other statements from the phony Lucy in which she fully endorses the Vatican II sect's line on Fatima, thus proving that she is an impostor. In 2001, in an article printed in *L'Osservatore Romano*, "Sr. Lucy" was specifically asked about the consecration of Russia and even "Fr." Gruner's attempts to still get it done. This interview was reported around the world:

> VATICAN CITY, DEC 20, 2001 (Vatican Information Service): "With reference to the third part of the secret of Fatima, she **["Sr. Lucy"] affirmed that she had attentively read and meditated upon the booklet published by the Congregation for the Doctrine of the Faith and confirmed everything that was written there**. **To whoever imagines that some part of the secret has been hidden, she replied: 'Everything has been published; no secret remains.'** To those who speak and write of new revelations she said: "There is no truth in this. If I had received new revelations I would have told no-one, but I would have communicated them directly to the Holy Father." Sister Lucy was asked: **'What do you say to the persistent affirmations of Fr. Gruner who is gathering signatures in order that the pope may finally consecrate Russia to the Immaculate Heart of Mary, which has never been done?'** She replied: **'The Carmelite Community has rejected the forms for gathering the signatures. I have already said that the consecration that Our Lady desired was accomplished in 1984 and was accepted in Heaven.'"** [83]

Of course, the Grunerites will claim that this interview was fabricated or distorted, but then they are admitting that there is a conspiracy! If the Vatican will go that far, it is certainly conceivable that it would implant an impostor; and, as we saw, the claim that all of these statements from "Sr. Lucy" endorsing the phony third secret are just fabrications is blown away by the video evidence in which anyone could see her endorse the Vatican's version of the third secret at Fatima in 2000.

A bizarre picture of "Sr. Lucy" kissing John Paul II's hand immediately after receiving "Communion"

Another point worth mentioning is "Sr. Lucy's" bizarre activity when receiving "Communion" from John Paul II at the aforementioned 2000 "beatification" ceremony at Fatima (the same one where she clearly endorsed the Vatican's version of the third secret). "Sr. Lucy" first extended her hands, as if she wanted to receive "Communion" in the hand. Being too smart for that, and knowing that it would blow the entire scheme, John Paul II hesitated, and extended his hand to give her "Communion" on the tongue. But immediately after receiving "Communion," "Sr.

Lucy" grabbed John Paul II's hand and kissed it (as pictured above). This is totally bizarre, for "Sr. Lucy" had every chance to pay her respects to the antipope, but apparently she couldn't even wait until after her thanksgiving for "Communion" and "Mass" had ended! The real Sr. Lucy would never have done this – thus interrupting her Communion and thanksgiving. **It's clear that the impostor Sr. Lucy was simply overzealous in playing her part of filial devotion to the antipope, and jumped the gun by grabbing his hand immediately after "Communion."**

Q. So what do you think happened to the real Sr. Lucy? A. They clearly eliminated her at some point. Whenever that may have occurred, there is no doubt that the woman playing the part of "Sr. Lucy" since Vatican II was not the real one. Readers can take this for what it's worth (and it is not essential in any way to the facts above which prove that there was indeed an impostor Sr. Lucy), but a few years back we received a very disturbing letter. We received a letter from a woman (a traditional Catholic convert) whose family was involved in the higher-echelons of the Illuminati and Freemasonry. We also spoke to this woman both before and after she sent it. There was much more in the letter and in the telephone conversations that added context and credibility to her claim, but we can only give a portion of the letter below. As hard as this may be to believe, **we really did receive the following letter and speak at length with this woman** (she asked that we withhold her name for obvious reasons):

> "Dear Brothers of Holy Family Monastery… As I told you on the phone I have some very dark relatives… [a world famous Freemason] is the brother of [x- name removed to preserve anonymity of author] who was married to my Grand Aunt. All of my relatives on my mother's side were 33rd degree Illuminati Freemasons. My Grandparents were in Eastern Star… I know I must sound like a screaming weirdo by now. I am not… When I was five my Mother hosted a gathering. There are many things that went on that are too gruesome to put in print about these gatherings. They are basically sacrificing to Satan to put it briefly. I had a new baby brother named [x]… My mother didn't know ahead of time [that x] was to be part of the 'ceremonies'. They were going to put him in what looked like a large brass wok [and torture him] in order to tell the future. …[thankfully, this didn't happen because of intervening events]… [But] **One of the things that was said that awful day was they had just killed sister Lucy (I thought they were talking about a sister I didn't know I had that they had killed). When I asked they said 'No stupid…she's a nun.'** It only made sense years later what this meant. It was 1958, late Oct when this happened. [I remember because my brother had just been born]. I know that I sound like a mad woman but it is the truth…"

We have spoken with this woman at length; she is a traditional Catholic convert, and we believe she is telling the truth. But regardless of whether one accepts this testimony or not, the fact is that there was an impostor Sr. Lucy. There is no doubt about this; the evidence is undeniable. The Vatican conveniently kept her alive until 97 years old, until it had revealed the phony third secret and she had finished playing her part, then a few years later she "died" and her cell was ordered sealed by "Cardinal" Ratzinger.

There are so many souls who have dismissed the evidence against the Vatican II apostasy and the New Mass simply because they saw that "Sr. Lucy" accepted them. We always informed them that they cannot dismiss facts of the Faith based on what they think another person believes.

> Galatians 1:8-9- "But though we, or an angel from heaven, preach a gospel to you besides that which we have preached to you, let him be anathema. As we said before, so now I say again: If anyone preach to you a gospel, besides that which you have received, let him be anathema."

Alas, but lacking true Faith, they chose to follow man instead of God, and were actually following a complete impostor.

THE FALSE MESSAGE OF "FR." NICHOLAS GRUNER

Prior to examining this issue in detail, like almost everyone else, we also held the popular position on the consecration of Russia: that the conversion of Russia necessarily means that the nation of Russia would be converted to the Catholic Faith, resulting in an astonishing reign of universal peace and Catholic renewal. We held it because that's what every person writing on Fatima was saying, and there was really no reason to question it. However, as shown in this article, after studying the basis for this position, we came to discover that there is no basis for this position, and that it finds no proof in the words of Our Lady; on the contrary, a vastly different and much more plausible position does find its evidence in the words of Our Lady.

There are many people who have held, and do hold, the erroneous position on the consecration and conversion of Russia in good Faith. (And strictly speaking, one is free to hold whatever opinion he feels inclined to on this matter, since it is not a matter of Catholic doctrine – *even though the evidence presented in this article shows that the position of Nicholas Gruner on this issue is false*.) Those who have held it in bad faith would be those who have dismissed the facts from the teaching of the Church on the present apostasy, and remained with the Vatican II sect or the New Mass, simply because they believed that one of the Vatican II "popes" must consecrate Russia.

That being said, we believe that the Fatima Enterprise of "Fr." Nicholas Gruner has become a colossus with the assistance of the Devil. His enterprise has been hugely important to the Devil in distracting souls from the real issues of the Faith to get a phony antipope to consecrate Russia. Even if Russia had not already been consecrated, it's a fact that the Vatican II antipopes are not Catholic and therefore have no authority to do it anyway. Thus, "Fr." Gruner's massive apostolate attempting to get the Vatican II antipopes to consecrate Russia is a waste on two fronts: 1) he is trying to get non-Catholic, manifestly heretical antipopes to do the consecration, when they can't; and 2) his entire position on the consecration of Russia is wrong. **Think of all the wasted time, resources and effort. Think – most importantly – of the souls who have been misled** and distracted and have obstinately accepted the Vatican II antipopes because (through their own lack of love of the truth) they dismissed the facts from the Magisterium, and held on to the Vatican II antipopes because they believed that one of them must consecrate Russia.

We hear from these people very frequently, and we've always assured them that they cannot dismiss facts from the teaching of the Magisterium based on their question of who will fulfill a prophecy. We always told them that against a fact there is no argument (heretics cannot be popes), and truth cannot contradict truth, and therefore there is a good answer to their question about the consecration, even if one didn't have it at the time. But alas, they dismissed all the facts from the teaching of the Magisterium, and accepted the Vatican II apostates because of their false idea that one of them must consecrate Russia. Now they can see not only that the sedevacantist position doesn't contradict the message of Fatima in any way, but that their position was actually a deception that has kept them mired in darkness on the present situation. "Fr." Gruner has actually become the fourth largest employer in Ft. Erie, Ontario based on his apostolate!

That "Fr." Gruner's apostolate has been assisted by the Devil finds corroboration in his devilish mixture of truth with error – of Catholicism with apostasy. We see this so clearly in the next quote about the apostasy in the Church.

> "Fr." Gruner, "God Have Mercy on us all," Crusader 71: **"In the Third Secret it is foretold, among other things, that the great Apostasy in the Church will begin at the**

top.' These are the very words of Cardinal Ciappi (personal Papal Theologian to Pope John Paul II). The result of "the great Apostasy" starting "at the top" is corruption of the clergy and the laity in doctrine, in morals and in liturgy… **God is very angry with His people because He is not only sending us bad priests, <u>He has also apparently sent us bad bishops and bad Cardinals too</u>**… Pope John Paul II at Fatima, on May 13, 2000 told us that: 'The message of Fatima is a call to conversion, alerting humanity to have nothing to do with the 'dragon' whose tail swept down a third of the stars of Heaven and cast them to the earth.' (Apoc. 12:4) To put that statement in plain English, Pope John Paul II is saying as follows: <u>Do not follow the one-third of the Cardinals, one-third of the Catholic bishops, and one-third of the Catholic priests</u>, who have been dragged down by the devil from their exalted position of leading the faithful to Heaven. In other words, **<u>the Holy Father is telling us what the Message of Fatima is warning us about today. That is that one-third of the clergy (who are the stars of Heaven) have been dragged down by the devil and his co-workers</u>** — the Masons, communists, homosexual networks — and are now working for the devil himself; not for God, not for the Church of Christ, but for the devil."

This really encapsulates "Fr." Gruner's evil methods and evil apostolate. Here we see Gruner discussing the truth of how it is predicted that the apostasy in the Church will begin "at the top." Who could that be? Obviously it would apply first and foremost to John Paul II, the man who claimed to be the pope (claimed to be the top of the Church) and led the entire apostasy by his idolatrous prayer gatherings at Assisi, his massive false ecumenism all over the world, etc. But while telling people about this truth (that the apostasy will begin at the top, or what *seems to be the top* of the Church), does he then warn them about the man to be most aware of, John Paul II? No, instead he does just the opposite: he then leads them directly to John Paul II – the one they should be most aware of regarding the apostasy – by quoting him as if he is their ally against the apostasy of the bishops and priests! This is totally wicked, even more so, in certain ways, than other more overt forms of wickedness, since it mixes truth with error (apostasy with Catholicism) and is more effective in leading conservatives back to the sources of the apostasy, the Vatican II antipopes. That is why he has been able to effectively mislead and distract so many with a false message on Fatima.

In addition to his deadly mixture of truth with error, one of the ways by which "Fr." Gruner's apostolate has become so influential is by propaganda. Here are some of the things that you can find on the website of his apostolate: His website (Fatima.org) calls his magazine "Our Lady's magazine." It states: "Click here to read more about **Our Lady's magazine**…"! Boy, who would want to disagree with or not support "Our Lady's magazine" – the magazine of Our Lady herself!

He calls his book service "Our Lady's Book Service"! Wow, we wish we could have the privilege of being "Our Lady's Book Service." He calls his radio program "**Our Lady's** Radio Program"! And – yes, you guessed it – he calls his apostolate, not just a Fatima apostolate, but "Our Lady's Apostolate"! His website states: "Shortly following the formation of <u>**Our Lady's Apostolate**</u>, Father Gruner began publishing the Fatima Crusader magazine. In 1980, Pope John Paul II directly encouraged Father Gruner in his Fatima work and the periodical has grown…"

Wow, he must be some "priest" to run "Our Lady's Apostolate" – the apostolate of Our Lady herself! – as well as *her* radio program, *her* magazine and *her* book service. Does anyone fail to see how presumptuous – and arguably blasphemous – this is? Oh, never mind… it's okay… I almost forgot… Gruner is, according to his apostolate (i.e. "Our Lady's" Apostolate), "the Fatima Priest"!

The Impostor Sister Lucy

In truth, this is simply propaganda from a <u>false prophet</u>, and that is why "Fr." Gruner has had such an influence on what people think about Fatima and the present situation. Propaganda is defined as an "…organized scheme, for propagation of a doctrine or practice." To dub almost every aspect of his apostolate "Our Lady's" is an organized scheme on the part of his apostolate to build itself up as the voice of Our Lady herself.

Besides being wickedly presumptuous, this propaganda brainwashes people just like the propaganda from the mainstream media. When they hear this stuff over and over – this is "Our Lady's apostolate" and "Our Lady's magazine" and "Our Lady's Book Service" – they are often brainwashed to follow everything he says on Fatima, support him vigorously (for who wouldn't want to support Our Lady?) or consider Gruner to be Our Lady's personal representative. Since people are so gullible, it has been a major factor in how big his apostolate has become. That is why his apostolate <u>continues to use this type of propaganda so often</u>. For instance, in a recent appeal for support, Gruner said:

> "Remember, **it is not I, Father Gruner, but Our Lady of Fatima Who [sic] asks you! Please do everything you can.**"[84]

This is why so many have been brainwashed not to consider anything on this issue that doesn't conform to "Fr." Gruner's views. By the way, Gruner stated in one of his letters that he wants to send the book *Fatima Priest* (which is the story of his life) to every "bishop" in the world! What a waste. The book *Fatima Priest*, which is replete with pictures of Gruner from throughout his life including as a baby, which is basically all about him and what a hero he supposedly is, has been translated into various languages to spread the "Good News" of Nicholas Gruner around the world.

All of this explains why Gruner consistently promoted pictures of Antipope John Paul II in his magazine for years (in a positive light) after he was aware of John Paul II's apostasy. For Gruner, it wasn't about telling people the truth; it was about keeping himself popular and seen as a hero with a somewhat mainstream "Catholic" audience – by promoting John Paul II and Fatima at the same time. Only a <u>very wicked man</u> would not have denounced John Paul II once he became aware of his apostasy, and that's exactly what Nicholas Gruner is.

Endnotes for Section 43:

[1] William Thomas Walsh, *Our Lady of Fatima*, Doubleday (1990 reprint of 1954 edition), pp. 81-82.
[2] Frere Michel de la Sainte Trinite, *The Whole Truth About Fatima*, Buffalo, NY: Immaculate Heart Publications, 1989, Vol. 1, p. 498.
[3] Mark Fellows, *Fatima in Twilight*, Niagra Falls, NY: Marmion Publications, 2003, p. 119.
[4] Frere Michel de la Sainte Trinite, *The Whole Truth About Fatima*, Vol. 3, p. 333.
[5] John Vennari, "It Doesn't Add Up," *The Fatima Crusader*, Constable, NY, Issue #70.
[6] Frere Michel de la Sainte Trinite, *The Whole Truth About Fatima*, Vol. 2, p. 420.
[7] Frere Michel de la Sainte Trinite, *The Whole Truth About Fatima*, Vol. 3, p. 741.
[8] Frere Michel de la Sainte Trinite, *The Whole Truth About Fatima*, Vol. 2, p. 464.
[9] Frere Michel de la Sainte Trinite, *The Whole Truth About Fatima*, Vol. 2, p. 465.
[10] Frere Michel de la Sainte Trinite, *The Whole Truth About Fatima*, Vol. 2, p. 732.
[11] *Le Nouvelliste de Lyon*, Jan. 26, 1938.
[12] Frere Michel de la Sainte Trinite, *The Whole Truth About Fatima*, Vol. 3, p. 190
[13] Warren H. Carroll, *The Rise and Fall of the Communist Revolution*, Christendom Press, 1995, p. 310.
[14] Joint Baltic American Committee, http://www.jbanc.org/65joint.html
[15] http://store.yahoo.com/jbanc2000/newsun.html
[16] Frere Michel de la Sainte Trinite, *The Whole Truth About Fatima*, Vol. 3, p. 505.
[17] Warren H. Carroll, *The Rise and Fall of the Communist Revolution*, p. 306.

[18] Frere Michel de la Sainte Trinite, *The Whole Truth About Fatima*, Vol. 3, pp. 193-194.
[19] Frere Michel de la Sainte Trinite, *The Whole Truth About Fatima*, Vol. 3, pp. 255-256.
[20] Frere Michel de la Sainte Trinite, *The Whole Truth About Fatima*, Vol. 2, p. 764.
[21] Frere Michel de la Sainte Trinite, *The Whole Truth About Fatima*, Vol. 2, pp. 576-577.
[22] Frere Michel de la Sainte Trinite, *The Whole Truth About Fatima*, Vol. 2, p. 564.
[23] Quoted by Frere Michel de la Sainte Trinite, *The Whole Truth About Fatima*, Vol. 2, p. 539.
[24] Warren H. Carroll, *The Rise and Fall of the Communist Revolution*, pp. 364-365.
[25] Warren H. Carroll, *The Rise and Fall of the Communist Revolution*, p. 285.
[26] Warren H. Carroll, *The Rise and Fall of the Communist Revolution*, p. 286.
[27] Warren H. Carroll, *The Rise and Fall of the Communist Revolution*, p. 288.
[28] *The Whole Truth About Fatima*, Vol. 3, p. 192.
[29] *The Whole Truth About Fatima*, Vol. 3, p. 123.
[30] *The Whole Truth About Fatima*, Vol. 2, p. 732.
[31] *The Whole Truth About Fatima*, Vol. 2, p. 457.
[32] Warren H. Carroll, *The Rise and Fall of the Communist Revolution*, p. 169.
[33] Warren H. Carroll, *The Rise and Fall of the Communist Revolution*, p. 116.
[34] *The Whole Truth About Fatima*, Vol. 2, p. 454.
[35] *The Whole Truth About Fatima*, Vol. 2, p. 451.
[36] *The Whole Truth About Fatima*, Vol. 2, p. 565.
[37] Warren H. Carroll, *The Rise and Fall of the Communist Revolution*, p. 142.
[38] Warren H. Carroll, *The Rise and Fall of the Communist Revolution*, p. 243.
[39] Warren H. Carroll, *The Rise and Fall of the Communist Revolution*, pp. 243-245.
[40] Warren H. Carroll, *The Rise and Fall of the Communist Revolution*, pp. 248-249.
[41] Warren H. Carroll, *The Rise and Fall of the Communist Revolution*, p. 318.
[42] Warren H. Carroll, *The Rise and Fall of the Communist Revolution*, pp. 224-225.
[43] Warren H. Carroll, *The Rise and Fall of the Communist Revolution*, pp. 227-228.
[44] Warren H. Carroll, *The Rise and Fall of the Communist Revolution*, p. 228.
[45] Warren H. Carroll, *The Rise and Fall of the Communist Revolution*, pp. 240-241.
[46] *The Whole Truth About Fatima*, Vol. 2, pp. 543-544.
[47] *The Whole Truth About Fatima*, Vol. 3, p. 333.
[48] William Thomas Walsh, *Our Lady of Fatima*, p. 52 (note 1).
[49] *The Whole Truth About Fatima*, Vol. 1, p. 235.
[50] *The Whole Truth About Fatima*, Vol. 2, p. 465.
[51] Quoted in *The Whole Truth About Fatima*, Vol. 2, pp. 543-544.
[52] *The Whole Truth About Fatima*, Vol. 3, p. 333.
[53] *The Whole Truth About Fatima*, Vol. 2, p. 732.
[54] http://en.wikipedia.org/wiki/Soviet_Union#History
[55] Warren H. Carroll, *The Rise and Fall of the Communist Revolution*, p. 778.
[56] http://www.answers.com/topic/union-of-soviet-socialist-republics
[57] http://www.fatima.org/news/newsviews/perestoi.asp
[58] http://en.wikipedia.org/wiki/Poland#History
[59] Warren H. Carroll, *The Rise and Fall of the Communist Revolution*, pp. 735-736.
[60] Warren H. Carroll, *The Rise and Fall of the Communist Revolution*, pp. 736-737.
[61] Warren H. Carroll, *The Rise and Fall of the Communist Revolution*, p. 738.
[62] Warren H. Carroll, *The Rise and Fall of the Communist Revolution*, p. 738.
[63] Warren H. Carroll, *The Rise and Fall of the Communist Revolution*, pp. 738-740.
[64] Warren H. Carroll, *The Rise and Fall of the Communist Revolution*, pp. 740-741.
[65] Warren H. Carroll, *The Rise and Fall of the Communist Revolution*, pp. 741-742.
[66] Warren H. Carroll, *The Rise and Fall of the Communist Revolution*, pp. 742-743.
[67] Warren H. Carroll, *The Rise and Fall of the Communist Revolution*, pp. 529-530.
[68] Warren H. Carroll, *The Rise and Fall of the Communist Revolution*, p. 494.
[69] Warren H. Carroll, *The Rise and Fall of the Communist Revolution*, pp. 529-530.
[70] *The Whole Truth About Fatima*, Vol. 2, pp. 543-544.
[71] *The Whole Truth About Fatima*, Vol. 2, p. 465.
[72] William Thomas Walsh, *Our Lady of Fatima*, p. 222.
[73] *The Whole Truth About Fatima*, Vol. 3, p. 712.

[74] *The Whole Truth About Fatima*, Vol. 3, p. 552.
[75] Mark Fellows, *Fatima in Twilight*, p. 334.
[76] Frere Michel de la Sainte Trinite, *The Whole Truth About Fatima*, Vol. 3, pp. 837-838.
[77] William Thomas Walsh, *Our Lady of Fatima*, p. 82.
[78] *The Whole Truth About Fatima*, Vol. 3, pp. 550-551.
[79] Frere Michel de la Sainte Trinite, *The Whole Truth About Fatima*, Vol. 3, pp. 748-749.
[80] Francis Alban, *The Fatima Priest*, Good Counsel Publications, 1997, Intro page.
[81] William Thomas Walsh, *Our Lady of Fatima*, p. 11.
[82] Mark Fellows, *Fatima in Twilight*, p. 327.
[83] Vatican Information Service, Dec. 20, 2001.
[84] "Fr." Gruner appeal letter from Monday, May 1, 2006, The Fatima Center, Constable, NY.

START OF PART IV – CONCLUDING SECTIONS

44. Is the Vatican II sect the Whore of Babylon prophesied in the Apocalypse?

Apocalypse 17:4- "And **the woman was clothed round about with purple and scarlet**, and gilt with gold, and precious stones and pearls, having a golden cup in her hand, full of the abomination and filthiness of her fornication."

None of the points which follow are necessary to prove that the Vatican II sect and its antipopes are not Catholic. The doctrinal evidence covered throughout this book proves this in detail. However, the points which follow are interesting and enlightening as they help to further explain why this catastrophic crisis is occurring, and what to make of it.

Apocalypse 17:1: "And there came one of the seven angels, who had the seven vials, and spoke with me, saying: Come, I will show thee the condemnation of **the great harlot, who sitteth upon many waters**…"

Chapters 17 and 18 of the Apocalypse make striking prophecies about the "great harlot" or the "Whore of Babylon" which will arise in the last days from the city of seven hills. Rome was constructed on seven hills. This is why throughout history Rome has been identified as **the city of seven hills** mentioned in the Apocalypse. Based on this, Protestants throughout the centuries have accused the Catholic Church of being the Whore of Babylon. But the Protestants are wrong, of course, because the Catholic Church is the immaculate Bride of Christ, the one true Church He founded. What **the Whore of Babylon describes, however, is** *a counterfeit Bride – a Counter-Catholic Church* – which arises in the last days in order to deceive Catholics (the true faithful), tread upon the faith and commit spiritual fornication.

1. The whore sits upon many waters.

As we saw already, the great harlot sits upon many waters. The Apocalypse clues us in as to what these waters are.

> Apocalypse 17:15- "And he said to me: **The waters which thou sawest, where the harlot sitteth, are peoples, and nations, and tongues.**"

"Peoples, nations, and tongues" are suggestive of global influence, something which has influence in all ends of the earth. Immediately Rome and the Catholic Church come to mind. The Catholic Church's universal mission has incorporated faithful from all peoples, nations and tongues.

> Pope Pius XII, *Fidei donum* (# 46), April 21, 1957: "Now, **our holy Mother the Church is indeed the Mother 'of all nations, of all peoples**, as well as of individual persons…"[1]

And since Rome is the headquarters of the universal Church, **if Rome were taken over by an antipope who imposed a new religion, it could then influence almost all of the peoples, nations and tongues into its spiritual infidelity**. That is why the harlot sits upon peoples, nations and tongues. In fact, the Council of Trent infallibly confirms our hunch – that the waters upon which the harlot sits are connected with the almost universal expanse that a final days, *counterfeit Catholic Church* would have if an antipope or set of antipopes successfully overtook Rome – with alarming specificity.

> Pope Pius IV, *Council of Trent*, Session 22, On the Holy Sacrifice of the Mass: "The holy synod then admonishes priests that it has been prescribed by the Church to mix water with the wine to be offered in the chalice, not only because the belief is that Christ the Lord did so, but also because there came from His side water together with blood, since by this mixture the sacrament is recalled. **And since in the Apocalypse of the blessed John the peoples are called waters [Apoc. 17:1, 15], the union of the faithful people with Christ, their head, is represented.**"[2]

Notice that the Council of Trent infallibly declares that the waters of Apoc. 17:1,15 represent the union of the faithful people with Christ; in other words, the Catholic Church. **The great harlot sits upon these waters!** Therefore, it is of the Catholic faith that the great harlot sits upon the Catholic Church, that is, she impedes, obstructs, suppresses and attempts to substitute for her. **This is a perfect description of the false Church that arose with Vatican Council II**, which has successfully deceived most of the world into thinking that it is the true Catholic Church.

Understanding that the "waters" of the Apocalypse represent the peoples, nations, and tongues of the Catholic Church, could be the key to understanding other important verses in this book. For example, Apoc. 18:17 talks about how the shipmasters and the mariners wept over the destruction of the great city.

> Apocalypse 18:17- "For in one hour are so great riches come to nought; and **every shipmaster, and all that sail into the lake, and mariners, and as many as work in the sea**, stood afar off, And cried, seeing the place of her burning, saying: What city is like to this great city?"

The shipmasters, mariners and those that work in the sea represent those who work with souls in the Catholic Church; that is, priests, religious, etc. They weep over the desolation of Rome and wonder how in such a short time she has been brought down.

2. The whore sits upon the city of seven mountains.

> Apocalypse 17:9- "And here is the understanding that hath wisdom. The seven heads are **seven mountains, upon which the woman sitteth**, and they are seven kings."

As stated already, Rome was constructed on seven hills. Since the great harlot sits upon the city of seven hills, the great harlot sits upon Rome itself – the center of unity in the Catholic Church and the home of the Roman Pontiffs.

> Pope Benedict XIV, *Apostolica Constitutio* (# 4), June 26, 1749:
> "**... the Catholic Church is signified by the City of Rome alone,** in which the bodily presence of this Apostle [Peter] is carefully reverenced..."[3]

Interestingly, <u>Rome only gives way to the great harlot in the last days</u> – i.e., after the Vatican II revolution. This is why the harlot is only mentioned in the book of the Apocalypse. And this is why Sacred Scripture speaks of the "fall" of Babylon.

> Apocalypse 18:2- "And he cried out with a loud strong voice, saying: **Babylon the great is fallen, is fallen**; and <u>is become</u> the habitation of devils, and the hold of every unclean spirit, and the hold of every unclean and hateful bird."

Babylon has historically been regarded as a code name for Rome.

> 1 Peter 5:13- "The Church that is in **Babylon**, elected together with you, saluteth you: and so doth my son Mark."

Scripture scholars understand that St. Peter was writing this epistle from Rome, which he calls "Babylon." Therefore, Rome is Babylon and Babylon has fallen. But if it has fallen, then it once stood strongly. And is this not true? For prior to its fall, Rome (Babylon) was the bulwark of Catholicism and the center of Christianity - the great city.

> Apocalypse 17:18- "And the woman which thou sawest, is the great city, which hath kingdom over the kings of the earth."

Some may ask: "If Rome is the 'great city,' why does Apocalypse 11:8 say that the great city is the place where Our Lord was crucified, which is Jerusalem?" The answer is that it doesn't actually say that:

> Apoc. 11:8 - "[the two witnesses] shall lie in the street of *the great city, **which spiritually is called Sodom and Egypt, <u>even where</u> their Lord was crucified.***"

Notice that, contrary to what some have claimed, the Apocalypse doesn't clearly state that the two witnesses (which some believe describe Peter and Paul) are killed in the city where Our Lord was crucified. Notice that the passage could very well mean that the great city *is called Sodom and Egypt even where their Lord was crucified*. In other words, the great city, Rome, is referred to as

"Sodom" and "Egypt" as far away as Jerusalem (where their Lord was crucified) because of its immoralities! This makes sense when we consider that Rome was notorious for its corruption. Hence, this passage doesn't clearly prove, as some have suggested, that Jerusalem must be the great city.

Another consideration is that the Mystical Body of Christ is being crucified in and from Rome at present, so in that sense it would also be accurate to say that Rome is the place where Our Lord is crucified in His Mystical Body.

The great city is Rome. Historically, no other city has ruled over the kings of the Earth as has Rome, which has a spiritual and ecclesiastical primacy which all nations must be subject to.

> Pope Leo XII, *Quod Hoc Ineunte* (# 6), May 24, 1824:
> "Come therefore to this holy Jerusalem, a priestly and royal city which the sacred seat of Peter has made the capitol of the world. **Truly it rules more widely by divine religion than by earthly domination.**"[4]

And whether the kings of the earth want to accept it or not, all human creatures must be subject to the spiritual power of the Catholic Church, which (when there is a true pope) is exercised from Rome.

> Pope Boniface VIII, *Unam Sanctam*, Nov. 18, 1302:
> "Now, therefore, **we declare, say, determine and pronounce that for every human creature it is necessary for salvation to be subject to the Roman pontiff.**"[5]

So the fall of the great city is the fall of Rome from the Catholic faith. It's not the fall of the Catholic Church, for the Catholic Church can exist without Rome. It can be reduced to a remnant, just as it is predicted by Our Lord when He speaks about the end of the world (Luke 18:8). Rome, on the other hand, can't exist without Catholicism. Without it, she becomes nothing more than "the habitation of devils, and the hold of every unclean spirit, and the hold of every unclean and hateful bird" (Apoc. 18:2).

> *Our Lady of La Salette*, Sept. 19, 1846, an approved apparition of the Catholic Church:
> "Rome will lose the Faith and become the seat of the Anti-Christ."

3. The whore is a woman.

> Apocalypse 17:6-7 -"And I saw **the woman** drunk with the blood of the saints, and with the blood of the martyrs of Jesus. And I wondered, when I had seen her, with great admiration. And the angel said to me: Why dost thou wonder? I will tell thee the mystery of **the woman**, and of the beast which carrieth her, which hath the seven heads and ten horns."

If it is true that the Whore of Babylon is the phony Catholic Church that began with the Vatican II revolution (as the evidence in this book overwhelmingly shows), it would make sense that this apocalyptic entity is described as a woman, in order to contrast her with another woman – her antithesis – the Catholic Church.

The Whore of Babylon

> Pope Boniface VIII, *Unam Sanctam*, Nov. 18, 1302: "'One is my dove, my perfect one. **One she is** of her mother, the chosen of her that bore her' [Cant. 6:8]; which represents the one mystical body whose head is Christ, of Christ indeed, as God."[6]

4. The whore is a mother.

> Apocalypse 17:5- "And on her forehead a name was written: A mystery; Babylon the great, **the mother of the fornications**, and the abominations of the earth."

Catholics have always referred to the Church as their mother.

> Pope Leo XIII, *Satis Cognitum* (# 16), June 29, 1896:
> "Let us love the Lord our God; let us love His Church; the Lord as our Father, **the Church as our Mother.**"[7]

> Pope Pius XI, *Mortalium Animos* (# 11), Jan. 6, 1928:
> "For if, as they continually state, they long to be united with Us and ours, why do they not hasten to enter the Church, **'the Mother** and mistress **of all Christ's faithful'?**"[8]

> Pope Pius XII, *Mystici Corporis Christi* (# 66), June 29, 1943:
> "**Certainly the loving Mother is spotless** in the Sacraments, by which she gives birth to and nourishes her children; in the faith which she has always preserved inviolate..."[9]

In fact, the Roman Church is specifically called the "mother and mistress" of all the churches (i.e. all the particular churches in communion with the universal Catholic Church).

> Pope Leo XIII, *Exeunte Iam Anno* (# 2), Dec. 25, 1888:
> "… **the Roman Church, mother and mistress of all Churches**..."[10]

It's quite obvious that the Apocalypse describes the Whore of Babylon as the "mother of the fornications" because the Counter Church overtakes *Rome*, where a true pope normally presides over *the Mother Church*. Rome has become the mother fornicator in an almost universal counterfeit Catholic Church of the last days. And we see this in action: the apostasy and spiritual fornication of the Counter Church *starts in Rome* and then spreads to all of the local churches in the counterfeit sect. For example: the religious indifferentism practiced in Rome is spread to the rest of the false Church.

Thus, as the Catholic Church is our loving Mother, the whore is the Mother of the fornications. And as the Catholic Church is the Mother of all Christ's faithful, the whore is the Mother of Christ's unfaithful, that is, those who have abandoned the Church and accepted the new Vatican II religion.

5. The whore is clothed in purple and scarlet.

> Apocalypse 17:4- "And **the woman was clothed round about with purple and scarlet**, and gilt with gold, and precious stones and pearls, having a golden cup in her hand, full of the abomination and filthiness of her fornication."

The Whore of Babylon 564

A cardinal clothed round about in scarlet; a bishop clothed round about (i.e. around the waist) in purple

Apocalypse 18:16- "And saying: Alas! alas! that great city, **which was clothed with fine linen, and purple, and scarlet**, and was gilt with gold, and precious stones, and pearls."

This is perhaps one of the most revealing verses in the Apocalypse. **In the Catholic Church, bishops wear purple and cardinals wear scarlet (red)!** Notice that they are clothed "round about" (around their waists) in these colors.

Cardinals (in scarlet at the top) and bishops (in purple at the bottom) at the Vatican

By choosing to describe the Whore of Babylon as a woman "clothed with fine linen, and purple, and scarlet," God is giving us <u>a clear indication</u> that the whore is <u>clothed</u> in the colors of the true episcopate and cardinalate. God is giving us a clear indication that the whore is clothed in these colors because **externally she gives all the appearances of being the true Church of Christ –** she **has dioceses, a hierarchy, the property of the Church, vestments, ceremonies, "sacraments," a "pope," etc. –** <u>but inwardly she is a fraud</u>. This is a perfect description of the Church of the Vatican II sect, the end-time Counter Church, which is clothed with the colors of Catholicism (and appears to most to be just that) but inwardly is a false apostate religion.

6. The whore has a golden cup in her hand.

Apocalypse 17:4- "And the woman was clothed round about with purple and scarlet, and gilt with gold, and precious stones and pearls, **having a golden cup in her hand**, full of the abomination and filthiness of her fornication."

Priests offering the Holy Sacrifice of the Mass in the Catholic Church are required to use a chalice of gold, if possible. It's no coincidence that the whore has a golden cup in her hand. The whore, **as usual, is mimicking, acting and pretending to be the Catholic Church; but she is not.** A

The Whore of Babylon

Catholic priest offers the golden chalice full of the Precious Blood of Our Lord and Savior Jesus Christ. **The whore offers a cup (chalice) full of abomination and filthiness – the invalid wine of the New Mass!**

In particular, this verse is referring to the *Novus Ordo Missae* (the New Mass), which does not contain the Blood of Jesus Christ, but an offering which is an abomination in His sight.

> Apocalypse 18:6- "Render to her as she also hath rendered to you; and double unto her double according to her works: **in the cup wherein she hath mingled**, mingle ye double unto her."

The word mingle means to mix.[11] In the Catholic Mass, the Church mingles the water with the wine in the chalice.

> Pope Eugene IV, *Council of Florence*, Session 8, Nov. 22, 1439, "Exultate Deo": "For blessed Alexander, the fifth Pope after blessed Peter, says: 'In the offerings of the sacraments which are offered to the Lord within the solemnities of Masses, let only bread and **wine mixed with water be offered as a sacrifice**. For either wine alone or water alone must not be offered in the chalice of the Lord, **but both mixed**, because it is read that both, that is, blood and water, flowed from the side of Christ.' *Then also, because it is fitting to signify the effect of this sacrament, which is the union of the Christian people with Christ.* For water signifies the people, according to the passage in the Apocalypse: 'the many waters... are many people' [Apoc. 17:15]... *Therefore,* **when wine and water are mixed** *in the chalice the people are made one with Christ, and the multitude of the faithful is joined and connected with Him in whom it believes.*"[12]

The symbolism of Apocalypse 18:6 – mingling in a cup – couldn't be more obvious without giving away the mystery of the verse. It's an obvious reference to the Mass, which has been completely perverted by the harlot. She has nothing left to offer to God in her cup but filthiness and abomination (Apoc. 17:4). Furthermore, this verse (18:6) points to a specific point in the Mass, the mixing of wine and water. This action of mixing signifies the union of the Christian people with Christ (the Catholic Church), as Pope Eugene IV defined at the Council of Florence. As we have shown, this is the precise signification which has been removed from the consecration of the New Mass, rendering it invalid!

In one and the same verse, therefore, God is revealing that the whore is conducting massive spiritual fornication in areas which regard the Catholic Mass and the Catholic Church as a whole. It is a startling description of the Vatican II sect: the end-time Counter-Church.

7. The whore is characterized by fornication and whoredom.

> Apocalypse 17:1-2- "Come, I will show thee the condemnation of **the great harlot**, who sitteth upon many waters, With whom the kings of the earth **have committed fornication**; and they who inhabit the earth have been made drunk with the wine of **her whoredom**."

The Whore of Babylon

> Apocalypse 18:3- "Because all nations have drunk of the wine of the wrath of **her fornication**; and **the kings of the earth have committed fornication with her**; and the merchants of the earth have been made rich by the power of her delicacies."

It's simply a fact that when the term fornication is used in Holy Scripture, many times it describes idolatry and spiritual infidelity.

> Exodus 34:16- "Neither shalt thou take of their daughters to wife for thy son, lest after they themselves have committed fornication, **they make thy sons also to commit fornication with their gods**."

> Judges 2:17- "**Committing fornication with strange gods**, and adoring them. They quickly forsook the way, in which their fathers had walked: and hearing the commandments of the Lord, they did all things contrary."

Many other passages could be given to show that Scripture describes spiritual infidelity and idolatry as fornication, whoredom and harlotry. When a "great harlot" committing world-wide fornication is spoken of in this context, it clearly indicates apostasy from the one true Faith. As we have proven in this book, apostasy from the one true Faith and an acceptance of false gods/idolatrous religions is exactly what most characterizes the Vatican II Counter Church and the Vatican II apostasy. It has put the demonic "gods" of the pantheon of world religions on a par with the true God of the Catholic Church.

This fornication which begins from apostate Rome and its antipopes (above) has been spread and imbibed all over the Earth (below), as we've shown.

The interreligious apostasy of the Counter Church spreads from Rome to the universities, etc., as we see here[13]

The Whore of Babylon is guilty of spiritual fornication to such an extent that this is the action which characterizes her title - the "great harlot." By such a description, God is directly contrasting the whore with the Catholic Church; for the Church **is a woman who is characterized by her unwavering fidelity to her Spouse, Jesus Christ**.

> Pope Pius XI, *Mortalium Animos* (# 10), Jan. 6, 1928: "During the lapse of centuries, the mystical Spouse of Christ has never been contaminated, nor can she ever in the future be contaminated, as Cyprian bears witness: '**The Bride of Christ cannot be made false to her Spouse: she is incorrupt and modest. She knows but one dwelling, she guards the sanctity of the nuptial chamber chastely and modestly.**'"[14]

So just as the whore is notorious for her impurity, the Catholic Church is known for her chastity.

> Pope St. Siricius, epistle (1) *Directa ad decessorem* to Himerius, Feb. 10, 385: "And so He has wished the beauty of the Church, whose spouse He is, **to radiate with the splendor of chastity**, so that on the day of judgment, when He will have come again, **He may be able to find her without spot or wrinkle** [Eph. 5:27] as He instituted her through His apostle."[15]

The Church is "the immaculate Bride of Christ." The "great harlot" represents nothing but the greatest mockery of the immaculate Bride of Christ in history.

> Pope Hadrian I, *Second Council of Nicaea*, 787: "...**Christ our God, when He took for His Bride His Holy Catholic Church, having no blemish or wrinkle, promised he would guard her and assured His holy disciples saying, I am with you every day until the consummation of the world.**"[16]

8. The whore has separated from her Spouse.

> Apocalypse 18:7- "As much as she hath glorified herself, and lived in delicacies, so much torment and sorrow give ye to her; **because she saith in her heart: I sit a queen, and am** no widow; and sorrow I shall not see."

In another amazing verse, the Apocalypse tells us that the whore says to herself, "I sit a queen and am no widow." She isn't a widow because her (former) Spouse is not dead.

> Apocalypse 1:17-18- "And when I had seen him, I fell at his feet as dead. And he laid his right hand upon me, saying: Fear not. I am the First and the Last, And alive, and was dead, **and behold I am living forever and ever**, and have the keys of death and of hell."

The Church's Spouse is Jesus Christ. The whore, being *a counterfeit Church that has broken from the Catholic Church*, therefore had Jesus Christ as her Spouse until she separated herself from Jesus Christ by leaving His traditions and teachings. Instead of being a faithful spouse, the whore has become her own queen, who is happy imposing on others her own will and glory, her own teachings and religion.

But whereas the whore has separated herself from the Catholic Church by forming a religion and a "Church" of her own, the Bride of Christ – the Catholic Church – always maintains union with Her Spouse, even if most of the world has left her to join the whore.

> Pope Pius XII, *Mystici Corporis Christi* (# 89), June 29, 1943:
> "This opinion is false; for **the divine Redeemer is most closely united not only with His Church, which is His beloved Spouse**, but also with each and every one of the faithful, and He ardently desires to speak with them heart to heart, especially after Holy Communion."[17]

9. The light of the lamp shall shine no more in the whore.

Apocalypse 18:23- "**And the light of the lamp shall shine no more at all in thee; and the voice of the bridegroom and the bride shall be heard no more at all in thee**: for thy merchants were the great men of the earth, for all nations have been deceived by thy enchantments."

The "light of the lamp" is a reference to the sanctuary lamp found in Catholic churches. **This lamp signifies Christ's real presence in the Eucharist**. This lamp can hardly be found in Vatican II churches. In most cases, it has been moved to the side or to the back of the church. But more than the displacement of the sanctuary lamp, Apocalypse 18:23 is indicating that Christ's real presence (the valid Eucharist) is no longer found in the Vatican II Church.

"The voice of the bridegroom and the bride" in Apocalypse 18:23 is a reference to Christ and His Church.

> Pope Pius XII, *Mystici Corporis Christi* (# 86), June 29, 1943: "... **he [St. Paul] brings Christ and His Mystical Body into a wonderfully intimate union, he nevertheless distinguishes one from the other** *as Bridegroom and Bride* (Eph. 5:22-23)."[18]

If there were any doubt about who the Bridegroom and the Bride are, Pope Pius XII obliterates it by quoting St. Paul. Jesus Christ is the Bridegroom, and His Mystical Body, the Church, is His immaculate Bride. When the Apocalypse makes reference to the voice of the Bridegroom and the Bride, it's another confirmation that the Whore of Babylon is the Vatican II sect – the Counter Church, which has abandoned the teaching (or voice) of the Bridegroom (Jesus Christ) and of the Bride (His Church).

10. The voice of the pipe is no longer heard in the whore.

> Apocalypse 18:22- **"And the voice of harpers, and of musicians, and of them that play on the pipe, and on the trumpet, shall no more be heard at all in thee**..."

Few people today know that "trumpets and harps were the standard instruments for liturgical music in St. John's day, as organs are today in the west."[19] By including the three primary instruments of Catholic liturgical music throughout history, St. John is warning us that traditional Catholic liturgical music as a whole will "no more be heard at all" in the whore. And hasn't this come true?

We've already shown that since Vatican II, Gregorian chant, our beautiful musical tradition, has been replaced by every type of secular music and instrument under the sun.

It's so bad now that one could enter a modern "Catholic" Church and hear anything from boisterous drums to electric guitars. One could walk into one of these churches and even be subjected to rock music. Yet, what's perhaps most disappointing about all of this is that most people don't realize that these modern "Catholic" churches aren't Catholic at all, but belong entirely to the Whore of Babylon.

11. All the world is drunk with the wine of her whoredom.

> Apocalypse 18:3- "Because all nations have drunk of **the wine of the wrath of her fornication**; and the kings of the earth have committed fornication with her."

> Apocalypse 14:8- "And another angel followed, saying: That great Babylon is fallen, is fallen; **which made all nations drink of the wine of the wrath of her fornication**."

> Apocalypse 16:19- "And great Babylon came in remembrance before God, to give her **the cup of the wine of the indignation of His wrath**."

> Apocalypse 17:1-2- "Come, I will shew thee the condemnation of the great harlot, who sitteth upon many waters. With whom the kings of the earth have committed fornication; **and they who inhabit the earth, have been made drunk with the wine of her whoredom.**"

The Whore of Babylon is condemned repeatedly for fornication having to do with wine. Why? As we've shown, it's the change to the wine portion of the consecration that renders the New Mass invalid!

> Pope St. Pius V, *De Defectibus*, chapter 5: "The words of Consecration, which are the form of this Sacrament, are these: *For this is my Body.* And: *For this is the Chalice of my Blood, of the new and eternal testament: the mystery of faith, which shall be shed for you and for many unto the remission of sins.* **Now if one were to remove, or change anything in the form of the consecration of the Body and Blood, and in that very change of words the [new] wording would fail to mean the same thing, he would not consecrate the Sacrament.**"

The reason that the whore is condemned for wine violations is because invalidating changes have been made to the WINE PORTION of the words of consecration in the New Mass. See the earlier section on the New Mass for the full discussion. These changes to the wine portion of the consecration invalidate both consecrations. The Vatican II Church has truly "*made all nations drink of the wine* of the wrath of her fornication" (Apoc. 14:8).

12. The whore is drunk with the blood of the saints and martyrs.

> Pope Leo XIII, *Au milieu des sollicitudes* (#11), Feb. 16, 1892: "[Many times]… **Christians, by the mere fact of their being such, and for no other reason, were forced to choose between apostasy and martyrdom**, being allowed no alternative."[20]

> Apocalypse 17:6- "**And I saw the woman drunk with the blood of the saints, and with the blood of the martyrs of Jesus.** And I wondered when I had seen her, with great admiration."

> Apocalypse 18:24- "**And in her was found the blood of prophets and of saints**, and of all that were slain upon the earth."

The whore can be said to be drunk with the blood of the saints on many levels. The first that comes to mind is ecumenism as it is practiced by the Vatican II sect. Prior to Vatican II, ecumenism referred to the apostolic endeavor to convert the world to Catholicism. Today, it refers to the effort to bring all religions together as one without conversion, while respecting all religions as essentially equal.

> Pope Leo XIII, *Custodi Di Quella Fede* (# 15), Dec. 8, 1892:
> "**Every familiarity should be avoided, not only with those impious libertines who openly promote the character of the sect, but also with those who hide under the mask of universal tolerance, <u>respect for all religions</u>**, and the craving to reconcile the maxims of the Gospel with those of the revolution. **These men seek to reconcile Christ and Belial**, the Church of God and the state without God."[21]

Ecumenism goes directly against the divinely revealed truth that the gods of the non-Catholic religions are devils (Psalm 95:5; 1 Cor. 10:20), and it puts Christ on a level with Lucifer. Throughout this book we've exposed the false ecumenism of the Vatican II sect. The Vatican II sect considers false religions more or less good and praiseworthy. Thus, it blasphemes the memory of the saints and martyrs whose flesh was torn with iron hooks, bodies were fed to the lions, and heads were chopped off because they refused to compromise their faith one iota or say that "all religions are more or less good and praiseworthy." It also mocks all the sacrifices of all the saints who gave up their lives for the priesthood, for religious life, for missionary work. All of it was unnecessary, according to the Vatican II sect.

> Pope St. Gregory the Great: "**The holy universal Church teaches that it is not possible to worship God truly except in her and asserts that all who are outside of her will not be saved.**"[22]

Because Margaret Clitherow refused to accept the Anglican sect and its "Mass" – but rather invited Catholic priests into her home against the penal laws – she was martyred by being crushed to death under a large door loaded with heavy weights. This style of execution is so painful that it is called "severe and harsh punishment." **She suffered it all because she wouldn't accept Anglicanism**. The Vatican II sect, however, teaches that Anglicans are fellow "Christians" who don't need conversion, and whose invalid "bishops" are actually true bishops of the Church of Christ. The Vatican II sect teaches that her martyrdom was pointless. It is thus drunk with the blood of the saints and martyrs.

How many martyrs, such as St. Thomas More, gave their lives for one article of the Catholic faith? Ecumenism renders their blood-shedding acts worthless, pointless and meaningless.

> Pope Leo XIII, *Satis Cognitum* (# 8), June 29, 1896: "It was thus the duty of all who heard Jesus Christ, if they wished for eternal salvation, not merely to accept His doctrine as a whole, **but to assent with their entire mind to all and every point of it, since it is unlawful to withhold faith from God even in regard to one single point.**"[23]

This is why the Vatican II Church is said to be drunk with the blood of martyrs and of saints (Apoc. 17:6; 18:24), and all those who support this antichrist activity now headed by Benedict XVI are drunk as well.

What's also fascinating is that the Apocalypse mentions that <u>the martyrs cried out from under the altar</u>.

> Apocalypse 6:9- "And when he had opened the fifth seal, **<u>I saw under the altar the souls of them that were slain for the word of God, and for the testimony which they held. And they cried out with a loud voice, saying</u>:** How long, O Lord (holy and true) dost thou not judge and revenge our blood on them that dwell on the Earth?"

It is prescribed that **Catholic Mass is to be said on altars which contain the relics of martyrs**! Thus, it makes perfect sense that the martyrs, whose lives are being mocked by the Vatican II sect's ecumenism and endorsement of false religions, are crying out from "under the altar"! They are crying out not only at the interreligious ecumenism which mocks their lives, but also at the liturgical abominations which occur directly over their relics in the New Mass. This striking point from Scripture should also show Protestants that the Catholic Church is the one true Church.

> Apocalypse 18:20, God's Judgment on the Whore- "Rejoice over her, thou heaven, and ye holy apostles and prophets; for God hath judged your judgment on her."

Conclusion on the Whore of Babylon

It's quite obvious, in our opinion, that the Vatican II sect is the Whore of Babylon prophesied in Scripture. And contrary to what the Protestant heretics believe, the fact that ecclesiastical Rome's apostasy from the Catholic faith in the last days is predicted in Scripture proves rather than disproves the authenticity of the Catholic Church. For the tribulation of the last days will be <u>one which focuses on deceiving the true faithful</u>, and undermining the true Faith.

> Apocalypse 11:2- "But the court, which is without the temple, cast out, and measure it not: because it is given unto the Gentiles, **and the holy city they shall tread under foot two and forty months.**"

It should be noted that "two and forty months" (Apoc. 11:2), "a thousand two hundred and sixty days" (Apoc. 12:6), and "a time, and times, and half a time" (Apoc. 12:14) and 3 and 1/2 years are regarded by some scholars as symbolic of any period of persecution.

> Luke 21:34-35- "And take heed to yourselves, lest perhaps your hearts be overcharged with surfeiting and drunkenness, and the cares of this life, and that day come upon you suddenly. **For as a snare it shall come upon all that sit upon the face of the whole earth.**"

A snare is a device used to catch animals. Now, if the snare of the last days involves a counterfeit Catholic Church set up from Rome, and a spiritual invasion of the holy city (Rome), then the "animal" that the devil is trying to catch is Traditional Catholicism. This is another proof that the Catholic religion is the one and only true religion.

It is our hope that this scriptural evidence against the Vatican II Church will strengthen Catholics in their opposition to it. The biblical prophecies which pinpoint our present situation also enable Catholics to have a better understanding of how God views the developments and events of the last 50 or so years.

But most of all, the Apocalypse uncovers the false resistance to this apostasy, even among the so-called traditionalists, who advocate a position in reference to this harlot church which demands that they remain united to its antipopes and the Vatican II sect. Such a false "We resist you..." places them right in the very bosom and womb of the harlot. By their own profession, they are still obstinately united to the "mother of the fornications." They still confuse the great harlot with the immaculate Bride of Christ. They still taint a pure and unsullied resistance to the harlot by sticking themselves in the midst of her abominable dominion.

> Apocalypse 18:4-5- "And I heard another voice from heaven, saying: **Go out from her, my people**; that you be not partakers of her sins, and that you receive not of her plagues. For her sins have reached unto heaven, and the Lord hath remembered her iniquities."

If they don't completely break with the great harlot, these people will lose their souls in the eternal fire for blaspheming the Church of Christ the King, which has no fellowship with the works of darkness, no part with the unbeliever, and no concord with the woman of iniquity. Though much of the world has been engulfed by the great harlot, the immaculate Bride of Our Lord still exists in all her purity, though she has been reduced to a remnant and forced underground. This woman, the remnant Catholic Church in the last days, is described in chapter 12 of the Apocalypse after the vision of the woman clothed with the sun, Our Lady of Fatima.

> Apocalypse 12:6- "And *the woman* **fled into the wilderness**, where she had a place prepared by God, that there they should feed her a thousand two hundred and sixty days."

> Apocalypse 12:14- "And **there were given to** *the woman* **two wings of a great eagle, that she might fly into the desert** unto her place, where she is nourished for a time and times, and half a time, from the face of the serpent."

If we have not joined already, we must enter this remnant Catholic Church in the wilderness. We must maintain "the faith once delivered to the saints" (Jude 1:3), and come closer to God by receiving the true sacraments, and practicing devotion to the Immaculate Heart of Mary and the holy rosary.

> Apocalypse 12:17- "And the dragon was angry against the woman: and went to make war with the rest of her seed, who keep the commandments of God, and have the testimony of Jesus Christ."

> Apocalypse 12:12- "Here is the patience of the saints, who keep the commandments of God, and the faith of Jesus."

Endnotes for Section 44:

[1] *The Papal Encyclicals*, by Claudia Carlen, Raleigh: The Pierian Press, 1990, Vol. 4 (1939-1958), p. 327.
[2] Denzinger, *The Sources of Catholic Dogma*, B. Herder Book. Co., Thirtieth Edition, 1957, no. 945.
[3] *The Papal Encyclicals*, Vol. 1 (1740-1878), p. 28.
[4] *The Papal Encyclicals*, Vol. 1 (1740-1878), p. 206.
[5] Denzinger 468.

[6] Denzinger 468.
[7] *The Papal Encyclicals*, Vol. 2 (1878-1903), p. 403.
[8] *The Papal Encyclicals*, Vol. 3 (1903-1939), p. 318.
[9] *The Papal Encyclicals*, Vol. 4 (1939-1958), p. 50.
[10] *The Papal Encyclicals*, Vol. 2 (1878-1903), p. 403.
[11] *The Oxford Illustrated Dictionary*, Second edition, Oxford: Clarendon Press, 1985, p. 538.
[12] Denzinger 698.
[13] www.georgetown.edu
[14] *The Papal Encyclicals*, Vol. 3 (1903-1939), p. 317.
[15] Denzinger 89.
[16] *Decrees of the Ecumenical Councils*, Sheed & Ward and Georgetown University Press, 1990, Vol. 1, p. 133.
[17] *The Papal Encyclicals*, Vol. 4 (1939-1958), p. 55.
[18] *The Papal Encyclicals*, Vol. 4 (1939-1958), p. 54.
[19] Scott Hahn, *The Lamb's Supper*, Doubleday, 1999, p. 120.
[20] *The Papal Encyclicals*, Vol. 2 (1878-1903), p. 279.
[21] *The Papal Encyclicals*, Vol. 2 (1878-1903), p. 304.
[22] *The Papal Encyclicals*, Vol. 1 (1740-1878), p. 230.
[23] *The Papal Encyclicals*, Vol. 2 (1878-1903), p. 392.

45. The Antichrist Code: The Shocking truth that John Paul II was preaching that Man is God – the Doctrine of Antichrist – right in the Vatican

John Paul II in Israel, sitting in a chair with an upside-down cross over his head, on March 24, 2000. For those who would attempt to justify this outrageous and very revealing action by pointing out that St. Peter was crucified upside-down, we respond that this is a futile attempt to defend the indefensible. When John Paul II did this, it was not one of St. Peter's feast days, nor was any commemoration of St. Peter made at all. The upside-down cross is one of the biggest symbols in satanism, as evidenced by its use by occultists, satanic rock groups, and ritual murderers. That's why John Paul II was sitting with this symbol over his head.

Pope St. Pius X, *E Supremi Apostolatus*, Oct. 4, 1903: "While, on the other hand, and this according to the same apostle is **the distinguishing mark of Antichrist, man has with infinite temerity put himself in the place of God**."[1]

John Paul II, *Redemptor Hominis* (# 10), March 4, 1979: "IN REALITY, THE NAME FOR THAT DEEP AMAZEMENT AT MAN'S WORTH AND DIGNITY IS THE GOSPEL, THAT IS TO SAY: THE GOOD NEWS. IT IS ALSO CALLED CHRISTIANITY."[2]

The Doctrine of Antichrist

John Paul II in Detroit, prior to becoming an antipope, wearing an upside-down cross vestment

Contents of this Section:
Our Lady Prophesied that Rome would lose the Faith and become the Seat of Antichrist
Antichrist Defined
Antipope John Paul II Preached:
    Each Man Must Take Possession of the Incarnation
    The Gospel is the Good News of Man
    Man is the Christ, the Son of the Living God
    The Truth About Man is that he is Christ
    And the Word became Flesh in Every Man
    The Incarnation is the Truth About Man
    The Mystery of the Word Made Flesh is the Mystery of Man
    Mary is Blessed because she had faith in Man
    Every man is the Christ Child Born on Christmas
    The Epiphany is the Manifestation of Man
    Man is the Way
    Man is the Truth
    Man is the Life
    Each Man is the Eucharist
    Each Man is the Crucified Christ
    Man is Indeed God
    Man is the Man from Above
    Man's true reality is that he is God
    Man is the Messiah

The New Evangelization
Man must discover that he is God
The Rosary of Man
The Unsearchable Riches of Christ are Everyone's Property
Man is the Risen Christ
Antichrist Revealed

1. Our Lady Prophesied that Rome will become the Seat of Antichrist

As we've seen, on Sept. 19, 1846, the Blessed Virgin Mary appeared in La Salette, France, and foretold that:

> *"Rome will lose the faith and become the Seat of the Antichrist… the Church will be in eclipse."*

Our Lady specifically predicted that Rome would lose the Catholic faith, fall into apostasy from the true Church of Christ and become the Seat of the Antichrist. But what is antichrist?

2. Antichrist defined

In all of Sacred Scripture, the word *antichrist* is only mentioned four times. The word *antichrist* is not mentioned at all in the Apocalypse and it is not mentioned by St. Paul (who only uses the terms "son of perdition" and "man of sin"). The word *antichrist* is only mentioned by St. John the Apostle in his epistles.

Therefore, in looking for the definition of *Antichrist*, we must first look to St. John's epistles, not the Apocalypse; for St. John uses and defines the word *Antichrist* and the Apocalypse does not. Out of the four times that St. John uses the word *Antichrist*, he only defines it twice. The two definitions that St. John gives for Antichrist are the most important pieces of evidence that exist in identifying who the Antichrist actually is, because Sacred Scripture is the inspired, infallible and inerrant Word of God. Therefore, Sacred Scripture's definition of Antichrist is infallibly the correct one.

> 1 John 2:22 – "Who is a liar, but **he who denieth that Jesus is the Christ? He is antichrist**, who denieth the Father, and the Son."

> 1 John 4:2-3 – "Every spirit that confesseth that Jesus Christ is come in the flesh, is of God: **And every spirit that dissolveth Jesus is not of God: and this is Antichrist**, of whom you have heard that he cometh…"

Both definitions of Antichrist deal with a denial of the truth about *who Jesus Christ is*. The truth about Our Lord Jesus Christ and the truth about the Most Holy Trinity are the very foundations of the Christian religion. They are the most important truths in the universe.

This is why the early councils of the Catholic Church condemned with the utmost vigor even the slightest deviation from the truth about Jesus Christ or the Trinity. And this is why the greatest enemies of Jesus Christ in history were not those men who caused Christ's followers temporal harm, but those who were most effective and blasphemous in attacking the truth about Jesus Christ – which is the very foundation of one's eternal salvation.

Thus, in defining "Antichrist," <u>Sacred Scripture refers to a specific attack on the truth about Jesus Christ, a specific attack on the truth about the God-man</u>. Sacred Scripture refers specifically to the dissolving of Jesus (1 John 4:2-3) and the denial that Jesus is the Christ (1 John 2:22). These two things serve as the distinguishing characteristic of the Antichrist, according to Sacred Scripture, and these two things clearly refer to an attack on the truth of the Incarnation of the Son of God.

One of the first and most notorious men in Church history to pervert the doctrine of the Incarnation was the 5th century heretic Nestorius, who was condemned by the Council of Ephesus in 431. The case of the heretic Nestorius is very important in identifying the Antichrist and how it has overtaken the Vatican, as we will see, because Nestorius's heresy was the specific heresy which fits the Bible's definition for Antichrist.

Nestorius was the heretic who tried to dissolve Jesus (1 John 4:2-3), and he did so by perverting the truth of the Incarnation.

> Pope Pius XI, *Lux Veritatis* (# 37), Dec. 25, 1931: "…all these, **no less than Nestorius, make a temerarious attempt to 'DISSOLVE CHRIST,'**…"[3]

Pope Pius XI here confirms that Nestorius's heresy was the specific doctrine of Antichrist – it was an attempt to dissolve the Person of Jesus Christ, which is the mark of Antichrist, according to Scripture. Keep this fact in mind (that Nestorius's doctrine of the "dissolving of Jesus" was the specific doctrine of Antichrist as described by Sacred Scripture), as it will become especially relevant soon.

But what was this doctrine of Nestorius? How did Nestorius "DISSOLVE" Jesus and in so doing become what St. John defines as "Antichrist"? In order to understand Nestorius's doctrine, we must very briefly repeat the Catholic truth of the Incarnation.

The Catholic Church teaches that the eternal Word – the Son of God – the Second Person of the Most Holy Trinity – assumed a human nature and truly became a man. St. John 1:14: *"And the Word was made flesh, and dwelt among us."*

Our Lord Jesus Christ is the eternal Word made flesh. He is truly God and He is also truly man. **He is one Christ** – One Divine Person with two natures.

> Pope St. Leo the Great, *Council of Chalcedon*, 451, ex cathedra: "… we all with one voice teach the confession of one and same Son, our Lord Jesus Christ: the same perfect in divinity and perfect in humanity, the same truly God and truly man, of a rational soul and a body… one and same Christ… a single person and subsistent being; <u>He is not parted or divided into two persons</u>, but is one and the same only-begotten Son, God, Word, Lord Jesus Christ…"[4]

But Nestorius rejected that Our Lord Jesus Christ is one person. Nestorius blasphemously dissolved Jesus into two persons. Nestorius blasphemously held that the Son of God did not become man in the Incarnation, but rather that the Son of God united himself in a certain way with a man named Jesus.

> **WE REPEAT, NESTORIUS DID NOT HOLD THAT THE SON OF GOD BECAME MAN IN THE INCARNATION, BUT RATHER <u>THAT THE SON OF GOD UNITED HIMSELF IN A CERTAIN WAY WITH A MAN NAMED JESUS</u>.** Does this sound familiar?

> Antipope John Paul II, *Redemptor Hominis* #13, March 4, 1979: "… by his Incarnation, he, **the Son of God, <u>in a certain way united himself with EACH MAN</u>.**"[5]

> Antipope John Paul II, *Homily*, July 2, 1986: "**… the Son of God**, incarnate in the womb of the Virgin Mary, **'has in a certain way united himself with each man.'**"[6]

> Antipope John Paul II, *Homily*, April 8, 1987: "… **by his incarnation the Son of God has united himself in a certain way with EACH PERSON.**"[7]

> Antipope John Paul II, *Letter to Families* (# 2): "… the Son of God, who in the Incarnation 'united himself in some sense with every man.'"[8]

And by holding that the Son of God did not become man, but rather <u>united Himself with a man named Jesus in the Incarnation</u>, Nestorius dissolved or divided Our Lord Jesus Christ into two persons.

> Pope St. Leo the Great, Dogmatic Letter to Flavian, 449: "Let Nestorius, therefore, be anathematized… **he made one person of the flesh, and another of the Godhead, AND DID NOT PERCEIVE THAT THERE WAS BUT ONE CHRIST…**"[9]

And by dissolving or dividing Our Lord Jesus Christ into two persons, Nestorius's Antichrist doctrine logically resulted in the worship of two Christs, and introduced, as a consequence, **THE WORSHIP OF MAN!**

> Pope Vigilius, *Second Council of Constantinople*, 553: "**The holy synod of Ephesus… has pronounced sentence against the heresy of Nestorius**… and all those who might later… adopt the same opinions as he held… They express these falsehoods against the true dogmas of the Church, **OFFERING WORSHIP TO TWO SONS**, trying to divide that which cannot be divided, **AND INTRODUCING TO BOTH HEAVEN AND EARTH THE OFFENCE OF THE WORSHIP OF MAN**. But the sacred band of heavenly spirits worship along with us only one Lord Jesus Christ."[10]

In this incredible quotation, the dogmatic *Second Council of Constantinople* teaches that the blasphemous dissolving of Jesus into two persons by Nestorius's view of the Incarnation, <u>resulted in the worship of two sons</u>, and introduced as a consequence **THE WORSHIP OF MAN**. We repeat, **NESTORIUS'S HERETICAL VIEW OF THE INCARNATION RESULTED IN THE WORSHIP OF TWO SONS, AND INTRODUCED, AS A CONSEQUENCE, THE WORSHIP OF MAN**. This was the very doctrine described by St. John as the doctrine of the Antichrist. Does it sound familiar?

Antipope John Paul II, *Redemptor Hominis* (# 10), March 4, 1979: "IN REALITY, THE NAME FOR THAT DEEP AMAZEMENT AT <u>MAN'S WORTH AND DIGNITY IS THE GOSPEL,</u>

THAT IS TO SAY: THE GOOD NEWS. IT IS ALSO CALLED CHRISTIANITY."[11]

Yes, Antipope John Paul II preached the heresy of Nestorius – the very doctrine of the Antichrist. He preached the dissolving of Jesus in the Incarnation, which results in the worship of multiple Christs and the worship of man!

Here, in his very first encyclical, *Redemptor Hominis*, Antipope John Paul II explicitly defined the Gospel, the Good News and Christianity as the deep amazement at man. **The Gospel is the Life of Jesus Christ!** By saying that the deep amazement at each man is the Gospel, the Good News and Christianity, Antipope John Paul II indicated that each man is Jesus Christ whom Christians worship. And this worship of each man as Christ springs from Antipope John Paul II's teaching that the Son of God united Himself with each man in the Incarnation!

Furthermore, while the similarity between Nestorius and Antipope John Paul II is undeniable, there is a crucial difference between the two. There is a crucial difference between the preliminary Antichrist, Nestorius, and Antipope John Paul II, whose doctrine represents the fulfillment of Our Lady's prophecy that Rome will become the Seat of the Antichrist. The difference is that Antipope John Paul II's preaching was six billion times worse. Nestorius dissolved Jesus into two (resulting in the worship of two Christs), while Antipope John Paul II dissolved Jesus into six billion, which resulted in the worship of six billion Christs.

> Antipope John Paul II, *General Audience*, Jan. 25, 1984: "**Christ, the Son of God, by becoming flesh, assumes the humanity of every man**… At this point he becomes united with every person… **In the Encyclical *Redemptor Hominis* I wrote that 'the name for that deep amazement at man's worth and dignity is the Gospel, that is to say, the Good News. It is also called Christianity.'**"[12]

Here we have Antipope John Paul II illustrating his dissolving of Jesus (his doctrine of the Antichrist) and his worship of man with cause and effect precision. He tells us that because the Son of God was united with each man in the Incarnation, that is, because the Son of God **was dissolved into each man in the Incarnation,** the name for **Christianity is the deep amazement at each man**; because by virtue of that event, every man is Jesus Christ. Every man is truly Son of God and truly man. We will prove in this article that this doctrine of the Antichrist, that each man became the Son of God in the Incarnation and is therefore Jesus Christ, is what Antipope John Paul II preached to the world.

3. Each man must take possession of the Incarnation

Just prior to defining Christianity as the deep amazement at man in his first encyclical *Redemptor Hominis*, Antipope John Paul II wrote the following:

> Antipope John Paul II, *Redemptor Hominis* (# 10): "**The man who wishes to understand himself thoroughly**… **he must 'appropriate' and assimilate the whole of the reality of the Incarnation** and Redemption **in order to find himself.** If this profound process takes place within him, he then bears fruit not only of adoration of God but also of deep wonder at himself."[13]

To appropriate something is to "*take possession of it*."[14] To assimilate something is to absorb it. Therefore, Antipope John Paul II is saying here that man must take possession of the Incarnation (that is, he must take possession of the fact that God became man) in order to find himself. This means that man must understand that he is a God-man in order to find himself.

When this happens in man, according to Antipope John Paul II, man will not only possess adoration of God, "but also of deep wonder at himself," because he will learn that he too is Christ, the Son of God who has become man. This is why Antipope John Paul II defined Christianity as the deep amazement at each man in the very next paragraph of this encyclical (quoted already).

> Antipope John Paul II, *Redemptor Hominis* (# 10), March 4, 1979: "The man who wishes to understand himself thoroughly… **he must 'appropriate' and assimilate the whole of the reality of the Incarnation** and Redemption in order to find himself… IN REALITY, THE NAME FOR **THAT DEEP AMAZEMENT AT MAN'S WORTH AND DIGNITY IS THE GOSPEL,** THAT IS TO SAY: THE GOOD NEWS. IT IS ALSO CALLED CHRISTIANITY."[15]

Moreover, Antipope John Paul II repeated his important message (about taking possession of the Incarnation in order to find man) numerous times in his writings (*Catechesi Tradendae* # 61; *Veritatis Splendor* # 8), since, as we have already shown, it is the foundation for the entire Gospel of Antichrist.

So at least three times in his writings, Antipope John Paul II taught that man must take possession of the Incarnation in order to find himself. And immediately after the first time he mentions this in *Redemptor Hominis*, Antipope John Paul II confirms his real meaning by defining Christianity as the deep amazement at each man, confirming that this worship of each man flows directly from the Incarnation.

4. The Gospel is the Good News of man

Antipope John Paul II defined the Gospel as the deep amazement at man in his first encyclical and numerous other times. But Antipope John Paul II also defined the Gospel as the Good News of Jesus Christ. He defined it both ways because his message was that every man *is* Jesus Christ.

> Antipope John Paul II, *Address*, March 7, 1983: "*The Gospel is a person*: it is Jesus Christ."[16]

> Antipope John Paul II, *Homily*, June 1, 1980: "Not only is the Gospel message addressed to man, but it is a great Messianic message about man; it is the revelation to man of the complete truth about himself…"[17]

> Antipope John Paul II, *Redemptoris Missio* (# 13): **"Jesus himself is the 'Good News,'** … **he proclaims the 'Good News' not just by what he says or does, but by what he is."**[18]

> Antipope John Paul II, *Homily*, June 4, 1997: **"The Gospel, by proclaiming the Good News of Jesus, announces also the Good News of man**…"[19]

> Antipope John Paul II, *On Christ's Lay Faithful* (# 7), Dec. 30, 1988: "…*Jesus Christ himself, is the 'good news'*…"[20]

> Antipope John Paul II, *Homily*, May 9, 1988: **"The Gospel is the revelation of God… And it is also the revelation of the truth about man**, about his dignity… We call it Good News or 'Good Tidings'…"[21]

The Doctrine of Antichrist 584

Antipope John Paul II preached to the world that man and Jesus are one and the same, and that the Gospel is the truth about Jesus *and also* the truth about each man. The next quotation, in fact, is particularly revealing.

> Antipope John Paul II, *Address to Members of U.S. Congress*, Jan. 8, 2001: "In the years of my ministry, but especially in the Jubilee Year just ended, I have invited all to **turn to Jesus in order** *to discover in new and deeper ways the truth of man* … **To see the truth of Christ is to experience with deep amazement the worth and dignity of every human being**, which is the Good News of the Gospel … (cf. Redemptor Hominis, n. 10)."[22]

First of all, notice the reference to *Redemptor Hominis* 10 that Antipope John Paul II made. *Redemptor Hominis* 10 is where Antipope John Paul II originally defined the Gospel and Christianity as the deep amazement at man.

> Antipope John Paul II, *Redemptor Hominis* (# 10), March 4, 1979: **"IN REALITY, THE NAME FOR THAT DEEP AMAZEMENT AT MAN'S WORTH AND DIGNITY IS THE GOSPEL, THAT IS TO SAY: THE GOOD NEWS. IT IS ALSO CALLED CHRISTIANITY."**[23]

Secondly, just before giving that reference, Antipope John Paul II says that to see the truth of Christ is to experience with deep amazement the worth and dignity of every human being. In other words, TO SEE THE TRUTH OF CHRIST IS TO EXPERIENCE EVERY MAN, according to Antipope John Paul II, and this is the Good News of the Gospel. This means that every man is Jesus Christ.

> Galatians 1:8-9- "But though we, or an angel from heaven, preach a gospel to you besides that which we have preached to you, let him be anathema. As we said before, so now I say again: If anyone preach to you a gospel, besides that which you have received, let him be anathema."

5. Man is the Christ, the Son of the Living God

In the 16th Chapter of St. Matthew's Gospel is recorded one of the most important events in the history of Christianity.

> "And Jesus came into the parts of Cesarea Philippi: and he asked his disciples, saying: Whom do men say that the Son of man is? But they said: Some John the Baptist, and others Elias, and others Jeremias, or one of the prophets. Jesus saith to them: But whom do you say that I am. Simon Peter answering said: **Thou art Christ, the Son of the Living God.**"

In this dramatic moment in salvation history, St. Peter professed the truth that lies at the heart of the Gospel. He professed correctly that Jesus is the Christ, the Son of the Living God.

In his very first homily, Antipope John Paul II addressed these words spoken by St. Peter about Our Lord Jesus Christ.

> Antipope John Paul II, Very First Homily, Forever Marking the Beginning of his Pastoral Ministry, Sunday, Oct. 22, 1978: "'1. *You are the Christ, the Son of the living God*' (Mt. 16:16). These words were spoken by Simon,

son of Jonah, in the district of Caesarea Philippi… These words mark the beginning of Peter's mission in the history of salvation…

"2. On this day and in this place these same words must again be uttered and listened to: '***You are the Christ, the Son of the living God***.' Yes, Brothers and sons and daughters, these words first of all… please listen once again, today, in this sacred place, to the words uttered by Simon Peter. In those words is the faith of the Church. ***In those same words is the new truth, indeed, the ultimate and definitive truth about man: the Son of the living God – 'You are the Christ, the Son of the living God.'***"[24]

In his first ever homily as antipope in 1978, <u>in the very speech which will forever mark the beginning of his pastoral ministry</u>, Sunday, Oct. 22, 1978, Antipope John Paul II proclaimed to the world that MAN is the Christ, the Son of the Living God! He even said that this is a "new truth" – a new truth which he is here to reveal. *"Thou art the Christ, the Son of the Living God,"* spoken by St. Peter about Our Lord Jesus Christ are the words which describe the truth about man, according to Antipope John Paul II.

And it is no accident that Antipope John Paul II made this proclamation in his very first homily as antipope. He was here to preach man in the place of Christ, so he was setting forth his Antichrist doctrine from the very beginning. People cannot underestimate the significance of this speech.

> Pope St. Pius X, *E Supremi Apostolatus*, Oct. 4, 1903: "While, on the other hand, and this according to the same apostle is **the distinguishing mark of Antichrist, man has with infinite temerity put himself in the place of God**."[25]

The distinguishing mark of Antichrist, man in the place of God, was the distinguishing mark of Antipope John Paul II. He was here to substitute the Gospel of Jesus Christ with a gospel of man as Christ; he was here to substitute the truth about Jesus Christ with the truth about man.

6. The Truth about man is that he is Jesus Christ

In Antipope John Paul II's writings, one will find countless references to man. But in his writings one will also find countless references to "the truth about man" and "the whole truth about man." We now know what Antipope John Paul II meant when he referred to this "truth about man." It was that the truth about man is that he is Jesus Christ.

> Antipope John Paul II, *Homily*, Dec. 17, 1991: "Dear brothers and sisters, **look to Christ, the Truth about man**…"[26]

Here Antipope John Paul II explicitly tells us that Christ is the Truth about man. This means that the truth about man is that he is Jesus Christ.

> Antipope John Paul II, *General Audience*, Feb. 22, 1984: "… **so that consciences can be freed in the full truth of man, who is Christ**…"[27]

In issue #5 of our magazine, we quote many other texts where John Paul II indicates – sometimes in a very crafty way – that the "truth about man" is that he is Christ. We refer you to those texts and the video on our website (www.mostholyfamilymonastery.com), as we must move on.

7. And the Word became flesh in every man

In John 1:14, we read about the Incarnation of the Son of God, *"And the Word was made flesh, and dwelt among us."* Here is what Antipope John Paul II had to say about these words.

> Antipope John Paul II, *Encyclical on the Holy Ghost* (# 50): "'**The Word became flesh.' The Incarnation of God the Son signifies the taking up into unity with God not only of human nature, but in this human nature, in a sense, everything that is 'flesh': the whole of humanity** …"[28]

Here Antipope John Paul II quotes the words of John 1:14, and says that the Word becoming flesh means the taking up of <u>all flesh</u>, the whole of humanity. This literally means that the Son of God became all flesh, the whole of humanity. And this is why Antipope John Paul II says the following:

> Antipope John Paul II, *Evangelium Vitae* (# 104): "**It is precisely in the 'flesh' of every person that Christ continues to reveal himself** … so that *rejection of human life*, in whatever form that rejection takes, is *really a rejection of Christ.*"[29]

Here Antipope John Paul II confirms his doctrine as he set it forth in the *Encyclical on the Holy Ghost* #50. Because the Word became flesh <u>in all of humanity</u>, it is in the flesh of EVERY PERSON that Christ reveals Himself. Every person is the Word made flesh, according to Antipope John Paul II. Notice how he even puts the word "flesh" in quotation marks, indicating specifically that every person is "the Word made flesh" of John 1:14.

8. The Incarnation is the Truth about Man

> Antipope John Paul II, *Homily in St. Louis*, Jan. 27, 1999: "*In the Incarnation, God fully reveals himself in the Son* … **The Incarnation also reveals the truth about man.**"[30]

This means that man is the Incarnate Word.

> Antipope John Paul II, *Angelus Address*, Jan. 4, 1981: "**The coming of God to the world, the birth of God in a human body, is a penetrating and dazzling truth. It is a way along which man, as he walks, rediscovers himself.**"[31]

This means that each man discovers that he is God in a human body.

> Antipope John Paul II, *Homily*, Dec. 14, 1999: "**By fixing our gaze on the mystery of the Incarnate Word… man discovers himself.**"[32]

Here Antipope John Paul II blatantly asserts that by looking at the God-man, man discovers himself.

9. The mystery of the Word made flesh is the mystery of man

> Antipope John Paul II, *Address*, Jan. 14, 1999: **"And in reality it is only in the mystery of the Word made flesh that the mystery of man truly becomes clear."**[33]

Antipope John Paul II uttered this statement hundreds of times. He told us that it is only in the MYSTERY of the Word made flesh – that is to say, only in the mystery of the God-man – that the mystery of each man becomes clear, because each man is the God-man, according to the doctrine of Antichrist which he preached. Notice that Antipope John Paul II did not say that it is in the *teaching* of the Word made flesh that the mystery of man is made clear, but rather in the *mystery* of the Incarnate Word – the mystery of the God-man Himself – Our Lord Jesus Christ.

> Antipope John Paul II, *Veritatis Splendor* (# 2), August 6, 1993: **"In fact, *it is only in the mystery of the Word Incarnate that light is shed on the mystery of man.*"**[34]

> Antipope John Paul II, *Encyclical on Faith and Reason* (# 12): **"…only in the mystery of the incarnate Word does the mystery of man take on light."**[35]

> Antipope John Paul II, *Homily*, Oct. 25, 1991: **"In reality it is only in the mystery of the Word made flesh that the mystery of man truly becomes clear…"**[36]

10. Mary is Blessed because she had faith in Man

In Luke 1:45 Elizabeth speaks to Mary:

> *"And blessed art thou that hast believed, because those things shall be accomplished that were spoken to thee by the Lord."*

In Luke 1:45, we read that Elizabeth praised Mary for her faith in the Lord. Here is what Antipope John Paul II said about this event.

> Antipope John Paul II, *Homily*, May 31, 1980: "On the threshold of the house of Zachariah, Elizabeth said to Mary: **'Blessed are you, you who believed'** (Luke. 1:45). Let us do honor to maternity, because **faith in man is expressed in it**… **IT IS NECESSARY TO BELIEVE IN MAN, from the beginning. BLESSED ARE YOU, MARY, YOU WHO BELIEVED.**"[37]

Luke 1:45 tells us that Mary believed the Lord. In a homily commenting on Luke 1:45 Antipope John Paul II tells us that Mary believed in man from the beginning. He was clearly saying that the Lord in whom Mary believed is each man.

11. Every man is the Christ Child born on Christmas

Just as Antipope John Paul II declared that man is the Christ, the Son of the Living God, in his very first homily, and just as he declared that Christianity, the Good News and the Gospel are the deep amazement at each man in his first encyclical, so too did this Antichrist have a message for the world in his very first Christmas address as antipope.

> Antipope John Paul II, *Urbi et Orbi*, Dec. 25, 1978: "I am addressing this message to every human being, to man in his humanity. **Christmas is the feast of man.**"[38]

The definition of Christmas is the following: "**Christmas** – *Christ's Mass, the common English name for the feast of the birthday of our Lord*…"[39] Christmas is the feast of Jesus Christ's birth. So, why do we find Antipope John Paul II, in his first Christmas address, proclaiming to every human being that Christmas is "the feast of **man**"? It is precisely because he was totally Antichrist, who was here to preach man in the place of Christ. And this Antichrist continued to preach his message on Christmas for many years to come.

> Antipope John Paul II, *Urbi et Orbi*, Dec. 25, 1979: "**Christmas is the feast of *all the children of the world* – all of them…**"[40]

> Antipope John Paul II, *Homily*, Dec. 25, 1993: "**Christmas is the feast of every human being**…"[41]

> Antipope John Paul II, *Urbi et Orbi*, Dec. 25, 1978: "**Accept the full truth concerning man that was uttered on Christmas night**; accept this dimension of man that was opened for all human beings on this Holy Night…"[42]

No truth concerning man was uttered on Christmas night. The only truth that was uttered concerned the birth of the Savior: "*For, this day, is born to you a Savior, who is Christ the Lord, in the city of David*" (Luke 2:11). If Christmas night also brought forth the "full truth concerning man," as Antipope John Paul II said, then the full truth concerning man is that he is Jesus Christ.

> Antipope John Paul II, *Evangelium Vitae* (# 1): "'… for to you is born this day in the city of David a Savior, who is Christ the Lord' (Lk. 2:10-11). **The source of this 'great joy' is the birth of the Savior; but Christmas also reveals the full meaning of every human birth**…"[43]

> Antipope John Paul II, *Urbi et Orbi*, Dec. 25, 1978: "**If we celebrate with such solemnity the birth of Jesus, it is to bear witness that every human being** is somebody unique and unrepeatable."[44]

Here Antipope John Paul II admits that **the solemn celebration of Christmas is simply to bear witness to every human being**.

> Antipope John Paul II, *Homily*, Dec. 25, 1985: "**The Lord's birth is the light of the Meaning:** the light of the rediscovered meaning of all things. And **above all the meaning of man…**"[45]

In this incredible homily on Christmas, 1985, Antipope John Paul II declared that the Lord's birth is the meaning of man, bluntly telling us that man is the Lord who is born on Christmas.

12. The Epiphany is the Manifestation of Man

The word "Epiphany" means a manifestation of God. Even Antipope John Paul II acknowledged this.

The Doctrine of Antichrist 589

> Antipope John Paul II, *Angelus Address*, Jan. 2, 1983: "**As is well known, Epiphany means the manifestation of Jesus to the people**, the revelation of the Messiah awaited for centuries…"[46]

But watch how this Antichrist also defined that every baby is an epiphany of God.

> Antipope John Paul II, *Angelus Address*, Jan. 11, 1998: "**Every baby who comes into the world is an 'epiphany' of God**…"[47]

This indicates, by his own definition – and consistent with all of his other preaching – that every baby who comes into the world is God.

In Apocalypse 3:14, Our Lord Jesus Christ calls Himself the "Amen," the faithful and true witness. Antipope John Paul II says that each man is the *Amen*.

> Antipope John Paul II, *Familiaris Consortio* (# 30), Nov. 22, 1981: "… the Church stands for life: **IN EACH HUMAN LIFE she sees the splendor of that 'Yes,' that 'Amen,' who is Christ Himself**."[48]

13. Man is The Way

In John chapter 14, we read the following:

> *"Thomas saith to Jesus: Lord, we know not whither thou goest; and how can we know the way? Jesus saith to him: I am the Way…"*

In one of the most striking verses in all of Sacred Scripture, Jesus Christ tells us that He (Jesus) is the Way. What did Antipope John Paul II tell us?

> Antipope John Paul II, *Address*, Feb. 9, 2001: "**The human being is the way**…"[49]

> Antipope John Paul II, Encyclical *On Human Work* (# 1), September 14, 1981: "… **man is the primary and fundamental way**… it is necessary to return constantly to this way…"[50]

> Antipope John Paul II, *Address in Poland*, June 14, 1999: "**Man is the primary and fundamental way**…"[51]

> Antipope John Paul II, *Address*, April 7, 1998: "… **man is the first way**…"[52]

> Antipope John Paul II, June 21, 2002: "… in the Encyclical *Redemptor Hominis*, I wanted to repeat that **the human person is the primary and principal way**…"[53]

> Antipope John Paul II, *Letter to Families* (# 1), Feb. 2, 1994: "… **man is the way…**"[54]

Jesus Christ told us very clearly He (Jesus) is the Way. Antipope John Paul II told us that man is the Way. Antipope John Paul II preached that man is the Way when Jesus alone is the Way, **precisely because he was Antichrist**, and he preached man in the place of Christ.

And there is no doubt that Antipope John Paul II was fully aware that he was putting man in the place of God when he preached that man is the way. He was fully aware of the fact that Jesus

Christ alone is the Way. Yes, this man who spoke 14 languages fluently, who was the most seen person in the world, who traveled more miles than anyone in history, and spoke to more people than anyone in history, was fully aware that Jesus Christ is the Way.

> Antipope John Paul II, *Catechesi Tradendae* (# 5), Oct. 16, 1979: "**It is Jesus who is 'the way,** and the truth, and the life,' (Jn. 14:6) ..."[55]

> Antipope John Paul II, *Catechesi Tradendae* (# 22), Oct. 16, 1979: "... **Christ, who is the way...**'"[56]

> Antipope John Paul II, *On the Lay Faithful* (# 34), Dec. 30, 1988: "**Christ is for you the Way...**"[57]

> Antipope John Paul II, *Homily*, April 8, 2001: "**For Jesus alone is the Way...**"[58]

Antipope John Paul II knew very well that Jesus alone is the Way, and yet he also preached over and over again that man is the Way. Antipope John Paul II was preaching to us that there is no contradiction between the two statements – that man and Christ are interchangeable because they are the same.

Antipope John Paul II, *Homily*, Dec. 10, 1989: "... make straight the way of the Lord <u>and of man</u>, WHICH is the path of the Church."[59]

In addressing this incredible homily, we must recall the words of St. John the Baptist in the Gospel. St. John the Baptist preached before Christ's coming:

> John 1:23- "*I am the voice of one crying in the wilderness, <u>make straight the way of the Lord</u>.*"

But Antipope John Paul II told us to make straight the way of the Lord AND OF MAN. His meaning is blatantly obvious! His meaning is that man is the Lord. In fact, notice the final phrase in this incredible quotation from Antipope John Paul II. He does not tell us to make straight the WAYS of the Lord and of man, which ARE the path of the Church. Rather he says, "*make straight <u>THE WAY</u> of the Lord and of man, <u>WHICH IS</u> the path of the Church.*" They are a single way, according to Antipope John Paul II.

> Antipope John Paul II, *Letter to Families* (# 23): "May we always be enabled to follow **the One who is 'the way,** and the truth, and the life' (Jn. 14:6)."[60]

> Antipope John Paul II, *Redemptor Hominis* (# 13), March 4, 1979: "**<u>Jesus Christ is the chief way for the Church</u>.**"[61]

> Antipope John Paul II, *Redemptor Hominis* (# 22): "For in this the Church also recognizes **the way for her daily life, <u>WHICH IS EACH PERSON</u>.**"[62]

Notice, once again, the clear message of substitution in these last two quotations from the same encyclical.

14. Man is the Truth

In John 14:6, Our Lord Jesus Christ identifies Himself not only as the Way, but also as the Truth.

> "*I am the Way, **and the Truth**...*" (Jn. 14:6)

Jesus Christ tells us that He is the Truth. What does Antipope John Paul II tell us?

> Antipope John Paul II, *Veritatis Splendor* (# 84): "**Pilate's question: 'What is truth?' reflects the distressing perplexity of a man who often no longer knows who he is**..."[63]

Here this Antichrist tells us that Pilate's question "*what is truth*" reflects the perplexity of a man who no longer knows WHO HE IS! Antipope John Paul II was here attempting to put his satanic gospel of Hell right in our faces. He was trying to put it right in our faces that man is the truth – that each man is really the Christ that Pilate couldn't recognize – and that Pilate himself (when he failed to perceive the truth that was in his very presence, the truth that is Our Lord Jesus Christ) *failed to perceive who man is*!

Besides "the Truth," one of Our Lord Jesus Christ's primary titles is "the Word."

> John 1:1- "In the beginning was the Word, and the Word was with God, and the Word was God."

Antipope John Paul II acknowledged this fact in his *Encyclical on the Holy Ghost* # 36.

> Antipope John Paul II, *Encyclical on the Holy Ghost* (# 36), May 18, 1986: "...**the Word, the eternal Son.**"[64]

But watch how Antipope John Paul II applied this title of Our Lord to man in *the very next paragraph of this encyclical*.

> Antipope John Paul II, *Encyclical on the Holy Ghost* (# 37): "Here we find ourselves at the very center of what could be called **the 'anti-Word,' that is to say the 'anti-truth.' For the truth about man becomes falsified**: who man is..."[65]

In the *Encyclical on the Holy Ghost* #36, Antipope John Paul II told us that Jesus Christ is the Word, the Eternal Son. Here, in #37 of the same encyclical, **Antipope John Paul II tells us that the "anti-Word" and the "anti-truth" are a falsification of the truth about man** – a falsification about *who man* is. This clearly means that man is the Word, the Truth, the Son of God.

15. Man is the Life

In John 14:6, Our Lord Jesus Christ identifies Himself not only as the Way and the Truth, but also as the Life.

> "*I am the Way, and the Truth, **and the Life**...*" (Jn. 14:6)

Jesus Christ tells us that He is the Life. St. John the Evangelist confirms this truth by describing Our Lord Jesus Christ as "the word of life" and the "life eternal" in his first epistle.

1st John Chapter 1 - "That which was from the beginning, which we have heard, which we have seen with our eyes, which we have looked upon, and our hands have handled, **of the word of life**. For **the life** was manifested; and we have seen and do bear witness, and declare unto you **the life eternal**, which was with the Father, and hath appeared to us."

In this profound passage of Sacred Scripture, St. John identifies that Jesus Christ is the Life Eternal, as Our Lord Himself told us. But what does Antichrist say? In fact, what does Antichrist say about the very passage of Sacred Scripture that we just quoted (the first chapter of St. John's first epistle)?

Antipope John Paul II, *Evangelium Vitae* (# 30), March 25, 1995: **"The deepest and most original meaning of this meditation on what revelation tells us ABOUT HUMAN LIFE was taken up by the Apostle John in the opening words of his First Letter**: 'That which was from the beginning, which we have heard… **concerning the Word of life** – the life was made manifest, and we saw it, and testify to it, and proclaim to you **the eternal life which was with the Father and was made manifest to us** …"[66]

Here Antipope John Paul II is quoting word for word the opening passage of St. John's first epistle, where St. John describes hearing and seeing Jesus Christ: the Word of Life. He tells us that this passage about Our Lord Jesus Christ is actually what revelation tells us about **HUMAN LIFE**! It is not possible for Antipope John Paul II to have preached that man is Jesus Christ any more clearly!

And Antipope John Paul II knew exactly what he was saying when he attributed this verse about Our Lord to man, because just 50 paragraphs later in the same encyclical, *Evangelium Vitae*, Antipope John Paul II again quoted the same verse of Scripture – but this time with the correct meaning!

Antipope John Paul II, *Evangelium Vitae* (# 80.1): "*'That which was from the beginning, which we have heard, which we have seen with our eyes … concerning the Word of life…'* **Jesus is the only Gospel: we have nothing further to say or any other witness to bear.**"[67]

So, in one encyclical, Antipope John Paul II quoted the opening words of St. John's first epistle two different times; and one time he says that it tells us about human life and one time he says it tells us about Jesus Christ. But, as we have shown, in the preaching of Antichrist this is no contradiction. In his preaching to speak of the "Life eternal" **is** to speak of man, and to speak of man **is** to speak of the "Life eternal."

16. Each man is the Eucharist

Antipope John Paul II, *Angelus Address*, May 29, 1983: "The thought of the Eucharist was present at every meeting, **not only because there is contained in the Eucharist that which the life of every man has most deeply**…"[68]

The Doctrine of Antichrist

Our Lord Jesus Christ, Body, Blood, Soul and Divinity is contained in the Eucharist. Antipope John Paul II says that what is contained in the Eucharist the life of every man has most deeply. This clearly means that each man has the Body, Blood, Soul and Divinity of Christ because each man is Christ.

> Antipope John Paul II, *Redemptor Hominis* (# 20): **"The Eucharist is the Sacrament in which our new being is most completely expressed ..."**[69]

17. Each man is the Crucified Christ

> Antipope John Paul II, *Homily*, June 11, 1982: **"When we look at the cross, we see in it the passion of man: the agony of Christ."**[70]

> Antipope John Paul II, *Address*, March 28, 1982: "My pastoral visit, so near to Holy Week, thus becomes **a meditation on the 'Passion of Christ' and on the 'Passion of Man.'"**[71]

> Antipope John Paul II, *On the Meaning of Suffering* (# 20): **"Man, discovering through faith the redemptive suffering of Christ, also discovers in it his own sufferings..."**[72]

Man does not discover his own sufferings in Christ's sufferings because man is not Christ. But this is what Antichrist John Paul II was preaching.

> Antipope John Paul II, *Speech in the Colosseum*, April 10, 1998: **"As we contemplate Christ dead on the Cross,** *our thoughts turn to the countless injustices and sufferings which prolong his passion in every part of the world.* **I think of the places where man is insulted..."**[73]

When we contemplate Christ dead on the Cross, we don't think of the places where man is insulted, because man is not the Crucified Christ.

> Antipope John Paul II, *General Audience*, Jan. 12, 1994: "**Even though St. Paul reminds us that 'Christ being raised from the dead will never die again; death no longer has dominion over him' (Rom. 6:9), death still continues to be a part of human existence**. We are witnesses to a process of death in the Balkans, and, unfortunately, powerless witnesses at that. *Christ continues to die* amid the tragic events taking place in that part of the world, and that was the subject of our shared reflection. **Christ continues his agony in so many of our brothers and sisters**: in men, women and children, in the young and in the old, **in so many Christians and Muslims, in believers and non-believers.**"[74]

Antipope John Paul II begins by admitting that Christ will never die again (Rom. 6:9). He then tells us that death continues to be a part of human existence. He then tells us that Christ continues to die, in Christians and Muslims, in believers and non-believers. His train of thought is not difficult to follow: though Christ will never die again, man still dies – thus Christ dies because man is Christ. He even stresses that Christ continues to die in Muslims and non-believers, which further confirms that he preaches that man is Christ.

> Antipope John Paul II, *Homily*, Oct. 1, 1999: **"He,** *Emmanuel,* **God-with-us, was crucified in the concentration camps and the gulags; he knew affliction under bombardment in the trenches;** he suffered wherever the inalienable dignity of man, of every human being, was humiliated, oppressed and violated."[75]

The Doctrine of Antichrist

The term *Emmanuel* (God with us) is very specific. It applies to one Person. Our Lord Jesus Christ is *Emmanuel* (Isaias 7:14; Mt. 1:23). And Our Lord Jesus Christ was crucified *once* for our sins. By describing each man as Emmanuel, Antipope John Paul II was specifically indicating that each man is God with us.

It's quite obvious that Antipope John Paul II preached that every man is the crucified Christ, the Savior of the World. But there is one place in his encyclical *Evangelium Vitae* that is particularly interesting on this topic, as it demonstrates the deception and subtlety that Antichrist uses in his diabolical preaching.

> Antipope John Paul II, *Evangelium Vitae* (# 50.2), speaking of the darkness on Good Friday: "**But the glory of the Cross is not overcome by this darkness; rather, it shines forth ever more radiantly and brightly, and is revealed as the center, meaning and goal of all history and of every human life.**"[76]

Here, Antipope John Paul II says that **the glory of the Cross is revealed as the meaning of EVERY HUMAN LIFE.** Keep this in mind as we read the next quote from *Evangelium Vitae*.

> Antipope John Paul II, *Evangelium Vitae* (# 50.3): "Jesus is nailed to the Cross… It is thus, at the moment of his greatest weakness, that **the Son of God is revealed for who he is: on the cross his glory is made manifest.**"[77]

Here, Antipope John Paul II tells us that **by the glory of the Cross the Son of God is revealed for who He is**. But he just told us, one paragraph before this, that the glory of the Cross is the meaning of EVERY HUMAN LIFE. This means, by way of logical equation, that the **Son of God = the meaning of every human life**. To illustrate this, we will look again at his words.

- The glory of the Cross is the meaning of every human life (Evangelium Vitae # 50.2).
- The glory of the Cross reveals the Son of God (Evangelium Vitae # 50.3).
- Conclusion: The Son of God is the meaning of every human life.

18. Man is indeed God

> Antipope John Paul II, *Ecclesia in America* (# 29): "Prayer leads Christians little by little to acquire a contemplative view of reality… **to contemplate God in every person** …"[78]

> Antipope John Paul II, *Homily*, August 10, 1985: "**Today, in consecrating your cathedral, we ardently desire that it become a 'true temple of God and man…'**"[79]

This quotation proves that Antipope John Paul II preached the worship of man as God, by calling for the transformation of the temple of God into a temple of God and MAN.

> Antipope John Paul II, *Homily*, Aug. 9, 1980: "… **the first and principal intention of every organization and every state: respect and love for man!**"[80]

> Antipope John Paul II, *Address*, April 13, 1979: "… the conscience of all humanity, which proclaims **the cause of man as the main purpose of all progress.**"[81]

The Doctrine of Antichrist

> Antipope John Paul II, *Address to University Teachers*, Sept. 9, 2000: "<u>Each of you could say</u>, with the ancient philosopher: 'I am searching for man!'"[82]

> Antipope John Paul II, *Homily*, Jan. 1, 1986: "**It is necessary for man to be sure of man.**"[83]

> Antipope John Paul II, *Homily*, June 21, 1986: "**Yes! Man! The Church does not rest as long as man is threatened in his dignity…**"[84]

> Antipope John Paul II, *Message to Conference on Culture*, March 10, 1986: "… the East and the West could be combined to develop **a truly universal and humanitarian outlook based on faith in man.**"[85]

> Antipope John Paul II, *Angelus Address*, April 20, 1980: "… **man** is offended and humiliated: **man,** the sublime creature of God, **who cannot, who must not, be offended.**"[86]

Remember, just as Nestorius preached that Jesus Christ is two persons: the Son of God and a man named Jesus, so did Antipope John Paul II preach that <u>every man is two persons: the Son of God and a mere man</u> (i.e., Nestorianism applied to every man). This is why he can speak in one sentence about man being a creature of God while at the same time he can indicate that man is God <u>who cannot, who must not be offended</u>.

19. Man is the Man from Above

In John 8:23 we read the following,

> *"And he (Jesus) said to them: You are from beneath, I am from above. You are of this world, I am not of this world. Therefore I said to you, that you shall die in your sins. For if you believe not that I am He, you shall die in your sin."*

In this profound verse of St. John's Gospel, Our Lord Jesus Christ describes **Himself as <u>the one from above</u>. He describes man as the one from below**. Keep this in mind as we read the following words from Antipope John Paul II.

> Antipope John Paul II, *Homily*, March 30, 1982: "Looking at himself, man discovers also – as Christ says in the dialogue with the Pharisees – what is 'from below' and what is 'from above.' **Man discovers within himself (this is a constant experience) the man 'from below' and the man 'from above'** not two men, but almost two dimensions of the same man, <u>the man that is each one of us</u>: of you, he, she."[87]

Here, Antipope John Paul II tells us with *almost astonishing boldness* that each man is the man from above and the man from below! But in the very passage that Antipope John Paul II is commenting on (Christ's dialogue with the Pharisees in John 8:23), **Jesus defines Himself as the one "from above" and man as the one "from below."** It is undeniable that Antipope John Paul II was saying that each man – each one of us – is also Christ, the man from above of John 8:23!

20. Man's True Reality is that he is God

> Antipope John Paul II, *Evangelium Vitae* (# 36): "**When God is not acknowledged AS GOD, the profound meaning of man is betrayed**..."[88]

This means that the profound meaning of man is that he is God.

> Antipope John Paul II, *Address to French Ambassador*, Oct. 24, 1998: "**Humanism is a common ideal for all the French; it states that nothing is more beautiful nor greater than man...**"[89]

> Antipope John Paul II, *Urbi et Orbi*, Dec. 25, 1985: "**What is grace? Grace is precisely the manifestation of God**. God's opening of himself to man. **God**, while remaining in the inscrutable fullness of **his divine Being, the Being One and Three**, opens himself to man, makes himself a Gift to man, whose Creator and Lord he is. **Grace is God as "our Father." It is the Son of God as the Son of the Virgin. It is the Holy Spirit**, at work in the human heart with the infinite abundance of his gifts. **Grace is Emmanuel: God with us. God in our midst**. Grace is God for us through Bethlehem night, through the Cross on Calvary, through the Resurrection, through the Eucharist, through Pentecost, through the Church - Christ's Body. **Grace is, also, man**..."[90]

Antipope John Paul II told us that grace is God and that grace is also man.

> Antipope John Paul II, *Veritatis Splendor* (# 58), Aug. 6, 1993: "**The importance of this interior *dialogue of MAN WITH HIMSELF* can never be adequately appreciated. But it is also a *dialogue of man with God*...**"[91]

Here Antipope John Paul II says that a dialogue of man with himself is a dialogue of man with God.

> Antipope John Paul II, *Veritatis Splendor* (# 10), Aug. 6, 1993: "**What man is** and what he must do **becomes clear as soon as God reveals himself.**"[92]

Here, Antipope John Paul II tells us in sly fashion that "*what man is*" becomes clear as soon as God reveals Himself, which means that what man is is God Himself revealed.

> Antipope John Paul II, *Encyclical on the Holy Ghost* (# 47), May 18, 1986: "... **it is the reality of God that reveals and illustrates the mystery of man**..."[93]

The reality of God is that God is! Therefore, Antipope John Paul II is saying that **man's mystery is revealed in the fact that God is, which means that man is God.**

> Antipope John Paul II, *General Audience*, Sept. 15, 1982: "**Jerusalem can become also the city of man** ..."[94]

> Antipope John Paul II, *Address to Bishops of Rwanda*, Sept. 17, 1998: "... their blood will be a gospel seed... **They will help you not to despair of man**..."[95]

> Antipope John Paul II, *Evangelium Vitae* (# 3), March 25, 1995: "Therefore **every threat to human dignity** and life must necessarily be felt in the Church's very heart; it **cannot but affect her at the core of her faith in the redemptive Incarnation** of the Son of God..."[96]

Here Antipope John Paul II says that every threat to human dignity <u>cannot but</u> affect faith in the Incarnation. Why would that be? Well, if every man became God in the Incarnation, as Antipope John Paul II preached, then every threat to man affects faith in the Incarnation.

> Antipope John Paul II, *Urbi et Orbi*, March 31, 1991: "**Let respect for man be total… Every offense against the person is an offense against God…**"[97]

> Antipope John Paul II, *World Day of Prayer for Peace* (Assisi, Italy), Jan. 24, 2002: "**To offend against human beings is, most certainly, to offend against God.**"[98]

> Antipope John Paul II, *Homily*, June 24, 1988: "… **God wishes to encounter in man the whole of creation.**"[99]

Here Antipope John Paul II indicates that in man one can find the whole of creation.

21. Man is the Messiah

> Antipope John Paul II, *Homily*, Sept. 12, 1982: "**And the meaning of human life**, the meaning it has in the eternal plan of love, **cannot be understood except through <u>that 'Messianic contest' which Jesus of Nazareth carried on one day with Peter and which he continues to carry on with every man</u> and with all of mankind**. Christianity is the religion of the 'Messianic contest' with mankind and for mankind."[100]

Here Antipope John Paul II says that Peter and all of mankind carried on and continue to carry on a "Messianic contest" with Jesus Christ. The word *Messiah* means "the savior." A "Messianic contest" is, therefore, a contest between saviors! What this homily of Antipope John Paul II means is that there exists a competition between every man and Jesus Christ about who is the Savior! **And only in this Messianic competition can the meaning of human life be understood**, according to the Antichrist Antipope John Paul II, because every man is the Messiah.

> Antipope John Paul II, *General Audience (or Urbi et Orbi)*, Dec. 25, 1987, speaking of **Mary, the Mother of God**: "**Within her is the world** which awaits its God. Within her is the creature completely opened before its Creator. **Within her is the history of every human being everywhere on earth…**"[101]

Antichrist Antipope John Paul II tells us that within the Mother of God is the history of every human being. **But within Mary there was only Jesus Christ**, the Son of the living God. By saying that every human being everywhere on Earth was in the womb of the Mother of God, Antipope John Paul II was indicating that every human being everywhere on Earth is Jesus Christ.

22. The New Evangelization

Antichrist wants to evangelize the world to man, making everything more human, because all of humanity is Christ, according to his gospel.

> Antipope John Paul II, *Homily*, May 15, 1982: "**Education… is intended to 'humanize' man.**"[102]

> Antipope John Paul II, *Homily*, July 7, 1980: **"The true apostle of the Gospel is he who humanizes and evangelizes at the same time..."**[103]

And in trying to convert the world to man as Christ, this Antichrist often explicitly equated becoming more human with becoming more divine; that is to say, he explicitly equated becoming more like man with becoming more like God.

> Antipope John Paul II, *Address to the Slovenians*, May 18, 1996: "In this way you will help change the world; <u>you will make it more human and thus more divine</u>."[104]

Here Antipope John Paul II says that to be more like man is thus (therefore) to become more like God, indicating that man is God.

> Antipope John Paul II, *Incarnationis mysterium* (# 2): "…**the Church opens to all people the prospect of being 'divinized' <u>and thus of becoming more human</u>**."[105]

Here again, Antipope John Paul II explicitly says that to become more divine is thus (therefore) to become more human, therefore equating God with man.

> Antipope John Paul II, *Address to Portuguese Bishops*, Nov. 30, 1999: "**In fact, by his Incarnation, he, the Son of God, has in a certain way united himself with each man…** the Christian way of life not only gives meaning to what exists, but also opens 'to all people **the prospect of being divinized and thus of becoming more human**.'"[106]

Here again Antipope John Paul II equates being divinized with becoming more human, and he bases it again on the Incarnation.

23. Man must discover that he is God

> Antipope John Paul II, *Homily*, March 6, 1988: "**Yes, God is 'jealous' *for that divine element which exists in man* …'<u>You shall not have other gods before me</u>. You shall love your God with all your heart, with all your mind, and with all your strength.' <u>Otherwise, you, man, shall not discover yourself!</u>**"[107]

Antipope John Paul II quotes the first commandment about worshipping God and he says that **if you don't worship God you will not discover yourself!**

> Antipope John Paul II, *Angelus Address*, March 7, 1982: **"What value, then, does Christ's call to conversion and belief in the Gospel have? What meaning do reconciliation with God and penance have** in the ongoing mission of the Church? However and also perhaps **above all the call is addressed to man, to every man, that he may again find himself! That he may believe in himself."**[108]

This is an amazing *Angelus Address*, even for one thoroughly possessed by the spirit of Antichrist. In it, Antipope John Paul II asks: "What is the meaning of reconciliation with God," and "What is the value of conversion and belief in the Gospel?" **He answers his own questions by stating that above all it is for man to find himself and believe in himself!** Therefore, <u>conversion, belief in the Gospel, and reconciliation with God equal man finding himself and believing in himself</u>. Man is God, according to the doctrine of Antichrist.

> Antipope John Paul II, *Ecclesia in America* (# 67): "… Jesus Christ, the human face of God and the divine face of man."[109]

> Antipope John Paul II, *Homily*, Feb. 26, 2000: "**In revealing himself on the Mountain and giving his Law, <u>God revealed man to man himself</u>**."[110]

There you have it! Here Antipope John Paul II says that by revealing <u>Himself</u> on Mt. Sinai, God revealed man to man himself!

24. The Rosary of Man

> Antipope John Paul II, *Document on the Rosary*, Oct. 2002: "**Anyone who contemplates Christ through the various stages of his life cannot fail to perceive in him the truth about man.**"[111]

This means that Christ is the truth about man.

> Antipope John Paul II, *Document on the Rosary*, Oct. 2002: "**It could be said that each mystery of the Rosary, carefully meditated, sheds light on the mystery of man.**"[112]

25. The Unsearchable Riches of Christ are everyone's property

> Ephesians 3:8- "To me, the least of all the saints, is given this grace, to preach among the Gentiles, **the unsearchable riches of Christ.**"

In Ephesians 3:8, St. Paul says that he was given the grace to preach the unsearchable riches of Christ to the Gentiles. St. Paul was referring to the attributes of Our Lord Jesus Christ, the Son of God. Christ's attributes as the Son of God are unsearchable and unfathomable. But Antipope John Paul II told us that these unsearchable riches of Christ are actually the property of each man.

> Antipope John Paul II, *Redemptor Hominis* (# 11), March 4, 1979: "… in short, helping everyone to get to know 'the unsearchable riches of Christ,' since these riches are for every individual <u>AND ARE EVERYBODY'S PROPERTY</u>."[113]

26. Each man is the Risen Christ

> Antipope John Paul II, *Address to International Symposium on Jan Hus*, Dec. 17, 1999: "**In contemplating the truth about man, we turn inevitably to the figure of the risen Christ. He alone teaches and embodies completely the truth of man….**"[114]

Antipope John Paul II could hardly have been more blunt. He says that to contemplate the truth about man is to turn inevitably to the risen Christ. The truth about man, therefore, is that man is the risen Christ.

> Antipope John Paul II, *Regina Caeli*, April 28, 2002, On the Risen Christ: "**His radiant countenance of glory fully reveals to us the truth of God <u>and the truth of man</u>.**"[115]

This again proves the point we've been making throughout this section on Antipope John Paul II's preaching. It proves that Antipope John Paul II was totally possessed by the spirit of Antichrist, that he preached the exact doctrine of Antichrist, and that one of his main goals was to replace the truth about Christ (the most important truth in the universe) with the truth about man.

> Antipope John Paul II, *Address to Missionaries of Precious Blood,* September 14, 2001: "And at the moment of Easter this joy came to its fullness as the light of divine glory shone on the face of **the Risen Lord, whose wounds shine forever like the Sun. This is the truth of who you are, dear Brothers**…"[116]

No comment necessary!

27. Antichrist Revealed

Read God's infallible definition of Antichrist in Sacred Scripture:

> 1 John 4:2-3 – "Every spirit that confesseth that Jesus Christ is come in the flesh, is of God: **And every spirit that dissolveth Jesus is not of God: and this is Antichrist**, of whom you have heard that he cometh, **and he is now already in the world.**"

Notice that Antichrist is a spirit that was in the world *in St. John's time*. That means that Antichrist has been around since the time of Christ. Antichrist is a spirit that occupies different people since the time of Christ and until His Second Coming; **but there will be a unique manifestation and personification of that spirit at the end of the world – at the time of or just before the Second Coming – which will be a major sign of the end.** And what does God's word say about this spirit and personification of Antichrist? It is a spirit that *dissolves* Jesus, and *denieth that Jesus is the Christ*.

> 1 John 2:22 – "Who is a liar, but **he who denieth that Jesus is the Christ? He is antichrist,** who denieth the Father, and the Son."

This is a commemorative coin with John Paul II's image which was put out by the Vatican. Notice the 3 stars with six points each, which gives you: 6, 6, 6.

We have proven that Antipope John Paul II's distinguishing teaching is this very thing; his distinguishing teaching is that the Son of God was dissolved into every man in the Incarnation, making every man Christ, thus dissolving Jesus and denying that Jesus is the Christ. At the very least, one can say that Antipope John Paul II was totally possessed with the spirit of Antichrist and that he preached exactly the doctrine of Antichrist. John Paul II exemplified and personified the spirit of Antichrist; it came out of him with astounding diabolical precision.

What's also fascinating is how Antipope John Paul II's own Catechism defines the Antichrist.

> Antipope John Paul II, *New Catechism of the Catholic Church*, # 675: "**The supreme religious deception is that of the Antichrist, a pseudo-messianism <u>by which man glorifies himself in place of God and of his Messiah come in the flesh</u>**."[117]

Antipope John Paul II's own Catechism could not have described his doctrine better! It accurately pinpoints that the deception of Antichrist is <u>a false or pseudo-messianism in which MAN replaces the Son of God come in the flesh</u>! This religion of Antichrist is not only preached by Antipope John Paul II as his distinguishing mark, but it is actually practiced in the liturgy of his Vatican II church.

By attempting to put Christ to death in the Mass and by replacing it with a non-Catholic counterfeit service, Paul VI definitely represented the fulfillment of Antichrist in the Vatican, as prophesied by Our Lady of La Salette.

Paul VI and Benedict XVI also represented Antichrist in the Vatican

The Doctrine of Antichrist

Our Lady of La Salette, Sept. 19, 1846: **"Rome will lose the Faith and become the seat of the Anti-Christ… the Church will be in eclipse."**

The New Mass of the Vatican II counterfeit church <u>puts man in the place of God</u> – the doctrine of Antichrist – by having the priest face man instead of God during the liturgy, and by orienting the entire worship toward man instead of toward God.

The New Mass, the liturgy of Antipope John Paul II's counterfeit Catholic Church, is attempting to indoctrinate the masses into idolatry and the worship of man, just as Antipope John Paul II preached it to the people in his encyclicals and speeches.

While Benedict XVI doesn't yet teach the dissolving of Jesus to the same extent as John Paul II, it's quite interesting that he covers Sacred Scripture's other definition for Antichrist – the denial of Jesus as the Christ! Benedict XVI represents Antichrist in the Vatican by putting the denial of Jesus Christ on a par with the acceptance of Him, as we've shown.

Benedict XVI, *God and the World*, 2000, p. 209: "<u>It is of course possible to read the Old Testament so that it is not directed toward Christ; it does not point quite unequivocally to Christ</u>. And if Jews cannot see the promises as being fulfilled in him, this is not just ill will on their part, but genuinely because of the obscurity of the texts… <u>There are perfectly good reasons, then, for denying that the Old Testament refers to Christ and for saying, No, that is not what he said</u>. And there are also good reasons for referring it to him – that is what the dispute between Jews and Christians is about."[118]

John Paul II preached the dissolving of Jesus (one definition of Scripture for Antichrist), while **Benedict XVI preaches that He might not be the Christ (the second definition for Antichrist)!** Thus, Our Lady's prophecy has been fulfilled. The Vatican II sect is the Counter Church of the Antichrist; it has been installed by a series of antichrists who are preaching a new Gospel of respect for false religions, religious indifferentism, acceptance of the false gods of the East, acceptance of the heresies of Protestantism and Eastern Orthodoxy – which has resulted in a spiritual wasteland and a myriad of bad fruits.

Catholics should take heart in these prophetic warnings that Heaven has given us, which have clearly foreseen our days. We should have confidence knowing that God is still with His Church, as He will be until the consummation of the world (Mt. 28), and He will never allow it to be completely destroyed or fall into any error. There will always remain a remnant of Catholics who hold to the full deposit of the faith and do not compromise with heresy, even though God has allowed Satan, as a punishment for the sins of men in these last days, the power to invade and take over the countless schools, seminaries, colleges, universities, chapels and buildings that once belonged to the true Catholic Church.

God has allowed Satan to take these structures to himself, and implant in them a non-Catholic apostate religion which is not Catholic, but still retains the name. We must oppose and have no part with this counterfeit Catholic Church, which has been created by Satan. We must have no part with its false Mass, its false sacraments, its heretical antipopes and "bishops." We must inform ourselves and others of the correct positions to take in this regard, which have been set out in this book based on the teaching of the Catholic Church. We must try to bring people back to the true Catholic Church which was founded by Jesus Christ, which can never be destroyed, which has been reduced to a remnant in this time of the Great Apostasy, and to which all must belong in order to be saved.

Besides completely rejecting its heresies, its false Council and its antipopes, what can Catholics do about this situation?

Endnotes for Section 45

[1] *The Papal Encyclicals*, by Claudia Carlen, Raleigh: The Pierian Press, 1990, Vol. 3 (1903-1939), p. 6.
[2] *The Papal Encyclicals*, Vol. 5 (1958-1981), p. 252.
[3] *The Papal Encyclicals*, Vol. 3 (1903-1939), p. 471.
[4] *Decrees of the Ecumenical Councils*, Sheed & Ward and Georgetown University Press, 1990, Vol. 1, p. 86.
[5] *The Papal Encyclicals*, Vol. 5 (1958-1981), p. 254.
[6] *L' Osservatore Romano* (the Vatican's Newspaper), July 21, 1986, p. 6.
[7] *L'Osservatore Romano*, May, 11, 1987, p. 15.
[8] *L'Osservatore Romano*, Feb. 23, 1994, p. 5.
[9] *The Papal Encyclicals*, Vol. 3 (1903-1939), p. 468.
[10] *Decrees of the Ecumenical Councils*, Vol. 1, p. 110.
[11] *The Papal Encyclicals*, Vol. 5 (1958-1981), p. 252.
[12] *L'Osservatore Romano*, Jan. 30, 1984, p. 3.
[13] *The Papal Encyclicals*, Vol. 5 (1958-1981), pp. 251-252.
[14] *The Oxford Illustrated Dictionary*, p. 34.
[15] *The Papal Encyclicals*, Vol. 5 (1958-1981), p. 252.
[16] *L'Osservatore Romano*, April 11, 1983, p. 11.
[17] *L'Osservatore Romano*, June 16, 1980, p. 9.
[18] *The Encyclicals of John Paul II*, Huntington, IN: Our Sunday Visitor Publishing Division, 1996, pp. 504-505.
[19] *L'Osservatore Romano*, June 18, 1997, p. 4.
[20] *Christifideles Laici*, Post-Synodal Apostolic Exhortation of John Paul II, Dec. 30, 1988, Pauline Books & Media, p. 22.
[21] *L'Osservatore Romano*, May 30, 1988, p. 7.
[22] *L'Osservatore Romano*, Jan. 10, 2001, p. 3.
[23] *The Papal Encyclicals*, Vol. 5 (1958-1981), p. 252.
[24] *L'Osservatore Romano*, Nov. 2, 1978, p. 1.
[25] *The Papal Encyclicals*, Vol. 3 (1903-1939), p. 6.
[26] *L'Osservatore Romano*, Jan. 8, 1992, p. 9.

[27] *L'Osservatore Romano*, Feb. 27, 1984, p. 1.
[28] *The Encyclicals of John Paul II*, p. 316.
[29] *The Encyclicals of John Paul II*, p. 893.
[30] *L'Osservatore Romano*, Feb. 3, 1999, p. 8.
[31] *L'Osservatore Romano*, Jan. 12, 1981, p. 2.
[32] *L'Osservatore Romano*, Jan. 12, 2000, p. 7.
[33] *L'Osservatore Romano*, Jan. 27, 1999, p. 8.
[34] *The Encyclicals of John Paul II*, p. 675.
[35] *Fides et Ratio*, Encyclical Letter of John Paul II, Sept. 14, 1998, Pauline Books & Media, p. 21.
[36] *L'Osservatore Romano*, Nov. 11, 1991, p. 2.
[37] *L'Osservatore Romano*, June 16, 1980, p. 3.
[38] *L'Osservatore Romano*, Jan. 1, 1979, p. 1.
[39] *A Catholic Dictionary*, edited by Donald Attwater, Rockford, IL: Tan Books, 1997, p. 95.
[40] *L'Osservatore Romano*, Jan. 7, 1980, p. 1.
[41] *L'Osservatore Romano*, Jan. 5, 1994, p. 3.
[42] *L'Osservatore Romano*, Jan. 1, 1979, p. 1.
[43] *The Encyclicals of John Paul II*, p. 792.
[44] *L'Osservatore Romano*, Jan. 1, 1979, p. 1.
[45] *L'Osservatore Romano*, Jan. 6, 1986, p. 2.
[46] *L'Osservatore Romano*, Jan. 3-10, 1983, p. 2.
[47] *L'Osservatore Romano*, Jan. 14, 1998, p. 1.
[48] *Familiaris Consortio*, Apostolic Exhortation of John Paul II, Nov. 22, 1981, Pauline Books & Media, p. 48.
[49] *L'Osservatore Romano*, March 21, 2001, p. 6.
[50] *The Encyclicals of John Paul II*, p. 167.
[51] *L'Osservatore Romano*, June 30, 1999, p. 7.
[52] *L'Osservatore Romano*, April 22, 1998, p. 3.
[53] *L'Osservatore Romano*, July 3, 2002, p. 10.
[54] *L'Osservatore Romano*, Feb. 23, 1994, p. 5.
[55] *Catechesi Tradendae*, Apostolic Exhortation of John Paul II, Oct. 16, 1979, Boston, MA: Pauline Books & Media, p. 6.
[56] *Catechesi Tradendae*, pp. 19-20.
[57] *Christifideles Laici*, Post-Synodal Apostolic Exhortation of John Paul II, Dec. 30, 1988, Pauline Books & Media, p. 85.
[58] *L'Osservatore Romano*, April 11, 2001, p. 2.
[59] *L'Osservatore Romano*, Jan. 22, 1990, p. 6.
[60] *L'Osservatore Romano*, Feb. 23, 1994, p. 16.
[61] *The Papal Encyclicals*, Vol. 5 (1958-1981), p. 254.
[62] *The Papal Encyclicals*, Vol. 5 (1958-1981), p. 270.
[63] *The Encyclicals of John Paul II*, p. 743.
[64] *The Encyclicals of John Paul II*, p. 299.
[65] *The Encyclicals of John Paul II*, p. 300.
[66] *The Encyclicals of John Paul II*, pp. 819-820.
[67] *The Encyclicals of John Paul II*, p. 869.
[68] *L'Osservatore Romano*, June 6, 1983, p. 2.
[69] *The Papal Encyclicals*, Vol. 5 (1958-1981), p. 265.
[70] *L'Osservatore Romano*, July 5, 1982, p. 12.
[71] *L'Osservatore Romano*, April 5-12, 1982, p. 7.
[72] *Salvifici Doloris*, Apostolic Letter of John Paul II, Feb. 11, 1984, Pauline Books & Media, p. 32.
[73] *L'Osservatore Romano*, April 15, 1998, p. 4.
[74] *L'Osservatore Romano*, Jan. 19, 1994, p. 19.
[75] *L'Osservatore Romano*, Oct. 6, 1999, p. 5.
[76] *The Encyclicals of John Paul II*, p. 838.
[77] *The Encyclicals of John Paul II*, p. 838.
[78] *Ecclesia in America*, Post-Synodal Apostolic Exhortation of John Paul II, Jan. 22, 1999, Pauline Books & Media, p. 49.
[79] *L'Osservatore Romano*, Sept. 2, 1985, p. 3.

[80] *L'Osservatore Romano*, Sept. 1, 1980, p. 4.
[81] *L'Osservatore Romano*, April 17, 1979, p. 11.
[82] *L'Osservatore Romano*, Sept. 13, 2000, p. 2.
[83] *L'Osservatore Romano*, Jan. 6, 1986, p. 6.
[84] *L'Osservatore Romano*, August 4, 1986, p. 10.
[85] *L'Osservatore Romano*, March 17, 1986, p. 2.
[86] *L'Osservatore Romano*, April 28, 1980, p. 2.
[87] *L'Osservatore Romano*, May 10, 1982, p. 6.
[88] *The Encyclicals of John Paul II*, p. 825.
[89] *L'Osservatore Romano*, Nov. 11, 1998, p. 4.
[90] *L'Osservatore Romano*, Jan. 6, 1986, p. 1.
[91] *The Encyclicals of John Paul II*, p. 722.
[92] *The Encyclicals of John Paul II*, p. 681.
[93] *The Encyclicals of John Paul II*, p. 312.
[94] *L'Osservatore Romano*, Sept. 20, 1982, p. 7.
[95] *L'Osservatore Romano*, Sept. 30, 1998, p. 7.
[96] *The Encyclicals of John Paul II*, p. 793.
[97] *L'Osservatore Romano*, April 2, 1991, p. 1.
[98] *L'Osservatore Romano*, Jan. 30, 2002, p. 6/7.
[99] *L'Osservatore Romano*, Aug. 29, 1988, p. 10.
[100] *L'Osservatore Romano*, Oct. 11, 1982, p. 3.
[101] *L'Osservatore Romano*, Jan. 4, 1988, p. 1.
[102] *L'Osservatore Romano*, July 5, 1982, p. 4.
[103] *L'Osservatore Romano*, August 4, 1980, p. 8.
[104] *L'Osservatore Romano*, June 5, 1996, p. 9.
[105] *L'Osservatore Romano*, Special Insert – *Incarnationis mysterium*, Dec. 2, 1998.
[106] *L'Osservatore Romano*, Dec. 15, 1999, p. 9.
[107] *L'Osservatore Romano*, March 21, 1988, p. 5.
[108] *L'Osservatore Romano*, March 15, 1982, p. 2.
[109] *Ecclesia in America*, p. 48.
[110] *L'Osservatore Romano*, March 1, 2000, p. 2.
[111] *L' Osservatore Romano*, Oct. 23, 2002, p. 5.
[112] *L' Osservatore Romano*, Oct. 23, 2002, p. 5.
[113] *The Papal Encyclicals*, Vol. 5, p. 253.
[114] *L'Osservatore Romano*, Dec. 22, 1999, p. 3.
[115] *L'Osservatore Romano*, May 1, 2002, p. 1.
[116] *L'Osservatore Romano*, Sept. 19, 2001, p. 10.
[117] *The Catechism of the Catholic Church*, by John Paul II, no. 675.
[118] Benedict XVI, *God and the World*, San Francisco, CA: Ignatius Press, 2000, p. 209.

46. What Catholics can and should do in the present apostasy

First, if you're not a Catholic, you need to become a traditional Catholic as soon as possible, since there is no salvation outside the one Church Christ has established. The information in this book shows that the Devil's assault in the final days is on the one Church established by Christ; it is the Devil's attempt to establish a counterfeit of the true Church. This counterfeit Church has reduced the true Catholic Church to a remnant in the last days. Non-Catholics should contact us for more information about how to convert; the profession of faith for converts to the Catholic Faith is given below.

Where to go to Mass or Confession?

This is probably the most frequent question that we receive and it is the hardest to answer. This is because there is hardly a solid Catholic priest to be found in the entire country today. We offer some guidelines here, and our opinion. Obviously, **no Catholic may attend the New Mass under any circumstances**. No Catholic may receive sacraments from a "priest" ordained in the new rite of ordination of Paul VI.

Attending Mass on Sunday and Holy Days is the Church's law, **which is only obligatory if the Church provides you with a true traditional Mass and a truly Catholic priest within a reasonable distance. Many Catholics throughout history were in situations where they had no Mass to attend or no Mass which was offered by an acceptable priest. They were thus forced to stay home.** Hence, it's not a sin to stay home on Sundays and sanctify the day by praying your Rosary if there is no acceptable traditional Mass option in your area, which is the case for many Catholics today in this time of the Great Apostasy. Those who only have a New Mass in their area would therefore have to stay home on Sundays. Contact us for more information on this question about possible traditional Mass locations, and consult our website (www.mostholyfamilymonastery.com).

If a person has committed mortal sin and needs to go to Confession, he can go to a Novus Ordo priest who was ordained in the Traditional Rite of Ordination (before 1968) as long as the priest says "I absolve you from your sins in the name of the Father and of the Son and of the Holy Ghost." This can be done if a person needs to go to Confession.

Profession of Faith for New Converts and People Leaving the Novus Ordo (the New Mass)

If you are a convert, make the Council of Trent's Profession of Faith for converts.

Profession of Catholic Faith for Converts

Promulgated solemnly by Pope Pius IV and the Council of Trent

- I, N., with firm faith believe and profess each and every article contained in the symbol of faith which the holy Roman Church uses; namely:
- I believe in one God, the Father almighty, maker of heaven and earth, and of all things visible and invisible; and in
- one Lord Jesus Christ, the only-begotten Son of God, born of the Father before all ages; God from God, light from light, true God from true God; begotten not made, of one substance (consubstantial) with the Father, through whom all things were made;
- who for us men and for our salvation came down from heaven, and was made incarnate by the Holy Spirit of the Virgin Mary, and was made man.
- He was crucified also for us under Pontius Pilate, died, and was buried; and
- He rose again the third day according to the Scriptures, and ascended into heaven;
- He sits at the right hand of the Father, and He shall come again in glory to judge the living and the dead, and of His kingdom there will be no end.
- And I believe in the Holy Ghost, the Lord, and giver of Life, who proceeds from the Father and the Son; who equally with the Father and the Son is adored and glorified; who spoke through the prophets.
- And I believe that there is one, holy, Catholic, and apostolic Church.
- I confess one baptism for the remission of sins; and I hope for the resurrection of the dead, and the life of the world to come. Amen.
- **I resolutely accept and embrace the apostolic and ecclesiastical traditions and the other practices and regulations of that same Church.**
- In like manner I accept Sacred Scripture according to the meaning which has been held by holy Mother Church and which she now holds. It is Her prerogative to pass judgment on the true meaning and interpretation of Sacred Scripture. And I will never accept or interpret it in a manner different from the unanimous agreement of the Fathers.
- I also acknowledge that there are truly and properly seven sacraments of the New Law, instituted by Jesus Christ our Lord, and that they are necessary for the salvation of the human race, although it is not necessary for each individual to receive them all.
- I acknowledge that the seven sacraments are: Baptism, Confirmation, Eucharist, Penance, Extreme Unction, Holy Orders, and Matrimony; and that they confer grace; and that of the seven, Baptism, Confirmation, and Holy Orders cannot be repeated without committing a sacrilege.
- I also accept and acknowledge the customary and approved rites of the Catholic Church in the solemn administration of these sacraments.
- I embrace and accept each and every article on Original Sin and Justification declared and defined in the most holy Council of Trent.
- I likewise profess that in Mass a true, proper, and propitiatory sacrifice is offered to God on behalf of the living and the dead, and that the Body and Blood together with the Soul and Divinity of our Lord Jesus Christ is truly, really, and substantially present in the most holy Sacrament of the Eucharist, and that there is a change of the whole substance of the bread into the Body, and of the whole substance of the wine into the Blood; and this change the Catholic Church calls transubstantiation.
- I also profess that the whole and entire Christ and a true Sacrament is received under each separate species.
- I firmly hold that there is a purgatory, and that the souls detained there are helped by the prayers of the faithful.

- I likewise hold that the saints reigning together with Christ should be honored and invoked, that they offer prayers to God on our behalf, and that their relics should be venerated.
- I firmly assert that images of Christ, of the Mother of God ever Virgin, and of the other saints should be owned and kept, and that due honor and veneration should be given to them.
- I affirm that the power of indulgences was left in the keeping of the Church by Christ, and that the use of indulgences is very beneficial to Christians.
- I acknowledge the holy, Catholic, and apostolic Roman Church as the mother and teacher of all churches; and...
- I unhesitatingly accept and profess all the doctrines (especially those concerning the primacy of the Roman Pontiff and his infallible teaching authority) handed down, defined, and explained by the sacred canons and ecumenical councils and especially those of this most holy Council of Trent (and by the ecumenical Vatican Council I). And at the same time:
- **I condemn, reject, and anathematize everything that is contrary to those propositions, and all heresies without exception that have been condemned, rejected, and anathematized by the Church.**
- **I, N., promise, vow, and swear that, with God's help, I shall most constantly hold and profess this true Catholic faith, outside which no one can be saved** and which I now freely profess and truly hold. With the help of God, I shall profess it whole and unblemished to my dying breath; and, to the best of my ability, I shall see to it that my subjects or those entrusted to me by virtue of my office hold it, teach it, and preach it. So help me God and His holy Gospel. – *end of Profession*

If there is a specific sect to which you belonged, add at the end that you also reject that heretical sect. If you are a person who has been involved in the Vatican II/Novus Ordo apostasy, you should also make that same profession of Faith from the Council of Trent. If there were particular dogmas that you denied (such as Outside the Church There is No Salvation), then add at the end of the Profession that you reject anything contrary to that particular dogma. The convert would then need to make a Confession to a validly ordained priest (see New Rite of Ordination section) mentioning all mortal sins that he or she has committed, including belonging to and/or spreading and supporting a non-Catholic sect.

People leaving the Novus Ordo also need to make a Confession (to a validly ordained priest, see New Rite of Ordination section) that they attended a non-Catholic service and for however long they attended. If they participated in other things at the Novus Ordo (e.g. were a lay-minister, dressed immodestly, etc.) or accepted false ecumenism or denied some other dogma, these things should also be mentioned in Confession. This must be done before receiving Communion at the Traditional Mass (if there is an acceptable one for you to attend in your area).

Baptism and Conditional Baptism: The form of baptism is: "I baptize you in the name of the Father, and of the Son, and of the Holy Ghost."

If there is some doubt about the validity of your baptism, the conditional form of baptism is: "*If you are baptized, I do not baptize you again, but if you are not yet baptized [pour water on the head, making sure it touches the skin] I baptize you in the name of the Father, and of the Son, and of the Holy Ghost.*" Since there are barely any true Catholic priests in the whole country, you can have a Catholic friend perform a conditional baptism, and you can baptize your own children.

Pope Eugene IV, Council of Florence, "Exultate Deo," 1439: "In case of necessity, however, not only a priest or a deacon, but even a layman or woman, yes even a pagan and a heretic can baptize, so long as he preserves the form of the Church and has the intention of doing what the Church does."[1]

Also, please contact us if you need a summary of the Catholic Catechism.

PRAYING THE ROSARY AND DEVOTION TO OUR LADY

For those who are Catholic, devotion to Our Lady and the Hail Mary are essential. Catholics must come to learn and understand the power of devotion to Our Lady and the Hail Mary. This will give them the spiritual armor to ward off the attacks of the Devil, and the light to see the truth of what's really going on.

St. Louis De Montfort (+1710): "Blessed Alan de la Roche who was so deeply devoted to the Blessed Virgin had **many revelations from her** and we know that he confirmed the truth of these revelations by a solemn oath. Three of them stand out with special emphasis: **the first, that if people fail to say the Hail Mary (the Angelic Salutation which has saved the world)** out of carelessness, or because they are lukewarm, or because they hate it, **this is a sign that they will probably and indeed shortly be condemned to eternal punishment**."[2] (*The Secret of the Rosary*, p. 45)

St. Louis De Montfort (+1710): "… **there are some very sanctifying interior practices for those whom the Holy Ghost calls to high perfection. These may be expressed in four words: to do all things *by* Mary, *with* Mary, *in* Mary and *for* Mary; so that we may do them all the more perfectly *by* Jesus, *with* Jesus, *in* Jesus and *for* Jesus.**"[3] (*True Devotion to Mary* #257)

St. Louis De Montfort (+ c. 1710): "**By this practice [the True Devotion to Mary which he teaches], faithfully observed, you will give Jesus more glory in a month than by any other practice, however difficult, in many years…**"[4] (*True Devotion to Mary* #222)

St. Louis De Montfort: "… many others have proved invincibly, from the sentiments of the Fathers (among others, St. Augustine, St. Ephrem, St. Cyril of Jerusalem, St. Germanus, St. John Damascene, St. Anselm, St. Bernard, St. Bernardine, St. Thomas and St. Bonaventure), **that devotion to Mary is necessary to salvation, and that… it is an infallible mark of reprobation to have no esteem and love for the holy Virgin.**"[5] (*True Devotion to Mary* # 40)

Regarding the Holy Rosary, Sister Lucia told Father Fuentes in a famous 1957 interview:

"Look, Father, **the Most Holy Virgin in these last times in which we live has given a new efficacy to the recitation of the Holy Rosary**. She has given this efficacy to such an extent that there is no problem, no matter how difficult it is, whether temporal or above all, spiritual, in the personal life of each one of us, of our families, of the families of the world, or of the religious communities, or even of the life of peoples and nations that cannot be solved by the Rosary. **There is no problem I tell you, no matter how difficult it is, that we cannot resolve by the prayer of the Holy Rosary. With the Holy Rosary, we will save ourselves. We will sanctify ourselves. We will console Our Lord and obtain the salvation of many souls.**"

What Catholics should do

We recommend that Catholics pray the entire 15-decade Rosary each day, if possible. One set of mysteries at three different times in the day is the recommendation of St. Louis De Montfort as a good way to get that accomplished. Frankly, many Catholics who are home most of the day are not getting this accomplished, when they easily could. They are missing out on tremendous graces and the opportunity to help save other souls by their prayers.

We also urge all Catholics to obtain and read the following books. If one reads and meditates upon the four last things (Death, Judgment, Heaven and Hell), one will most likely avoid sin. He will avoid the occasions of sin and live a good life. We consider the following books to be essential for a proper spiritual formation; we believe that one will gain more from reading them than many other books.

> *True Devotion to Mary* by St. Louis De Montfort
> -*The Secret of the Rosary* by St. Louis De Montfort
> -*Preparation for Death* by St. Alphonsus (abridged version)
> -*Our Lady of Fatima* by William Thomas Walsh (get to know and live the message Our Lady delivered at Fatima)

All of these books are available from Tan Books (1-800-437-5876). We don't endorse all of their books or their theological positions, however.

Copyright © 2007: Most Holy Family Monastery. All rights reserved. The sections in this book are the intellectual property of Bro. Michael Dimond and Bro. Peter Dimond of Most Holy Family Monastery.

* Bolding, underlining and italicization, which are used throughout this book, are not necessarily that of the quoted author or entity and are usually our own.

Most Holy Family Monastery
4425 Schneider Rd.
Fillmore, NY 14735
1-800-275-1126; 585-567-4433; fax: 585-567-8352
www.mostholyfamilymonastery.com

Endnotes for Section 46:

[1] Denzinger, *The Sources of Catholic Dogma*, B. Herder Book. Co., Thirtieth Edition, 1957, no. 696.
[2] St. Louis De Montfort, *The Secret of the Rosary*, Rockford, IL: Tan Books, 1999, p. 45.
[3] St. Louis De Montfort, *True Devotion to Mary*, Bay Shore, NY: The Montfort Fathers, 1946, p. 188.
[4] St. Louis De Montfort, *True Devotion to Mary*, p. 167.
[5] St. Louis De Montfort, *True Devotion to Mary*, p. 26.

Videos, Audios, & MP3's

Video List for our tapes   #videos   Cost for videos

Video	#videos	Cost for videos
1) The Amazing Heresies of Benedict XVI		
2) Why the New Mass and New Rite of Ordination are Invalid		
3) Why John Paul II Cannot be the Pope		
4) The Amazing Heresies of Paul VI		
5) Vatican II: Council of Apostasy		
6) The Communist and Masonic Infiltration of America & the Catholic Church		
7) Creation and Miracles, Past and Present		
8) Death and the Journey Into Hell		
9) Abortion, Rock Music, and Freemasonry Exposed		
10) Freemasonry's Vast Influence over America		

if you want our 2 books, booklet and other written info add $4.00 →

if you want 4 audios (of our choice) and our MP3 disc add $2.00 →

Shipping: Included

Total:

VIDEO PRICES FOR THOSE IN US: Any 10 videos listed above for $15.00, or $2.00 for 1 video, or any 20 or more videos are $1.00 a copy (all prices include shipping)

VIDEO PRICES FOR THOSE IN CANADA: All 10 videos listed above for $35.00, or $6.00 for 1 video, or any 6 videos for $20.00, any 25 videos for $65.00, any 40 videos for $85.00, or any 75 videos for $155.00 (all prices include shipping)

VIDEO PRICES FOR OUTSIDE US or CANADA: All 10 videos listed above for $70.00, or $20.00 for 1 video, or any 6 videos for $55.00, or any 25 videos for $130.00 (all prices include shipping)

AUDIO TAPE List	# of Audio Tapes	Cost
1) Debate: Are the Post Vatican II Claimants to the Papacy True Popes? Tape 1		
2) Debate: Are the Post Vatican II Claimants to the Papacy True Popes? Tape 2		
3) Exorcisms		
4) Outside the Catholic Church there is Absolutely No Salvation		
5) A Soldier Encounters an Angel and Story of Claude Neumann		
6) Hell, and the Brown Scapular		
7) Prayer, the Great Means of Grace		
8) The Amazing Heresies of Benedict XVI		
9) Why John Paul II Cannot be the Pope		
10) The Amazing Heresies of Paul VI		
11) Why the New Mass and New Rite of Ordination are Invalid		
12) Abortion, Rock Music, and Freemasonry Exposed		
13) Creation and Miracles, Past and Present		
14) Death and the Journey Into Hell		
15) Vatican II: Council of Apostasy		
16) Communist & Masonic Infiltration of America & Catholic Church		
17) The Amazing Heresies of Benedict XVI & Why the New Mass & Rite of Ordination are Invalid		
	Shipping:	Included
	Total:	

Audio Tape Specials for those in the US: Any 12 audio tapes (includes binder & color cover) for $10.00, or audios 1 to 16 (includes binder & color cover) for $14.00, or $2.00 an audio tape, or any 15 audio tapes for $10.00, any 25 audio tapes for $15.00, any 50 audio tapes for $27.00, or any 75 audio tapes for $35.00 (all prices include shipping)

Audio Tape Specials for those outside the US: Any 12 audio tapes (includes binder and color cover) for $30.00, or audios 1 to 16 (includes binder and color cover) for $40.00, or $4.00 an audio tape, or any 11 audio tapes for $25.00, any 25 audio tapes for $45.00, any 50 audio tapes for $55.00, or any 75 audio tapes for $63.00 (all prices include shipping)

MP3's

Get all of the programs listed above (1-16) and other radio programs on one MP3 disc for $2.00. Two or more copies are $1.00 a piece (all prices include shipping).

	# of MP3 disc	Total
MP3disc		

Flyer List: # copies   cost

Flyer	# copies	cost
1) The Amazing Heresies of Benedict XVI (new)		
2) Outside the Catholic Church there is Absolutely No Salvation (new)		
3) 202 Heresies of Vatican II		
4) Is the New Mass Valid?		

Flyer prices: 10 copies for $3.00, 30 copies for $5.00, 75 copies for $10.00, 150 copies for $15.00, 250 copies for $20.00 (prices include shipping)

Shipping: Included

Total:

OUT THE TRUTH ABOUT WHAT REALLY HAPPENED TO THE CATHOLIC CHURCH SINCE VATICAN COUNCIL II

The most complete exposé of the post-Vatican II apostasy from the Catholic Faith that has ever been produced (contains almost 200 color photos)

	# of copies	Shipping	Total:
The Truth about What Really Happened to the Catholic Church after Vatican II (658 page book)		Included	

The Truth about What Really Happened to the Catholic Church book Prices for those in US: 1 Book for $10.00, 2 for $14.00, or 6 copies for $30.00, or for larger quantities please call us (all prices include shipping). Outside US: 1 Book for $20.00; larger quantities please call (all prices include shipping).

DVD List (numbers 1, 2 and 3 contain all 10 programs on 3 DVDs!)

	#DVDs	Cost for DVDs
1 1A) The Amazing Heresies of Benedict XVI 1B) Why the New Mass and New Rite of Ordination are Invalid 1C) Creation and Miracles, Past and Present 1D) Death and the Journey Into Hell *(4 programs on 1 DVD!)*		
2 2A) Why John Paul II Cannot be the Pope 2B) The Amazing Heresies of Paul VI 2C) Vatican II: Council of Apostasy *(3 programs on 1 DVD!)*		
3 3A) The Communist and Masonic Infiltration of America and the Catholic Church *(3 programs on 1 DVD!)* 3B) Freemasonry's Vast Influence over America 3C) Abortion, Rock Music, and Freemasonry Exposed		
4 4A) Creation and Miracles, Past and Present 4B) Death and the Journey Into Hell *(2 programs on 1 DVD!)*		

DVD PRICES FOR THOSE IN US: 1 to 6 copies of any DVDs listed above are $2.00 a copy, or 7 or more copies of any DVDs are $1.00 a copy (all prices include shipping)

if you want our 2 books, booklet and other written info add $4.00
if you want 4 audios (of our choice) and our MP3 disc add $2.00

Shipping: Included
Total:

DVD PRICES FOR THOSE IN CANADA: Any 3 DVDs for $10.00, any 7 DVDs listed above for $19.00, or $6.00 for 1 DVD, or any 16 DVDs for $40.00, any 25 DVDs for $55.00, any 40 DVDs for $85.00, any 75 DVDs for $155.00 or any 120 DVDs for $240.00 (all prices include shipping)

DVD PRICES FOR OUTSIDE US & CANADA: Any 3 DVDs for $16.00, any 7 DVDs listed above for $25.00, or $6.00 for 1 DVD, or any 16 DVDs for $60.00, any 25 DVDs for $80.00, any 40 DVDs for $150.00, or any 75 DVDs for $175.00 (all prices include shipping)

Book on the life and miracles of Padre Pio (88 pages)

	#of copies	Shipping	Total:
Padre Pio: A Catholic priest who worked miracles and bore the wounds of Jesus		Included	

Booklet prices for those in the US: 1 booklet for $2.00, 5 to 9 copies are $1.00 a copy, 10 or more copies are 50 cents a copy (all prices include shipping) Special prices for Padre Pio booklets: 100 for $35.00 or 180 for $50.00 (all prices include shipping)

Booklet prices for those in Canada: 1 booklet for $5.00, 15 or more booklets are $1.00 a copy (all prices include shipping)
Booklet prices for outside the US/Canada: 1 booklet for $7.00, 15 or more booklets are $1.00 a copy (all prices include shipping)

The best book on this Catholic dogma! (a 286 page book)

	#of copies	Shipping	Total:
Outside the Catholic Church There Is Absolutely No Salvation		Included	

Outside the Catholic Church Book Prices for those in US: 1 Book for $4.00, 10 copies for $25.00, or 24 copies for $50.00 (all prices include shipping)
Outside the Catholic Church Book Prices for those outside US: 1 Book for $8.00, 10 copies for $50.00, or 24 copies for $120.00 (all prices include shipping)

One of the best DVDs on the events of 911 (DVD: 1 hour 34 minutes)

	#of DVDs	Cost	Shipping	Total:
911 In Plane Site (The Director's Cut) by Dave VonKleist		$12.00 in US / $20.00 outside US	included	

This DVD is amazing, stunning, incredible! It is one of the best DVDs produced on what really happened on 9/11. It provides <u>video evidence</u> utterly refuting the media's lie about the events of 9/11 and allows you to draw your own conclusion. It is probably one of the most important DVDs on a purely secular topic ever produced.

Best video ever produced exposing Rock music! (3 1/2 hours)

	#of copies	Cost	Shipping	Total:
Rock-n-Roll Sorcerers of the New Age Revolution video (not available in DVD)		$15.00 in US /$22.00 outside US	included	

Other Items (available in both video and DVD)

	#of Videos	Cost for Videos	#of DVDs	Cost for DVDs	Shipping:	Total:
Jesus and the Shroud of Turin (1 hour) The best film produced on the Shroud of Turin		$7.00 a copy in US / $12.00 a copy outside US		$7.00 a copy in US / $12.00 a copy outside US	included	
The Exodus Revealed (1 hour) Shows incredible evidence of Moses's crossing of the Red Sea		$7.00 a copy in US / $12.00 a copy outside US		$7.00 a copy in US / $12.00 a copy outside US	included	

The best book in the world that disproves evolution

	#of copies	Cost	Shipping	Total:
In the Beginning (328 page color book) by Dr. Walt Brown		$25.00 a copy in US / $40.00 a copy outside US	included	

This amazing book totally refutes evolution from all aspects of science, and shows how the Biblical Flood not only occurred, but is earth's defining geological event. It contains many color pictures, figures and charts, and is well worth the price. This book is somewhat deep and technical at times, but for those interested in the detailed arguments disproving evolution and proving the Flood, it is a tremendous read: the best, most devastating and scholarly work on this topic.

Name:

Address:

City/St/Zip:

Visa/MC/Discover: Exp Date:

Most Holy Family Monastery * 4425 Schneider Rd. Fillmore, NY. 14735 * 800-275-1126 / 585-567-4433 (24 hour fax 585-567-8352)

www.mostholyfamilymonastery.com Now watch all our videos free online!